Autodesk Revit Architecture 2015 for Architects and Designers

(11th Edition)

CADCIM Technologies
525 St. Andrews Drive
Schererville, IN 46375, USA
(www.cadcim.com)

Contributing Author
Sham Tickoo
Professor
Purdue University Calumet
Hammond, Indiana, USA

CADCIM Technologies

Autodesk Revit Architecture for Architects and Designers
Sham Tickoo

Published by CADCIM Technologies, 525 St Andrews Drive, Schererville, IN 46375 USA. © Copyright 2014 CADCIM Technologies. All rights reserved. No part of this publication may be reproduced or distributed in any form or by any means, or stored in the database or retrieval system without the prior permission of CADCIM Technologies.

ISBN   978-1-936646-71-5

NOTICE TO THE READER

Publisher does not warrant or guarantee any of the products described in the text or perform any independent analysis in connection with any of the product information contained in the text. Publisher does not assume, and expressly disclaims, any obligation to obtain and include information other than that provided to it by the manufacturer.

The reader is expressly warned to consider and adopt all safety precautions that might be indicated by the activities herein and to avoid all potential hazards. By following the instructions contained herein, the reader willingly assumes all risks in connection with such instructions.

The publisher makes no representation or warranties of any kind, including but not limited to, the warranties of fitness for particular purpose or merchantability, nor are any such representations implied with respect to the material set forth herein, and the publisher takes no responsibility with respect to such material. The publisher shall not be liable for any special, consequential, or exemplary damages resulting, in whole or part, from the reader's use of, or reliance upon this material.

www.cadcim.com

DEDICATION

*To teachers, who make it possible to disseminate knowledge
to enlighten the young and curious minds
of our future generations*

*To students, who are dedicated to learning new technologies
and making the world a better place to live in*

SPECIAL RECOGNITION

*A special thanks to Mr. Denis Cadu and the ADN team of Autodesk Inc.
for their valuable support and professional guidance to
procure the software for writing this textbook*

THANKS

*To the faculty and students of the MET department of
Purdue University Calumet for their cooperation*

To employees at CADCIM Technologies for their valuable help

Online Training Program Offered by CADCIM Technologies

CADCIM Technologies provides effective and affordable virtual online training on various software packages including Computer Aided Design and Manufacturing (CAD/CAM), computer programming languages, animation, architecture, and GIS. The training is delivered 'live' via Internet at any time, any place, and at any pace to individuals as well as students of colleges, universities, and CAD/CAM training centers. The main features of this program are:

Training for Students and Companies in a Classroom Setting

Highly experienced instructors and qualified Engineers at CADCIM Technologies conduct the classes under the guidance of Prof. Sham Tickoo of Purdue University Calumet, USA. This team has authored several textbooks that are rated "one of the best" in their categories and are used in various colleges, universities, and training centers in North America, Europe, and in other parts of the world.

Training for Individuals

CADCIM Technologies with its cost effective and time saving initiative strives to deliver the training in the comfort of your home or work place, thereby relieving you from the hassles of traveling to training centers.

Training Offered on Software Packages

CADCIM provides basic and advanced training on the following software packages:

CAD/CAM/CAE: CATIA, Pro/ENGINEER Wildfire, Creo Parametric, SolidWorks, Autodesk Inventor, Solid Edge, NX, AutoCAD, AutoCAD LT, Customizing AutoCAD, EdgeCAM, and ANSYS

Computer Programming: C++, VB.NET, Oracle, AJAX, and Java

Animation and Styling: Autodesk 3ds Max, Autodesk 3ds Max Design, Autodesk Maya, eyeon Fusion, Adobe Flash, Adobe Premiere, Foundry NukeX, Autodesk Softimage, Pixologic ZBrush, and Autodesk Alias

Architecture and GIS: Autodesk Revit Architecture, AutoCAD Civil 3D, Autodesk Revit Structure, Revit MEP, AutoCAD MEP, and AutoCAD Map 3D

For more information, please visit the following link:

http://www.cadcim.com

Note

If you are a faculty member, you can register by clicking on the following link: *http://www.cadcim.com/Registration.aspx*. The student resources are available at *http://www.cadcim.com*. We also provide **Live Virtual Online Training** on various software packages. For more information, write us at sales@cadcim.com

Table of Contents

Dedication   iii
Preface   xvii

Chapter 1: Introduction to Autodesk Revit Architecture 2015

Introduction to Autodesk Revit Architecture	1-2
Autodesk Revit Architecture as a Building Information Modeler	1-2
Basic Concepts and Principles	1-3
Understanding the Parametric Building Modeling Technology	1-4
Terms used in Autodesk Revit Architecture	1-4
Creating a Building Model using Parametric Building Elements	1-6
Visibility/Graphics Overrides, Scale, and Detail Level	1-7
Extracting the Project Information	1-8
Creating an Architectural Drawing Set	1-8
Creating an Unusual Building Geometry	1-8
Flexibility of Creating Special Elements	1-8
Creating Structural Layouts	1-9
Working on Large Projects	1-9
Working in Large Teams and Coordinating with Consultants	1-9
Starting Autodesk Revit Architecture 2015	1-9
User Interface	1-12
Invoking Tools	1-12
Title Bar	1-12
Ribbon	1-12
Application Frame	1-14
Status Bar	1-16
View Control Bar	1-16
Options Bar	1-17
Type Selector	1-17
Drawing Area	1-17
Project Browser	1-18
Keyboard Accelerators	1-18
Properties Palette	1-19
Dialog Boxes	1-19
Multiple Document Environment	1-20
Interoperability of Autodesk Revit Architecture	1-20
Building Information Modeling and Autodesk Revit Architecture 2015	1-21

Autodesk Revit Architecture Help	1-21
Using the Revit Architecture 2015 Help Enhanced	1-22
Worksharing Using Revit Server	1-23
Working with BIM 360 New	1-24
Sharing Models with BIM 360	1-24

Chapter 2: Starting an Architectural Project

Introduction	2-2
Starting a New Architectural Project Enhanced	2-2
Project Units	2-3
Length Unit	2-4
Area Unit	2-5
Volume Unit	2-5
Angle Units	2-5
Slope Unit	2-5
Currency Unit	2-6
Mass Density Unit	2-6
Snaps Tool	2-6
Dimension Snaps Area	2-7
Object Snaps Area	2-8
Temporary Overrides Area	2-9
Saving a Project	2-9
Saving the Project File	2-9
Using the Save Tool	2-11
Configuring Global Settings	2-11
General Tab Enhanced	2-12
User Interface Tab	2-13
Graphics Tab	2-14
File Locations Tab	2-15
Rendering Tab	2-16
Check Spelling Tab	2-17
SteeringWheels Tab	2-18
ViewCube Tab	2-19
Macros Tab	2-20
Closing a Project	2-21
Exiting Autodesk Revit Architecture	2-21
Opening an Existing Project	2-21
Opening an Existing Project Using the Open Tool	2-22
Model Display Tools	2-25
Using the Zoom Tools	2-25
Using the Orient Options	2-26
Navigation Tools	2-27
Other Display Options	2-31
Tutorial 1 Apartment 1	2-32
Tutorial 2 Club	2-35
Self-Evaluation Test	2-39
Review Questions	2-40

Table of Contents

Exercise 1 Apartment 2 — 2-41
Exercise 2 Elevator and Stair Lobby — 2-41

Chapter 3: Creating Walls

Introduction	3-2
Creating a Building Project	3-2
Sequence of Creating a Building Model	3-2
Understanding Wall Types	3-3
Creating Architectural Walls	3-4
Working With Stacked Walls New	3-17
Creating a Stacked Wall	3-18
Adding Interior Walls	3-18
Adding Wall Sweeps and Wall Reveals	3-21
Wall Sweeps	3-21
Wall Reveals	3-23
Tutorial 1 Apartment 1	3-26
Tutorial 2 Club	3-32
Tutorial 3 Apartment 1 - Interior Walls	3-38
Tutorial 4 Club - Interior Walls	3-44
Tutorial 5 Office - Stacked Wall	3-49
Self-Evaluation Test	3-57
Review Questions	3-58
Exercise 1 Apartment 2	3-59
Exercise 2 Elevator and Stair Lobby	3-60
Exercise 3 Club-Interior Walls	3-61

Chapter 4: Using Basic Building Components-I

Introduction	4-2
Adding Doors in a Building Model	4-2
Adding Doors	4-2
Understanding Door Properties	4-4
Adding a Door to a Wall	4-7
Adding Windows in a Building Model	4-9
Adding Windows	4-10
Understanding Window Properties	4-10
Adding a Window to a Wall	4-13
Doors and Windows as Wall Openings	4-15
Openings in the Wall	4-16
Tutorial 1 Apartment 1	4-16
Tutorial 2 Club	4-27
Self-Evaluation Test	4-33
Review Questions	4-34
Exercise 1 Apartment 2	4-35
Exercise 2 Elevator and Stair Lobby	4-36
Exercise 3 Club - Hall 2	4-37

Chapter 5: Using the Editing Tools

Introduction	5-2
Creating a Selection Set	5-2
Selecting Multiple Elements	5-2
Selecting Elements Using Advanced Tools	5-3
Restoring the Selection	5-4
Using the Filter tool Enhanced	5-4
Moving and Copying Elements	5-7
Moving the Elements by Changing the Temporary Dimensions	5-7
Moving the Elements by Dragging	5-7
Moving the Elements by Dragging the End-Joint Components	5-8
Moving the Elements by Selecting and Dragging	5-8
Using the Move Tool	5-9
Using the Copy Tool	5-10
Trimming and Extending Elements	5-10
Using the Trim/Extend to Corner Tool	5-11
Using the Trim/Extend Single Element Tool	5-12
Using the Trim/Extend Multiple Elements Tool	5-13
Cutting and Pasting Elements	5-14
Cutting Elements	5-14
Copying Elements to the Clipboard	5-15
Pasting Elements from the Clipboard	5-15
Rotating Elements	5-15
Mirroring Elements Enhanced	5-17
Mirroring Elements using the Mirror -Pick Axis Tool	5-17
Mirroring Elements using the Mirror - Draw Axis Tool	5-18
Creating an Offset	5-19
Creating an Array of Elements	5-21
Linear Array	5-22
Radial Array	5-24
Matching Elements	5-25
Aligning Elements and Working with Constraints	5-26
Deleting Elements	5-27
Splitting Element	5-27
Splitting with Gap	5-29
Splitting Faces	5-29
Grouping Element	5-29
Creating Groups by Selecting Elements in the Project Views	5-30
Creating Groups Using the Group Editor	5-30
Creating a Detail Group	5-31
Creating Model and Attached Detail Groups Enhanced	5-31
Placing Groups	5-32
Swapping Groups	5-33
Modifying Groups	5-33
Excluding Elements from a Group	5-34
Saving and Loading Groups	5-34
Converting Groups to Linked Models	5-35

Deleting Groups	5-36
Creating Similar Elements	5-36
Pinning and Unpinning Elements Enhanced	5-37
Scaling Elements	5-37
Using Diagnostic Tools	5-38
Measuring Distance between References and Along an Element	5-38
Selecting Elements Using the Element ID	5-39
Assemblies New	5-40
Creating Assemblies	5-40
Editing Assemblies	5-41
Creating Assembly Views and Sheets	5-41
Tutorial 1 Apartment 1	5-41
Tutorial 2 Club	5-47
Tutorial 3 Office- Assembly Views	5-43
Self-Evaluation Test	5-61
Review Questions	5-62
Exercise 1 Apartment 2	5-63
Exercise 2 Club	5-64
Exercise 3 Elevator and Stair Lobby	5-65
Exercise 4 Office	5-66

Chapter 6: Working with Datum Plane and Creating Standard Views

Introduction	6-2
Working with Levels	6-2
Understanding Level Properties	6-3
Adding Levels	6-6
Modifying Level Parameters	6-8
Hiding Elements in a View	6-10
Controlling the Visibility of Levels	6-11
Working with Grids	6-11
Creating Grids	6-11
Modifying Grids	6-16
Grid Properties	6-18
Customizing the Grid Display	6-21
Controlling the Visibility of Grids	6-22
Reference Planes	6-23
Work Planes	6-23
Setting a Work Plane	6-23
Controlling the Visibility of Work Planes	6-24
Working with Project Views	6-25
Viewing a Building Model	6-25
Visibility/Graphic Overrides of an Element	6-26
Visibility/Graphic Overrides of an Element Category	6-27
Making Elements Transparent	6-28
Using the Temporary Hide/Isolate Tool	6-29
Plan Views	6-30
Elevation Views	6-31
Section Views	6-34

Using the Scope Box Tool	6-39
Tutorial 1 Apartment 1	6-41
Tutorial 2 Club	6-50
Self-Evaluation Test	6-57
Review Questions	6-58
Exercise 1 Apartment 2	6-59
Exercise 2 Elevator and Stair Lobby	6-60

Chapter 7: Using Basic Building Components-II

Introduction	7-2
Creating Architectural Floors	7-2
Sketching the Floor Boundary	7-4
Creating Roofs	7-7
Creating Roofs by Footprint	7-7
Creating Roofs By Extrusion	7-10
Modifying Roof Properties and Editing Shapes	7-14
Shape Editing Tools for Structural Floors	7-18
Modify Sub Elements	7-18
Add Point	7-19
Adding Split Line	7-20
Pick Supports	7-20
Reset Shape	7-20
Creating Ceilings	7-20
Creating an Automatic Ceiling	7-21
Sketching a Ceiling	7-21
Using the Pick Walls Method	7-22
Modifying a Ceiling	7-22
Rooms	7-24
Adding Rooms	7-24
Calculating Room Volumes	7-28
Cutting Openings in a Wall, Floor, Roof, and Ceiling	7-29
Joining Walls with Other Elements	7-32
Using the Attach Top/Base and Detach Top/Base Tools	7-32
Tutorial 1 Apartment 1	7-33
Tutorial 2 Club	7-38
Self-Evaluation Test	7-47
Review Questions	7-48
Exercise 1 Apartment 2	7-49
Exercise 2 Elevator and Stair Lobby	7-49

Chapter 8: Using Basic Building Components-III

Introduction	8-2
Using Components in a Project	8-2
Adding Components	8-2
Adding Stairs	8-6
Adding Stair By Component	8-6

Converting a Stair Component to a Sketch	8-13
Adding Stairs by Sketching Runs	8-13
Adding Stairs by Sketching the Boundary and Riser Lines	8-15
Modifying Stairs Properties	8-18
Adding Railings	8-20
Adding Railings by Sketching the Path	8-20
Modifying Railing Properties	8-20
Modifying Railing Joints	8-21
Adding Ramps	8-21
Using Curtain Systems in a Project	8-23
Creating a Curtain Wall Using the Wall: Architectural Tool	8-24
Creating a Curtain Wall by Picking Lines	8-25
Creating a Curtain System on a Face	8-25
Adding Curtain Grids	8-26
Modifying Curtain System Panels	8-28
Adding Doors and Awnings to a Curtain System	8-28
Adding Mullions	8-29
Copying Elements from One Level to Another	8-29
Using the Pasting Tools	8-30
Tutorial 1 Apartment 1	8-31
Tutorial 2 Club	8-39
Tutorial 3 Elevator and Stair Lobby	8-42
Self-Evaluation Test	8-50
Review Questions	8-51
Exercise 1 Apartment 2	8-52

Chapter 9: Adding Site Features

Introduction	9-2
Working with Site Features	9-2
Creating a Toposurface Enhanced	9-3
Creating Topographical Subregions	9-6
Splitting a Topography	9-6
Merging Toposurfaces	9-7
Creating a Topography Using Imported Data	9-8
Setting the Site Properties	9-9
Adding Property Lines	9-10
Sketching Property Lines	9-11
Creating Property Lines Using Distances and Bearings	9-11
Creating Building Pads	9-13
Adding Site Components	9-16
Adding Parking Components	9-18
Adding Labels to Contours	9-18
Tutorial 1 Site Plan	9-19
Self-Evaluation Test	9-38
Review Questions	9-39
Exercise 1 Site Plan	9-40
Exercise 2 Museum Site Plan	9-41

Chapter 10: Using Massing Tools

Introduction	10-2
Understanding Massing Concepts	10-2
Creating the Massing Geometry	10-3
Creating a Massing Geometry in the Family Editor	10-4
Editing a Massing Geometry in the Family Editor	10-10
Creating Cuts in a Massing Geometry Using the Family Editor	10-11
Placing the Massing Geometry in a Project	10-13
Creating the In-Place Mass in a Project	10-14
Massing in Conceptual Design Environment	10-15
Interface of the Conceptual Design Environment	10-15
Creating Masses in Conceptual Design Environment	10-16
Creating Building Elements from the Massing Geometry	
Using Building Maker Tools	10-21
Creating Walls by Selecting Faces	10-21
Creating Floors by Selecting Faces	10-21
Creating Roofs by Selecting Faces	10-22
Creating Curtain Systems by Selecting Faces	10-23
Controlling the Visibility of a Massing Geometry	10-24
Adding other Building Elements	10-24
Creating Families	10-25
Creating In-Place Families	10-26
Creating Families Using Standard Family Templates	10-26
Tutorial 1 Office Building 2	10-36
Tutorial 2 Architectural Column	10-52
Self-Evaluation Test	10-67
Review Questions	10-68
Exercise 1 Office Towers	10-69
Exercise 2 Stadium	10-71

Chapter 11: Adding Annotations and Dimensions

Introduction	11-2
Adding Tags	11-2
Tagging Elements by Category	11-3
Tagging All Elements in a View	11-6
Tagging Treads or Risers	11-8
Room Tags	11-9
Room Separation	11-9
Tagging Rooms	11-11
Keynotes	11-11
Loading Keynote File	11-12
Placing Keynotes	11-13
Adding Keynote Legends	11-15
Adding Symbols	11-16
Adding Dimensions	11-16
Types of Dimensions	11-17
Dimensioning Terminology	11-19

Table of Contents

Adding Permanent Dimensions	11-21
Adding Alternate Dimension Units	11-25
Baseline and Ordinate Dimensions	11-26
Editing Dimensions	11-27
Controlling the Display of Tick Marks and Dimension Arrows	11-29
Creating Linear Wall Dimensions Automatically	11-30
Adding Spot Dimensions	11-31
Placing a Spot Dimension	11-31
Modifying Spot Dimension Properties	11-32
Converting Temporary Dimensions to Permanent Dimensions	11-32
Tutorial 1 Apartment 1	11-34
Self-Evaluation Test	11-44
Review Questions	11-44
Exercise 1 Club	11-45
Exercise 2 Elevator and Stair Lobby	11-46
Exercise 3 Building 1	11-47

Chapter 12: Creating Project Details and Schedules

Project Detailing in Autodesk Revit Architecture	12-2
Creating Details Using a Building Model	12-2
Callout View	12-3
Displaying the Callout View	12-5
Modifying Callout View Properties	12-5
Adding Details to the Callout View	12-7
Crop Regions	12-8
Model Crop Region	12-9
Annotation Crop Region	12-9
Creating Drafted Details	12-15
Creating a Drafting View	12-15
Drafting a Detail	12-16
Line Style Settings	12-16
Using Line Weights	12-17
Using Line Patterns	12-18
Adding Text Notes	12-19
Creating Text Notes	12-20
Editing Text Notes	12-21
Creating a Model Text	12-23
Revision Clouds	12-25
Creating the Revision Cloud	12-25
Adding a Revision Tag	12-26
Using Schedules in a Project	12-28
Generating a Schedule	12-28
Exporting Schedule to Excel Sheet	12-32
Creating a Legend View	12-34
Tutorial 1 Apartment 1 - Callout View	12-35
Tutorial 2 Apartment 1 - Schedules	12-47
Tutorial 3 Road Section Detail	12-51
Self-Evaluation Test	12-58

Review Questions	12-59
Exercise 1 Club - Drafted Detail	12-60
Exercise 2 General - Sketch Detail	12-60
Exercise 3 Club - Schedules	12-61

Chapter 13: Creating Drawing Sheets and Plotting

Introduction	13-2
Creating Drawing Sheets	13-2
Adding a Drawing Sheet to a Project	13-2
Adding Views to a Drawing Sheet	13-5
Modifying View Properties	13-6
Panning the Viewports Added to the Sheet	13-8
Adding Schedules to a Drawing Sheet	13-8
Modifying a Building Model in a Drawing Sheet	13-10
Creating Guide Grid New	13-10
Duplicate Dependent Views	13-11
Creating Dependent Views	13-12
Adding Matchline to Dependent Views	13-13
Adding Views to Sheet New	13-14
Adding View Reference New	13-15
Printing in Autodesk Revit Architecture	13-15
Printing Drawing Sheets and Project Views	13-16
Selecting and Modifying the Printer Settings	13-17
Using the Print Setup Dialog Box	13-19
Previewing the Print Setup	13-21
Tutorial 1 Apartment 1	13-22
Self-Evaluation Test	13-27
Review Questions	13-27
Exercise 1 Club	13-28
Exercise 2 Urban House	13-30

Chapter 14: Creating 3D Views

Introduction	14-2
Three-Dimensional (3D) Views	14-2
Creating Orthographic Views	14-3
Dynamically Viewing Models Using Navigation Tools	14-4
Using the Orient Tool	14-11
Generating Perspective Views	14-12
Locking and Unlocking 3D Views	14-17
Using the Section Box	14-18
Tutorial 1 Apartment 1	14-19
Tutorial 2 Club	14-24
Self-Evaluation Test	14-28
Review Questions	14-29
Exercise 1 Apartment 1	14-30
Exercise 2 Office Building 1	14-31

Exercise 3 Office Building 2	14-32
Exercise 4 Hotel Building	14-33

Chapter 15: Rendering Views and Creating Walkthroughs

Rendering in Revit Architecture	15-2
Rendering Workflow	15-2
Introduction to Materials	15-5
Applying Lights	15-15
Using Decals and Entourages	15-17
Rendering Settings	15-21
Creating a Walkthrough	15-26
Creating the Walkthrough Path	15-26
Editing and Playing the Walkthrough	15-27
Recording a Walkthrough	15-30
Autodesk 360 | Rendering	15-31
Rendering in Cloud *Enhanced*	15-32
Accessing Render Gallery	15-33
Tutorial 1 Apartment 1	15-33
Tutorial 2 Office Building 2	15-49
Self-Evaluation Test	15-55
Review Questions	15-55
Exercise 1 Club	15-56
Exercise 2 Apartment 1 - Morning View	15-56
Exercise 3 Hotel Building - Walkthrough	15-57

Chapter 16: Using Advanced Features

Introduction	16-2
Creating Structural Components	16-2
Creating Structural Walls	16-3
Creating Structural Columns	16-5
Adding Structural Beams and Braces	16-7
Cutting Openings in Beams, Braces, and Columns	16-8
Generating Multiple Design Options	16-9
Generating Design Options for a Project	16-10
Presenting Design Options	16-11
Using Area Analysis Tools	16-12
Area Schemes	16-12
Area Plans	16-13
Area Schedules	16-15
Color Schemes	16-17
Creating Color Schemes	16-17
Modifying Color Scheme	16-21
Masking Regions	16-21
Adding Masking Regions to a Project	16-22
Adding Masking Region to a Detail Family	16-22
Adding Masking Regions to a Model Family	16-23
Creating Displaced Views	16-23

Using Project Phasing Tools	16-24
Understanding Phasing Concepts	16-24
Linking Building Models and Sharing Coordinates	16-26
Linking or Importing Models	16-27
Linking Revit Models	16-30
Nested Linked Models	16-31
Converting Linked Models to Groups - Binding Links	16-33
Managing Links	16-35
Including Elements of Linked Models in Schedules	16-36
Applying the Color Schemes of the Host Model to Rooms and Areas of the Linked Models	16-36
Copying Linked Model Elements	16-37
Worksharing Concepts	16-37
Worksharing Using Workset Tools	16-38
Process of Worksharing	16-38
Saving Methodology in Worksharing	16-44
Element Ownership Concepts	16-44
Purging Unused Element Families	16-45
Transferring Project Standards	16-45
Organizing the Project Browser	16-47
Generating Shadows	16-47
Revit Architecture Solar Studies	16-47
Generating Still Solar Study	16-48
Creating an Animated Solar Study	16-51
Point Cloud	16-54
Inserting a Point Cloud File	16-54
Point Cloud Visibility	16-54
Using a Point Cloud File in a Project	16-55
Revit Architecture Interoperability	16-55
Interoperability with Autodesk 3ds Max and Autodesk 3ds Max Design	16-55
Interoperability with Google SketchUp	16-56
Publishing Tips in Revit Architecture 2015	16-58
Tutorial 1 Apartment 1	16-59
Tutorial 2 Apartment Complex	16-71
Self-Evaluation Test	16-82
Review Questions	16-82
Exercise 1 Apartment 2	16-83
Exercise 2 Apartment Complex	16-85
Student Project- City Mall	**SP-1**
Index	**I-1**

Preface

Autodesk Revit Architecture 2015

Welcome to the world of Autodesk Revit Architecture. This textbook introduces the users to the spectacular realm of one of the most powerful software in the architectural quiver, Autodesk Revit Architecture. This textbook is a gateway to power, skill, and competence in the field of architectural and interior presentations, drawings, and documentations.

This textbook is specially meant for professionals and students of architecture and interior design, facilities planners, and CAD professionals who are associated with the building construction and allied fields in the construction industry.

Special emphasis has been laid to explain new concepts, procedures, and methods in Revit Architecture by using sufficient text and graphical examples. The accompanying tutorials and exercises, which relate to the real world projects, help you understand the usage and abilities of the tools available in Autodesk Revit Architecture.

The main features of this textbook are as follows:

- **Project-based Approach**
  The author has adopted the project-based approach and the learn-by-doing theme throughout the textbook. This approach helps the users learn the concepts and procedures easily.

- **Real-World Designs as Projects**
  The author has used real-world building designs and architectural examples as projects in this textbook so that the users can correlate them to the real-time designs.

- **Tips and Notes**
  Additional information related to various topics is provided to the users in the form of tips and notes.

- **Learning Objectives**
  The first page of every chapter summarizes the topics that will be covered in that chapter. This will help the users to easily refer to a topic.

- **Self-Evaluation Test, Review Questions, and Exercises**
  Every chapter ends with Self-Evaluation test so that the users can assess their knowledge of the chapter. The answers to Self-Evaluation Test are given at the end of the chapter. Also, the Review Questions and Exercises are given at the end of each chapter and they can be used by the Instructors as test questions and exercises.

- **Heavily Illustrated Text**
  The text in this book is heavily illustrated with around 900 line diagrams and screen capture images that support the command sections and tutorials.

Symbols Used in the Textbook

Note   The author has provided additional information to the users about the topic being discussed in the form of notes.

Tip   Special information and techniques are provided in the form of tips that helps in increasing the efficiency of the users.

New   This symbol indicates that the command or tool being discussed is new in the current release of Autodesk Revit Architecture.

Enhanced   This symbol indicates that the existing command or tool being discussed has been enhanced in the current release of Autodesk Revit Architecture.

Formatting Conventions Used in the Textbook

Please refer to the following list for the formatting conventions used in this textbook.

- Names of tools, buttons, options, browser, palette, panels, and tabs are written in boldface.

  Example: The **Wall: Architecture** tool, the **Modify** button, the **Build** panel, the **Architecture** tab, the **Properties** palette, the **Project Browser**, and so on.

- Names of dialog boxes, drop-downs, drop-down lists, list boxes, areas, edit boxes, check boxes, and radio buttons are written in boldface.

  Example: The **Options** dialog box, the **Wall** drop-down of **Build** panel in the **Architecture** tab, the **Name** edit box of the **Name** dialog box, the **Chain** check box in the **Options Bar**, and so on.

- Values entered in edit boxes are written in boldface.

  Example: Enter **Brick Wall** in the **Name** edit box.

- Names of the files are italicized.

  Example: *c14_Club_tut2.rvt*

- The methods of invoking a tool/option from the ribbon, Application Menu, or the shortcut keys are given in a shaded box.

  Ribbon: Home > Build > Wall drop-down > Wall
  Application Menu: New
  Shortcut Keys: CTRL+N

- When you select an element or a component, a contextual tab is displayed depending upon the entity selected. In this textbook, this contextual tab is referred to as **Modify | (Elements / Components)**.

    Ribbon: Modify | (Elements / Components) > Modify > Move
    Shortcut Key: MV

Naming Conventions Used in the Textbook

Tool

If you click on an item in a panel of the ribbon and a command is invoked to create/edit an object or perform some action, then that item is termed as **tool**.

For example:
Wall: Architectural tool, **Window** tool, **Railing** tool
Filled Region tool, **Trim/Extend to Corner** tool, **Rotate** tool
Link Revit tool, **Detail Line** tool

If you click on an item in a panel of the ribbon and a dialog box is invoked wherein you can set the properties to create/edit an object, then that item is also termed as **tool**, refer to Figure 1.

Figure 1 Tools in the ribbon

For example:
Load Family tool, **Materials** tool, **Project Units** tool
Design Options tool, **Visibility/Graphics** tool

Button

The item in a dialog box that has a 3d shape like a button is also termed as **Button**. For example, **OK** button, **Cancel** button, **Apply** button, and so on. If the item in a ribbon is used to exit a tool or a mode, it is also termed as button. For example, **Modify** button, **Finish Edit Mode** button, **Cancel Edit Mode** button, and so on; refer to Figure 2.

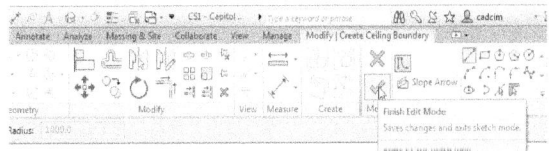

Figure 2 Choosing the **Finish Edit Mode** button

Dialog Box

In this textbook, different terms are used to indicate various components of a dialog box. Refer to Figure 3 for the terminologies used for referring to the componnts of a dialog box.

Preface

Figure 3 Different components of a dialog box

Drop-down

A drop-down is the one in which a set of common tools are grouped together for performing an action. You can identify a drop-down with a down arrow on it. The drop-downs are given a name based on the tools grouped in them. For example, **Wall** drop-down, **Component** drop-down, **Region** drop-down, and so on, refer to Figure 4.

Figure 4 Choosing a tool from the drop-down

Drop-down List

A drop-down list is the one in which a set of options are grouped together. You can set various parameters using these options. You can identify a drop-down list with a down arrow on it. For example, **Type Selector** drop-down list, **Units** drop-down list, and so on; refer to Figure 5.

Figure 5 Selecting an option from the **Type Selector** drop-down list

Options

Options are the items that are available in shortcut menus, drop-down lists, dialog boxes, drop-down lists, and so on. For example, choose the **Zoom In Region** option from the shortcut menu displayed on right-clicking in the drawing area; refer to Figure 6.

Free Companion Website

It has been our constant endeavor to provide you the best textbooks and services at affordable price. In this endeavor, we have come out with a free Companion website that will facilitate the process of teaching and learning of Autodesk Revit Architecture 2015. If you purchase this textbook, you will get access to the files on the Companion website.

The following resources are available for the faculty and students in this website:

Faculty Resources
- **Technical Support**
  You can get online technical support by contacting *techsupport@cadcim.com*.

Figure 6 Choosing an option from the shortcut menu

- **Instructor Guide**
  Solutions to all review questions and exercises in the
  textbook are provided in this guide to help the faculty members test the skills of the students.

- **PowerPoint Presentations**
  The contents of the book are arranged in PowerPoint slides that can be used by the faculty for their lectures.

- **Part Files**
  The part files used in illustration, tutorials, and exercises are available for free download.

- **Learning Resources**
  Additional Learning Resources at:
  http:/revitxperts.blogspot.com and *http:/youtube. com/cadcimtech*

Student Resources

- **Technical Support**
  You can get online technical support by contacting ***techsupport@cadcim.com***.

- **Part Files**
  The part files used in illustrations and tutorials are available for free download.

Visit the following link to access the student resources:
http://www.cadcim.com

Stay Connected

You can now stay connected with us through Facebook and Twitter to get the latest information about our textbooks, videos, and teaching/learning resources. To get such updates, follow us on Facebook (www.facebook.com/cadcim) and Twitter (@cadcimtech). You can also subscribe to our YouTube channel (www.youtube.com/cadcimtech) to get the information about our latest video tutorials.

If you face any problem in accessing these files, please contact the publisher at *sales@cadcim.com* or the author at *stickoo@purduecal.edu* or *tickoo525@gmail.com*

Chapter 1

Introduction to Autodesk Revit Architecture 2015

Learning Objectives

After completing this chapter, you will be able to:
- Understand the basic concepts and principles of Revit Architecture 2015.
- Understand different terms used in Revit Architecture.
- Know the parametric behavior of Revit Architecture.
- Use different components of the User Interface screen of Revit Architecture.
- Access the Revit 2015 Help and Autodesk WikiHelp.
- Know Worksharing using Revit Server.

INTRODUCTION TO Autodesk Revit Architecture

Welcome to the realm of Autodesk Revit Architecture, a powerful building modeler that has changed the outlook of the building industry about computer aided designs. Autodesk Revit Architecture is a design and documentation platform that enables you to use a single, integrated building information model to conceptualize, design, and finally document a project. Its integrated parametric modeling technology is used to create the information model of a project, and to collect and coordinate information across all its representations. In Autodesk Revit Architecture, drawing sheets, 2D views, 3D views, and schedules are a direct representation of the same building information model. Using its parametric change engine, you can modify a design at any stage of a project. The change in the project is automatically made and represented in all its views, resulting in the development of better designs, along with an improved coordination. The use of Autodesk Revit Architecture provides a competitive advantage and a higher profitability to architects and building industry professionals.

Autodesk Revit Architecture AS A BUILDING INFORMATION MODELER

The history of computer aided design and documentation dates back to the early 1980s when architects began using this technology for documenting their projects. Realizing its advantages, information sharing capabilities were developed, especially to share data with other consultants. This led to the development of object-based CAD systems in the early 1990s. Before the development of these systems, objects such as walls, doors, windows were stored as a non-graphical data with the assigned graphics. These systems arranged the information logically, but were unable to optimize its usage in a building project. Realizing the advantages of the solid modeling tools, the mechanical and manufacturing industry professionals began using the information modeling CAD technology. This technology enabled them to extract data based on the relationship between model elements.

In 1997, a group of mechanical CAD technologists began working on a new software for the building industry. The Building Information Modeling (BIM) provided an alternative approach to building design, construction, and management. This approach, however, required a suitable technology to implement and reap its benefits. In such a situation, the use of parametric technology with the Building Information Modeling approach was envisaged as an ideal combination. They developed a software that was suitable for creating building projects. This led to the development of a software that later came to be known as Autodesk Revit Building, and has now been changed to Autodesk Revit Architecture.

Autodesk Revit Architecture is a building design and documentation platform, in which a digital building model is created using the parametric elements such as walls, doors, windows, and so on. All the building elements have inherent relationship with one another, which can be tracked, managed, and maintained by the computer.

BASIC CONCEPTS AND PRINCIPLES

Autodesk Revit Architecture enables you to envisage and develop a building model with actual 3D parametric building elements. It provides a new approach to the architectural thought and the implementation process. In a way, it replicates the way architects conceive a building. For example, 2D CAD platforms mostly use lines to represent all elements, as shown in Figure 1-1. However, in Autodesk Revit Architecture, you can create a building model using 3D elements such as walls, floors, doors, and windows, as shown in Figure 1-2.

Figure 1-1 CAD project created using 2D lines and curves

Figure 1-2 Autodesk Revit Architecture project created using parametric building model

Using these 3D elements, you can visualize the architectural or interior project with respect to its scale, volume, and proportions. This enables you to study design alternatives and develop superior quality design solutions. Autodesk Revit Architecture automates routine drafting and coordination tasks and assists in reducing errors in documentation. This, in turn, saves time, improves the speed of documentation, and lowers the cost for users.

Understanding the Parametric Building Modeling Technology

A project in Autodesk Revit Architecture is created using the in-built parametric building elements. The term parametric refers to the relationship parameters between various building elements. Some relationships are made by Autodesk Revit Architecture itself, and others by the user. For example, doors, which have an inherent parametric relationship with walls cannot be created without first creating a host wall. A door always moves with the host wall. Similarly, floors too are parametrically linked to walls. When you move walls, the floor extents are also modified automatically. Each building element has in-built bidirectional associativity with many other elements in the project.

A building information model is created using different interdependent parametric building elements such as walls, floors, roof, ceiling, stairs, ramps, curtain walls, and so on. As they are bidirectionally associated elements, any change made in one element is automatically adopted by others. The integrated building information model thus created contains all the data for a project. You can then create project presentation views such as plans, sections, elevations, and so on for documentation. As you modify the model while working in certain views, Autodesk Revit Architecture's parametric change engine automatically updates other views. This capability is, therefore, the underlying concept in Autodesk Revit Architecture.

Autodesk Revit Architecture's parametric change engine enables you to modify design elements at any stage of the project development. As changes are made immediately and automatically, it saves the time and effort of coordinating them in all other associated views, which, for most projects, is an inevitable part of the design process. Autodesk Revit Architecture's capability to coordinate between various aspects of the building design provides immense flexibility in the design and development process along with an error-free documentation.

Autodesk Revit Architecture also provides a variety of in-built parametric element libraries that can be selected and used to create a building model. It also provides you with the flexibility of modifying properties of these elements or create your own parametric elements, based on the project requirement.

Terms Used in Autodesk Revit Architecture

Before using Autodesk Revit Architecture, it is important to understand the basic terms used for creating a building model. Various terms in Autodesk Revit Architecture such as project, level, category, family, type, and instance are described next.

Autodesk Revit Architecture Project

A project in Autodesk Revit Architecture is similar to an actual architectural or interior project. In an actual project, the entire documentation such as drawings, 3D views, specifications, schedules, cost estimates, and so on are inherently linked and read together. Similarly, in Autodesk Revit Architecture, a project not only includes the digital 3D building model but also its parametrically associated documentation. Thus, all the components such as the building model, its standard views, architectural drawings, and schedules combine together to form a complete project. A project file contains all the project information such as building elements used in a project, drawing sheets, schedules, cost estimates, 3D views, renderings, walkthroughs, and so on. A project file also stores various settings such as environment, lighting, and so on. As data is stored in the same file, it becomes easier for Autodesk Revit Architecture to coordinate the entire database.

Introduction to Autodesk Revit Architecture 2015

Levels in a Building Model
In Autodesk Revit Architecture, a building model is divided into different levels. These levels may be understood as infinite horizontal planes that act as hosts for different elements such as roof, floor, ceiling, and so on. The defined levels in a building model can, in most cases, relate to different floor levels, or stories of the building project. Each element that you create belongs to a particular level.

Subdivisions of Elements into Categories and Subcategories
Apart from building elements, an Autodesk Revit Architecture project also contains other associated elements such as annotations, imported files, links, and so on. These elements have been divided into following categories:

Model Category : Consists of various building elements used in creating a building model such as wall, floor, ceiling, roof, door, window, furniture, stairs, curtain systems, ramps, and so on

Annotation Category : Consists of annotations such as dimensions, text notes, tags, symbols, and so on

Datum Category : Consists of datums such as levels, grids, reference planes, and so on

View Category : Consists of interactive project views such as floor plans, ceiling plans, elevations, sections, 3D views, renderings, and walkthroughs

In addition to these four categories, other categories such as **Imported**, **Workset**, **Filter**, and **Revit Categories** can also exist if the project has imported files, enabled worksets, or linked Autodesk Revit Architecture projects, respectively.

Families in Autodesk Revit Architecture
Another powerful concept in Autodesk Revit Architecture is family. A family is described as a set of elements of the same category that can be grouped together based on certain common parameters or characteristics. Elements of the same family may have different properties, but they all have common characteristics. For example, **Double Hung** is a single window family, but it contains different sizes of double hung windows. Family files have a *.rfa* extension. You can load additional building component families from the libraries provided in Autodesk Revit Architecture package.

Families are further divided into certain types. Type or family type, as it is called, is a specific size or style of a family. For example, **Double Hung : 36" x 48"** is a window type. All uses of the same family type in a project have same properties. Family and family types can also be used to create new families using the **Family Editor**.

Instances are the actual usage of model elements in a building model or annotations in a drawing sheet. A family type created in a new location is identified as an instance of the family type. All instances of the same family type have same properties. Therefore, when you modify the properties of a family type, the properties of all its instances also get modified. The family categorization of Revit elements is given below:

Model Category : Wall
Family : Basic Wall
Family type : Brick on Mtl. Studs
Instance : Particular usage of a family type

The hierarchy of building elements in Autodesk Revit Architecture plays an important role in providing the flexibility and ease of managing a change in the building model. Figure 1-3 shows the hierarchy of categories and families in a typical Autodesk Revit Architecture project. The following is another example of the terms described in this section.

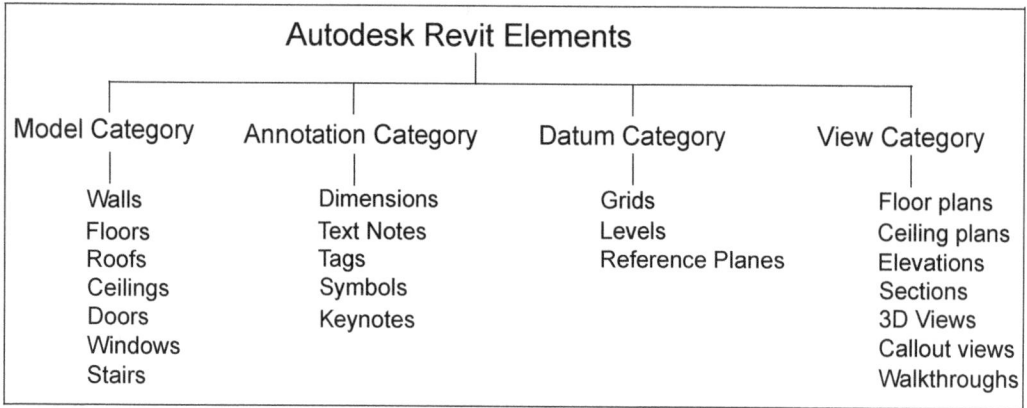

Figure 1-3 Hierarchy of Autodesk Revit Architecture categories and families

Creating a Building Model Using Parametric Building Elements

Another classification of categories of elements followed in Autodesk Revit Architecture is based on their usage. Autodesk Revit Architecture uses five classes of elements: host, component, annotation, view, and datum. Hosts are the element categories that form the basic structure of a building model and include model elements such as walls, floor, roof, and ceiling. Components are the elements that are added to host elements or act as stand-alone elements such as doors, windows, and furniture. Annotations are the 2D, view-specific elements that add content to the project documentation such as dimensions, tags, text notes, and so on. Views represent various orientations of a building model such as plans, elevations, sections, 3D views, and so on. Datum refers to the reference elements that assist you in creating a building model, which include grids, levels, reference planes, and so on.

There is no specific methodology available for creating a building model in Autodesk Revit Architecture. It provides you with the flexibility of generating building geometry based on the project requirement, design complexity, and other factors. However, the following steps describe a general procedure that may be followed for creating an architectural building model using the in-built parametric elements provided in Autodesk Revit Architecture.

The first step is to create the exterior walls of a building at the predefined lowest level (level 1). Next, create interior walls at that level and add components to the building model. Then, define the upper levels based on the story height of the building. You can also link the control height of the walls to the levels and extend the exterior walls to their full height. Next, create floors and roof using the defined levels. Add the site topography to the building model and then add site components to complete the building project. You can then create drawing sheets with the desired views for its presentation. Autodesk Revit Architecture also provides tools to create rendered 3D views and walkthroughs. Figure 1-4 shows an example of a building section with various building elements and annotations.

Figure 1-4 Building section showing building elements and levels

Visibility/Graphics Overrides, Scale, and Detail Level

Autodesk Revit Architecture enables you to control the display and graphic representation of a single element or the element category of various elements in project views by using the visibility and graphics overrides tools. You can select a model category and modify its linetype and detail level. This can also be done for various annotation category elements and imported files. These settings can be done for each project view based on its desired representation. You can also hide an element or an element category in a view using the **Hide in View** and **Isolate** tools. You can override the graphic representation of an element or an element category in any view using the **Visibility/Graphics** tool.

The scale is another important concept in an Autodesk Revit Architecture project. You can set the scale for each project view by selecting it from the available list of standard scales such as 1/16"=1'0" (1:192), 1/4"=1'0" (1:48), 1"=1'0" (1:12), 1/2"=1'0" (1:24), and so on. As you set a scale, Autodesk Revit Architecture automatically sets the detail level appropriate for it. There are three detail levels provided in an Autodesk Revit Architecture project: **Coarse**, **Medium**, and **Fine**. You can also set the detail level manually for each project view. Each detail level has an associated linetype and the detail lines associated with it. The details of annotations such as dimensions, tags, and so on are also defined by the selected scale.

Extracting the Project Information

A single integrated building information is used to create and represent a building project. You can extract project information from a building model and create area schemes, schedule, and cost estimates, and then add them to the project presentation.

Autodesk Revit Architecture also enables you to export the extracted database to the industry standard Open Database Connectivity (ODBC) compliant relational database tables. The use of the building information model to extract database information eliminates the error-prone method of measuring building spaces individually.

Creating an Architectural Drawing Set

After creating the building model, you can easily arrange the project views by plotting them on drawing sheets. Drawing sheets can also be organized in a project file based on the established CAD standards followed by the firm. In this manner, the project documentation can easily be transformed from the conceptual design stage to the design development stage and finally to the construction document stage. The project view on a drawing sheet is only a graphical representation of the building information model and therefore, any modification in it is immediately made in all the associated project views, keeping the drawings set always updated.

Creating an Unusual Building Geometry

Autodesk Revit Architecture also helps you conceptualize a building project in terms of its volume, shape, and proportions before working with the actual building elements. This is possible by using the **Massing** tool, which enables you to create quick 3D models of buildings and conduct volumetric and proportion study on overall masses. It also enables you to visualize and create an unusual building geometry. The same massing model can then be converted into a building model with individual parametric building elements. It provides continuity in the generation of building model right from sketch design to its development.

Flexibility of Creating Special Elements

Autodesk Revit Architecture provides a large number of in-built family types of various model elements and annotations. Each parametric element has the associated properties that can be modified based on the project requirement.

Autodesk Revit Architecture also enables you to create the elements that are designed specifically for a particular location. The in-built family editor enables you to create new elements using family templates. This provides you with the flexibility of using in-built elements for creating your own elements. For example, using the furniture template, you can create a reception desk that is suitable for a particular location in the design.

Creating Structural Layouts

Autodesk Revit Architecture's structural tools enable you to add structural elements to a building model. An extensive in-built library of structural elements has been provided in Autodesk Revit Architecture. You can add structural columns, beams, walls, braces, and so on to the project. Thus, structural consultants can also incorporate their elements in the basic architectural building model and check for inconsistency, if any.

Working on Large Projects

In Autodesk Revit Architecture, you can work on large projects by linking different building projects together. For a large project that consists of a number of buildings, you can create individual buildings as separate projects and then link all of them into a single base file. The database recognizes the linked projects and includes them in the project representation of the base file.

For example, while working on a large campus of an educational institution, you can create separate project files for academic building, administration area, gymnasium, cafeteria, computer centre, and so on, and then link them into the base site plan file. In this manner, large projects can be subdivided and worked upon simultaneously.

Working in Large Teams and Coordinating with Consultants

Worksets, in Autodesk Revit Architecture, enable the division of the building model into small editable set of elements. The worksets can be assigned to different teams working on the same project and then their work can easily be coordinated in the central file location. The effort required to coordinate, collaborate, and communicate the changes between various worksets is taken care of by computer. Various consultants working on a project can be assigned a workset with a set of editable elements. They can then incorporate their services and modify the associated elements.

For example, a high rise commercial building project can be divided into different worksets with independent teams working on exterior skin, interior walls, building core, toilet details, finishes, and so on. The structural consultants can be assigned the exterior skin and the core workset, in which they can incorporate structural elements. Similarly, the rest of the teams can work independently on different worksets.

STARTING Autodesk Revit Architecture 2015

When you turn on your computer, the operating system is automatically loaded. You can start Autodesk Revit Architecture by double-clicking on the **Revit Architecture 2015** icon on the desktop. Alternatively, choose the **Start > All Programs > Autodesk > Revit Architecture 2015 > Revit Architecture 2015** from the taskbar, as shown in Figure 1-5; the user interface screen of Revit Architecture 2015 will be displayed, as shown in Figure 1-6.

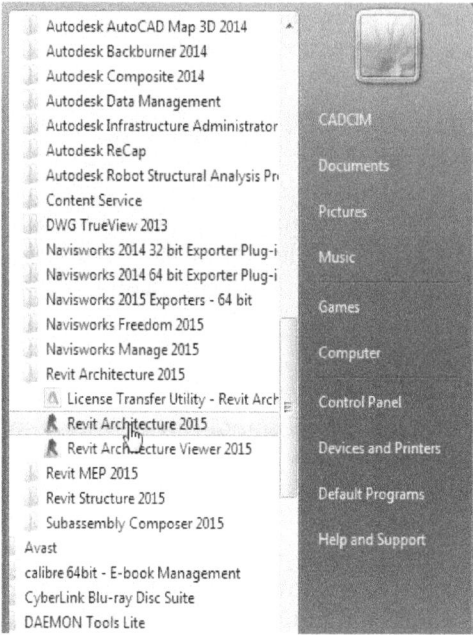

Figure 1-5 Starting Autodesk Revit Architecture 2015 using the taskbar

Note
The path for starting Autodesk Revit Architecture depends on the Operating System being used.

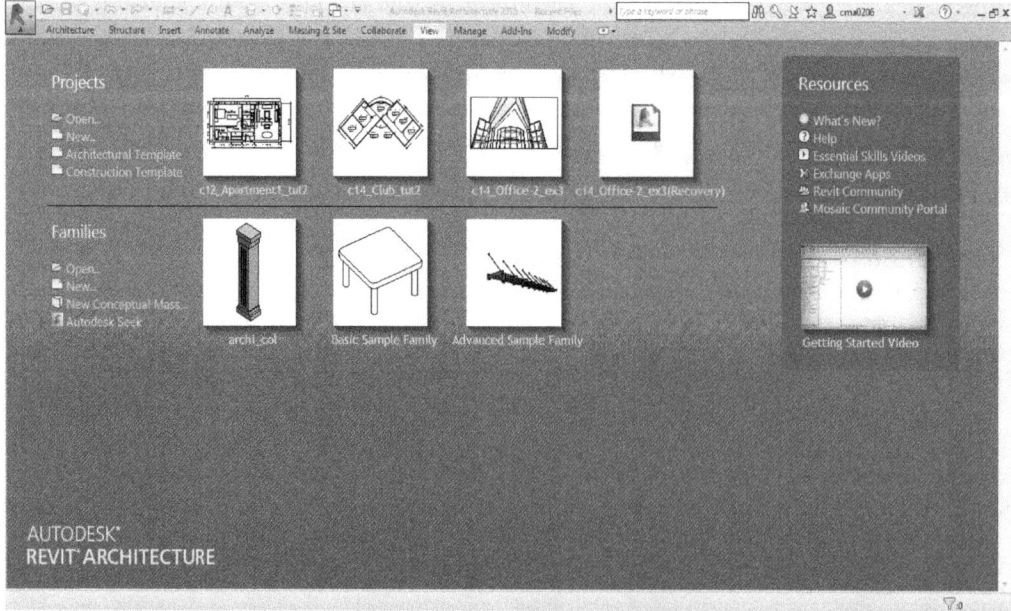

Figure 1-6 The interface screen of Autodesk Revit Architecture 2015

Introduction to Autodesk Revit Architecture 2015

The interface screen has three sections: **Projects**, **Families**, and **Resources**. The options in the **Projects** section are used to open an existing project, a new project, and an existing template. The options in the **Families** section are used to open a new or an existing family. You can also invoke the Conceptual Mass environment from this section to create a conceptual mass model. If you choose the **Autodesk Seek** option from the **Families** section, you will be directed to the *http://seek.autodesk.com/localeTaxBrowse.htm?category=en_us:adsk:revit-arch&locale=en-us&globaldd =globaldropdown.option.b* link and the **Autodesk® Revit Architecture Web Library - US Edition** page will open. From this page, you can download various components for your project.

In the **Resources** section of the interface screen, you can choose the **What's New?** option to get information about the new tools and features in Autodesk Revit Architecture 2015. In addition, you can choose the **Help** option from the **Resources** section to view help resources related to Revit software. On choosing the **Help** option, you will be directed to *http://help.autodesk. com/view/RVT/2015/ENU/* link and the **Autodesk WikiHelp** page with the **Revit 2015** page will open. In the **Community Learning** section, there are two areas: **Browse Help** and **Add Knowledge**. In the **Browse Help** area, you can choose various links to access help documents related to Revit 2015 release. For example, to access information related to additions and enhancements in Revit 2015 release, you can choose the **New in Revit 2015** link. On doing so, the **New in Revit 2015** page will be displayed with various links. You can know about various enhancements through these links. In the **Revit 2015** page, you can use various options in the **Add Knowledge** area to contribute resources in the form of articles, tutorials, and videos to the Autodesk WikiHelp.

In the **Resources** section of the Autodesk Revit Architecture 2015 interface screen, you can choose **Essential Skills Videos** to get basic information about using Revit Architecture. These videos and their associated information help you to learn about the complete software. Moreover, you can choose the **Exchange Apps** option to access various add-ons that can be used to enhance the productivity of Revit. On choosing this option, the **Autodesk Exchange| Apps** page will be displayed. In this page, various links, are available as add-ons which can be used in Revit applications. In **Revit Community** of the **Resources** section, you can access information related to various communities and their contribution in form of articles, tutorials, and videos. The **Mosaic Community Portal** in the **Resources** section is used to open the mosaic projects on the web. The mosaic projects is an initiative of Autodesk, which is an online peer-to peer (P2P) resource for Autodesk Revit and AutoCAD Civil 3D users.

In the **Projects** section, choose the **Open** option; the **Open** dialog box will be displayed. Browse to the desired location in the dialog box and select the file. Now, choose the **Open** button to open the file.

To open a new project file, choose the **New** option from the **Projects** section. Alternatively, choose **New > Project** from the **Application Menu**; the **New Project** dialog box will be displayed. In this dialog box, you can select the desired template from the **Template file** drop down or you can browse the other template files, by choosing the **Browse** button from the **Choose Template** dialog box. In this dialog box, make sure that the **Project** radio button is selected, and then choose the **OK** button; a new project file will open and the interface screen will be activated.

USER INTERFACE

In Autodesk Revit Architecture 2015 has ribbon interface. The ribbon, which contains task-based tabs and panels, streamlines the architectural workflow and optimizes the project delivery time. In Autodesk Revit Architecture 2015, when you select an element in the drawing area, the ribbon displays a contextual tab that comprises of tools corresponding to the selected element. The interface of Autodesk Revit Architecture is similar to the interfaces of many other Microsoft Windows based programs. The main parts in the Revit interface are **Ribbon**, **Options Bar**, **Project Browser**, **Drawing Area**, **Status Bar**, and **View Control Bar**, as shown in Figure 1-7.

*Figure 1-7 The **Autodesk Revit Architecture 2015** user interface screen*

Invoking Tools

To perform an operation, you can invoke the required tools by using any one of the following two options:

Ribbon: You can invoke all necessary tools from the ribbon.

Shortcut Keys: Some tools can also be invoked by using the keys on the keyboard.

Title Bar

The Title bar, docked on the top portion of the user interface, displays the program's logo, program's name, name of the current project, and the view opened in the viewing area. **Project 1- Floor Plan: Level 1** is the default project and view.

Ribbon

The ribbon, as shown in Figure 1-8, is an interface that is used to invoke tools. When you open a file, the ribbon is displayed at the top in the screen. It comprises of task-based tabs

Introduction to Autodesk Revit Architecture 2015

and panels, refer to Figure 1-8, which provide all the tools necessary for creating a project. The tabs and panels in the ribbon can be customized according to the need of the user. This can be done by moving the panels and changing the view states of the ribbon (changing the ribbon view state is discussed later in this chapter). The ribbon has three types of buttons are available in: general button, drop-down button, and split button. These buttons can be used from the panels.

Figure 1-8 Different components of a ribbon

Moving the Panels

In the ribbon, you can move a panel and place it anywhere on the screen. To do so, press and hold the left mouse button on the panel label in the ribbon, drag it to desired place on the screen. Next, use the tools of the moved panel and place the panel back to the ribbon. To do so, place the cursor on the moved panel and choose the **Return Panels to Ribbon** button from the upper right corner of this panel, as shown in Figure 1-9; the panel will return to the ribbon.

*Figure 1-9 Choosing the **Return Panels to Ribbon** button*

Changing the View States of the Ribbon

The ribbon can be displayed in three view states by selecting any of the following four options: **Minimize to Tabs**, **Minimize to Panel Titles**, **Minimize to Panel Buttons**, and **Cycle through all**. To use these options, move the cursor and place it over the second arrow on the right of the **Modify** tab, refer to Figure 1-10 in the ribbon; the arrow will be highlighted. Now, click on the down arrow; a flyout will be displayed, as shown in Figure 1-10. In this flyout, you can choose the **Minimize to Tabs** option to display only the tabs in the ribbon. If you choose the **Minimize to Panel Titles** option, the ribbon will display the titles of the panels along with the tabs. You can choose the **Minimize to Panel Buttons** option to display the panels as buttons in the ribbon along with tabs.

Figure 1-10 Various options in the flyout for changing the view state of the ribbon

Tip: *Tooltips appear when you rest the cursor over any tool icon in the ribbon. The name of the tool appears in the box, assisting you to identify each tool icon.*

Note

*If the ribbon is changed to a different view state, place the cursor over the first arrow at the right of the **Modify** tab, the **Show Full Ribbon** tooltip will be displayed. Click on the arrow; the full ribbon will be displayed.*

The following table describes various tabs in the ribbon and their functions:

Tab	Description
Architecture	Contains tools for creating architectural elements for a project
Structure	Contains tools for creating structural elements in a project
Create	This tab is available in family editor. It contains tools that are used to create a family
Insert	Contains tools to insert or manage secondary files such as raster image files or CAD files
Annotate	Contains tools for documenting a building model such as adding texts and dimensions
Massing & Site	Contains tools for modeling and modifying conceptual mass and site elements
Analyze	Contains tools for energy analysis of the project
Collaborate	Contains tools for collaborating the project with other team members (internal and external)
View	Contains tools used for managing and modifying the current view and also for switching views
Manage	Contains tools for specifying the project and system parameters and project settings
Modify	Contains tools for editing elements in the model

Contextual Tabs in the Ribbon

These tabs are displayed when you choose certain tools or select elements. These tabs contain a set of tools or buttons that relate only to a particular tool or element. For example, when you invoke the **Window** tool, the **Modify | Place Window** contextual tab is displayed. This tab shows ten panels: **Select, Properties, View, Measure, Geometry, Clipboard, Create, Modify, Mode,** and **Tag**. The **Select** panel contains the **Modify** tool. The **Properties** panel contains the **Properties** button and the **Type Properties** tool. The **Mode** panel has some necessary tools that are used to load model families or to create the model of a window in a drawing. The other panels, apart from those discussed above, contain the tools that are contextual and are used to edit elements when they are placed in a drawing or selected from a drawing for modification.

Application Frame

The application frame helps you manage projects in Autodesk Revit Architecture. It consists of **Application** button, **Application Menu**, **Quick Access Toolbar**, **InfoCenter**, and **Status Bar**. These are discussed next.

Application Button

The **Application** button is displayed at the top-left corner of the Revit interface. This button is used to display as well as close the **Application Menu**.

Application Menu

The **Application Menu** contains the tools that provide access to many common file actions such as **Open**, **Close**, and **Save**. Click the down arrow on the **Application** button to display the **Application Menu**, as shown in Figure 1-11. Alternatively, press ALT+F to display tools in the **Application Menu**.

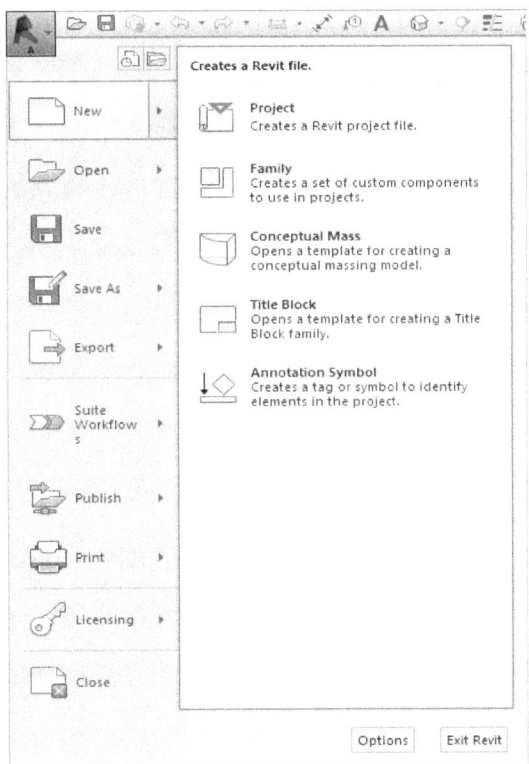

Figure 1-11 The Application Menu

Quick Access Toolbar

The **Quick Access Toolbar**, as shown in Figure 1-12, contains the options to undo and redo changes, open and save a file, create a new file, and so on.

By default, the **Quick Access Toolbar** contains the following options: **Open**, **Save**, **Redo**, **Undo**, and others. You can customize the display of the **Quick Access Toolbar** by adding more tools and removing the unwanted tools. To add a tool or a button from the panel of the ribbon to the **Quick Access Toolbar**, place the cursor over the button; the button will be highlighted. Next, right-click; a flyout will be displayed. Choose **Add Quick Access Toolbar** from the flyout displayed; the highlighted button will be added to **Quick Access Toolbar**. The **Quick Access Toolbar** can be customized to re-order the tools displayed in it. To do so, choose the down arrow next to the **Switch Windows** drop-down, refer to Figure 1-12; a flyout will be displayed. Choose the **Customize Quick Access Toolbar** option located at the bottom of the flyout; the **Customize Quick Access Toolbar** dialog box will be displayed. Use various options in this dialog box and choose the **OK** button; the **Customize Quick Access Toolbar** dialog box will close and the tools in the **Quick Access Toolbar** will be re-ordered.

Figure 1-12 The Quick Access Toolbar

InfoCenter

You can use the **InfoCenter** to search the information related to Revit Architecture (Help), display the **Subscription Center** panel for subscription services and product updates, and display the **Favorites** panel to access saved topics. Also in the **InfoCenter**, you can use the **Autodesk 360** and the **Exchange Apps** options to log-in to **Autodesk 360** and **Autodesk Exchange Apps** pages. Figure 1-13 displays various tools in **InfoCenter**.

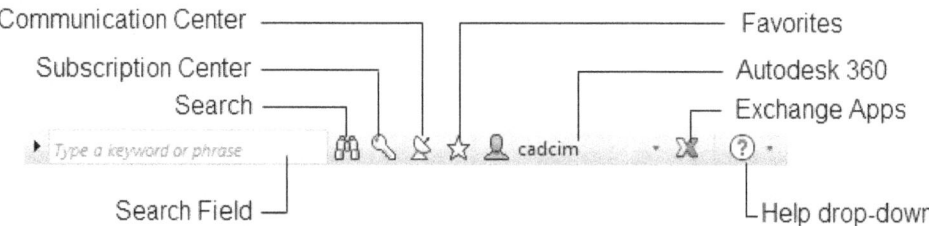

Figure 1-13 The InfoCenter

Status Bar

The **Status Bar** is located at the bottom of the interface screen. When the cursor is placed over an element or component, the **Status Bar** displays the name of the family and type of the corresponding element or components. It also displays prompts and messages to help you use the selected tools.

View Control Bar

The **View Control Bar** is located at the lower left corner of the drawing window, as shown in Figure 1-14. It can be used to access various view-related tools. The **Scale** button shows the scale of the current view. You can choose this button to display a flyout that contains standard drawing scales. From this flyout, you can then select the scale for the current view. The **Detail Level** button is used to set the detail level of a view. You can select the required detail level as **Coarse**, **Medium**, and **Fine**. Similarly, the **Visual Style** button enables you to set the display style. The options for setting the display style are: **Wireframe**, **Hidden Line**, **Shaded**, **Consistent Colors**, **Realistic**, and **Raytrace**.

Figure 1-14 The View Control Bar

Options Bar

The **Options Bar** provides information about the common parameters of component type and the options for creating or editing. The **Options Bar** changes its appearance based on the type of component selected or being created. You can also modify the properties of the component by entering a new value in the edit box for the corresponding parameter in the **Options Bar**. For example, the **Options Bar** for the **Wall** tool displays various options to create a wall, as shown in Figure 1-15.

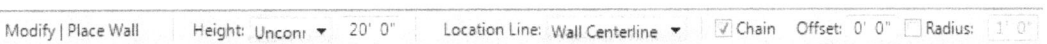

*Figure 1-15 The **Options Bar** with different options to create a wall*

Type Selector

The **Type Selector** drop-down list is located in the **Properties** palette of the currently invoked tool. For example, if you invoke the **Wall** tool, all the properties of the wall will be displayed in the **Properties** palette. In the **Properties** palette, you can use the **Type Selector** drop-down list to select the required type of the wall. The options in the **Type Selector** drop-down list keep on changing based on the current function of the tool or the elements selected. When you place an element or a component in a drawing, you can use the **Type Selector** drop-down list to specify the type of element or component. You can also use this drop-down list to change the existing type of a selected element to a different type. In Autodesk Revit Architecture, you can add the **Type Selector** drop-down list to the **Quick Access Toolbar**. To do so, right-click on the **Type Selector** drop-down list in the **Properties** palette and choose the **Quick Access Toolbar** option from the flyout displayed.

Drawing Area

The Drawing Area is the actual modeling area where you can create and view the building model. It covers the major portion of the interface screen. You can draw various building components in this area using the pointing device. The position of the pointing device is represented by the cursor. The Drawing Area also has the standard Microsoft Windows functions and buttons such as close, minimize, maximize, scroll bar, and so on. These buttons have the same function as that of the other Microsoft Windows-based programs.

Project Browser

The **Project Browser** is located below the ribbon. It displays project views, schedules, sheets, families, and groups in a logical, tree-like structure, as shown in Figure 1-16, and helps you open and manage them. To open a view, double-click on the name of the view; the corresponding view will be displayed in the drawing area. You can close the **Project Browser** or dock it anywhere in the drawing area.

Note
If the Project Browser is not displayed on the screen, choose the View tab from the ribbon and then click on the User Interface drop-down from the Windows panel. Next, select the Project Browser check box from the flyout displayed.

The **Project Browser** can be organized to group the views and sheets based on the project requirement. For example, while working on a large project with a number of sheets, you can organize the **Project Browser** to view and access specific sheets.

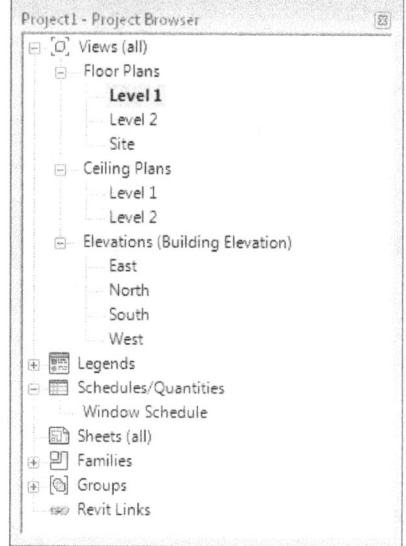
Figure 1-16 The Project Browser

Note
In the Project Browser, you can expand or collapse the view listing by selecting the '+' or '-' sign, respectively. The current view in the drawing window is highlighted in bold letters. The default project file has a set of preloaded views.

Keyboard Accelerators

In Autodesk Revit Architecture, accelerator keys have been assigned to some of the frequently used tools. These keys are shortcuts that you can type through the keyboard to invoke the corresponding tool. Accelerator keys corresponding to a tool appear as a tooltip when you move the cursor over the tool. In Autodesk Revit Architecture 2015, you can export all commands (even if they do not have shortcut keys assigned) to a XML file. You can further edit the XML file to assign shortcut keys to commands, and then import them back to be used in Revit.

Properties palette

The **Properties** palette, as shown in Figure 1-17, is a modeless interface, which displays the type and element properties

Figure 1-17 The Properties palette

of various elements and views in a drawing. The **Properties** palette is dockable and resizable, and it supports multiple monitor configurations. The **Properties** palette is displayed in the Revit interface by default and it shows the instance properties of an active view. When you select an element from a drawing, the **Properties** palette displays its instance properties. You can also access the **Type Properties** of the selected element from the **Properties** palette. To do so, choose the **Edit Type** button from the palette; the **Type Properties** dialog box will be displayed. In this dialog box, you can change the **Type Properties** of the selected element. In the **Properties** palette, you can assign a type to a selected element in a drawing from the **Type Selector** drop-down list. In Revit Architecture, you can toggle the display of the **Properties** palette in its interface. Choose the **Properties** button in the **Properties** panel of the **Modify** tab to hide it. Similarly, you can choose the **Properties** button to display the palette if it is not visible in the interface.

DIALOG BOXES

Certain Autodesk Revit Architecture tools when invoked, display a dialog box. A dialog box is a convenient method of accessing and modifying the parameters related to that tool. For example, when you choose **Save As > Project** from **Application Menu**, the **Save As** dialog box will be displayed, as shown in Figure 1-18. A dialog box consists of various parts such as dialog label, radio buttons, text or edit boxes, check boxes, slider bars, image box, and tool buttons, which are similar to other windows-based programs. Some dialog boxes contain the [...] button. On choosing such buttons, another related dialog box will be displayed. There are certain buttons such as **OK**, **Cancel**, and **Help**, which appear at the bottom of most of the dialog boxes. The names of the buttons imply their respective functions. The button with a dark border is the default button.

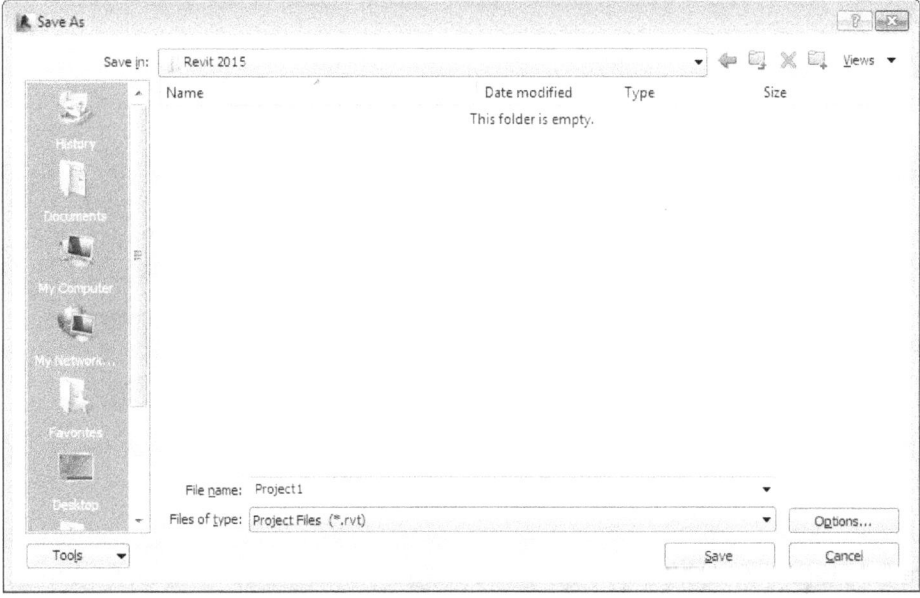

Figure 1-18 The **Save As** *dialog box*

MULTIPLE DOCUMENT ENVIRONMENT

The multiple document environment feature allows you to open more than one project at a time in a single Autodesk Revit Architecture session. This is very useful when you want to work on different projects simultaneously and make changes with reference to each other.

Sometimes, you may need to incorporate certain features from one project into the other. With the help of multiple document environments, you can open multiple projects and then use the **Cut**, **Copy**, and **Paste** tools from the **Clipboard** panel of the **Modify (type of element)** tab to transfer the required components from one project to another. These editing tools can also be invoked by using the CTRL+C and CTRL+V keyboard shortcuts.

To access the opened projects, choose the **Switch Windows** drop-down from the **Windows** panel of the **View** tab; a menu will be displayed showing the name of different project files opened, as shown in Figure 1-19. Like other Microsoft Windows-based programs, you can select and view the opened projects using the **Cascade** and **Tile** tools from the **Windows** panel of the **View** tab. The cascaded view of projects, as shown in Figure 1-20.

Figure 1-19 Selecting an option from the Switch Windows drop-down

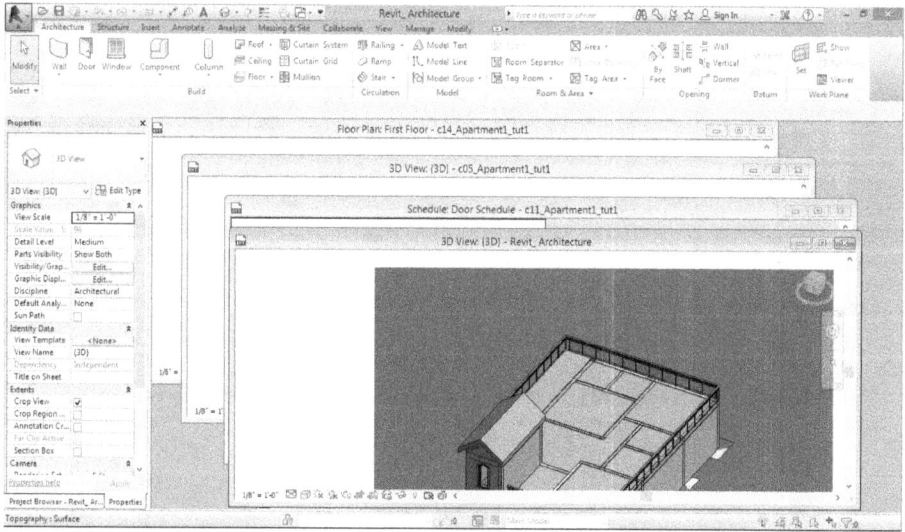

Figure 1-20 The cascaded view of the projects

INTEROPERABILITY OF Autodesk Revit Architecture

The models or geometries created in Revit Architecture can easily be exported to AutoCAD based programs, such as 3ds Max and Max Design in the DWG file format. This enables you to visualize and create photorealistic exterior and interior renderings for your project designs. You can also transfer drawings from Revit Architecture to Google SketchUp to visualize your projects in a better way.

Revit Architecture 2015 follows a wide range of industry standards and supports various CAD file formats such as DWG, DXF, DWF, DGN, FBX, and SAT. For image files, it supports JPG, TIFF, BMP, PNG, AVI, PAN, IVR, and TGA file formats. Besides these, the formats that are supported by Revit Architecture include ODBC, HTML, TXT, gbXML, XLS, and MDB. Revit Architecture is compatible with any CAD system that supports the DWG, DXF, or DGN file format. Revit Architecture can import the models and geometries as ACIS solids. This enables designers to import models from AutoCAD Architecture and AutoCAD MEP (Mechanical, Electrical, and Plumbing) software and to link and import 3D information to Revit Architecture. This feature makes Autodesk Revit Architecture 2015 an efficient, user-friendly, and compatible software.

In Autodesk Revit Architecture 2015, you can directly link the Revit files into 3ds Max Design and load selected views in it. You can also override material in 3ds Max Design and retain its settings when you reload Revit link file. Also, in 3ds Max Design, you can add high level of detail to curved objects to make them smooth. In Autodesk Revit Architecture 2015, the interoperability with V8 Microstation has been introduced. The V8 Microstation files can be imported to the Revit project. In addition to these, mapping functionality for levels, lines, line weights, patterns, and texts and fonts has been added to the export DGN workflow.

BUILDING INFORMATION MODELING AND Autodesk Revit Architecture 2015

Building Information Modeling (BIM) is defined as a design technology that involves the creation and use of coordinated, internally consistent, and computable information about a building project in design and construction. BIM covers spatial relationships, geographic information, quantities, and properties of building components. Using this technology, you can demonstrate the entire life cycle of a building project starting from the process of construction, facility operation, and information about quantities and shared properties of elements. BIM enables the circulation of virtual information model from the design team to contractors and then to the owner, thereby adding changes and their knowledge to update the model at each stage of transfer. The ability to keep information up-to-date and make it available in an integrated digital environment enables the architects, owners, builders, and engineers to have clear vision of the project before the commencement of actual construction. It enables them to make better and faster decisions as well as to improve the quality and profitability of projects. Autodesk Revit Architecture 2015 is a specially designed platform based on BIM. Revit Architecture 2015 is the best example of the BIM technology. Revit Architecture's parametric model represents a building as an integrated database of coordinated information. In Revit, change anywhere is change everywhere. Any change made in your project at any stage is reflected in the entire project, and also, due to the parametric behavior of elements, the project is updated automatically according to the changes made anywhere in the project. Also, the integration of Revit Architecture with the available in-built commercial tools such as solar studies, material takeoffs, greatly simplifies the project design and reduces the time consumed by these analyses, thereby enabling faster decision making.

Autodesk Revit Architecture HELP

Autodesk Revit Architecture provides help to easily understand various tools and methods used in it. In Autodesk Revit Architecture 2015, you can access online help documentation.

To access the help feature, click on the **Help** down arrow on the right of the **InfoCenter**; a flyout containing help options will be displayed, as shown in Figure 1-21. Various options to access the help are discussed next.

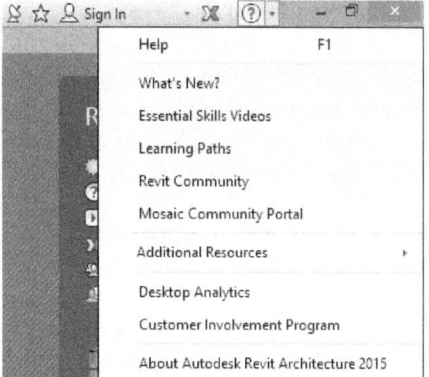

Figure 1-21 A drop-down menu displaying help options

Using the Revit Architecture 2015 Help

You can access Revit Architecture 2015 help when you are online. To do so, choose the **Help** tool from the InfoCenter bar; the **Revit Help** page will be displayed, as shown in Figure 1-22. In this page, there are two tabs that contain information of help topics. These tabs are discussed next.

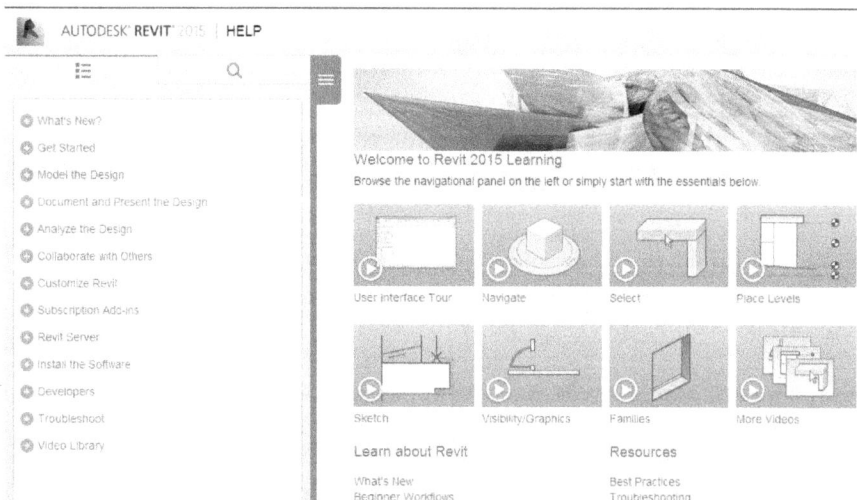

*Figure 1-22 The partial view of the **Revit Help** page*

Contents Tab

By default, this tab is chosen in the **Revit Help** page. In this tab, the **New in Revit 2015** link is selected by default. As a result, the **New in Revit 2015** page is displayed with the information about the new and enhanced features that are introduced in Autodesk Revit Architecture

2015. Information related to various features such as Platform Enhancement, Architectural Enhancement, MEP Enhancement, Structural Enhancement, and Revit Server is displayed in this page.

In the **Contents** tab, various options such as **What's New**, **Introduction to Revit**, **Start a Project**, and so on will be displayed. You can use these options to access information on the new features introduced, how to start a project and so on.

The subscription feature links such as **Revit Server**, **Essential Skill Videos**, **Technical Support** and **Legal Notices** help you to know about the add-ons that are available to the subscribers.

Search Tab

In Autodesk Revit Architecture, you can access the help files. To do so, choose the **Search** tab; a page that will help you to search topics in Revit will be displayed. Type a keyword in the **Search help for** edit box and choose the **Search** button; the topics related to the search will be displayed in the area below the edit box. In the **Search method** area, you can use various options to do advanced searches regarding the related topics in Revit.

WORKSHARING USING REVIT SERVER

Worksharing is a method of distributing work among team involved in a project, and accomplishing it within the stipulated period of time. In worksharing, each person involved in the project is assigned a task that has to be accomplished by proper planning and by coordinating with the other members of the team.

In a large scale building project, worksharing helps in finishing a project in time and meeting the quality requirements that are set during the process. Generally, in a large scale building project, worksharing is based on the specialization of work. The professionals such as structural engineers, architects, interior architects, and MEP engineers are involved in their respective fields to accomplish the project. So, the distribution of work at the primary stage is made on the basis of the area of specialization. Each professional has his own set of work to perform for the accomplishment of the project.

In Autodesk Revit Architecture 2015, you can apply server-based worksharing with the help of Revit Server, which is a server application. Revit Server uses a central server and multiple local servers for collaborating across a Wide Area Network (WAN). The central server hosts the central model of a workshared project and remain accessible to all team members over the Wide Area Network. Similarly, the local server is accessible to all team members in a Local Area Network (LAN). The local server hosts a local updated copy of the central model. In the Worksharing environment, the team members are not aware of the local server, as it is transparent in their daily operations. Refer to Figure 1-23 for the network model of Revit Server.

In Worksharing environment, a team member starts working on the local model of the central model. The local model will be saved in the computer of the team member. As the team member works, the local server requests updated information from the central model on the central server using available network capacity to transfer the data over the WAN. The updated version of the model is stored on the local server, so the updates are readily available when a team member requests them.

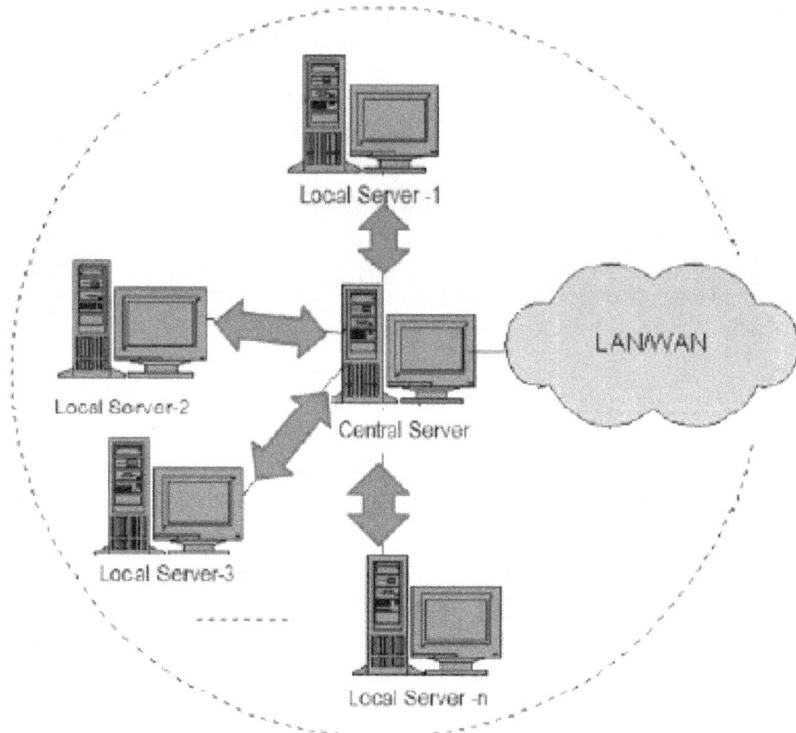

Figure 1-23 The Network model of Revit Server

WORKING WITH BIM 360

In Revit Architecture 2015, BIM 360 has been introduced as an add-in. BIM 360 is a cloud based BIM management and collaboration solution. It is used for publishing models on the BIM 360 cloud and for sharing latest project information within a team. This add-in allows you to perform several functions such as opening model from BIM 360 Glue to Architecture, appending models from BIM 360 Glue to the current model in Arcitecture, and sharing models with BIM 360 Glue. These functions are discussed next.

Sharing Models With BIM 360

In BIM 360, you can use the **Glue** tool to share models with the BIM 360 cloud, which can be shared further within a team. To share model with the cloud, first load the desired model in Revit Acrhitecture and ensure that you are signed in to the autodesk account then choose the **Glue** tool from the **BIM 360** panel in the **Add-Ins** tab; the **BIM 360 GLUE** apps page will be displayed. Next, you need to sign in with your Autodesk ID and password, and specify a name for the BIM 360 page. Now, you will be registered to the BIM 360 page. Follow the instructions mentioned on the apps page and install BIM 360 cloud application. When the installation gets over Autodesk BIM 360 app page will be displayed with the project. Close the dialog box and open the Revit software.

Introduction to Autodesk Revit Architecture 2015

Note
*If you are not signed in to Autodesk account then on choosing the **Glue** tool, the **Autodesk-Sign In** dialog box will be displayed and will prompt you to sign in .*

In Revit, if you are signed in to the autodesk account then on choosing the **Glue** tool, the **Select Project** dialog box will be displayed, as shown in Figure 1-24. Select the **Sample Project** and then choose the **Next** button in the dialog box; the **Select Views** dialog box will be displayed, as shown in Figure 1-25.

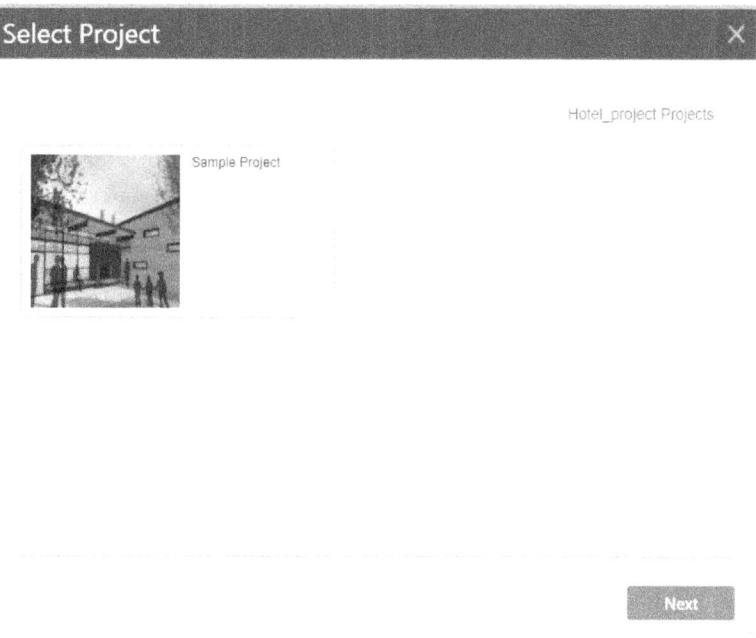

*Figure 1-24 The **Select Project** dialog box*

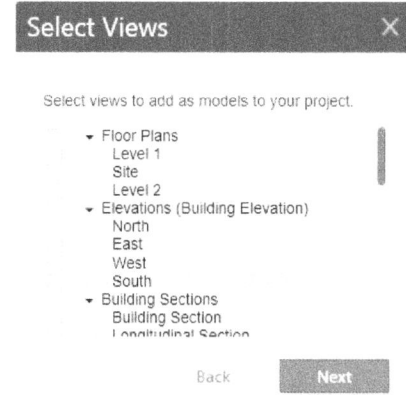

*Figure 1-25 The **Select Views** dialog box*

In this dialog box, select the check box corresponding to the required view and then choose the **Next** button; the **Review and Confirm** dialog box will be displayed, as shown in Figure 1-26.

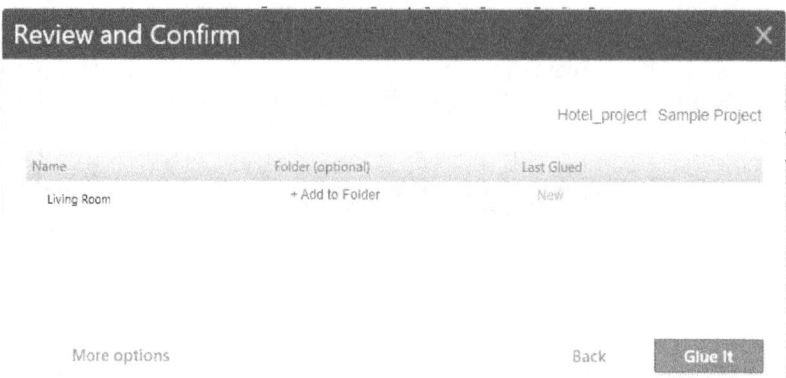

*Figure 1-26 The **Review and Confirm** dialog box*

In this dialog box, you can select the required folder from the **Folder** column. To select the folder click under the **Folder(optional)** column; the **Add to Folder** dialog box will be displayed, as shown in Figure 1-27. In this dialog box, select the required folder and choose the **Select** button; the **Add to Folder** dialog box will be closed and the **Review and Confirm** dialog box will be displayed. In the **Review and Confirm** dialog box, choose the **Glue It** button; the **Gluing in Progress** message box will be displayed. Choose the **OK** button; the message box will be closed. After sometime, the **Gluing Complete** message box will be displayed. Choose the **OK** button; the model will be shared with the BIM 360 cloud.

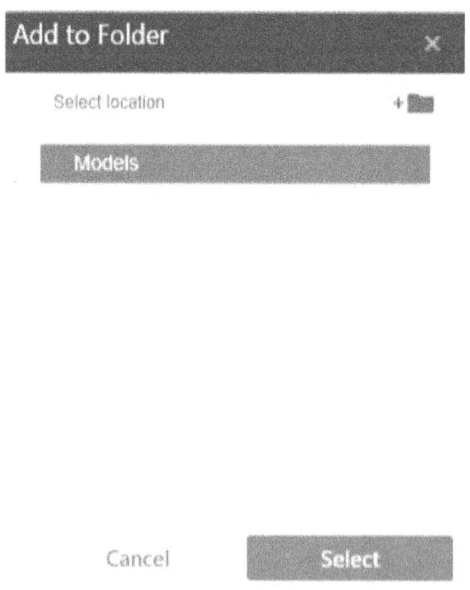

*Figure 1-27 The **Add to Folder** dialog box*

Chapter 2

Starting an Architectural Project

Learning Objectives

After completing this chapter, you will be able to:
- *Start a new architectural project.*
- *Set units of various measurement parameters for a project.*
- *Understand the concept of snaps, dimensions, and object snaps.*
- *Save a project.*
- *Modify parameters and settings of a project.*
- *Close project and exit Revit 2015.*
- *Open an existing project.*
- *Explore the building model using viewing tools.*
- *Use the Navigation tools.*

INTRODUCTION

In Autodesk Revit Architecture, you can work on structural, architectural, and MEP (Mechanical, Electrical and Plumbing) projects on a single platform. The chapters in this textbook are specially written for professionals in architectural and space design field. In this chapter, you will learn about the tools and the processes involved in starting up a new architectural project.

STARTING A NEW ARCHITECTURAL PROJECT

Application Menu: New > Project
Shortcut Key: CTRL+N

In Autodesk Revit Architecture, a project is considered as a single database that contains all information related to building design. Starting from geometry to construction data, each project file contains the complete information of the building design. In a building design, the three-dimensional models drawn using this software are called BIM (Building Information Model). BIM is a process involving the generation and management of digital representation of physical and functional characteristics of places.

In Autodesk Revit, to start an architectural project, choose the **Application** button; the **Application Menu** will be displayed. From the **Application Menu**, choose **New > Project**, as shown in Figure 2-1. On doing so, the **New Project** dialog box will be displayed, as shown in Figure 2-2. Using this dialog box, select an existing .*rte* template file format that can be used in the new project.

Figure 2-1 Choosing the **Project** Option

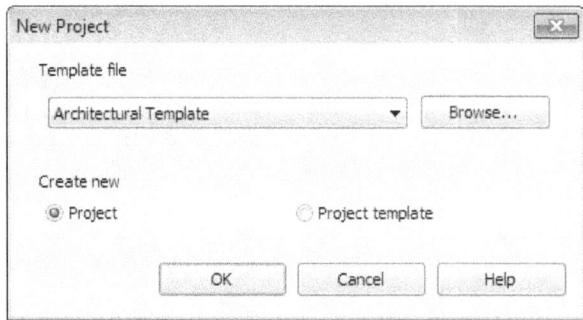

Figure 2-2 The **New Project** *dialog box*

Starting an Architectural Project

A template file can be defined as a template which has various project parameters such as units and views, already saved in it. On using the template file, the new project file will adopt the same parameters as the template file. The difference between a template file and a project file is that the template file has a *.rte* extension, whereas the project file has a *.rvt* extension. You can either select any of the template files provided in Autodesk Revit Architecture or create your own file. Any project file can be saved as a template file.

In the **New Project** dialog box, select the desired template file from the drop-down list in the **Template file** area. By default, the **Architectural Template** option is selected. To select a different template file which is not available in the drop-down list, choose the **Browse** button. On doing so, the **Choose Template** dialog box will be displayed. In this dialog box, browse to the **US Imperial** or **US Metric** folder, select a template file, and then choose the **Open** button; the selected template file will be added to the drop-down list in the **Template file** area.

In the **Create new** area of the **New Project** dialog box two radio buttons will be displayed: **Project** and **Project template**. The **Project** radio button is selected by default. As a result, you will work on a new project. Alternatively, if you select the **Project template** radio button, you will work on a new project template.

Note
*If you select the **None** option from the drop-down list in the **New Project** dialog box, a new project file will be created without a template file but with the default settings of Autodesk Revit Architecture.*

PROJECT UNITS

Ribbon: Manage > Settings > Project Units
Shortcut Key: UN

 Units are important parameters in a project. While installing Autodesk Revit Architecture, you are prompted to set the default unit as Imperial (feet and inches) or Metric (meter). The default selection of units helps you open project with the specified/selected unit system. However, you can change the default unit set system. To set units, choose the **Project Units** tool from the **Settings** panel of the **Manage** tab; the **Project Units** dialog box will be displayed, as shown in Figure 2-3. Project units are grouped into six disciplines: **Common**, **Structural**, **HVAC**, **Electrical**, **Piping**, and **Energy**. Each discipline has a set of measurement parameters. You can select any of these disciplines from the **Discipline** drop-down list of this dialog box. In this drop-down list, the **Common** option is selected by default. As a result, various measurement parameters such as **Length**, **Area**, **Volume**, **Angle**, **Slope**, **Currency**, and **Mass Density** will be displayed in the **Project Units** dialog box. The **Format** column in the dialog box displays the current unit format for the corresponding parameter. You can preview and select the possible digit grouping and decimal separators from the **Decimal symbol/digit grouping** drop-down list located at the lower left corner of the dialog box, refer to Figure 2-3. The options for settings various measurement units are discussed next.

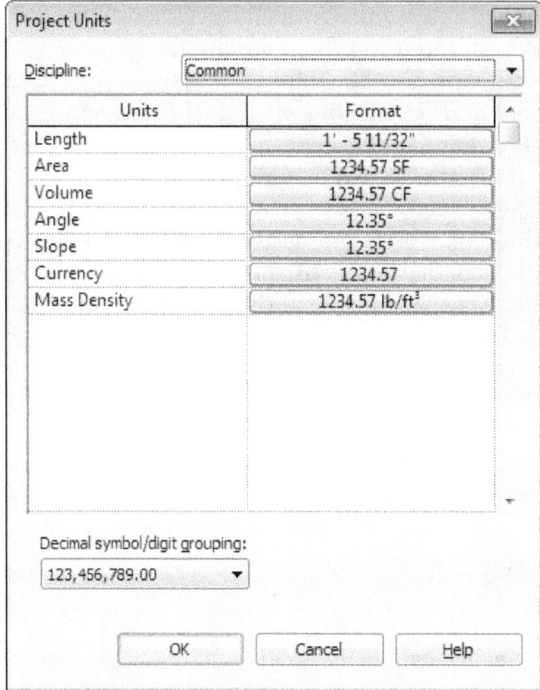

*Figure 2-3 The **Project Units** dialog box*

Length Unit

To assign a unit for measuring the lengths of building elements in your project, click in the **Format** column corresponding to the **Length** parameter; the **Format** dialog box will be displayed, as shown in Figure 2-4. This dialog box displays different units of length and their settings. You can select the desired unit from the **Units** drop-down list in the dialog box. After selecting the desired unit, you can specify the rounding value for the selected unit. To do so, select the desired option from the **Rounding** drop-down list in the **Format** dialog box. Note that by default, the **Rounding increment** edit box in the **Format** dialog box is inactive. To make it active, select the **Decimal feet** or **Decimal inches** option from the **Units** drop-down list and then select the **Custom** option from the **Rounding** drop-down list. The default value in the **Rounding increment** edit box is 1. You can change this value by entering a value in this edit box. Similarly, the **Unit symbol** drop-down list will be inactive for the **Feet and fractional inches**, **Fractional inches**, and **Meters and Centimeters** options of the **Units** drop-down list. From the **Unit symbol** drop-down list, you can select the measurement symbol that will be added to the unit of length. For example, you can select '**m**' as the measurement symbol after all metric length measurement. In case, you select **Feet and fractional inches** from the **Units** drop-down list in the **Format** dialog box, then you need to select the **Suppress spaces** check box to remove spaces in the dash when a length string is expressed in feet and fractional inches to denote a particular measurement.

Starting an Architectural Project

Tip: *While selecting a rounding value from the **Rounding** drop-down list in the **Format** dialog box, you should consider the extent of detailing that may be required for the project. For projects that require too much detailing, a lower rounding value may be set. This parameter, however, can be modified at any stage during the project development.*

*Figure 2-4 The **Format** dialog box*

Area Unit

To assign a unit for measuring the areas of building elements, click in the **Format** column for the **Area** parameter; the **Format** dialog box will be displayed. In this dialog box, you can set the unit for measuring an area by selecting an option from the **Units** drop-down list. This drop-down list contains various options such as **Square feet**, **Square meters**, **acres**, and so on. By default, the **Square feet** option is selected in this drop-down list. The settings for rounding, rounding increment, and units can be done by selecting the desired option from the respective drop-down list and edit boxes.

Volume Unit

The units for volume can be set similar to that of the length and area. You can set the unit for the volume measurement by selecting any of the options from the **Units** drop-down list in the **Format** dialog box of the **Volume** parameter.

Angle Unit

The units for angle can be set by the **Units** drop-down list in the **Format** dialog box of the **Angle** parameter.

Slope Unit

To specify the unit for the slope measurement, click in the **Format** column for the **Slope** parameter; the **Format** dialog box will be displayed. In this dialog box, you can specify the desired unit settings by selecting the required option from the **Units** drop-down list. The default option for the Imperial unit setting in the drop-down list is **Rise /12"**.

Currency Unit

The currency unit is used to set the unit of currency for its usage in the cost and estimation schedules. To set the unit of currency, invoke the **Project Units** dialog box and then choose the button displayed in the **Format** column corresponding to the **Currency** parameter; the **Format** dialog box will be displayed. From this dialog box, you can select the required type of currency symbol from the **Unit symbol** drop-down list.

Mass Density Unit

The mass density of building elements is required for structural analysis. In Autodesk Revit Architecture, you can assign a unit for measuring mass density. To assign the unit of mass density, invoke the **Project Units** dialog box. In the **Format** column of this dialog box, choose the button corresponding to the **Mass Density** parameter; the **Format** dialog box will be displayed. In this dialog box, you can select different units from the **Units** drop-down list. Also, you can assign a unit symbol for the selected unit. To do so, click on the **Unit symbol** drop-down list and then select any of the options displayed.

Tip: *As soon as you change the units and choose the **OK** button to close the **Format** dialog box, the numbers and units shown for each measurement parameter in the **Project Units** dialog box are modified to the new settings. You can modify their settings and format any time during the project.*

Note
*You can format the display of units represented on the screen using the **Project Units** dialog box. The actual values for these units in the project may be different. For example, if you set the wall length rounding to the nearest 1', the wall may show this rounded value, but the actual length of the wall might be in fractional feet.*

SNAPS TOOL

Ribbon: Manage > Settings > Snaps

The **Snaps** tool is one of the most productive tools available while creating and editing elements in a building model. This tool represents the ability of the cursor to snap or jump to the preset increments or specific object properties of various elements such as endpoint, midpoint, and so on. Invoke the **Snaps** tool from the **Settings** panel of the **Manage** tab; the **Snaps** dialog box will be displayed, as shown in Figure 2-5. This dialog box has three areas: **Dimension Snaps**, **Object Snaps**, and **Temporary Overrides**. These areas are discussed next.

Note
*The settings in the **Snaps** dialog box apply to all the projects opened in the session and are not saved in a particular project.*

Starting an Architectural Project

Tip: *The values that you will enter for dimension snapping should be set based on the scale and the amount of detailing required for the project. You may set smaller increments for working on a detail or a small portion of a building.*

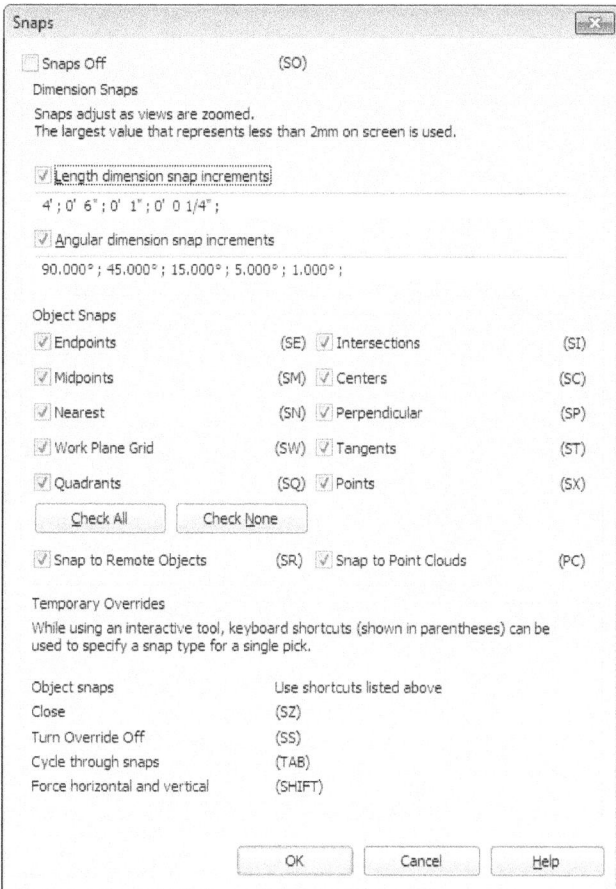

*Figure 2-5 The **Snaps** dialog box*

Dimension Snaps Area

In this area, you can set increments for placing elements or components in a project view. You can set increments for the length and angle dimensions. To set the increment of length dimension, select the **Length dimension snap increments** check box if it is not selected by default, and then enter the increment values in the edit box below it. The default values entered in this edit box are: **4'**; **0'6"**;**0'1"**; **0'1/4"**; for Imperial (**1000** ; **100** ; **20** ; **5** ; for Metric). Note that every incremental value is separated by a semicolon (;). You can also set increments by typing the values separated by a semicolon. For example, to create an interior layout plan in which the length of the partitions is in 5'(1524 mm) modules, counter top width is 2'(609.6 mm), and the thickness of partitions is 4"(101.6 mm), you can enter the values for the dimension snaps as 5'; 2';4" for Imperial (1524; 609.6;101.6 for Metric). This will enable the cursor to move in these increments and help create the layout with relative ease.

In the **Dimension Snaps** area, snap increments for angular dimensions can be set by selecting the **Angular dimension snap increments** check box and then entering suitable values in the edit box below this check box. This setting is quite useful for projects that have radial geometry.

Tip: *The **Snaps** tool is frequently used not only while creating various building elements but also while editing and placing them. By using this feature efficiently, you can also improve the performance and accuracy of your project besides making modeling much simpler.*

Object Snaps Area

In the **Object Snaps** area, you can specify various object snaps for using them in a project. Object snapping refers to the cursor's ability to snap to geometric points on an element such as endpoints, midpoint, perpendicular, and so on. It is useful for creating and editing elements. The advantage of using object snapping is that you can locate the appropriate point on a drawing object. When enabled, the appropriate object snap is displayed as soon as the cursor is near to an element. For example, it is virtually impossible to pick the exact endpoint to start a wall from an endpoint of an already drawn wall. But when you enable the **Endpoints** object snap, the cursor automatically jumps or snaps to the endpoint of this wall. This helps to start the new wall from the endpoint. This, besides making the drawing accurate, later helps in adding dimensions to the project.

Note
The object snapping works only with the objects that are visible on the screen. A tooltip, with the same name as the object snap, is also displayed when you bring the cursor close to the snap point.

Various object snaps modes available in the **Object Snaps** area are: **Endpoints**, **Midpoints**, **Nearest**, **Work Plane Grid**, **Quadrants**, **Intersections**, **Centers**, **Perpendicular**, **Tangents**, **Points**, **Snap to Remote Objects**, and **Snap to Point Clouds**.

The use of each object snap corresponds to its respective name. The **Work Plane Grid** snap option enables you to snap to a point on a reference plane already defined in the model. For example, you can place a furniture component exactly on the floor by snapping to the floor level reference plane. You can snap to the object that is closest to the cursor using the **Snap to Remote Objects** option. You can also snap points of a point cloud data object by selecting the **Snap to Point Clouds** check box. Each object snap mode has a geometrical shaped marker to identify it from the other object snaps. For example, the endpoint object snap is indicated by a square, midpoint by a triangle, nearest by a cross, and so on. To use an object snap mode, move the cursor over the object. You will notice a marker that appears as you move it close to the snap point. To select the appropriate snap point, click when the corresponding marker or tooltip is displayed.

In Autodesk Revit Architecture, all the enabled object snaps work simultaneously. You can turn off all the snap options including the dimension snaps and object snaps by clearing the **Snaps Off** check box located at the top of the **Snaps** dialog box. Alternatively, you can type **SO** on the keyboard to turn them off and on while using a tool. The **Check All** and **Check None** buttons can be used to enable or disable the object snaps, respectively.

Starting an Architectural Project   2-9

Temporary Overrides Area

The options in the **Temporary Overrides** area provide you the alternative of overriding snaps setting for a single use only. For example, if you have not selected the **Endpoints** object snap in the **Snaps** dialog box and you want to use this option while working with a tool, you need not open the **Snaps** dialog box and set this option. Instead, you can type the shortcut, **SE** in this case, to temporarily activate the endpoint object snap. Once you have used this object snap option, snapping to the endpoint is automatically turned off.

You can toggle between various object snap options available at the same location using the TAB key on the keyboard. Hold down the SHIFT key to create the elements vertically or horizontally. This restricts the movement of the cursor in the orthogonal directions only. Once you release the SHIFT key, the cursor resumes its movement in all directions. You can select the **Snaps Off** check box to disable all types of snapping.

SAVING A PROJECT

You must save your work before closing a project or exiting the Autodesk Revit Architecture 2015 session. You have the option of saving the project file in a permanent storage device, which may be a hard disk or a removable disk. Also, you must save your work at regular intervals to avoid loss due to any error in the computer's hardware or software.

Saving the Project File

Application Menu:	Save As > Project
Shortcut Key:	CTRL+S

To save the project file to the desired location, click the **Application** button to display the **Application Menu** and then choose **Save As > Project** from the **Application Menu**; the **Save As** dialog box will be displayed, as shown in Figure 2-6. Alternatively, you can save the project file by choosing the **Save** button from the **Quick Access Toolbar**. In the **Save As** dialog box, the **Save in** drop-down list displays the current drive and path in which the project file will be saved. The list box below the **Save in** drop-down list shows all folders available in the current directory. The **File name** edit box can be used to enter the name of the file to be assigned to the project. The **Places List** area in the left of the **Save As** dialog box contains shortcuts for the folders that are frequently used.

 Tip: *The selection of large number of backup files for storing may use a lot of resources on the hard disk.*

*Figure 2-6 The **Save As** dialog box*

Using the Options Button

You can use different features for saving a file by choosing the **Options** button from the **Save As** dialog box. On choosing this button, the **File Save Options** dialog box will be displayed, as shown in Figure 2-7. Using the **Maximum backups** edit box from this dialog box, you can specify the maximum number of backup files that you need to store for the project. In Autodesk Revit Architecture, by default the non-workshared projects have three backup files and the workshared projects have twenty backup files. The options in the **Thumbnail Preview** area enable you to specify the image to be used as the preview of the project file that can be used at the time of opening a project file. You can specify the view of the model to be used as a preview image by selecting an option from the **Source** drop-down list. The **Active view/sheet** is the default option for previewing a project file. For example, to make the **Floor Plan: Level 1** the preview image, select it from the drop-down list. Whenever you select this project file, the preview will always show the **Floor Plan: Level 1**, irrespective of the last active view.

Select the **Regenerate if view/sheet is not up-to-date** check box to see the preview with the latest modifications. Selecting this check box will update the preview image on closing the project file.

Note
*Autodesk Revit Architecture updates the preview image continuously. Therefore, selecting the **Regenerate if view/sheet is not up-to-date** check box can consume considerable resources.*

Starting an Architectural Project

Figure 2-7 The **File Save Options** *dialog box*

Using the Save Tool

To save a project, choose the **Save** tool from the **Application Menu**, as shown in Figure 2-8, the **Save As** dialog box is displayed. In this dialog box, you can enter a file name and save the file by choosing the **Save** tool. If we are saving the project for the first time, the **Save As** dialog box is displayed. Alternatively, you can save your project by choosing the **Save** button from the **Quick Access Toolbar**. As you save your project file, Autodesk Revit Architecture 2015 updates it automatically without prompting you to re-enter the file name and path.

Figure 2-8 *Choosing the* **Save** *tool from the* **Application Menu**

 Note
Once the project is saved using the **Save As** *tool, you do not need to re-enter the file parameters to save it again.*

CONFIGURING GLOBAL SETTINGS

In Autodesk Revit Architecture 2015, you can configure global settings by using the **Options** dialog box. This dialog box can be invoked by choosing the **Options** button from the **Application Menu**. The **Options** dialog box shown in Figure 2-9, contains nine tabs: **General**, **User**

Interface, **Graphics**, **File Locations**, **Rendering**, **Check Spelling**, **SteeringWheels**, **ViewCube**, and **Macros**. The options of these tabs are discussed next.

General Tab

The **General** tab is chosen by default in the **Options** dialog box. This tab contains the following areas: **Notifications**, **Username**, **Journal File Cleanup**, **Worksharing Update Frequency**, and **View Options**, refer to Figure 2-9. These areas are discussed next.

Notifications Area

The **Notifications** area provides you the option for setting reminders to save work at regular intervals. In this area, you can set the time interval at which Autodesk Revit Architecture will remind you to save the project file. The default value for the **Save reminder interval** parameter is **30 minutes**. You can specify the time interval by selecting the interval option from the drop-down list corresponding to the **Save reminder interval** parameter. If you do not want a reminder, you can select the **No reminders** option from the drop-down list. Similarly, you can set the value for the **Synchronize with Central reminder interval** parameter.

Figure 2-9 Various areas in the **General** tab

Username Area

In Autodesk Revit Architecture, if you are not signed in as a user of autodesk account, then the Username will not be displayed. To enter a name in the **Username** area, you need to sign in to Autodesk 360. When you sign in, your autodesk ID will be used as a username.

Tip: *If you are not logged into an Autodesk account, you can directly enter a username.*

Starting an Architectural Project

Journal File Cleanup Area

Journal files are the text files that are used to resolve technical problems that may occur during the Autodesk Revit Architecture session and they record every step during the session. Whenever you encounter any technical problem with the software, you can run this file to detect the problem as well as recover the lost files or steps that had caused the problem. In Autodesk Revit Architecture, these files are saved at the following default location: *C:\Users\<Username>\ AppData\Local\Autodesk\Revit\Autodesk Revit Architecture 2015\Journals* for Windows 7/8 and for Window Vista users *C:\Documents and Settings\<Username>\Local Settings\Application* for Windows XP users. These files are saved each time you close the Autodesk Revit Architecture 2015 session. As such the quantity of these files keeps on increasing until you remove these files from their location. To retain certain files and clean others, you can use the **Journal File Cleanup** area in the **General** tab of the **Options** dialog box. This area contains two spinners: **When number of journals exceeds then** and **Delete journals older than (days)**. You can set the required values in these spinners to retain the files that are recently created. For example, if you need to delete journal files if their number exceeds 15 and if they were created before 30 days. Then, in such a situation, set the value in the **When number of journal exceeds** spinner to **15** and the value in the **Delete journals older than (days)** spinner to **30**.

Worksharing Update Frequency Area

In this area, you can set the time interval for updating the project in a worksharing environment. To set the update frequency for worksharing, you can set the slider between **Less Frequent** and **More Frequent**.

View Options Area

In this area, you can set the default view discipline for the project. To do so, select an option from the **Default view discipline** drop-down list. The list of options available in this drop-down list are: **Architectural**, **Structural**, **Mechanical**, **Electrical**, **Plumbing**, and **Coordination**.

User Interface Tab

The **User Interface** tab contains two areas: **Configure** and **Tab Switching Behavior**. You can specify the options for the display of Autodesk Revit Architecture user interface. You can do so by selecting the **Dark** or **Light** option from the **Active theme** drop-down list in this area. To customize the use of shortcut keys in a project you can choose the **Customize** button corresponding to the **Keyboard Shortcuts** parameter. You can also choose the **Customize** button corresponding to the **Double-click options**, the **Customize Double-click Settings** dialog box will be displayed, as shown in Figure 2-10. In the **Configure** area, you can select an option from the **Tooltip assistance** drop-down list to set the extent of the tip that will displayed with the cursor when it is close to a tool. The options in this drop-down list are **None**, **Minimal**, **Normal**, and **High**. By default, the **Normal** option is selected in this drop-down list. Note that the tooltip will appear more frequently in your drawing if you select **High** in the **Tooltip assistance** drop-down list. In the **Configure** area, the **Enable Recent Files page at startup** check box is selected by default. As a result, the recent files will be displayed on starting the Autodesk Revit Architecture software. You can clear this check box if you do not want to display the recent files at the startup. In the **Tab Switching Behavior** area, you can specify the tab to be displayed once you clear a selection or exit a tool. In this area, the **Project environment** drop-down list contains two options: **Stay on the Modify tab** and **Return to the**

previous tab. Select the **Stay on the Modify tab** option to display the options in the **Modify tab** after exiting a tool or clearing a selection. Alternatively, you can select the **Return to the previous tab** option to display the last used tab after exiting a tool or clearing a selection. In the **Tab Switching Behavior** area, the **Display the contextual tab on selection** check box is selected by default. As a result, the contextual tab is displayed once you select a tool from the Autodesk Revit Architecture interface.

Tip: *When you rest the cursor on the project file name, a tooltip appears, which provides you the information regarding the type and size of the project file.*

*Figure 2-10 The **Customize Double-click Settings** dialog box*

Graphics Tab

The options in the **Graphics** tab enable you to configure the display card of your computer to improve the display performance. You can also use this tab to assign colors to selections, highlights and alerts, and enable anti-aliasing for 3D views. In the **Graphics Mode** area of this tab, the **Use Hardware Acceleration (Direct 3D)** check box is selected by default. As a result, the hardware accelerators are enabled. Hardware accelerators help display the larger models faster on refreshing the views. In addition, the hardware accelerators help you speed up the process of switching between the windows of views. In Autodesk Revit Architecture, the **Use Optimized View Navigation** check box in the **Graphics Mode** area is selected, by default. As a result, certain features in the Autodesk Revit Architecture interface that affect the display of the model elements are barred. The selection of the check box will result in the improvement of the performance of the display while navigating a 2D view or a 3D view using the following methods of navigation: Using the **ViewCube**; Using the tools in the **Navigation Bar**; Navigating by scrolling the mouse wheel; and while using the Keyboard shortcuts.

Starting an Architectural Project

The following table shows the list of features barred for Visual Styles:

Feature	Visual Styles			
	Hidden Line	Shaded	Consistent Colors	Realistic
Edges	-----------	Barred	Barred	Barred
Fill Patterns	Barred	Barred	Barred	Barred
Shadows	Barred	Barred	Barred	Barred
Structural Hidden Lines	Barred	Barred	Barred	Barred
Mechanical Hidden Lines	Barred	Barred	Barred	Barred

In the **Graphics Mode** area, the **Smooth lines with anti-aliasing** check box is selected to display the views as aliased. On selecting this check box, the **Allow control for each view in the Graphics Display Options dialog** and **Use for all views (control for each view is disabled)** options will be enabled. The selection of the **Allow control for each view in the Graphics Display Options dialog** check box will allow to control the aliasing using the **Graphic Display Options** dialog box for each view. The **Graphic Display Options** dialog box can be invoked using the options in the **Visual Styles** menu of the **Status Bar**. On selecting the **Use for all view (control for each view is disabled)** option enables to view the sketched lines as a smooth lines in all views.

Note
*While navigating a camera view in the **Wireframe** view style, the fill patterns are not displayed in the model.*

In the **Colors** area of the **Graphics** tab, select the **Invert background** check box to toggle the color of the background and elements. The **Selection** parameter specifies a color that an element acquires when it is selected. The default color is **RGB 000-059-189**. To use any other color, click the button on the right of the **Selection** parameter to display the **Color** dialog box and then select the desired color. The **Pre-selection** parameter specifies the color of the highlighted elements. To use any other color for highlighting the element, click the button on the right of the **Selection** parameter and select the desired color from the **Color** dialog box displayed. Autodesk Revit Architecture uses the **Alert** button to highlight elements when an error occurs. In the **Colors** area, the **Semi-transparent** check box is selected by default. As a result, you can make the selected elements semi-transparent and you can view the elements behind the selection. In the **Temporary Dimension Text Appearance** area, you can select an option from the **Size** drop-down list to specify the size of the text to be used in temporary dimensions. In this area, you can set the background of the text in the temporary dimensions. To do so, select the **Opaque** or **Transparent** option from the **Background** drop-down list.

File Locations Tab
The options in the **File Locations** tab can be used to display the link of the default template files present in the project. The options in this tab can also be used to set the path for the

template files, user files, family template files that are accessed frequently, and the root path for the point clouds. Figure 2-11 shows various options in this tab. The path for these files is set at the time of installing Autodesk Revit Architecture. However, you can modify the location by choosing the corresponding **Browse** button and specifying a new path. The default template file location can be changed, in case you wish to use a custom made template file for your projects. Autodesk Revit Architecture uses the default path for user files for saving or opening a project. You can also specify the default path for family template files and for the point clouds by using the corresponding **Browse** button.

*Figure 2-11 Options in the **File Locations** tab*

Rendering Tab

The **Additional Render Appearance Path** section in the **Options** dialog box specifies the path for the additional image files that defines texture, bump map, custom color for the render appearance, which can be used in the project. These image files are not present in the software and therefore, you need to specify their paths to use them. To do so, choose the **Add Value** button in the **Additional Render Appearance Paths** area and specify the required path in the displayed field or choose the **Browse** button; the **Browse for Folder** dialog box will be displayed. In this dialog box, select the desired path and choose the **Open** button to add the path to the field. In the **ArchVision Content Manager Location** area of the **Rendering** tab, you can specify the location of the licensed additional RPC content from Archvision. In this area, the **Network** radio button is selected by default. As a result, you can provide the address of the licensed Archvision content in a network, so that more than one user can access the content. To provide the network location of the RPC content, you can specify the IP address or the machine name in the **Address** edit box. Also, you can specify the port used by the Archvision Content Manger in the edit box next to the **Address** edit box. By default, the value entered in the edit box for the port is **14931**. Alternatively, you can select the **Local** radio button in the **ArchVision Content Manager Location** area of the **Rendering** tab, if the additional RPC content is available in the local drive of the computer. On selecting the **Local**

Starting an Architectural Project

radio button, you can specify the location of the local ACM executable file (*rcpACMapp.exe*) in the **Executable Location** edit box. To browse for the local ACM executable file, you can choose the **Browse** button; the **Browse for Template File** dialog box will be displayed. Select the desired executable file and then choose the **Open** button; the path of the file will be added and displayed in the **Executable Location** edit box. In the **Archvision Content Manager** area, you can choose the **Get More RPC** button to connect to *http://www.archvision.com/products/plugin* page and get additional RPC required for the project.

Check Spelling Tab

This tab provides you with the option to run spell check in the text and then rectify the errors. You can choose the **Check Spelling** from the **Options** dialog box to display its options. Various self-explanatory settings can be selected from the **Settings** list. You can choose the **Restore Defaults** button available below the **Settings** list to revert back to the default settings. In the **Main Dictionary** area of this tab, you can select the type of dictionary to be used as main dictionary for the spelling check from the **Autodesk Revit** drop-down list. Apart from the main dictionary, you can also use additional dictionaries such as the personal and building industry dictionaries. This facilitates the use of various personal and industry related terms in the text matter of the project. There are many words that are not included in the main dictionaries but are frequently used in the building industry. For example, the abbreviation for architecture 'archi' is not available in the main dictionaries. The additional building industry dictionary has many such words and abbreviations that can be used in the text matter of the project without being prompted for errors while checking spellings. You can also add or remove words from your personal and building industry dictionary. Choose any of the **Edit** buttons available in the **Additional Dictionaries** area to view the list of words. You can enter or remove any word from these lists using the cursor and keyboard. To run spell check in your drawing, choose the **Check Spelling** tool from the **Text** panel in the **Annotate** tab; the **Check Spelling** dialog box will be displayed, as shown in Figure 2-12, wherein you can rectify the spelling errors in the text by selecting the correct spelling and then choosing the **Change** button in the dialog box, refer to Figure 2-12. Alternatively, you can press the F7 key to display the **Check Spelling** dialog box, refer to Figure 2-12, and then make necessary corrections in the text.

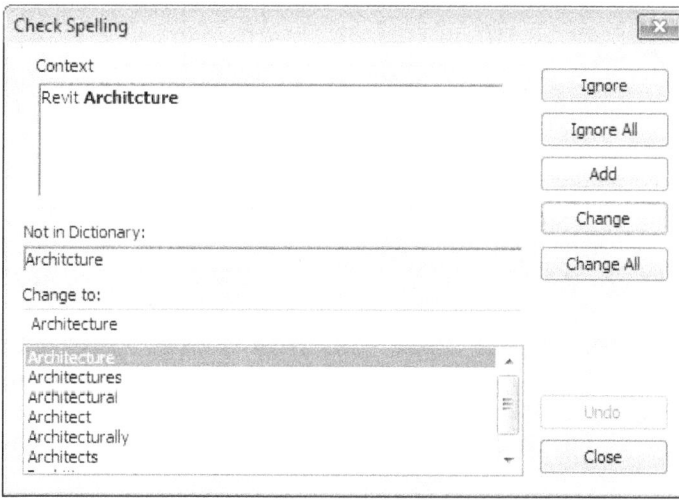

Figure 2-12 *The* **Check Spelling** *dialog box*

SteeringWheels Tab

The options in the **SteeringWheels** tab in the **Options** dialog box are used to control the visibility, appearance, and operational tools of different types of SteeringWheels. This tab has seven different areas of control to use the SteeringWheels, as shown in Figure 2-13. These areas are discussed next.

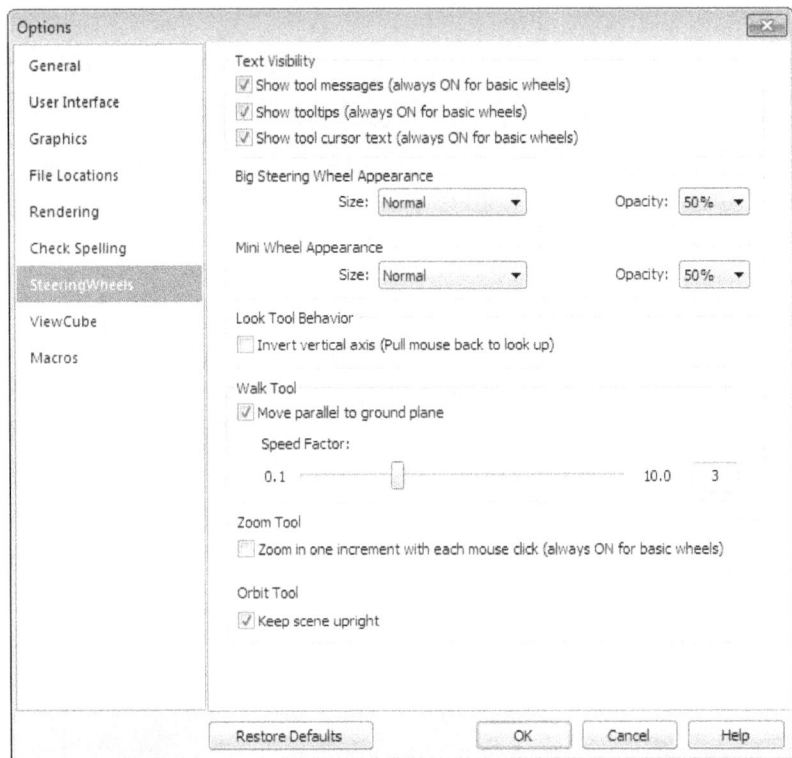

*Figure 2-13 The **SteeringWheels** tab of the **Options** dialog box*

Text Visibility Area

You can control the display of tool messages, tooltips, and tool cursor of the SteeringWheels by using the options in the **Text Visibility** area of the **SteeringWheels** tab. In this area, the **Show tool messages** check box is selected by default. As a result, the visibility of tool messages in SteeringWheels is enabled. To display the tooltips along with the SteeringWheels, select the **Show tooltips** check box in this area. Similarly, to control the display of the cursor text when a tool is active, use the **Show tool cursor text** check box. Select this check box to display the cursor text when the tool is active.

Big Steering Wheel Appearance and Mini Wheel Appearance Areas

To set the size of the SteeringWheels, select the required option from the **Size** drop-down list in the corresponding areas and set its size to small, normal, or large. Similarly, you can set the transparency of the SteeringWheels by selecting the required option from the **Opacity** drop-down list.

Starting an Architectural Project   2-19

Look Tool Behavior and Walk Tool Areas

In the **Look Tool Behavior** area of the **SteeringWheels** tab, select the **Invert vertical axis** check box to change the movement of the view along the vertical axis while using the **Look** tool. Note that on selecting the check box, the view will move in the same direction as that of the cursor. In the **Walk Tool** area of the **SteeringWheels** tab, use the **Speed Factor** slider to change the speed of the walk while using the **Walk** tool of the SteeringWheels. Select the **Move parallel to ground plane** check box if it is not selected by default, to constrain the movement angle of the walk to ground plane.

Zoom Tool and Orbit Tool Areas

Select the **Zoom in one increment with each mouse click** check box in the **Zoom Tool** area to enable the zooming operation with a single click. In the **Orbit Tool** area, ensure that the **Keep scene upright** check box is selected. This helps maintaining the perpendicularity between the sides of the model and the ground plane while using the **Orbit** tool.

ViewCube Tab

The options in the **ViewCube** tab in the **Options** dialog box are used to edit various settings of the ViewCube. It has four different areas to modify the ViewCube: **ViewCube Appearance**, **When Dragging the ViewCube**, **When Clicking on the ViewCube**, and **Compass**, as shown in Figure 2-14. These areas are discussed next.

Figure 2-14 The ViewCube tab of the Options dialog box

ViewCube Appearance Area

The appearance and display of the ViewCube can be controlled by the **ViewCube Appearance** area in the **ViewCube** tab.

In the **ViewCube Appearance** area, the **Show the ViewCube** check box is selected by default, so the ViewCube will be visible. If you clear this check box, the ViewCube will disappear and all options of the **ViewCube** in the **ViewCube Appearance** area will be deactivated.

In the **ViewCube Appearance** area, you can use various drop-down lists to align, resize, and change the transparency of the ViewCube. You can select an option from the **Show in** drop-down list to specify whether the ViewCube will be displayed in all 3D views or only in the active view. The **On-screen position** drop-down list is used to position the ViewCube on the screen. Similarly, you can resize the ViewCube by selecting the required option from the **ViewCube size** drop-down list. You can also set the opacity of the inactive ViewCube by selecting various options from the **Inactive Opacity** drop-down list.

When Dragging the ViewCube Area

In this area, the **Snap to closest view** check box is selected by default. As a result, the closest ViewCube view orientation will be snapped.

When Clicking on the ViewCube Area

Select the **Fit-to-view on view change** check box in the **When Clicking on the ViewCube** area to fit the view on screen while changing the viewing direction. The **Use animated transition when switching views** check box is selected by default in this area that enables the view to change in animation. Clearing this check box will result in the change of view without any animation, when using the ViewCube. Select the **Keep scene upright** check box to keep the sides of the ViewCube and the sides of the view perpendicular to the ground plane. Clear the check box to turn around the model in full 360-degree swing. Clearing this check box can be useful when you are editing a family.

Compass Area

The **Show the compass with the ViewCube** check box in the **Compass** area is selected by default. As a result, the compass along with the ViewCube will be visible in the drawing.

In the **ViewCube** tab, you can choose the **Restore Defaults** button to restore the default settings that were changed in its different areas.

Macros Tab

The options in the **Macros** tab can be used to set the security level for the **Macros** used in the project. The options in this tab are available in two areas: **Application Macro Security Settings** and **Document Macro Security Settings**. The various options in these areas are discussed next.

Application Macro Security Settings Area

In this area, the **Enable application macros** radio button is selected by default. As a result, the application macros in the project are enabled. To disable the application macros, select the **Disable application macros** radio button.

Document Macro Security Settings Area

In this area, the **Ask before enabling document macros** radio button is selected by default. As a result, the document macros are disabled, but you will be prompted to enable them whenever you open a project that contains a macro. To enable the document macros, select the **Enable document** macros radio button. Similarly, to disable a document macros in the project, select the **Disable document macros** radio button.

*Tip: If you disable the macros by selecting the **Disable application macros** radio button in the **Macros** tab of the **Options** dialog box, you will still be able to modify the code, although the modifications in the code will not change the current status of the macros.*

CLOSING A PROJECT

To close a project, choose the **Application** button and then select the **Close** option from the **Application Menu** displayed, as shown in Figure 2-15. If you have already saved the latest changes, the project file will be closed. Otherwise, Autodesk Revit Architecture will prompt you to save the changes through the **Save File** confirmation box. You can save the changes by choosing the **Yes** button or discard them by choosing the **No** button. You can also choose the **Cancel** button to return to the interface and continue working on the project file. You can also use the **Close** button (**X**) in the drawing window to close the project.

Figure 2-15 Choosing the Close option

EXITING AUTODESK REVIT ARCHITECTURE

To exit the Autodesk Revit Architecture 2015 session, choose the **Exit** button from the **Application Menu**. Even if the project is open, you can still choose the **Exit Revit** button to close the file and exit Autodesk Revit Architecture 2015. In case, the project has not been saved, it enables you to save the work through the **Save File** message box, as shown in Figure 2-16. If you choose the **No** button, all the changes that were not saved will be lost. You can also use the **Close** button (**X**) in the main Autodesk Revit Architecture window (in the title bar) to end the Autodesk Revit Architecture 2015 session.

Figure 2-16 The Save File message box

OPENING AN EXISTING PROJECT

To open an existing project, you can use various options, such as the **Open** tool or the Windows explorer. These options are discussed in detail in the next section.

Opening an Existing Project Using the Open Tool

To open an existing project file, choose **Open > Project** from the **Application Menu**, as shown in Figure 2-17. Alternatively, you can open a project by choosing the **Open** button from the **Quick Access Toolbar** or by pressing CTRL+O. On doing so, the **Open** dialog box will be displayed, as shown in Figure 2-18. In this dialog box, you can open a particular project file by accessing the appropriate folder using the **Look in** drop-down list.

Figure 2-17 Choosing the **Project** option from the **Application Menu**

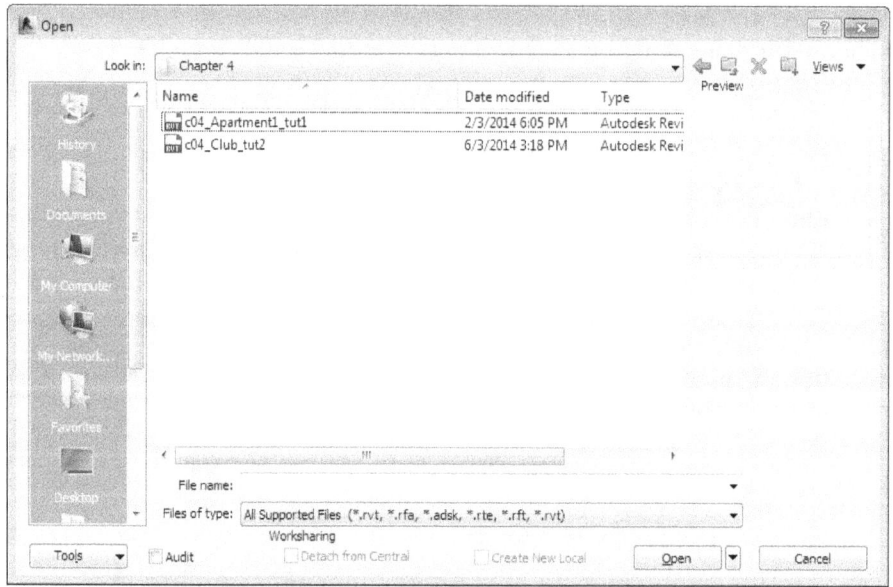

Figure 2-18 The **Open** dialog box

Tip: *The **Preview** image acts as a thumbnail to identify a project file. You must select the view that will help you identify the project file easily.*

The **Preview** area of the **Open** dialog box shows the preview of the selected project file. It helps you select a particular file by viewing its contents; even if you are not sure about the file name. The window icons such as the **Views** menu, placed along with the **Look in** drop-down list, help you select a project file based on its size, type, and the date when it was last saved.

Starting an Architectural Project 2-23

On choosing the **Thumbnails** option from the **Views** menu, you can preview the contents of the project files inside the selected folder in the file list area, refer to Figure 2-19.

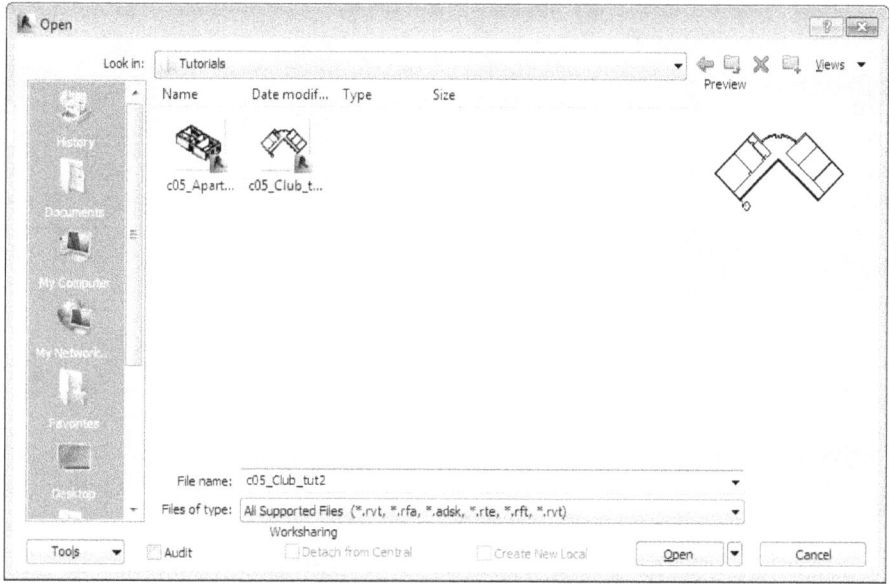

Figure 2-19 Previewing the files in the **Open** dialog box

The **Places** list is located on the left in the **Open** dialog box. You can add or remove folders from the **Places** list by choosing the **Options** button from the **Application Menu**. On doing so, the **Options** dialog box will be displayed. Choose the **File Locations** tab from the dialog box, and then choose the **Places** button from it; the **Places** dialog box will be displayed, as shown in Figure 2-20.

Figure 2-20 The **Places** dialog box

The **Places** dialog box contains two columns: **Library Name** and **Library Path**. You can add or remove folders in the libraries list to create a list of frequently accessed folders. The four buttons on the left of the **Places** dialog box can be used to create or delete a library, or move it up and down in the list. To create a new library, choose the **Add Value** button, which is the third button from the top; a new library will be added to the defined path. By default, the name of the new library in the **Library Name** section will be **NewLibrary2**. Change the name of the new library and then click in the **Library Path** column to display the browse button. Choose the browse button and select the folder to be added in the libraries list using the **Browse for Folder** dialog box. Choose the **Open** button after selecting the folder; the new folder gets added to the list. If required, choose the upward arrow button in the **Places** dialog box to move the folder up to the top of the list. Similarly, you can choose the down arrow button to move it down. To delete any library, select the library and choose the **Remove Value** button. Choose the **OK** button in the **Places** dialog box to exit, and then close the **Options** dialog box. When you invoke the **Open** tool next time, the new folder icon will be displayed in the places list.

Once the file to be opened has been selected, its name will be displayed in the **File Name** edit box of the **Open** dialog box and its preview will be displayed in the **Preview** area.

Note
*If you try opening an already opened file, which has been modified in the Autodesk Revit Architecture 2015 session, a message box appears, prompting you to close the file first and reopen it. In case you open a file that has been created using an older version of Autodesk Revit Architecture, the **Program Upgrade** message box is displayed. It mentions that the file is being upgraded to the latest file format and that this is a onetime process. Once the file is opened, it gets upgraded to Autodesk Revit Architecture 2015 version.*

Tip: *The names of the recently opened files are displayed in the **Application Menu**. On starting Autodesk Revit Architecture, you can click on the name of the project file that you wish to open.*

Using the Windows Explorer to Open an Existing Project

Apart from using the **Open** tool from the Autodesk Revit Architecture interface, you can also open files directly from the **Windows Explorer** by using the methods discussed next.

A file can be opened by double-clicking on its icon in the **Windows Explorer**. It opens the project file in the latest Autodesk Revit Architecture session. If Autodesk Revit Architecture is not running, double-click on the file icon to start Autodesk Revit Architecture and then open the file. Another method of opening a project file is by dragging the project file icon from the **Windows Explorer** and dropping it into the drawing window of the Autodesk Revit Architecture interface. You can also select, drag, and drop more than one file in the drawing window. In this case, Autodesk Revit Architecture prompts you to open the files in separate windows. Choose the **OK** button to open all files in the same Autodesk Revit Architecture session.

Tip: *By default, the preview of a file is the last active view or sheet at the time it was last saved. You can set the preview to a particular view by using the **Options** button in the **Save As** dialog box.*

Starting an Architectural Project 2-25

MODEL DISPLAY TOOLS

As described earlier, in Autodesk Revit Architecture, you can create the building model using the 3D parametric elements. Various tools are provided to view the building model. Based on the requirement, you can use these tools to navigate and edit elements in the building model.

Using the Zoom Tools

The **Zoom** tools are used to enlarge or reduce a project view in the viewing area. To use these tools, you need to display the **Navigation Bar** in your drawing. Generally, the **Navigation Bar** is displayed by default. If it is not displayed, choose the **User Interface** drop-down from the **Window** panel of the **View** tab; a drop-down list will be displayed, as shown in Figure 2-21. From the drop-down list, select the **Navigation Bar** check box if it is not selected; the **Navigation Bar** will be displayed in the viewing area. In the **Navigation Bar**, click on the down arrow below the **Zoom All to Fit** tool; a cascading menu will be displayed, as shown in Figure 2-22. This cascading menu displays different zooming options, which are discussed next.

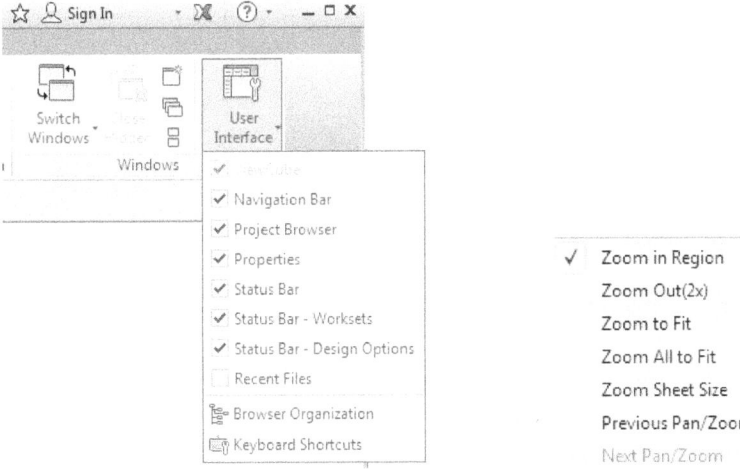

Figure 2-21 A drop-down menu displayed on clicking the **User Interface** drop-down

Figure 2-22 Different zooming options in the cascading menu

Zoom In Region

This tool is used to zoom in a specified area or window. When you invoke the **Zoom In Region** tool from the **Navigation Bar**, the cursor is replaced by a magnifying glass. To zoom into an area, you need to define a rectangular window by picking its diagonally opposite corners. You can click at a point to specify the start point of the window. When you move the cursor, a dynamic rectangular window is created whose one corner is the specified point and the other corner is attached to the cursor. Move the cursor across the area you want to enlarge. When the area is enclosed in the rectangle, click to specify the diagonally opposite corners of the zoom window. The specified portion of the current view is enlarged. For example, to work on the stairs of a building plan, you can invoke the **Zoom In Region** tool and click to specify the two opposite corners of the window, as shown in Figure 2-23. The resulting enlarged view is shown in Figure 2-24.

Figure 2-23 Specifying the corners of the zoom window

Figure 2-24 The resulting enlarged view

Zoom Out(2X)m
This tool is used to zoom out of the existing view by twice the size of the current view. This means, when you invoke this tool, the new view will show twice the length and width of the original view.

Zoom To Fit and Zoom All to Fit
The **Zoom To Fit** tool is used to display all the contents of the project in the current view. On invoking this tool, the drawing window will adjust to show all the elements that have been created in a view. If there are multiple windows open with different zoom factors, invoke the **Zoom All to Fit** tool to perform **Zoom To Fit** in all the windows.

Zoom Sheet Size
The **Zoom Sheet Size** tool is used to fit the drawings in the default sheet size displayed in the **Paper** tab of the printer's **PDF Report Writer's Properties** dialog box. This dialog box will be displayed on choosing the **Properties** button in the **Print** dialog box. To invoke the **Print** dialog box, choose the **Application Button**; the **Application Menu** will be displayed. Choose the **Print** option or enter a shortcut key CTRL+P.

Previous Pan/Zoom and Next Pan/Zoom
The **Previous Pan/Zoom** tool reverts back to the last displayed view using zoom or pan, whereas the **Next Pan/Zoom** tool is a toggle tool to show the next displayed view.

Using the Orient Options
In Autodesk Revit Architecture, you can view a building model in 3D from the preset viewpoints using the **Orient** options.

To use the **Orient** options, activate the 3D view by choosing the **Default 3D View** tool from **View > Create > 3D View** drop-down. Alternatively, you can activate the 3D view by

Starting an Architectural Project

double-clicking on {**3D**} under the **3D Views** head in the **Project Browser**. On doing so, the current view will orient to the default 3D view along with the ViewCube displayed at the upper-right corner of the drawing area. Now, place the cursor over the ViewCube and right-click; a shortcut menu will be displayed, as shown in Figure 2-25. Now, in the shortcut menu, click on the **Orient to a Direction** option; a cascading menu will be displayed, as shown in Figure 2-26. From this cascading menu, select the appropriate view that will be displayed in the drawing window.

Figure 2-25 Options in the shortcut menu of the **ViewCube**

Figure 2-26 Options in the cascading menu of the **Orient to a Direction** option

Navigation Tools

Navigation tools in Autodesk Revit Architecture help you navigate and maneuver into your model in different directions and views. The two navigation tools, **SteeringWheels** and **ViewCube**, are discussed next.

ViewCube

The **ViewCube** tool is an interactive 3D navigation tool that appears in all 3D views of a Autodesk Revit Architecture project. By default, the **ViewCube** tool is visible at the top right corner of your drawing area.

The **ViewCube** navigation tool comprises of a cube, a compass ring at the base with various directions marked on it, and a home icon that helps you set the default view, as shown in Figure 2-27. The **ViewCube** navigation tool is displayed in your drawing area either in the active or inactive state, as shown in Figures 2-28 and 2-29. By default, the ViewCube is in its inactive state and it appears partially transparent over your drawing area. Therefore it prevents the obstruction of the view of your model. Whereas, in its active state, the ViewCube appears opaque and distinct and obstructs the view of your model. You can change the size, on-screen placement, visibility of the compass, and the inactive opacity of the ViewCube as per your requirement. To do so, choose the **ViewCube** tab from the **Options** dialog box as discussed earlier. In the **ViewCube** tool, there are twenty-six defined areas comprising faces, edges, and corners. The twenty-six defined areas can be divided into three categories, corner, edge, and face, as shown in Figure 2-30. Out of the twenty-six defined areas, six areas represent the standard orthographic views of a model such as top, bottom, front, back, left, and right. The standard orthographic views are set by clicking on one of the faces on the ViewCube. The other twenty areas are defined to access the angular views of a model.

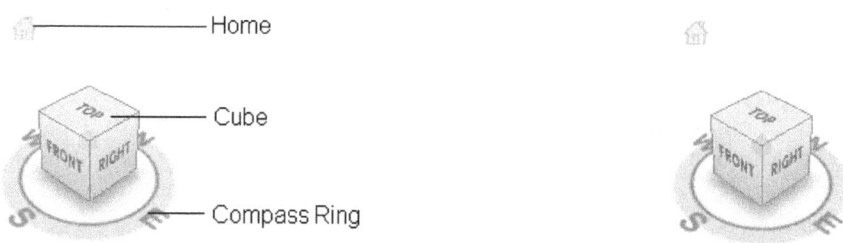

Figure 2-27 The ViewCube and its various components

Figure 2-28 The ViewCube in the active state

When you move the cursor on the faces, edges, or vertices of an active **ViewCube**, the corresponding area gets highlighted in dark-gray color. These highlighted regions are called hotspots. While using the ViewCube, you can click on these hotspots to orient your view as per your requirement.

 Tip: *You can link the **Navigation Bar** to the **ViewCube**. To do so, choose the **Customize** button located at the bottom of the **Navigation Bar**; a flyout will be displayed. Click on the **Docking positions** option in the flyout; a cascading menu will be displayed. From the cascading menu, choose the **Link to ViewCube** option; the **Navigation Bar** will be linked to the **ViewCube** displayed.*

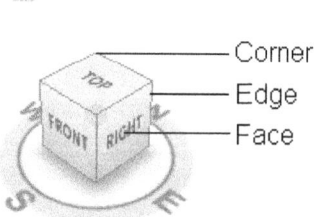

Figure 2-29 The ViewCube in the inactive state

Figure 2-30 Different areas on the ViewCube

SteeringWheels

The **SteeringWheels** navigation tools are tracking menus that comprise of multiple navigation features in a single interface. Using the features in these tools, you can pan, zoom, walk, look, and adjust the view of your model as per your requirement. The **SteeringWheels** tool is divided into different sections known as wedges. Each wedge represents a unique function for navigation.

To activate the **SteeringWheels** navigation tool in your model, press the F8 key. The **SteeringWheels** tool will appear according to the state of view in which you are working. If you are currently working in a 2D view, you can use the **2D SteeringWheels** tool. Similarly, you can use the **3D SteeringWheels** tool when you are working in the 3D view.

Starting an Architectural Project

In Autodesk Revit Architecture, you can access various types of SteeringWheels from the **Navigation Bar**. In the **Navigation Bar**, click on the down arrow below the default **Full Navigation Wheel** tool; a shortcut menu with various types of Steering Wheels will be displayed, as shown in Figure 2-31. To navigate the 2D view, you can use the 2D navigation wheel, as shown in Figure 2-32. The 2D navigation wheel has three navigation tools, **Zoom**, **Pan**, and **Rewind**. **Zoom** is a common navigation tool for enlarging or reducing the viewing scale of the model. You can use the **Pan** tool for traversing across the model view. The **Rewind** tool can be used to see the views of the previous zooming states which are saved temporarily.

Figure 2-31 Shortcut menu displaying various types of SteeringWheels

Figure 2-32 The 2D **Steering Wheels** navigation tool

The 3D **SteeringWheels** navigation tools help you navigate through your 3D views. Based on the size and appearance, the 3D SteeringWheels is categorized into two groups, Mini Steering Wheels and Big SteeringWheels.

The Mini SteeringWheels are classified into three types, **Mini Tour Building Wheel**, **Mini View Object Wheel**, and **Mini Full Navigation Wheel**, as shown in Figure 2-33. The **Mini View Object Wheel** has four distinct navigation tools, **Pan**, **Zoom**, **Rewind**, and **Orbit**. Similarly, the **Mini Tour Building Wheel** comprises of four unique navigation options, **Up/Down**, **Look**, **Walk**, and **Rewind**. The **Full Navigation Wheel** comprises of eight wedges with each wedge defining a unique navigation function. The **Mini Full Navigation Wheel** combines all the functions of the **Mini View Object Wheel** and the **Mini Tour Building Wheel**. The Big SteeringWheels has similar classification as that of the Mini SteeringWheels, as shown in Figure 2-34, and it has same navigation tools as that in the Mini SteeringWheels with the only difference in their appearances on screen.

As you put your cursor over any of the navigation tools, the tooltips and messages are displayed, as shown in Figure 2-35. The tooltips inform you regarding the tool that you want to use and provide instruction for using it. You can control the visibility of the tooltips and the tool messages while using the SteeringWheels by using the **Options** dialog box, as discussed earlier in this chapter.

While using the **SteeringWheels** navigation tool, you can activate the available navigation tools by clicking and holding the left mouse button over any one of the wedges. After holding the left mouse button and dragging it over the drawing area, you can use the selected navigation tool for reorienting your view. Now, to exit the selected navigation tool, release the left mouse button.

Figure 2-33 Types of Mini SteeringWheels for 3D Views

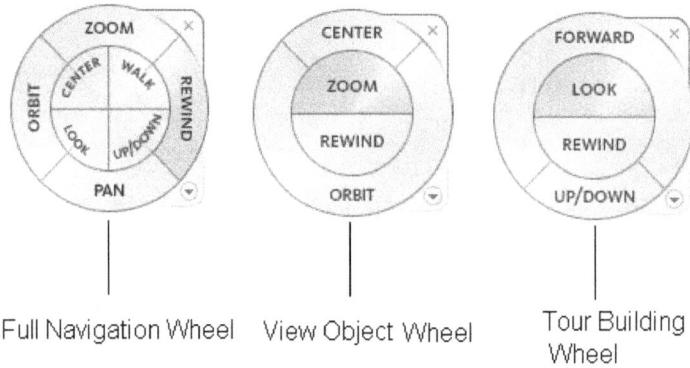

Figure 2-34 Appearance of Big SteeringWheels

Figure 2-35 Appearance of the tooltip displayed with the **SteeringWheels**

Other Display Options

Autodesk Revit Architecture provides five options to view the building model in different modes of shading. You can select these options by clicking on the **Visual Style** button from the **View Control Bar** and then selecting the desired option from the shortcut menu that will be displayed. There are six options that are available in the shortcut menu and are discussed next.

Wireframe : Displays the model with all lines and edges without surfaces.

Hidden Line : Displays the model with lines and edges that are visible.

Shaded : Displays the building model with the surfaces shaded with respect to the material shading and default lighting effect.

Consistent Colors : Displays the building model in different consistent colors, making the model more aesthetic.

Realistic : Displays the realistic view of the model with textures visible in the elements. In this view style, you can specify and visualize the effect of artificial lights and photographic exposure lighting schemes in the project. The use of this style is helpful for quick presentation, where you do not want to render the image using mental ray.

Ray Trace : Displays the real time ray trace render view. As you select, an option from the **View Control Bar**, Autodesk Revit starts rendering the model in a photorealistic Style. Initially, the render quality is low, but it improves after sometime.

Note
By default, these options affect the current view only. However, you can save the shading effects by saving the shaded view in the project file.

TUTORIALS

In the tutorials of this chapter, you will start two projects: an apartment complex and a club building. However in the subsequent chapters of this textbook, some portions of these two projects will be completed in tutorials and the rest will given as exercises and need to be completed. The tutorials and exercises form a sequence, and therefore, to complete these projects, you need to complete both the tutorials and exercises in the previous chapters. The following tutorials will familiarize you with the tools and concepts discussed in this chapter such as starting Autodesk Revit Architecture, opening a new project, setting units, setting snaps, saving and closing the project.

Tutorial 1   Apartment 1

In this tutorial, you will create a new project file for the *Apartment 1* project with the following parameters.   **(Expected time: 15 min)**

1. Template file-
   - For Imperial   *default.rte*
   - For Metric   *DefaultMetric.rte*
2. Project Units-
   - For Imperial   **Feet and fractional inches**, Rounding- **To the nearest 1/2"**.
   - For Metric   **Milimeters**,   Rounding- **0 decimal places**.
3. Length dimension snap increment-
   - For Imperial   **5' ;2'6"; 3"; 0'1/2"**.
   - For Metric   **1524; 762; 76; 13** .
4. File name to be assigned-
   - For Imperial   *c02_Apartment1_tut1.rvt*
   - For Metric   *M_c02_Apartment1_tut1.rvt*

The following steps are required to complete this tutorial:

a. Start an Autodesk Revit Architecture 2015 session.
b. Use the template file for the project.
   - For Imperial   *default.rte*
   - For Metric   *DefaultMetric.rte*
c. Set the project units using the **Format** dialog box.
   - For Imperial   **Feet and fractional inches**
   - For Metric   **Milimeters**
d. Set the length dimension snap increment using the **Snaps** dialog box.
   - For Imperial   **5'; 2'6" ;3"; 0'1/2"**
   - For Metric   **1524; 762; 76; 13**
e. Set **Endpoint, Midpoint, Nearest, Perpendicular, Work Plane Grid, Snap to Remote Objects**, and **Intersection** as the object snaps in the **Snaps** dialog box.
f. Save the project using the **Save As** tool.
   - For Imperial   *c02_Apartment1_tut1.rvt*
   - For Metric   *M_c02_Apartment1_tut1.rvt*
g. Close the project using the **Close** tool.

Starting Autodesk Revit Architecture 2015

1. Start Autodesk Revit Architecture 2015 by choosing **Start > All Programs >Autodesk > Autodesk Revit Architecture 2015 >Autodesk Revit Architecture 2015**. As a result, the program is loaded and the user interface screen is displayed.

2. Choose the **Application** button; the **Application Menu** is displayed. Choose **New > Project** from this menu; the **New Project** dialog box is displayed.

Using the Template File

To use the template file for the project, you need to access the appropriate folder and then select the required template file.

Starting an Architectural Project   2-33

1. In the **New Project** dialog box, choose the **Browse** button from the **Template file** area; the **Choose Template** dialog box is displayed, showing a list of the template files available in the **US Imperial** folder.

2. In the **Choose Template** dialog box, select the **default** template file from the **US Imperial Folder** (for Metric **DefaultMetric** template file from the **US Metric** folder), refer to Figure 2-36 and then choose the **Open** button; the **Choose Template** dialog box closes and the selected template file is applied to the new project.

3. Ensure that the **Project** radio button is selected in the **New Project** dialog box. Next, choose the **OK** button from the dialog box; the *default.rte* (for Metric *DefaultMetric.rte*) template file is loaded. Notice that the **Project Browser** now shows different levels and views that have already been created in the selected template.

Figure 2-36 The **Choose Template** *dialog box with the* ***default.rte*** *file selected*

Setting Units
1. To set units for the project, choose the **Project Units** tool from the **Settings** panel of the **Manage** tab; the **Project Units** dialog box is displayed.

2. Click in the **Format** column next to the **Length** parameter; the **Format** dialog box is displayed.

3. In the **Format** dialog box, select the required option from the **Units** drop-down list, if it is not selected by default.
         For Imperial   **Feet and fractional inches**
         For Metric   **Milimeters**

4. Click on the **Rounding** drop-down list in this dialog box and select the required option, as shown in Figure 2-37.
   For Imperial   **To the nearest 1/2"**
   For Metric   **Millimeters**

5. Choose the **OK** button; the **Project Units** dialog box is displayed. Choose the **OK** button; the specified units are applied and the dialog box is closed.

*Figure 2-37 Selecting the **To the nearest 1/2"** option in the **Format** dialog box*

Setting the Dimension and Object Snaps

To set the dimension and object snaps, use the **Snaps** tool. These settings are made based on the type of the project and the amount of detailing required.

1. Choose the **Snaps** tool from the **Settings** panel of the **Manage** tab; the **Snaps** dialog box is displayed. In the **Length dimension snap increments** edit box, enter the required values.
   For Imperial   **5';2'6";3"; 0'1/2";**
   For Metric   **1524; 762; 76; 13**

2. In the **Object Snaps** area, clear the **Quadrants**, **Centers**, **Tangents**, and **Points** check boxes. Leave the other check boxes selected. Choose the **OK** button; the settings are applied and the **Snaps** dialog box is closed.

Saving the Project

The project parameters set in the previous steps are an integral part of the project file. To save this project file with these settings, use the **Save** tool.

1. To save the project, choose the **Save** tool from the **Application Menu**. As you are saving the project for the first time, the **Save As** dialog box is displayed.

Starting an Architectural Project

2. In this dialog box, browse to the *C* drive and then create a folder with the name **Autodesk Revit Architecture_2015**.

3. Open the *Autodesk Revit Architecture_2015* folder and then create a sub-folder with the name *c02*. Next, open the created folder and save the file with the name, refer to Figure 2-38.
   For Imperial   *c02_Apartment1_tut1*
   For Metric   *M_c02_Apartment1_tut1*

   Notice that the **File of type** drop-down list shows **Project Files (*.rvt)** as the default option.

4. Choose the **Save** button to save the project with the name c02_Club_tut2.rvt. The project is saved at the specified location.

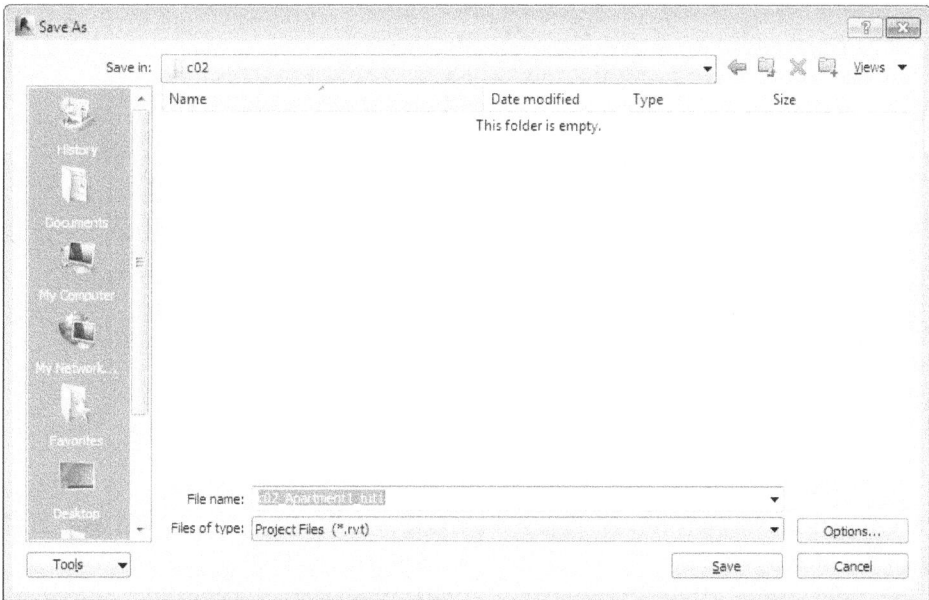

Figure 2-38 Saving the project using the Save As dialog box

Closing the Project

1. To close the project, choose the **Close** option from the **Application Menu**.

Tutorial 2   Club

In this tutorial, you will create a new project file for the *Club* project using the following project parameters.   (**Expected time: 15 min**)

1. Template file-
   For Imperial   *Commercial-Default.rte*
   For Metric   *DefaultMetric.rte*
2. Project Units-
   For Imperial   **Feet and fractional inches**.
   For Metric   **Millimeters**

3. Length dimension snap increment-
   For Imperial   **10';2'6";1'; 0'3"**.
   For Metric   **3048; 762; 305; 76** .
4. Object snaps to be set- all available object snaps.
5. File name to be assigned-
   For Imperial   *c02_Club_tut2.rvt*
   For Metric   *M_c02_Club_tut2.rvt*

The following steps are required to complete this tutorial:

a. Start an Autodesk Revit Architecture 2015 session.
b. Use the template file by accessing the **US Imperial** templates folder.
   For Imperial   *Commercial-Default.rte*
   For Metric   *Construction-DefaultMetric.rte*
c. Set the project units using the **Project Units** dialog box.
   For Imperial   **Feet and fractional inches**
   For Metric   **Millimeters**
d. Set the length dimension snap increment in the **Snaps** dialog box.
   For Imperial   **10';2'6";1'; 0'3"**
   For Metric   **3048; 762; 305; 76**
e. Select the option for rounding.
   For Imperial   **To the nearest 1/4"**
   For Metric   **0 decimal places**
f. Enable all the object snaps using the **Snaps** dialog box.
g. Save the project using the **Save As** tool.
   For Imperial   *c02_Club_tut2.rvt*
   For Metric   *M_c02_Club_tut2.rvt*
h. Close the project using the **Close** tool.

Starting Autodesk Revit Architecture 2015 and Opening a New Project

1. Start a new Autodesk Revit Architecture 2015 session by double-clicking on the Autodesk Revit Architecture shortcut icon on the desktop. On doing so, the user interface screen is displayed. In case, the Autodesk Revit Architecture 2015 session is already running, this step can be ignored and the project file can be opened directly.

2. Choose **New > Project** from the **Application Menu**; the **New Project** dialog box is displayed.

Using the Template File

As given in the project parameters, you need to use the *Commercial-Default.rte* template file for Imperial and *DefaultMetric.rte* for this project.

1. In the **New Project** dialog box, choose the **Browse** button; the **Choose Template** dialog box is displayed. In this dialog box, select the **Commercial-Default** template file from the **US Imperial Templates** folder (**DefaultMetric** from US Metric folder) and then choose

Starting an Architectural Project

Open; the selected template file is assigned to the project. Next, choose **OK**; the template file is loaded.

Notice that the **Project Browser** now shows several levels that are preloaded in the template file.

Setting Units

You can set units for various measurement parameters using the **Project Units** dialog box.

1. Choose the **Project Units** tool from the **Settings** panel of the **Manage** tab; the **Project Units** dialog box is displayed, as shown in Figure 2-39.

Figure 2-39 The **Project Units** *dialog box*

2. Click in the **Format** column next to the unit **Length**; the **Format** dialog box is displayed. In this dialog box, make sure that the **Feet and fractional inches** option for Imperial or **Millimeters** option for Metric (default option) is selected in the **Units** drop-down list.

3. Next, select the required option from the **Rounding** drop-down list.
   For Imperial **To the nearest 1/4"**
   For Metric **0 decimal places**

4. Choose **OK** to return to the **Project Units** dialog box. Next, choose the **OK** button to apply the settings and return to the user interface screen.

Setting Dimensions and Object Snaps

In this section of the tutorial, you need to access and modify the settings in the **Snaps** dialog box. Further, you need to specify the dimension snap increment and enable all the object snap options.

1. Choose the **Snaps** tool from the **Settings** panel of the **Manage** tab; the **Snaps** dialog box is displayed, as shown in Figure 2-40.

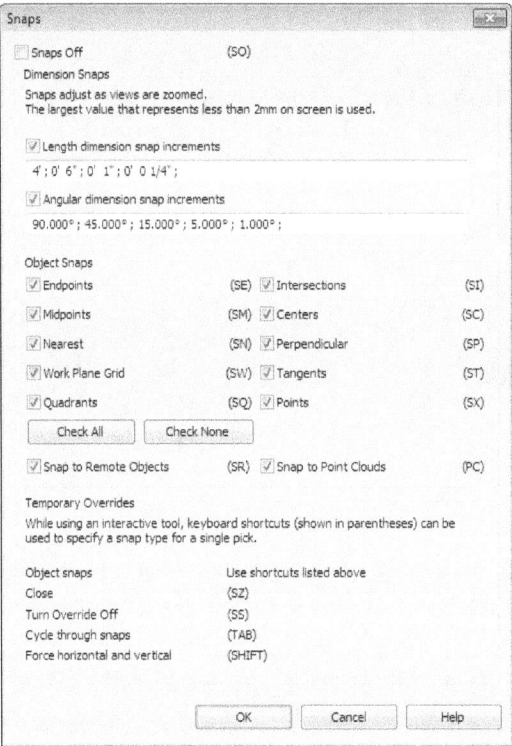

Figure 2-40 The **Snaps** *dialog box*

2. In the **Object Snaps** area, ensure that all the check boxes for snapping are selected.

3. In the **Length dimension snap increments** edit box, enter required values.
    For Imperial   **10';2'6";1'; 0'3";**
    For Metric   **3048; 762; 305; 76**
    Choose the **OK** button; the settings are applied and the **Snaps** dialog box is closed.

Saving the Project

In this section, you will save the project and the settings using the **Save** dialog box.

1. To save the project with the specified settings, choose **Save As > Project** from the **Application Menu**; the **Save As** dialog box is displayed.

Starting an Architectural Project 2-39

2. Browse to the *c02* sub-folder in the *Autodesk Revit Architecture_2015* folder and enter the required file name in the **File name** edit box. Notice that the **File of type** drop-down list shows **Project Files (*.rvt)** as the default option.
   For Imperial   **c02_Club_tut2**
   For Metric   **M_c02_Club_tut2**

3. Choose the **Save** button to save the project. The project is saved at the specified location.

Closing the Project

1. To close the project, choose the **Close** option from the **Application Menu**.

   The file is closed and this completes Tutorial 2 of Chapter 2.

Self-Evaluation Test

Answer the following questions and then compare them to those given at the end of this chapter:

1. You can open only one Autodesk Revit Architecture project at a time. (T/F)

2. In Autodesk Revit Architecture, all the enabled object snaps work together. (T/F)

3. While saving a project file for the first time, the **Save As** dialog box is displayed on choosing the **Save** tool from the **Application Menu**. (T/F)

4. A project file can be opened by double-clicking on the file name in the **Windows Explorer**. (T/F)

5. You can save any project file as a template file. (T/F)

6. The keyboard shortcut for the **Save** tool is _____.

7. To specify the location of the default template file, you can use the _____ tab of the **Options** dialog box.

8. The _____ button in the **Save As** dialog box can be used to specify the maximum number of backup(s) for a project file.

9. The _____ option of Autodesk Revit Architecture enables you to override the snap settings for a single pick only.

10. You can add folders to the _____ list in the **Save As** dialog box to access the frequently used folders directly.

Review Questions

Answer the following questions:

1. You can modify the project unit settings anytime during a project. (T/F)

2. The file name and path of a project have to be specified each time you save a project. (T/F)

3. You cannot control the visibility of the tooltip assistant. (T/F)

4. The **Save reminder interval** drop-down list available in the **General** tab of the **Options** dialog box is used to specify the time interval between the reminder prompts to save a project file. (T/F)

5. If changes made to a project file have not been saved, Autodesk Revit Architecture prompts you to save the changes when you choose the **Close** tool from the **Application Menu**. (T/F)

6. You cannot control the display of tool messages, tooltips, and tool cursor of the SteeringWheels. (T/F)

7. You can add words to revit dictionaries for checking spellings. (T/F)

8. Which of the following is not an object snap option?

   a) **Endpoint**   b) **Work Plane Grid**
   c) **Dimension**   d) **Centers**

9. Which of the following keys can be used to toggle between the object snap options available at the same point?

   a) TAB   b) CTRL
   c) ALT   d) F3

10. Which of the following shortcut keys is used to activate the SteeringWheels?

    a) F2   b) F6
    c) CTRL   d) F8

Starting an Architectural Project

11. Which three conditions are inherited by new projects from the project template?

    a) Levels
    c) Families
    b) Workflow Settings
    d) Library Structure.

12. Which of the following boxes helps to set the units?

    a) **Format**
    c) **Options**
    b) **Snaps**
    d) **Project Information**

Exercises

Exercise 1   Apartment 2

Create a new project file for the *Apartment 2* project with the following parameters: **(Expected time: 15 min)**

1. Template file-
   - For Imperial   **default.rte**
   - For Metric   **DefaultMetric.rte**
2. Project Units-
   - For Imperial   **Feet and fractional inches**
   - For Metric   **Millimeters**
3. Length dimension snap increment-
   - For Imperial   **5';2'6";3"; 0'1/2"**
   - For Metric   **1524 ;762;76; 13**
4. File name to be assigned-
   - For Imperial   *c02_Apartment2_ex1.rvt*
   - For Metric   *M_c02_Apartment2_ex1.rvt*

Exercise 2   Elevator and Stair Lobby

Create a new project file for the *Elevator and Stair Lobby* project with the following parameters: **(Expected time: 15 min)**

1. Template file-
   - For Imperial   **default.rte**
   - For Metric   **DefaultMetric.rte**
2. Project Units-
   - For Imperial   **Feet and fractional inches**
   - For Metric   **Millimeters**
3. Length dimension snap increment-
   - For Imperial   **5';1';3"; 0'1"**
   - For Metric   **1524; 305; 76; 25**
4. File name to be assigned-
   - For Imperial   *c02_ElevatorandStairLobby_ex2.rvt*
   - For Metric   *M_c02_ElevatorandStairLobby_ex2.rvt*

Answers to Self Evaluation Test
1. F, **2.** T, **3.** T, **4.** T, **5.** T, **6.** CTRL+S, **7.** File Locations, **8.** Options, **9.** Temporary Overrides, **10.** Places

Chapter 3

Creating Walls

Learning Objectives

After completing this chapter, you will be able to:
- *Understand the concept of walls.*
- *Understand the properties of walls.*
- *Use the sketching tools to create walls.*
- *Work with stacked wall.*
- *Create exterior and interior walls based on the given parameters.*
- *Create wall sweeps and wall reveals.*

INTRODUCTION

In the previous chapter, you learned about various tools and options to start, open and save an architectural project in Revit Architecture. In this chapter, you will learn about various tools and options to create different types of walls. You will also learn about the functions and parameters of different types of walls. Moreover, you will learn various options to modify the properties of an architectural wall and its type properties will be discussed in detail. Also, you will learn about various tools that are used to add modifiers, such as sweep and reveal to a wall.

CREATING A BUILDING PROJECT

In Revit, the term 'project' comprises not only the physical building model but also its associated documentation such as drawings, views, schedules, areas, and so on. The first step in creating a project is to create the building model. In Autodesk Revit Architecture, you can create it using the following two methods:

Method 1: Create a building model using individual building elements such as walls, windows, doors, floors, roofs, and so on.

Method 2: Create a conceptual mass of a building model using the massing tools and conceptualize the overall building shape and volume before working with individual elements.

> **Tip:** *You can also use a combination of above two methods. You can generate a building mass using the massing tools and then convert it into a building model with individual building elements using the building maker tools.*

The selection of method depends on different project parameters such as project magnitude, building shape, building technology, current documentation stage of a project, industry parameters, and so on. The use of the massing tools to create a building geometry and the usage of individual building components to develop a building model will be described later.

Autodesk Revit Architecture provides you with several tools to add individual building elements such as wall, floor, roof, and so on for creating a building model. Several predesigned element types have been provided for each building element in Autodesk Revit Architecture libraries. You have the flexibility to either use the predesigned element types or create your own element type to create a building model.

Sequence of Creating a Building Model

The sequence of using building elements for creating a building model depend on various parameters such as building type, building volume, building shape, and so on. For most of the building projects, the sequence given below may be adopted.

Step 1: Start the model by creating the exterior walls of the building at Level 1 (lowest level).

Step 2: Create interior walls at the desired locations.

Creating Walls

Step 3: Add doors and windows to the exterior and interior walls at the desired location.

Step 4: Add the floor to the building model.

Step 5: Add the roof to the building model.

Step 6: Add the structural or architectural grid and structural elements.

Step 7: Add stand-alone components such as furniture items and plumbing fixtures.

Step 8: Add text and annotations to different spaces.

Step 9: Create dimensions for different parameters of the project.

Step 10: Create project details and documentation.

Step 11: Create the rendered 3D views and walkthrough.

In Revit, each building element is considered a three-dimensional parametric entity. This means, on adding elements, you also add the related information and specification about them. One of the most important elements in a building model is the wall. It defines the basic spatial arrangement of the building and that acts as the host for doors and windows.

Understanding Wall Types

Autodesk Revit Architecture provides you with several predefined wall types such as **Exterior**, **Interior**, **Retaining**, **Foundation**, **Curtain**, and **Stacked Wall**, based on their usage.

Exterior Wall Type

This category constitutes the wall types that are primarily used for generating the exterior skin of the building model. It has predefined wall types such as **Brick on CMU**, **Brick on Mtl. Stud**, **CMU Insulated**, and so on.

Interior Wall Type

The interior walls are used as the interior partitions in a building project. These walls are non-bearing in character. The predefined interior walls provided in Autodesk Revit Architecture have a dry wall construction with a metal stud frame and varying thickness.

Retaining Wall Type

As the name suggests, the primary function of the retaining walls is to retain the earth. You can either use the retaining walls provided in the program or set the function of any wall type as retaining. For example, you can select a wall from the drawing and select **Retaining - 12" Concrete** for Imperial or (**Retaining 300mm Concrete** for Metric) from the **Properties** palette. On doing so, the current wall type will be changed to retaining wall.

Foundation Wall Type

The walls that form the foundation or substrate of the main building structure belong to this category. To create a foundation wall, the **Foundation - 12" Concrete** option for Imperial (**Foundation- 300mm Concrete** for Metric) is provided as the predefined foundation wall type in the **Properties** palette.

Curtain Wall Type

These wall types has predefined curtain walls or screen walls that consist of panels and mullions.

Stacked Wall Type

A stacked wall is a wall that is made of different types of walls stacked vertically on top of each other.

This software provides you with the flexibility of creating your own wall type. The walls that you will create can have different parameters which can be modified, depending on their usage. In Revit, you can create both architectural and structural walls. An architectural wall does not contain analytical properties like the structural walls. In the next section, various techniques to create and modify architectural walls are discussed.

Creating Architectural Walls

Ribbon: Architecture > Build > Wall drop-down > Wall: Architectural
Shortcut Key: WA

In this section, you will learn the method of creating and editing architectural walls. In Autodesk Revit Architecture, each wall type has specific predefined properties such as its usage, composition, material, characteristics, finish, height, and so on. You can select the wall type based on its specific usage in the project. Walls, like most other model elements, can be created in a plan view or a 3D view.

To create an architectural wall, first you need to invoke the **Wall: Architectural** tool and then select the appropriate wall type and specify various properties. To do so, choose the **Wall: Architectural** tool from the **Build** panel of the **Architecture** tab, refer to Figure 3-1; the **Modify | Place Wall** tab will be displayed. Select an exterior or interior wall type from the **Type Selector** drop-down list in the **Properties** palette, as shown in Figure 3-2. Next, from the **Properties** palette, specify and edit various properties of the wall to be created. Various wall properties and the process to specify them are discussed next.

Figure 3-1 Invoking the **Wall: Architectural** tool from the **Build** panel

Creating Walls 3-5

 Tip: *Besides the* **Properties** *palette, wall types are also listed under the* **Families** *head in the* **Family Browser**. *Left-click on the arrow sign next to the* **Families** *head to view the families available in Autodesk Revit Architecture. Click the arrow symbol next to the* **Walls** *subhead and then the one next to the* **Basic Wall** *subhead to display various basic wall types. Select and right-click on any wall type to display a shortcut menu with the options that can be used for editing.*

Figure 3-2 Selecting the wall type from the **Type Selector** *drop-down list*

Specifying Architectural Wall Properties

In Autodesk Revit Architecture, wall, like other elements, has two sets of properties, type and instance. These set of properties control the appearance and the behavior of the element concerned.

Specifying Instance Properties

After invoking the **Wall: Architectural** tool, the instance properties of the wall will be displayed in the **Properties** palette, as shown in Figure 3-3.

The **Properties** palette contains the **Type Selector** drop-down list. You can select the family and the type of the proposed wall, respectively from this drop-down list. This palette shows various instance properties and their corresponding values for the specified instance of the element. The options in this palette depend on the type and instance of the selected element or the element to be created as well as on the options selected in the **Type Selector** drop-down list. The properties of exterior walls are displayed in different categories such as **Constraints**, **Structural**, **Dimensions**, **Identity Data**, and **Phasing** each representing a set of properties corresponding to the title. You can use the twin arrows on the extreme right of the title to collapse the table of properties for each title. Some of the important parameters are discussed next.

Figure 3-3 The partial view of the **Properties** palette for the **Exterior - Brick on CMU** wall type

In the **Properties** palette, the **Location Line** parameter indicates the reference line used for creating a wall. In 3D environment, the location line in a wall refers to a plane that does not get modified even if the wall parameters are changed. To assign a value to the **Location Line** parameter, click in the value field corresponding to this parameter; a drop-down list will be displayed. Click on the drop-down list to view the available options. The options in the drop-down list are given next.

Wall Centerline	-	Center line of the entire composite wall
Core Centerline	-	Center line of the structural core of the wall
Finish Face: Exterior	-	Exterior face of the wall as the location line
Finish Face: Interior	-	Interior face of the wall as the location line
Core Face: Exterior	-	Exterior face of the core
Core Face: Interior	-	Interior face of the core

The location line is indicated by a dashed line, which appears while sketching a wall segment. For example, on selecting **Wall Centerline** as the location line parameter, you will notice a dashed line in the middle of the wall, as shown in Figure 3-4. When you select **Finish Face: Interior**, it appears on the interior face of the wall, see Figure 3-5.

Creating Walls

Figure 3-4 Wall on selecting the **Wall Centerline** option

Figure 3-5 Wall on selecting the **Finish Face: Interior** option

Note
When a design is developed, you may need to modify certain parameters of the exterior wall such as its thickness and composition, based on the final selection of materials and their specifications. Considering this flexibility, the location line parameter enables you to create walls.

In Autodesk Revit Architecture, you can specify the height of walls by applying the base and top constraints with respect to the levels defined in the project. This means, if you set the base and height parameters of a top story and apply these constraints, all walls will be sketched with the same base and the top. To create a wall segment that is not related to these components and levels, you can type the desired height in the column of the **Unconnected Height** instance parameter. The default value for the unconnected height is 20' 0".

The various instance parameters for walls and their usage are given next. The values of some of the instance parameters will be available only after an instance is created. The instance parameters of the wall are given in the table below.

Instance Parameter	Description
Location Line	Line or reference plane for sketching the wall
Base Constraint	Level or reference plane of the base of a wall
Base is Attached	Check box showing whether or not the base of the wall is attached to any other element
Base Offset	Height of a wall from its base constraint
Base Extension Distance	Distance of the base of the layers in a wall
Top Constraint	Whether the wall height is defined by specified levels or is unconnected
Image	Specifies the image file corresponding to a wall instance. This parameter can be used in the wall schedule to display the image of the wall instance.
Unconnected Height	Explicit height of a wall
Top Offset	Distance of the top of a wall from the top constraint
Top Extension Distance	Distance of the top of a layer on a wall
Room Bounding	Whether the wall constitutes the boundary of a room
Related to Mass	Whether the wall relates to a massing geometry

Structural Usage	Defines the specific structural usage of a wall
Length	Indicates the value of the length of a wall
Area	Indicates the value of the surface area of a wall
Volume	Indicates the value of the volume of a wall
Comments	Specific comments that give description of a wall
Mark	To add a unique value or label to each wall
Phase Created	Phase in which a wall is created
Phase Demolished	Phase in which a wall was demolished

Tip: *The selection for the **Location Line** parameter should be based on your design intent. For example, to create walls defined by exact interior dimensions, you can select **Finish Face: Interior** as the location line value. Once this parameter is selected, any addition or reduction of wall thickness in the project will be made towards its outer face.*

Specifying Type Properties

The type properties of a wall specify the common parameters shared by certain elements in a family. Any changes made in the type properties of a wall element will affect all individual elements of that family in the project. To modify the type properties of an element, invoke the **Wall: Architectural** tool; the **Modify | Place Wall** tab will be displayed. In this tab, choose the **Type Properties** tool from the **Properties** panel; the **Type Properties** dialog box will be displayed, as shown in Figure 3-6. Using this dialog box, you can modify the type properties of the selected wall type such as **Structure**, **Function**, **Coarse Scale Fill Pattern**, and so on. In Autodesk Revit Architecture, in the **Type Properties** dialog box, you can view the Analytical Properties of the wall such as the **Thermal Mass**, **Thermal Resistance**, and **Heat Transfer Coefficient**. The Analytical Properties that you can edit are: **Absorptance** and **Roughness**. In the **Type Properties** dialog box, you can also define the composition of the wall type. To do so, choose the **Edit** button in the **Value** column of the **Structure** parameter; the **Edit Assembly** dialog box will be displayed. In the **Edit Assembly** dialog box, choose the **Preview** button; a preview box will be displayed. The preview box will display sectional detail of the selected wall type, as shown in Figure 3-7

Creating Walls

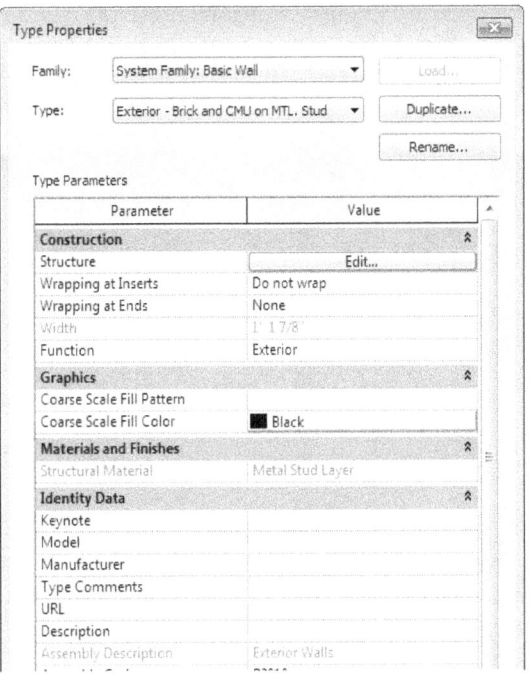

Figure 3-6 *The partial view of the **Type Properties**
dialog box with the **Exterior-Brick on CMU** wall type*

In Autodesk Revit Architecture, a wall is a composite building element and can consist of several layers. The **Layers** area in the **Edit Assembly** dialog box displays multiple layers of the selected wall, each with a specific function, material, and thickness. The layer on the top of the table represents the exterior side of a wall and the last layer represents the in face. The **Layers** area, refer to Figure 3-7, displays the selected wall type. In this case, it is **Exterior- Brick on Mtl. Stud**. This wall type has nine layers. Each layer of the composite wall is assigned a specific function and priority based on its usage. The layers available in Autodesk Revit Architecture can be broadly classified into the categories given next.

Structure [1]- Consists of main supporting element of the structure such as concrete, brick, wood, metal stud, and so on.

Substrate [2] - Consists of material that functions as substructure, such as foundation and plywood.

Thermal/Air Layer - Indicates the air cavity or the thermal insulation layer.

Membrane Layer - A zero thickness layer primarily for the prevention against water vapor penetration.

Finish 1 [4] - Exterior finish such as metal, brick, and stone.

Finish 2 [5] - Interior finish such as paint, gypsum wall board, and so on.

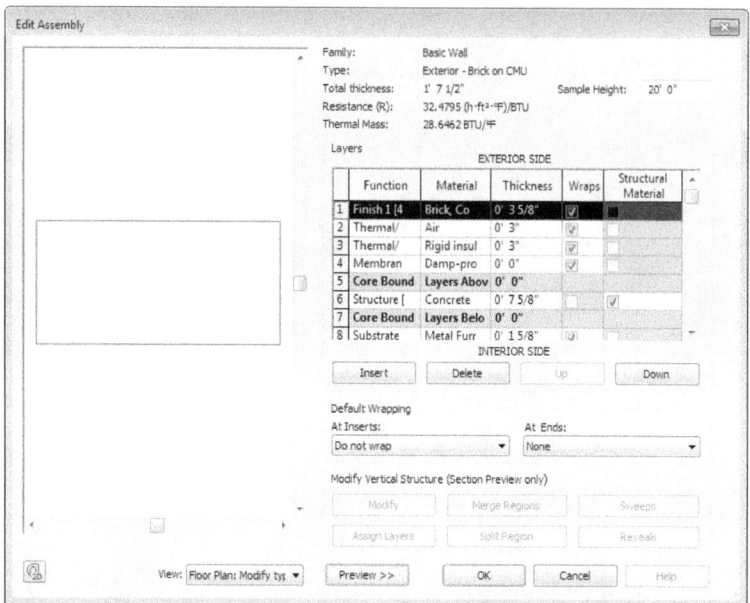

*Figure 3-7 The **Edit Assembly** dialog box with the **Preview** button chosen*

Note
The numbers placed next to certain layers show the priority set of the layer and enables Autodesk Revit Architecture to work out the joinery detail of wall segments at corners and intersections according to the priority. When joined, a higher priority layer takes precedence over a lower priority layer.

In the **Edit Assembly** dialog box, the **Material** column displays the material specification, whereas the **Thickness** column displays the thickness of each layer. The total thickness of this composite wall is the sum of thickness of all layers. In the present case, the total thickness of wall is **1'1 7/8" (350 mm)** which is given beside the **Total thickness** parameter on the top of the dialog box. You can click on the **View** drop-down list and select **Section: Modify type attributes** to view the section of the wall.

Note
*The **View** drop-down list will only be visible if you choose the **Preview** button in the **Edit Assembly** dialog box.*

Autodesk Revit Architecture enables you to add and remove layers by using the **Insert** and **Delete** buttons, respectively, provided in the **Layers** area in the **Edit Assembly** dialog box. To shift the layers, choose the **Up** and **Down** buttons. You can also create your own layers. You will learn more about materials, layers, and composite walls in the later chapters. The **Default Wrapping** area in the **Edit Assembly** dialog box has two drop-down lists namely, **At Inserts** and **At Ends**. The options in these drop-down lists allow wrapping of a compound wall at the end and at the inserts (for doors and windows). From the **At Inserts** drop-down list, you can select any of the following options: **Exterior**, **Interior**, **Both**, and **Do not wrap**. Similarly, from the **At Ends** drop-down list, you can select any of the following options: **Exterior**, **Interior**, or **None**. The wrapping in the walls can be

Creating Walls

viewed in a plan view. The Figures 3-8 through 3-11 illustrate the effects of different types of wrapping options on the wall.

Figure 3-8 The wall created with the **Do not wrap** option selected from the **At Inserts** drop-down list in the **Default Wrapping** area

Figure 3-9 The wall created with the **Exterior** option selected from the **At Inserts** drop-down list in the **Default Wrapping** area

 Tip: *While creating a new wall type, you can specify whether a wall is an exterior or interior wall. To do so, invoke the **Type Properties** dialog box of the wall to be created and click in the **Value** field of the **Function** parameter; a drop-down list will be displayed. From this drop-down list, you can select the **Exterior** option to assign exterior wall type function to the selected wall. Similarly, you can select the **Interior** option to assign the interior wall type function to the wall.*

Figure 3-10 The wall created with the **None** option selected from the **At Ends** drop-down list in the **Default Wrapping** area

Figure 3-11 The wall created with the **Exterior** option selected from the **At Ends** drop-down list in the **Default Wrapping** area

Sketching Walls

The next step after selecting the wall type from the **Properties** palette is to select the sketching tool. Autodesk Revit Architecture provides several sketching tools, such as **Line, Rectangle**, and others to sketch the walls of different shapes. These tools, along with the **Options Bar**, can be invoked from the **Draw** panel in the **Modify | Place Wall** tab, as shown in Figure 3-12.

*Figure 3-12 Wall sketching tools available in the **Draw** panel*

Using Sketching Tools

In Autodesk Revit, you can access different sketching tools from the **Draw** panel and the **Options Bar** in the **Modify | Place Wall** tab. On invoking these tools, you can sketch different wall profiles. The procedure to do so is discussed next.

Sketching Straight Wall Profiles. You can sketch straight walls using the **Line** sketching tool by specifying the start point and the endpoint of the wall segment. To specify the location of the start point, click anywhere in the drawing area. Now, move the cursor in the drawing area, you will notice that a wall segment is starting from the specified point and the dimension that changes dynamically appears on it. This dimension is called the temporary dimension or listening dimension, and it shows the length and angle of the wall segment at any given location of the cursor, as shown in Figure 3-13. Also, notice that the cursor moves in increments by the value set in the **Dimension Snaps** area of the **Snaps** dialog box (See Setting Snaps topic, Chapter 2). The angle subtended by the wall on the horizontal axis is also displayed and it keeps changing dynamically as you move the cursor to modify the inclination of the wall. Also notice that, on bringing the cursor near the horizontal or the vertical axis, a dashed line will appear on the wall segment. This is called the alignment line and it helps you sketch the components with respect to the already created components. You will also notice that a tooltip is displayed indicating that the wall segment being sketched is horizontal, as shown in Figure 3-14.

Figure 3-13 Length and angle of the wall segment

Figure 3-14 Sketching a horizontal wall

Creating Walls 3-13

Autodesk Revit Architecture provides you the flexibility of specifying the length of the walls in different ways. The first option is to specify the starting point of the wall, move the cursor in the desired direction, and click when the angle and the temporary dimension attain the required values. The second option is to sketch the wall and then modify its length and angle to the exact value. For example, to sketch a 18'0"(5486mm) long horizontal wall after specifying the starting point, you can move the cursor to the right until you see a dashed horizontal line parallel to the sketched wall. Click when the temporary dimension shows 20'0"(6096 mm) approximately. Note that the length of the wall may not be exactly 18'0"(5486 mm). You can now use the wall controls to modify the dimensions of the wall to its exact value.

To modify the wall, select the wall segment and view its control and properties. As you select the wall segment, it gets highlighted in blue and the symbols appear in blue above the wall segment, as shown in Figure 3-15

The exact dimension of the sketched wall is visible in the dimension text of the temporary dimension. The conversion control symbol, which appears below the dimension value, is used to convert the temporary dimension into a permanent dimension. The two blue arrows, which also appear on the upper face of the wall, indicate the flip control symbol for the sketched walls. They appear on the side interpreted as the exterior face of the wall. By default, the walls drawn from the left to right have the external face on the upper side and the walls drawn from the top to bottom have it on the right side. You can flip the orientation of the wall by clicking on the arrows symbol. Alternatively, you can place the cursor over the flip control symbol and notice the change in its color. After the color of the flip control changes, press SPACEBAR to flip the wall. The two blue dots that appear at the two ends of the wall segments are the drag control symbols. You can use them to stretch and resize the walls. To set the wall to the exact length, click on the temporary dimension; an edit box will appear showing the current dimension of the wall segment. Now, you can change the length of the wall by entering the desired value in the edit box. For example, you can enter **14' 8"(4470 mm)** in the edit box, as shown in Figure 3-16. Next, press ENTER; the length of the wall will be modified to 14' 8"(4470 mm).

Figure 3-15 *Highlighted wall displaying its various controls*

Alternatively, you can create a straight wall by typing the dimension of the length before choosing the endpoint. As soon as you start typing the length, an edit box appears above the dimension line. Enter the value of the length and press ENTER to create a wall segment of the specified length. To sketch a wall at a given angle, sketch it at any angle and then click on the angular dimension symbol; an edit box will appear. In the edit box, you can enter the exact angular dimension from the horizontal axis to which the wall will be inclined.

Figure 3-16 Specifying the length of the wall

Note
*The **Project Browser** shows **Level 1** in bold letters. This indicates that the wall has been sketched in that level.*

Sketching Rectangular Wall Profiles. You can invoke the **Rectangle** tool from the **Draw** panel in the **Modify | Place Wall** tab to sketch a rectangular wall profile. After you invoke the **Rectangle** tool, click on the screen to specify the location of one corner of the rectangular wall to be drawn. Next, move the cursor away from the point; a rectangular wall profile will be displayed along with the temporary dimension between the two parallel walls. Now, move the cursor to the desired location and when the temporary dimension attains the desired value, click to specify the diagonally opposite corner of the profile; the rectangular wall will be created along with the temporary dimensions displayed. Alternatively, you can also create a rectangular wall profile by sketching it using some rough dimension and then modifying its size. This can be done by clicking on the temporary dimension of the sketched profile and entering the exact distance in the edit box, as shown in Figure 3-17. The size of the rectangle will be modified to the exact values.

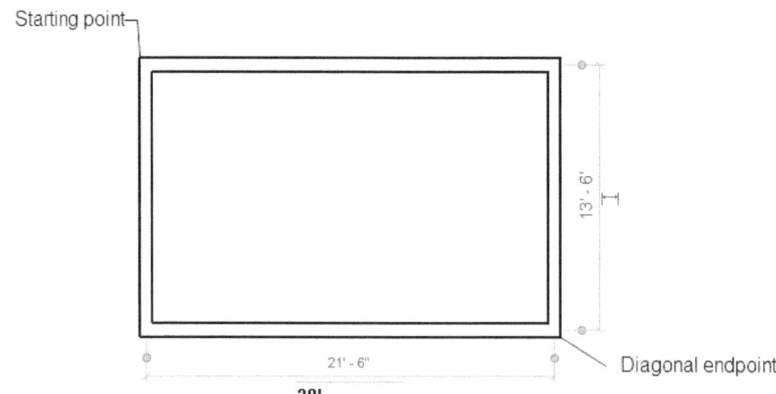

Figure 3-17 Creating and modifying a rectangular wall profile

Sketching Polygonal Wall Profiles. You can sketch a polygonal wall profile using either the **Inscribed Polygon** or **Circumscribed Polygon** tool from the **Draw** panel in the **Modify | Place Wall** tab. To draw an inscribed polygon, invoke the **Inscribed Polygon** tool or to draw a circumscribed polygon, invoke the **Circumscribed Polygon** tool. When you invoke any of these tools, various options for polygon creation are displayed in the **Options Bar**. In the **Options Bar**, you can specify the number of sides of the polygon in the **Sides** edit box. The polygonal profile can be created by specifying the radius of the

Creating Walls

inscribed or circumscribed circle. To draw an inscribed polygon, choose the **Inscribed Polygon** tool from the **Draw** panel in the **Modify | Place Wall** tab and then specify the desired number of sides, height (if unconnected), and offset value in the respective edit boxes in the **Options Bar**. Next, click in the drawing area to specify the center of the polygon. Then, drag the cursor and click again to get the desired radius; the inscribed polygon will be created. Similarly, a circumscribed polygon can also be created by choosing the **Circumscribed Polygon** tool from the **Draw** panel in the **Modify | Place Wall** tab.

Sketching Circular Wall Profiles. The **Circle** tool in the list box can be used to sketch circular wall profile. To sketch a circular wall profile, invoke the **Circle** tool from the **Draw** panel of the **Modify | Place Wall** tab and click in the drawing area to specify the center point of the circular wall. You will notice that a circular wall profile is extending dynamically with the specified point as the center and the other end attached to the cursor, as shown in Figure 3-18. The temporary radial dimension will also be displayed. Click when the desired value for the radius is displayed. Alternatively, before clicking on the second point, type the value for the radius of the circular profile. As you type, the value will be displayed in the edit box. Press ENTER to complete the profile. Notice that the dimension that you entered is the distance of the center point to the location line of the profile.

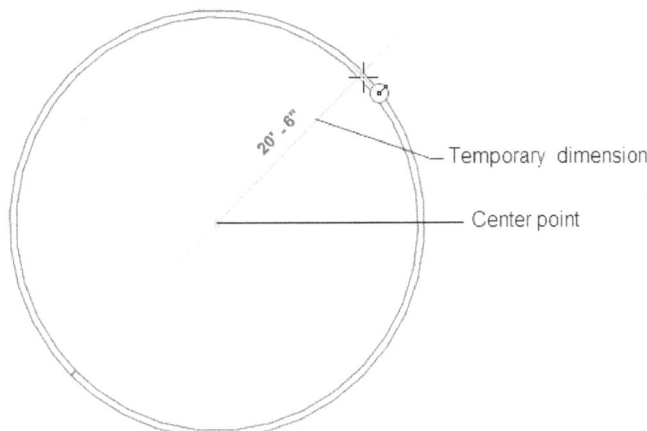

*Figure 3-18 Sketching the **Circular wall** profile*

Sketching Start-End-Radius Arc Profiles. The **Start-End-Radius Arc** tool in the **Draw** panel of the **Modify | Place Wall** tab enables you to sketch an arc wall by specifying the start point, end point, and the intermediate point that determines the radius of the arc. To create an arc wall, invoke the **Start-End-Radius Arc** tool from the **Draw** panel of the **Modify | Place Wall** tab; you will be prompted to specify the start point of the proposed arc wall. Specify the start point by clicking in the drawing area. Now, you will be prompted to specify the endpoint of the curved wall. Specify the endpoint of the curved wall; a curved wall with a variable radius stretches dynamically between the two specified points. Specify the location of the third point between the two specified points to specify the subtended angle or the radius of the arc. As you specify the third point, the angular and radial temporary dimensions are displayed along with the curve on the screen.

Next, click in the drawing area to specify the third point; the curved wall will be sketched. You can also modify the sketched wall to the desired curvature parameters such as radius, angle subtended, orientation, and so on. To modify the curvature, select the sketched wall, click on the parameter such as the angular dimension and enter the new value, as shown in Figure 3-19. You can also use the drag controls to increase or decrease the extent of the wall. The central blue dot can be used to stretch the wall, keeping the subtended angle constant.

Sketching Center-ends Arc Wall Profiles. You can sketch a curved wall by specifying its center point and two endpoints. To do so, choose the **Center-ends Arc** tool from the **Draw** panel in the **Modify | Place Wall** tab. Next, click in the drawing area to specify the location of the center point and then move the cursor. Click when the desired value of the radius is displayed. You can also type the radius value and then press ENTER. The point that you specify will be taken as the start point of the wall. Next, click in the drawing area again to specify the endpoint of the arc wall. Note that the curved wall segment can be extended up to 180-degree. When the angle exceeds 180-degree, the wall will flip the side. Once the wall is sketched, you can select it and modify its parameters such as its subtended angle and radius. You can also modify the curvature keeping the radius fixed by using the drag controls, refer to Figure 3-20.

Figure 3-19 Sketching and modifying a curved wall profile

Figure 3-20 Sketching a curved wall profile using the **Center-ends Arc** sketching tool

Sketching Tangent End Arcs Wall Profiles. To sketch a curved wall profile that starts tangentially from an existing wall, invoke the **Tangent End Arc** tool from the **Draw** panel in the **Modify | Place Wall** tab and click at the endpoint of an existing wall to specify the start point. After specifying the start point, move the cursor to the desired distance and click to define the curved wall profile.

Sketching Fillet Arc Wall Profiles. To create a curved fillet wall between the two existing walls, choose the **Fillet Arc** tool in the **Draw** panel of the **Modify | Place Wall** tab. Now, one by one, click on the two walls to create a fillet close to the desired fillet end. On doing so, a fillet wall will appear, showing its possible locations, as shown in Figure 3-21. Click to specify the location of the fillet. Once the fillet wall is sketched, you can modify its radius by clicking on it and typing its value. Notice that the walls are automatically trimmed after placing the fillet arc.

Using the Chain Option. Select the **Chain** check box in the **Options Bar** to create a continuous wall profile with a number of wall segments. It enables you to create a continuous wall with wall segments connected end to end. The end point of the previous wall becomes the start point of the next wall. To enable the **Chain** option, select the check box before or while sketching the wall profile. You can also use this option while using different sketching tools.

*Figure 3-21 Sketching a fillet arc wall profile using the **Fillet Arc** tool*

Using the Offset Option. The **Offset** edit box can be used to create a wall that starts at a specified offset distance from a point defined in an existing element. You can enter the offset distance value in the **Offset** edit box provided in the **Options Bar**. However, the shape of the resulting wall depends on the sketching tool selected. After entering the offset value and selecting the sketching option, click near the element to define the offset distance. When you move the cursor, the wall will start at the specified distance from the selected point. For example, this option can be used for creating boundary walls that are placed at a specific distance from the building profile.

Using the Radius Option. The **Radius** edit box in the **Options Bar** is used to specify the radius while sketching a circular, curved, or a fillet wall. You can type the value of the radius in the **Radius** edit box before or after invoking the desired sketching tool.

Tip: *An appropriate sketching option should be selected based on the desired wall profile. You can also sketch walls using a combination of available sketching tools.*

WORKING WITH STACKED WALLS

In Autodesk Revit Architecture, besides basic wall and curtain wall there is a special kind of wall called a stacked wall. A stacked wall is a wall created using two or more basic wall that are stacked on top of another to form a complex design. These walls are assembled in such a way that the entire facade acts as a single wall. In the next section, you will learn about various options that are used to create a stacked wall and then add it to the project.

Creating a Stacked Wall

To create a stacked wall, choose the **Wall: Architectural** tool from **Architecture > Build > Wall** drop-down; the **Modify | Place Wall** tab with the instance parameters in the **Properties** palette will be displayed. In the **Properties** palette, select the stacked wall type from the **Type-Selector** drop-down list. After selecting the stacked wall type, choose the **Edit Type** button from the **Properties** palette; the **Type Properties** dialog box will be displayed.

In the **Type Properties** dialog box, choose the **Duplicate** button to create a new type of stacked wall; the **Name** dialog box will be displayed. In this dialog box, enter a desired name and choose the **OK** button; the **Type Properties** dialog box will be displayed and the created type will be updated in the **Type** drop-down list. Now, you are required to edit the structural properties to form a new type. Choose the **Edit** button corresponding to the **Structure** parameter; the **Edit Assembly** dialog box will be displayed. In this dialog box, select the type of wall from the **Name** column. In the **Height** column, you need to specify the height of the walls. By default, the height of first wall is **Variable**. If you want to make other wall types as variable, select the desired wall type; the **Variable** button will be activated. Choose the **Variable** button to change the wall to variable. If you want to insert a row then choose the **Insert** button and to delete a row, choose the **Delete** button. You can use the **Preview** button to preview the stacked wall. Next, choose the **OK** button twice; the **Edit Assembly** and the **Type Properties** dialog boxes will be closed and will be selected in the **Type Selector** drop-down list. Now, you can use the stacked wall to create the building.

ADDING INTERIOR WALLS

In Autodesk Revit Architecture, interior walls form a separate family of wall types. They differ from the exterior wall types based on their usage, material specifications, and non load-bearing character. Several predefined interior wall types are provided in the Autodesk Revit Architecture libraries.

To view the interior wall types, choose the **Wall: Architectural** tool from **Architecture > Build > Wall** drop-down; the instance parameters of the wall will be displayed in the **Properties** palette. From this palette you can select different types of walls available in Revit. The wall types that may be used as interior walls have been assigned the prefix **Interior**. Based on the project requirement, you can select the appropriate interior wall type from the drop-down list. For example, **Interior- 5" Partition (2-hr)** is a type of interior wall for Imperial (**Interior- 135mm Partition (2-hr)** for Metric) with a 2-hour fire rating and can be selected from the **Properties** palette, as shown in Figure 3-22.

To view and specify the properties of an interior wall type, you can use the **Properties** palette, as shown in Figure 3-23. This palette shows various parameters of the selected wall such as **Unconnected Height, Location Line, Structural Usage, Top Constraint**, and so on. You can modify these parameters by entering a new value or selecting the required value from the corresponding value field in the **Properties** palette.

Creating Walls

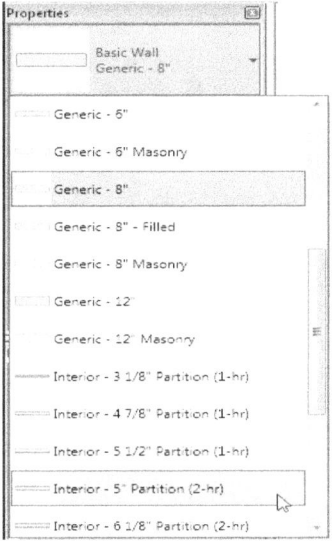

Figure 3-22 Selecting the interior wall type from the **Properties** palette

Figure 3-23 The **Properties** palette for the **Interior - 5" Partition (2-hr)** wall type

 Tip: *After creating a wall, right click on any end of the wall; a shortcut menu will be displayed. Choose the **Disallow Join** option from the shortcut menu to prevent the wall end from joining with other walls.*

The sketching tools explained earlier (for exterior walls) can also be used for sketching interior walls. When you sketch the interior walls, the top constraint of the interior walls is automatically set to a level above the current level.

Tip: *The **Location Line** parameter in the **Properties** palette of the selected walls is useful for creating interior walls. You can create interior walls at some specified distance from another existing wall using the **Finish Face: Interior** option.*

Note
The interior walls do not create a neat junction with the exterior walls as they have different composition and characteristics.

Walls are the host elements for other building elements such as doors and windows. Therefore, deleting walls will delete all their dependent elements as well.

The basic composition of an interior wall type can be viewed by choosing the **Type Properties** tool from the **Properties** panel in the **Modify | Place Wall** tab. On doing so, the **Type Properties** dialog box will be displayed, showing different type parameters of the selected wall type.

To view the structural composition of a wall type, choose the **Edit** button in the **Structure** type parameter; the **Edit Assembly** dialog box will be displayed, showing layers for the corresponding wall type. For example, the **Interior-5" Partition (2-hr)** for Imperial or (**Interior-135mm Partition (2-hr)** for Metric) wall type comprises of seven layers with different materials and thickness. You can use the **Insert** and **Delete** buttons to modify the wall type. You can choose the **Preview** button to display the graphic view of the **Interior - 5" Partition(2 -hr)** for Imperial (**Interior - 135mm Partition(2 -hr)** for Metric) wall type in the preview area, as shown in Figure 3-24.

*Figure 3-24 The **Edit Assembly** dialog box for the **Interior - 5" Partition (2-hr)** wall type*

Creating Walls   3-21

 Tip:: *In Autodesk Revit, you can add a structural wall to a project by choosing the **Wall: Structural** tool from **Architecture > Build > Wall** drop-down. The structural wall has analytical properties that can be used for structural analysis.*

ADDING WALL SWEEPS AND REVEALS

In an architectural project, wall sweep and wall reveal acts as modifiers in a wall. Each type of wall sweep and wall reveal has predefined properties. You can select and use any type of wall sweep and wall reveal based on its usage in project. Wall sweep is used to add a baseboard, crown moulding or other type of decorative horizontal or vertical projections to a wall. Wall reveal is used to add a decorative horizontal or vertical cutout to a wall. Wall sweep and wall reveal provide advancement to the building model by adding skirtings, projections and cutout through a building.

 Note
Wall sweep and wall reveal can be added to a wall only in 3D view or in elevation view.

Wall Sweeps

Ribbon: Architecture > Build > Wall drop-down > Wall: Sweep

To add details to a wall, you can add a wall sweep by using the **Wall Sweep** tool. Wall Sweep can be selected either in an elevation view or in 3D view. Choose the **3D View** tool from the **Quick Access Toolbar**, the user interface will be displayed. Next, invoke the **Wall: Sweep** tool from the **Build** panel of the **Architecture** tab, as shown in Figure 3-25. On doing so, the **Modify | Place Wall Sweep** tab will be displayed. In the **Placement** panel of this contextual tab, the **Horizontal** tool is selected by default. As a result, the wall sweep will be added horizontally to the face of the wall. Select the required type of the wall sweep from the **Type Selector** drop-down list. Now, move the cursor over the face of the wall; a preview of the wall sweep along with the temporary dimensions will be displayed on the wall face. Click at the desired level of elevation; a wall sweep will be created, as shown in Figure 3-26. After adding the wall sweeps at desired faces of the wall, press ESC, or choose the **Modify** button from the **Select** panel to exit from the contextual tab. Similarly, you can add a vertical wall sweep at the face of the wall. To create a vertical wall sweep, choose the **Vertical** tool from the **Placement** panel.

After adding the wall sweep to the wall, you can change the properties of the sweep such as its profile. To change the profile of the sweep invoke the **Edit Type** button from the **Properties** palette; the **Type Properties** dialog box will be displayed. Now, choose the **Duplicate** button from the upper left corner of this dialog box; the **Name** dialog box will be displayed. In this dialog box enter the desired name in the **Name** edit box and choose the **OK** button to return to the **Type Properties** dialog box. In **Type Properties** dialog box, you can select the desired wall sweep type from the **Profile** drop-down list by clicking on the value field of the corresponding parameter. You can edit the **Subcategory of Walls** by clicking on the corresponding value field of the **Type Parameter** area.

Tip: *You can add more options to the **Type-Selector** drop-down list by loading more families of profile into the drawings. To load more options, choose the **Load Family** tool from the **Load From Library** panel of the **Insert** tab; the **Load Family** dialog box will be displayed. In this dialog box, the predefined family profiles are available in **Profiles > Wall folder**.*

The methods to modify other **Type Properties** are discussed next :

*Figure 3-25 Invoking the **Wall: Sweep** tool from the **Build** panel*

Figure 3-26 Wall sweep added to the wall

Modifying Type Properties

The **Type Properties** dialog box displays various type parameters of wall sweep such as **Constraints**, **Construction**, **Material and Finishes**, and **IFC Parameters**. To edit the parameters, click in the **Value** field corresponding to any of the parameters under these heads

Creating Walls

and then specify a desired value to it. To edit the material properties of the wall sweep click in the **Value** field corresponding to the **Material** parameter: a browse button will be displayed. Choose the browse button; the **Material Browser** dialog box will be displayed. You can use various options in this dialog box to specify the desired material for the wall sweep. Choose the **OK** button: the **Material Browser** dialog box will be closed and the specified material will be assigned to the wall sweep type.

Now, to create a copy of the original sweep type you can choose the **Duplicate** button from the top right corner in the **Type Properties** dialog box. On doing so, the **Name** edit dialog box will be displayed, and you will be prompted to assign a new name to the duplicate copy. Enter a name in this edit box and choose the **OK** button; a new sweep type is created which inherits the properties of the parent sweep type. Now, you can modify its parameters, as desired. The **Rename** button is also available on the top right corner, this button is used to give a new name to the selected sweep type without changing its properties.

Now, you will learn to modify the instance properties of the sweep type.

Modifying Instance Properties

You can modify various instance properties of the wall sweep by using the parameters in the **Properties** palette. The modification in these properties results in the change of the properties of only that particular instance in the project. The description of various instance parameters are given next:

Instance Parameter	Description
Offset From Wall	Copies or moves a selected element to a specified distance from Wall face
Level	Level or reference plane of the base of a wall sweep and the properties shown only for Horizontal Sweep
Offset From Level	Specifies distance of sweep from level
Length	Indicates the length of a wall sweep
Comments	Describes about the Wall Sweep
Mark	Add a mark or label to each sweep
Phase Created	Phase in which a wall sweep is created
Phase Demolished	Phase in which a wall sweep was demolished

Wall Reveals

Ribbon: Architecture > Build > Wall drop-down > Wall: Reveal

To complete the design of our wall, you need to add decorative cutout in the wall. To do so, you can use the wall reveal. To add a wall reveal, you need to be in an elevation view or in 3D view and then invoke the **Wall: Reveal** tool from the **Build** panel of the **Architecture** tab, refer to Figure 3-27; the **Modify | Place Reveal** tab will be displayed. In this contextual tab, select the desired orientation of the wall reveal by choosing either the **Horizontal** or **Vertical** tool from the **Placement** panel. Next, select the type of the wall reveal from the **Type Selector** drop-down list and then move the cursor over the face of the wall; a preview of the wall reveal with the temporary dimension will be displayed along the wall face. Click at desired level of elevation; a wall reveal will be added, as shown in Figure 3-28. You can add the wall reveal to other walls by clicking on their faces. After adding the wall reveal at desired faces of the wall, press **ESC** or choose the **Modify** button from the **Select** panel to exit the contextual tab. After adding the wall reveal to the wall, you can change the properties of the reveal such as its profile. To change the profile of the reveal, invoke the **Edit Type** button from the **Properties** palette; the **Type Properties** dialog box will be displayed. Choose the **Duplicate** button from the upper left corner of this dialog box; the **Name** dialog box will be displayed. In this dialog box, enter the desired name in the **Name** edit box and choose the **OK** button to return to the **Type properties** dialog box. In this dialog box, you can select the desired **Wall Reveal** type from the **Profile** drop-down list by clicking on the value field of this dialog box. You can edit the **Subcategory of Walls** by clicking on the corresponding value field in the **Type Parameter** area.

*Figure 3-27 Invoking the **Wall: Reveal** tool from the **Build** Panel*

Figure 3-28 Wall reveal added to the wall

Creating Walls

3-25

Now, you will learn to modify the properties of wall reveal i.e. **Type Properties** and **Instance Properties**.

Modifying Type Properties

To modify the type properties of the selected **Wall Reveal** type, choose the **Edit Type** button from the **Properties** palette; the **Type Properties** dialog box for the selected reveal type will be displayed.

The **Type Properties** dialog box displays the value of various parameters of **Wall Reveal**. The various type parameters described as:

Parameter	Description
Default Setback	By default, the default setback value in the edit box is 0'0". Wall reveal changes with the change in the value from positive to negative. The setback helps in making reveal type near windows and door trims.
Profile	Wall reveal is created by the profile family.

Modifying Instance Properties

To modify the instance properties of the selected **Wall Reveal** type, choose the reveal from the drawing window the **Properties** palette displays the **Instance Properties** of that reveal type. The various instance parameters are described next:

Instance Parameter	Description
Offset From Wall	Copies or moves a selected element to a specified distance from Wall face
Level	Level or reference plane of the base of a wall reveal and the properties shown only for Horizontal Sweep
Offset From Level	Specified distance of reveal from level
Length	Indicates the length of a wall reveal

Tip: *Wall sweep and wall reveal type can also be used directly by invoking the **Edit Type** button in the **Properties** palette of the wall. It is to be used only when sweep type or reveal type is required to be done throughout the building model along with the wall.*

TUTORIALS

The following tutorials are designed to familiarize you with the concepts of invoking the **Wall: Architectural** tool, selecting the wall type, modifying the wall properties, using the sketching tools, and sketching a wall with the given parameters.

All the files used in the tutorials can be downloaded from the cadcim website. These files are compressed in zip file format and are required to be extracted before using them in the tutorials. The path of the files is as follows: *Textbooks > Civil/GIS > Revit Architecture > Autodesk Revit Architecture 2015 for Architects and Designers*. For example, the tutorial file, *c02_Apartment_tut1.rvt* that is used in Tutorial 1 of Chapter 3 is compressed in the *C02_Revit Architecture.zip file*.

Tutorial 1   Apartment 1

In this tutorial, you will create the exterior walls of a two-room apartment based on the sketch plan shown in Figure 3-29. The dimensions have been given only for reference and are not to be used in this tutorial. The project file and the parameters to be used for creating the exterior walls are given next.   **(Expected time: 30 min)**

1. Project file-
   For Imperial   *c02_Apartment_tut1.rvt*
   For Metric   *M_c02_Apartment_tut1.rvt*
2. Exterior wall type- **Basic Wall: Exterior - Brick on Mtl. Stud**.
3. Location line parameter- **Wall Centerline**; Top Constraint- **Up to Level 2.**

The following steps are required to complete this tutorial:

a. Open the *Apartment 1* project file created in Tutorial 1 of Chapter 2.
b. Invoke the **Wall**: **Architectural** tool from the ribbon.
c. Select the exterior wall type **Exterior - Brick on Mtl. Stud** from the **Properties** dialog box.
d. Modify **Top Constraint- Up to level: Level 2** and **Location Line - Wall Centerline** as wall properties using the **Properties** palette, refer to Figure 3-30.
e. Invoke the **Line** sketching tool and then sketch the exterior walls based on the given parameters, refer to Figures 3-31 through 3-38.

Figure 3-29 Sketch plan for creating exterior walls for the Apartment 1 project

Opening the Project File

Choose **Open > Project** from the **Application Menu** and open the *c02_Apartment1_tut1.rvt* (*M_c02_Apartment1_tut1.rvt for Metric*) project file. You can also download this file from

Creating Walls   3-27

http://www.cadcim.com. The path of the file is as follows: *Textbooks > Civil/GIS > Revit Architecture > Autodesk Revit Architecture 2015 for Architects and Designers.*

Invoking the Wall: Architectural Tool and Selecting the Wall Type

To start sketching the wall, you must invoke the **Wall: Architectural** tool from the ribbon and select the wall type to be used (**Exterior - Brick on Mtl. Stud** in this case).

1. Invoke the **Wall: Architectural** tool from **Architecture > Build > Wall** drop-down; the **Modify | Place Wall** tab is displayed.

2. In the **Type Selector** drop-down list of the **Properties** palette, select the **Exterior - Brick on Mtl. Stud** wall type.

Modifying Properties of the Exterior Wall

After selecting the wall type, you need to modify the instance properties of the wall type using the **Properties** palette.

Note
*The default.rte or (DeafultMetric.rte for Metric) template file used for this project has two predefined levels: **Level 1** and **Level 2**.*

1. In the **Properties** palette, ensure that the **Location Line** parameter has **Wall Centerline** as the default value. Click on the column adjacent to the **Top Constraint** instance parameter; a drop-down list is displayed. Select **Up to level: Level 2** from this drop-down list, and choose the **Apply** button, as shown in Figure 3-30.

> **Tip:** *If the **Properties** palette is not displayed in the User interface screen by default, choose the **Properties** check box from the **Views > Windows > User-Interface** drop-down.*

*Figure 3-30 Setting the **Top Constraint** parameter using the **Properties** palette*

Sketching the First Exterior Wall Segment

To sketch a wall, you need to choose an appropriate sketching tool from the **Draw** panel in the **Modify | Place Wall** tab. The exterior walls of the given sketch of the *Apartment 1* project can be created using the **Rectangle** tool. You will however use the **Line** option to learn and understand the usage of this tool for sketching the straight walls.

1. Ensure that the **Line** tool is chosen in the **Draw** panel in the **Modify | Place Wall** tab and the **Chain** check box is cleared in the **Options Bar**.

2. To specify the start point of the first wall segment, click between the four inward arrow keys. Next, move the cursor toward the right hand side. On doing so, a wall segment starts from the specified point with temporary dimension appearing on it. The dimension changes dynamically as you move the cursor. This shows the length of the wall segment at any given location of the cursor.

3. Right click in the drawing area; a shortcut menu is displayed. Choose the **Zoom In Region** option from the shortcut menu and zoom into the area to get a closer view of the sketched wall segment, as shown in Figure 3-31 (for zooming techniques, refer to Chapter 2- Starting an Architectural Project).

Figure 3-31 *The temporary dimensions displayed on the wall*

4. Move the cursor on the horizontal axis such that a dashed line appears at the central axis of the wall segment, as shown in Figure 3-32. Notice the two-sided arrow attached to the endpoint of the wall. This indicates that the wall segment being sketched is horizontal. A tooltip indicating the horizontal alignment is also displayed with two-sided arrow.

Figure 3-32 *Sketching a horizontal wall segment*

5. Move the cursor to the right until the temporary dimension shows a value more than 40'- 0"(12192 mm), as shown in Figure 3-33. Click at this location as the endpoint of the wall segment and press ESC twice; the wall is created. Note that, if the dimension is not displayed, you need to click on the created wall to display the dimension. Press ESC.

Figure 3-33 *The sketched horizontal wall with its controls*

Note
You can create a wall of exactly 40'0"(12192 mm) length using the dimension snaps set in the **Snaps** *dialog box. The only purpose of creating a wall of length more than the desired length is to explain how to modify the length of the sketched wall to the exact value.*

Modifying the Length of the Sketched Exterior Wall

You will now modify the length of the sketched wall to the actual dimension, as given in the *Apartment 1* sketch.

Creating Walls   3-29

1. Select the created wall and click on its temporary dimension; an edit box appears showing the current dimension of the wall segment.

2. Enter **40' (12192 mm)** in the edit box, as shown in Figure 3-34 and then press ENTER; the length of the wall is modified to 40'0"(12192 mm). Press ESC to exit the **Modify | Walls** tab.

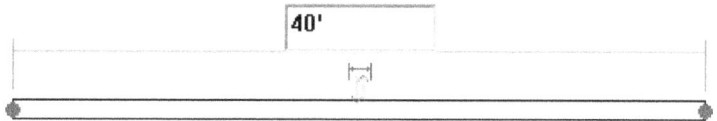

Figure 3-34 Modifying the length of a wall segment using temporary dimensions

Tip: To exit the current tool, you can also right-click and choose **Cancel** from the shortcut menu displayed.

Note
By default, the exterior faces of the walls drawn from the left to right is on the upper face, and those drawn from top to bottom is on the right face. Similarly, the exterior face of the walls drawn from right to left is on the lower face, and those drawn from the bottom to top on the left side. Hence, you can minimize the use of the **flip** tool by sketching the walls in the appropriate direction.

Sketching Other Exterior Wall Segments

In this section, you need to create other exterior wall segments using the **Endpoint** object snap tool.

1. Choose the **Wall: Architectural** tool from **Architecture > Build > Wall** drop-down. Now, bring the cursor close to the right endpoint of the first wall segment. When the cursor shows a square box at the endpoint (indicating the **Endpoint** object snap), as shown in Figure 3-35, click to specify the start point of the second wall segment.

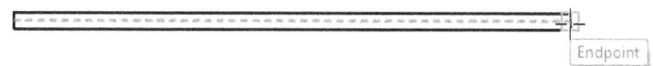

Figure 3-35 Starting a second exterior wall segment using the **Endpoint** object snap option

2. As you move the cursor, wall starts to get created dynamically, with one end attached to the specified point and the other end attached to the cursor. Move the cursor vertically downward. A dashed vertical line is visible inside the wall segment. Now, enter **20'0"(6096 mm)** as the value of the length; an edit box is displayed with the dimension that you have entered, as shown in Figure 3-36. Press ENTER; the second wall segment is sketched exactly to 20'0"(6096 mm) length.

Notice that the intersection of the first and second wall segments has been intuitively filled or completed.

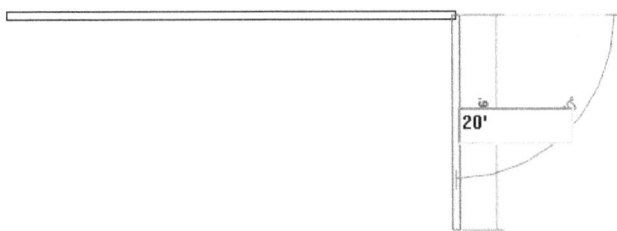

Figure 3-36 *Creating the second exterior wall segment*

3. To draw the third wall segment, select the **Chain** check box from the **Options Bar**.

4. Move the cursor close to the endpoint of the second wall segment and click when the endpoint object snap is displayed. On doing so, the third wall segment starts from this specified point. Move the cursor horizontally toward the left. Now, hold the SHIFT key while moving the cursor.

Notice that the cursor can now move only in the orthogonal directions (in the horizontal and vertical direction). When the length of the wall segment is around 40'0"(12192 mm), a vertical dashed line originates from the start point of the first wall segment. The alignment line shows the point on the third wall segment that is in plumb with the first point. An intersection snap symbol indicated by an X appears at this point, as shown in Figure 3-37.

Figure 3-37 *Creating the third wall segment*

5. Click to specify the location of the endpoint of the third wall segment when the intersection snap symbol is displayed.

6. As you have enabled the **Chain** option, the next wall segment automatically starts from the last specified point. Move the cursor vertically upward and enter **25'(7620 mm)**, as shown in Figure 3-38, and then press ENTER. The fourth wall segment is created.

Creating Walls 3-31

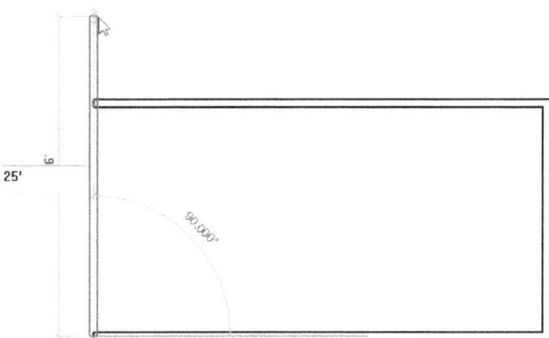

Figure 3-38 Sketching the fourth exterior wall segment

7. Press ESC twice to exit the **Wall: Architectural** tool.

Note
The purpose of creating a wall more than the desired length is only to explain how to stretch the wall to the exact length.

Stretching the Wall Segment

You will now stretch the wall segment to change its length to the desired dimension by using the drag controls.

1. Select the fourth wall segment to display its controls. The two blue dots at its two endpoints are the drag controls. Move the cursor near the upper dot; the color of the drag control symbol changes, as shown in Figure 3-39. Press and hold the left mouse button at this point and drag the cursor vertically downward and bring it close to the start point of the first wall segment. On doing so, the endpoint object snap is displayed at the intersection of two walls and the tooltip shows **Endpoint and Vertical**.

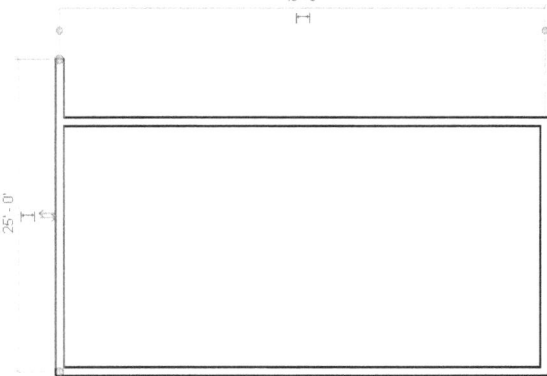

Figure 3-39 Using the drag control to modify the length of wall

2. Release the left mouse button at the intersection point and click; the first and fourth wall segments are joined at the corner with their ends completed.

   Note that if these wall segments do not join at the corner on releasing the left mouse button, you need to click at their intersection.

3. Press ESC to remove the wall segment from the selection set. The external wall profile is completed for this tutorial, as shown in Figure 3-40.

Figure 3-40 The completed exterior wall profile

4. Choose **Save As > Project** from the **Application Menu**; the **Save As** dialog box is displayed. Enter **c03_Apartment1_tut1** (**M_c03_Apartment1_tut1**) in the **File name** edit box and then choose **Save**.

   This completes the creation of the external wall segments for the *Apartment 1* project.

Tutorial 2 — Club

Create the exterior walls of the club building whose sketch plan is shown in Figure 3-41. The dimensions given are to be measured from the exterior faces and are not to be created. The parameters to be used for creating the exterior walls of the club building are given next.

(Expected time: 30 min)

1. Project file-
   For Imperial   *c02_Club_tut2.rvt*
   For Metric   *M_c02_Club_tut2.rvt*
2. Exterior wall type- **Exterior - Split Face and CMU on Mtl. Stud**.
3. Unconnected height of walls- **15'0"** (**4572 mm**).
4. All inclined walls are at 45-degree to the horizontal axis.

   The following steps are required to complete this tutorial:

a. Open required the project file.
   For Imperial   *c02_Club_tut2.rvt*
   For Metric   *M_c02_Club_tut2.rvt*
b. Invoke the **Wall: Architectural** tool.

Creating Walls

3-33

c. Select the exterior wall type:
   For Imperial   **Exterior - Split Face and CMU on Mtl. Stud**
   For Metric   **Exterior - Brick on Mtl. Stud**
d. Set the unconnected height to **15'0"** or **4572mm**.
e. Change the **Location Line** parameter to **Finish Face: Exterior**, refer to Figure 3-41.
f. Select the **Line** sketching option and sketch the inclined wall profile using the **Chain** option, refer to Figures 3-43 through 3-49.
g. Use the **Center-ends Arc** sketching option to create the curved wall, refer to Figures 3-46 and 3-47.

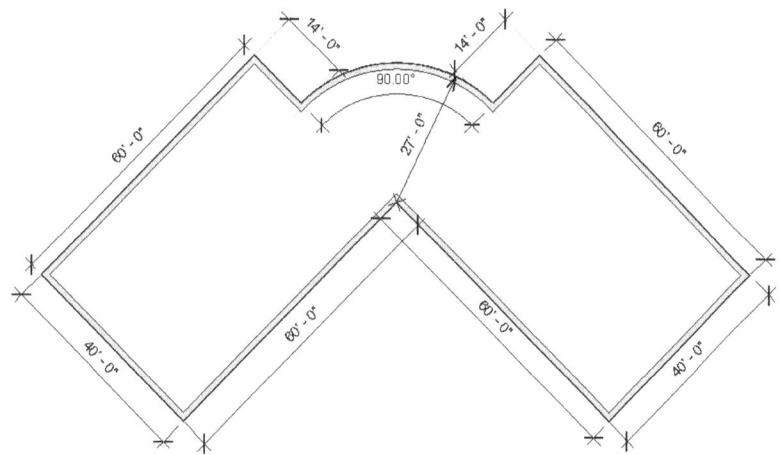

Figure 3-41 Sketch plan for the Club project

Opening an Existing Project

Choose **Open > Project** from **Application Menu** and open the *c02_Club_tut2.rvt (M_c02_Club_tut2.rvt* for Metric) project file created in Tutorial 2 of Chapter 2. You can also download this file from *http://www.cadcim.com*. The path of the file is as follows: *Textbooks > Civil/GIS > Revit Architecture > Autodesk Revit Architecture 2015 for Architects and Designers*.

Invoking the Wall: Architectural Tool and Selecting the Wall Type

First, you will invoke the **Wall: Architectural** tool from the ribbon and then select the specified exterior wall type, as given in the project parameters.

1. Choose the **Wall: Architectural** tool from the **Architecture > Build > Wall** drop-down; the **Modify | Place Wall** tab is displayed.

2. In the **Properties** palette, select the required option from the **Type Selector** drop-down list.
   For Imperial   **Exterior - Split Face and CMU on Mtl. Stud**
   For Metric   **Exterior - Brick on Mtl. Stud**

Modifying Properties of the Exterior Wall

Next, you will use the **Properties** palette to modify the unconnected height to 15'0" or 4572mm. The dimensions given in the sketch are exterior wall face dimensions. Therefore, you need to set the **Location Line** parameter to **Finish Face: Exterior**.

1. In the **Properties** palette, click in the value field corresponding to the **Unconnected Height** parameter and replace the current value with **15'0" (4572mm)**.

2. Click in the value field of the **Location Line** parameter and select the **Finish Face : Exterior** option from the drop-down list displayed, as shown in Figure 3-42. Choose the **Apply** button to accept the specified values.

Sketching the Inclined Exterior Walls

Start creating the exterior wall profile by first sketching the inclined walls in a sequence such that the exterior face of the wall is on the external side. You need to select the **Chain** check box to sketch the continuous wall profile. Once you have created the first inclined wall, the other parallel and perpendicular walls can easily be created using the alignment lines and different object snaps options.

Figure 3-42 Selecting the **Finish Face : Exterior** option for the **Location Line** parameter

1. To create the straight wall, choose the **Line** tool in the **Draw** panel of the **Modify | Place Wall** tab, if it is not chosen by default.

2. In the **Options Bar**, select the **Chain** check box, if it is not selected.

3. To start sketching the first inclined wall segment, click inside the four arrow keys in the drawing window and move the cursor upward toward the right and then move it to an inclination such that the angle subtended at the horizontal axis is 45 degrees.

4. Enter the value **14' (4267 mm)** to specify the length of the first wall segment; the value is displayed in the edit box, as shown in Figure 3-43. Press ENTER to create the first wall segment of the specified length.

5. As the **Chain** check box is selected in the **Options Bar**, the second wall segment will start from the last specified point. Now, move the cursor downward toward the right and right-click to invoke the shortcut menu. Next, choose **Snap Overrides > Perpendicular** from the shortcut menu displayed; the perpendicular snap symbol appears at the end

Creating Walls   3-35

of the wall. Enter **60'(18288 mm)**, see Figure 3-44; a wall is created perpendicular to the first inclined wall.

Figure 3-43 Sketching the first inclined wall segment

Figure 3-44 Sketching the second inclined wall segment

6. Similarly, for creating the next wall, move the cursor downward to the left and choose the perpendicular snap override as in step 5. Enter **40'(12192 mm)** as length, as shown in Figure 3-45. Now, press ENTER to create the third inclined wall.

7. To create the next wall, move the cursor upward toward the left and invoke the perpendicular snap override as in step 5. Enter **60' (18288 mm)** as the length of the wall segment and press ENTER to create the fourth inclined wall segment, as shown in Figure 3-46.

Figure 3-45 Sketching the third inclined wall segment

Figure 3-46 Sketching the fourth inclined wall segment

8. Similarly, create the fifth inclined wall segment of 60'(18288 mm) length, as shown in Figure 3-47.

9. Next, create the connected wall segment of 40'(12192 mm) length, as shown in Figure 3-48.

Figure 3-47 Sketching the fifth inclined wall segment

Figure 3-48 Sketching the sixth inclined wall segment

10. Now, create the next two wall segments of lengths 60'(18288 mm) and 14'(4267 mm) to complete the inclined wall exterior profile, as shown in Figure 3-49.

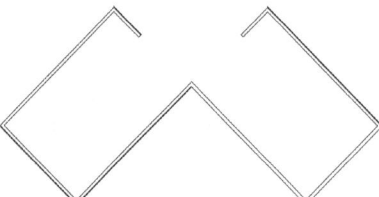

Figure 3-49 The sketched inclined wall exterior profile

11. Press the ESC key to discontinue the wall at this point and finish sketching the inclined walls.

Sketching the Curved Exterior Wall

Next, you will sketch the curved exterior wall profile based on the given parameters. You need to use the **Center-ends Arc** tool to create the curved wall segment.

1. Choose the **Center-ends Arc** tool in the **Draw** panel of the **Modify | Place Wall** tab. Move the cursor in the drawing window and click on the outer intersection of the inclined walls to specify the center of the curved wall, refer to Figure 3-50.

2. Move the cursor near the endpoint of the last sketched inclined wall segment. When 135-degree is displayed as the angular dimension, enter the value **27' (8230 mm)** as the radius of the curved wall and press ENTER, as shown in Figure 3-50. On doing so, the curved wall with the specified radius starts from the specified point.

 Note
*While tracking the wall, if the perpendicular or other snapping symbol does not appear, you can right-click and choose **Snap Overrides**; a cascading menu will be displayed. Choose any snapping option from the cascading menu. On doing so, the desired snapping symbol will appear for the specified point or action.*

Creating Walls 3-37

3. Move the cursor toward the right and click when the cursor snaps to the endpoint of the inclined wall, as shown in Figure 3-51. Now, press ESC twice to complete the exterior wall profile, as shown in Figure 3-52.

Figure 3-50 Starting the curved wall segment

Figure 3-51 Completing the curved wall segment

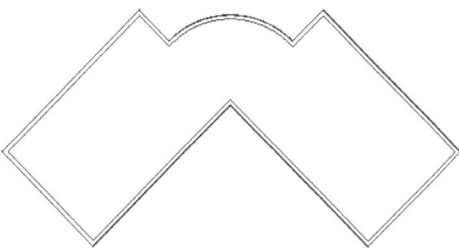

Figure 3-52 Completed layout of the exterior walls for the Club project

4. Choose the **Default 3D View** tool from **View > Create > 3D View** drop-down; a 3D view of the building model is displayed, as shown in Figure 3-53.

5. From the **View Control Bar**, choose the **Visual Style** button; a flyout is displayed. Choose the **Shaded** option from the flyout.

6. Under the **Floor Plans** head in the **Project Browser**, double-click on **Level 1** to return to the plan view.

Figure 3-53 3D view of the completed exterior wall profile

7. Choose **Save As > Project** from **Application Menu**; the **Save As** dialog box is displayed. Enter **c03_Club_tut2** (**M_c03_Club_tut2** for Metric) in the **File name** edit box and then choose **Save**.

This completes the tutorial for creating the exterior wall profile for the *Club* project.

Tutorial 3 — Apartment 1 - Interior Walls

In this tutorial, you will add interior walls to the apartment plan created in Tutorial 1 of this chapter. The interior walls to be created are the intermediate walls among various rooms, as shown in the plan sketch in Figure 3-54. The dimensions and text have been given for reference and are not to be created. The project file name and the parameters to be used for different elements are given next.

(Expected time: 30 min)

1. Project file-
   - For Imperial   *c03_Apartment1_tut1.rvt*
   - For Metric   *M_c03_Apartment1_tut1.rvt*
2. Interior wall type- **Interior - 5" Partition (2-hr)**.
3. Location line parameter- **Wall Centerline**.

The following steps are required to complete this tutorial:

a. Open the *Apartment 1* project file created earlier in this chapter.
b. Invoke the **Wall: Architectural** tool and select the required interior wall.
   - For Imperial   **Interior - 5" Partition (2-hr)**
   - For Metric   **Interior - 135mm Partition (2-hr)**
c. Set the location line parameter as **Location Line- Wall Centerline**.
d. Select the **Line** sketching tool to sketch the straight walls.
e. Sketch the interior walls based on the given parameters, refer to Figures 3-56 through Figure 3-62.
f. Edit the interior walls location to achieve clear internal distances, refer to Figures 3-63 and Figure 3-65.

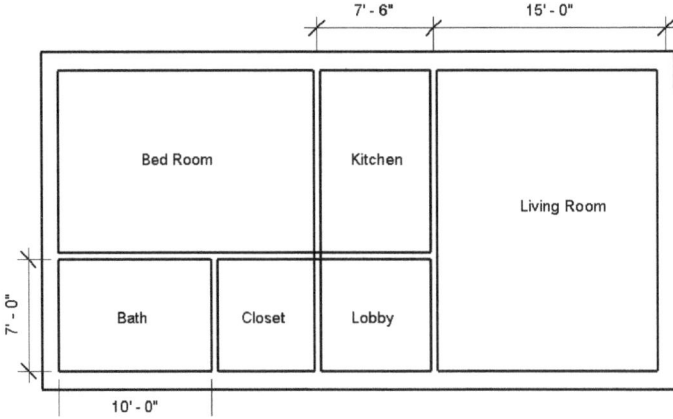

Figure 3-54 Layout of internal walls for Apartment 1 project

Creating Walls   3-39

Opening the Project and Invoking the Wall: Architectural Tool
1. Choose **Open > Project** from the **Application Menu** and open the *c03_Apartment1_tut1.rvt (M_c03_Apartment1_tut1.rvt)* project created earlier in this chapter. You can also download this file from *http://www.cadcim.com*. The path of the file is as follows: *Textbooks > Civil/GIS > Revit Architecture > Autodesk Revit 2015 for Architects and Designers*.

2. Invoke the **Wall: Architectural** tool from **Architecture > Build > Wall** drop-down.

Selecting the Interior Wall Type
1. On invoking the **Wall: Architectural** tool, the wall instance parameters are displayed in the **Properties** palette. In this palette, select the required option from the **Type Selector** drop-down list, as shown in Figure 3-55.
   For Imperial   **Interior-5" Partition (2-hr)**
   For Metric   **Interior - 135 mm Partition (2-hr)**

2. In the **Options Bar**, select the **Wall Centerline** option from the **Location Line** drop-down list, if it is not selected by default. Also, clear the **Chain** check box.

Sketching the First Interior Wall
After selecting the interior wall type, start sketching the interior walls. Notice that the **Line** tool is chosen as the default tool for sketching the walls.

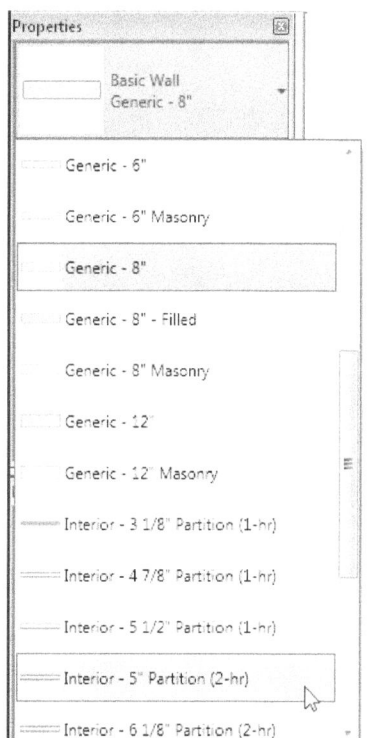

1. Move the cursor near the top right endpoint of the wall structure and start moving the cursor toward left along the top horizontal wall. You will notice that a temporary dimension appears which changes dynamically as you move the cursor away from it. This dimension shows the distance of the cursor from the nearest wall segment.

2. Type **15'(4572 mm)** from the keyboard, as shown in Figure 3-56. Now, press ENTER; the starting point of the first interior wall is specified.

3. Next, move the cursor vertically downward near the lower exterior wall segment. When the **Vertical and Nearest** symbol appears, as shown in Figure 3-57, click to specify the location of the endpoint of the wall segment; the first interior wall segment is sketched.

Figure 3-55 Selecting the Basic Wall : Interior - 5"Partition (2-hr) wall type

Sketching Other Interior Walls
Next, you will sketch the other horizontal and vertical interior walls by specifying their start point and endpoint using different object snap options.

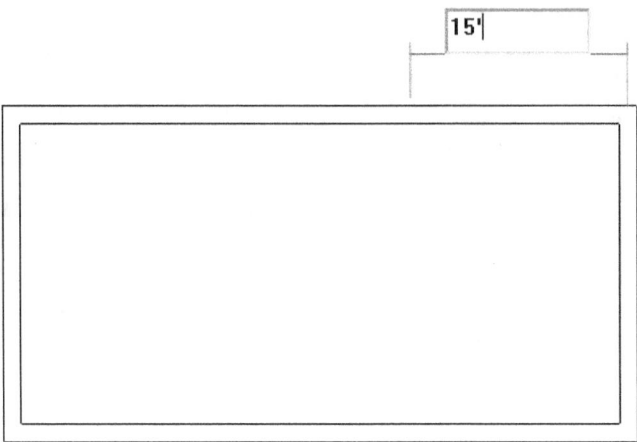

Figure 3-56 Specifying the distance for starting the first interior wall segment

Figure 3-57 Specifying the endpoint of the first interior wall segment

1. To sketch the second interior wall, move the cursor to the upper endpoint of the interior wall you just created and then move the cursor horizontally toward the left. When the temporary dimension and the intersection object snap appears, enter **7'6"(2286 mm)**, as shown in Figure 3-58. Now, press ENTER; the start point of the second interior wall segment is specified on the upper horizontal exterior wall.

Figure 3-58 Specifying the starting point of the second interior wall

Creating Walls   3-41

2. Press SHIFT and move the cursor downward. You will notice that the cursor moves parallel to the vertical axis while moving it downward. Click near the lower external wall when the **Vertical and Nearest** symbol appears, as shown in Figure 3-59.

   Next, you will sketch the interior walls of the bath. Since the internal dimensions have been provided for the interior walls, you will first sketch them using the wall center lines and later move them to get the exact clearance distance of the walls.

3. Move the cursor to the lower left corner and then move it vertically upward. When the temporary dimension appears, enter **7'0"(2134 mm)** and then press ENTER to specify the starting point of the third interior wall, as shown in Figure 3-60.

Figure 3-59 Sketching the second interior wall

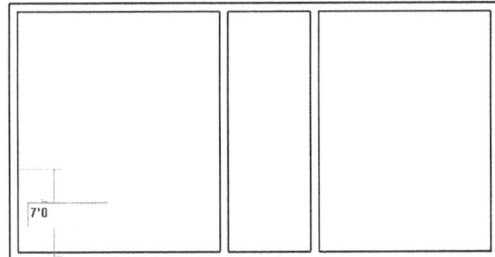

Figure 3-60 Specifying the distance for sketching the third internal wall

4. Press SHIFT and move the cursor horizontally toward the right until it reaches the first vertical interior wall. When the **Horizontal and Nearest** object snap symbol appears, click to specify the location of the endpoint of the third interior wall, as shown in Figure 3-61, the wall segment is created.

Figure 3-61 Sketching the third interior wall segment

5. Similarly, move the cursor near the lower left corner and then move it horizontally toward the right. When the temporary dimension and the intersection object snap appears, enter the value **10'0"**, as shown in Figure 3-62, and then press ENTER.

6. Press and hold the SHIFT key and move the cursor vertically upward until it reaches the horizontal interior wall. When the **Vertical and Nearest** symbol appears, click to specify the endpoint of the wall. Now, press ESC twice to finish the sketch of the wall.

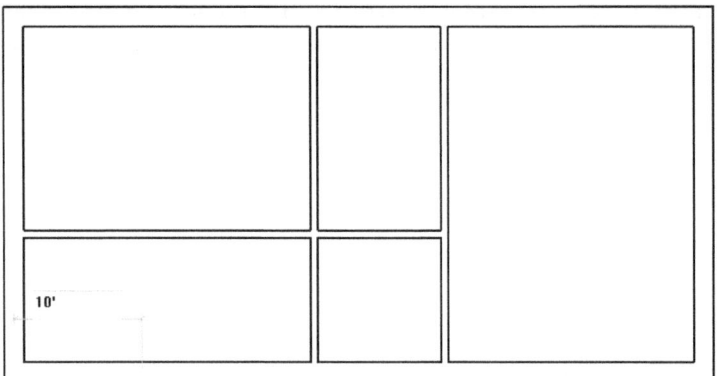

Figure 3-62 Sketching the interior walls of the bath

Moving Walls Using Witness Lines

As the dimension of the bath walls will be measured from the centerline of the external walls, you need to move the interior walls of the bath such that the internal dimensions are 7'0"X10'0" as specified in the sketch. Use the witness lines and specify these dimensions.

1. Select the last created interior wall from the drawing; the selected interior wall shows the centerline distances and its controls.

2. Three blue dots define the extents of the dimensions. Click on the dot on the extreme left; the dot and dimension witness line moves to the interior face of the exterior wall, as shown in Figure 3-63.

3. Similarly, click twice on the next blue dot on the right to move it to the inner face of the third interior wall.

4. Now, click on the temporary dimension, enter the value **10'(3048 mm)** and then, press ENTER; the interior wall is moved to the desired distance 10'-0" from the interior face of the exterior wall, as shown in Figure 3-64.

Creating Walls   3-43

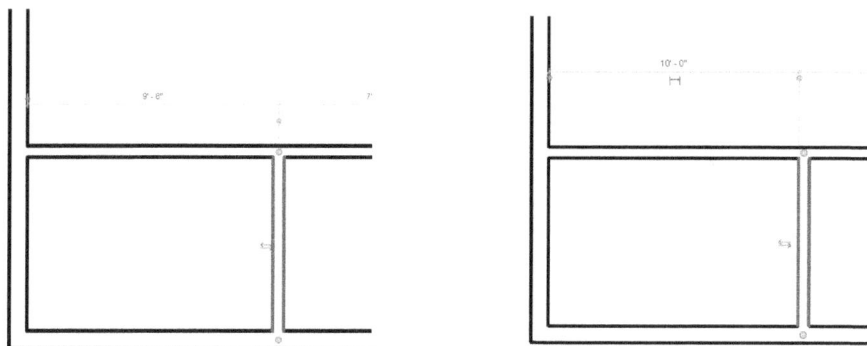

Figure 3-63 The square dot moved   *Figure 3-64* The adjusted inner wall distance

5. Similarly, to move the horizontal interior wall (common for the bath, kitchen and the closet), select it and move both the witness lines toward the inner face by clicking on the blue dots.

6. Now, click on the blue dots of temporary dimension from the lower external wall and the upper interior wall. Enter the value **7'(2134 mm)**, as shown in Figure 3-65 and press ENTER. On doing so, the interior wall is moved to the desired location. Now, press ESC to exit the **Modify | Walls** tab.

   This completes the interior wall layout for the *Apartment 1* project, refer to Figure 3-65.

Figure 3-65 Entering the value to adjust the dimension of the horizontal interior wall

7. To view the building model in 3D, choose the **Default 3D View** tool from **View > Create > 3D View** drop-down. On doing so, the 3D view of the building model is displayed along with the **ViewCube** tool.

8. Now, choose the **Visual Style** button from the **View Control Bar**; a flyout is displayed. Choose the **Shaded** option from this flyout; the 3D view is displayed and with shading with edges visible, as shown in Figure 3-66.

Figure 3-66 *3D view of the Apartment 1 building model*

9. Choose **Save As > Project** from **Application Menu**; the **Save As** dialog box is displayed. Enter **c03_Apartment1_tut3** in the **File name** edit box and then choose **Save**.

Tutorial 4   Club - Interior Walls

Create the interior walls of the left portion of the club building whose exterior wall profile was created in Tutorial 2 earlier in this chapter. Create the walls based on the sketch plan shown in Figure 3-67. The dimensions are given for the centerlines of the walls and are displayed only for drawing purpose. You do not need to dimension or add text to the building. The project file name and the parameters to be used for different elements are given below.

(Expected time: 30 min)

1. Project file-
     For Imperial   *c03_Club_tut2.rvt*
     For Metric   *M_c03_Club_tut2.rvt*
2. Interior wall type -
     For Imperial   **Interior - 6 1/8" Partition (2-hr)**.
     For Metric   **Interior - 138mm Partition (1-hr)**.
3. Unconnected height of walls- **12'0"(3658 mm)**.
4. Location Line- **Wall Centerline**.
5. Inclined walls are parallel to the external walls and perpendicular to each other.

Creating Walls

Figure 3-67 Sketch plan for creating the interior wall of the left portion of the Club project

The following steps are required to complete this tutorial:

a. Open the project file.
   For Imperial   *c03_Club_tut2.rvt*
   For Metric   *M_c03_Club_tut2.rvt*
b. Invoke the **Wall: Architectural** tool and select the required wall type, refer to Figure 3-68.
   For Imperial   **Interior - 6 1/8" Partition (2-hr)**.
   For Metric   **Interior - 138mm Partition (1-hr)**.
c. Set the unconnected height to **12'0"(3658 mm)**.
d. Ensure that the location line parameter is set to **Wall Centerline**.
e. Select the **Line** sketching option to create the straight walls.
f. Sketch the interior walls based on the given parameters, refer to Figures 3-69 through 3-75.

Opening the Existing Project and Invoking the Wall: Architectural tool

1. Open the *c03_Club_tut2.rvt (M_c03_Club_tut2.rvt)* project file by choosing **Open > Projects** from the **Application Menu**. You can also download this file from *http://www.cadcim.com*. The path of the file is as follows: *Textbooks > Civil/GIS > Revit Architecture > Autodesk Revit 2015 for Architects and Designers*.

2. Click twice on **Level 1** under the **Floor Plans** head in the **Project Browser** and invoke the **Wall: Architectural** tool from **Architecture > Build > Wall** drop-down.

Selecting the Interior Wall Type

Before creating the interior walls, you need to select the wall type using the **Properties** palette.

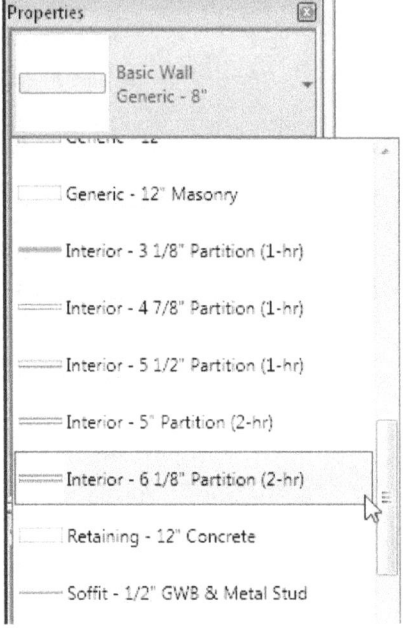

1. Select the required option from the **Type Selector** drop-down list in the **Properties** palette, as shown in Figure 3-68.
   For Imperial   **Interior - 6 1/8" Partition (2-hr)**.
   For Metric   **Interior - 138mm Partition (1-hr)**

2. Click in the value field corresponding to the **Top Constraint** parameter to display a drop-down list and ensure that the **Unconnected** option is selected in it.

3. Next, click on the value field corresponding to the **Unconnected Height** parameter, and replace the current value by entering the new value **12'0"** (**3658 mm**) in the cell.

4. Choose the **Apply** button to apply the changes made.

Figure 3-68 Selecting the interior wall type from the Properties palette

Sketching the Interior Walls

The interior walls to be created are straight in nature. Therefore you can use the **Line** tool from the **Draw** panel to create them.

1. Make sure that the **Wall Centerline** option is selected from the **Location Line** drop-down list in the **Options Bar**.

2. Clear the **Chain** check box in the **Options Bar**, if it is selected.

3. Move the cursor close to the lower left corner, marked as 6, refer to Figure 3-69, and traverse upward along the centerline of extreme left wall of the building profile. When the temporary dimension appears, enter the value **10'(3048 mm)** and press ENTER to start the interior wall profile from the specified point, as shown in Figure 3-69.

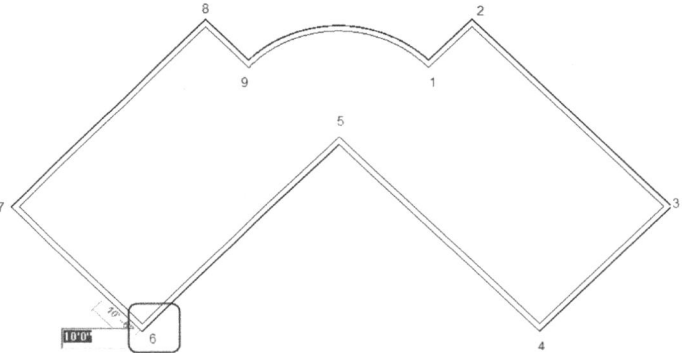

Figure 3-69 Specifying the start point of the first interior wall

Creating Walls 3-47

4. Move the cursor 45 degrees upward to the right. When a dashed line appears, enter the value **59'(17983 mm)**, as shown in Figure 3-70 and then press ENTER.

Figure 3-70 Sketching the first interior wall of the Club project

5. Start the next wall from the endpoint of the last wall by clicking on its endpoint. Move the cursor upward toward the left such that it subtends an angle of 135 degrees with the horizontal and reaches the exterior wall displaying the **Nearest** object snap, as shown in Figure 3-71. Click to specify the endpoint of the wall.

6. Similarly, to start the next interior wall, bring the cursor close to the starting point of the last created wall (marked as 10), refer to Figure 3-71. Then, move the cursor away along the center of the wall that is connected to the last created wall until the temporary dimension appears. When the temporary dimension appears, enter the value **10'0"(3048 mm)** and press ENTER to specify the start point of the wall.

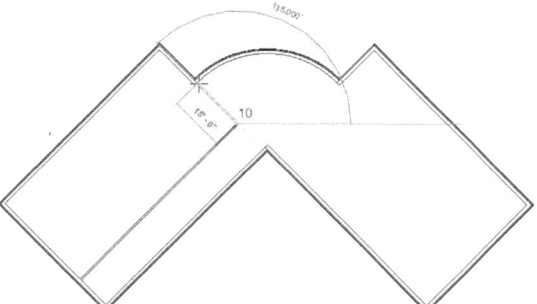

Figure 3-71 Sketching the second interior wall

7. Move the cursor upward towards the left such that it subtend an angle of 135 degrees with the horizontal until it reaches the exterior wall and the **Nearest** object snap is displayed, as shown in Figure 3-72. Click to specify the endpoint of the wall.

8. Create the next wall by moving the cursor away from the specified point. Next, move it downward towards the right. When the temporary dimension appears, enter the value **9'(2743 mm)** and press ENTER to start the wall, as shown in Figure 3-73.

Figure 3-72 Sketching the third interior wall

Figure 3-73 Specifying the distance of the fourth interior wall

9. Move the cursor upward toward the right. Click on the exterior wall to specify the endpoint of the interior wall when the **Nearest** object snap is displayed.

10. To create the next wall, bring the cursor close to the midpoint of the first interior wall until the midpoint object snap appears, as shown in Figure 3-74. Click on the drawing to start the wall.

11. Move the cursor up toward the left upto the exterior wall such that it subtend an angle of 135 degrees with the horizontal and click when the **Nearest** object snap appears on the exterior wall, as shown in Figure 3-75. Click to specify the endpoint; the wall is created.

    This completes the interior wall layout for the left portion of the *Club* project.

Figure 3-74 Starting the fifth interior wall from the midpoint of the first interior wall

Figure 3-75 Completing the interior walls

12. Choose the **Modify** button to exit the tool selection.

13. Choose **Save As > Project** from **Application Menu**; the **Save As** dialog box is displayed. Enter **c03_Club_tut4** in the **File name** edit box and then choose **Save**.

14. Now, choose **Close** from **Application Menu** to close the file.

Tutorial 5 Office-Stacked Wall

In this tutorial, you will create stacked walls and also add interior walls to the house plan. The interior walls to be created are the intermediate walls of the rooms, as shown in the plan sketch in Figure 3-76. The dimensions and text have been given for reference and are not to be created. The project file name and the parameters to be used for different elements are given next.

(Expected time: 45 min)

1. Project file-
     For Imperial   *default*.rte
     For Metric   *DefaultMetric*.rte
2. Interior wall type-
     For Imperial   **Interior - 5 1/2" Partition (1-hr)**
     For Metric   **Interior - 138 mm Partition (1-hr)**
3. Location line parameter- **Wall Centerline**.

The following steps are required to complete this tutorial:

a. Open the project file.
     For Imperial   *default.rte*
     For Metric   *DefaultMetric.rte*
b. Invoke the **Wall: Architectural** tool and select the required wall type from the **Type Selector** drop-down list.
     For Imperial   **Stacked Wall Exterior - Brick over CMU w Metal Stud**
     For Metric   **Render on Brick on Block w Metal Stud**
c. Edit the wall type as **Stacked wall Exterior- EIFS over CMU w Metal Stud**.
d. Set the location line parameter as **Location Line- Wall Centerline**.
e. Select the **Rectangle** sketching tool to sketch the exterior walls.
f. Sketch the interior walls based on the given parameters.
g. Edit the interior walls location to achieve clear internal distances.

Figure 3-76 Layout of internal walls for House project

Opening a New Project

1. Choose **New > Project** from **Application Menu**; the **New Project** dialog box is displayed.

2. In this dialog box, choose the **Browse** button; the **Choose Template** dialog box is displayed.

3. In the **Choose Template** dialog box, select the required template file.
       For Imperial   *default.rte*
       For Metric   *DefaultMetric.rte*
   Then, choose the **Open** button; the selected template file is loaded in the **New Project** dialog box.

4. Now, choose the **OK** button; the selected template file is loaded.

Invoking the Wall: Architectural Tool and Selecting the Wall Type

In this section, you will create a stacked wall type.

1. Choose the **Wall: Architectural** tool from **Architecture > Build > Wall** drop-down; the **Modify | Place Wall** tab is displayed.

2. In the **Properties** palette, select the required option from the **Type Selector** drop-down list.
       For Imperial   **Stacked Wall Exterior - Brick Over CMU w Metal Stud**
       For Metric   **Stacked Wall Exterior - Brick Over Block w Metal Stud**

Modifying Exterior Wall Type

In this section, you will use the **Type Properties** dialog box to edit the wall type and the **Properties** palette to modify the unconnected height to 18'0"(5486 mm).

1. In the **Properties** palette, choose the **Edit Type** button; the **Type Properties** dialog box is displayed.

2. In this dialog box, choose the **Duplicate** button; the **Name** dialog box is displayed. Enter required name in the **Name** edit box.
       For Imperial   **Exterior- EIFS Over CMU w Metal Stud**
       For Metric   **Exterior- Render on Brick on Block w Metal Stud**
   Then, choose the **OK** button.

3. Choose the **Edit button** corresponding to the **Structure** parameter; the **Edit Assembly** dialog box is displayed.

4. In this dialog box, click on the first row under the value field of the **Name** column and select the required option from the drop-down list displayed.
       For Imperial   **Exterior- EIFS on Metal Stud**
       For Metric   **Exterior- Render on Brick on Block**
   Ensure that **Variable** is selected under the **Height** column.

Creating Walls 3-51

5. Similarly, click on the second row under the value field of the **Name** column and select the required option from the drop-down list displayed and enter the height as **5' (1524 mm)** under the **Height** column.

   For Imperial   **Exterior- CMU on Metal Stud**
   For Metric   **Exterior- Block on Metal Stud**

6. Choose the **Preview** button to view the wall type; a preview pane is displayed.

7. Now, choose the **OK** button from the **Edit Assembly** dialog box and the **Type Properties** dialog boxes to close them.

8. In the **Properties** palette, click in the value field corresponding to the **Unconnected Height** parameter and replace the current value with **18'0"(5486 mm)**.

9. Click in the value field of the **Location Line** parameter and select the **Finish Face : Exterior** option from the drop-down list displayed. Choose the **Apply** button to accept the specified values.

Sketching the Exterior Walls

In this section, you will learn to create the exterior walls.

1. To create the exterior wall, choose the **Rectangle** tool from the **Draw** panel of the **Modify | Place Wall** tab, if it is not chosen by default.

2. To start sketching the first inclined wall segment, click inside the four arrow keys in the drawing window and move the cursor downward toward the right and click again; a rectangle is created with temporary dimensions displayed along with it, as shown in Figure 3-77.

Figure 3-77 Rectangle drawn with its temporary dimensions

3. Press ESC twice to exit the currently selected tool.

4. Now, select the upper horizontal wall; the **Modify | Stacked Wall** tab is displayed.

5. In the **Options Bar**, choose the **Activate Dimensions** button; the dimension are activated for vertical side.

6. Click on the vertical temporary dimension and enter **45'**(13716 mm) in the edit box displayed, as shown in Figure 3-78 and press ENTER.

Figure 3-78 Entering vertical dimension in the edit box

7. Now, select the left wall and then activate the dimension using the **Activate Dimension** button from the **Options Bar**.

8. Click on the horizontal temporary dimension and enter **60'(18288 mm)** for the horizontal wall, as shown in Figure 3-79. Press ENTER.

Figure 3-79 Entering horizontal dimension in the edit box

Creating Walls

Selecting the Interior Wall Type

Before creating the interior walls, you need to select the wall type using the **Properties** palette.

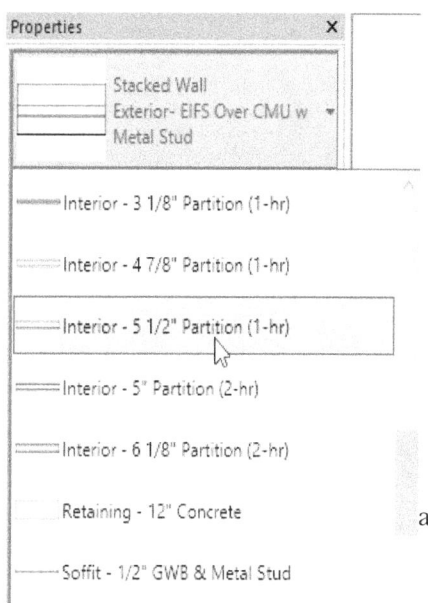

1. Choose the **Wall: Architectural** tool from **Architecture > Build > Wall** drop-down.

2. Select the required option from the **Type Selector** drop-down list in the **Properties** palette, as shown in Figure 3-80.
   For Imperial **Interior - 5 1/2" Partition (1-hr)**
   For Metric **Interior- 138mm Partition (1-hr)**

3. Click in the value field corresponding to the **Top Constraint** parameter to display drop-down list and ensure that the **Unconnected** option is selected in it.

4. Next, click on the value field corresponding to the **Unconnected Height** parameter, and replace the current value by entering the new value **18'(5486 mm)** in the cell.

Figure 3-80 Selecting the interior wall type from the **Properties** palette

5. Choose the **Apply** button to apply the changes made.

Sketching Interior Walls

In this section, you will sketch the horizontal and vertical interior walls by specifying their start point and endpoint using different object snap options.

1. To sketch the interior wall, move the cursor to the upper left corner of the exterior wall and then move the cursor horizontally toward the right. Enter **13'(3962 mm)**, as shown in Figure 3-81, when the temporary dimension and the intersection object snap appears. Now, press ENTER; the start point of the interior wall segment is specified on the upper horizontal exterior wall.

Figure 3-81 Entering the value in the edit box

2. Press SHIFT and move the cursor downward. You will notice that the cursor moves parallel to the vertical axis while moving it downward. Click near the lower external wall, as shown in Figure 3-82 when the **Vertical and Nearest** symbol appears.

   Next, you will sketch the other interior walls.

Figure 3-82 Straight wall created till the lower exterior wall

3. Move the cursor to the bottom of the wall just drawn and then move it vertically upward. When the temporary dimension appears, enter **5'0"(1524 mm)** and then press ENTER; the starting point of the third interior wall is specified, as shown in Figure 3-83.

Creating Walls 3-55

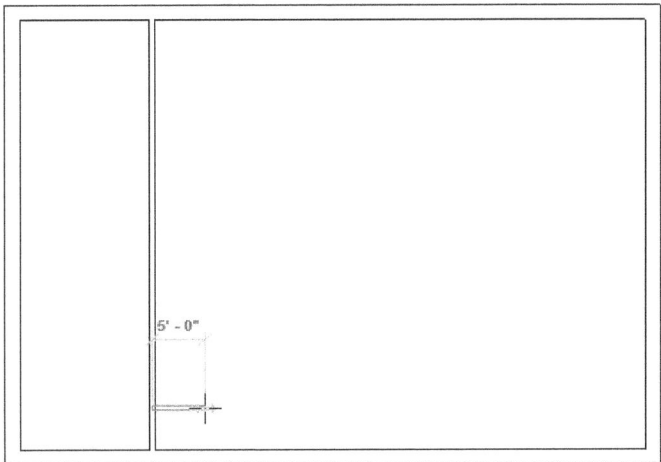

Figure 3-83 Specifying the starting point of third interior wall

4. Press SHIFT and move the cursor horizontally toward the right. When temporary dimension appears, enter **13'(3962 mm)** and then press ENTER; the wall segment is created.

5. Now, click on the wall you just created and move the cursor vertically upward and click on the upper external wall, as shown in Figure 3-84.

Figure 3-84 Created wall is extended to the upper exterior wall

6. Move the cursor near the upper right corner and then move it vertically downward. When the temporary dimension and the intersection object snap appears, enter the value **10'0"(3048 mm)** and then press ENTER.

7. Press and hold the SHIFT key and move the cursor horizontally towards left until it reaches the vertical interior wall. Next, click to specify the endpoint of the wall, as shown in Figure 3-85. Now, press ESC twice to finish the sketch of the wall.

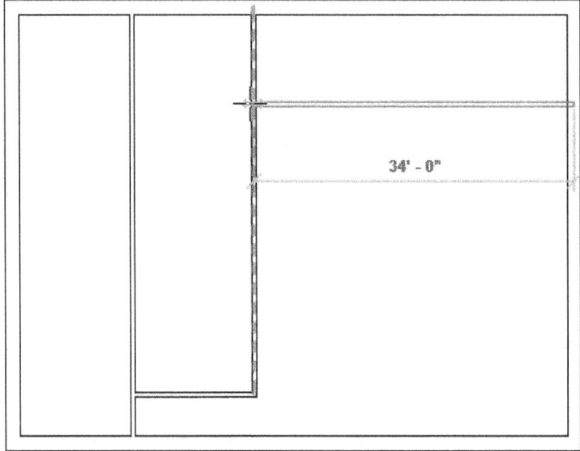

Figure 3-85 *Horizontal wall created at the distance of 10' from the outer exterior wall*

8. Similarly, sketch other walls as shown in Figure 3-86.

Figure 3-86 *Selecting the interior wall type from the **Properties** palette*

9. To view the building model in 3D, choose the **Default 3D View** tool from **View > Create > 3D View** drop-down. On doing so, the 3D view of the building model is displayed along with the **ViewCube** tool.

Creating Walls

10. Now, choose the **Visual Style** button from the **View Control Bar**; a flyout is displayed. Choose the **Shaded** option from this flyout; the 3D view is displayed with shading and with edges visible, as shown in Figure 3-87.

11. Choose **Save As > Project** from **Application Menu**; the **Save As** dialog box is displayed. Enter **c03_office_tut5** in the **File name** edit box and then choose **Save**.

Figure 3-87 *3D view of a building with the shaded edges*

Self-Evaluation Test

Answer the following questions and then compare them to those given at the end of this chapter:

1. You can modify the instance properties of a wall type in the **Properties** palette. (T/F)

2. When you modify the instance properties of a wall, the instance properties of all the similar wall types used in the project are modified. (T/F)

3. You can create a wall type of your choice by combining various layers. (T/F)

4. By default, when you sketch a wall from left to right, the lower face becomes the external face. (T/F)

5. A stacked wall is comprised of one or more _____ wall types.

   a) Generic   b) Simple
   c) Basic   d) Complex

6. You can use the _____ to view the instance parameters of an element.

   a) Properties palette   b) Project Browser
   c) Filter   d) Type Selector

7. Which value of the Structural Usage parameter will turn a structural wall into an architectural wall?

   a) Bearing
   c) Structural combined
   b) Non-bearing
   d) Shear

8. The _____ option enables you to sketch continuous and end to end connected wall segments.

9. To create a wall starting at a specified distance from a point on an existing element, you can use the _____ option from the **Options Bar**.

10. You can select a wall type from the _____ drop-down list.

Review Questions

Answer the following questions:

1. Which of the following sketching tools can be used to create a straight wall?

   a) **Lines**
   c) **Fillet Arc**
   b) **Circles**
   d) **Center-ends Arc**

2. Which of the following keys can be used to constrain the cursor such that it moves along the orthogonal direction only?

   a) TAB
   c) ALT
   b) SHIFT
   d) F3

3. Which of the following sketching tools can be used to create a curved wall?

   a) **Polygon**
   c) **Fillet Arc**
   b) **Line**
   d) **Rectangle**

4. The **Location Line** parameter is an instance property of a wall. (T/F)

5. The value of the **Function** parameter in the **Type Properties** dialog box for an exterior wall is **Exterior**. (T/F)

6. You can add or delete layers of a composite wall type to create a new wall type. (T/F)

7. Once a wall is sketched, its dimension and angle cannot be modified. (T/F)

8. The **Chain** option can be enabled or disabled without exiting the **Wall: Architectural** tool. (T/F)

Creating Walls

9. The usage of the wall can be changed by modifying the value of the **Function** parameter. (T/F)

10. While using the **Wall: Architectural** tool, if you invoke any other tool, the **Wall: Architectural** tool will be exited (T/F)

11. The _____ dimension appears after you specify the start point of a wall and move the cursor.

12. You can use the _____ option to create a curved wall by specifying the center and the endpoints.

Exercises

Exercise 1   Apartment 2

Create the exterior and interior walls of the *Apartment 2*, based on Figure 3-88. The thick walls are the exterior walls and the thin walls are the interior walls. The dimensions and texts are not to be added. The project parameters for this exercise are given next.

(Expected time: 30 min)

1. Project file -
   - For Imperial   *c02_Apartment2_ex1.rvt*.
   - For Metric   *M_c02_Apartment2_ex1.rvt*.
2. Exterior wall type- **Exterior - Brick on Mtl. Stud**.
3. Interior wall type-
   - For Imperial   **Basic Wall: Interior - 5" Partition (2-hr)**.
   - For Metric   **Basic Wall: Interior - 135mm Partition (2-hr)**.
4. Height of the wall- **Top Constraint - Up to Level 2**.
5. Location line parameter for the exterior walls- **Wall Centerline**.
6. Name of the file to be saved-
   - For Imperial   **c03_Apartment2_ex1**
   - For Metric   **M_c03_Apartment2_ex1**

Figure 3-88 The sketch plan for creating the exterior and interior walls for the Apartment 2 project

Exercise 2   Elevator and Stair Lobby

Create the exterior walls of the *Elevator and Stair Lobby* project, based on Figure 3-89. Do not add dimensions or texts as they are given only for reference. The project parameters for this exercise are given next. **(Expected time: 30 min)**

1. Project file -
    For Imperial   *c02_ElevatorandStairLobby_ex2.rvt*
    For Metric   *M_c02_ElevatorandStairLobby_ex2.rvt*
2. Exterior wall type - **Basic Wall Exterior Brick on Mtl. Stud**.
3. Height of the wall - **Top Constraint- Up to Level 2**.
4. Location line parameter - **Wall Centerline**.
5. Name of the file to be saved -
    For Imperial   **c03_ElevatorandStairLobby_ex2**.
    For Metric   **M_c03_ElevatorandStairLobby_ex2**.

Creating Walls 3-61

Figure 3-89 Sketch plan for creating the exterior walls for the Elevator and Stair Lobby project

Exercise 3   Club-Interior Walls

Create the interior walls of Hall 2 of the *Club* project based on Figure 3-90. Do not dimension the sketch as these are given only for reference. The project parameters for this exercise are given next.   **(Expected time: 30 min)**

1. Project file -
   - For Imperial   *c03_Club_tut4.rvt*
   - For Metric   *M_c03_Club_tut4.rvt*
2. Interior wall type-
   - For Imperial   **Basic Wall: Interior - 6 1/8" Partition (2-hr)**.
   - For Metric   **Basic Wall: Interior - 138mm Partition (1-hr)**.
3. Unconnected height of walls- **12'0"(3658 mm)**.
4. Location Line- **Wall Centerline**.
5. Inclined walls are parallel to the external walls and perpendicular to each other.
6. Name for saving the file-
   - For Imperial   **c03_Club_ex3**.
   - For Metric   **M_c03_Club_ex3**.

Figure 3-90 Sketch plan for sketching the interior walls of right portion for the Club project

Answers to Self-Evaluation Test
1. T, 2. F, 3. T, 4. F, 5. Basic, 6. **Properties** palette, 7. Structural Combined, 8. Chain, 9. Offset, 10. Type Selector

Chapter 4

Using Basic Building Components-I

Learning Objectives

After completing this chapter, you will be able to:
- *Understand the concept of doors.*
- *Understand various properties of doors.*
- *Add doors to the exterior and interior walls.*
- *Understand the concept of windows.*
- *Understand various properties of windows.*
- *Add windows to a building model.*
- *Create door and window openings in walls.*
- *Add openings to the walls.*

INTRODUCTION

In the previous chapter, you learned to create various types of exterior and interior walls in a building profile. Similar to walls, the positioning of doors and windows also play an important role in designing a building profile. In this chapter, you will learn the process of selecting and adding doors and windows to a building model. Autodesk Revit Architecture has several in-built families of doors and windows which help in adding different types of doors and windows in a building model. In Revit Architecture, doors and windows act as hosted components that can be added to any type of wall. In this chapter, you will also learn to use these components and modify their properties.

ADDING DOORS IN A BUILDING MODEL

A door is one of the most frequently used components in a building model. It helps in accessing various exterior and interior spaces in a project. Autodesk Revit Architecture provides a variety of predefined door types. You can access these door types by using the options from the **Type Selector** drop-down list of the **Properties** palette. You can also load other door types from the **US Imperial** or **US Metric** folder. A wall acts as a host element for doors. This means that a door can be placed only if there exists a wall. When you add a door to a wall, Autodesk Revit Architecture intuitively creates an opening in it. The procedure for adding doors to a building model is described next.

Adding Doors

You can add doors to a building model by using the **Door** tool. You can invoke this tool from the **Build** panel, as shown in Figure 4-1. Alternatively, you can type **DR** to invoke this tool.

Figure 4-1 Invoking the **Door** tool from the **Build** panel

To add a door, invoke the **Door** tool; the **Modify|Place Door** tab will be displayed in the ribbon. In this tab, select the desired door type from the **Type Selector** drop-down list in the **Properties** palette, as shown in Figure 4-2. This drop-down list displays the in-built door types. Next, after selecting a door type, click on the desired location of a wall to add the door. After adding the door to the building model, you can view and modify its properties. To do so, select the door; the instance properties of the door will be displayed in the **Properties** palette, as shown in Figure 4-3. You will learn more about adding doors to a wall further in this chapter.

Now, to modify the type properties of the selected door type, choose the **Edit Type** button from the **Properties** palette; the **Type Properties** dialog box for the selected door type will be displayed, as shown in Figure 4-4. In this dialog box, change the parameters as per your requirement and then choose the **Preview** button to view the graphical image of the selected door type.

Using Basic Building Components-I

Figure 4-2 Selecting the door type from the **Properties** palette

Figure 4-3 The instance properties displayed for the **Single-Flush: 34" x 84"** door type

Figure 4-4 The **Type Properties** dialog box

Understanding Door Properties

The **Type Properties** dialog box displays the values of different parameters of a door. The type parameters are arranged under various heads based on their properties such as **Construction**, **Materials and Finishes**, **Dimensions**, **Identity Data**, and **IFC Parameters**. The parameters associated with each property are listed under each head. For example, the **Dimensions** head includes the dimensional type parameters associated with the door type such as, **Height**, **Width**, **Trim Width**, and so on. You have the option of either using the default values for these parameters or modifying them to the desired values. However, before modifying the type properties of a predefined door type, it is recommended to create a copy of the original door type and modify the desired properties of the new door type. The **Duplicate** button available on the top right corner in this dialog box is used to create a copy of the door type. When you choose this button, the **Name** edit box will be displayed, prompting you to assign a name to the new door type. Enter a name in this edit box and choose the **OK** button; a new door type is created which inherits the properties of the parent door type. Now, its parameters can be modified as desired. Use the **Rename** button to give a new name to the selected door type. You can use the **Load** button provided on the top right corner of the dialog box to load a door type of the required family from the additional libraries.

Note

Renaming a door type does not alter its properties. For example, if you rename 34"x 84" to 36"x 84", its width will still remain 34", irrespective of its name.

Door Type Properties

If you change the type properties of a door, the properties of all instances of that door type in the project will also change. The door type properties are described in the table given next:

Parameter Name	Description
Function	Specifies the function of Door. You can set the door function value to Interior or Exterior. This value will be used at the time of scheduling
Wall Closure	Specifies the Wall Closure for the door type. In this case, you can set the layer wrapping for the door type
Construction Type	Specifies the type of construction for the door
Door Material	Specifies the finished material of the door panel. You can select the material of the door panel by clicking on the browse button in the value field. It displays **Material Browser - Door - Panel** dialog box. You can select the desired material from the **Name** list of the displayed dialog box
Frame Material	Specifies the finish material of the door frame and can be selected from the **Name** list of the **Material Browser-Door -Frame** dialog box displayed on clicking the browse button of the value field

Height	Used to set the height of the door by editing in the value field
Trim Projection Ext	Specifies the thickness of the trim projection on the exterior side
Trim Projection Int	Specifies the thickness of the trim projection on the interior side
Trim Width	Specifies width of the trim at both sides of door
Width	Specifies width of the door and can be set to desired value
Rough Width	Specifies width of the door type used for scheduling or exporting
Rough Height	Specifies height of the door type used for scheduling or exporting
Assembly Code	Specifies the **Assembly Code** for the specified door type that can be selected from the hierarchical list
Keynote	This parameter is available for all model elements, detail components, and materials under identity data. You can add or edit the door keynote from the **Keynote** dialog box by clicking on the browse button in the value field of this parameter
Model	Specifies the name to be given to the model door type
Manufacturer	Specifies the name of the manufacturer of the door type
Type Comments	Specifies the comments entered for the door type. You can enter or select the additional information or comments to be added to the door type from the drop-down list, primarily for including in schedules
URL	Specifies the web link of the door type manufacturer
Description	Specifies the description of the door type
Assembly Description	Specifies the description of the assembly of the door type
Type Mark	Specifies a unique value that may be generated in a sequence of creation of the door type
Fire Rating	Specifies the fire rating of the door type. You can edit the fire rating of the door type by clicking in the value field corresponding to the fire rating parameter
Cost	Specifies the cost of the door primarily used for costing purpose

Analytic Construction	Specifies the Heat Transfer Coefficient, Thermal Resistance, Solar Heat Gain Coefficient, and Visual Light Transmittance. The values of these options are set by default for the materials available in the **Analytic Construction** drop-down list
Heat Transfer Coefficient	Helps in calculating heat transfer by convection or phase change between a solid or a liquid
Thermal Resistance	Measures temperature difference
Solar Heat Gain Coefficient	Specifies the Solar Heat Gain Coefficient for the door type. Solar radiations entering through a door directly absorbed and released inward
Visual Light Transmittance	Specifies the amount of visible light that passes through a glazing system

Some of the properties of the door are shown graphically in Figure 4-5.

Figure 4-5 *The door properties*

Door Instance Properties

The door instance properties, available in the **Properties** palette, refer to the instance properties of a particular door. On changing these properties, the properties of only a particular instance in the project are changed. The description of various instance parameters is given in the table next:

Parameter Name	Description
Sill Height	Specifies the distance or height of the sill of the door from the specified level
Frame Type	Specifies the type of frame used for the door instance

Using Basic Building Components-I

Frame Material	Specifies the material used for the frame of the instance
Finish	Specifies the finish applied to the door and frame
Image	Specifies the image file corresponding to the door instance. This parameter can be used in the door schedule to display the image of the door instance
Comments	Specifies the comments for the door instance. It can be selected from the drop-down list
Mark	Specifies the mark of the selected door
Phase Created	Specifies whether the door is a part of the new construction or an existing construction
Phase Demolished	Specifies whether the door is a part of the existing building or a new structure, or none
Head Height	Specifies the height of the top of the door from the specified level

Adding a Door to a Wall

Doors can be added to a wall in the plan, section, elevation or a 3D view by clicking at the desired location on the wall. After invoking the **Door** tool and selecting the door type, move the cursor over the wall on which it is to be added. The '**+**' symbol over the cursor indicates that an element is being added. You will notice that the door symbol appears when the cursor is moved over the wall. When the cursor comes close to the upper or the lower face of the wall, the door symbol appears on it, as shown in Figure 4-6. Also, a temporary dimension appears depicting the distance of the center of the door opening from the adjacent walls or wall edges.

Figure 4-6 Adding a door to a wall

Using the temporary dimensions displayed, you can add the door at the desired location. Alternatively, you can first add the door at an approximate location on the wall and then modify its location to the exact dimension. When a door is added, an opening is automatically created in the wall and the edges are also completed, as shown in Figure 4-7. After selecting the door, you will notice that the horizontal and vertical twin arrow symbols appear in the door along with a tag number. To flip the swing-side of the door, click on the twin arrow key that appears parallel to the wall edge. To shift the door to the other side of the wall, click on the twin arrow key that appears perpendicular to the wall edge (vertical, in this case).

To move the added door to the exact dimension, click on the particular temporary dimension text and enter the exact value, as shown in Figure 4-8. The door shifts to the desired location.

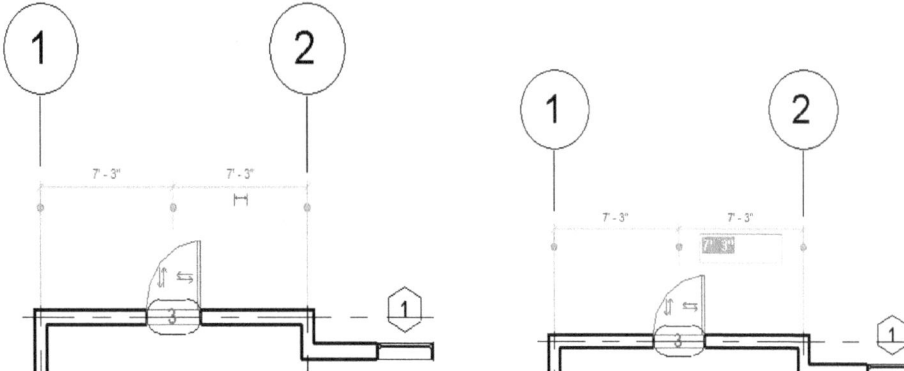

Figure 4-7 A door added along with its controls   *Figure 4-8* Specifying the exact location of the door

 Tip: *To flip the swing of the door, select the door and press the SPACEBAR. Each time you press the SPACEBAR, the door will cycle through all the four possibilities.*

 Note
A door can be placed in any type of wall regardless of the height of the door. Autodesk Revit Architecture 2015 displays alert messages if the door is not placed appropriately.

In Autodesk Revit Architecture, when doors are inserted, door tags are generated automatically. They assist in marking the doors and later arranging them in the form of a schedule. The door type tag number increases sequentially when you place a door by using the **Door** tool or when you copy and paste it into the building model. You can, however, give a specific mark or tag to doors individually. The visibility of door tags can be controlled by using the **Visibility/Graphics Overrides for Floor Plan** dialog box. This dialog box can be invoked by typing **VG**, or by selecting the desired door from the drawing and choosing the **Visibility/Graphics** tool in the **Graphics** panel in the **View** tab. Next, if you want to hide the door tags, choose the **Annotation Categories** tab from the **Visibility/Graphics Overrides for Floor Plan** dialog box and clear the **Door Tags** check box. When you invoke the **Door** tool, the option for adding a horizontal or vertical door tag becomes available in the **Options Bar**. You can set the orientation of the door tags to horizontal or vertical by selecting the **Horizontal** or **Vertical** option from the drop-down list displayed in the **Options Bar**.

To change a door type, select the particular instance; the properties and the type of the selected door will be displayed in the **Properties** palette. In the **Properties** palette, select a new door type from the **Type Selector** drop-down list; the selected door will be replaced with the new door type.

In Autodesk Revit Architecture, you can create a new door type by using various tools. To create a new door type, choose the **Model In-place** tool from the **Mode** panel of

Using Basic Building Components-I 4-9

the **Modify | Place Door** tab; the **Name** dialog box will be displayed. In this dialog box, enter a name in the **Name** edit box and choose the **OK** button; the dialog box will be closed and the **Modify** tab will be displayed. Using the tools from this tab, you can create the doors that are specifically designed for that instance.

Note
*On invoking the **Model In-place** tool, the family editor mode will be activated. In this mode, you can use various massing tools from the **Architecture** tab to create an in-place door assembly.*

Apart from the door types available in the **Type Selector** drop-down list, you can use other door types from additional libraries. To access them, choose the **Load Family** tool in the **Mode** panel of the **Modify | Place Door**; the **Load Family** dialog box will be displayed. Additional door types are available in the **Doors** sub folder of the **US Imperial** folder. Select a door type to view its image in the **Preview** area, as shown in Figure 4-9. After selecting the door type, choose the **Open** button. The selected family of doors will be added to the **Type Selector** drop-down list in the **Properties** palette for that project.

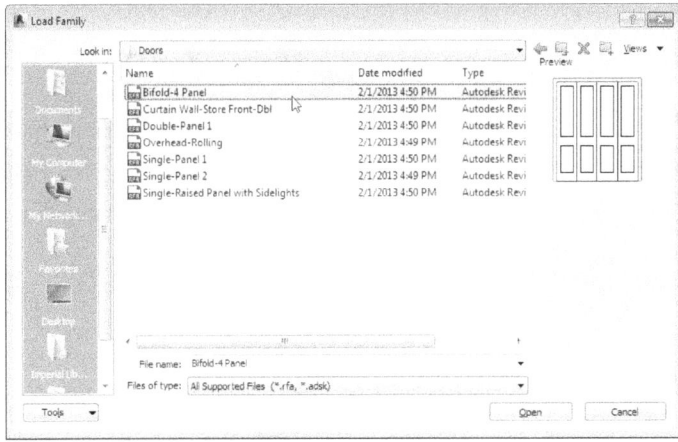

*Figure 4-9 Using the **Load Family** dialog box to load additional door types*

Tip: *Using the **Options Bar**, you can set certain parameters before placing the components. For example, before placing the door, you can set the horizontal or vertical position of door tags and select the leader as well.*

ADDING WINDOWS IN A BUILDING MODEL
Windows form an integral part of any building project. Autodesk Revit Architecture provides several in-built window types that can be easily used and added to the building model. Like doors, windows are also dependent on the walls that act as their host element.

Adding Windows

Ribbon: Architecture > Build > Window
Shortcut Key: WN

In Autodesk Revit Architecture, you can add windows to a building model by using the **Window** tool. To do so, invoke the **Window** tool from the **Build** panel of the **Architecture** tab, as shown in Figure 4-10; the **Modify | Place Window** tab will be displayed. In this tab, select the window type from the **Type Selector** drop-down list in the **Properties** palette, as shown in Figure 4-11. To add a building model, move the cursor over the wall and click to place it either in the upper face or in the lower face. After adding the window, you can view or change its instance parameters. To do so, select the window from the drawing; the **Properties** palette will be displayed, as shown in Figure 4-12. You can use this palette to view and modify various instance parameters of the selected window such as its Level, Head Height, Sill Height, and others. To modify and view the type parameters of the window, choose the **Edit Type** button in the **Properties** palette; the **Type Properties** dialog box will be displayed. In this dialog box, choose the **Preview** button to view the graphical image of the selected window type, as shown in Figure 4-13.

Figure 4-10 Invoking the **Window** tool from the **Build** panel

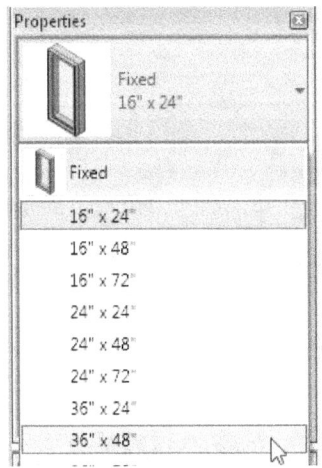

Figure 4-11 Selecting the window type from the **Type Selector** drop-down list

Figure 4-12 The **Properties** palette for the **Fixed: 36" x 48"** window type

Understanding Window Properties

The **Type Properties** dialog box displays the type parameters for different components of a window such as **Glass Pane Material**, **Sash Material**, **Default Sill Height**, **Width**, **Height**,

Using Basic Building Components-I 4-11

and so on. You can click in the value column of each parameter and select from the available options or use the **Load** button provided on the top right corner of the dialog box to load a window family type from the additional libraries. The **Duplicate** button is used to create a copy of the window type with a different name. The new window inherits the properties of the parent window type and its parameters can be modified. By using the **Rename** button, you can give a new name to the selected window type. The window type properties are discussed next.

Figure 4-13 The **Type Properties** dialog box for the **Fixed: 36" x 48"** window type with the **Preview** button chosen

Window Type Properties

When you change the type properties of a window type, the properties of all instances of that window type in the project will also change. Various type parameters and their corresponding descriptions are given in the following table:

Parameter Name	Description
Wall Closure	Specifies layer wrapping for the window type
Construction Type	Specifies the construction type of the window
Glass Pane Material	Specifies the finish and material of the glass pane and can be selected from the **Material Browser-Glass** dialog box. This dialog box is displayed on clicking the browse button in the value field
Sash Material	Specifies the material assigned to the sash of the window
Height	Specifies the height of the window
Default Sill Height	Specifies the distance of the window from the bottom of the wall, its default value is 3'0". The default value of this parameter can be edited by clicking in the value field of the corresponding parameter

Width	Specifies the width of the window
Window Inset	Specifies the inset of the window from the wall face
Rough Width	Specifies the width used for scheduling or exporting
Rough Height	Specifies the height used for scheduling or exporting
Keynote	This parameter is available for all model elements, detail components, and materials under identity data
Model	Specifies the name to be given to the window type
Manufacturer	Specifies the name of the manufacturer of the window type
Type Comments	Additional information or comments to be added to the window type, primarily for creating schedules
URL	Specifies the weblink of the manufacturer
Description	Specifies the description of the window type
Assembly Description	Specifies the description of the assembly
Type Mark	Specifies the unique value assigned to each window
Cost	Specifies the cost of the window, primarily for costing purpose

Figure 4-14 shows the window properties such as height, width, and sill height.

Figure 4-14 Graphic showing the window properties

Window Instance Properties

The parameters given in the **Properties** palette displays the window instance properties, and these prameters can be changed to change the instance properties of the selected window. The instance properties of a window are given in the table below.

Using Basic Building Components-I

Parameter Name	Description
Level	Shows the level to which the window belongs and can be used to move the window to a different level
Sill Height	Specifies the distance or height of the sill of the window from the specified level
Image	Specifies the image file corresponding to the window instance. This parameter can be used in the door schedule to display the image of the window instance
Comments	Specifies the window instance that is not covered in the type properties
Mark	Specifies or modifies the mark of the selected window
Phase Created	Specifies whether the window is part of a new construction or an existing construction
Phase Demolished	Specifies whether the window is a part of an existing building or new structure
Head Height	Specifies the height of the top of the window from the specified level

Adding a Window to a Wall

To add a window to a wall, invoke the **Window** tool from the **Architecture** tab of the ribbon and select the window type from the **Type Selector** drop-down list in the **Properties** palette. Next, move the cursor close to the wall on which it needs to be added. The window symbol appears when the cursor is moved over the wall. When the cursor comes close to the lower face of the wall, the window appears on that face. The window appears on the upper face when the cursor comes near to it, as shown in Figure 4-15. Also, notice a temporary dimension, which depicts the distance of the center of the window opening from the adjacent walls or wall edges. You can use the temporary dimensions to add the window by clicking at the appropriate location on the wall. Autodesk Revit Architecture automatically creates an opening in the wall and the edges also get completed, as shown in Figure 4-16.

Figure 4-15 Adding a window to an existing wall

You will also notice a twin arrow symbol on the window, along with a tag number. Click on the symbol to flip the orientation of the window. The flip arrow symbol will appear on the side that is interpreted as the inner side of the window. You can specify the exact position of the window with respect to the adjacent walls or edges after placing it at the approximate location. To specify the dimensional location of a window, click on the particular temporary dimension text and type the exact dimension, as shown in Figure 4-17. The window will shift to the desired location.

Figure 4-16 *Window added to an existing wall*

Window tags are automatically generated in Autodesk Revit Architecture. Unlike doors, however, each window of the same type bears the same tag. Different window types have preassigned marks, which can be changed using the **Type Properties** dialog box. Window tags are used for creating the window schedule.

Figure 4-17 *Changing the location of the added window*

Tip: *The depth of the window is automatically created based on the thickness of the host wall. If you change the type of the host wall of a window, the depth of the associated window will change accordingly.*

Note

As you place windows in a project, the tag number assigned to them increase by one. You can also give them a specific tag number individually.

Similar to the door tags, the visibility of the window tags can also be controlled in the drawing. To hide the window tags, invoke the **Visibility/Graphics for Floor Plan** dialog box and choose the **Annotation Categories** tab from it. Next, clear the **Window Tags** check box.

Note

*On clearing the **Window Tags** check box in the **Annotation Categories** of the **Visibility/Graphics for Floor Plan** dialog box, the tags although become hidden, but will still remain a part of the project.*

In Autodesk Revit Architecture, you can create the windows that are specifically designed for a location or an instance. To do so, choose the **Model In-place** tool from the **Mode** panel of the **Modify | Place Window** tab; the **Name** dialog box will be displayed. In this dialog box, enter the name of the window type in the **Name** edit box and choose the **OK** button; the dialog box will be closed and the **Modify** tab will be displayed. Now, the family editor mode will be activated, and in this mode, you can use various tools to create the in-place window. Apart from the window types displayed in the **Type Selector** drop-down list, you can access other window types as well. To add other window types in the **Type Selector** drop-down list, choose the **Load Family** tool from the **Mode** panel of the **Modify | Place Window** tab; the **Load Family** dialog box will be displayed. In this dialog box, add additional window types from the **Library > US Imperial > Windows** folder. Alternatively, you can use the **Revit Architecture Web Content Library** to download more window types to your project.

DOORS AND WINDOWS AS WALL OPENINGS

Autodesk Revit Architecture also provides in-built opening types for door and windows. These types are available in the **Openings** subfolder of the **Libraries > US Imperial** folder for Imperial (**Libraries > US Metric** folder for Metric) that can be accessed from the **Load Family** dialog box .To invoke this dialog box, choose the **Load Family** tool from the **Load from Library** panel of the **Insert** tab.

To add an opening for the door, invoke the **Load Family** dialog box and then from the **Openings** subfolder, select any of the following family types such as: For Imperial- **Opening with Trim**, **Opening**, **Opening-Door**, **Passage Opening-Cased**, **Opening-Window-Round**, **Passage Opening-Elliptical Arch**, and **Opening-Window-Square** or For Metric **M_Opening with Trim**, **M_Opening**, **M_Opening-Door**, **M_Passage Opening-Cased**, **M_Opening-Window-Round**, **M_Passage Opening-Elliptical Arch**, and **M_Opening-Window-Square**. After selecting any of the family type, choose the **Open** button in the **Load Family** dialog box; the selected family will be loaded in the project. Now, to place the selected opening type in the wall, choose the **Place a Component** tool from **Architecture > Build > Component** drop-down; the **Modify|Place Component** tab will be displayed. In the **Properties** palette, ensure that the desired opening type is selected in the **Type Selector** drop-down list. Next, click in a desired location in the wall to insert the door opening. In the **Properties** palette, you can also edit the width and height of the door opening.

Similar to adding a door opening, you can insert a window opening. To do so, invoke the **Load Family** dialog box and then select any of the two family types from the **Openings** sub folder: **Opening with Trim** or **Opening**. To place the window opening in the wall you will follow the same method as used for inserting the door opening.

OPENINGS IN THE WALL

Ribbon: Architecture > Opening > Wall

You can create rectangular openings in a curved or straight wall. To cut an opening in a wall, you can use a plan, elevation, or sectional view. Generally, the sectional or elevation view is preferred as locating and placing such views are easy. To cut a rectangular opening in a wall, open a preferred elevation or a section view in which the host wall of the opening is visible. (You will learn about creating the elevation and section views in Chapter 6 of this textbook). Next, choose the **Wall Opening** tool from the **Opening** panel of the **Architecture** tab and then select the wall that will host the opening. Next, click in the desired area in the wall to mark the start point or the first corner point of the rectangular opening. As you move the cursor, a rectangle with its temporary dimensions appears. Click at the desired point in the wall to mark the other corner point of the rectangular opening. Now, you can use the temporary dimensions displayed on the opening to modify the placement of the opening. Next, choose the **Modify** button from the **Select** panel to exit the tool. After exiting the tool, you can select the created opening to modify its properties such as its height, top offset, base offset, and so on from the **Properties** palette.

Tip: *Press the shortcut keys SM to snap the inserts to the midpoint of the wall. This is known as jump snap.*

TUTORIALS

Tutorial 1   Apartment 1

In this tutorial, you will add doors and windows to the apartment project file created in Tutorial 3 of Chapter 3. Refer to Figure 4-18 for adding these elements. The dimensions and the text have been given for reference and are not to be added. The project file name and parameters to be used are given next.   **(Expected time: 30 min)**

1. Project file-
    For Imperial   *c03_Apartment1_tut3.rvt*
    For Metric   *M_c03_Apartment1_tut3.rvt*

2. Door types to be used
    For Imperial   1- **Single - Flush: 30"x 84"**
                        2 and 3- **Single Decorative 2 - 36"x 84"**
                        4- **Bifold-4 Panel - 60"x 84"**
                        Door openings- **Passage Opening-Cased** resize to **7'0"**
    For Metric   1- **M_Single - Flush: 0762 x 2134 mm**
                        2 and 3- **M_Single Decorative 2 - 0762 x 2134 mm**
                        4- **M_Bifold-4 Panel - 1525 x 2134 mm**
                        Door openings- **Passage Opening-Cased** resize to **2134 mm**

Using Basic Building Components-I 4-17

3. For Imperial   Window types to be used
    1- **Fixed: 24"x48"**
    2- **Fixed: 48"x48"** (with modified width)
   For Metric   Window types to be used
    1- **Fixed: 0610 x 1220 mm**
    2- **Fixed: 1220 x 1220 mm** (with modified width)

The following steps are required to complete this tutorial:

a. Open the file created in Chapter 3.
    For Imperial   *c03_Apartment1_tut3.rvt*
    For Metric   *c03_Apartment1_tut3.rvt*
   Invoke the **Door** tool.
b. Add doors at approximate locations, refer to Figures 4-19 through 4-24.
c. Load and add door openings, refer to Figure 4-25.
d. Place the door openings to the exact location based on the given parameters, refer to Figure 4-26 and Figure 4-27.
e. Invoke the **Window** tool. Select the window type by using the **Type Selector** drop-down list.
f. Place the windows at approximate locations.
g. Place the windows at the exact location as per the given dimensions, refer to Figures 4-28 through 4-34.

Figure 4-18 Sketch for adding doors and windows to the Apartment 1 project

Opening the Existing Project and Invoking the Door Tool

First, you need to open the specified project and invoke the **Door** tool from the **Architecture** tab.

1. Choose **Open > Project** from the **Application Menu** and open the *c03_Apartment1_tut3.rvt* for Imperial or *M_c03_Apartment1_tut3.rvt* for Metric project file created in Tutorial 3 of Chapter 3.

You can also download this file from *http://www.cadcim.com*. The path of the file is as follows: *Textbooks > Civil/GIS > Revit Architecture > Autodesk Revit Architecture 2015 for Architects and Designers*.

2. Double-click on **Level 1** under the **Floor Plans** head in the **Project Browser**; the floor plan view is displayed.

3. Invoke the **Door** tool from the **Build** panel of the **Architecture** tab; the **Modify| Place Door** tab is displayed.

4. On invoking the **Door** tool, the properties of the door to be added are displayed in the **Properties** palette. In the palette, select the type of door from the **Type Selector** drop-down list.
    For Imperial   **Single - Flush: 30" x 84"**
    For Metric   **M_Single - Flush: 0762 x 2134 mm**

5. Ensure that the **Tag on Placement** tool is chosen from the **Tag** panel of the **Modify | Place Door** tab.

Adding Doors

In this section, you need to add doors at the approximate location and then modify its location by specifying the exact dimension. You will also use the **Load Family** tool to load the desired door type in the project.

1. Move the cursor close to the interior wall of the Bath area to display the door symbol, as shown in Figure 4-19. Notice that as you move the cursor, the side of the door is changed. Click on the interior wall; the door is created at the specified location.

2. To move the door to the exact location, choose the **Modify** button in the **Select** panel of the **Modify | Doors** tab. Next, select the door added in the drawing; the selected door gets highlighted in blue with the controls and the related temporary dimensions are displayed in it.

3. Since the location of the door is given with reference to the upper interior wall, click on the upper temporary dimension, and then enter **2'0"(610 mm)**, as shown in Figure 4-20. Next, press ENTER; the door moves to the specified location.

4. To place the door type 2, invoke the **Door** tool from the **Build** panel of the **Architecture** tab; the **Modify | Place Door** tab is displayed.

5. Choose the **Load Family** tool in the **Mode** panel of this tab; the **Load Family** dialog box is displayed.

Using Basic Building Components-I 4-19

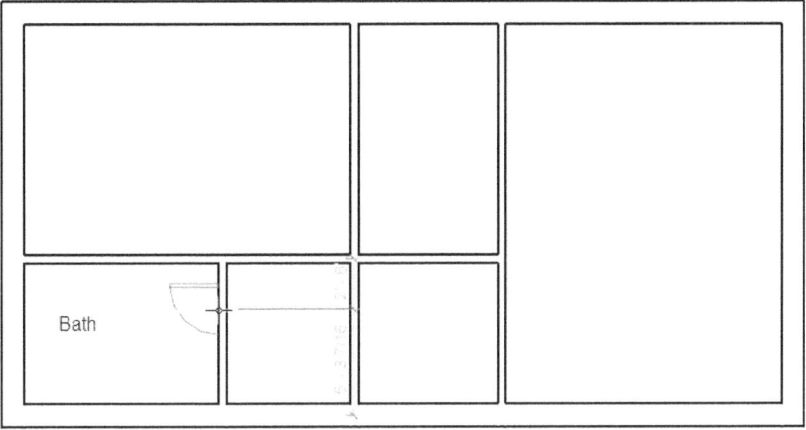

Figure 4-19 Specifying the location of the bath door

Figure 4-20 Moving the door to the exact location

6. In this dialog box, choose the **Doors** subfolder from the **US Imperial** folder. Next, select the required door family.
   For Imperial   **Single Decorative 2**
   For Metric   **M_Single Decorative 2**
   Next, choose the **Open** button.

7. In the **Type Selector** drop-down list, select the door type, as specified in the project parameters.
   For Imperial   **Single Decorative 2 - 36" x 84"**
   For Metric   **M_Single Decorative 2 - 0762 x 2134 mm**

8. Move the cursor near the interior wall common to the Lobby and the Kitchen areas, as shown in Figure 4-21, and click to add the kitchen door close to this location.

Figure 4-21 Adding the door to the kitchen area

9. Choose the **Modify** button from the **Select** panel. Next, select the door inserted in the drawing; the door gets highlighted and its controls are displayed.

   Notice that the door placed has the swing on the right side whereas the sketch shows a left side opening door, so you need to flip the swing side.

10. Click on the horizontal arrow key to flip the swing side. The swing side of the door is changed, as shown in Figure 4-22.

11. Click on the right side dimension to set it to **5'6" (1677 mm)**, as specified in the sketch plan.

12. Add the door of the same type in the bedroom area at a distance of **4'4" (1320 mm)** from the internal wall, as shown in Figure 4-23.

13. To create the entrance door of the apartment, choose the **Load Family** tool from the **Mode** panel of the **Modify | Place Door** tab; the **Load Family** dialog box is displayed. In this dialog box, add the **Bifold- 4 Panel** for Imperial (**M_Bifold- 4 Panel** for Metric) family type from the **Doors** subfolder in the **US Imperial** folder.

Figure 4-22 Using the flip control to change the swing side of the door

Using Basic Building Components-I 4-21

Figure 4-23 Specifying the location of the door in the bedroom area

14. Ensure that the **Bifold-4 Panel - 60"x 84"** option for Imperial or **M_Bifold-4 Panel - 1525 x 2134 mm** option for Metric is selected in the **Type Selector** drop-down list, and then add the door to the lobby area, as per the sketch plan, refer to Figure 4-24. While adding the door, you can use the spacebar to flip the door swing side.

15. After adding the door, choose the **Modify** button and select the recently created door; the temporary dimension is displayed. Click on the left of the temporary dimension and then enter the value **3'9"(1143 mm)**, as shown in Figure 4-24, to move the door to the exact location as given in the sketch plan. Now, press ESC to exit the **Modify | Doors** tab.

Figure 4-24 Specifying the location of the entrance door

Adding Door Openings

Next, you need to create two door openings in the lobby walls as given in the sketch plan. The openings can be loaded as door families but are added to the model as components.

1. Choose the **Insert** tab and then choose the **Load Family** tool from the **Load from Library** panel; the **Load Family** dialog box is displayed.

2. In the **Load Family** dialog box, select the **Passage Opening-Cased** family from the **Openings** sub-folder of the **US Imperial** folder or select the **M_Passage Opening-Cased**

family from the **Openings** sub-folder of the **US Metric** folder. Next, choose the **Open** button to load this family; the **Passage Opening - Cased** family is added as a component type.

3. Invoke the **Place a Component** tool from **Architecture > Build > Component** drop-down; the **Modify | Place Component** tab is displayed.

4. Select the **Passage Opening - Cased 36" x 84"** option for Imperial or **M_Passage Opening - Cased 915 x 2134 mm** for Metric from the **Type Selector** drop-down list in the **Properties** palette, if it is not selected by default.

5. Move the cursor near the location shown in Figure 4-25 and then click to specify the location for the center of the opening. The opening is created.

Figure 4-25 Adding openings

6. Now to modify the width of the opening, choose the **Modify** button from the **Select** panel. Select the recently created opening from the drawing; the **Modify | Generic Models** tab is displayed.

7. In this tab, choose the **Type Properties** tool from the **Properties** panel; the **Type Properties** dialog box is displayed.

8. Choose the **Duplicate** button; the **Name** dialog box is displayed. In this dialog box, enter **48" x 84"** for Imperial or **1220 x 2134 mm** for Metric in the **Name** edit box. Next, choose the **OK** button to close the **Name** dialog box.

9. Click in the **Value** field of the **Width** parameter and enter **4'0"** (**1219 mm**) as the new value.

10. Choose the **OK** button in the **Type Properties** dialog box to close it.

Figure 4-26 Specifying the exact location of the opening

11. To move the opening to the exact location, click on its temporary dimension, and enter **5'0"**(**1524 mm**), as shown in Figure 4-26. Next, press ENTER and ESC to accept the value entered and exit the editing mode.

Using Basic Building Components-I   4-23

12. Similarly, create the opening of the same size on the opposite wall to complete the creation of doors and opening for the *Apartment 1* project. After adding them, the layout plan of the project will look similar to the plan shown in Figure 4-27.

Figure 4-27 Layout plan with all doors and openings added

 Tip: *Doors and door openings can also be added in 3D view, sections, and elevations. You should, however, choose the appropriate view to place the door. You can use the temporary dimensions to place the door at the exact location. In case you add a door incorrectly (for example, if the door is not entirely placed on the wall), Autodesk Revit displays a message, alerting you about the conflict and prompting you to take an appropriate action.*

Adding Windows

The procedure of adding windows is quite similar to that of adding doors. Invoke the **Window** tool, select the window type, and add the window at an approximate location. You can then modify its location based on the sketch provided next in this tutorial.

1. Invoke the **Window** tool from the **Build** panel of the **Architecture** tab; the **Modify | Place Window** tab is displayed.

2. Ensure that the **Tag on Placement** tool is chosen from the **Tag** panel of the **Modify | Place Window** tab.

3. Click on the **Type Selector** drop-down list to view the in-built window types. To create the window number 1, select **Fixed 24" x 48"** for Imperial or **M_Fixed: 0610 x 1220 mm** for Metric from the drop-down list.

4. Move the cursor close to the exterior wall of the kitchen to display the window symbol, as shown in Figure 4-28. Add the window by clicking on the inner face of the exterior wall. The window is created at the specified location.

Figure 4-28 *Adding the kitchen window to the exterior wall*

5. To move the window to the exact location, choose the **Modify** button from the **Select** panel and then select the window from the drawing; it gets highlighted in blue and its controls are displayed.

6. Click on the left temporary dimension and enter **3'9"(1143 mm)**, as shown in Figure 4-29. Press ENTER; the window is moved to the specified location. Similarly, add another window of the same type near the external wall of the bath by invoking the **Window** tool from the **Build** panel, refer to Figure 4-18.

7. After adding the window in the external wall of the bath, you need to move it to the exact location. To do so, select the window; it is highlighted in blue. Click on the lower temporary dimension; an edit box is displayed. Enter **4'0"(1220 mm)** in the edit box, refer to Figure 4-30, and then press ENTER. The window is moved to the desired location. Press the ESC key and exit.

Figure 4-29 *Specifying the exact location of the window*

Figure 4-30 *Specifying the location of the bath window*

Using Basic Building Components-I 4-25

Now, you need to add the windows of type 2 to the drawing. These windows have a modified width of 4'0"(1220 mm). To add these windows, select the **Fixed: 24" x 48"** for Imperial or **M_Fixed: 0610 x 1220 mm** for Metric window type and create the window type duplicate. Modify window width to 4'0"(1220 mm) by using the **Type Properties** dialog box and add the window at the desired location.

8. Invoke the **Window** tool from the **Build** panel of the **Architecture** tab; the **Modify | Place Window** tab is displayed.

9. In the **Type Selector** drop-down list, select the **Fixed: 24" x 48"** (**M_Fixed: 1220 x 1220 mm** for Metric) window type. Next, choose the **Edit Type** button in the **Properties** palette; the **Type Properties** dialog box is displayed.

10. In this dialog box, choose the **Duplicate** button; the **Name** dialog box is displayed. In the **Name** edit box, enter **48" x 48" (1220 x 1220 mm)** and then choose the **OK** button.

11. In the **Value** field for the **Width** type parameter, enter **4'0"(1220 mm)** and then choose the **Apply** and **OK** to close the **Type Properties** dialog box and return to the drawing window.

    Notice that the **Fixed: 48" x 48"** (**M_Fixed: 1220 x 1220 mm** for Metric) window type is added to the **Type Selector** drop-down list.

12. Move the cursor near the exterior wall of the bedroom and click to place the window. Press ESC twice to exit.

13. Now, select the added bedroom window; the window gets highlighted in blue color and its controls are displayed. Click on the temporary dimension displayed at the left and enter **8'9" (2667 mm)** to specify the location of the bedroom window, as shown in Figure 4-31. The window is moved to the desired location. Similarly, add the windows of the same type to the walls of the living room and specify their respective locations based on the sketch plan given, refer to Figures 4-32 and 4-33.

Figure 4-31 Specifying the location of the bedroom window

14. To change the window tag numbers, move the cursor over the number in any of the window tags marked 2 (tag number may vary) and double-click; an edit box is displayed. Enter **1** in the edit box and press ENTER; the **Revit** message box is displayed. Choose **Yes** in the message box; the window tag is renamed. Similarly, replace the other window tags marked 2 with the tag mark 1 and those marked 10 with the tag mark 2, refer to Figure 4-34. You will notice that the tag marks of other instances of the same window type are immediately modified.

Figure 4-32 Specifying the location of the first living room window

Figure 4-33 Adding the second living room window using temporary dimensions

This completes the tutorial of creating doors and windows for the *Apartment 1* project. The Level 1 plan should look similar to the plan shown in Figure 4-34.

Figure 4-34 Completed project plan with renamed window tags

15. To view the plan in 3D, choose the **Default 3D View** tool from the **View > Create > 3D View** drop-down; the 3D view of the project is displayed, as shown in Figure 4-35.

16. Choose **Save As > Project** from **Application Menu**; the **Save As** dialog box is displayed. Enter the desired name in the **File name** edit box.
    For Imperial   **c04_Apartment1_tut1**
    For Metric   **M_c04_Apartment1_tut1**
Choose **Save**; the file is saved.

Using Basic Building Components-I 4-27

17. Choose **Close** from **Application Menu** to close the project file.

Figure 4-35 *3D view of the Apartment 1 project*

Tutorial 2   Club

In this tutorial, you will add doors and windows to Hall 1 and Lounge of the *Club* project created in Exercise 3 of Chapter 3. The centerline dimensions of the location of the doors and windows are given in Figure 4-36. You will create the doors and windows of Hall 2 in Exercise 2 later in this chapter. Use the following project file and parameters for this tutorial.   **(Expected time: 30 min)**

1. Project file-
   - For Imperial   *c03_Club_ex3.rvt*
   - For Metric   *M_c03_Club_ex3.rvt*

2. Door types to be used
   - For Imperial   1, 2, and 3- **Single- Glass 1- 36" x 84"**
                               4- **Single- Flush: 36" x 84"**
                               5- **Double- Glass 2 - 72"x 84"**
   - For Metric   1, 2, and 3- **M_Single- Glass 1- 0915 x 2134 mm**
                               4- **M_Single- Flush: 0915 x 2134 mm**
                               5- **M_Double- Glass 2 - 1830 x 2134 mm**

3. Window types to be used
   - For Imperial   1- **Fixed: 36" x 48"**
   - For Metric   1- **M_Fixed: 0915 x 1220 mm**

Figure 4-36 Sketch plan for adding doors and windows to the Club project

The following steps are required to complete this tutorial:

a. Open the file created in Chapter 3.
    For Imperial   *c03_Club_ex3.rvt*
    For Metric   *M_c03_Club_ex3.rvt*
  Invoke the **Door** tool.
b. Select the door type by using the **Type Selector** drop-down list.
c. Add the door at approximate locations, refer to Figures 4-37 through 4-44.
d. Change the placement of the door to the desired location.
e. Invoke the **Window** tool and select the window type using the **Type Selector** drop-down list.
f. Add the window at approximate locations, refer to Figures 4-45 through 4-47.
g. Modify the placement of windows to the exact location, based on the given sketch plan.

Opening the Existing Project and Invoking the Door Tool

First, you need to open the *Club* project and then invoke the **Door** tool.

1. Choose **Open > Project** from the **Application Menu** and for Imperial open the *c03_Club_ex3.rvt* (for Metric open the *M_c03_Club_ex3.rvt* project file) project file created in Exercise 3 of Chapter 3. You can also download this file from *http://www.cadcim.com*. The path of the file is as follows: *Textbooks > Civil/GIS > Revit Architecture > Autodesk Revit Architecture 2015 for Architects and Designers*.

2. Invoke the **Door** tool from the **Build** panel of the **Architecture** tab; the **Modify | Place Door** tab is displayed. Alternatively, type **DR**.

Selecting a Door Type

Select the door type 1 and add it to the project. The project parameters indicate that the door type is to be loaded from the **US Imperial** folder. To access the **US Imperial** folder, choose the **Load Family** tool from the **Mode** panel of the **Modify | Place Door** tab.

1. Choose the **Load Family** tool from the **Mode** panel in the **Modify | Place Door** tab; the **Load Family** dialog box is displayed.

2. In this dialog box, open the **Doors** folder and select the door type **Single-Glass 1**. Choose **Open** to load the family of this door type; various door types of the loaded door family are added to the **Type Selector** drop-down list.

3. In the **Type Selector** drop-down list, select the **Single-Glass 1: 36" x 84"** option for Imperial or **M_Single-Glass 1- 0915 x 2134 mm** option for Metric, if it is not selected by default.

Adding Doors

You can add a door at its exact location by clicking at an approximate point in its host wall and then modifying its location by specifying the exact dimension. First you need to add the door type 1 and then the other door types.

1. Move the cursor close to the interior wall face to display the door symbol, as shown in Figure 4-37. Notice that the side of the door changes as you move the cursor.

2. Place the door by clicking on the interior wall and then press ESC twice to exit. On doing so, the door is added to the exact location.

Figure 4-37 Adding the door

3. To move the door to the exact location, select the door; it gets highlighted in blue and its controls are displayed.

4. As the location of the door is given with reference to the interior wall, click on the right temporary dimension and enter **2'0"(610 mm)**, as shown in Figure 4-38. Press ESC to exit the setting of dimensions. The door moves to the desired location.

Note
Depending on the placement of the cursor, the door side and swing might not be same as desired. If required, click on the flip control arrows or the door swing arrows to achieve the desired orientation.

5. Add the next door using the same door type by clicking at the approximate location, as shown in Figure 4-39. Press ESC twice.

Figure 4-38 Editing the location of the door   *Figure 4-39* Adding next door

6. Click on the temporary dimension between the door center and the interior wall and enter the value **2'0"(610 mm)** in the edit box, as shown in Figure 4-40. The door moves to the desired location.

7. Add another door at the location shown in Figure 4-41. You may need to use the flip arrows to orient the door swing in the desired direction.

8. To place the next door type, select **Single: Flush - 36" x 84"** option for Imperial or **M_Single-Flush: 0915 x 2134 mm** option for Metric from the **Type Selector** drop-down list, as specified in the project parameters.

9. Move the cursor near the interior wall and click to add the door close to the location, as shown in Figure 4-42. Press ESC to exit.

Figure 4-40 Editing the location of the next door

Figure 4-41 Specifying the location of the next door

Using Basic Building Components-I   4-31

10. Choose the **Modify** button from the **Select** panel in the **Modify | Place Door** tab and select the door added last in the drawing; it gets highlighted in blue and its controls are displayed.

11. Click on the right side dimension and enter **2'0"(610 mm)**, as shown in Figure 4-42.

12. To create the entrance door, invoke the **Door** tool again and then choose the **Load Family** tool from the **Mode** panel; the **Load Family** dialog box is displayed. In the dialog box, load **Double-Glass 2** from the **US Imperial > Doors** folder.

Figure 4-42 Adding a new door type

13. Select the **Double-Glass 2: 72" x 84"** door type for Imperial or **M_Double-Glass 2 - 1830 x 2134 mm** for Metric from the **Type Selector** drop-down list in the **Properties** palette, if it is not selected by default.

14. Move the cursor near the main door location, as shown in Figure 4-43. Press SPACEBAR to flip the swing side of the door to the desired side, if required, and click to create the door.

15. Click on the temporary dimension and set the angle to 46 degrees, as shown in Figure 4-44. Press ENTER.

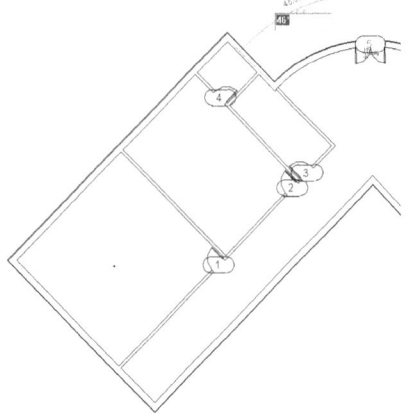

Figure 4-43 Adding the entrance door   *Figure 4-44* Specifying the angular dimension

16. Press ESC twice to exit the selection.

Adding Windows

The procedure for adding windows is similar to that for adding doors. After invoking the **Window** tool and selecting the required window type, click at the approximate location to add it. The location can then be modified to the exact dimension, as specified in the sketch plan.

1. Choose **Window** from the **Build** panel of the **Architecture** tab; the **Modify | Place Window** tab is displayed.

2. Select the **Fixed 36" x 48"** option for Imperial **M_Fixed: 0915 x 1220 mm** for Metric from the **Type Selector** drop-down list in the **Properties** palette.

3. Move the cursor close to the exterior wall of Hall 1 to display the window symbol, as shown in Figure 4-45. Add the window by clicking on the exterior wall.

 Tip: *If tags are displayed with doors and windows then choose the **Tag on Placement** tool from the **Tag** panel of the **Modify|Place Window** tab.*

Figure 4-45 Moving the cursor near the wall of Hall 1 to add window

4. Next, to move the window to the exact location, choose the **Modify** button from the **Select** panel. Then, select the window, click on the lower temporary dimension, and enter **4'0"(1219 mm)**, as shown in Figure 4-46. The window moves to the desired location.

5. Repeat step 1 through step 3 to add another window by clicking near the left end of the curved wall, refer to Figure 4-47.

6. Select the window created and enter **6** as the angular dimension, as shown in Figure 4-47. The window moves to the desired location.

Using Basic Building Components-I   4-33

7. Next, select the window tag and click on the tag number; an edit box is displayed. Enter **1** in the edit box and press ENTER; the **Revit Architecture** message box is displayed. Choose **Yes**; the window tag is renamed.

   This completes the tutorial of adding doors and windows to the *Club* building project.

Figure 4-46 Editing the location of the window   *Figure 4-47* Adding windows

8. Choose **Save As > Project** from the **Application Menu** and enter the required name in the **File name** edit box of the **Save As** dialog box.
   For Imperial   **c04_Club_tut2**
   For Metric   **M_c04_Club_tut2**
   The project file is saved.

9. Choose **Close** from the **Application Menu** to close the project file.

Self-Evaluation Test

Answer the following questions and then compare them to those given at the end of this chapter:

1. You can add a door or a window to a project without creating a wall. (T/F)

2. The type parameters of a door can be modified in the **Properties** palette. (T/F)

3. You can change the swing side of a door after adding it to a wall. (T/F)

4. You can add windows in the plan view only. (T/F)

5. The door and window tags are automatically created in Autodesk Revit Architecture. (T/F)

6. In the **Type Properties** dialog box, the **Rename** button is used to change the name of a door or a window. (T/F)

7. A loaded door type can be selected from the _____ drop-down list.

8. You can import and load additional door and window types by choosing the _____ button from the **Modify | Place Component** tab of the ribbon.

9. Using the _____ button in the **Type Properties** dialog box, a copy of an existing door type can be created.

10. The _____ type parameter indicates the height of a door.

11. Which of the following parameters of doors is an instance property?

    a) **Frame Material**　　　　　　b) **Thickness**
    c) **Level**　　　　　　　　　　　d) **Fire Rating**

12. Which of the following shortcut keys is used for invoking the **Visibility/ Graphics Overrides** dialog box?

    a) **VO**　　　　　　　　　　　　b) **VD**
    c) **VG**　　　　　　　　　　　　d) **VB**

Review Questions

Answer the following questions:

1. The door tag mark cannot be changed after the door is created. (T/F)

2. When you add a door or a window to a wall, Autodesk Revit Architecture automatically creates an opening in the host wall. (T/F)

3. Door tags increases automatically as you add doors to a project. (T/F)

4. You cannot control the visibility of the door and the window tags in the plan view. (T/F)

5. When you modify the width of a door type, its name is automatically modified. (T/F)

6. You can modify the width and height of a window in the **Properties** palette. (T/F)

7. While adding windows, you need to specify the thickness of the window with respect to the thickness of the wall. (T/F)

8. After placing a door at an approximate location on the wall, it can be modified to the exact location. (T/F)

Using Basic Building Components-I 4-35

9. Which of the following parameters of the window cannot be modified in the **Properties** palette?

   a) **Level**
   c) **Head Height**
   b) **Assembly Code**
   d) **Mark**

10. Which of the following keys can be used to flip the swing side of a door before adding it to a wall?

    a) TAB
    c) ALT
    b) SPACEBAR
    d) ESC

11. Which of the following tab contains the Window tool?

    a) **Design**
    c) **Architecture**
    b) **Modify**
    d) **Insert**

12. Which of the following is a door instance parameter?

    a) **Level**
    c) **Door**
    b) **Thickness**
    d) **Material Height**

Exercises

Exercise 1   Apartment 2

Add doors, windows, and openings to the *Apartment 2* project, created in Exercise 1 of Chapter 3, refer to Figure 4-48. The dimensions and text need not to be mentioned. Use the following project parameters: **(Expected time: 30 min)**

1. Project file-
   For Imperial   *c03_Apartment2_ex1.rvt*
   For Metric   *M_c03_Apartment2_ex1.rvt*

2. Door types to be used:
   For Imperial   Bath and kitchen doors- **Single - Flush: 36" x 84"**
                   Bedroom door- **Single Decorative - 36" x 84"**
                   Lobby door- **Bifold-4 Panel - 36" x 84"**
                   Door openings in dining (dashed lines)- **4'0" x 7'0"**
                   using **Passage-Opening Cased : 36"x 84"**
                   Distance of the door centerlines from wall centerlines- **2'0"**
   For Metric   Bath and kitchen doors- **M_Single - Flush: 0915 x 2134 mm**
                   Bedroom door- **M_Single Decorative 2- 0915 x 2134 mm**
                   Lobby door- **M_Bifold-4 Panel - 0915 x 2134 mm**
                   Door openings in dining (dashed lines)- **1220 x 2134 mm**
                   using **M_Passage-Opening Cased : 0915 x 2134 mm**
                   Distance of the door centerlines from wall centerlines- **610 mm**

3. Window types to be used
   - For Imperial   Bedroom and living room windows - **Fixed: 36" x 48"**
     Bath and kitchen windows- **Fixed: 24" X 48"**
   - For Metric   Bedroom and living room windows - **M_Fixed: 0915 x 1220 mm**
     Bath and kitchen windows- **M_Fixed: 0610 X 1220 mm**
4. File name to be saved-
   - For Imperial   **c04_Apartment2_ex1**
   - For Metric   **M_c04_Apartment2_ex1**

For the distance of window centerlines from wall centerlines refer to Figure 4-48.

Figure 4-48 Sketch plan for adding doors and windows to the Apartment 2 project

Exercise 2   Elevator and Stair Lobby

Add doors, windows, and openings to the *Elevator and Stair Lobby* project created in Exercise 2 of Chapter 3, refer to Figure 4-49. Do not add text or dimensions as they are given for reference only. Use the following project parameters.   **(Expected time: 30 min)**

1. Project File-
   - For Imperial   *c03_ElevatorandStairLobby_ex2.rvt*
   - For Metric   *M_c03_ElevatorandStairLobby_ex2.rvt*

2. Door types to be used-
   - For Imperial   **Single - Flush: 36" x 84"**,
     Distance of door centerlines from wall centerlines- **2'6"**
     Door openings - **4'0" x 7'0"**
     Passage Opening-Cased- 36" x 84"
   - For Metric   **M_Single - Flush: 0915 x 2134 mm**
     Distance of door centerlines from wall centerlines- **762 mm**
     Door openings - **1220 x 2134 mm**
     Passage Opening-Cased- 0915 x 2134 mm

Using Basic Building Components-I

3. Window types to be used:
   - For Imperial   **Fixed: 36" x 48"**
   - For Metric   **M_Fixed: 0915 x 1220 mm**

4. File name to be saved-
   - For Imperial   **c04_ElevatorandStairLobby_ex2**
   - For Metric   **M_c04_ElevatorandStairLobby_ex2**

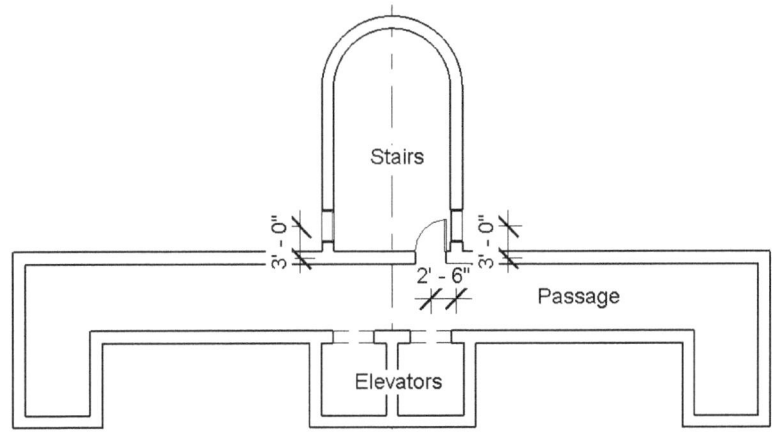

Figure 4-49 Sketch plan for adding doors, windows, and openings to the Elevator and Stair Lobby project

Exercise 3   Club - Hall 2

Add doors, windows and openings to Hall 2 of the *Club* project created in Tutorial 2 of this chapter, refer to Figure 4-50. The dimensions and text are given for reference and are not to be created. Use the following project parameters: **(Expected time: 30 min)**

1. Project-
   - For Imperial   *c04_Club_tut2.rvt*
   - For Metric   *M_c04_Club_tut2.rvt*

2. Door types to be used:
   - For Imperial   D1- **Single- Glass 1 - 36" x 84"**
   - For Metric   D1- **M_Single- Glass 1 - 0915 x 2134 mm**

3. Window types to be used:
   - For Imperial   W1- **Fixed: 36" x 48"**
   - For Metric   W1- **M_Fixed: 0915 x 1220 mm**

4. File name to be saved-
   - For Imperial   **c04_Club_ex3**
   - For Metric   **M_c04_Club_ex3**

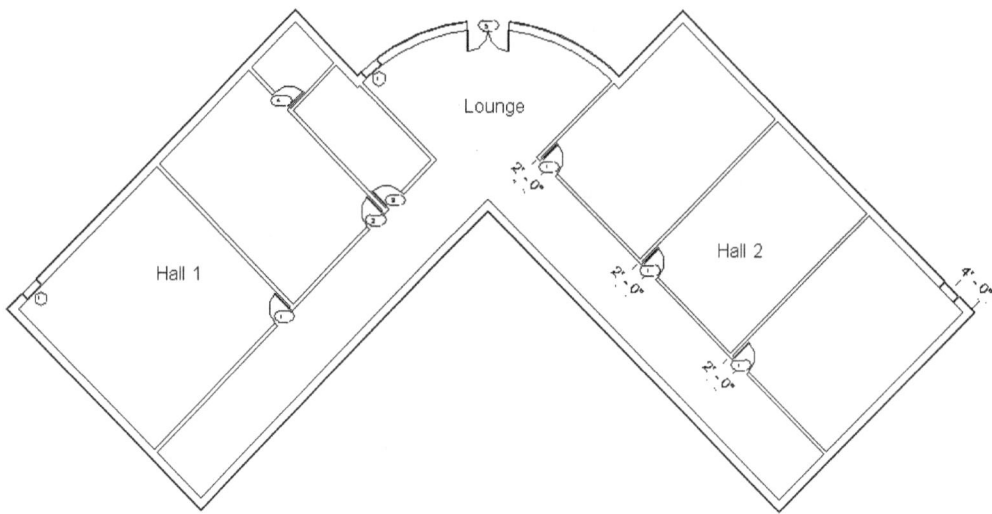

Figure 4-50 Sketch plan for adding doors and windows to Hall 2 of the Club project

Answers to Self-Evaluation Test
1. F, 2. F, 3. T, 4. F, 5. T, 6. T, 7. Type Selector, 8. Load Family, 9. Duplicate, 10. Height, 11. Frame Material, 12. VG.

Chapter 5

Using the Editing Tools

Learning Objectives

After completing this chapter, you will be able to:
- *Create a selection set of elements.*
- *Use the tools in the Status Bar.*
- *Move and copy elements.*
- *Use the Trim and Extend tools.*
- *Use the Cut and Paste tools.*
- *Use the Rotate, Mirror, and Offset tools.*
- *Create an array of elements using the Array tool.*
- *Use the Match, Align, Delete, Lock, and Group tools.*
- *Split walls using the Split Elements and Split with Gap tools.*

INTRODUCTION

In the previous chapter, you learned to create building elements such as walls, doors, and windows. You will now learn to use various editing tools provided in Autodesk Revit Architecture. You can use these tools to add specific design requirements to the elements that you have created. You will now learn to select and edit elements using object controls and editing tools such as **Move**, **Copy**, **Trim**, **Extend**, **Cut**, **Delete**, **Rotate**, **Mirror**, **Array**, **Align**, **Match**, and so on. You will also learn to use different tools located in the **Status Bar**.

CREATING A SELECTION SET

In order to edit an element or a group of elements, you must first select them. To create a selection set, first you need to exit the currently invoked tool. To do so, choose the **Modify** button from the **Select** panel of the contextual tab or type **MD** to exit the current tool. After exiting the current tool, move the cursor near to the element that you wish to select. On doing so, you will notice that it gets highlighted and its description is displayed in the **Status Bar**. For example, on highlighting a door, you might see **Doors: Single : Flush:34"X84"** displayed in the **Status Bar**. In case, there are elements in proximity of the element to be selected, press the TAB key to cycle between them. Click to select the element when it is highlighted. By default a selected element will appear semi-transparent and blue in color. In the next sections, you will learn different methods of selecting multiple elements, restoring the selected elements, and removing elements from a selection.

Selecting Multiple Elements

The methods of selecting multiple elements are discussed next.

Using the CTRL Key

You can press and hold the CTRL key and click on elements to add them to the current selection set. In case, you need to make multiple selections of the same type, release the CTRL key and when the elements are highlighted, press the TAB key.

Using the Selection Window

You can select elements by defining a selection window. To define a selection window, you need to click at a point in the drawing area which is close to the elements you desire to select. Next, drag the cursor to form a rectangle. You will notice that on dragging the cursor from left to right, the rectangle is formed in continuous lines and the elements that are completely inside it are selected, as shown in Figure 5-1. If you drag the cursor from right to left, a dashed rectangle appears and all items that are partially or fully inside it are selected, as shown in Figure 5-2.

Using the TAB Key (For Walls)

You can use the TAB key to select the walls that are joined together and form a continuous chain. To use this method, first highlight one of the wall and then press the TAB key. All the walls that are joined to the chosen wall are highlighted for selection.

Note
The usage of the TAB key for the selection of walls has certain limitations. It cannot be used if the walls are not properly joined to each other.

Using the Editing Tools

Tip: *On defining the selection window, you will notice that the color of the selected elements has changed and the element has become transparent, thereby making the selection easier.*

Figure 5-1 Defining a selection window from left to right

Figure 5-2 Defining a selection window from right to left

Using the Select All Instances Option

The **Select All Instances** option is used to select all instances of an element type used in the project. To use this option, select a single instance and then right-click to display a shortcut menu. Now, click on the **Select All Instances** option in the shortcut menu, a flyout will be displayed. From the flyout, you can either select the **Visible in View** option or the **In Entire Project** option. On choosing the **Visible in View** option from the flyout, the elements which have instances similar to that of the selected element in the current view will get selected. Alternatively, if you choose the **In Entire Project** option from the flyout, the elements which have instances similar to that of the selected element in the project will get selected. You can also select an element and type **SA** to select all its instances in the project.

Selecting Elements Using Advanced Tools

In Autodesk Revit, besides the basic selection tools discussed in the earlier chapters, you can use the advanced selection tools for selecting and modelling process. These advanced tools are available in the **Status Bar**, as shown in Figure 5-3. These tools are discussed next.

Figure 5-3 The tools in the **Status Bar**

Select Links

In a project, you may require to select an entire linked model or an individual element inside the linked model. To do so, choose the **Select Links** tool from the **Status Bar** and then select the complete model or an individual part of the linked model.

 Tip: *To select an individual element in a model, move and place the cursor on it and then press the TAB key; the element gets highlighted. Now, click on the highlighted element to select it.*

Select Underlay Elements

You can select the elements which are not part of the current plan view. To do so, choose the **Select Underlay Elements** tool from the **Status Bar**. Next, place the cursor on the element; the element will get highlighted. Now, click on the highlighted element to select it. You can disable this tool by choosing it again.

Select Pinned Elements

You can select or deselect the pinned elements by using the **Select Pinned Elements** tool.

Select Elements by Face

This tool is used to select an element by enabling the selection of an element by face. To select an element using this tool, choose the **Select Elements by Face** tool from the **Status Bar**. Next, click at any point on the face of an architectural element such as a wall, floor and so on to select it. You can disable this tool by choosing it again.

Restoring the Selection

A selection, cleared intentionally or unintentionally, can easily be restored by using several methods. One of the options for restoring the previous selection is to choose the **Modify** button from the contextual tab and then right-click in the drawing area; a shortcut menu will be displayed. From the shortcut menu, choose the **Select Previous** option, the previous selection will be restored. Alternatively, press CTRL+Left Arrow to restore the previous selection.

Using the Filter tool

You can use the **Filter** tool to filter the currently selected elements in your project. Select different types of elements to filter; the **Modify | Multi-Select** tab will be displayed. Now, choose the **Filter** tool from the **Filter** panel of the **Modify | Multi-Select** tab; the **Filter** dialog box will be displayed along with a list of categories of the currently selected elements, as shown in Figure 5-4. Alternatively, click on the filter icon displayed at the extreme right corner of the **Status Bar** to invoke the **Filter** dialog box.

In Revit Architecture, the **Filter** dialog box displays the count of the selected elements in each category, and the total number of elements currently selected at the bottom of the dialog box. You can clear the relevant check boxes to remove the elements corresponding to a specific family from the current selection. You can use the **Check All** button or the **Check None** button to select or clear all check boxes in the element categories displayed in the dialog box.

Using the Editing Tools

In Autodesk Revit, you can edit a selection set from a list using the **Edit** tool from the **Selection** panel of the **Modify | Multi-Select** tab. Choose the **Edit** tool; the **Filters** dialog box will be displayed, as shown in Figure 5-5. In this dialog box, choose the **New** button; the **Filter Name** dialog box will be displayed. In the **Name** edit box of the dialog box, enter a desired name of the entity to be selected and then choose the **OK** button. On doing so, the **Filters** dialog box will be displayed. In this dialog box, the name of the created filters will be displayed in the **Filters** area. Click on the desired filter name that you will edit. Next, in the **Categories** area, you can click on the **Filter list** drop-down list; a list of check boxes will be displayed. By default, all the check boxes are selected in the list. Clear all the check boxes except the **Architecture** check box. As a result, the categories that are relevant to the architectural properties will be displayed in the list box of the **Categories** area. If the filter rule for the selection requires the inclusion of the mechanical, electrical, structural, piping, or electrical properties, you can select the other check boxes such as **Structure**, **Electrical**, **Mechanical**, or **Piping** from the list. The selection of multiple check boxes in the list will enable you to broaden the filter rule for selecting the elements in the drawings by the properties common to them. For example, if you are required to select walls, pipes, and columns of the same cost, in that case then you need to select the **Architecture** and **Piping** check boxes from the list displayed on clicking the **Filter list** drop-down list.

*Figure 5-4 The **Filter** dialog box displaying a list of categories*

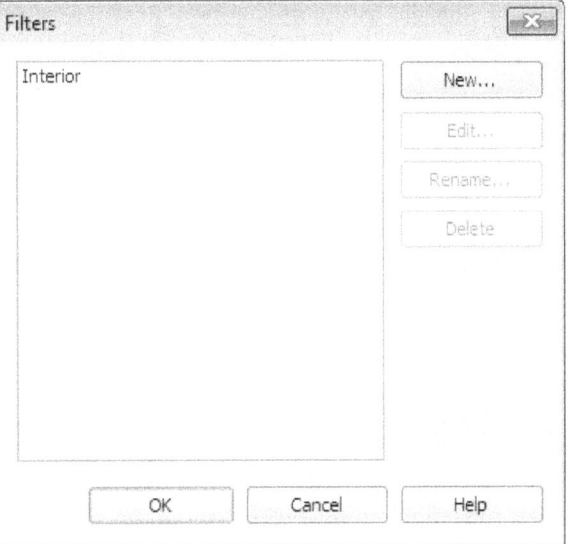

*Figure 5-5 The **Filters** dialog box*

On selecting the required check boxes, the categories common to the selected check boxes will be displayed in the list box below the **Filter list** drop-down list. From the list box, select the check boxes of the categories you require to add in the filter rules. After selecting the categories, you can use various options in the **Filter Rules** area to define the filter.

To define the filter rules, select the required parameter from the **Filter by** drop-down list in the **Filter Rules** area. If the desired parameter does not exist in the drop-down list you can create a parameter of your own. To do so, choose the button next to the **Filter by** drop-down list; the **Project Parameters** dialog box will be displayed. Choose the **Add** button; the **Parameter Properties** dialog box will be displayed. In this dialog box, select the **Project parameter** radio button and select the desired options from the **Discipline, Type of Parameter**, and **Group Parameter under** drop-down lists. When the **Shared Parameter** radio button is selected, the **Discipline** and **Type of Parameter** drop-down lists will get deactivated.

Note

*Project parameters in the **Parameter type** area can appear in schedules but not in tags whereas, Shared parameters can appear in schedules as well as in tags.*

In the **Parameter Data** area of the **Parameter Properties** dialog box, select the **Type** radio button to make the created parameter as a type parameter. You can select the **Instance** radio button to make the parameter as instance parameter in the project.

In the **Parameter Properties** dialog box, select the appropriate options from the **Categories** area to select the categories under which you want to display the created parameter and then choose the **OK** button; the **Parameter Value** dialog box will be displayed. In this dialog box, enter a desired value in the **Value** column corresponding to the created parameter and choose the **OK** button; the **Parameter Value** dialog box will be closed and the parameter defined will be added to the **Project Parameters** dialog box. Now choose the **OK** button to close the **Project Parameter** dialog box and return to the **Filters** dialog box.

In the **Filters** dialog box, you can now select the created parameter from the **Filter by** drop-down list and select the filter operators from various drop-down lists in the **Filter Rules** area to define the filter rules. After defining the filter rules in the **Filters** dialog box, choose the **OK** button; the **Filters** dialog box will be closed and you will return to the **Filters** dialog box that contains the name of the filters created. In the **Filters** dialog box, you can use the **Rename** button to change the name of the filter displayed in the list. You can delete any filter from the list by using the **Delete** button. You can use the **New** button to create a new filter definition. To close the **Filters** dialog box, choose the **OK** button.

In the **Modify | Multi-Select** tab, you can choose the **Save** tool to save the current selection set. On choosing the **Save** tool; the **Save Selection** dialog box will be displayed. In this dialog box, enter the name of the selection set in the **Name** edit box and then choose the **OK** button; the current selection set will be saved. You can retrieve the saved selection by choosing the **Load** tool from the **Selection** panel of the **Modify | Multi-Select** tab.

Note

*In Autodesk Revit platform, the **Filter** icon is located at the lower right corner on the **Status Bar**. The number displayed next to the **Filter** icon indicates the number of currently selected elements.*

MOVING AND COPYING ELEMENTS

Moving and copying elements are frequent tasks that you need to perform while working in a project. In Revit platform, there are different options or methods by which you can perform these tasks. You can perform both copying and moving task at the same time. The methods used for moving and copying elements are described next.

Moving the Elements by Changing the Temporary Dimensions

When you create an element, its temporary dimension from a nearby object is also displayed. As explained in Chapters 3 and 4, you can move the element by changing this dimension. Click the temporary dimension and enter the new value to move the element to the desired location. For example, a door can be moved by specifying its new value from the adjacent wall or door (see Chapter 4).

Moving the Elements by Dragging

Dragging is a method used to move elements to the desired location. To drag an element, choose the **Modify** button from the **Select** panel and then select the element from the drawing. After making selection, move the cursor over the element, click and hold the left mouse button. Next, move the cursor toward the desired location. You will notice that the image of the selected element moves along with the cursor, as shown in Figure 5-6. When the element reaches the desired location, release the left mouse button; the element is moved to the new location, as shown in Figure 5-7. Some elements such as walls, can be moved only in a particular direction. The SHIFT key may be pressed to remove this constraint. Other elements can be moved in all directions. You can restrict the direction of movement of elements by pressing the SHIFT key.

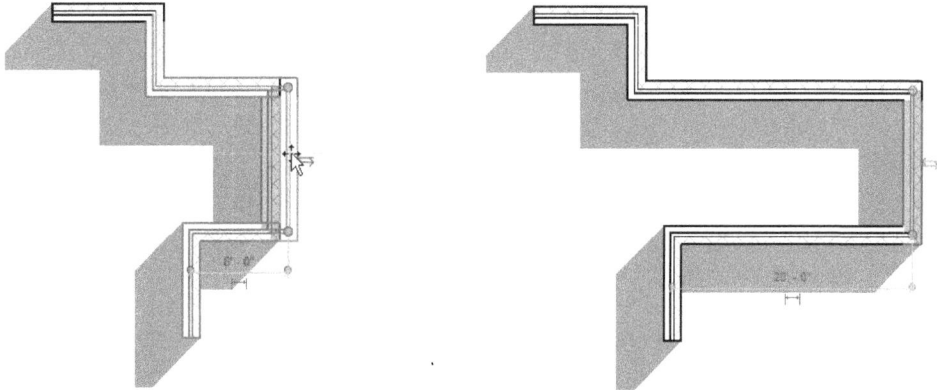

Figure 5-6 Moving the walls by dragging   *Figure 5-7* Moved wall with completed edges

Note
In case of walls, the joined walls adjust and get completed automatically, refer to Figure 5-7.

Moving the Elements by Dragging the End-Joint Components

You can drag and move more than two components simultaneously, provided they have a common joint by using the drag control symbol. This feature is applicable for the line based components such as walls, beams, or braces. To drag the common joined elements, select one of the members of the common joint from the drawing and right-click; a shortcut menu will be displayed. Choose the **Select Joined Elements** option from the shortcut menu. All the members joined at the common end will be highlighted displaying the circular shaped drag controls, as shown in Figure 5-8. Bring the cursor at the common joint; the **Drag Wall End** tooltip will be displayed. Drag the common joint to a new location, as shown in Figure 5-9. You will notice that all the components joined to that common joint have been dragged. Doors and windows can be moved along their host walls only by picking and dragging them to the new location on the host wall. Autodesk Revit Architecture closes the old opening and automatically creates the opening at the new location.

Figure 5-8 *Three walls joined at a common end*   *Figure 5-9* *Dragging the end-joined walls simultaneously*

Moving the Elements by Selecting and Dragging

You can modify the location of an element by pressing and dragging the cursor over it. To do so, choose the **Drag Element On Selection** tool and place the cursor on the desired element; the element gets highlighted. Now, press and drag the elements and the element will get relocated.

Note
*It is recommended that the **Drag Elements On Selection** tool is disabled to avoid accidental displacement of the elements.*

Using the Move Tool

Ribbon: Modify | (Elements / Components) > Modify > Move
Shortcut Key: MV

The usage of the **Move** tool is similar to that of dragging, with the only difference that the preview of the elements is not displayed. It is more useful for moving elements by a specific distance, thereby increasing the accuracy of the building model. To move elements, select them; a contextual tab will be displayed. Note that the name of the contextual tab will depend on the element type selected from the drawing. Invoke the **Move** tool from the **Modify** panel of the contextual tab, or type **MV**; the selected elements will be highlighted inside a dashed rectangle and the **Constrain**, **Disjoin**, and **Multiple** check boxes will be displayed in the **Options Bar**. These options have been discussed in the table given next.

Constrain	The selection of this check box, restricts the movement of the selected element along its collinear or perpendicular vectors.
Disjoin	By selecting this check box, you can break the association of an element with its associated elements and move it to a new location. For example, by selecting this check box from the **Options Bar**, you can move a wall without moving the joined wall. You can also move the elements from their current host element to another host element. For example, you can easily move a door or window from one wall to another. This option can be effectively used if the **Constrain** check box is cleared.
Multiple	The selection of this check box enables the creation of multiple copies of the elements by clicking at the desired location. It is enabled only when the **Copy** check box is selected.

Note
*The **Move** tool, like other editing tools such as **Copy**, **Rotate**, **Mirror**, **Array**, and **Scale** is only available after a selection is made. You can access these tools from the contextual tabs such as **Modify / Walls**, **Modify / Windows**, and others. The name of the contextual tab will depend upon the type of element or component you select.*

After invoking the **Move** tool, click in the drawing area to specify the start point for moving. Next, move the cursor to the desired location and click to specify the endpoint; the element will move to a new location. To move elements by a specific distance, enter the displacement value, after specifying the first point. An edit box is displayed with the specified value, as shown in Figure 5-10. Press ENTER to move the selected element by the specified value.

Figure 5-10 Moving elements through a specific distance

Using the Copy Tool

Ribbon: Modify | (Elements / Components) > Modify > Copy
Shortcut Key: CO

 The usage of the **Copy** tool is similar to that of the **Move** tool. After invoking the **Copy** tool, click in the drawing window to specify the start point and then move the cursor to the desired distance. To specify the endpoint, click at the appropriate location. You can also specify the distance between the original and copied elements by entering the value.

Creating Multiple Copies of an Element

You can create several copies of the elements using the **Multiple** option from the **Options Bar** of the **Copy** tool. To do so, invoke the **Copy** tool and then select the **Multiple** check box in the **Options Bar**. To specify the start point, click in the drawing window. Move the cursor and click at the desired locations. Each successive click would results in the copy of the original element. Alternatively, you can enter the distance value in the edit box between the currently selected and next elements to create copies at a desired distance. The multiple copy option remains active until you choose some other tool or press the ESC key twice.

> **Tip:** *While copying elements, the specified distance should be in the direction of the new location. You can also use negative values to specify the distance in the direction opposite to that of the cursor movement.*

TRIMMING AND EXTENDING ELEMENTS

You can trim or extend one or more elements to a boundary defined by the element of the same type. You can also extend or trim (if the elements intersect) the elements that are not-parallel to create a corner. You can trim or extend a reference line or a wall to another reference line or wall. In Autodesk Revit Architecture, you can trim and extend elements by

Using the Editing Tools

using three tools namely: **Trim/Extend to Corner**, **Trim/Extend Single Element**, and **Trim/Extend Multiple Elements**. You can use these tools with walls, lines, beams, or braces. These tools are discussed next.

Using the Trim/Extend to Corner Tool

Ribbon: Modify > Modify > Trim/Extend to Corner

This tool is used to extend a wall to another wall or to trim to any extended portion of building element at the apparent intersection to form a corner. For example, to extend the vertical wall to the horizontal wall, as shown in Figure 5-11, to make a corner elbow, invoke the **Trim/Extend to Corner** tool from the **Modify** panel. Now, select the first element to be trimmed or extended, in this case, the horizontal wall. If you want to retain its left portion, then click anywhere on the wall on the left region of the apparent intersection, as shown in Figure 5-12. To select the next wall to trim or extend, move the cursor near the vertical wall. As you move the cursor, you will notice that a dashed line appears, showing the corner that will be formed, refer to Figure 5-13. When you click on the vertical wall, it is extended and the horizontal wall is trimmed to form the desired corner, refer to Figure 5-14.

Figure 5-11 Vertical wall extended to the horizontal wall

Figure 5-12 Selecting the first wall to be trimmed/extended on the side to be retained

Tip: *Similar to walls, you can use the **Trim/Extend to Corner** tool also while working with lines (for example, while creating 2D details for your project).*

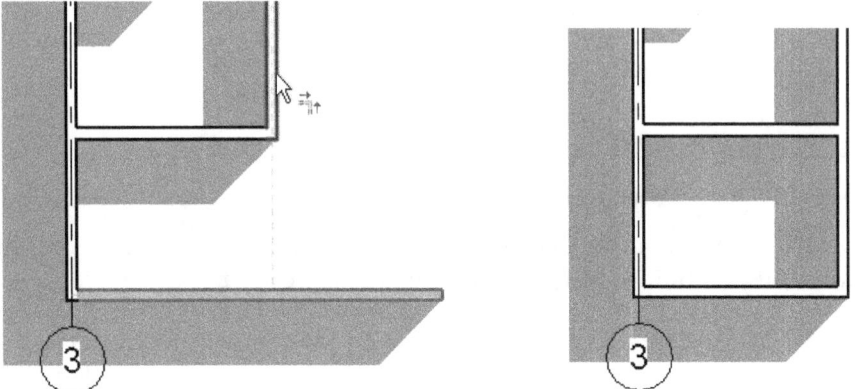

Figure 5-13 Selecting the second wall to trim/extend   *Figure 5-14* Trimmed and extended walls

Using the Trim/Extend Single Element Tool

Ribbon: Modify > Modify > Trim/Extend Single Element

This tool enables you to extend or trim an element by defining a reference line or boundary. Using this tool, you can trim a wall or extend a wall to another wall without creating a corner at the intersection. You can also select the desired side of the wall to be retained. For example, use this option to trim the vertical wall at its intersection with the horizontal wall so that the lower portion of the vertical wall is retained. Invoke the **Trim/Extend Single Element** tool from the **Modify** panel and then select the horizontal wall as the cutting boundary. It is highlighted in red. To retain the lower portion of the inclined wall, move the cursor near it until a dashed line appears, refer to Figure 5-15. The profile that is created will be displayed as a dashed line. Click on the lower side of the vertical wall to retain the lower portion. The wall is trimmed at the specified boundary, as shown in Figure 5-16. The **Trim/Extend Single Element** tool can also be used to extend an element to another element. For example, to extend a horizontal wall up to the vertical wall, invoke the tool and then select the latter as the defining boundary. On moving the cursor near the wall to be extended, you will notice that a dashed line appears, as shown in Figure 5-17. Now, click to extend the vertical wall up to the horizontal wall, as shown in Figure 5-18.

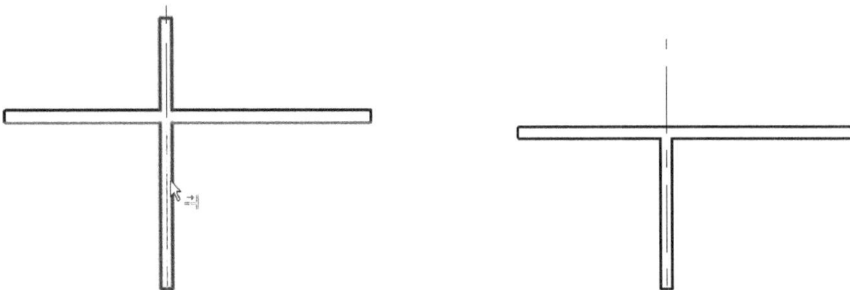

Figure 5-15 Selecting the wall to be trimmed by clicking on the portion to be retained   *Figure 5-16* Trimmed wall

Using the Editing Tools 5-13

Figure 5-17 The dashed line on the wall to be extended

Figure 5-18 The extended wall

Using the Trim/Extend Multiple Elements Tool

Ribbon: Modify > Modify > Trim/Extend Multiple Elements

The **Trim/Extend Multiple Elements** tool enables you to extend or trim a number of elements using a common boundary or edge, which can be defined by clicking on an element. After specifying the boundary, select the elements to be extended or trimmed. Autodesk Revit Architecture intuitively extends or trims them at the defined boundary. For example, you may need to extend and trim multiple vertical and inclined walls using the horizontal wall as the boundary such that the lower portions of the walls are retained. To do so, invoke the **Trim/Extend Multiple Elements** tool from the **Modify** panel. On doing so, you will notice that a symbol of this tool appears along with the cursor. Then, click on the horizontal wall to define the cutting boundary and you will see it highlighted. To retain the lower portion of the wall, move the cursor near it until a dashed line appears, as shown in Figure 5-19. Now, click to trim the wall at the specified boundary. Similarly, you can click on the other inclined wall at the lower portion to trim it, refer to Figure 5-20. Without discontinuing the trim tool, move the cursor near the vertical wall which you want to extend, as shown in Figure 5-21, and then click on it. The wall is extended to the horizontal wall. To extend the next wall, move the cursor near it and click when the dashed line appears, as shown in Figure 5-22. Alternatively, you can use a selection box to select multiple elements to trim or to extend to a defined boundary.

Figure 5-19 Selecting the wall to be trimmed

Figure 5-20 Selecting the inclined wall to be trimmed by clicking on the portion to be retained

Figure 5-21 Selecting the wall to be extended

Figure 5-22 Selecting the next wall to be extended

> **Tip:** *While selecting walls or lines for extending and trimming, ensure that the portion of the element to be retained is clicked. In trimming, the portion of the element on the other side of the intersection is removed.*

CUTTING AND PASTING ELEMENTS

Using various cut and paste tools, you can cut some elements and then paste them at another location. You can use these tools efficiently to speed up your work and reduce the time for creating new elements. Various cutting and pasting tools are discussed next.

Cutting Elements

Ribbon: Modify | (Elements / Components) > Clipboard > Cut to Clipboard
Shortcut Keys: CTRL+X

 The **Cut to Clipboard** tool is used to remove one or more elements from the project. The selected elements that are cut using this tool are copied on the clipboard where they stay until another selection is cut. When you cut an element and paste it to the clipboard, the existing selection is overwritten by the new one. These elements can then be pasted into the same or another project. The **Cut to Clipboard** tool becomes available only after a selection is made in the drawing. To create a selection set, you can use any selection tool described earlier in this chapter. Select the element(s) that you want to cut from the drawing area and choose the **Cut to Clipboard** tool from the **Clipboard** panel of the contextual tab. Alternatively, press the CTRL+X keys. On doing so, the selected elements will be removed from the project and pasted on the clipboard.

Copying Elements to the Clipboard

Ribbon: Modify | (Elements / Components) > Clipboard > Copy to Clipboard
Shortcut Keys: CTRL+C

This tool is used to create a copy of the selected elements on the clipboard and retain the original ones in the current project. Select the elements or components that you desire to copy from the drawing area and invoke the **Copy to Clipboard** tool from the **Clipboard** panel of the contextual tab. Alternatively, press the CTRL+C keys. A copy of the selected elements will be created on the clipboard.

Pasting Elements from the Clipboard

Ribbon: Modify | (Elements / Components) > Clipboard > Paste drop-down > Paste from Clipboard
Shortcut Key: CTRL+V

The **Paste from Clipboard** tool, which is used to add one or more elements from the clipboard to the project, becomes available only after the element(s) have been cut or copied to it earlier. The selection can be pasted on the current view or a different view. To paste the elements from the clipboard to the drawing, invoke the **Paste from Clipboard** tool from the **Clipboard** panel. Alternatively, press the CTRL+V keys to paste the selected elements on the drawing view. You can then paste the element(s) at the desired location. To paste a single element, such as a door or a window on the clipboard, move the cursor to the desired location on the wall and click; the copied door or window will be placed in the host wall. If there are a number of elements in the pasted selection, they will appear in the preview box. If they are pasted into the same project, a temporary dimension will be displayed. This indicates the distance and direction of the cursor from the original selection. You can enter the value of the dimension and the angle to paste the elements. Alternatively, to paste the elements graphically, move the box to the desired location and click. Once these elements are pasted, they remain selected as a group in a dashed rectangular box and the **Modify | Model Groups** tab is displayed. Using this tab, you can use other editing tools such as **Move**, **Copy**, **Rotate**, **Align**, and so on to modify them. In the **Options Bar**, choose the **Activate Dimensions** button to view the dimensions of the pasted elements from the nearby element(s). After completing the pasting procedure, choose the **Finish** button from the **Edit Pasted** panel to return to the **Architecture** tab (default mode). To abort the pasting operation after the entities have been pasted and while the group of elements is selected, choose the **Cancel** button in the **Modify | Model Groups** tab. On doing so, the recently pasted group of elements will be removed from the project and you will exit from the **Paste from Clipboard** tool.

ROTATING ELEMENTS

Ribbon: Modify (Elements / Components) > Modify > Rotate
Shortcut Keys: RO

The **Rotate** tool is used to rotate elements about a specified axis or point. You can rotate an element about an axis perpendicular to its plan, elevation, and section views. In 3D view, elements rotate about an axis perpendicular to the current work plane. This tool is available only after the elements have been selected.

Note
*The **Rotate** tool has its limitations. For example, walls cannot be rotated in the elevation view. Dependent elements such as doors and windows cannot be rotated without their host elements.*

Select the element(s) or component(s) from the drawing that you need to rotate and invoke the **Rotate** tool from the **Modify** panel. Alternatively, you can type **RO** to invoke the **Rotate** tool. On invoking the **Rotate** tool, a rotation symbol is displayed at the center of the selected element(s). It represents the perpendicular axis or the center about which the elements will be rotated. You can snap to the symbol and drag it to the desired center of rotation.

Once the center of rotation has been specified, a ray is generated from this point, which moves along the direction of the cursor. Click at the desired start point of the rotation to display a line indicating its direction. You can use various object snap options to specify the start point of the rotation. Once the starting point has been specified, another line rotates with the cursor. A preview box, indicating the selected elements, also rotates with it. Now, move the cursor to the required angle and click in the drawing area to specify the second point of rotation. On doing so, the element will rotate toward a new direction. On rotating the entities, you will notice that a temporary angular dimension is displayed. You can enter the exact value of the angle of rotation, if required. This rotates the element to the specified angle. When you invoke the **Rotate** tool, five options are displayed in the **Options Bar**, as shown in Figure 5-23.

*Figure 5-23 Rotate options available in the **Options Bar***

Before rotating, you can select the **Disjoin** check box to break the association between the selected elements and the other associated elements. For example, you can independently rotate a wall that is joined to the other walls. The **Copy** option enables you to create a rotated copy of the selected element while retaining its original location. The **Angle** option can be used to rotate the elements by a specific angle. You can enter the value of the angle of rotation in the edit box. In the **Options Bar**, you can drag the rotation symbol or use the **Place** button to move the center of rotation to a different location. After you place the center of rotation you can choose the **Default** button to move the center of rotation to its default location. For example, to rotate a furniture element about its center by an angle of 90-degrees, click on the furniture element to select it. Next, invoke the **Rotate** tool from the **Modify** panel of the **Modify | Furniture** tab; the rotate symbol will be displayed at the center of the furniture element and a ray will be generated from it, as shown in Figure 5-24. You can now move the center of rotation to a different location. To do so, choose the **Place** button and move the rotation symbol at the center of the bottom edge of the furniture element and click; the rotation symbol moves to the new location and the ray is now generated from this point, as shown in Figure 5-25. Next, move the cursor horizontally right and click when the generated ray will be parallel to the top and bottom edges of the furniture element, refer to Figure 5-26. To rotate the furniture element by 90-degrees angle, move the cursor counter-clockwise and click when the temporary dimension shows the desired angle value. As a result, the selected furniture element will rotate about the specified rotation point, as shown in Figure 5-27.

Figure 5-24 A ray generating from the center of the furniture element

Figure 5-25 Dragging the center of rotation

Figure 5-26 Snapping the rotation line using the object snap

Figure 5-27 Using the temporary dimensions to rotate the element

MIRRORING ELEMENTS

In Autodesk Revit Architecture, you can create a mirror image of elements selected from the drawing about an axis defined by an imaginary line passing through the two specified points. You can use various tools to mirror the selected elements. Using these tools, you can create a symmetrical profile and also create a copy of the elements which are equidistant from the specified axis. You can mirror elements using any of the two tools, **Mirror- Pick Axis** or **Mirror- Draw Axis**. These tools are available only after the elements to be mirrored have been selected. To mirror the element(s) in the drawing, select them and then choose **Mirror - Pick Axis** tool or **Mirror - Draw Axis** tool from the **Modify** panel of the contextual tab. Alternatively, you can type **MM** or **DM** to mirror elements. Note that when you type **MM**, the **Mirror - Pick Axis** tool is invoked and on typing **DM**, the **Mirror - Draw Axis** tool is invoked. On invoking these tools, you will be prompted to select the axis of reflection from the drawing area. Also, you will notice that the **Options Bar** displays the **Copy** option. By default, this option is selected, and therefore you will be able to create a mirrored copy of the elements. Clear the **Copy** check box if you do not require a copy. The two options to mirror the elements are discussed next.

Mirroring Elements Using the Mirror - Pick Axis Tool

Ribbon: Modify | (Elements / Components) > Modify > Mirror - Pick Axis
Shortcut Keys: MM

 The **Mirror - Pick Axis** tool is represented symbolically by a cursor symbol and can be used to select an element defining the mirror axis. To use this tool, select the desired

element(s) from the drawing and then choose the **Mirror - Pick Axis** tool from the **Modify** panel; the mirror symbol will appear with the cursor in the drawing area. Next, move the cursor over the element that will define the mirror axis and click when the appropriate object snap appears. Figure 5-28 shows a floor plan with various elements selected for mirroring and the vertical gridline as the mirror axis. Figure 5-29 shows the elements created after mirroring.

Note
*Using the **Mirror - Pick Axis** tool, you can only select a line or a reference plane that the cursor can snap to. You cannot mirror elements about an imaginary axis created in the open space.*

Tip: *For mirroring elements about an inclined axis, you can create a line inclined at the appropriate angle and then use the **Mirror - Pick Axis** tool to select it as the mirror axis.*

Figure 5-28 Elements selected for mirroring

Mirroring Elements Using the Mirror - Draw Axis Tool

Ribbon: Modify (Elements / Components) > Modify > Mirror - Draw Axis

The **Mirror - Draw Axis** tool is represented by a pencil with the mirror symbol. You can use this tool to mirror element(s) in the drawing about an axis that is defined by specifying two points in the drawing area. To use this tool, select the element(s) to be mirrored from the drawing and then choose the **Mirror - Draw Axis** tool from the **Modify** panel. Alternatively, type **DM**. Next, click in the drawing area to specify the start point of the mirror line; a ray will emerge from the specified point. Move the cursor to the desired location and click to specify the second point; the selected elements will be mirrored about the line which represents the mirror axis. Figure 5-30 shows the inclined mirror axis defined by the two points. Figure 5-31 shows the mirrored elements about the specified inclined mirror axis.

Using the Editing Tools

Figure 5-29 The floor plan after mirroring the elements

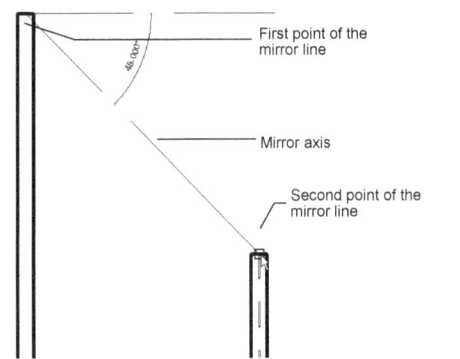

Figure 5-30 Using the **Draw Mirror Axis** tool to define the mirror axis

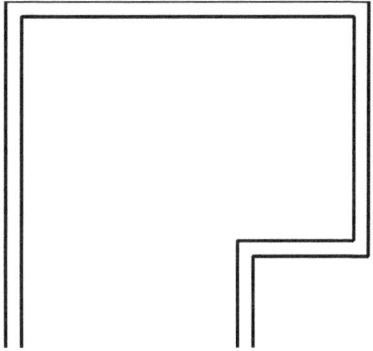

Figure 5-31 Sketched profile with the mirrored elements

CREATING AN OFFSET

Ribbon: Modify > Modify > Offset
Shortcut Key: OF

The **Offset** tool is used to create a copy of the selected element at a specified distance from the original element. You can select a single element or multiple elements. The selection can be made even after invoking this tool. By default, Autodesk Revit Architecture creates a copy of the selected element while creating an offset. To offset an element, invoke the **Offset** tool from the **Modify** panel of the **Modify** tab. Alternatively, you can type **OF** to invoke the **Offset** tool. On invoking the **Offset** tool, you will notice that the **Options Bar** displays the **Copy** check box. By default, this check box is selected. As a result, you will be able to create a copy of the element at the offset distance. Clear the **Copy** check box, if you do not require a copy. In this case, the object selected will be shifted to the offset distance and no copy will be created. The **Options Bar** also shows two radio buttons, **Graphical** and **Numerical**, which can be used to specify the mirror axis. The use of these options is discussed next.

Tip: *After creating the offset, the **Offset** text box in the **Options Bar** displays the distance through which the offset was created.*

The **Graphical** radio button is selected to specify the offset distance graphically in the drawing window. After selecting the elements and this option, click in the drawing area to specify the start point of the offset distance. A preview image of the selected element is displayed. Now, click again to specify the second point. The selected element is copied at a distance and in the direction defined by the two specified points. As you move the cursor to specify the second point, the temporary dimension is displayed. To specify the exact offset distance, move the cursor in the appropriate direction and enter the offset value, as shown in Figure 5-32. Figure 5-33 shows the offset element is created.

Figure 5-32 Specifying the offset distance using the **Graphical** option

Figure 5-33 Offset wall created at the specified distance

Tip: *To create a copy of the selected element to offset, you can also press and hold the CTRL key, if the **Copy** check box is not selected.*

The selection of the **Numerical** radio button from **Options Bar** provides you the flexibility to create an offset by specifying the offset distance in the **Offset** edit box. This value must be a positive number. You can select the **Numerical** radio button to offset single element or a chain of elements. After specifying the offset distance, as you move the cursor near the element, a preview image profile of the selected element at the specified offset distance is displayed in the form of a dashed line. You have the option of changing the offset distance at this stage. You will notice that as you move the cursor over the element, the preview image flips sides. To select a chain of elements, press TAB when the preview image appears. All the connected elements are selected and the preview will change accordingly. Figure 5-34 shows the connected wall profile with its preview offset image. Click to offset the walls, when you see the preview image on the desired side. The offset is created at the specified distance entered in the **Offset** edit box. Figure 5-35 shows the offset wall profile created.

Note

You can offset elements only in the same work plane and not the elements created as in-place families.

Using the Editing Tools

Figure 5-34 Previewing the offset and selecting a chain of walls using the TAB key

Figure 5-35 An offset wall profile created at the specified distance

In case, the wall selected for the offset has other dependent elements such as doors and windows, they are also copied and created in the offset. Figures 5-36 and 5-37 show a wall profile with the doors, windows, and its resultant offset.

Figure 5-36 Selecting the wall profile with the doors and windows inserted

Figure 5-37 Resulting offset with inserts copied at the specified offset distance

CREATING AN ARRAY OF ELEMENTS

Ribbon: Modify | (Elements / Components) > Modify > Array

The **Array** tool creates copies of the selected element in a rectangular or radial pattern. It is available only after the elements are selected for an array. You can use any of the methods discussed earlier in this chapter to create a selection. Autodesk Revit Architecture provides you the option of arraying multiple elements that are associated as a group. Select the element(s) that you want to array from the drawing and then invoke the **Array** tool from the **Modify** panel. Alternatively, you can type **AR** to invoke the array tool. On invoking the **Array** tool, you will notice that the **Options Bar** displays certain array options. From the **Options Bar**, select the **Group and Associate** check box to create a group of the selected elements, which are then copied as a group rather than individual elements. Clear this check box, if you want to array elements individually. The two options available for creating an array are discussed next.

Linear Array

Linear, the default array option, can be used to create copies of the selected elements in a rectangular or linear pattern. In the **Options Bar**, additional options are available for creating an array. In the **Number** edit box, enter the number of copies you want to create. You can select the **2nd** radio button to specify the distance between items in the array. The **Last** option is used to specify the entire distance of the array. The items specified are then placed equidistantly between the first and the last specified points. You can use the **Activate Dimension** button to view various dimensions of the elements.

You can specify various options in the **Options Bar** either before or during the creation of an array. Using the 2nd radio button, click at any point in the drawing window to specify the start point of the array distance. As you move the cursor in the desired direction, a temporary dimension is displayed. You have the option to either enter the value of the distance in that direction or simply move the cursor to the appropriate location and click. Autodesk Revit creates the array of the selected elements by calculating the distance and direction between the two specified points. After the second point is specified, you are prompted to enter the number of items for the array in an edit box. The number of items specified in the **Options Bar** appears as the default value. You have the option of overriding it and specifying a new number. An array of the selected items is created with the specified distance between each group of items. Figure 5-38 shows the selected elements and the distance between each element being specified. The preview of the array to be created is shown in Figure 5-39. You can use the **Constrain** check box in the **Options Bar** to restrict the movement of the cursor in orthogonal directions only. This helps in creating a horizontal or vertical linear array.

Figure 5-38 Specifying the distance and the angle for creating an array

Figure 5-39 The preview image of the arrayed items

You can select the **Last** radio button from the **Options Bar**, to create an array of elements between two points. Figure 5-40 shows the selection of the start point for specifying the array distance and the selected window to be arrayed. Move the cursor to the total distance that needs to be divided, as shown in Figure 5-41. As you click to specify the endpoint of the array distance, an edit box appears displaying the number of items in the array. You can specify the number in it, as shown in Figure 5-42, and press ENTER to complete the procedure. An array of the selected window is created on the wall, as shown in Figure 5-43.

Using the Editing Tools 5-23

Figure 5-40 Specifying the start point of the distance to array the selected window

Figure 5-41 Specifying the endpoint of distance to array

Figure 5-42 Specifying the number of items in an array

Figure 5-43 Array of windows created on the wall

 Tip: *Autodesk Revit displays error messages, if the elements cannot be arrayed. For example, if the specified angle or the number of items do not fit into the length of the wall, or overlap each other, a suitable warning message is displayed to help you modify the settings accordingly.*

Radial Array

You can create radial arrays using the **Radial** option available in the **Options Bar**. The other setting options available in the **Options Bar** such as **Group and Associate**, **Number**, **Move to: 2nd** and **Last** are the same as those given for the **Linear** option. The **Angle** edit box is provided to specify the angle about which the array is to be created. If the **Move to: 2nd** option is selected, the angle specified becomes the angle between each items, whereas if the **Move to: Last** option is selected, the number of items are created by equally dividing the specified angle. The procedure for creating a radial array is similar to that of using the **Rotate** tool, described earlier in this chapter. After selecting the element(s) of array and choosing the **Radial** option, you will notice that a rotational symbol is displayed at the center of the selection, which you can drag to the location to be used as the center of the array. Figure 5-44 shows a wall profile, in which the window is selected for an array with the center of the circular wall as its center. Next, click to specify the start point of the angle of the array. The example shows the creation of multiple windows within a specified angle. You can choose the **Move to: Last** option for this purpose. Move the cursor radially and click to specify the end point of the angle, as shown in Figure 5-45. An edit box is displayed prompting you to enter the number of items to be created between the specified angles, as shown in Figure 5-46. After specifying the number, press ENTER to complete the procedure. Figure 5-47 shows the resultant radial array of the windows. You will notice that the number of items are displayed in blue. You can click on it and enter a new value, if required. The two controls at the end of the arc can be used to resize it. The middle control can be used to modify the radius of the radial array, while the central control lets you drag it.

Figure 5-44 *Specifying the first point of the angle with the center of circular wall for the radial array of the selected window*

Using the Editing Tools

Figure 5-45 Specifying the second point of the angle for the radial array

Figure 5-46 Specifying the number of items for the radial array

Figure 5-47 The resulting radial array with the last item highlighted

MATCHING ELEMENTS

Ribbon: Modify > Clipboard > Match Type Properties
Shortcut Keys: MA

In Autodesk Revit, you can use the **Match Type Properties** tool to copy the properties of a source element and transfer them to another element belonging to the same family. For example, you can select a wall and then another wall and match its properties with the first wall.

To match the property of a source element to another element of the same family, invoke the **Match Type Properties** tool from the **Clipboard** panel. After invoking this tool, you will notice that as you move the cursor in the drawing window, it changes to a paint brush. To select a type of element to match, move the paint brush near the element and click. The empty paint brush changes into a filled one indicating that the element type has been selected. To match another element of the same family type as the first selection, move the dropper over it and click. The dropper empties, indicating that the element type has been changed. In case of walls, the matching wall type does not change the instance parameters. Autodesk

Revit Architecture has the improved feature of matching multiple family elements to a selected element of the same family.

ALIGNING ELEMENTS AND WORKING WITH CONSTRAINTS

Ribbon: Modify > Modify > Align
Shortcut Keys: AL

The **Align** tool is used to arrange elements in a collinear manner. You can choose an element that acts as a reference line or a plane, along which the other elements can be aligned. When you align them, a padlock key will be displayed, which represents the alignment constraint. Using this key, you can lock or unlock the alignment of the walls. Once you lock the alignment, the walls move together. The **Align** tool can be used only in plan or elevation views. In Autodesk Revit Architecture, you can use the **Align** tool to align multiple elements in your project at once. Invoke the **Align** tool from the **Modify** panel. In the **Options Bar**, the **Multiple Alignment** check box can be selected to align a number of elements to a common line. While aligning walls, you can choose to align the wall centerlines or wall faces by selecting the appropriate option from the **Prefer** drop-down list in the **Options Bar**. To select the reference line, click when the appropriate line is displayed. Figure 5-48 shows a wall profile and a wall centerline being selected as the reference line. To align another wall, you can move the cursor over it and click when the centerline snap is displayed. The second wall gets aligned to the first wall, as shown in Figure 5-49. You can click the padlock key to lock the alignment of these two walls. To align them to the third wall, select them as the reference line, as shown in Figure 5-50. Since you have locked the alignment of the first two walls, both of them are aligned to the third wall centerline, as shown in Figure 5-51. You can click the padlock key to lock the alignment of all the three horizontal walls. You can also use the **Multiple Alignment** option and use one wall centerline as the reference line to align the other two walls.

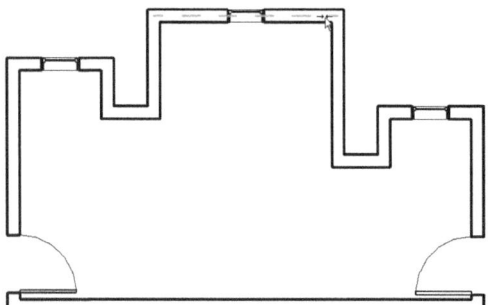
Figure 5-48 *Selecting the wall centerline as the alignment line*

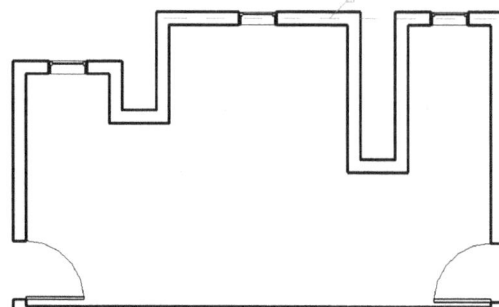
Figure 5-49 *The second wall aligned to the specified alignment line*

Using the Editing Tools

Figure 5-50 Specifying the reference line to align the walls

Figure 5-51 The resulting aligned walls

DELETING ELEMENTS

Using the **Delete** tool, you can remove the selected elements from the project. The deleted elements are permanently removed and are not pasted on the clipboard. The tool is available only after the elements have been selected. To invoke the **Delete** tool, select the element you want to delete, the contextual tab will be displayed. From the **Modify** panel of the contextual tab, choose the **Delete** tool; the selected elements will be deleted from the drawing. Alternatively, you can press the DELETE key or type **DE** to delete the selected elements.

SPLITTING ELEMENT

Ribbon: Modify > Modify > Split Element
Shortcut Keys: SL

The **Split Element** tool is used to break a wall or a line into two parts at a specified point. Once a wall or a line is split, the parts can be edited independently. Invoke the **Split Element** tool from the **Modify** panel and select the element that you desire to split from the drawing. The **Options Bar** has the **Delete Inner Segment** check box, which you can select to delete the inner segment created between the two consecutive splits. On moving the cursor in the drawing window, you will notice that it changes to a cutting tool. Now, move the cursor over the wall or a line until the temporary dimension is displayed. You can move the cursor to the desired distance, as shown in Figure 5-52, and then click to specify the point of the split. A temporary dimension, indicating the location of the split, will be displayed. Click on it and enter the value of the distance, as shown in Figure 5-53. As a result, the split moves to the specified location. Similarly, you can click to specify the location of the second split, as shown in Figure 5-54. If the **Delete Inner Segment** check box is selected, the portion of the wall between these two split points is automatically removed, as shown in Figure 5-55; otherwise, the single wall is now split into three portions, each with a specified length. The walls can be split in the elevation or 3D view along a horizontal line. You can view the elevation by clicking the appropriate elevation name from the **Project Browser**. To split the wall, move the cursor and click to specify the location of the split. You can split the wall at the predefined levels by snapping to the reference lines or at any other level by clicking at the appropriate height.

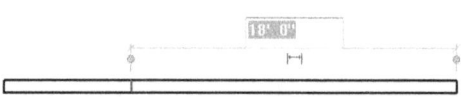

Figure 5-52 Specifying the point of the split

Figure 5-53 Specifying the distance of the split by entering a value

Figure 5-54 Specifying the second point to split the wall segment

Figure 5-55 Single wall segment split at two points after selecting the **Delete Inner Segment** check box from **Options Bar**

To split a wall segment of a double story building at Level 2 in the elevation view, invoke the **Split Element** tool and move the cursor till it snaps to the Level 2 reference line. Click to split the wall into two portions. When a wall is split at the reference line, the base constraint for its upper portion is set to Level 2. And, the top constraint of its lower portion is set to Level 1. You can also split the wall at a location other than the reference line. For example, to split the middle portion of a wall in the elevation view, invoke the **Split Element** tool and click at the location shown in Figure 5-56; the wall will split horizontally into two. Now, click at another location to separate the middle segment. Next, click at a suitable place in the middle segment to split it vertically into two. You can now select and delete the lower portion of this middle wall to create an opening, as shown in Figure 5-57.

Figure 5-56 Specifying the location of the split for the middle wall segment

Figure 5-57 The resulting wall after removing the lower portion of the split middle wall

Using the Editing Tools 5-29

SPLITTING WITH GAP

Ribbon: Modify > Modify > Split with Gap

The **Split with Gap** tool is used to split a wall into two separate walls with a defined gap defined between them. To split a wall, invoke the **Split with Gap** tool from the **Modify** panel; the cursor will change to a cutting tool. In the **Options Bar**, enter a value in the **Joint Gap** edit box to set the spacing between two consecutive splits. Note that you can enter a value between 0 1/16" and 1' in the **Joint Gap** edit box. Next, move and place the cursor over the wall that you want to split. Click at the desired point in the wall; the wall will split into two separate walls with a gap value specified in the **Joint Gap** edit box.

SPLITTING FACES

Ribbon: Modify > Geometry > Split Face

The **Split Face** tool is used to split a face of a wall or a column into two separate regions. The splitting of the face of a wall or a column into different regions will help in applying different materials to each region. To split the face of a wall or column, invoke the **Split Face** tool from the **Geometry** panel; the cursor will change to a selection mode. Move the cursor toward the face of a wall or column and click when the face is highlighted. On doing so, the **Modify | Split Face > Create Boundary** tab will be displayed. From the **Draw** panel of this tab, choose a desired sketching tool and sketch the boundary line that will split the face. After sketching the boundary, choose the **Finish Edit Mode** button from the **Mode** panel; the face of the wall or column will be divided into two different regions and you can apply materials to them.

GROUPING ELEMENT

Ribbon: Architecture > Model > Model Group drop-down > Create Group

Grouping elements enables you to associate a single or a number of elements as a single entity or group. Once grouped, the elements act as a single entity. They can be selected as a single element so that you can move or copy a number of elements as a single unit. Each instance of the group acts as a single unit and any modifications made in the group are propagated in all its instances. For example, you may create a group with a cluster of walls, windows, and doors, and then create their multiple instances. When you modify the door type in one group, the change will reflect in all instances of the group. You can create three types of groups, model groups for the model elements, detail groups for the view-specific elements, and attached detail groups for view-specific elements associated with a specific model group. You can create groups either by selecting the elements first and then grouping them, or by creating groups first and then later adding the elements to the groups by selecting them from the project views. To create groups, invoke the **Create Group** tool from the **Model** panel of the **Architecture** tab; the **Create Group** dialog box will be displayed in which you can enter the name of the group.

Note
*If you invoke the **Create Group** tool after selecting the elements, the **Create Model Group** dialog box will be displayed.*

*You can invoke the **Create Group** tool from the **Create** panel of the **Modify|(Elements/Components)** tab. Alternatively, type GP.*

Creating Groups by Selecting Elements in Project Views

You can create a group by selecting only the model elements from the project views or using the **Group Editor**. To create groups of elements, select the elements to group and then choose the **Create Group** tool from the **Create** panel of the **Modify | Multi-Select** tab; the **Create Model Group** dialog box will be displayed, as shown in Figure 5-58. Alternatively, after selecting the elements to be grouped, choose the **Create Group** tool from **Architecture > Model > Model Group** drop-down; the **Create Model Group** dialog box will be displayed.

Note
*While creating a group, if you have selected one element type, the corresponding **Modify / (Elements / Components)** tab will be displayed instead of the **Multi-Select** tab.*

In the **Create Model Group** dialog box, specify the name of the group in the **Name** edit box and choose the **OK** button; the name of the created group will be automatically displayed under the **Group** heading in the **Project Browser**. The default name given to a model group is **Group 1** and the number in it increments as more groups are created. You can rename a group by selecting and right-clicking its name and choosing **Rename** from the shortcut menu.

*Figure 5-58 The **Create Model Group** dialog box*

Creating Groups Using the Group Editor

This option allows you to create groups prior to the selection of the elements. You can create the **Model** group or the **Annotation** group based on the requirement and later on, select the elements from the project views and add them to the groups. To do so, choose the **Create Group** tool from **Architecture > Model > Model Group** drop-down; the **Create Group** dialog box will be displayed, as shown in Figure 5-59. In this dialog box, specify the name of the group in the **Name** edit box. The **Group Type** area in this dialog box displays two radio buttons for creating a group, **Model** and **Detail**. Specify the type of group by selecting the **Model** or **Detail** radio button and then choose the **OK** button; the screen will turn in the edit mode with a yellow background and the **Edit Group** panel will be displayed in the **Architecture** tab. Figure 5-60 shows the options in the **Edit Group** panel. In the **Edit Group** panel, you can choose the **Add** button to add elements into a group. On choosing the **Add** button, the add (**+**) symbol will appear with the cursor. You can select the elements from the project view to

Using the Editing Tools

group them. If there are no elements in the project view, you can create the elements using different tools from the **Build** panel in the **Architecture** tab. The elements will be automatically grouped. You can remove the elements from the existing group, attach details, and even view properties of the group using the respective buttons from the toolbar. Choose the **Finish** button after adding elements to the group.

Figure 5-59 The **Create Group** dialog box

Figure 5-60 The options in the **Edit Group** panel

Creating a Detail Group

Revit allows you to group all detail lines, fill regions, and the detail components separately. You will learn about them in Chapter 12 of this textbook. To group detail components, select them in the drawing and choose the **Create Group** tool from **Annotate > Detail > Detail Group** drop-down; the **Create Detail Group** dialog box will be displayed. Specify the name of the detail group in the **Name** edit box and choose the **OK** button; the name of the detail group will be displayed in the **Groups > Detail** head in the **Project Browser**.

Note
If you select incorrect components to add to a particular type of group, Revit Architecture will display a warning about the components that cannot be grouped together. For example, you cannot add tags, dimensions, and spot dimensions in a group of detail components.

Creating Model and Attached Detail Groups

Autodesk Revit allows you to group all the dimensions, tags, and the detail components as an attachment to the model group. This attached group consists of dimensions, tags, detail lines, or detail components that refer to the model group. To create an attached detail group, select the model elements and detail elements simultaneously using a crossing window; the **Modify | Multi-Select** tab will be displayed. Choose the **Create Group** tool from the **Create** panel; the **Create Model Group and Attached Detail Group** dialog box will be displayed, as shown in Figure 5-61. Enter the name of the model group in the **Name** edit box of the **Model Group** area. Next, enter a name of the detail group in the **Name** edit box of the **Attached Detail Group** area and choose the **OK** button; the attached detail group will be created consisting of the detail components, dimensions, and detail elements. The details will be attached automatically to the required model group and displayed in the **Project Browser** under the model group that it belongs to.

You can create a new group by duplicating an existing group. You can also modify the group without affecting the parent group. To create a duplicate group, select the group of which you want to create a duplicate in the **Project Browser** and right-click; a shortcut menu will be displayed. Choose **Duplicate** from the shortcut menu; a new group will be added in the **Project Browser** under the parent group. You can rename the group, if required.

*Figure 5-61 The **Create Model Group and Attached Detail Group** dialog box*

Alternatively, to create a duplicate group, select the group of which you want to create a duplicate and then choose the **Type Properties** tool from the **Properties** panel of the **Modify | Multi-Select** tab; the **Type Properties** dialog box is displayed. Choose the **Duplicate** button and name the group in the **Name** dialog box displayed. Choose the **OK** button; the group will be added to the **Project Browser** with the new name.

Tip: *You can group elements belonging to different families such as walls, doors, windows, furniture, and so on into a single group. If dependent elements are grouped without their respective hosts, Autodesk Revit will display relevant error messages when these groups are used in the project.*

Note
*In Revit Architecture 2015, the Detail Group behave as clipped element instead of pinned elements. As on selecting the detail group a clipped symbol will appear and will get selected even if the **Select Pinned Element** option is disabled in the **Status Bar**. Whereas, on selecting the Model Group and Detail Group together and making it a pinned element, then the Detail group will act as a pinned element and will not get selected on disabling the **Select Pinned Elements** option.*

Placing Groups

Once a group is created, you can easily place its instances in the project by dragging the group from the **Project Browser**. Select the required **Detail** or the **Model** group from the **Project Browser**, drag and drop it at the desired location in the drawing area, and then click to place it. Alternatively, to place a model group choose the **Place Model Group** tool from **Architecture > Model > Model Group** drop-down; the **Modify | Place Group** tab will be displayed. Select the required group from the **Type Selector** drop-down list and click in the drawing area to place the model group.

Tip: *The origin and rotation axis controls of the group are useful in positioning and swapping them. Their efficient use can save a lot of time and effort for repositioning them frequently.*

Alternatively, to place a detail group, choose the **Place Detail Group** tool from **Annotate > Detail > Detail Group** drop-down; the **Modify | Place Group** tab will be displayed. Now, select the desired detail group from the **Type Selector** drop-down list and click in the drawing area to place the detail group.

While placing a model group that has an attached detail group, you can control the display of the attached detail group. To do so, you need to place an instance of a model group that has a detail group attached with it in the drawing, and then select it; the **Modify | Model Groups** tab will be displayed. Now, choose the **Attached Detail Groups** tool from the **Group** panel; the **Attached Detail Group Placement** dialog box will be displayed. In the **Attached detail groups** area, the list of attached detail groups, along with their corresponding check boxes, will be displayed. You can select or clear the desired check box(es) to display or hide the detail group(s) along with the model group(s), when placed. Now, choose **OK**; the **Attached Detail Group Placement** dialog box will close and the selected model group will display or hide the attached detail group depending on whether the corresponding check box of the detail is selected or cleared in the **Attached Detail Group Placement** dialog box.

Once a group is placed in a drawing, you can position it at the appropriate location by moving or dragging it. Autodesk Revit provides the origin and rotation controls to set the position of the group. The origin control defines the base point of the grouped elements, whereas the rotation axis defines the rotation of the group. You can drag the two controls to the required location. By doing so, the orientation or position of the group will not change.

Swapping Groups

You can easily replace one group with another group. To do so, select a group from the drawing area; the **Modify | Model Groups** tab will be displayed. In the **Type Selector** drop-down list, the name of the available groups will be displayed. You can click on the **Model Group** drop-down list and select a different group to replace the selected group.

In case of swapping an attached detail group, Revit has the ability to update and replace the attached detail group of the old group with the attached detail group of the swapped group having the same name. Revit Architecture also displays a warning indicating the elements for which the reference could not be found out.

Modifying Groups

You can modify a group by ungrouping it. To modify a group, select it from the drawing; the **Modify | Model Groups** tab will be displayed. The **Group** panel of this tab displays the **Edit Group**, **Ungroup**, and **Link** buttons. On choosing the **Ungroup** button, the elements in the selected group will get disassociated and ungrouped. Using the **Edit Group** button, you can add or remove elements from the group and also attach details to it. When you choose this button, the screen will enter into the edit mode displaying the **Edit Group** panel, as shown earlier in Figure 5-60. The **Add** and **Remove** buttons can be chosen to add and remove elements from the group, respectively. After editing, choose the **Finish** button to complete the modifications. The **Cancel** button provides the option of discarding the modifications and returning to the **Modify | Model Groups** tab. You can use different editing tools on the grouped elements such as **Move**, **Copy**, **Mirror**, **Cut**, **Paste**, **Rotate**, and so on.

Excluding Elements from a Group

You can exclude elements from the group if some elements of a group overlap with the elements of the other group while placing them together. If the elements host some other elements such as doors and windows, Revit Architecture will automatically rehost the elements in the adjacent walls. To exclude an element from a group, place the cursor over the element that you want to exclude. Next, press TAB to highlight it, and click; a blue color icon will be displayed as shown by the cursor in Figure 5-62. When you place the cursor on the icon, a tooltip will be displayed prompting you to click on the icon to exclude the selected element. Click on the icon and press ESC; the element will be excluded from the group, and will not be displayed in the drawing. Alternatively, to exclude an element from the group select the element in the drawing as explained above and right-click; a shortcut menu will be displayed. Choose **Exclude** from the shortcut menu; the element will disappear from the drawing and will be excluded from the group. The elements that are excluded will not be visible in the drawing and will not be included in the schedule. To restore the excluded elements in the group, select the group and right-click; a shortcut menu will be displayed. Choose **Restore All Excluded** from the shortcut menu; the elements will be restored in the group and will be displayed in the drawing.

Figure 5-62 *Cursor showing an icon to exclude an element from the group*

 Tip: *You can use the shortcuts to exclude element from the group. For Example, select the element in the drawing and press EX, DELETE, or CTRL+X to exclude the selected element.*

Saving and Loading Groups

In Revit, you can save the group as the Revit file with *.rvt* extension. You can edit the groups independent of the project in which they are loaded. To save groups, choose **Save As > Library > Group** from **the Application Menu**; the **Save Group** dialog box will be displayed, as shown in Figure 5-63. Select the group to be saved from the **Group To Save** drop-down list and then save it using either the same name as the group name or enter a new name in the **File name** edit box. The group(s) will be saved with the assigned name with *.rvt* extension in case of a project file, or *.rfa* extension in case of a family file. The saved groups can also be loaded into another Autodesk Revit Architecture project that is open in the current session by choosing the **Load as Group into Open Projects** tool from **Architecture > Model > Model Group** drop-down; the **Load into Projects** dialog box will be displayed. In this dialog box, the list box displays the name of the project files, along with their check boxes, that are opened in the current session. To load the group(s) to a specified file, you can select the check box that is displayed along with the file name, from the list box. In the **Include** area of the **Load into Projects** dialog box, you can select the **Attached Details**,

Using the Editing Tools

Levels, or **Grids** check boxes, if you want to load the details, grids, and levels in the project with the group. The detail elements will be loaded in the project as attached detail groups. Now, choose **OK**; the **Load into Projects** dialog box will close and the window of the selected project file(s) will be displayed. Notice that the group(s) that you have loaded is displayed under the **Groups** head in **Project Browser**.

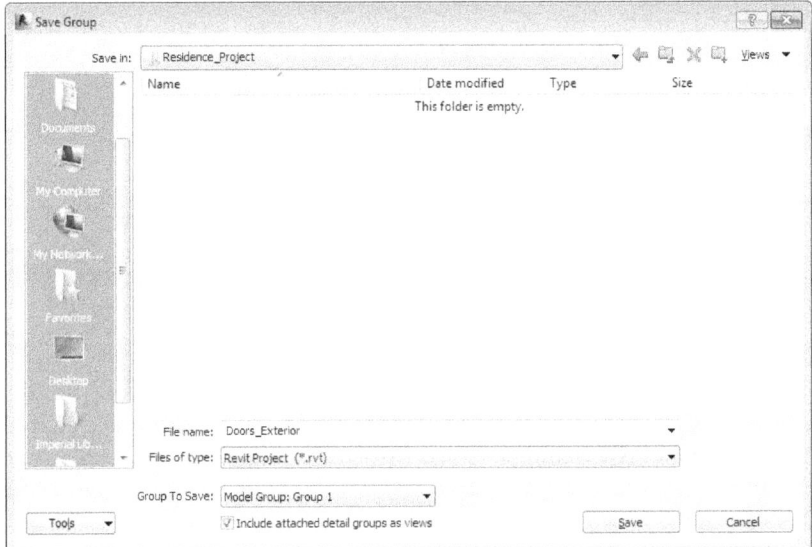

Figure 5-63 The **Save Group** *dialog box*

Converting Groups to Linked Models

To convert the groups to linked models, select the group to be converted to a linked model from the drawing; the **Modify | Model Groups** tab will be displayed. In this tab choose the **Link** tool from the **Group** panel; the **Convert to Link** dialog box will be displayed, as shown in Figure 5-64.

Figure 5-64 The **Convert to Link** *dialog box*

To create a new linked file, choose the **Replace with a new project file** button from the dialog box; the **Save Group** dialog box will be displayed. Specify the name in the **File name** edit box, browse to the required location, and choose the **Save** button to save the file. Choose the **Replace with an existing project file** button to replace the group with an already existing linked Revit model. On choosing this button, the **Open** dialog box will be displayed. Browse to the required location, select the existing file, and choose the **Open** button; the model group will be replaced by the existing linked file. You can choose the **Cancel** button to cancel the conversion.

If the name assigned to the linked group file already exists in the project then, Revit Architecture will display a message box, as shown in Figure 5-65. Choose the **Yes** button to replace the group file. On choosing the **No** button, the **Save As** dialog box will be displayed. Enter a new name for the linked group file to save the file with a different file name.

Figure 5-65 The message box prompting to replace the existing file

Deleting Groups

The created groups can be deleted only after all the instances of the group are deleted from the project. To delete all the instances of a group, right-click the group name in the **Project Browser** and select **Select All Instances > In Entire Project** from the shortcut menu. Then, choose the **Delete** button from the **Modify** panel of the contextual tab or press the DELETE key. The name of the group will be displayed even after all the instances are deleted. To delete the group from **Project Browser**, right-click its name and choose **Delete** from the shortcut menu. The **Delete** option is available only when all the instances of the group have been deleted from the project.

Tip: *You can also create nested groups with sub-groups within groups. When you ungroup a group with sub-groups, the association between the sub-groups is terminated. The **Ungroup** button can be used again to edit individual elements in the sub-group. To delete or edit an element in an instance of a group, you need to ungroup it first and then modify the desired element. After the necessary changes are made, the elements can be regrouped.*

CREATING SIMILAR ELEMENTS

Ribbon: Modify (Elements / Components) > Create > Create Similar
Shortcut Key: CS

Autodesk Revit provides the **Create Similar** tool to create and place copies of an element or a group at specified points. This tool is available only after a selection has been made. To create an element similar to an existing element in the drawing, select it; the **Modify | (Elements / Components)** tab will be displayed. Now, choose the **Create Similar** tool from the **Create** panel; the creation tool which was used to create the selected element will be invoked. Now, create the element of similar instance parameter as that of the selected element in your drawing. For example, if you select a window from the drawing and then invoke the **Create Similar** tool; the **Modify | Place Window** tab will be displayed with the window type similar to that of the selected window, which is selected in the **Type Selector**

Using the Editing Tools

drop-down list. Now, you can place windows, with similar instance parameter as that of the selected window in the drawing. Alternatively, to invoke the **Create Similar** tool, select the element and then right-click; a shortcut menu will be displayed. Next, choose **Create Similar** from the shortcut menu; the **Create Similar** tool will be invoked.

PINNING AND UNPINNING ELEMENTS

Ribbon: Modify | (Elements / Components) > Modify > Pin / Unpin
Shortcut Key: PN, UP

Elements can be pinned to their position using the **Pin** tool. To do so, select an element from the drawing; the **Modify | (Elements / Components)** tab will be displayed. Invoke the **Pin** tool from the **Modify** panel. Alternatively, you can type **PN** to invoke the **Pin** tool. Once pinned, a graphical pushpin symbol appears with the element, as shown in Figure 5-66, indicating that it is pinned and cannot be moved from its position. You can also pin the position with respect to other elements and groups. Click on the pin symbol to pin or unpin an element. For example, you can pin the position of columns with the intersecting grid lines. Once pinned, the column and the grid lines cannot be moved without first unpinning their position. You can use the **Unpin** tool to unpin the position constraint for the pinned elements. Note that the **Unpin** tool will replace the **Pin** tool after an element is pinned.

Figure 5-66 Group of windows pinned at their position

Note
The pin symbol is not visible after invoking other tools. The element or group must be selected to display the pin symbol.

In Revit Architecture 2015, you cannot delete the pinned elements. In case of multiple selections, if pinned elements are selected accidentally, then while deleting them Revit will warn you that the elements are pinned and can not be deleted. Also, it will instruct you to unpin the element.

SCALING ELEMENTS

Ribbon: Modify (Elements / Components) > Modify > Scale
Shortcut Key: RE

The **Scale** tool, used to modify the scale of a single or a selection of elements, is available only for walls, lines, images, *.dwg* and *.dxf* imports, reference planes and position of dimensions. After making a selection, invoke the **Scale** tool from the **Modify** panel. The **Options Bar** displays two radio buttons that can be selected for scaling, Graphical and Numerical.

You can select the **Graphical** radio button from the **Options Bar** to resize an element graphically. On selecting this radio button, you will be prompted to specify three points, first to specify the origin of scaling and the other two to define the scale vectors. Once the origin is specified, move the cursor and click to specify the length of the first vector. Move the cursor and click again to define the length of the second vector. Autodesk Revit Architecture calculates the proportion of the two vectors and resizes the selected element in the same proportion using the specified origin. The temporary dimensions displayed can also be used to resize the element to the desired scaling. For example, if the length of the first vector is 10' and the second vector is 15', the selected element is resized 1.5 times. Figure 5-67 shows a 10' long wall for which the left endpoint has been selected as the origin and the first vector whose length is 7'6". When you specify the length of the second vector as 15', as shown in Figure 5-68, Autodesk Revit Architecture calculates the proportion of the two vectors, 2 in this case, and scales the wall length to 20'.

   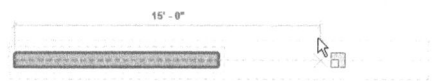

Figure 5-67 Specifying the first vector for resizing the wall segment   *Figure 5-68 Specifying the length of the second vector for resizing the wall segment*

You can select the **Numerical** radio button in the **Options Bar** and specify the numeric value of the scaling in the **Scale** edit box. You then need to specify the origin of the scaling by clicking it. Autodesk Revit Architecture instantly resizes the element by the specified scaling proportion. For example, when you resize a 10' long wall by a numerical factor of 2.5, its length is resized to 25'.

 Tip: *Scaling moves the position of the location line of the walls but it does not change its height or thickness. You can use either the location line or the face of the wall for specifying the origin point.*

USING DIAGNOSTIC TOOLS

Autodesk Revit provides tools to assist you in seeking information about the elements in the project. You can use these tools to measure distances and angles, get information of the element identification, and more.

Measuring Distance Between References and Along an Element

Ribbon: Modify > Measure > Measure drop-down > Measure Between Two References / Measure Along an Element

In this, you can use the measure tools to quickly measure and temporarily display the length (and angle from the horizontal, if applicable) of individual walls or lines that you select in the project view (plan and elevation). The dimensions generated by this tool will remain on the screen until you exit from the current tool or start the next measurement.

Using the Editing Tools

In Revit, you have two measuring tools: **Measure Between Two References** and **Measure Along an Element**. You can invoke the **Measure Between Two References** tool to find out the exact distance between any two points and also the angle of the distance vector with the horizontal. Invoke this tool from the **Measure** panel; you will be prompted to select the start point. Now, move the cursor to the desired point and click; the start point of the line to be measured will be specified. Now, move the cursor towards the second point; a temporary dimension appears between the specified point and the current location of the cursor. Now, click to specify the location of the second point and the end of the line to be measured. A temporary dimension, along with the angular dimension, is created between the two specified points. Notice that in **Options Bar**, the **Total Length** text box displays the running total for the length of the chain, if the **Chain** check box is selected.

For example, Figure 5-69 shows the temporary dimension created when the two diagonal endpoints of a rectangular wall profile are selected. This temporary dimension or the tape measure value remains on the screen until another measurement or tool is invoked.

Figure 5-69 *The temporary dimension displayed using the* **Measure Between Two References** *tool*

You can invoke the **Measure Along an Element** tool to display the length and angle of an element along its axis line. Invoke this tool from the **Measure** panel and then select an element from the drawing; the temporary dimensions will be displayed along the axis of the element.

 Tip: *While using the measure tools, you can use the object snaps to measure the distance accurately. The location line snaps can also be used to get this information.*

Selecting Elements Using the Element ID

In Autodesk Revit, each created element, group or annotation symbol is referred by a unique identification number. Error messages that are displayed refer to an element by its identification number. To display the identification of an element, select it from the drawing and then choose the **IDs of Selection** tool from the **Inquiry** panel of the **Manage** tab. On doing so, the **Element IDs of Selection** dialog box will be displayed, as shown in Figure 5-70. The **Id(s)** text box in this dialog box displays the identification number of the selected element.

You can invoke the **Select by ID** tool from the **Inquiry** panel of the **Manage** tab to identify and select an element by entering its identification number. On invoking this tool, the **Select Elements by ID** dialog box will be displayed, as shown in Figure 5-71. You can enter more than one Id using a ' ,' (comma) between them. Choose the **Show** button to preview the elements with the entered Ids in the drawing. Choose the **OK** button to create a selection of these elements.

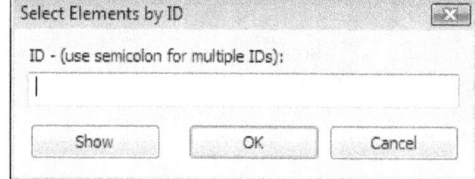

Figure 5-70 The **Id(s)** text box showing the Id of the selected elements

Figure 5-71 The **Select Elements by ID** dialog box

Note
When you select a chain of entities, the controls are displayed at joints and vertices. Select the control at the joint and drag it by pressing and holding the left mouse button. The joint remains intact.

ASSEMBLIES
In revit, you can combine multiple elements to form a single entity called an assembly. The assembly include elements like model elements, annotations, detail items, groups, images, and so on. These assemblies help in identifying, classifying and quantifying the unique element combinations in the model and are used for scheduling, tagging, and filtering.

The assemblies are listed as a type in the Project Browser. You can select the assembly type from the Project Browser and generate one or more types of isolated views of the assembly as well as parts lists, material takeoffs, and sheets. Assemblies can be placed in the project or assembly sheet views.

Creating Assemblies
To create an assembly, first select the elements that you want to include in the assembly; the **Modify|Multi- Select** tab will be displayed. Choose the **Create Assembly** tool from the **Create** panel of the **Modify|Multi-Select** tab; the **New Assembly** dialog box will be displayed. If the assembly includes elements of different categories like walls, doors and windows then the type name will depend on the option selected from the **Naming Category** drop-down list. If the assembly includes elements of same categories, the **Naming Category** drop-down list will be disabled and you can edit the type name in the **Type Name** edit box. Now, choose the **OK** button; the **New Assembly** dialog will be closed and the created assembly will be listed in the **Project Browser**.

Using the Editing Tools 5-41

Editing Assemblies

In Revit, you can add elements, remove elements or can perform edits on the assembly. To edit an assembly, select tit from the drawing area; the **Modify|Assemblies** dialog box will be displayed. In this tab, choose the **Edit Assembly** tool from the **Assembly** panel, you will enter into the editing mode and the floating **Edit Assembly** panel and origin with its planes in the drawing area will be displayed.

The origin determines the orientation of the assembly in relation to the project orientation. The planes of the origin helps in determining the orientation of assembly in the corresponding elevations while creating assembly views. On changing the type of an assembly instance, the origin of the new type is applied to that instance. When you select the assembly origin, the drag controls are displayed. You can use the drag controls to modify the origin.

This floating **Edit Assembly** panel will allow you to add or remove the elements from the drawing area. After adding or removing the desired elements from the assembly, choose the **Finish** button from the floating **Edit Assembly** panel, the created assembly will be modified.

You can remove the created assembly at any time from the project by choosing the **Disassemble** tool from the **Edit Assembly** panel of the **Modify|Assemblies** tab.

Creating Assembly Views and Sheets

You can create the assembly views and sheets for an assembly type. To create the assembly view, select the assembly; the **Modify|Assemblies** contextual tab will be displayed. Now, choose the **Create Views** tool from the **Assembly** panel of the **Modify|Assemblies** tab; the **Create Assembly Views** dialog box will be displayed. In this dialog box, you can set the view scale from the **Scale** drop-down list. You can also set your own scale value. To do so, choose the **Custom** option from the **Scale** drop-down list; the **Scale Value** edit box will be enabled. In the **Scale Value** edit box, you can set the scale value for the view. In the **Views to Create** area of the dialog box, all the check boxes are selected by default. As a result, all the views will be created for the assembly. For the assembly, you can create the schedules as well. To create a schedule, select the check box(es) from the **Schedule** drop-down list. You can include the sheets as well by selecting the required sheet from the **Sheet** drop-down list. You can also load the sheets, if required, by choosing the **Load** option from the **Sheet** drop-down list. Now, choose the **OK** button; the assembly views are created under the **Assembly** head in the **Project Browser**.

TUTORIALS
Tutorial 1   Apartment 1

In this tutorial, you will modify the *c04_Apartment1_tut1.rvt* project file created in Tutorial 1 of Chapter 4. You will copy, move, and mirror the windows to create the project, refer to Figure 5-72. Do not create the dimensions and text as they are given only for reference. Use the following project parameters: **(Expected time: 30 min)**

The following steps are required to complete this tutorial:

a. Open the required file created in Chapter 4.
    For Imperial   *c04_Apartment1_tut1.rvt*
    For Metric   *M_c04_Apartment1_tut1.rvt*
b. Create the window type W5 using the **Window** tool, refer to Figure 5-73.
c. Use the **Copy** tool to create the windows at the desired locations, refer to Figures 5-74 and 5-75.
d. Use the **Group** tool to group the twin windows W3, refer to Figures 5-76 and 5-77.
e. Use the **Mirror** tool to mirror windows, refer to Figures 5-78 and 5-79.

Figure 5-72 Sketch plan of the Apartment1 project

Opening the Project and Creating the Window

You need to open the specified project and add the left side bedroom window using the **Window** tool (see Adding Windows section in Chapter 4).

1. Choose **Open > Project** from the **Application Menu** and open the file created in Tutorial 1 of Chapter 4.
    For Imperial   *c04_Apartment1_tut1.rvt*
    For Metric   *M_c04_Apartment1_tut1.rvt*

    You can also download this file from *http://www.cadcim.com*. The path of the file is as follows: *Textbooks > Civil/GIS > Revit Architecture > Autodesk Revit Architecture 2015 for Architects and Designers.*

2. In the Project Browser, double-click on **Level 1** under the **Floor Plans** head.

Using the Editing Tools 5-43

3. Invoke the **Window** tool from the **Build** panel of the **Architecture** tab. Next, in the **Properties** palette, select the required option from the **Type Selector** drop-down list.
   For Imperial   **Fixed 16"x48"**
   For Metric   **Fixed 406 x 1220mm**

4. Click near the top exterior wall of the bed room to create a window and then modify the temporary dimensions, as shown in Figure 5-73. Press ESC twice to exit the **Window** tool.

Creating a Copy of the Window

Next, you need to copy the window type created in the previous section and then create another window at the specified distance.

1. Select the recently created window from the drawing area by clicking on it. On doing so, the **Modify | Windows** tab is displayed.

2. Invoke the **Copy** tool from the **Modify** panel; the window enclosed in the preview box is displayed, indicating that it has been selected for copying. Ensure that the **Constrain** check box is selected in the **Options Bar**.

Figure 5-73 Modifying dimension to add window to the Apartment 1 project

3. Move the cursor near the midpoint of the window you just created and click to specify the first point of the copy distance when the mid-point snap is displayed, as shown in Figure 5-74.

4. Move the cursor toward the right and type **2'0"(610 mm)** in the edit box displayed. Next, press ENTER; the window is copied at the specified distance, as shown in Figure 5-75. Now, press ESC to exit the **Modify | Windows** tab.

Figure 5-74 Specifying the first point of the copy distance   *Figure 5-75 Specifying the distance at which the copy of the window will be placed*

Grouping Windows

In this section, you will learn to create a group using the **Create Group** tool. Since these windows appear at the same distance at all occurrences in the project, you can group them as a single entity and then create the copies. Use the pick box option for selecting the windows and then use the **Create Group** tool to group them.

1. Using the pick box selection method, select the two windows; the two windows are highlighted, refer to Figure 5-76.

2. Invoke the **Create Group** tool from the **Create** panel of the **Modify | Windows** tab; the **Create Model Group** dialog box is displayed.

3. Specify **2XW3** as the name of the group in the **Name** edit box and choose the **OK** button.

The windows are grouped and a preview box is displayed. Also, the group origin controls are displayed, as shown in Figure 5-77.

Figure 5-76 Selecting the windows by using the pick box selection method   *Figure 5-77 Grouped windows with the group origin controls displayed*

Mirroring and Copying Windows

Now, the twin windows need to be mirrored and copied using the **Mirror - Pick Axis** tool. The sketch plan shows that the twin windows of the bedroom are equidistant from the center of the window tagged 2(W2). You will use this point to create a mirror axis to mirror the windows.

Using the Editing Tools

1. Invoke the **Mirror - Pick Axis** tool from the **Modify** panel in the **Modify | Model Groups** tab. The mirror tools are available because the created group are already selected and highlighted.

2. Move the cursor near the midpoint of the window tagged 2 (W2) until a vertical line is displayed, as shown in Figure 5-78. This line indicates the midpoint and the mirror axis. Click at this location; the windows are mirrored on the other side of the mirror axis, as shown in Figure 5-79.

Figure 5-78 Specifying the mirror axis to mirror the twin windows

Figure 5-79 Windows created after mirroring

Placing Grouped Windows

Next, you need to place the grouped windows on the exterior wall of the living room by dragging and dropping the group in the drawing.

1. In **Project Browser**, click on the '+' sign in the **Groups** node of the **Project Browser** to display the created groups. Click on the '+' sign corresponding to the **Model** sub-node; it displays **2XW3** as the group in the project.

2. To place this group in the project, click on the group name in the **Project Browser** and drag and drop it on the exterior wall of the living room, as shown in Figure 5-80. Click to place the group.

3. Select the placed group, as shown in Figure 5-81, and choose the **Activate Dimensions** button from the **Options Bar**. Click on the left dimension and enter **1'7"(483 mm)**; the group moves to the desired location.

Figure 5-80 Dragging and dropping a group from the **Project Browser**

Figure 5-81 Selecting the group to move to the desired location

4. Create a mirror image of the twin windows using the midpoint of the central window as the mirror axis. The windows are mirrored, as shown in Figure 5-82.

Figure 5-82 Mirrored windows

5. Repeat steps 1, 2, and 3 to place the window group on the upper side of the right exterior wall of the living room. Use the same distance parameter as specified in the sketch plan, refer to Figure 5-72. After placing the window group, create a mirror image of the group using the midpoint of the central window. Use the dimensions shown in Figure 5-72 to specify the exact location of the group. Press ESC to exit the **Modify | Model Groups** tab.

6. Choose **Save As > Project** from **the Application Menu**; the **Save As** dialog box is displayed.

   Enter the required file name in the **File name** edit box.
       For Imperial   **c05_Apartment1_tut1**
       For Metric   **M_c05_Apartment1_tut1**
   Choose the **Save** button; the file gets saved and the **Save As** dialog box is closed.

7. Choose **Close** from **the Application Menu** to close the project file.

Using the Editing Tools 5-47

The completed project will look similar to the project shown in Figure 5-83.

Figure 5-83 *The completed Apartment 1 project*

Tutorial 2 — Club

In this tutorial, you will modify Hall 1 and Lounge of the *Club* project created in Tutorial 2 of Chapter 4. You will move and copy the windows to their desired locations and modify their size and type, refer to Figure 5-84. Do not create the dimensions and text as they are only for reference. Use the following project parameters: **(Expected time: 30 min)**

1. Project File-
   For Imperial   *c04_Club_tut2.rvt*
   For Metric   *M_c04_Club_tut2.rvt*

2. Window types to be used:
   For Imperial   W1- **Fixed 36"x48"**
   For Metric   W1- **Fixed 0915 x 1220 mm**

The following steps are required to complete this tutorial:

a. Open the required file created in Chapter 4.
   For Imperial   *c04_Club_tut2.rvt*
   For Metric   *M_c04_Club_tut2.rvt*
b. Create an array of four windows of Hall 1 by selecting the **Linear** option of the **Array** tool, refer to Figures 5-85 and 5-86.
c. Create an array of windows of the Lounge by selecting the **Radial** option of the **Array** tool, refer to Figures 5-87 to 5-90.
d. Use the **Create Group** tool to group the four windows W1 as a single entity.
e. Use the **Mirror - Pick Axis** and **Mirror - Draw Axis** tools to mirror the grouped windows, refer to Figures 5-91 to 5-94.
f. Use the **Copy** tool to copy the grouped windows, refer to Figures 5-95 and 5-96.

Figure 5-84 Sketch plan for moving and copying the windows in the Club project

Opening an Existing Project and Creating an Array of Windows

In Figure 5-84, notice that the windows of Hall 1 appear in three clusters of four windows each in the sketch plan. The four windows are equidistant, 4'0"(1220 mm) apart. You can create them using the **Linear** option of the **Array** tool. Similarly, to create the four windows of the Lounge, use the **Radial** option.

1. Choose **Open > Project** from **the Application Menu** and open the desired file.
   For Imperial   c04_Club_tut2.rvt
   For Metric   M_c04_Club_tut2.rvt
   You can also download this file from *http://www.cadcim.com*. The path of the file is as follows: *Textbooks > Civil/GIS > Revit Architecture > Autodesk Revit Architecture 2015 for Architects and Designers*

2. Move the cursor on the lower left window tagged 1(W1) of Hall 1 and click to select the window.

3. Invoke the **Array** tool from the **Modify** panel of the **Modify | Windows** tab; the window is enclosed in a dashed rectangular box, indicating that it has been selected for creating an array.

4. In the **Options Bar**, ensure that the **Linear** button is chosen and the **2nd** radio button is selected in the **Move To** area. Also, ensure that the **Constrain** check box is cleared.

5. In the **Number** edit box of the **Options Bar**, enter **4**.

6. Now, move the cursor near the midpoint of the selected window and click when the midpoint object snap is displayed, as shown in Figure 5-85; the start point of the linear array is specified. Ensure that the **Group and Associate** check box is selected.

Using the Editing Tools 5-49

7. Move the cursor upward along the wall incline and enter the value **4'0"(1220 mm)**, as shown in Figure 5-86; a text box with the number of array elements is displayed.

Figure 5-85 Specifying the first point of the array distance

Figure 5-86 Entering the value of the array distance

8. Press ENTER to accept the value; an array is created. Notice that as you move the cursor, a preview box showing the location of the selected elements is displayed.

    Similarly, the windows of the Lounge can be created using the **Radial** option of the **Array**.

9. Move the cursor over the exterior window at the Lounge area tagged 1(W1), and click when it is highlighted; the window is selected.

10. Next, invoke the **Array** tool from the **Modify** panel of the **Modify | Windows** tab.

11. In the **Options Bar**, choose the **Radial** button. Also, ensure the **Group and Associate** check box is selected.

12. Select the **Last** radio button in the **Move to** area of the **Options Bar**. To create three windows, enter the value **3** in the **Number** edit box, if it is not entered by default.

    As the center of the required radial array is the center of the circular wall, you need to move the rotation point to it and then create the radial array.

13. In the **Options Bar**, choose the **Place** button and place the cursor at the center of the curved wall, as shown in Figure 5-87. Alternatively, you can move the cursor near the rotation key of the selected window and drag it to the center of the curved wall.
    Notice that the radial array line now originates from the new center point.

14. Move the cursor near the midpoint of the Lounge window and click when the **Midpoint** object snap is displayed, as shown in Figure 5-88; the start point of the radial array is specified.

Figure 5-87 Rotation key moved to the new rotation point

Figure 5-88 Specifying the first point of the array

15. Move the cursor clockwise along the curved wall and enter **27** as the temporary angular dimension, as given in the sketch plan and shown in Figure 5-89.

16. Next, press ENTER twice to accept the value specified for the angular dimension and the number of array elements; the radial array is created, as shown in Figure 5-90.

17. Choose the **Modify** button from the **Select** panel to exit the current selection.

Figure 5-89 Specifying the array angle

Figure 5-90 Radial array of the selected window

Grouping the Cluster of Windows

The sketch plan shows the cluster of four Hall 1 windows appearing together. Group them for the ease of copying. You can use the **Create Group** tool to group the array of windows.

1. Move the cursor near the four windows of the Hall 1 and select them using the CTRL Key.

2. Invoke the **Create Group** tool from the **Create** panel of the **Modify | Model Groups** tab; the **Create Model Group** dialog box is displayed. The default name of the group of windows in the dialog box is Group 1.

Using the Editing Tools

3. Specify **4XW1- Linear Windows** as the group name in the **Name** edit box.

4. Choose the **OK** button in the dialog box; the windows are grouped and the group name is displayed in the **Groups** node of the **Project Browser** in the **Model** subhead.

Mirroring the Grouped Windows

You need to mirror the grouped windows of Hall 1 and the radial windows of the Lounge using the **Mirror - Pick Axis** and **Mirror - Draw Axis** tools.

1. Move the cursor near the grouped windows of Hall 1 and click; the grouped windows are selected and highlighted, as shown in Figure 5-91.

2. Choose the **Mirror - Pick Axis** tool from the **Modify** panel of the **Modify | Model Groups** tab. Also, ensure that the **Copy** check box is selected in the **Options Bar**.

3. Move the cursor near the interior wall and click when the cursor snaps to the wall centerline; the wall centerline is selected as the mirror axis, as shown in Figure 5-92, and the grouped windows are mirrored to the other end of the exterior wall. Ignore the error that is displayed due to the conflicts between the interior wall and the window. Now, choose the **Modify** button from the **Select** panel or press ESC to exit the current selection.

Figure 5-91 Grouped windows selected and highlighted

Figure 5-92 Using the wall centerline as the mirror axis

Notice that the same window type is also placed on the lower left perpendicular wall. You can use the **Mirror - Draw Axis** tool to mirror the grouped windows to the perpendicular wall.

4. Click on the original grouped windows to select them.

5. Invoke the **Mirror - Draw Axis** tool from the **Modify | Model Groups** tab.

6. In the **Options Bar**, ensure that the **Copy** check box is selected.

7. Move the cursor to the intersection of the two perpendicular walls and click when the endpoint object snap is displayed; the first point of the mirror line is specified.

8. Move the cursor horizontally and click when the dashed line is displayed, as shown in Figure 5-93; the second point of the mirror axis is specified. Now, choose the **Modify** button from the **Select** panel to exit from the current selection.

9. The grouped windows are mirrored to the perpendicular wall, as shown in Figure 5-94. Similarly, mirror the three radial windows of the Lounge to the other side of the door using the **Mirror - Draw Axis** tool. Draw the vertical axis from the center of the curved wall as the mirror axis.

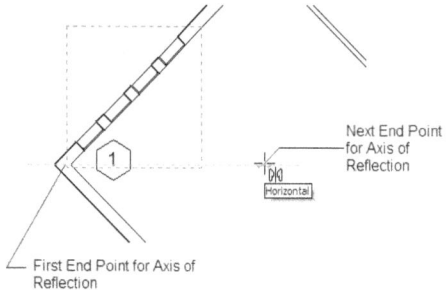

Figure 5-93 *Using the horizontal axis as the mirror reference line*

Figure 5-94 *Mirrored windows on the perpendicular wall*

Copying the Grouped Windows

You can use the **Copy** tool to copy the grouped windows of Hall 1.

1. Select the original grouped window of Hall 1.

2. Invoke the **Copy** tool from the **Modify | Model Groups** tab.

3. Select the group origin or the midpoint of the grouped windows as the start point of the copy distance.

4. Move the cursor upward along the external wall and choose the endpoint of the central internal wall as the second point of the copy distance, as shown in Figure 5-95. On doing so, the grouped window is copied at the desired location, as shown in Figure 5-96.

Using the Editing Tools   5-53

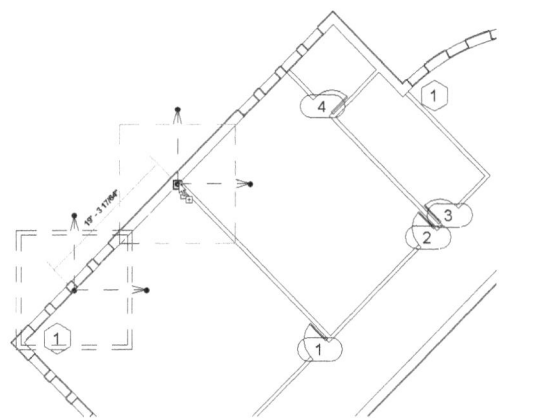

Figure 5-95 *Specifying the start and end*   *Figure 5-96* *Grouped windows copied*
points of the copy distance

5. Choose **Save As > Project** from **the Application Menu**; the **Save As** dialog box is displayed.
   Enter the required file in the **File name** edit box
       For Imperial   **c05_Club_tut2**
       For Metric   **M_c05_Club_tut2**
   Choose **Save**; the file is saved and the dialog box gets closed.

6. Choose **Close** from **the Application Menu** to close the project file.

   This completes Tutorial 2 for adding windows to the Club project.

Tutorial 3   Office-Assembly Views

In this tutorial, you will modify *Office* project. You will create, move, and copy the doors and windows to their desired locations and also create assembly of the stacked wall. Do not create the dimensions and text as they are only for reference. Use the following project parameters: **(Expected time: 30 min)**

1. Project File:
       For Imperial   *c03_Office_tut5.rvt*
       For Metric   *M_c03_Office_tut5.rvt*

2. Door types to be used:
       For Imperial   **Sliding-2 panel 72" x 84"**
                            Single-Glass 1 36" x 84"
       For Metric   **M_Sliding-2 panel 1830 x 2134 mm**
                            M_Single-Glass 1 0762 x 2134 mm

3. Window types to be used:
       For Imperial   W1- **Awning with Trim 36"x48"**
       For Metric   W1- **Awning with Trim 0915 x 1220 mm**

The following steps are required to complete this tutorial:

a. Open the required file.
   For Imperial   c03_Office_tut5.rvt
   For Metric   M_c03_Office_tut5.rvt

b. Add doors and windows to the project.
c. Copy and mirror windows.
d. Create assembly using the **Create Assembly** tool.

Figure 5-97 Sketch plan for adding and copying the doors and windows in the Office project

Opening the Project

In this section, you will open the existing project and also add the doors and windows to the *Office* project.

1. Choose **Open > Project** from **the Application Menu** and open the desired file.
   For Imperial   c03_Office_tut5.rvt
   For Metric   M_c03_Office_tut5.rvt
   You can also download this file from *http://www.cadcim.com*. The path of the file is as follows:
   Textbooks > Civil/GIS > Revit Architecture > Autodesk Revit Architecture 2015 for Architects and Designers

2. Double-click on **Level 1** under the **Floor Plans** head in the **Project Browser**; the floor plan view is displayed.

Using the Editing Tools

Adding Doors and Windows

In this section, you will add doors and copy and array the windows to the *Office* project.

1. Invoke the **Door** tool from the **Build** panel of the **Architecture** tab; the **Modify | Place Door** tab is displayed.

2. In this tab, choose the **Load Family** tool from the **Mode** panel; the **Load Family** dialog box is displayed.

3. Load the **Sliding-2 panel** and **Single Glass 1** door types from the **US Imperial > Doors** folder (**US Metric > Doors** folder for Metric); the loaded types are displayed in the **Type-Selector** drop-down list.

4. Select the required door type from the **Type-Selector** drop-down list.
   For Imperial   **Sliding-2 panel 72" x 82"**
   For Metric   **M_Sliding-2 panel 1830 x 2134 mm**

5. Now, place the door at the entrance, as shown in Figure 5-98.

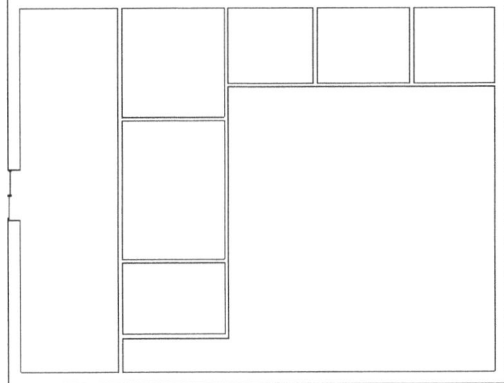

Figure 5-98 Entrance door placed

6. Select the desired door type from the **Type Selector** drop-down list.
   For Imperial   **Single Glass 1 36" x 84"**
   For Metric   **Single Glass 1 0762 x 2134 mm**

7. Place the doors, as shown in Figure 5-99.

Figure 5-99 Other doors in the building

8. Invoke the **Window** tool from the **Build** panel of the **Architecture** tab; the **Modify | Place Windows** tab is displayed.

9. Repeat the procedure followed in steps 2 and 3 and load the **Awning with Trim** window type from **US Imperial > Windows** folder for Imperial (**US Metric > Windows** folder for Metric).

10. Place the windows, as shown in Figure 5-100.

Figure 5-100 Windows are placed at a specified distance

11. Press ESC twice to exit the current selection tool.

Copying and Mirroring Windows

Here, you will copy and mirror the windows.

1. Choose the windows that you want to copy; the **Modify|Windows** tab is displayed.

2. Invoke the **Copy** tool from the **Modify** panel of the **Modify | Windows** tab; the window is enclosed in a dashed rectangular box, indicating that it has been selected for creating an array.

3. In the **Options Bar**, ensure that the **Multiple** check box is selected. Also, ensure that the **Constrain** check box is cleared.

4. Now, move the cursor near the midpoint of the selected window and click when the midpoint object snap is displayed; the start point of the copy is specified.

5. Move the cursor left along the wall and enter value **5'0" (524 mm)**, as shown in Figure 5-101 and then press ENTER.

Figure 5-101 Entering the value 5' in the edit box

6. Press ENTER to accept the value; a copy of the window is created. Notice that as you move the cursor, a preview box showing the location of the selected elements is displayed.

7. Repeat the procedure followed in steps 5 and 6 to place other windows, refer to Figure 5-102.

Figure 5-102 *Two other windows placed*

8. Select all the windows using the CTRL key; the windows get highlighted in blue and the **Modify| Windows** tab is displayed.

9. Now, choose the **Mirror-Pick Axis** tool from the **Modify** panel of the **Modify| Windows** tab.

10. Pick the axis when it gets highlighted in blue then click, refer to Figure 5-103; the windows are mirrored.

Figure 5-103 *Picking the axis of wall to mirror windows*

Using the Editing Tools   5-59

Creating Assemblies

Now, you will first create assemblies and then the views within that assembly.

1. Select the entire model which you have created; the **Modify| Multi-Select** tab is displayed.

2. In this tab, choose the **Filter** tool from the **Selection** panel; the **Filter** dialog box is displayed.

3. In this dialog box, choose the **Check None** button; all the check boxes are cleared.

4. Now, select the **Walls** check box and choose the **OK** button; the wall is highlighted in blue.

5. Choose the **Create Assembly** tool from the **Create** panel of the **Modify|Multi-Select** tab; the **New Assembly** dialog box is displayed.

6. In this dialog box, enter **Wall Assembly** in the **Type Name** edit box and choose the **OK** button; the assembly is created with the name **Wall Assembly** under the **Assemblies** head in the **Project Browser**.

7. Now, select the assembly from the drawing area, as shown in Figure 5-104; the **Modify|Assemblies** tab is displayed.

Figure 5-104 Selecting the assembly

8. Choose the **Create Views** tool from the **Assembly** panel of the **Modify|Assemblies** tab; the **Create Assembly Views** dialog box is displayed.

9. In this dialog box, ensure that all the check boxes are selected and then select the **Wall Schedule** check box from the **Schedule** drop-down list.

10. Select the **Load** option from the **Sheet** drop-down list; the **Load Family** dialog box is displayed.

11. In this dialog box, select the required titleblock from the **US Imperial > Titleblocks** folder for Imperial (**US Metric > Titleblocks** folder for Metric).
    For Imperial   **C 17 x 22 Horizontal**
    For Metric   **A2 Metric**

12. Choose the **Open** button; the sheet is loaded in the **Sheet** drop-down list.

13. Choose the **OK** button; the assembly views are displayed under the **Wall Assembly** head in the **Project Browser** and the view in the drawing area is changed.

14. Double-click on the **Detail View: Plan Detail** under the **Wall Assembly** head in the **Project Browser**; the plan detail view is displayed.

15. In the **Properties** palette, select the required option from the **View Scale** drop-down list.
    For Imperial   **3/32" = 1'-0"**
    For Metric   **1:100**

16. Double-click on **Sheet: A101 - Sheet** in the **Project Browser**; the sheet view is displayed.

17. Select **Detail View: Plan Detail** from the **Wall Assembly** head in the **Project Browser** and then drag it to the drawing area and place the view, as shown in Figure 5-105.

Figure 5-105 The *Detail View: Plan Detail* view placed on the sheet

Using the Editing Tools 5-61

18. Repeat the procedure followed in step 17 and place the **Schedule: Material Takeoff**, **Schedule: Part List 1** and **Schedule: Wall Schedule** views in the sheet view, as shown in Figure 5-106.

   After placing the schedule in the sheet, adjust the view by using the controls of schedule.

Figure 5-106 All assembly views arranged in sheet

19. Choose **Save As > Project** from the **Application Menu**; the **Save As** dialog box is displayed. Specify the file name in the **File name** edit box;
   For Imperial   **c05_Office_tut3**
   For Metric   **M_c05_Office_tut3**
   Choose **Save**; the file is saved and the dialog box is closed.

20. Choose **Close** from the **Application Menu** to close the project file.

Self-Evaluation Test

Answer the following questions and then compare them to those given at the end of this chapter:

1. If a pick box is defined by dragging the cursor from left to right, the elements that are entirely enclosed in it are selected. (T/F)

2. After highlighting one element, you can press the CTRL key to select a chain of walls joined with each other. (T/F)

3. You can create multiple copies of an element by using the **Move** tool. (T/F)

4. You can rotate elements only in the plan view. (T/F)

5. When you mirror walls, the inserted elements such as doors and windows are also mirrored. (T/F)

6. While using the **Offset** tool, you can select the _____ radio button to create an offset at a specified distance.

7. You can break a wall into a number of segments using the _____ tool.

8. Using the _____ tool, you can group a number of elements as a single entity.

9. You can use the _____ tool to measure the distance between any two points in a drawing window.

10. The _____ tool is used to copy the properties of a source element and transfer them to another element of the same family.

11. Which of the following panel contains the Create Views tool?

    a) **Assembly**   b) **Modify**
    c) **Create**   d) **Geometry**

Review Questions

Answer the following questions:

1. You can save groups and use them in other Autodesk Revit Architecture projects. (T/F)

2. Once an element is locked, it is not possible to move it without removing the lock constraint. (T/F)

3. In Autodesk Revit, you cannot create nested groups. (T/F)

4. You cannot modify the number of items in a radial array after they have been created. (T/F)

5. While rotating an element, you can move the center of rotation by dragging it to the desired location. (T/F)

6. Using the **Trim/Extend Multiple Elements** tool, you can trim or extend multiple elements. (T/F)

Using the Editing Tools

7. The **Filter** tool is used to restore the selection of elements. (T/F)

8. Which of the following tools is used to create copies of the selected elements?

    a) **Match**   b) **Array**
    c) **Lock**   d) **Group**

9. Which of the following keys should be kept pressed while adding elements to a selection?

    a) TAB   b) SHIFT
    c) CTRL   d) ESC

10. Which of the following tools can be used to restrict or lock the position of an element?

    a) **Align**   b) **Place Similar**
    c) **Copy**   d) **Pin Position**

11. Which of the following tab provide the **Select by ID** tool?

    a) **Insert**   b) **Modify**
    c) **View**   d) **Manage**

Exercises

Exercise 1   Apartment 2

Add windows to the exterior wall of the dining area of the *Apartment 2* project created in Exercise 1 of Chapter 4 based on Figure 5-107. The dimensions and text are given only for reference and need to be created. The parameters to be used for the project are given next.

(Expected time: 30 min)

1. Project-
    For Imperial   *c04_Apartment2_ex1.rvt*
    For Metric   *M_c04_Apartment2_ex1.rvt*
2. Window type to be added in the dining area-
    For Imperial   **Fixed: 24"X48"**
    For Metric   **Fixed: 0610 x 1220 mm**
3. Name of the file to be saved-
    For Imperial   **c05_Apartment2_ex1**
    For Metric   **M_c05_Apartment2_ex1**

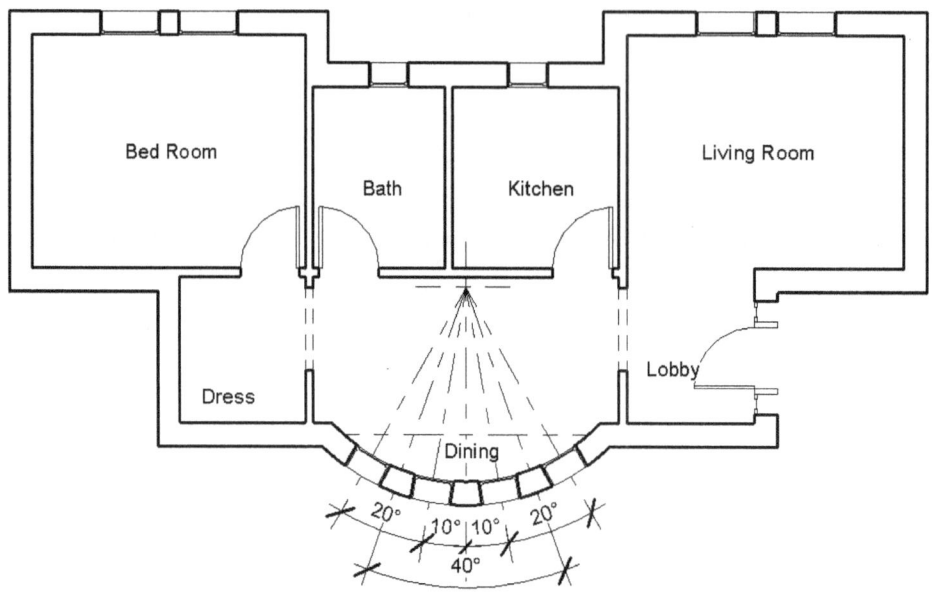

Figure 5-107 Sketch plan for adding windows to the Apartment 2 project

Exercise 2   Club

Add windows, as shown in Figure 5-108, to the Hall 2 of the *Club* project created in Tutorial 2 of this chapter. The dimensions and text have been given for reference and need not be created.   **(Expected time: 30 min)**

1. Project File-
   - For Imperial   *c04_Club_ex3*
   - For Metric   *M_c04_Club_ex3*
2. Window types to be used -
   - For Imperial   W1- **Fixed: 36" X 48"**
   - For Metric   W1- **Fixed: 0910 X 1220 mm**
3. Name of the file to be saved -
   - For Imperial   **c05_Club_ex2**
   - For Metric   **M_c05_Club_ex2**

Using the Editing Tools

Figure 5-108 Sketch plan for adding windows to Hall 2 of the Club project

Exercise 3   Elevator and Stair Lobby

Create windows for the *Elevator and Stair Lobby* project created in Exercise 2 of Chapter 4, based on Figure 5-109. The dimensions and text have been given for reference and are not to be created. The parameters to be used for the elements are given next.

(Expected time: 15 min)

1. Project -
   - For Imperial   c04_ElevatorandStairLobby_ex2.rvt
   - For Metric   M_c04_ElevatorandStairLobby_ex2.rvt
2. Window type to be used:
   - For Imperial   W2- **Fixed 24" X 48"**
   - For Metric   W2- **Fixed 0610 X 1220 mm**
3. Name of the file to be saved-
   - For Imperial   **c05_ElevatorandStairLobby_ex3**
   - For Metric   **M_c05_ElevatorandStairLobby_ex3**

Figure 5-109 Sketch plan for adding and creating windows for the Elevator and Stair Lobby project

Exercise 4   Office

Create the profile of an office building by using the tools learnt in this chapter. The exterior wall profile of the building is shown in Figure 5-110. The dimensions are given only for reference and need not be created. The parameters to be used for various elements are given next.

(Expected time: 15 min)

1. Project Name to be given-
   - For Imperial **c05_Office_ex4**
   - For Metric **M_c05_Office_ex4**
2. Template file-
   - For Imperial *Construction-Default*
   - For Metric *Construction-DefaultMetric*
3. Exterior wall type-
   - For Imperial **Basic Wall: Exterior - Brick on Mtl.Stud**
   - For Metric **Basic Wall: Exterior - Brick on Mtl.Stud**
4. Unconnected height of walls-
   - For Imperial **12'0"**
   - For Metric **3658 mm**
5. All inclined walls are at an angle of 45-degree to the horizontal axis.

Figure 5-110 Sketch plan of the exterior wall profile of the office building

Answers to Self-Evaluation Test

1. T, **2.** F, **3.** F, **4.** F, **5.** T, **6.** Numerical, **7.** Split Element, **8.** Create Group, **9.** Measure Between Two References, **10.** Match Type Properties

Chapter 6

Working with Datum Plane and Creating Standard Views

Learning Objectives

After completing this chapter, you will be able to:
• *Understand the concept of levels.*
• *Create multiple levels in a project.*
• *Understand the concept of using grids in a project.*
• *Create rectangular and circular grids in a project file.*
• *Use the Work Plane and Reference Plane tools in a project.*
• *Create a plan view in a project.*
• *Create and understand the usage of elevation view.*
• *Create section views and modify their properties.*
• *Use the Scope Box tool.*

INTRODUCTION

In the previous chapters, you learned to use editing tools to create groups and modify their properties in a project. In this chapter, you will learn to add datum elements and the procedure to create standard views in an architectural project. Datum elements, the non-physical elements, form the basic framework in a project. These datum elements include levels, reference planes, and grids. Depending on the complexity of a project, you can use some or all of these components to systematize and provide a reference to a building model. These elements are also used for editing a project and creating schedules, and other reference documentation for a project.

In Autodesk Revit, a standard view can be created and displayed with relative ease. Creating standard views in a project not only help in its presentation but also assist in creating and editing various building and stand-alone elements of a project.

WORKING WITH LEVELS

For a multistory building project, you need to specify floor levels within the building volume. Each floor level or story can contain a different set of building components. Levels, in a typical multistory building, may be understood as infinite horizontal planes that define each story. Autodesk Revit Architecture uses levels as references for level-hosted elements such as floor, roof, and ceiling. The distance between levels can be used to define the story-height of a building model, as shown in Figure 6-1. Autodesk Revit Architecture also provides flexibility to create a non-story level or a reference level such as sill level, parapet level, and so on. For example, a multistory office building may have different story heights for each floor. Building components such as exterior walls, windows, doors, and furniture may also differ on each floor. You can create levels based on the story height of a building. You can then create various building elements on each level such as an entrance door on the first floor level, bay windows on the second floor level, an elevator room on the roof level, and so on.

Figure 6-1 Levels displayed in a multistory building project

Working with Datum Plane and Creating Standard Views

When you use the default template file for creating a new project file, it loads two predefined levels, **Level 1** and **Level 2**, which are displayed in the elevation view or section view. You can view any of the elevation or section views using the **Project Browser**. Levels can be added, renamed, and modified at any time during the project development.

Tip: *In the conceptual design environment, the levels are displayed in 3D views. If you select a level in 3D view, the elevation and the name of the level will be displayed in the drawing area.*

Understanding Level Properties

A typical level is represented by a level line, level bubble, level name, level elevation, and so on, refer to Figure 6-2. Using these parameters and controls, you can modify the appearance of a level. The level name is a modifiable parameter that is used to refer to each level. The level elevation is the distance of the level from the base level. The visibility of the level bubble on either side of the level line can be controlled by using the bubble display control. The length alignment control can be used to align levels lines. Autodesk Revit provides the 2D or 3D extents control for datums when they are selected. This enables you to change their extents in one or multiple views in which they are visible. When a datum is in the 3D mode, any modifications made in the 3D view will be propagated in all views of a building model. On the other hand, the 2D mode can be used to modify a datum in a specific view, thereby making it view-specific.

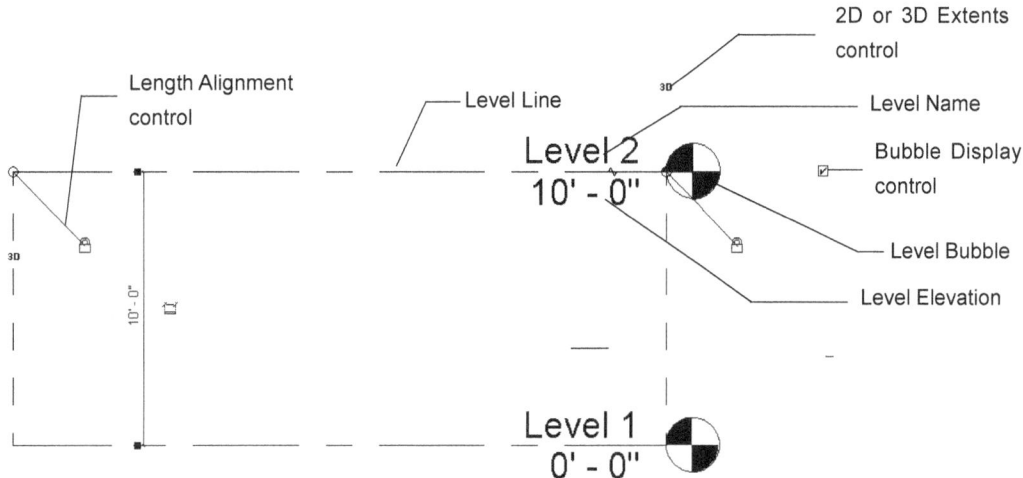

Figure 6-2 Various levels defined in the default template file

Note
A 3d extents of revit helps in modifying the levels in all views whereas a 2d extent helps in modifying a level in the current view.

Like other building elements used in an Autodesk Revit Architecture project, levels also have associated types and instance properties. You can view and modify the instance properties of a level in the **Properties** palette, refer to Figure 6-3. You can also use the **Properties** palette to view and modify the type properties of the selected level. To do so, choose the **Edit Type** button in the **Properties** palette; the **Type Properties** dialog box will be displayed, as shown in Figure 6-4. You can use this dialog box to modify and view the type properties of the selected level from the drawing.

*Figure 6-3 The **Properties** palette for a level*

*Figure 6-4 Partial view of the **Type Properties** dialog box for a typical level*

Level Type Properties

The type properties of a level can be viewed and modified in the **Type Properties** dialog box of a level. When you change the type properties of a level, all its instances are also modified.

Working with Datum Plane and Creating Standard Views 6-5

In the **Type Properties** dialog box of a level, you can modify the value of a parameter by clicking in its corresponding **Value** field and selecting a new value from the drop-down list or entering a new value in the field. Different level type properties are described in the table given next.

Parameter Name	Value and Description
Elevation Base	Describes the elevation base value with respect to the project or the shared origin.
Line Weight	Specifies the weight of the line defining the level. It can be specified by clicking in its value field and selecting a desired option from the drop-down list displayed.
Color	Specifies to the color of the level line. The default color selected is black. You can select other colors from the displayed **Color** dialog box which appears on clicking in the value field corresponding to this parameter.
Line Pattern	Used to set the linetype of the level line.
Symbol	Specifies the symbol indicating the level and can be chosen from the drop-down list. The **None** option can be specified if the level head is not required.
Symbol at End 1 Default	Check box is selected if a bubble is required at the left end of the level line.
Symbol at End 2 Default	Check box is selected if a bubble is required at the right end of the level line.

Level Instance Properties

When you change the instance properties of a level, the properties of only the selected instance are changed. The different level instance properties are described in the following table:

Parameter Name	Value and Description
Elevation	Specifies the vertical height of the level from the elevation base.
Story Above	Specifies the next building story for the level.
Computation Height	Specifies the computation height for a level. This value is used to compute the area, perimeter, and volume of a room.
Name	Specifies the name assigned to the level. You can enter any name based on the project requirement.

Structural	By default, the check box corresponding to this parameter is cleared. You can select the check box to define the level as structural. For example, the level defined for the top of a foundation can be a structural level.
Building Story	By default, the check box corresponding to this parameter is selected. As a result, you can define a level as a functional story or a floor in the project.
Scope Box	Specifies the scope box assigned to the level that controls its visibility in different views.

Adding Levels

Ribbon: Architecture > Datum > Level
Shortcut Key: LL

In Autodesk Revit Architecture, you can create multiple levels based on your project requirements. Note that the **Level** tool remains inactive in the **Datum** panel for all the plan views. The **Level** tool will only be active in an elevation or a section view. To create a level, invoke the **Level** tool from the **Datum** panel, as shown in Figure 6-5; the **Modify | Place Level** tab will be displayed. In this tab, choose any of the sketching options displayed in the **Draw** panel to create levels in your project. You can also invoke the **Level** tool by typing **LL**. In the **Modify | Place Level** tab, you can select a type of level from the **Type Selector** drop-down list to modify an existing level. This drop-down list has two types of levels, **Level: 1/4" Head** and **Level: No Head**. To make the level head visible, select the **Level: 1/4" Head** option. Else, select the **Level: No Head** option.

Figure 6-5 Choosing the **Level** tool from the **Datum** panel of the **Architecture** tab

In the **Draw** panel of the **Modify | Place Level** tab, you can use the **Line** (default selection) or **Pick Lines** tool to sketch a level line. In the **Options Bar**, the **Make Plan View** check box is selected by default. As a result, when you will add a level in a project view, its associated plan view/s will be created. To specify the associated view/s to the level, choose the **Plan View Types** button displayed next to the **Make Plan View** check box; the **Plan View Types** dialog box will be displayed. In the **Select view types to create** area of this dialog box, three associated views will be displayed namely, **Ceiling Plan**, **Floor Plan** and **Structural Plan**. All three views are selected by default. You can select any one of them or all options from the **Select view types to create** area and then choose **OK** to close the dialog box; the selected view/s will be associated with the level. Alternatively, if you clear the **Make Plan View** check box, the associated views

Working with Datum Plane and Creating Standard Views 6-7

will not be created. The **Offset** edit box in the **Options Bar** can be used to add a level at a specified distance from the selected point or element.

To add a level, invoke the **Level** tool and move the cursor near the existing levels. On doing so, the temporary dimensions are displayed, indicating the perpendicular distance between the nearest level and the cursor. To add a level at the specified distance from the existing level, specify the perpendicular distance value, as shown in Figure 6-6.

To sketch a level line, specify its start point and endpoint. The level elevation and the start point will be specified simultaneously. Click to specify the first point and move the cursor to the left or the right. You will notice that the level line, level name, and elevation appear and move with the cursor. On moving the cursor above the endpoint of the existing level line, a dashed alignment line will appear, indicating its alignment with the existing level, as shown in Figure 6-7. When the alignment line appears, click to specify the endpoint of the level line. You can also enter the elevation of the level by entering the value before specifying the start point.

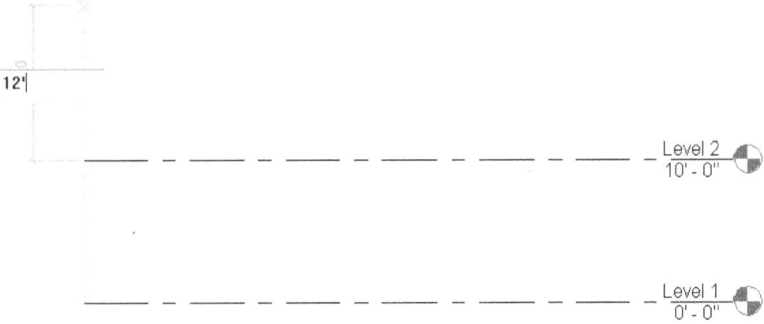

Figure 6-6 Specifying the distance of the new level from an existing level

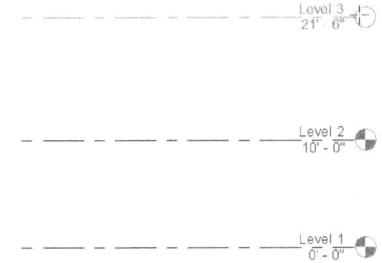

Figure 6-7 Using the alignment line to specify the endpoint of the level line

Note
Although you are required to specify the start point and the endpoint of the level lines, the levels corresponding to these lines are infinite horizontal planes. The placement of the level line can, however, be useful in the elevation and section views.

When you select a recently added level, it is highlighted and displays two square boxes, on the either side of the level, as shown in Figure 6-8. These boxes are used to control the visibility of the level bubble. They can be selected or cleared to make the bubble visible or invisible, respectively, at the desired side(s). The two small circles representing the drag controls for the level line can be used to increase or decrease its length by dragging. The padlocks act as the length alignment control for the alignment of all the level lines. When locked, the length of all the level lines is increased or decreased simultaneously. To modify the length of a single level line, unlock the control and then modify its length.

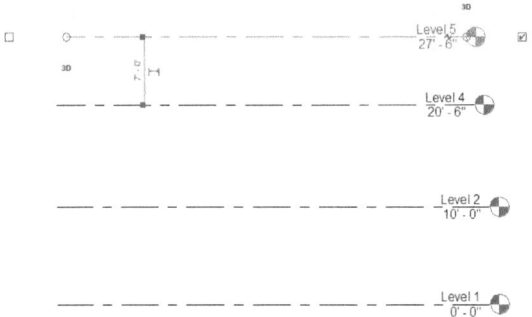

Figure 6-8 *The highlighted level with its constraints and controls*

Modifying Level Parameters

You can change a level type by selecting the level from the drawing and then selecting a different level type from the **Type Selector** drop-down list in the **Properties** palette. On doing so, the current level will be modified into the selected level. You can specify the properties of a level using the **Properties** palette before adding it. Some of the parameters of the level can also be modified by clicking on the level in the drawing window and entering the new value.

For example, after selecting a level, you can click on its name and assign a new name to it. As you start typing the new name, an edit box appears, with the new value, as shown in Figure 6-9. Also, Autodesk Revit prompts you to specify whether you want to rename all the associated views such as the floor plan, ceiling plan, and so on. If you choose to rename the views, the name of the associated views will change in the **Project Browser**. Similarly, you can modify the elevation of a level by selecting it and entering the new temporary dimension value, as shown in Figure 6-10. When you enter the new value, the level automatically moves to the specified elevation.

Working with Datum Plane and Creating Standard Views 6-9

Figure 6-9 Editing the name of the level   *Figure 6-10* Modifying the level elevation

 Tip: *It is recommended that you name the levels based on the floor such as first floor, second floor, roof, and so on. This helps in referring to their corresponding plan views and also helps in editing level hosted elements. The names assigned to the levels are also reflected in the schedules created for the project.*

You can also move levels by simply dragging them to the desired location. Click to select a level and drag the level(s) to the desired location. As you drag, the elevation level changes dynamically with respect to the cursor location. Hold the SHIFT key to move the level only in vertical direction. Next, release the mouse button at the appropriate location to complete the dragging process.

 Tip: *In addition to the level heads already loaded in Revit, you can load level heads from the **US Imperial > Annotations** folder path.*

When you move the cursor near a level, it will be highlighted. Right-click on the highlighted level line; a shortcut menu will be displayed with various options. You can choose the **Go to Floor Plan** option from the shortcut menu to open the corresponding floor plan for the level. On choosing the **Find Referring Views** option from the shortcut menu, the **Go To View** dialog box will be displayed. In this dialog box, select the desired view from the list of views and then choose the **Open View** button; the view in which the selected level is visible will be displayed.

 Tip: *When you select a level, its distance from the adjacent levels is displayed. Click on the corresponding temporary dimension and enter the new value to move the level to the new location.*

For certain levels, you may want to move the level bubble to a different location. When you select a level, you will notice that a break control appears below its name, next to the level bubble. This break control can be used to break the level line and move the level bubble away

from it. On clicking this control, you will observe that the level name and the level bubble are also moved to the new location and an extension line is created, as shown in Figure 6-11. You can then use the blue dots to place the level bubble at the appropriate location.

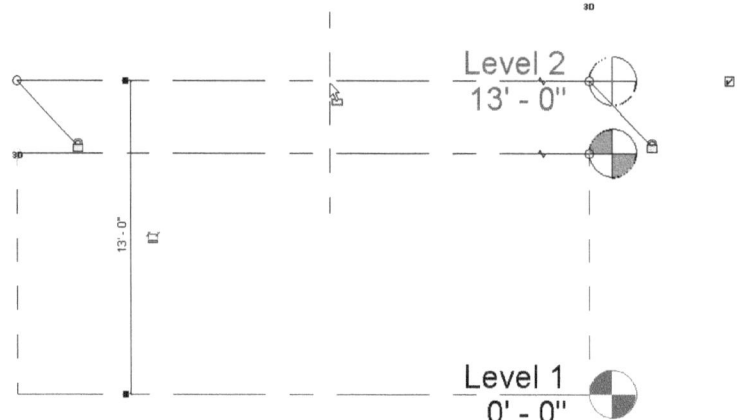

Figure 6-11 Moving the level to a different location

Tip: *To view the floor plan of a level, you can move the cursor over the bubble and double-click. As a result, the corresponding floor plan view will be displayed in the viewing area.*

HIDING ELEMENTS IN A VIEW

Revit allows you to hide elements and their categories, including annotations. You can also restore the visibility of hidden elements.

To hide an element in a view, select the view in which you want to hide a particular element or a category, select the element in the drawing, and then right-click to display a shortcut menu. In the shortcut menu, choose **Hide in View > Elements / Category** to hide an element or a category in the current view.

To restore the visibility of a hidden element or a category, choose the **Reveal Hidden Elements** button from the **View Control Bar**; the screen will enter the **Reveal Hidden Elements** mode with a magenta boundary and also a new panel **Reveal Hidden Elements** will be displayed in the ribbon. All hidden elements inside the magenta boundary will be displayed in magenta color. Select a hidden element and then choose the **Unhide Element** button from the **Reveal Hidden Elements** panel to restore the visibility of hidden element. Now, choose the **Toggle Reveal Hidden Elements Mode** button in the **Reveal Hidden Elements** panel to exit the **Reveal Hidden Elements** mode. Another method to restore the visibility of the hidden element (s) is to select the element(s) in the **Reveal Hidden Elements** mode and then right-click; a shortcut menu will be displayed. Choose **Unhide in View > Elements / Category** from the shortcut menu to restore the visibility of the hidden elements.

Tip: *After selecting the element (s) or a category in the **Reveal Hidden Elements** mode, you can type EU or VU to unhide the element (s) or the category in the current view.*

Working with Datum Plane and Creating Standard Views

Controlling the Visibility of Levels

You can control the visibility of one level or all levels in any of the project views. When you select a level and right-click, a shortcut menu is displayed, as shown in Figure 6-12. Choose **Hide in View > Category** from the shortcut menu; the level category will be hidden in the current view. To hide a particular level, choose **Hide in View > Elements** from the shortcut menu; only the selected level will be hidden in the current view. The level will, however, be displayed in all other views.

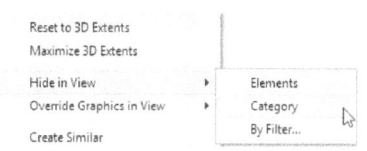

Figure 6-12 *Partial view of the shortcut menu displayed on selecting the level*

To hide all the levels in a project view, select any of the level in the project view. Next, choose the **Override by Category** tool from the **Modify| Levels > View > Override Graphics in View** drop-down; **the View Specific Category Graphics** dialog box will be displayed. Clear the **Visible** check box in this dialog box and choose **OK**; all levels will be hidden from the current view. You can use the **Scope Boxes** feature to control the visibility of levels. You will learn about this feature later in this chapter.

Tip: *After selecting the element, you can type EH or VH to hide an element or a category in the current view.*

WORKING WITH GRIDS

Ribbon: Architecture > Datum > Grid
Shortcut Key: GR

 Autodesk Revit provides you the option of creating rectangular or circular grids for your projects. Using these grids, you cannot only create building profiles easily but also place the structural elements at the specific locations and intersections.

Creating Grids

You can create the grid patterns based on the project requirements. Grid patterns can be rectangular or radial, depending on the project geometry. A rectangular grid pattern can be created using straight grid lines, whereas a radial grid pattern can be formed using arc grids. The created grids are visible in all plan, elevation, and section views.

To create a grid line, invoke the **Grid** tool from the **Datum** panel of the **Architecture** tab, as shown in Figure 6-13; the **Modify | Place Grid** tab and the **Properties** palette with the properties of grids will be displayed. The **Modify | Place Grid** tab, as shown in Figure 6-14, displays various options to draw and modify grids in a drawing. The **Draw** panel in this tab displays various tools to draw grids as lines and curves or to convert existing model lines into grids. In this **Properties** palette, you can modify the type and instance properties of the grid, before or after creating it. You can also change the type of grid by selecting a grid type from the **Type Selector** drop-down list.

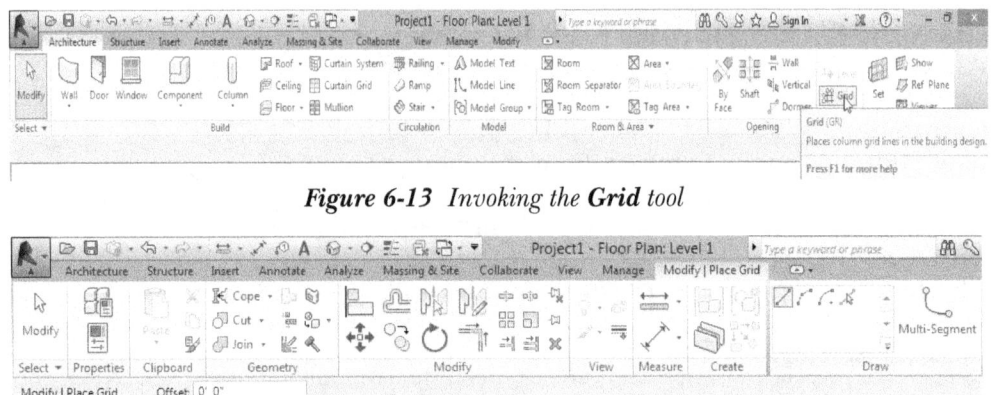

Figure 6-13 Invoking the **Grid** tool

Figure 6-14 Various options in the **Modify / Place Grid** tab

Creating Grids Using the Draw Tools

To create a straight grid line, select any floor plan view from the **Project Browser** and then choose the **Grid** tool from the **Datum** panel in the **Architecture** tab; the **Modify | Place Grid** tab will be displayed. The **Line** tool in the **Draw** panel is chosen by default. As a result, you can start sketching the grid line by clicking at the appropriate location to specify the start point and then moving the cursor to the desired direction. As you move the cursor, you will notice that a grid line is created with one end fixed at the specified point and the other end attached to the cursor. A temporary angular dimension indicating the angle of the line with the horizontal axis is also displayed, refer to Figure 6-15. Click to specify the endpoint of the grid line when the appropriate angular dimension is displayed. You can also sketch an arbitrary inclined grid line and then click on the angular dimension to enter a new value of the angle. To draw orthogonal grids, hold the SHIFT key and restrain the movement of the cursor to the horizontal and vertical axes. When you click to specify the endpoint, a grid is created and its controls are highlighted, as shown in Figure 6-16. The recently added grid is highlighted and it displays one square box on either side. These boxes are used to control the visibility of the grid bubble. They can be checked or cleared to make the grid bubble visible or invisible at the desired side(s). The two circles, one on the either corner, can be dragged to extend or reduce the extents of the grid line.

Figure 6-15 Sketching a grid line

Figure 6-16 A horizontal grid line with its controls

Working with Datum Plane and Creating Standard Views

Similarly, when you sketch a new grid line near an existing one, a temporary dimension indicating the distance between the two grid lines is displayed. You can enter the value of distance in the displayed edit box, refer to Figure 6-17. Alternatively, you can move the cursor to the desired distance using the temporary dimensions. Once this is done, click to specify the start point of the second grid line, Move the cursor horizontally to the right and when the alignment line appears, click to specify the endpoint of the grid line; the second grid line is created. Notice that the name of this grid is 2. Autodesk Revit automatically numbers the grid lines as they are created.

Figure 6-17 Specifying the distance of the second grid line

Similarly, you can draw other parallel grid lines as well. These lines will be numbered automatically as you draw them, as shown in Figure 6-18. The **Offset** edit box in the **Options Bar** can be used to create a grid line that starts at a specified offset distance from a point defined on an existing element. The offset distance can be specified in the edit box in **Options Bar**. The shape of the resulting grid line depends on the selected sketching tool.

To create vertical grid lines, specify the start point above the first grid line. Now, move the cursor vertically downward and click below the last horizontal grid line to specify the endpoint. The procedure adopted for creating multiple horizontal grid lines can be used to create multiple vertical grid lines.

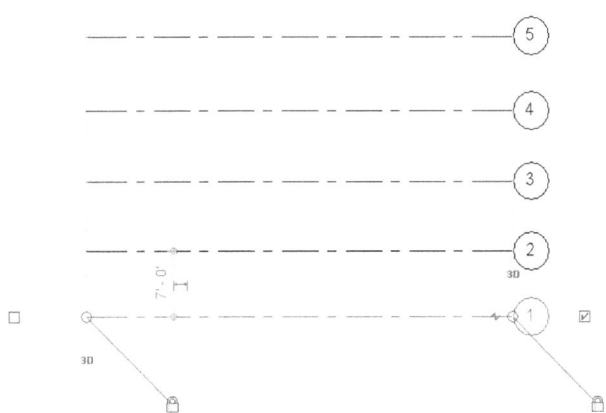

Figure 6-18 Parallel grid lines automatically numbered

In the same manner, you can create a rectangular grid pattern that is aligned at a given angle to the horizontal axis. You can also specify different angles for the grid lines and create the grid patterns based on the project requirement. Figure 6-19 shows some other examples of the rectangular grid patterns.

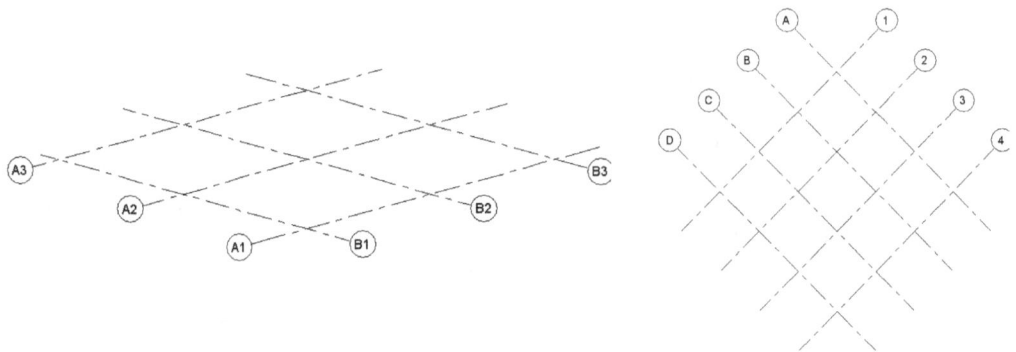

Figure 6-19 *Examples of the rectangular grid patterns*

In the **Draw** panel of the **Modify | Place Grid** tab, you can use the **Start-End-Radius Arc** and **Center-ends Arc** tools to create curved or radial grid patterns. The procedure of creating the curved grid lines using these options is similar to the sketching options for creating walls (see Chapter 3). You can create multiple curved grids using the tools in the **Draw** panel and specifying their radius in the **Radius** edit box in the **Options Bar**. You can specify a value in the **Radius** edit box in the **Options Bar** only if you select the check box located before it. Figure 6-20 shows an example of radial grid patterns created using the semicircular and straight grid lines.

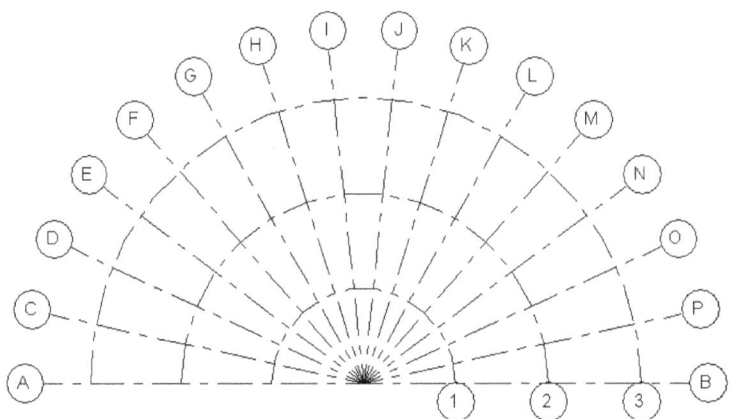

Figure 6-20 *An example of a radial grid pattern created using the semi-circular and straight grid lines*

Creating Grids Using the Multi-Segment Tool

You can use the **Multi-Segment** tool to sketch a multi-segmented grid in the project. To do so, choose the **Grid** tool from the **Datum** panel of the **Architecture** tab; the **Modify | Place Grid** tab will be displayed. In this tab, choose the **Multi-Segment** tool from the **Draw** panel; the **Modify | Edit Sketch** tab will be displayed. In the **Draw** panel of the tab, you can choose any of the sketching tools, displayed in the list box, to sketch the multi-segmented gridline.

Working with Datum Plane and Creating Standard Views 6-15

After choosing the desired sketching tool, you need to use various options in the **Options Bar** to control the creation of the gridline in the project. For example, select the **Chain** check box in the **Options Bar** to create grids in chain. In the **Offset** edit box, you can enter a value to specify the offset distance by which the grids will be offset from the clicked point in the drawing area. After setting the options in the **Options Bar**, click in the drawing area; a magenta colored gridline with a temporary dimension will emerge from the point at which you have clicked. Next, click in a desired point to create the first segment of the grid. Similarly, you can click on multiple points in the drawing area to create other segments. To finish the creation of the multi-segmented grids, choose the **Finish Edit Mode** button from the **Mode** panel of the **Modify | Edit Sketch** tab. Figure 6-21 shows a sketch with multi-segmented gridlines.

Figure 6-21 An example of the multi-segmented grids in a floor plan

Creating Grids Using the Pick Lines Tool

The **Pick Lines** tool is used to create grid lines that are aligned to the existing elements. When you select this tool from the **Draw** panel of the **Modify | Place Grid** tab and move the cursor near an existing element, the cursor snaps to certain object properties such as the interior face of the walls, centerlines of columns, and so on. Click when the desired property of the element is highlighted. Autodesk Revit automatically creates a grid line along the specified alignment of the element.

 Tip: *You can also use different editing tools such as **Copy**, **Array**, **Mirror**, **Move**, and so on to create grid patterns. Autodesk Revit Architecture numbers the grids intuitively. For example, if you array a grid named A, the new grids will sequentially be named as B, C, D, E, and so on.*

For example, to create grid lines for the interior wall profile, choose the **Pick Lines** tool from the **Draw** panel and move the cursor near the inclined exterior wall. As you move the cursor over the wall, it will snap to the interior and exterior faces. Click when the interior face is highlighted, as shown in Figure 6-22; a grid line aligned with the interior face of the wall will be created, as shown in Figure 6-23. Similarly, you can click on the other wall segments to create a grid pattern required for the building. Autodesk Revit also creates the curved grid lines, if a curved element is selected.

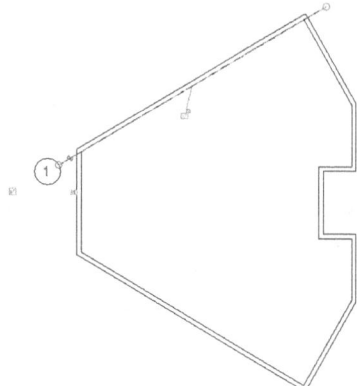

Figure 6-22 *Selecting the interior face to align the grid line*

Figure 6-23 *Grid line created along the interior face of the selected wall using the **Pick Lines** tool*

If the cursor does not snap to the wall centerline, the grid lines along the centerlines of the walls will be created using the **Offset** edit box in the **Options Bar**. Specify the distance of the centerline from the interior face in the **Offset** edit box and then use the **Pick Lines** tool to select the interior face. The grid line aligned to the centerline of the wall is shown in Figure 6-24. Similarly, you can create other grid lines for the building project using the **Pick Lines** tool, as shown in Figure 6-25.

 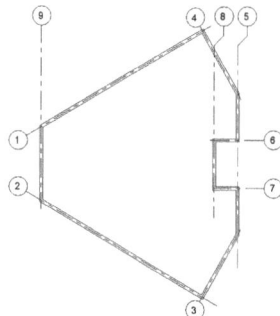

Figure 6-24 *Creating a grid line along the centerline of the wall using the **Offset** option*

Figure 6-25 *Grid lines created using the **Pick Lines** tool*

Modifying Grids

As mentioned earlier, parameters of grids can be modified before or after grids are created. To modify a grid after it is created, you need to select the grid and modify its properties from the **Properties** palette.

For example, after selecting a grid, you can click on its name and assign it a new name. Similarly, you can modify the distance between grids by selecting the temporary dimension and entering a new value, as shown in Figure 6-26. When you enter a new value, the grid automatically moves to the specified distance.

Working with Datum Plane and Creating Standard Views 6-17

Figure 6-26 Modifying the distance between grids

You can also move the grids by simply dragging them to the desired location. Click to select a single grid. Hold the CTRL key while clicking to select multiple grids. You can now drag the grid(s) to the desired location. Hold the SHIFT key to restrain the movement of the cursor in the orthogonal direction.

When you move the cursor near a grid, it gets highlighted. Now, right-click; a shortcut menu will be displayed with various options. These options are **Select Previous**, **Select All Instances**, **Create Similar**, **View Properties**, and so on.

For certain grids, you may need to move or offset the grid bubble to a different location. When you select a grid, a blue circle appears on each of its endpoints. The drag control, as mentioned earlier, controls the extents of the grid line. The grid line break control, which appears near the grid bubble, is used to create a grid bubble offset. You can click on this control and use the displayed drag controls to move the grid bubble to the desired location. The grid name also moves to the new location and an extension line is created. Figure 6-27 shows the newly created grid bubble offset.

 Tip: *The radial and rectangular array tools can be effectively used to create grid patterns suitable for the project.*

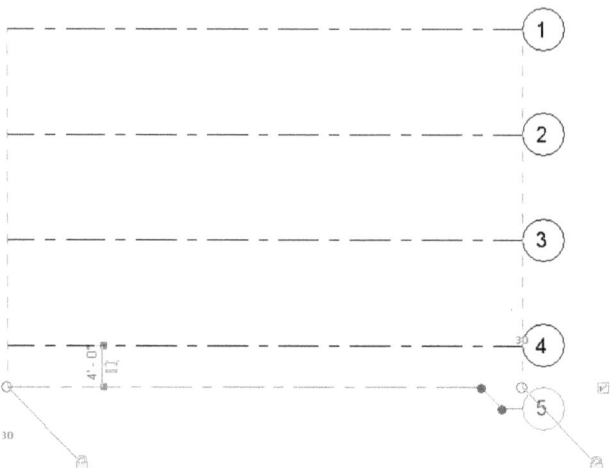

Figure 6-27 A grid bubble offset created

Grid Properties

Like levels, grids too have associated properties. A typical grid consists of a grid line, grid bubble, grid name, and other controls, as shown in Figure 6-28. The usage of the controls such as grid bubble visibility, 2D or 3D extents, and grid bubble break is similar to the usage described for levels.

To view and modify the properties of a grid, select it; the instance parameter of the selected grid will be displayed in the **Properties** palette. In this palette, choose the **Edit Type** button; the **Type Properties** dialog box will be displayed, as shown in Figure 6-29. You can use this dialog box to view and modify the type properties of the selected grid. The type properties of grids and their description are discussed next.

 Tip: *It is recommended that you draw the grid lines with the endpoints aligned to each other. You can use the alignment line that is displayed when the cursor is moved to its proximity. The* **Lock** *constraints can be used to drag the extents of the single or multiple grid lines.*

Working with Datum Plane and Creating Standard Views 6-19

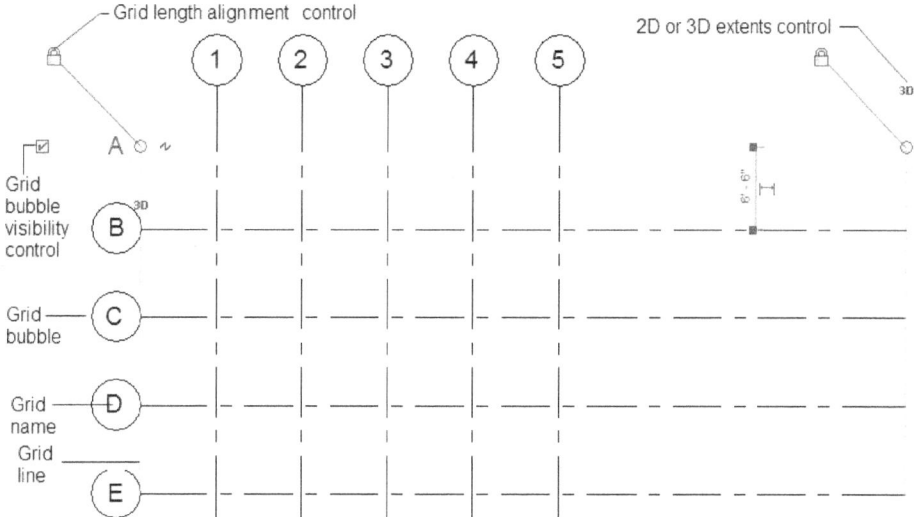

Figure 6-28 A typical grid line pattern with its controls

Figure 6-29 Partial view of the **Type Properties** dialog box of a grid

Grid Type Properties

When the **Type Properties** of a grid is changed, the properties of all instance parameters related to it are also changed. You can click in the value field and select a new value from the drop-down list or enter a new value in that field. The properties of grid types are described next.

Parameter Name	Value and Description
Symbol	Specifies the display of the symbol at the end of the grid line. You can control the display of the symbol by selecting various options from the drop-down list
Center Segment	Specifies the display type of the center segment of the grid line. You can select **Continuous**, **None** or **Custom** from the drop-down list
Center Segment Weight	Specifies the line weight of the center segment, if the **Center Segment** parameter is set to **Custom**
Center Segment Color	You can assign a color to the center segment, if the **Center Segment** parameter is set to **Custom**
Center Segment Pattern	Specifies the line type of the segment at the center, if the **Center Segment** parameter is set to **Custom**. You can select various line patterns from the drop-down list
End Segment Weight	Specifies the line weight of the grid line, if the **Center Segment** parameter is set to **Continuous**. You can set the line weight of the end segments if the **Center Segment** parameter is set to **None** or **Custom**
End Segment Color	Specifies the color assigned to the grid line, if the **Center Segment** parameter is set to **Continuous**. You can set the color of the end segments if the **Center Segment** parameter is set to **None** or **Custom**
End Segment Pattern	Specifies the line type of the grid line if the **Center Segment** parameter is set to **Continuous**. You can set the line type of the end segments if the **Center Segment** parameter is set to **None** or **Custom**
End Segments Length	Specifies the length of each end segment as measured in the sheet if the **Center Segment** parameter is set to **None** or **Custom**
Plan View Symbols End 1(Default)	Specifies the default status for the visibility of the symbol at end 1 of the grid line in plan view. By default, the check box is cleared. If you select the check box, the visibility of the symbol at end 1 in the plan view will be turned on

Working with Datum Plane and Creating Standard Views

Plan View Symbols End 2(Default)	Specifies the default status for the visibility of the symbol at end 2 of the grid line in the plan views. By default, the check box is selected. If you clear the check box, the visibility of the symbol at end 2 in the plan view is turned off
Non-Plan View Symbols (Default)	Specifies the default status for the visibility of the grid line in the sections and elevations, other than in the plan views. You can control the visibility of the symbol at the top and bottom of the grid line by selecting various options from the drop-down list

Note
In the **Type Properties** *dialog box, the* **Center Segment Weight**, **Center Segment Color**, *and* **Center Segment Pattern** *options will be available only when you choose the* **Custom** *option in the* **Center Segment** *drop-down list.*

Grid Instance Properties
When the instance properties of a grid are changed, only the properties of the selected instances are changed. The instance properties of grids are given next.

Parameter Name	Value and Description
Name	Specifies the name assigned to the grid. You can enter any name, based on the project requirement
Scope Box	Specifies the scope box assigned to the grid that controls its visibility in different views

Customizing the Grid Display
In Revit, you can customize the grid display according to your need. You can change the color, line weight, and line type of the entire grid line or part of the grid line such as center segment and end segment. At the same time, you can change the display of symbols at the end of the grid line.

Changing the Continuous Grid Line
A grid line is said to be continuous when the **Center Segment** parameter in the **Type Properties** dialog box is set to **Continuous**. You can change the line type, line weight, and color of the end segments using various options available in the **Type Properties** dialog box. Similarly, you can change the display of a symbol at the ends of the grid, using the other options available in the **Type Properties** dialog box.

Creating a Grid Line with Central Gap

In a grid line, you can create a gap between the two end segments. To do so, set the **Center Segment** parameter in the **Type Properties** dialog box to **None**, as shown in Figure 6-30. Simultaneously, you can change the display properties of the end segments, as discussed above. To create a grid, ensure that the **1/4" Bubble Custom Gap** (**6.5mm Bubble Custom Gap**) option is selected in the **Type-Selector** drop-down list.

Figure 6-30 *The grid line with a central gap*

Creating a Grid Line with Center Segment

A grid line will appear with the center and end segments that have different display properties such as line color, line weight, and line pattern. To create a grid line with center segment, select **Grid : 1/4" Bubble** or the **Grid : 1/4" Bubble Custom Gap** option from the **Type Selector** drop-down list and choose the **Edit Type** button; the **Type Properties** dialog box will be displayed. In the **Type Properties** dialog box, select the **Custom** option corresponding to the **Center Segment** parameter. Now in the **Type Properties** dialog box, use various parameters to change the display properties such as color, lineweight, and line pattern for the end and center segments of a grid. Figure 6-31 shows a grid line with the center segment having a different line pattern as compared to its end segments.

Figure 6-31 *The grid line with a center segment*

Controlling the Visibility of Grids

You can control the visibility of a grid or all grids in any of the project views. To control the visibility of a grid, select it and right-click, a shortcut menu will be displayed. Choose **Hide in View > Category** from the shortcut menu; the grid category will be hidden in the current view. Similarly, you can also hide one particular grid by choosing **Hide in View > Elements** from the shortcut menu. On doing so, the selected grid will be hidden in the current view. The grid will, however, be displayed in all other views.

Alternatively, you can control the visibility of grids by using the **Visibility/Graphic Overrides** dialog box. To invoke this dialog box, select a grid from the drawing; the **Modify | Grids** tab will be displayed. In the **View** panel of this tab, click on the **Override Graphics in View** drop-down and choose the **Override by Category** tool from the list displayed; the **View-Specific Category Graphics** dialog box will be displayed. In this dialog box, choose the **Open the Visibility Graphics dialog....** button; the **Visibility/Graphic Overrides for Floor Plan** dialog box will be displayed. In the **Annotation Categories** tab of this dialog box, clear the check box for the visibility of grids; the visibility of all grids will turn off in the current view. You can also control the visibility of grids using the Scope Box feature. You will learn more about this feature later in this chapter.

REFERENCE PLANES

Ribbon: Architecture > Work Plane > Ref Plane
Shortcut Key: RP

Reference planes are useful while sketching and adding building elements to a design. They can be used as datum planes to act as a guideline for creating elements. They can also be used effectively for creating new family elements. To create a reference plane, choose the **Ref Plane** tool from the **Work Plane** panel. On invoking the **Ref Plane** tool; the **Modify | Place Reference Plane** tab will be displayed. Select the tools from the **Draw** panel and start drawing the reference plane in the drawing. Alternatively, you can type **RP** to invoke the **Ref Plane** tool.

After invoking the tool, click at the desired location in the drawing window to start a line that defines the reference plane. Now, move the cursor to the new location and release the left button to specify the endpoint of the reference line; the reference plane will be created. To assign the reference plane a name, select it from the drawing. Next in the **Properties** palette, enter the name of the selected reference plane in the value field of the **Name** instance parameter.

WORK PLANES

As the name suggests, the work plane is a plane that can be used for sketching elements. In Autodesk Revit, you can create and edit only those elements that are in the current work plane. The work plane can be horizontal, vertical, or inclined at any specified angle. Each generated view has an associated work plane. This plane is automatically defined for some standard views such as floor plans. For others such as sections, elevations, and 3D views, you can set the work plane based on the location of the elements that are to be created or edited. The concept of work planes is especially useful for creating elements in elevations, sections, or inclined planes.

Setting a Work Plane

You can set a work plane based on your project requirement. To set a work plane, choose the **Set** tool from the **Work Plane** panel in the **Architecture** tab; the **Work Plane** dialog box will be displayed, as shown in Figure 6-32. It shows the current work plane and assists you in specifying the parameters to set a new work plane. The **Name** radio button has a drop-down list of available views. Select an available work plane from the drop-down list, which contains the names of levels, grids, and named reference planes. You can select the **Pick a plane** radio button in the **Work Plane** dialog box to set a work plane along an existing plane. On selecting this radio button and choosing the **OK** button in this dialog box, you will be prompted to select an existing plane in the drawing to which you want to align the work plane. The existing plane can be a face of a wall, floor, or roof. You can also select the **Pick a line and use the work plane it was sketched in** radio button from this dialog box to create a work plane that is coplanar with the plane on which the selected line was created.

*Figure 6-32 The **Work Plane** dialog box*

Note
*In the project environment of Autodesk Revit, you can choose the **Viewer** tool from the **Work Plane** panel of the **Architecture** tab to display the **Workplane Viewer** window. In this window, you can modify the workplane dependent element easily.*

Controlling the Visibility of Work Planes

You can control the visibility of the current work plane by choosing the **Show** button from the **Architecture** tab. As a result, the work plane appears as a grid in the current view, as shown in Figure 6-33. To hide it, choose the **Show** button again.

Figure 6-33 The display of the work plane as a grid

You can also set the grid spacing for a work plane by selecting it from the drawing. On doing so, the work plane gets highlighted. Specify the spacing by entering the new value in the **Spacing** edit box in **Options Bar**. You can snap to the work plane grid using the object

Working with Datum Plane and Creating Standard Views

snap tools. For example, these tools can be used to create wall profiles based on a square grid or a flooring pattern for an inclined ramp.

 Tip: *The drop-down list, next to the **Name** radio button in the **Work Plane** dialog box shows all levels, grids, and reference planes that have been created in the project. If you select a plane that is perpendicular to the current view, the **Go to View** dialog box will be displayed and you can select the appropriate view from it.*

WORKING WITH PROJECT VIEWS

While working on the building model, you may need to view its different exterior and interior portions in order to add or edit the elements in the design. Revit provides various features and techniques that can be used to view the building model. In this section, you will recapitulate some concepts introduced earlier and also learn about the tools that will help you in working with the views.

Viewing a Building Model

The default template file has certain predefined standard project views, which are displayed in the **Views** head of the **Project Browser**, as shown in Figure 6-34. These include floor plans, ceiling plans, and elevations. To open any of these views, double-click on the name; the corresponding view will be displayed in the viewing area. You can control the visibility of the **Project Browser** by selecting the **Project Browser** check box from **View > Windows > User Interface** drop-down.

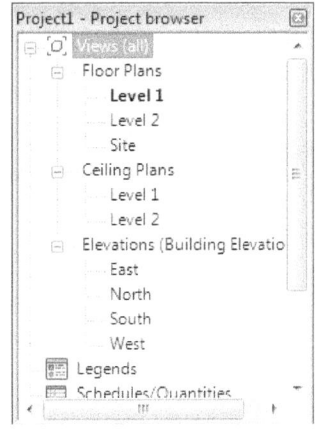

Figure 6-34 The **Project Browser** *showing the standard building views*

When you open a new project, the viewing area displays four inward arrow symbols in the floor plan view, which indicate the four side elevations: North, East, South, and West. You can use these symbols to view the appropriate building elevation by double-clicking on them.

Apart from these standard building views, you can use different viewing tools to view the building model from various angles. As described earlier (see Chapter 2), you can use the **Zoom** tool by choosing it from the navigation bar to zoom-in or zoom-out of the current view. You can also use the **Orient** tool to view the model using the preset standard viewpoints. The **SteeringWheels** and **ViewCube** tools assist you in navigating and viewing the model with various options. You can pan, zoom, walk, and change viewpoints using these tools.

To restrict the visibility of certain categories of elements, choose the **Visibility/Graphics** tool from the **Graphics** panel of the **View** tab; the **Visibility/Graphic Overrides** dialog box for the specific view will be displayed. The **Model Categories** tab of this dialog box contains a list of model elements such as walls, doors, windows, and so on, whereas the **Annotation Categories** tab contains annotations such as dimensions, door tags, and so on. You can clear the category of elements that you want to hide from the current view using this dialog box.

Visibility/Graphic Overrides of an Element

You can override the visibility and graphics of any element in a view. To do so, select an element and right-click; a shortcut menu will be displayed. Choose **Override Graphics in View > By Element** from the shortcut menu; the **View-Specific Element Graphics** dialog box will be displayed, as shown in Figure 6-35. The options in this dialog box are discussed next.

Visible

The **Visible** check box controls the visibility of an element in a view. The check box is selected by default. Clear the check box to hide the selected element in the view.

Tip: *You can also use the keyboard shortcuts VV and VG to open the Visibility/Graphics Overrides dialog box.*

Figure 6-35 The View-Specific Element Graphics dialog box

Halftone

Select the **Halftone** check box to adjust and blend the line color of an element with the background color.

Projection Lines

To view different options in the **Projection Lines** area, choose the arrow button located on the left of this area; the area will be expanded. In the expanded area, you can use any of the following options: **Weight**, **Color**, and **Pattern**. To set the line weight of the projection lines, you can select options from the **Weight** drop-down list. Similarly, to change the color of the projection lines, choose the button located on the right of the **Color** option; the **Color** dialog box will be displayed. Select the required color from the dialog box. Now, choose the **OK** button to close the dialog box. You can also change the pattern of projection lines. To do so, choose the button on the right of the **Pattern** option; the **Line Patterns** dialog box will be displayed. Select the required pattern of the projection lines from this dialog box. Next, choose the **OK** button to close the dialog box.

Surface Patterns

Choose the arrow button on the left of this option to expand the **Surface Patterns** area. You can change the visibility of the surface pattern by clearing the **Visible** check box. Select the color and pattern of the surface in the same way as explained earlier for the projection lines.

Working with Datum Plane and Creating Standard Views

Surface Transparency

Choose the arrow button on the left of the **Surface Transparency** area to expand it. In this area, you can change the transparency of the selected element by moving the **Transparency** slider or by entering a suitable value in the edit box displayed next to the slider. Note that higher the value you enter in the edit box, more transparent will be the object.

Cut Lines

Choose the arrow button on the left of the **Cut Lines** area to expand it. In this area, you can change the weight, color, and pattern of the cut lines, as explained earlier for the **Projection Lines** area. Once you have edited the graphic settings of an element in the **View Specific Element Graphics** dialog box, choose the **Apply** and the **OK** button to apply the settings and close the dialog box.

Cut Patterns

Expand the **Cut Pattern** area by choosing the arrow button on its left. In the expanded area, change the visibility, color, and pattern of the cut patterns. Once you have edited the visibility settings of an element in the **View Specific Element Graphics** dialog box, choose the **Apply** and then the **OK** button to apply the settings and close the dialog box.

Visibility/Graphic Overrides of an Element Category

To edit the visibility and graphics of an element category, open the required project view. Next, select an element of the required category and right-click; a shortcut menu will be displayed. Choose **Override Graphics in View > By Category** from the shortcut menu; the **View-Specific Category Graphics** dialog box for the loaded view will be displayed. In this dialog box, choose the **Open the Visibility Graphics** button, the **Visibility/Graphic Overrides for Floor Plan** dialog box will be displayed, refer to Figure 6-36.

The dialog box contains the tabs to edit the visibility and graphic display of the models, annotations, and imported elements. Choose the required tab to edit the visibility and graphics of the selected category. In the **Visibility** column, clear or select the visibility check box available on the left of the category name to edit the visibility in the view. To specify overrides to a category, click on the name of the category in the **Visibility** column of the **Visibility/ Graphics Overrides for Floor Plan** dialog box; the **Overrides** button will be displayed for the respective columns in the specified tab. To override patterns for the selected category, choose the **Override** button displayed in the **Patterns** column corresponding to the selected category; the **Fill Pattern Graphic** dialog box will be displayed. Set the visibility, color, and pattern for the **Visible**, **Color**, and **Pattern** options in the dialog box and choose the **OK** button. Similarly to override the transparency, of the selected object, choose the **Override** button displayed in the **Transparency** column; the **Surfaces** dialog box will be displayed. In this dialog box, you can use the **Transparency** slider to control the transparency of the selected element.

Similarly, click in the required columns in the **Visibility/Graphics Overrides for Floor Plan** dialog box to edit the graphic display of the category. Select the check boxes in the **Halftone** column if required. You can set the detail level of the selected category in the **Detail level** column. To do so, click in the **Detail Level** column and choose the down arrow displayed on the left. Select the detail level from the **Detail Level** drop-down list. Choose the **Apply** button to view the changes in the visibility and graphic display of the selected category. Choose the **OK** button to retain the changes and close the **Visibility/Graphics Overrides for Floor Plan** dialog box.

Figure 6-36 The *Visibility/Graphic Overrides for Floor Plan* dialog box

Making Elements Transparent

Revit provides you with a tool to make elements transparent so that you can see through an object. This tool can be used to view the interior of a building from the top, even after adding roofs or ceilings.

To make an element transparent, select the element and right-click; a shortcut menu will be displayed. Choose **Override Graphics in View > By Element** from the shortcut menu; the **View Specific Element Graphics** dialog box will be displayed. In this dialog box, choose the arrow on the left of the **Surface Transparency** area; the options in this area will be displayed. In this area, you can use the **Transparency** slider to control the transparency of the selected object. You can also increase the transparency by moving the slider towards right. Alternatively, you can enter a desired value in the edit box, next to the **Transparency** slider, to control the transparency of the selected element. After setting the transparency in the **Surface Transparency** area, choose the **OK** button; the selected element will become transparent and you will be able to see through it. Although the element becomes transparent, the edges and surface pattern of the element will still be visible. You can view the change before and after using the Transparency slider, refer to Figures 6-37 and 6-38.

Working with Datum Plane and Creating Standard Views

Figure 6-37 *Elements before selecting the* **Transparent** *check box*

Figure 6-38 *Elements after selecting the* **Transparent** *check box*

Using the Temporary Hide/Isolate Tool

The **Temporary Hide/Isolate** tool can be used to hide or isolate elements temporarily from a project view. This tool will be available only after a selection has been made. Select the element or elements that you need to hide or isolate in the project view and then choose the **Temporary Hide/Isolate** tool from the **View Control Bar**; a cascading menu will be displayed.

You can hide or isolate elements or their categories using the tools given in the cascading menu. The cascading menu contains six tools. On choosing any of the tools from it, a cyan color border will be displayed in the drawing area, indicating that the elements in the drawing are in the **Temporary Hide/Isolate** mode. You can choose the **Hide Element** tool from the cascading menu, as shown in Figure 6-39, to hide the selected element in a view. On choosing the **Isolate Element** tool, only the selected elements will be displayed while the rest will be hidden in the view. The **Hide Category** tool is used to hide all the elements of the category of the selected element. The **Isolate Category** is used to display only the elements belonging to the category of the selected element in the view.

Figure 6-39 *Choosing the* **Hide Element** *tool*

The **Reset Temporary Hide/Isolate** tool is used to revert to the original view without saving the temporary hide or isolate changes in the view. The **Apply Hide/Isolate to view** option is used to hide or isolate the temporary hidden or isolated elements permanently in the view. After you choose this tool, the blue boundary becomes invisible and the temporarily hidden or isolated elements and categories are permanently hidden or isolated. On hiding or isolating an element or category, the sunglasses symbol of the **Temporary Hide/Isolate** tool in the **View Control Bar** is highlighted in the same color as that of the boundary, indicating that certain elements have been hidden temporarily. When you choose the **Reset Temporary Hide/Isolate** option, the sunglasses symbol is no longer highlighted.

Revealing and Unhiding Elements

To reveal and unhide the hidden elements in the view, choose the bulb icon from the **View Control** bar to invoke the **Reveal Hidden Elements** tool. On doing so, a magenta color border will be displayed and the hidden elements will be highlighted in the same color. Select the required elements and choose the **Unhide Element** or the **Unhide Category** button from the **Reveal Hidden Elements** panel in the **Architecture** tab. Now, again you need to click the bulb icon to exit the **Reveal Hidden Elements** mode. You can also exit by choosing the **Toggle Reveal Hidden Elements Mode** button from the **Reveal Hidden Elements** panel of the **Architecture** tab. You will notice that all the hidden elements and categories will be displayed in the view.

Plan Views

In Autodesk Revit, you can use the floor and ceiling views to view the building model plan. By default, Autodesk Revit opens the floor plan view when you create a new project. The default template file contains two floor plans and two corresponding ceiling plans. These views are enlisted under the **Floor Plans** and **Ceiling Plans** heads in the **Project Browser**.

Adding a Plan View

As described earlier, when you add levels in the project view, Autodesk Revit automatically adds their corresponding floor and ceiling plan views in the **Project Browser**. To create new plan views for the added levels that do not contain associated plans in the **Project Browser**, choose the **Floor Plan** tool from **View > Create > Plan Views** drop-down; the **New Floor Plan** dialog box will be displayed, as shown in Figure 6-40.

Figure 6-40 *The* ***New Floor Plan*** *dialog box*

In the **New Floor Plan** dialog box, the **Floor Plan** option is selected by default in the **Type** drop-down list, refer to Figure 6-40. You can edit the existing type or create a new type by choosing the **Edit Type** button. On choosing the **Edit Type** button; the **Type Properties** dialog box will be displayed. In this dialog box, you can edit various type parameters for the existing view type or choose the **Duplicate** button and create a new type. Choose the **OK** button to return to the **New Floor Plan** dialog box. In this dialog box, you can select the appropriate level to create the plan view in the list box displayed. You can also select multiple levels by holding the SHIFT key. The **Do not duplicate existing views** check box can be cleared to

Working with Datum Plane and Creating Standard Views 6-31

create a plan view for a level that has an already existing plan view. The duplicate view is created and added in the **Project Browser** with the suffix (1). The number in the brackets increments as more copies of the plan view are added. The appropriate scale for the new view can be selected from the **Scale** drop-down list.

Note
*While creating a level, if you have cleared the **Make Plan View** check box in the **Options Bar**, then its corresponding plan view will not be created.*

Modifying the Plan View Properties

To modify the view properties of a plan view or any other project view, select the project view from the **Project Browser**; the properties of the selected view will be displayed in the **Properties** palette. Using this palette, you can modify the parameters related to the current view such as **View Scale**, **Display Model**, **Detail Level**, **View Name**, and so on. The **View Range** parameter in the **Extents** category controls the visibility and appearance of the elements in the view by defining the extent of horizontal plane of the view. The crop region parameter defines the boundary of a view and can be turned on or off using the **Crop Region Visible** check box. You can also access the tools related to the visibility settings of the view using the **View Control Bar** available near the bottom left corner of the drawing window.

Elevation Views

An elevation view refers to the view of the building model from four sides, North, East, South, and West. The four side elevation views are automatically created by Autodesk Revit when the default template file is used. Using the elevation view, you cannot only visualize the building from its exterior but also create the views of the interior walls of various internal spaces.

For example, for a residential building, you can easily view the four side elevations and also create the elevation views of the walls of the interior spaces such as kitchen and bathroom. In the plan view, the elevation is represented by the elevation symbol pointing in the direction of the elevation view side.

Creating an Elevation View

To create an elevation view, invoke the **Elevation** tool from **View > Create > Elevation** drop-down; the **Properties** palette for the elevation will be displayed. In this palette, select the type of elevation from the **Type Selector** drop-down list. From this drop-down list, you can select any of the two options: **Building Elevation** or **Interior Elevation**. To create an exterior elevation, select the **Building Elevation** option and move the cursor in the viewing area in the drawing. On doing so, the elevation symbol will appear. On moving the cursor near the exterior walls, you will notice that the arrow head of the elevation symbol has changed its alignment perpendicular to the wall, as shown in Figure 6-41. Now, click when the elevation arrow head symbol points toward the desired direction; the new elevation view will be created and added to the list of elevations in the **Project Browser**. Revit Architecture automatically numbers the elevation names. When you select the elevation symbol created, its controls are displayed, as shown in Figure 6-42.

Figure 6-41 Placing the elevation symbol for creating the exterior view

Figure 6-42 Controls of the elevation symbol

Similarly, to create an elevation view of the interior walls of an interior space of a building model, invoke the **Elevation** tool and select the **Interior Elevation** option from the **Type Selector** drop-down list. Next, move the cursor near the interior wall in the interior space; the elevation symbol will appear. Place this symbol inside the space, as shown in Figure 6-43. When you select the elevation symbol, its controls are displayed. Using the check box(es) in these controls, you can create the elevation of the desired walls, as shown in Figure 6-44. The rotate symbol can be used to rotate the elevation symbol in the desired direction.

You can also set the width of the elevation view using the clip plane control. When you click the arrow head of the elevation symbol, the clip plane is displayed as a blue line with the drag control dots on its two ends, as shown in Figure 6-45. You can drag them to resize the width of the elevation view. For the interior elevation views, Autodesk Revit automatically extends the clip plane to the extents of the room. You can drag the blue dots to increase or decrease the extents of the elevation view, as shown in Figure 6-46.

Note

*In Revit, elevations are added in **Project Browser** under two different headings, **Elevations (Building Elevation)** and **Elevations (Interior Elevation)**. All the exterior elevations are added under the **Elevations (Building Elevation)** heading and all the interior elevations are added under the **Elevations (Interior Elevation)** heading.*

Figure 6-43 Placing the elevation symbol for creating the interior elevation view

Figure 6-44 Adding the interior view by using the elevation controls

Working with Datum Plane and Creating Standard Views 6-33

Figure 6-45 The clip plane drag controls   *Figure 6-46* Dragged clip plane controls

To rename the elevation view created, right-click on the view name in the **Project Browser**; a shortcut menu will be displayed. Choose the **Rename** option from the shortcut menu; the **Rename View** dialog box will be displayed. In this dialog box, enter a name in the **Name** edit box and choose the **OK** button; the elevation view will be renamed.

There are various methods to display an elevation view. The first method is by double-clicking on the name of the elevation in the **Project Browser**. When you do so, the corresponding elevation view will be displayed in the drawing window. Second method to display the elevation view is to double-click on the arrow head of the elevation symbol to display its corresponding elevation view. The third method is to right-click on the elevation symbol to display a shortcut menu. Choose **Find Referring Views** from the shortcut menu; the **Go To View** dialog box is displayed, as shown in Figure 6-47. Next, select the view to be displayed from this dialog box and then choose the **Open View** button or double-click on the name of the view. The other method to display the elevation view is to select the arrow head of the elevation symbol and then right-click to display a shortcut menu. Next, choose the **Go to Elevation View** option from the shortcut menu displayed; the corresponding elevation will be displayed in the drawing area.

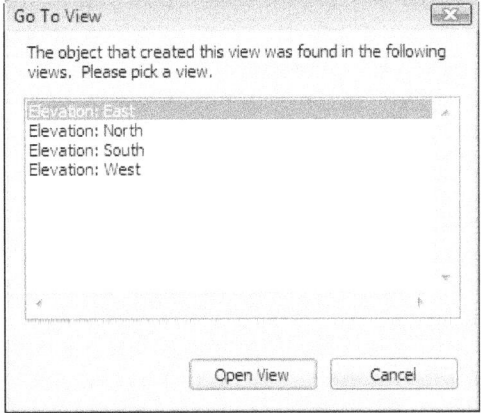

Figure 6-47 The **Go To View** dialog box

You can modify the properties associated with elevation views by using the **Properties** palette. This palette is displayed with instance parameters when you select the required view or when the required view is displayed in the drawing area.

Note
While working on the floor plan, if the created building model extends beyond the clip planes of the four side elevation views, the corresponding elevations no longer show the complete exterior views. An elevation view that is cut through the building model is displayed instead. You can drag the clip plane controls symbol beyond the extent of the building profile to retain the view as a complete exterior elevation view.

Tip: *You can also change the elevation view symbol by selecting it and then choosing the **Edit Type** button from the **Properties** palette to display the **Type Properties** dialog box. You can then select and modify different parameters to create the desired elevation view symbol.*

Section Views

Section views are generated by cutting sections through the building model. These views are created to display various wall elevations, floor heights, and special vertical features of the project. They are also useful in creating and editing elements added to the interior spaces of the building model.

For example, in an office building, to emphasize the salient features of the central atrium, you may need to show a section through the central atrium. Autodesk Revit enables you to create it with relative ease. You can also modify the sectional view to create a section that displays the interior spaces.

Creating a Section View

To create a section view, invoke the **Section** tool from the **Create** panel of the **View** tab. On doing so, the **Modify | Section** tab will be displayed. The options in the **Modify | Section** tab are used to specify the section type to be created and to specify the instance and its type properties. The section can be created in the plan, elevation, and section views. You can create different types of section views such as the building section, wall section, and detail section. You can choose the section view type to be created from the **Type Selector** drop-down list in the **Properties** palette. In the **Options Bar** you can use the **Reference other view** check box to create a reference section that acts as a reference for another view. Notice that the reference sections are not added as an additional section in the list of section views in the **Project Browser**.

To create a building section, invoke the **Section** tool from the **Create** panel and move the cursor to the viewing area; the cursor will change into a cross symbol, and you will be prompted to draw the section line in the current view. Click at the appropriate location to specify the start point. To create a section through the entire building, click near the exterior face of the building profile. As you move the cursor, a section line will appear with one end fixed at the specified point and the other end attached to the cursor. You can even create a section line at any angle. To create a horizontal or vertical section view, move the cursor horizontally or vertically across the building profile, as shown in Figure 6-48 and click to specify the endpoint. The section

Working with Datum Plane and Creating Standard Views

line along with its controls is shown in Figure 6-49. It is represented by a section head and a line. The section head indicates the direction toward which the section will be created.

Note that, the methods used for displaying the section views are similar to the ones described for the elevation view.

Figure 6-48 Specifying the start point and the endpoint of the vertical section line

Figure 6-49 The vertical section line and its controls

Modifying a Section View

After creating a section view, you can modify the location of the section line of the section view by dragging it, as shown in Figure 6-50. When you drag a section line, the corresponding section view is updated immediately, refer to Figure 6-51.

Figure 6-50 Dragging the section line

Figure 6-51 The updated section view

You can modify the parameters of the section view by using the controls available on the section view line. When selected, the created section line shows its controls. The twin arrow symbol represents the flip tool that can be used to flip the viewing side of the section view. By default, the section head appears on one side. The cyclic control on both the ends of the section line can be used to change the visibility of the section head and tail at the respective end. You can click on the symbol to hide or display them. Click on the break line symbol, which appears in the middle of the section line, to break it. You can then resize the two section lines to the required extent of the view. To rejoin the section line, click on the break line control again.

When you create a section view, Autodesk Revit intuitively creates its view depth, which is the extent of the view in the current view. It is represented by a dashed line the blue arrows as drag controls. To modify the view depth, drag the arrows to the desired location. The section view shows only those elements that are within the view depth. For example, Figure 6-52 shows the modified view depth with its corresponding updated section view. Notice that the west wall is not visible in the section view because it is not within the view depth.

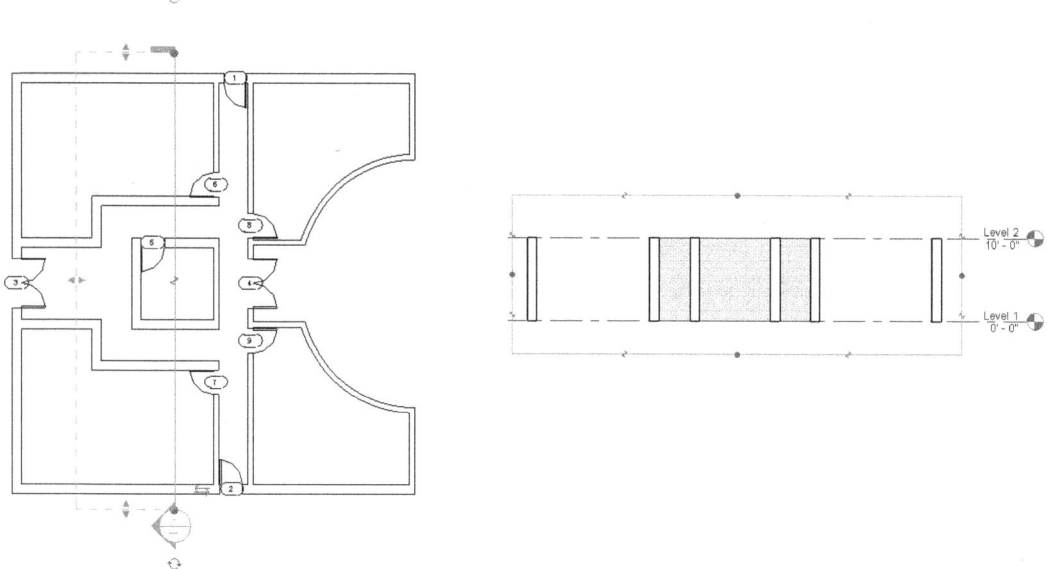

Figure 6-52 *The modified view depth with its corresponding updated section view*

To modify the properties of a section view, select its section line; the **Properties** palette will be displayed with the instance parameters of the section view, as shown in Figure 6-53. Using this palette, you can modify various instance properties such as **View Name**, **View Scale**, **Crop Region Visible**, and so on by clicking in the corresponding **Value** column and selecting a new value from the drop-down list if available, or by entering a new value in that field.

Working with Datum Plane and Creating Standard Views

*Figure 6-53 The **Properties** palette for a section view*

You can choose the **Edit Type** button to display the **Type Properties** dialog box and modify the type properties of the section view such as **Callout Tag**, **Section Tag**, and **Reference Label**.

 Tip: *By default, when you create a section line horizontally from the left to right, the section view faces upward, whereas if you create it from the right to left, it faces downward. Similarly, when you create it vertically from the bottom to top, the section view faces toward the left, whereas if you create it from the top to bottom, it faces toward the right.*

Creating a Segmented Section

Autodesk Revit enables you to split the section into segments that are orthogonal to the direction of the section view. This enables you to show different parts of the building model in the same section view.

To create a segmented section, create a straight section line in the drawing and then choose the **Split Segment** tool from the **Section** panel of the **Modify | Views** tab. On doing so, a split symbol will be attached to the cursor. Move it over the section line and click at the point from where you want to split it. Move the cursor perpendicular to the section line; it will break from the specified point and you can move the cursor in the desired direction to split the section line along the head or tail side. Click again to specify the location of the split. The segmented section will be created and the section view will be modified immediately, as shown in Figure 6-54.

Figure 6-54 The segmented section line with the modified section view

Controlling the Visibility of a Section Line

The section line is visible in plan, section, and elevation view, if the view range of the created views intersects the crop region of the current view. The section line created in one view is visible and created simultaneously in all the other views.

You can also control the visibility of the section line in the views. Select the section line, right-click, and choose the **Hide in View > Element** option from the shortcut menu. It becomes hidden in the current view.

Note

The section of elements is displayed when a section is cut through them. Sections through in-place elements are not available; therefore they are not displayed in the section view.

Creating a Detail and a Wall Section View

In Autodesk Revit, you can create different types of section views. The types of section views will depend upon the type you will select from the **Type Selector** drop-down list in the **Properties** palette. From the **Type Selector** drop-down list you can select any of the three different types of section views such as detail, building, or wall section view.

To create a detail section view from the building model, select the **Detail View : Detail** option from the **Type Selector** drop-down list of the **Properties** palette. Similarly, to create a building section or a wall section of the building model, select the **Section : Building Section** or the **Section : Wall Section** option from the **Type Selector** drop-down list. After clearing a wall section using the **Section : Wall Section** type, you will notice that its section view has been added to the list of sections under the subhead **Sections (Wall Sections)** in the **Project Browser** and you can display it by double-clicking on the section name. Similarly, a section view created as a building section or a detail section will be displayed in the subhead **Sections (Building Sections)** or **Detail Views (Detail)**, respectively. You will learn more about these views in the later chapters.

Working with Datum Plane and Creating Standard Views

Using the Scope Box Tool

With the **Scope Box** tool, Autodesk Revit provides you the option of controlling the visibility of the datum elements in the project views. As described earlier in this chapter, the datum planes have an infinite scope and extend throughout the project. Using the **Scope Box** tool, you can limit the boundary for the visibility of the datum planes. You can also specify the views in which these datum planes become visible.

Note
*The **Scope Box** tool is activated only in the plan view and it is view specific.*

Creating a Scope Box

The Scope box can be created in the plan view by invoking the **Scope Box** tool. You can invoke this tool from the **Create** panel of the **View** tab. Once this tool has been invoked, the **Options Bar** displays the **Name** and **Height** edit boxes. You can enter the name and height of the scope box using these edit boxes.

To create the Scope Box, move the cursor in the viewing area. It changes into a cross symbol, prompting you to draw the scope box in the plan view. To define the scope box, click on its upper left corner, move the cursor to the lower right corner, and then click to specify the diagonally opposite ends. The rectangle should be drawn in such a way that the elements that need to be visible are enclosed in it. The scope box with the assigned name is created. When it is selected, the drag controls are visible on it, as shown in Figure 6-55. These drag controls can be used to resize the scope box.

Figure 6-55 Drag controls displayed on selecting the scope box

Applying the Scope Box

The visibility of datum planes can be controlled by associating them with the scope box. You can select a datum such as a grid, a level, or a reference plane, and then in the **Properties** palette, click in the value column for the **Scope Box** parameter and select the name of the scope box from the drop-down list displayed. Now, choose the **Apply** button to apply the property to the selected datum. The datum now appears only in those views whose cutting planes intersect the scope box.

Controlling the Visibility of the Scope Box

The scope box can be resized to limit its visibility for certain views. Its visibility can also be controlled for each view. To control the visibility of the scope box, select it; the instance properties of the selected scope box will be displayed in the **Properties** palette. In the **Parameters** area of the palette, choose the **Edit** button displayed in the value field for the **Views Visible** parameter; the **Scope Box Views Visible** dialog box will be displayed. This dialog box lists all views types and view names available in the project. In the **Scope Box Views Visible** dialog box, the **Automatic visibility** column shows the current visibility of scope boxes for corresponding views. You can click in the value field in the **Override** column for a specific view. On doing so, a drop-down list will be displayed, as shown in Figure 6-56. The drop-down list has three options: **None**, **Visible**, and **Invisible**. You can select any of the options from the drop-down list displayed to override the automatic visibility setting.

Figure 6-56 Controlling the visibility of the scope boxes using the **Scope Box Views Visible** dialog box

Working with Datum Plane and Creating Standard Views   6-41

TUTORIALS

Tutorial 1   Apartment 1

In this tutorial, you will add levels and grids to the *c05_Apartment1_tut1.rvt (M_c05_Apartment1_tut1.rvt* for Metric*)* project. Also, you will create wall elevation for the kitchen walls and sections using the Figure 6-57 as reference. Do not create the dimensions and text as they have been given only for your reference. Use the following project parameters:

(Expected time: 30 min)

1. Rename Level 1 as **First Floor** and Level 2 as **Second Floor**

2. Levels to be added:
   - For Imperial **Third Floor- Elevation 20'0"**
   - **Fourth Floor- Elevation 30'0"**
   - **Roof Floor- Elevation 40'0"**
   - For Metric **Third Floor- Elevation 6000 mm**
   - **Fourth Floor- Elevation 9000 mm**
   - **Roof Floor- Elevation 12000 mm**

   Note that in the metric template level 2 is at 4000 mm. Change that level to 3000mm and then add further levels.

3. Grids and sections to be created using Figure 6-57 as reference. The horizontal section to be renamed as **Section X** and the vertical section as **Section Y**.

The following steps are required to complete this tutorial:

a. Open the file created in Chapter 5.
   - For Imperial *c05_Apartment1_tut1.rvt*
   - For Metric *M_c05_Apartment1_tut1.rvt*
b. Add levels using the **Level** tool, refer to Figures 6-58 through 6-61.
c. Add grids using the **Grid** tool, refer to Figures 6-62 through 6-64.
d. Create section views using the **Section** tool, refer to Figures 6-64 and 6-66.
e. Create and view the four interior wall elevations of the kitchen walls, refer to Figures 6-67 and 6-68.

Figure 6-57 Sketch plan for adding grids, sections, and elevations to the Apartment 1 project

Opening an Existing Project and Hiding Tags

Before starting this tutorial, you need to open the specified project, and then you need to hide the door and window tags to simplify the project view using the **Visibility/Graphics** tool.

1. To open the specified project, choose **Open > Project** from the **Application Menu** and then open the *c05_Apartment1_tut1.rvt* file (for Metric *M_c05_Apartment1_tut1.rvt*), created in Tutorial 1 of Chapter 5. You can also download this file from *http://www.cadcim.com*. The path of the file is as follows: *Textbooks > Civil/GIS > Revit Architecture > Autodesk Revit Architecture 2015 for Architects and Designers*.

2. Ensure that the **Floor Plans** view for Level 1 is opened. Next, to hide the doors and windows tags, choose the **Visibility/Graphics** tool from the **Graphics** panel of the **View** tab; the **Visibility/Graphics Overrides for Floor Plan** dialog box is displayed.

3. Choose the **Annotation Categories** tab from the dialog box and clear the check boxes for **Door Tags** and **Window Tags**.

4. Choose the **Apply** button to apply the changes and then the **OK** button to close the dialog box and return to the drawing window.

Adding Levels

In this section, you will learn to create levels in the elevation view.

1. Move the cursor to the **Project Browser** and double-click on **North** under the **Elevations (Building Elevation)** head. The north elevation with the existing levels is displayed in the drawing window. Make sure that the **Hidden Line** option is selected in the **Visual Style** menu of the **View Control Bar**. Select the levels and drag the endpoints of the level lines near the building profile; the view is adjusted, as shown in Figure 6-58.

Working with Datum Plane and Creating Standard Views 6-43

Figure 6-58 The north elevation view of the Apartment 1 project

2. Invoke the **Level** tool from the **Datum** panel of the **Architecture** tab.

Note
In the metric unit system, by default, the Level 2 is at 4000 mm. Shift the Level 2 to 3000mm by clicking on the value and entering the value as 3000.

3. Next, move the cursor near the left endpoint of the level line of Level 2 and when the alignment line appears, enter **10'0"(3000 mm)** as the distance of the new level from the Level 2, as shown in Figure 6-59.

Figure 6-59 Specifying the distance of the new level

4. Move the cursor toward right until the alignment line is displayed above the Level 2 bubble, as shown in Figure 6-60, and click to complete the level line. The new level line is created showing the level name as **Level 3**, and the elevation as **20'0"(6000 mm)**. Press ESC to exit.

Figure 6-60 Creating the new level line using the alignment line

5. Repeat the procedure followed in steps 3 and 4 to create two more levels, Level 4 and Level 5 above Level 3 at a distance of 10'0"(3000 mm) each. Press ESC twice to exit the **Level** tool.

   Notice that the **Project Browser** now shows the floor and ceiling plans for Level 3, Level 4, and Level 5.

6. To rename the levels, move the cursor over Level 1 under the **Floor Plans** head in the **Project Browser** and then right-click to display a shortcut menu.

7. Choose the **Rename** option from the shortcut menu; the **Rename View** dialog box is displayed.

8. In the **Rename View** dialog box, enter **First Floor** in the **Name** edit box and choose the **OK** button. Autodesk Revit prompts you to verify whether you want to rename the corresponding levels and views.

9. Choose the **Yes** button to rename the levels and views. Level 1 is renamed to **First Floor** in the elevation view.

10. Repeat the procedure followed in steps 6 through 9 to rename Level 2 as **Second Floor**, Level 3 as **Third Floor**, Level 4 as **Fourth Floor**, and Level 5 as **Roof**. Figure 6-61 shows all levels renamed in the north elevation.

Figure 6-61 North elevation showing the renamed levels

Working with Datum Plane and Creating Standard Views

Adding Grid Lines

You can use the plan view to add grids to the project using the **Grid** tool. Grids are automatically numbered as they are created. You will create grids in the sequence, as shown in the sketch plan.

1. Double-click on **First Floor** from the **Floor Plans** head in the **Project Browser** to display the ground floor plan in the drawing window.

2. Next, choose the **Grid** tool from the **Datum** panel of the **Architecture** tab; the **Modify | Place Grid** tab is displayed.

   Notice that the sketch plan shows the grid lines as the centerlines of walls. You can use the **Line** tool (default) from the **Draw** panel to create them.

3. Now, ensure that the **Line** tool is chosen in the **Draw** panel.

4. Move the cursor near the top left corner of the exterior wall profile and move the cursor up till a vertical extension line is displayed. Click to specify the start point of the grid line when the temporary dimension of 3'0"(900 mm) is displayed from the centerline of the exterior wall, as shown in Figure 6-62.

5. Move the cursor vertically downward and click outside the south wall to specify the endpoint of the grid line, as shown in Figure 6-63.

Note

*If grid lines are not visible in the drawing, choose the **Visibility/Graphics** tool from the **Graphics** panel of the **View** tab to display the **Visibility/Graphic Overrides for Floor Plan** dialog box. In the **Annotation Categories** tab of this dialog box, select the **Grids** check box.*

The same procedure can be followed to draw grid lines for the interior walls. As the thickness of the interior wall is 5"(127 mm), you can specify 2 1/2"(64 mm) as the offset distance to draw grid lines for the interior walls.

Figure 6-62 Specifying the start point of the grid line

Figure 6-63 Specifying the end point of the first vertical grid line

6. Repeat the procedure followed in steps 3, 4, and 5 to create other vertical and horizontal grid lines in the sequence of their numbers using the alignment line feature. After adding grid lines, press ESC twice to exit. Figure 6-64 shows the floor plan after adding grid lines.

7. To rename the grid 5, select it and then click on its name. The edit box with the current number is displayed.

8. Enter the value **A** in the edit box and press ENTER to rename the grid.

9. Repeat steps 7 and 8 to rename the grid 6 as **B**.

Note
*You can rename a grid by selecting it from the drawing and then entering a value corresponding to the value column for the **Name** parameter in the **Properties** palette. The entered value will be the new name of the grid.*

Working with Datum Plane and Creating Standard Views 6-47

Figure 6-64 The horizontal and vertical grids created for the wall centerlines

Creating Section Views

The Section views can be created by using the **Section** tool.

1. Choose the **Section** tool from the **Create** panel of the **View** tab.

2. Move the cursor near the midpoint of the west wall. Click to specify the start point of the section line, refer to Figure 6-65.

3. Move the cursor horizontally across the building plan until you cross the exterior face of the east wall, as shown in Figure 6-65. Click to specify the endpoint of the section line. The section view is created and the name **Section 1** is displayed in the **Sections (Building Section)** head in the **Project Browser**.

4. Repeat the procedure followed in steps 2 and 3 to create a transverse section through the apartment building, as shown in Figure 6-66. Choose a point outside the main entrance as the start point and move the cursor vertically upward beyond the exterior wall of the kitchen to specify the endpoint of the section line. As the bubble of the grid line 2 touches the section line, you can move the grid bubble using the **split and drag** tool.

5. Select the grid line 2 and click on the **Add Elbow** symbol displayed near the grid bubble.

6. Drag the two blue dots to a location outside the exterior wall, refer to Figure 6-66. Press ESC to exit.

Figure 6-65 *Creating a section line for the section view*

Figure 6-66 *The section lines created for the section views*

7. Click on the '**+**' symbol on the left of the **Sections (Building Section)** head in the **Project Browser** to display the section name created. Right-click on **Section 1** and then choose **Rename** from the shortcut menu; the **Rename View** dialog box is displayed.

8. Enter **Section X** in the **Name** edit box of the **Rename View** dialog box and then choose **OK**; the section view is renamed.

9. Similarly, rename **Section 2** as **Section Y**.

10. Double-click on **Section X** to display the corresponding section in the drawing window, as shown in Figure 6-67.

Working with Datum Plane and Creating Standard Views 6-49

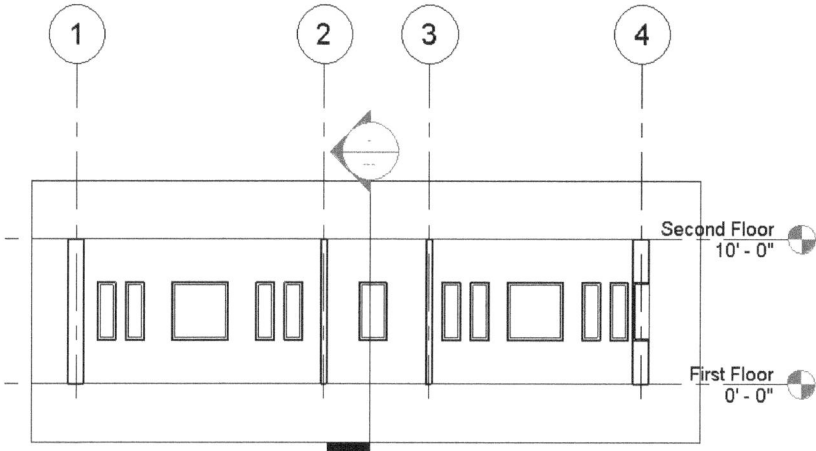

Figure 6-67 Section view of Section X

Creating Elevation Views

To create the interior wall elevation of the kitchen walls, use the **Elevation** tool. You can use the first floor plan view to create new elevations.

1. Double-click on the name **First Floor** in the **Floor Plans** head of the **Project Browser** to display the first floor plan in the drawing window.

2. Choose the **Elevation** tool from the **View > Create > Elevation** drop-down.

3. Move the cursor inside the kitchen area until the arrowhead points upward, toward the kitchen window and click to create the elevation.

4. Press the ESC key to exit the **Elevation** tool.

5. Select the elevation symbol to display its controls.

6. Click to select all the three cleared check boxes to create interior elevations. The new elevations are added under the **Elevations (Building Elevation)** head in the **Project Browser**.

7. Rename the corresponding elevation views as **Kitchen-North Wall**, **Kitchen-East Wall**, **Kitchen-South Wall**, and **Kitchen-West Wall** using the shortcut menu displayed on right-clicking the elevation views.

8. Double-click on the **Kitchen-North Wall** option in the **Project Browser** to display the corresponding elevation view. The crop-region can be picked by selecting the box. On selecting the box, drag controls appear. Drag the view crop region using the drag controls and grids of the kitchen area, as shown in Figure 6-68. Similarly, create the **Kitchen- South Wall** elevation, as shown in Figure 6-69.

Figure 6-68 Kitchen-North wall elevation   *Figure 6-69* Kitchen-South wall elevation

 Note
If the crop-region boundary is not visible in the drawing, then choose the **Show Crop Region** *button from the* **View Control Bar.**

9. Double-click on the **First Floor** under the **Floor Plans** head in the **Project Browser** to return to the floor plan view.

10. Choose **Save As > Project** from **the Application Menu**; the **Save As** dialog box is displayed. Enter **c06_Apartment1_tut1** in the **File name** edit box and then choose **Save** to save the project.

11. Choose the **Close** option from **the Application Menu**.

    This completes Tutorial 1 for adding levels, grids, and sections to the *Apartment 1* project.

Tutorial 2   Club

In this tutorial, you will add levels and grids to the *c05_Club_ex2.rvt(M_c05_Club_ex2.rvt)* project created in Exercise 2 of Chapter 5. Also, you will create sections in the sketch plan shown in Figure 6-70. Do not create dimensions and texts as they have been given only for reference. Use the following project parameter.

(Expected time: 30 min)

1. Rename Level 1 as the **First Floor** and move the Roof level to **15'0"(4572 mm)** elevation.
   Rename the Level 2 as **Roof** in Metric unit system.

2. Grids and sections to be created in the sketch plan shown in Figure 6-70.

Working with Datum Plane and Creating Standard Views

The following steps are required to complete this tutorial:

a. Open the file.
   For Imperial   *c05_Club_ex2.rvt*
   For Metric   *M_c05_Club_ex2.rvt*
b. Modify levels by dragging, refer to Figures 6-71 and 6-72.
c. Add grids using the **Grid** tool, refer to Figures 6-73 and 6-74.
d. Create section views using the **Section** tool, refer to Figure 6-75 through Figure 6-77.

Figure 6-70 Sketch plan for adding grids and creating section views for the Club project

Opening the Existing Project and Hiding Tags

To start with the tutorial, you need to open the Club project file and hide the door and window tags using the **Visibility/Graphics** tool.

1. Choose **Open > Project** from the **Application Menu** and open the required file.
   For Imperial   *c05_Club_ex2.rvt*
   For Metric   *M_c05_Club_ex2.rvt*
   You can also download this file from *http://www.cadcim.com*. The path of the file is as follows:
   Textbooks > Civil/GIS > Revit Architecture > Autodesk Revit Architecture 2015 for Architects and Designers.

2. Choose the **Visibility/Graphics** tool from the **Graphics** panel of the **View** tab; the **Visibility/Graphics Overrides for Floor Plan** dialog box for the plan view is displayed.

3. Choose the **Annotations Categories** tab and clear the check boxes for **Door Tags** and **Window Tags**.

4. In the **Visibility/Graphics Overrides for Floor plan** dialog box, choose the **Apply** and **OK** buttons to apply the changes and close it.

Modifying Levels

You can use the **Elevation** tool to display any exterior elevation of the project. You will open the north elevation and then drag the level to the specified distance.

1. Move the cursor to the **Project Browser** and double-click on **North** under the **Elevations (Building Elevation)** head. The north elevation is displayed within the existing levels in the drawing window.

2. Choose the **Zoom In Region** tool from the **Navigation Bar** to enlarge the right portion of the elevation showing the levels, as shown in Figure 6-71. Ensure that the **Hidden Line** option is chosen in the **View Control Bar** for Visual Style.

   Notice that the wall extends beyond the roof level line. This is because you have used the explicit parameter for the wall height. You can now move the level to the wall top.

Figure 6-71 Existing levels for the Club project

3. Move the cursor near the roof level line, and click when it gets highlighted. Drag it to the top of the wall. The elevation in the level bubble now shows **15' - 0" (4572 mm** for Metric) as its elevation from the base.

4. To rename the levels, move the cursor over **Level 1** in the **Project Browser** and right-click; a shortcut menu is displayed.

5. Choose the **Rename** option from the shortcut menu; the **Rename View** dialog box is displayed.

6. In this dialog box, enter **First Floor** in the **Name** edit box and choose the **OK** button. You are prompted to verify whether you want to rename the corresponding levels and views.

7. Choose the **Yes** button to rename the levels and views. The level is immediately renamed in the elevation view, as shown in Figure 6-72.

Working with Datum Plane and Creating Standard Views 6-53

Figure 6-72 Renamed levels and views for the Club project

Similarly, rename the level 2 as **Roof** in the Metric unit system.

Creating Grid Lines

You will use the plan view to add grids to the project using the **Grid** tool. The grids are automatically numbered as they are created. You will, however, rename them based on the names given in the sketch plan.

1. Double-click on **First Floor** from the **Floor Plans** head of the **Project Browser** to display the first floor plan in the drawing window.

2. Choose the **Grid** tool from the **Datum** panel of the **Architecture** tab.

   Notice that the sketch plan shows the grid lines as the centerlines of the walls. Use the **Line** tool to create grid lines at the centerline of the walls. You may need to zoom into the area for Autodesk Revit to snap to the wall centerlines.

3. Choose the **Line** tool, if it is not chosen by default in the **Draw** panel of the **Modify | Place Grid** tab.

4. Zoom into the west corner of Hall 1 and move the cursor near the exterior wall intersection, marked 1, refer to Figure 6-73. Use the TAB key to toggle between the object snaps at the intersection and click when a dashed line appears in the center of the wall on which the grid 1 is to be created, refer to Figure 6-74.

5. Move the cursor along the exterior wall and click when the cursor crosses the lower exterior wall intersection, as shown in Figure 6-73. The first grid line is created.

6. Repeat the procedure followed in steps 4 and 5 to create other grid lines for the external walls, as shown in the Figure 6-74. Press ESC twice to exit.

   The completed plan with grids will be similar to the one shown in Figure 6-74.

7. To rename the grid number 4, double-click on it; an edit box with the current grid number is displayed.

8. Enter the new value **A1** in the edit box to rename the grid.

*Figure 6-73 Grid line created using the **Line** tool in the **Draw** panel*

9. Repeat the procedure followed in steps 7 and 8 to rename all other grid numbers based on the sketch plan, refer to Figure 6-70.

Figure 6-74 Grids created for the Club project

Creating Section Views

The Section views can be created by using the **Section** tool.

1. Choose the **Section** tool from the **Create** panel of the **View** tab.

2. Move the cursor over the wall of the grid A1, refer to Figure 6-70 and drag it downward. When the temporary dimension appears, enter 20'(6000 mm) in the edit box displayed; the start point of the section line is specified. Now, drag it straight to draw the section across the building, refer to Figure 6-75.

Working with Datum Plane and Creating Standard Views   6-55

3. Move the cursor diagonally upward across the building plan until you cross the exterior face of the lobby wall. Click to specify the endpoint of the section line, as shown in Figure 6-75. The name, **Section 1** is displayed in the **Sections (Building Sections)** head in the **Project Browser**.

4. Repeat the procedure followed in steps 2 and 3 to create a transverse section through Hall 1 of the club building, as shown in Figure 6-76.

Figure 6-75 The section line created

Figure 6-76 Creating the second section line

5. Right-click on the name **Section 1** under the **Section (Building Section)** in the **Project Browser**, and then choose the **Rename** option from the shortcut menu displayed; the **Rename View** dialog box is displayed.

6. In the **Rename View** dialog box, enter **Section X** in the **Name** edit box and choose the **OK** button.

7. Repeat the procedure followed in steps 5 and 6 to rename **Section 2** as **Section Y**, as specified in the sketch plan.

8. Double-click on **Section X** in the **Project Browser** to display the corresponding section in the drawing window, as shown in Figure 6-77.

Figure 6-77 Displaying the section view for the Club project

9. Double-click on **First Floor** under the **Floor Plans** head in the **Project Browser** to display the floor plan of the first floor.

10. Choose **Save As > Project** from **the Application Menu** and enter the required name **c06_Club_tut2** (for Metric **M_c06_Club_tut2**) in the **File name** edit box of the **Save As** dialog box. Next, choose **Save**.

11. Choose **Close** from **the Application Menu** to close the file.

This completes Tutorial 2 for modifying levels, adding grids, and creating section views for the *Club* project.

Working with Datum Plane and Creating Standard Views

Self-Evaluation Test

Answer the following questions and then compare them to those given at the end of this chapter:

1. Which of the following grid properties can you modify?

   a) **Name** b) **Type**
   c) **Position** d) **Elevation**

2. The **Project Browser** shows a logical organization of all views, schedules, sheets, groups, linked Revit models, and other parts of the _____.

   a) Current project c) User interface
   b) Properties palette d) View control bar

3. Levels, once created, cannot be modified. (T/F)

4. You can control the visibility of a level head. (T/F)

5. When you move a level, its elevation is modified automatically. (T/F)

6. In Autodesk Revit Architecture, grids are numbered automatically. (T/F)

7. You cannot copy or array grids. (T/F)

8. Using the _____ tool, you can create grids by picking elements.

9. You can change the viewing side of a section by clicking on the _____ symbol.

10. You can select the _____ type of section from the **Type Selector** drop-down list to create a detail section view.

11. To assign a new name to a section view, right-click on the name of the view in the **Project Browser** and then choose the _____ option from the shortcut menu.

12. The _____ tool can be used to limit the visibility of a datum in a portion of a view.

Review Questions

Answer the following questions:

1. You can control the visibility of grids in each view. (T/F)

2. A work plane cannot be rotated or moved. (T/F)

3. You can align the elevation view based on the orientation of walls. (T/F)

4. Modifications made in any one view are propagated immediately to all other views. (T/F)

5. You can also create detail section views using the **Section** tool. (T/F)

6. Using the **Grid** tool, you can create radial grid patterns. (T/F)

7. The **Scope Box** tool can be used to limit the visibility of grids in a portion of a view. (T/F)

8. Which of the following tools is used to hide the elements belonging to the same category?

    a) **Delete**
    c) **Hidden Lines**
    b) **Hide/Isolate**
    d) **Zoom**

9. Which of the following keys needs to be held to add elements to a selection?

    a) TAB
    c) CTRL
    b) SHIFT
    d) ESC

10. Which of the following tools can be used to limit the visibility of a datum to a certain portion of a view?

    a) **Hide/Isolate**
    c) **Scope Box**
    b) **Hidden lines**
    d) **Dynamic View**

11. You must place an elevation tag to generate an elevation_____.

    a) View
    c) Element
    b) Parameter
    d) Sheet

12. Which of the following tools is used to turn off the visibility of any element in a view.

    a) **Visual styles**
    c) **Object styles**
    b) **Visibility/graphic overrides**
    d) **Display styles**

Exercises

Exercise 1 — Apartment 2

Add levels and grids to the *c05_Apartment2_ex1.rvt (M_c05_Apartment2_ex1.rvt* for Metric) project created in Exercise 1 of Chapter 5. Create the wall elevation for the dining room walls and also sections in the sketch plan shown in Figure 6-78. Do not create dimensions and texts as they are given only for your reference. Use the parameters given below.

(Expected time: 30 min)

1. Rename Level 1 as the **First Floor** and Level 2 as the **Second Floor**.
   In Metric unit system, shift the Level 2 to **3000** mm.
2. Levels to be added:
   For Imperial   **Third Floor- Elevation 20'0"**
                  Fourth Floor- Elevation 30'0"
                  Roof- Elevation 40'0"
   For Metric   **Third Floor- Elevation 6000 mm**
                  Fourth Floor- Elevation 9000 mm
                  Roof- Elevation 12000 mm
3. Grids and Sections to be created in the sketch plan shown in Figure 6-78. Name the horizontal section as **Section X1** and the vertical section as **Section Y1.**
4. Name of the file to be save-
   For Imperial   **c06_Apartment2_ex1**
   For Metric   **M_c06_Apartment2_ex1**

Figure 6-78 Sketch for adding grids and sections to the Apartment 2 project

Exercise 2 — Elevator and Stair Lobby

Add levels and grids to the *Elevator and Stair Lobby* project created in Exercise 3 of Chapter 5. Do not create the dimensions and texts as they are given only for reference. Use the following project parameters:

(Expected time: 30 min)

1. Rename Level 1 as **First Floor** and Level 2 as **Second Floor**
2. Levels to be added:
   For Imperial   **Third Floor- Elevation 20'0"**
                      Fourth Floor- Elevation 30'0"
                      Roof Floor- Elevation 40'0"
   For Metric   **Third Floor- Elevation 6000 mm**
                      Fourth Floor- Elevation 9000 mm
                      Roof- Elevation 12000 mm
3. Grids and Sections are to be created in the sketch plan shown in Figure 6-79. Name the horizontal section as **Section H** and the vertical section as **Section V**.
4. Name of the file to be saved-
   For Imperial   **c06_ElevatorandStairLobby_ex2**
   For Metric   **M_c06_ElevatorandStairLobby_ex2**

Figure 6-79 Sketch plan for creating grids and sections for the Elevator and Stair Lobby project

Answers to Self-Evaluation Test
1. F, 2. T, 3. T, 4. T, 5. F, 6. Pick Line, 7. Flip Section, 8. Detail View: Detail, 9. Rename, 10. Scope Box

Chapter 7

Using Basic Building Components-II

Learning Objectives

After completing this chapter, you will be able to:
- *Understand the concept of floor.*
- *Create floors using the Floor tool.*
- *Create roofs using the Roof tool.*
- *Use the shape editing tools for floor, roof, and slabs.*
- *Create ceilings using the Ceiling tool.*
- *Create openings in the floor, roof, and ceiling.*
- *Create rooms using the Room tool.*
- *Join walls with the other walls and roofs.*

INTRODUCTION

In the earlier chapters, you learned to use levels, grids, and datums in a project. Also, you have learned that elements such as walls, doors, windows, and so on can be added from the library of in-built elements provided in Autodesk Revit. This chapter describes creation of sketched elements such as floors, roofs, and ceilings in a project. For creating these sketched elements, you need to draw sketch.

CREATING ARCHITECTURAL FLOORS

Ribbon: Architecture > Build > Floor drop-down > Floor: Architectural

You can add a floor to the current level of a building model using the **Floor: Architectural** tool. You can invoke this tool from the **Build** panel of the **Architecture** tab. On invoking this tool, the **Modify | Create Floor Boundary** contextual tab will be displayed, as shown in Figure 7-1.

Figure 7-1 The *Modify | Create Floor Boundary* tab

You can use this tab to draw, annotate, and edit a floor boundary for your building model as well as to assign properties to it. The **Draw** panel of the **Modify | Create Floor Boundary** tab consists of various tools that are used to draw the floor sketches. These sketches define the boundary of the floor. To define the boundary of the floor, you can either pick the existing walls or sketch the boundary in the plan view by using lines or sketch the boundary in the 3D view, provided that the work plane is set to the plan view.

Similar to the other model components, the floor too has associated type and instance properties. Once you sketch the floor, the **Properties** palette will display the instance parameters of floor, as shown in Figure 7-2. The **Type Selector** drop-down list in this palette displays the floors available in Autodesk Revit Architecture's library, refer to Figure 7-2. This palette can be used to modify the instance properties of the floor such as the level at which the floor is to be created, the height offset of the floor from the specified level, and so on. To modify the type properties of a floor, choose the **Edit Type** button from the **Properties** palette; the **Type Properties** dialog box will be displayed, as shown in Figure 7-3. You can set the type parameters for the floor in it. You can also create a new floor type by using the **Duplicate** button. To edit the structural elements of the floor, choose the **Edit** button in the **Value** column for the **Structure** type parameter; the **Edit Assembly** dialog box will be displayed, showing the structure of the floor type with its different layers. In the **Edit Assembly** dialog box, the **Insert** or **Delete** button can be used to customize the new floor type based on the specific project requirement.

Note
The type and instance properties vary depending upon the floor type selected. Autodesk Revit Help provides a detailed explanation of all the properties associated with the floor types.

Using Basic Building Components-II

*Figure 7-2 The **Properties** palette displaying the instance parameters*

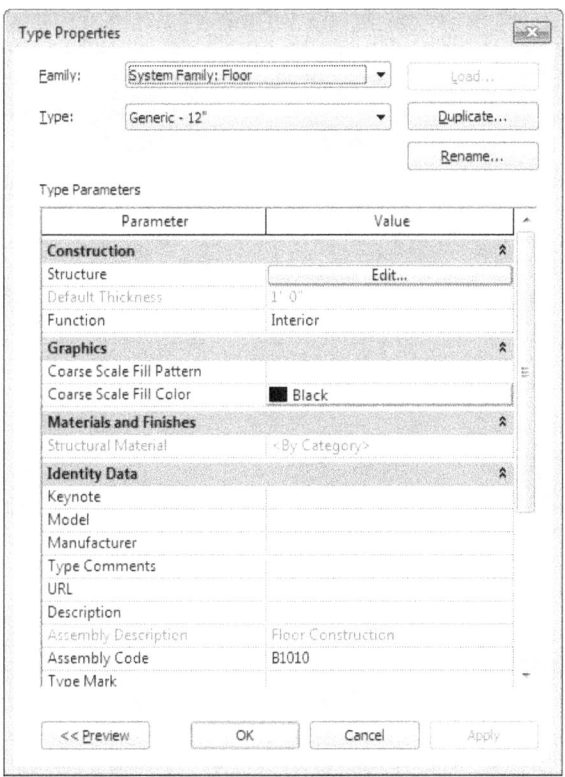

*Figure 7-3 The **Type Properties** dialog box*

Tip: *The **Preview** button in the **Type Properties** dialog box can be used to display a graphical image of the floor type which changes when you add or remove a layer in the floor structure.*

Sketching the Floor Boundary

To create a floor, you need to sketch its boundary. There are two methods to sketch a boundary. The first method is to pick the already created walls using the **Pick Walls** tool to define the floor boundary. The other method to define the floor boundary is to draw the floor profile using the draw tools such as line, rectangle, polygon, arc, and others from the **Draw** panel of the **Modify | Create Floor Boundary** tab.

By default, the **Pick Walls** tool is chosen in the **Draw** panel of the **Modify | Create Floor Boundary** tab. This tool can be used to sketch the floor for the spaces bound by the connected walls. The **Option Bar** displays the **Offset** edit box, which can be used to specify the offset distance of the floor sketch line from an existing wall. The **Extend into wall (to core)** check box is used to extend the floor to the wall core and assists in creating a joint between the floor and the wall core. If the **Pick Walls** tool is not chosen by default, then invoke this tool and move the cursor near the wall. You will notice that as the cursor is brought near the face of the wall, a dashed line appears along its inner or outer face. You can choose either of the faces of the wall to sketch the floor. Click when the dashed line appears at appropriate location; a magenta line with flip and drag controls as well as two parallel lines will be displayed on the wall, refer to Figure 7-4. The flip control can be used to flip the line between the two faces of the wall.

Similarly, you can select other walls to define the floor boundary. The sketched boundary must form a closed profile with all edges connected to each other.

Figure 7-4 A boundary line created from one of the wall faces while sketching the floor boundary

Using Basic Building Components-II 7-5

 Tip: *You can also use the TAB key to select a chain of wall segments to create the floor boundary.*

After completing the floor boundary, you can edit it by using the drag controls and various tools in the **Modify** panel of the **Modify | Create Floor Boundary** tab. For example, you can drag the sketched line of the floor boundary to a new location by using the drag controls, as shown in Figure 7-5. After the floor profile has been sketched, choose the **Finish Edit Mode** button from the **Mode** panel; the floor will be created and highlighted in blue. As the floor created will not be visible in the plan view, you can use the **Default 3D View** tool from the **Quick Access Toolbar** to view it.

Figure 7-5 *Dragging the sketched floor boundary*

 Tip: *In case the sketched profile does not form a closed loop, Autodesk Revit displays an error message informing that the lines are not connected. Also, you are prompted to specify whether you want to quit the sketching or continue editing the sketch. To rectify the error, you can choose the **Continue** option, make the correction, and then proceed.*

The other option to sketch the floor profile is to draw it using the sketching tools from the **Draw** panel. You can choose the appropriate sketching tool to sketch the floor boundary based on its shape. The functions of the sketching tools are the same as those used for creating a wall. When you use the **Line** tool, the **Chain** check box in the **Options Bar** can be selected to sketch the lines that are connected end-to-end. The **Offset** edit box in the **Options Bar** can be used to sketch lines at a specified offset distance from a point on an existing element. Using the editing tools in the **Modify** panel of the **Modify | Create Floor Boundary** tab, you can edit the sketched profile.

In the sketched floor boundary, you can provide slope. To do so, invoke the **Slope Arrow** tool from the **Draw** panel; a list box containing tools to draw the slope arrow will be displayed. The list box contains two tools: **Line** and **Pick Lines**. The **Line** tool is chosen by default in the display panel. You need to specify the start point and endpoint of the arrow in the drawing. After specifying the start point and endpoint, you can modify its instance properties in the **Properties** palette. Using this palette, you can modify the associated properties such as specification method to define the slope arrow, the level at which the tail of the slope arrow will rest, height offset at the tail of the arrow, and more. You can attain the desired slope in the floor using the instance properties in the **Properties** palette.

After you complete the profile and add specifications for the floor, choose the **Finish Edit Mode** button from the **Mode** panel; the floor will be created and the **Modify|Floors** tab will be displayed. In this tab, you can use various modification tools to modify the floor created. This tab consists of nine panels: **Properties**, **Clipboard**, **Geometry**, **View**, **Modify**, **Measure**, **Create**, **Mode**, **Draw** and **Work Plane**.

Tip: *You can also create a floor from a mass floor using the **Floor by Face** tool from **Architectural > Build > Floor** drop-down. The method of creating a mass floor from a massing object is explained in Chapter 10.*

In Autodesk Revit, you can also create a structural floor in a building model. The structural floor is capable of carrying loads and transferring it to other active structural members. It actively participates in the structural analysis of the building. This makes it different from the floor that you will add using the **Floor: Architectural** tool. To add a structural floor, you can invoke the **Floor: Structural** tool from **Architecture > Build > Floor** drop-down.

In an architectural floor, you can create a slab edge under the existing floor. To do so, invoke the **Floor: Slab Edge** tool from the **Floor** drop-down in the **Build** Panel of the **Architecture** tab. On invoking this tool, the **Modify|Place Slab Edge** tab will be displayed. Now, place the cursor at the desired edge of the floor; the edge will get highlighted. Click at the highlighted edge; slab under the floor will be created as shown in Figure 7-6. After clicking on the edge, two flip arrows will be displayed at the selected edge. You can flip the direction of the slab using these arrows. After doing so, you can change the properties in the **Properties** palette by modifying the type and instance properties of slab created. To modify the type properties, choose the **Edit Type** button from the **Properties** palette; the **Type Properties** dialog box will be displayed. In this dialog box, you can specify the desired values in the **Value** fields of the parameters either by entering a new value or selecting an option from the drop-down list in the **Type Properties** dialog box. Similarly, you can modify the instance properties of a slab by entering a new value or by selecting an option from the drop-down list displayed in the value field of the corresponding parameter.

Note
If you place a slab segment at the adjacent side of the existing slab edge, both the existing and the new segments will mitter and form a one continuous slab.

Using Basic Building Components-II

Figure 7-6 Slab edge displayed at one face

CREATING ROOFS

A roof is a structure that covers the uppermost part of a building. The primary function of a roof is to protect the building and its contents from rain. The other functions of a roof depend upon the nature of the structure that it is protecting. For dwellings, a roof can protect against heat, cold, sunlight, and wind.

In Autodesk Revit, you can create a roof structure using various tools displayed in the **Roof** drop-down in the **Build** panel of the **Architecture** tab, as shown in Figure 7-7. You can use the extrusions, or mass instances present in the drawing to create a roof.

Figure 7-7 Various tools displayed in the Roof drop-down

Creating Roofs by Footprint

Ribbon: Architecture > Build > Roof drop-down > Roof by Footprint

The roof footprint is a two dimensional sketch of the perimeter of a roof. In Autodesk Revit, you can create a roof footprint by drawing lines or picking walls that will define the perimeter of the roof to be created.

The sketch of the footprint, that is to be created, will be placed at the same level of the plan view where it was sketched. The sketch of the footprint should be a closed loop geometry that may also contain other closed loops, which will define the opening in the roof.

In Autodesk Revit, you can invoke the **Roof by Footprint** tool from **Architecture > Build > Roof** drop-down. On invoking this tool, the **Lowest Level Notice** dialog box will be displayed. This dialog box contains a drop-down list. From this drop-down list, you can select the required level to sketch the roofprint in which it will be created. By default, **Level 2** is selected in the drop-down list, as shown in Figure 7-8. Therefore, by default, Autodesk Revit sketches the footprint in **Level 2**. However, you can specify different levels in the drop-down list of the **Lowest Level Notice** dialog box and then choose the **Yes** button; the dialog box will be closed and the **Modify|Create Roof Footprint** tab will be displayed. The **Modify|Create Roof Footprint** tab contains tools to draw, annotate, edit, and change the properties of the roof to be created. To draw a footprint, choose the required drawing tools from the **Draw** panel of the **Modify|Create Roof Footprint** tab. In the **Draw**

Figure 7-8 Specifying the level to sketch the roof footprint

panel, the **Pick Walls** tool is chosen by default. You can use this tool to draw the footprint of the roof by selecting walls. Alternatively, you can use sketching tools such as line, rectangle, circle, or ellipse to draw the footprint from the **Draw** panel. While drawing the roof footprint, you can set the overhang distance of the roof by entering a value in the **Overhang** edit box in the **Options Bar**. You can also change the slope definition of the line that constitutes the footprint. To do so, select the **Defines slope** check box in the **Options Bar**. As such, when you draw the footprint, you can define the slope value of the line by clicking on it and changing the existing slope value in the edit box that will be displayed. You can also extend the roof to the wall core by selecting the **Extend to wall core** check box from the **Options Bar**. Figure 7-9 shows the completed roof footprint for a rectangular wall profile with a specified offset distance and a defined slope. After completing the sketch of the footprint, choose the **Finish Edit Mode** button in the **Mode** panel of the **Modify | Create Roof Footprint** tab; the **Modify|Roofs** tab will be displayed.

Note
*While drawing the roof for the first time in a project or while drawing it at the Level 1 the **Lowest Level Notice** dialog box will be displayed.*

In the **Modify | Roofs** tab, you can use various tools for modifying the created roof such as modifying the instance and type properties, editing the footprint, and other modification tools. After modifying the roof, press ESC to exit from the roof creation tool. Now, you can choose the **{3D}** option from the **Project Browser** to view the created roof, as shown in Figure 7-10. You can create a gable roof from the roof footprint by setting the two parallel lines of the roof footprint as sloping. To do so, select the roof that you want to create as a gable roof from the drawing; the **Modify | Roofs** tab will be displayed. In this tab, choose the **Edit Footprint** tool from the **Mode** panel; the **Modify | Roofs > Edit Footprint** tab will be displayed. Also, the footprints of the roof will be displayed in the drawing area.

Using Basic Building Components-II

Figure 7-9 Roof footprint of a rectangular wall profile

Figure 7-10 Hip roof created

Now, select a footprint line from the drawing and clear the **Defines slope** check box in the **Options Bar** to remove the slope parameter. Similarly, select the footprint line parallel to the previously selected line and remove the slope. Alternatively, to modify the slope of a footprint line, select it; the **Properties** palette will be displayed. In this palette, select or clear the **Defines Roof Slope** check box in the value column of the **Defines Roof Slope** parameter. Selecting the **Defines Roof Slope** check box helps you create a sloping edge of the roof footprint, whereas clearing the check box enables you to remove the slope. For example, for a given rectangular profile, you can select the longer edges of the roof footprint as sloping, as shown in Figure 7-11. Next, after setting the slopes for the footprint, choose the **Finish Edit Mode** button from the **Mode** tab to complete the sketch. The resulting roof shape resembles the illustration shown in Figure 7-12.

Figure 7-11 Sketching the roof footprint by longer edges

Figure 7-12 Resulting gable roof

A shed roof can be created by selecting only one edge of the roof footprint as the sloping side. Figure 7-13 shows the selected sloping side for the rectangular wall profile. The resulting roof is shown in Figure 7-14.

Figure 7-13 Specifying the sloping side   *Figure 7-14* Resulting shed roof

A flat roof is created if no line is assigned a sloping parameter. To create a flat roof, clear the **Defines slope** check box before sketching the roof footprint. Alternatively, enter the value **0** for the roof slope control while sketching the roof profile.

> **Note**
> *To select the roof, open the view in which it has been created because it might not be visible in the lowest plane. The sloping roof may appear to be cut off at a level because of the intersection of the roof and the work plane of the level. Double-click on **Site** in the **Floor Plans** head of the **Project Browser** to view the entire roof profile.*

Creating Roofs By Extrusion

Ribbon: Architecture > Build > Roof drop-down > Roof by Extrusion

The second method of creating a roof is by using the **Roof by Extrusion** tool. You can sketch the roof profile and then extrude it to create the roof by using this tool. The profile can be created in the elevation view by using a specific work plane. Also, the profile created must have a series of connected lines that do not form a closed boundary.

To create a roof by extrusion, invoke the **Roof by Extrusion** tool from the **Build** panel; the **Work Plane** dialog box will be displayed, as shown in Figure 7-15. In this dialog box, select the work plane for sketching the roof profile.

Using Basic Building Components-II

*Figure 7-15 Specifying the work plane for sketching the roof profile in the **Work Plane** dialog box*

You can choose an existing work plane by selecting the **Name** radio button and then selecting its name from the corresponding drop-down list. By default, the **Pick a plane** option is selected. You can also select an existing plane by using this option. When you select this option, Autodesk Revit Architecture prompts you to select a work plane or an element defining a plane to sketch the roof profile. The **Pick a line and use the work plane it was sketched in** radio button is used to select a line and use the work plane, in which it was sketched for sketching the roof profile. You can also create a work plane that is coplanar to the work plane of the file.

If the selected plane is perpendicular to the existing view, the **Go to View** dialog box will be displayed. In this dialog box, you can select a view from the different views available to set the work plane. For example, you can select the **East** or **West** elevation view option to make the sketch parallel to the screen or you can select the **3D View** option to place the roof sketch at an angle to the screen. On selecting a work plane, the **Roof Reference Level and Offset** dialog box will be displayed, as shown in Figure 7-16.

*Figure 7-16 The **Roof Reference Level and Offset** dialog box*

You can specify the base level of the roof by selecting the required option from the **Level** drop-down list. The default level in the drop-down list is the highest level in the project. The **Offset** edit box can be used to specify the offset distance of the roof from the base level. Specify a positive value to create the roof above the specified base level, and a negative value to create the roof below the specified base level. Then, choose the **OK** button in the **Roof**

Reference Level and Offset dialog box; a reference plane will be generated automatically at the offset distance from the specified level and the **Modify|Create Roof Extrusion Profile** tab will be displayed. From this tab, you can use various tools to draw, annotate, and modify a roof. To draw a profile, you can use the sketching tools available in the **Draw** panel. While or after sketching the roof profile, you can dimension it using various dimension tools that will be displayed in the **Dimension** panel. While sketching the roof profile, you can also use various editing tools such as **Trim**, **Extend**, **Align**, **Split**, and **Offset**. You can also modify the sketched profile by using various tools such as **Move**, **Copy**, **Mirror**, **Array**, **Scale**, and **Delete** in the **Modify** panel of the **Modify|Create Roof Extrusion Profile** tab.

After you sketch the roof profile, you can change the instance and type properties of the roof for which the profile will be created from the **Properties** palette. In this dialog box, you can change the family and the type of the roof to be created. To do so, select the desired family and then select its type from the **Type Selector** drop-down list. After selecting the desired family and its type for the roof, you can change various instance parameters like start and end values of the extrusion, the reference level, the offset of the level, and other parameters of the roof. To change values of these parameters, click on their respective value fields in the **Properties** palette, and change the existing value by entering a new value or by selecting a new option from the drop-down list. In the **Properties** palette, choose the **Edit Type** button; the **Type Properties** dialog box will be displayed. You can use this dialog box to change the type parameters of the roof such as structural, coarse scale fill and color, and the parameters that reveal the identity of the roof. After changing the type parameters in the **Type Properties** dialog box, choose the **OK** button to exit the dialog box and return to the drawing and editing mode of the roof with the **Modify | Create Extrusion Roof Profile** tab displayed.

Note
*For sketching the roof profile, you can draw reference planes at the specified work plane before you invoke the **Roof by Extrusion** tool. To draw reference planes, align your view with the desired elevation view, and then choose the **Reference Plane** tool from the **Work Plane** panel in the **Architecture** tab; you will enter the sketching mode. Sketch the desired reference planes, as shown in Figure 7-17, and then invoke the **Roof by Extrusion** tool. Now, you can sketch the roof profile using these reference planes, as shown in Figure 7-18.*

Figure 7-17 Sketching reference planes to sketch the roof profile

Using Basic Building Components-II

Figure 7-18 *Sketching the roof profile by using the reference planes*

Now, you can finish the sketch of the extrusion profile and the creation of the roof by choosing the **Finish Edit Mode** button from the **Mode** panel of the **Modify | Create Extrusion Roof Profile** tab. After you finish the sketching of the roof profile and create the roof view, you can use the **ViewCube** navigation tool to change the view to display the other views of the roof for better visualization.

 Note
For the sketch to be valid, the sketched profile should have lines and/or curves that are connected end-to-end. Also, it should not form a closed loop if it is to be extruded.

After creating the roof, you will notice that the walls do not go up to the roof soffit, as shown in Figure 7-19. To extend the unconnected walls to the roof soffit, select the walls; the **Modify | Walls** tab will be displayed. In this tab, choose the **Attach Top/Base** tool from the **Modify Wall** panel; the **Options Bar** for the attaching option will be displayed. The **Options Bar** displays two radio buttons: **Top** and **Base**. To attach the wall top to the roof, select the **Top** radio button. Similarly, to attach the selected wall base to the roof, select the **Base** radio button. After selecting the desired radio button, select the roof; the selected walls will be extended and attached to the roof soffit, as shown in Figure 7-20.

Figure 7-19 *Walls unattached to the roof soffit*   *Figure 7-20* *Extending and attaching the walls to the roof*

In Autodesk Revit, you can create and add soffit, fascia, or gutter to the created roof. You can invoke the tools to create these structures by choosing the **Roof Soffit/Fascia/Gutter** tool from the **Roof** drop-down in the **Build** panel of the **Architecture** tab.

Note
The examples given in this chapter are elementary in nature and their purpose is to explain the basic methods of creating roofs. Using the described techniques, you can experiment with roof shapes and forms to create roofs that are suitable for your project. Autodesk Revit Architecture empowers you to create a variety of dynamic roof forms using a combination of these tools.

Modifying Roof Properties and Editing Shapes

In Autodesk Revit, you can modify the properties and edit the shape of the roof that you have created for the building model. The properties of a roof can be classified into the following three categories:

a) **Roof Boundary Line Properties** - properties of the lines used in sketching the roof footprint such as length, slope angle, offset from the base, and so on.

b) **Roof Instance Properties** - instance properties of the selected roof such as maximum ridge height, base offset from level, and so on.

c) **Roof Type Properties** - properties of the roof, composition, and cost such as structure, thickness, material, and so on.

Tip: *You can combine different roof shapes and join or unjoin them by selecting the roof and then choosing the **Join Geometry/Unjoin Geometry** tool from the **Join** drop-down in the **Geometry** panel of the **Modify** tab.*

You can modify the roof instance and type properties by using the **Properties** palette. To modify these properties from the palette, select the desired roof; the properties related to it will be displayed in the **Properties** palette. You can select a roof type from the **Type Selector** drop-down list in this palette, as shown in Figure 7-21.

The **Properties** palette, as shown in Figure 7-22, lists various instance parameters under the following five main headings: **Constraints**, **Construction**, **Dimensions**, **Identity Data**, and **Phasing**.

Using Basic Building Components-II

Figure 7-21 Selecting an option from the *Type Selector* drop-down list

Figure 7-22 The **Properties** palette displaying various instance properties of a roof

Note
*The number of headings and parameters can increase depending upon the options selected from the **Type Selector** drop-down list in the **Properties** palette.*

The parameters under the **Constraints** head are used to specify the boundary and level constraints for the selected roof. The **Base Level** parameter is used to set the level for the footprint of the selected roof. To change this parameter, click in the corresponding **Value** field and select the desired level from the drop-down list displayed. By default, the top most level is selected. The **Room Bounding** parameter displays a check box in its corresponding value field. This check box is selected by default, which indicates that the selected roof is part of the room boundary. If this check box is cleared, it means the roof is not a part of the room boundary. The **Related to Mass** parameter contains a check box in its value field. If the check box is selected, it indicates that the selected roof is generated from an existing mass element in the drawing. The selection of the check box for the **Related to Mass** parameter is a read-only parameter and it depends upon the method by which the selected roof will be created. The **Base Offset From Level** parameter is used to specify the distance of the selected roof above or below the level where it is being sketched. To modify the existing value in the value field, click on it and enter a suitable value.

The parameters under the **Construction** head of the **Properties** palette are used to specify various values related to the construction of the roof. The parameters that can be used to specify values under this head are: **Rafter Cut**, **Fascia Depth**, **Rafter or Truss**, and **Maximum ridge height**. The **Rafter Cut** parameter specifies the rafter cut on the eave of the roof. For this parameter, you can specify any of the three values such as **Plumb Cut**, **Two-Cut Plumb**, and **Two-Cut Square**, by clicking on the corresponding field in the **Value** column and selecting the desired option from the drop-down list that will be displayed. The **Fascia Depth** parameter displays the length of the lines that will define the fascia on the selected roof. The **Rafter or Truss** parameter affects only those roofs that are created by picking walls. This parameter is used as a control for measuring the **Plate Offset from Base** property that can be specified as an instance property for a specific footprint of the roof. This parameter can be assigned any of the two values such as **Truss** and **Rafter** by clicking on its value field and selecting a desired option from the drop-down list displayed. If you select the **Rafter** option from the drop-down list, the **Plate Offset from Base** property will be measured from the inside of the wall that is associated with the roof. On selecting the **Truss** option from drop-down list, the **Plate Offset from Base** property will be measured from the outside of the wall that is associated with the roof. The **Maximum ridge height** parameter displays the maximum height of the top of the roof above the base level of the building model. The value displayed for this parameter is a read-only value.

The parameters under the **Dimensions** heading in the **Properties** palette are used to specify the dimensional properties of the selected roof such as **Slope**, **Thickness**, **Volume**, and **Area**. The **Slope** parameter is used to specify the slope of the selected roof. This parameter initially displays a value if there is a slope-defining line. If there is no slope-defining line, the parameter is blank and disabled. You can change its value by clicking in its value field and then entering a desired value. The **Thickness** parameter displays the thickness of the roof. Similarly, the **Volume** and **Area** parameters display the volume and area of the selected roof in their corresponding value fields. The values displayed in the **Value** field of the **Volume** and **Area** parameters are read-only and so you cannot change them.

The **Identity Data** and **Phasing** headings in the **Properties** palette of the selected roof contain the parameters that specify the values related to the identification and phasing information.

Tip: *You can add a glazed roof to your model. To do so, select the **Sloped Glazing : Sloped Glazing** option from the **Type Selector** drop-down list in the **Properties** palette, while adding or modifying a roof in a model.*

After specifying the instance parameters in the **Properties** palette, you can view and specify the type properties of the selected roof. To do so, choose the **Edit Type** button displayed in the **Properties** palette of the selected roof; the **Type Properties** dialog box will be displayed, as shown in Figure 7-23. In this dialog box, choose the **Edit** button displayed in the **Value** column of the **Structure** parameter; the **Edit Assembly** dialog box will be displayed. In this dialog box, you can modify various type parameters such as layer composition, material, thickness, and so on. Use the **Insert** and **Delete** buttons to add or remove layers in the existing assembly. The total thickness of the roof is calculated by adding the individual thickness of all layers. After specifying the type parameters, choose the **OK** button; the **Edit Assembly** dialog box will be closed. Now, choose the **OK** button again to return to the settings of the **Modify|Roofs** tab in your drawing.

Using Basic Building Components-II

Figure 7-23 The **Type Properties** *dialog box for the selected roof*

In the **Modify | Roofs** tab, you can use various editing tools such as **Copy**, **Rotate**, **Move**, and **Mirror** to edit or copy the roof created. You can also edit the geometry of the footprints of the selected roof. To do so, choose the **Edit Footprint** tool from the **Mode** panel; the **Modify | Roofs > Edit Footprints** tab along with the sketched profile of the selected roof in the sketched mode will be displayed. Now, you can modify the sketch profile by using the drag controls and other editing tools that are displayed in the **Modify | Roofs > Edit Footprints** tab.

For a roof generated using the **Roof by Footprint** tool, each line segment of the sketched footprint can be assigned a slope parameter individually to create sides with the desired slope. You can also specify the pitch for each sloping side of the roof. To define the slope, select the line; the **Properties** palette will be displayed. Next, enter the value of the instance parameters such as overhang, rise, and so on. You can enter the value of the rise per 12" of the horizontal length in the value column of the **Slope** parameter. After editing the profile of the selected roof, choose the **Finish Edit Mode** button from the **Mode** panel of the **Modify | Roofs > Edit Footprints** tab; Revit will exit from the footprint editing mode and the **Modify|Roofs** tab will be displayed. Press ESC to exit the displayed tab.

Note

The instance parameters displayed in the instance parameters table depend upon the roof type selected. You can experiment with these parameters to modify the roof to a desired shape.

SHAPE EDITING TOOLS FOR FLOORS

Autodesk Revit provides you with a set of shape editing tools. Using these tools, you can modify the horizontal surface of floors, roofs (without slope), and structural floors by adding slopes to the surfaces for draining. You can add slopes to the horizontal surfaces without defining the sloping edges. To do so, you need to add low or high elevation points to the horizontal surface of the selected floor, roof, or structural floor, thereby splitting the surface into subregions, which in turn slope into different directions. These tools basically belong to the Revit Structure program, but you can access these tools in Autodesk Revit.

To access the shape editing tools, select the floor, roof, or structural floor created in the drawing; the shape editing tools will be displayed in the **Shape Editing** panel of the **Modify | Floors** tab of the ribbon, as shown in Figure 7-24. The shape editing tools are **Modify Sub Elements**, **Add Point**, **Add Split Line**, **Pick Supports**, and **Reset Shape**. These tools are discussed next.

*Figure 7-24 The shape editing tools displayed in the **Shape Editing** panel*

Tip: *Autodesk Revit generates roofs based on the sketch profile and values of the instance and type parameters. In case the roof profile is not continuous or the inputs given are invalid, an error message is displayed. Based on the error description, you can take the necessary corrective actions.*

Modify Sub Elements

This tool helps you select and modify the points or edges on a selected slab, floor, or roof surface. On invoking the **Modify Sub Elements** tool from the **Shape Editing** panel, a green colored boundary line and green colored corner grips will be displayed at the corners, as shown in Figure 7-25.

On selecting an edge, the edge will be highlighted in blue color and a drag control symbol consisting of two arrows and a square will be displayed. Drag the arrows to move the selected point or edge vertically to different elevations. Drag the square control to move the selected point or edge in the horizontal direction. Figure 7-26 shows the drag control symbol displayed after selecting the left corner point and Figure 7-27 shows the floor after dragging the corner point vertically upward. Instead of dragging the selected point or the edge by using the drag controls, you can type the elevation value in the **Elevation** edit box in the **Options Bar**. On doing so, the selected point or the edge will move to the specified elevation value. If you select an edge, the drag control symbol will be displayed at the center of the edge. The edge can be modified by dragging the center point control to different elevations but the other two points of an edge will remain at the same elevation.

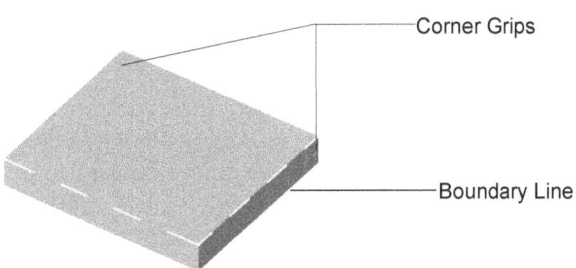

Figure 7-25 The boundary line and the corner grips displayed after selecting the floor

 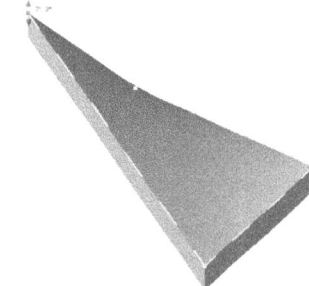

Figure 7-26 Drag control symbol displayed after selecting the left corner point

Figure 7-27 The floor after dragging the left corner point vertically upward

Note
The shape editing tools are available only after selecting the existing space floor, roof (without slope), or slab.

Add Point

This tool is used to assign a spot elevation by adding single or multiple points on the surface. These points are then used to modify the geometry of the selected slab, floor or roof. On invoking this tool, the **Elevation** edit box and the **Relative** check box will be displayed in the **Options Bar**. The **Relative** check box is selected by default, which means that the point will be added at a specified elevation relative to the surface to which it is added. You can specify the elevation value in the **Elevation** edit box. By default, the elevation value is **0'0"** which means that the points will be added on the surface on which they are created. On clearing the **Relative** check box, the points will be added on the surface at the elevation value displayed in the **Elevation** edit box. This value represents the project elevation. Figure 7-28 shows the floor after adding a point at the center and dragging the point vertically downward.

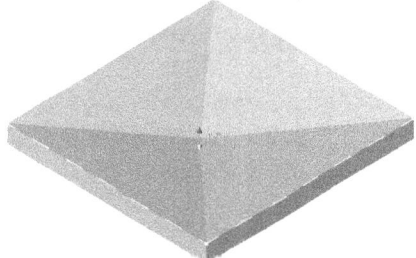

Figure 7-28 Adding a point at the center of the surface and then dragging the point

Add Split Line

This tool is used to split or divide the slab, floor, or roof surface into different sub regions by adding the split lines to the surface. These split lines act as edges and split the surface into different regions. You can then drag these split edges to different elevations, thereby providing slopes to these subregions. Each subregion created will slope independently in different directions. To add split lines, invoke this tool and select a vertex, edge, point, or face of the surface to start the split line. Select another vertex, point, or edge to complete the split line between the points, vertices, or edges. Figure 7-29 shows the floor shape after adding three split edges, one joining the two corners and the other two joining the centers of two edges.

Figure 7-29 The floor after adding three split lines and dragging them to different elevations

Pick Supports

This tool is used to select the beams to define the split lines. Invoke this tool and select the beams from the drawing for reference; a new split edge will be created using the elevations of the endpoints of the picked reference. The elevations will shift from the bottom face to the top face of the selected slab or roof according to the slab or roof thickness.

Reset Shape

This tool allows you to reset the geometry and shape of the slab, floor, or roof. After invoking this tool, the selected floor, roof, or slab reverts to the original shape.

CREATING CEILINGS

Ribbon: Architecture > Build > Ceiling

You can add a ceiling to a building model by using the **Ceiling** tool. To do so, invoke this tool from the **Build** panel; the **Modify | Place Ceiling** tab with various tools for creating the ceiling will be displayed. Since the ceilings are not visible in the floor plan, they are created in the ceiling plan. You can add a ceiling to a project using three different methods: by automatic ceiling, by sketching the ceiling, and by using the pick walls method.

Creating an Automatic Ceiling

The first method to add a ceiling to a project is by creating an automatic ceiling. To do so, choose the **Ceiling** tool from the **Build** panel; the **Modify | Place Ceiling** tab will be displayed. In this tab, the **Automatic Ceiling** tool is selected by default in the **Ceiling** panel. In the **Properties** palette, select the ceiling type from the **Type Selector** drop-down list. You can select different types of built-in ceiling that can be used from this list. Now, to add the ceiling to the entire room, open the ceiling plan, move the cursor inside the room, and click when the ceiling boundary is displayed. Autodesk Revit will automatically create the ceiling from the center of the room. For example, when you move the cursor inside the room for creating an automatic ceiling, its boundary is highlighted in red, as shown in Figure 7-30. Click to create the ceiling automatically. If you have created the ceiling in a floor plan, Autodesk Revit Architecture will display a warning indicating that the ceiling created will not be visible in it. You can then open the ceiling plan of the corresponding level to view the created ceiling, as shown in Figure 7-31. You can also open the section view through the room to view the cross-section of the ceiling.

Figure 7-30 Selecting the room to create an automatic ceiling

Figure 7-31 Automatic ceiling created

Sketching a Ceiling

You can sketch a ceiling boundary and create a ceiling. To do so, choose the **Ceiling** tool from the **Build** panel; the **Modify | Place Ceiling** tab will be displayed. In this tab, choose the **Sketch Ceiling** tool from the **Ceiling** panel; the **Modify | Create Ceiling Boundary** tab will be displayed. This tab contains various tools for sketching and modifying the ceiling boundary. To start the sketch of the ceiling boundary, choose the **Boundary Line** tool from the **Draw** panel; a list box containing various drawing tools will be displayed on the right of this panel, as shown in Figure 7-32. The **Line** tool is chosen by default in the **Draw** panel. You can use this tool and other drawing and modification tools displayed in the **Modify | Create Ceiling Boundary** tab to complete the sketch. Figure 7-33 shows a ceiling boundary that is sketched using various tools displayed in the **Modify| Create Ceiling Boundary** tab. After completing the sketch, choose the **Finish Edit Mode** button from the **Mode** panel of the **Modify | Create Ceiling Boundary** tab; the ceiling will be created within the sketched profile, as shown in Figure 7-34. Display the section view to view the ceiling in it. The ceiling will appear at a certain height from the floor level, as shown in Figure 7-35.

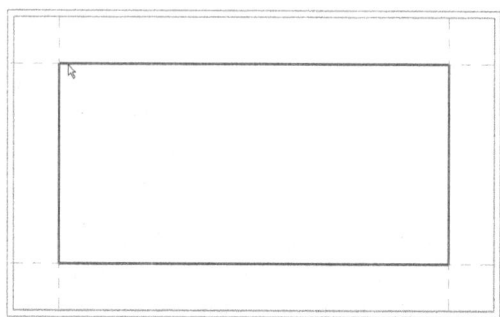

Figure 7-32 The list box containing the tools to sketch the boundary line

Figure 7-33 Sketching the ceiling boundary

Figure 7-34 Ceiling created within the sketched boundary

Figure 7-35 Ceiling displayed in the section view

Using the Pick Walls Method

The third method to create the ceiling is by picking the wall faces. This is a common method for creating ceilings. To create a ceiling by picking the wall faces, choose the **Ceiling** tool from the **Architecture** tab; the **Modify | Place Ceiling** tab will be displayed. In this tab, choose the **Sketch Ceiling** tool from the **Ceiling** panel; the **Modify | Create Ceiling Boundary** tab will be displayed. In this tab, choose the **Pick Walls** tool from the list box of the **Draw** panel; you will be prompted to pick the walls to define the boundary of the ceiling. Specify the offset value for the ceiling in the **Offset** edit box in the **Options Bar**. Select the **Extend into Wall (to core)** check box, if you want the offset to be measured from the core layer of the walls. Next, pick the walls to create the sketch for the ceiling. In the **Properties** palette, select the ceiling type from the **Type Selector** drop-down list. Next, choose the **Finish Edit Mode** button from the **Mode** panel of the **Modify | Create Ceiling Boundary** tab; the ceiling will be created.

Modifying a Ceiling

You can modify a ceiling after it has been created. To modify the ceiling, select it; the **Modify|Ceiling** tab will be displayed. From this tab, you can use various modification and editing tools to make changes on the selected ceiling. For editing the selected ceiling, you can use the editing tools such as **Copy**, **Rotate**, **Move**, and **Mirror**. You can also modify the properties of the selected ceiling based on its sketch. To do so, choose the **Edit Boundary** tool from the **Mode** panel; the **Modify | Ceiling > Edit Boundary** tab will be displayed and

Using Basic Building Components-II

the sketch mode will be activated for the selected ceiling in the drawing. Now, you can modify the sketch profile by using the drag controls and other editing tools. Select the edge(s) of the ceiling boundary; the instance properties for the selected edges(s) of the ceiling profile will be displayed in the **Properties** palette. In this palette, you can enter the required values of various instance parameters for the selected edge(s) of the ceiling boundary.

You can view and edit the instance properties of a ceiling. To do so, select the ceiling from the drawing; the instance properties of the ceiling will be displayed in the **Properties** palette. This palette displays the instance parameters of the selected ceiling such as the level, height offset from level, and so on, as shown in Figure 7-36.

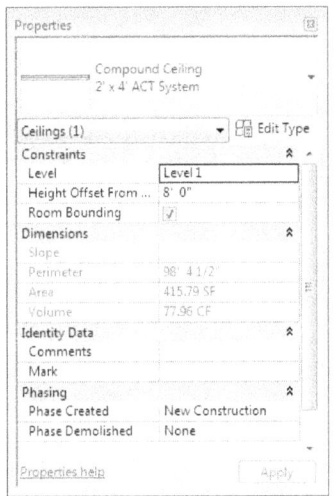

Figure 7-36 Partial view of the Properties palette with various instance properties

Being a level-based element, ceilings are created at a specified distance from the base level. This distance is specified in the **Height Offset From Level** instance parameter in the **Properties** palette. For example, to create a ceiling at 10' height from Level 2, you can select it as the value for the **Level** instance parameter and enter the value **10'** in the **Height Offset From Level** instance parameter.

The **Edit Type** button in the **Properties** palette is used to invoke the **Type Properties** dialog box. Choose the **Edit Type** button; the **Type Properties** dialog box for the selected ceiling type will be displayed, as shown in Figure 7-37. In the **Type Properties** dialog box, you can create a duplicate type as the new ceiling type. To do so, choose the **Duplicate** button; the **Name** dialog box will be displayed. In this dialog box, enter a name for the new ceiling type in the **Name** edit box and choose **OK**; the **Name** dialog box will close and new type of ceiling will be created. In the **Type Properties** dialog box, choose the **Edit** button in the **Value** column for the **Structure** type parameter to display the **Edit Assembly** dialog box. This dialog box displays the structure of the ceiling type with its various layers. The **Insert** or **Delete** button can be used to customize the new ceiling type based on the specific project requirement.

*Figure 7-37 The partial view of **Type Properties** dialog box for the selected ceiling type*

Note
*When you select the created ceiling in the section view and choose **Edit**, Autodesk Revit displays the **Go To View** dialog box. You can select the view that you want to open for editing the ceiling boundary sketch.*

ROOMS

Room is a part of Autodesk Revit building elements. Autodesk Revit provides you the flexibility of creating rooms independent of room tags. Rooms can be created only in the plan view. You can also add rooms from the room schedules. Rooms and areas have the same graphical representation.

Adding Rooms

Ribbon: Architecture > Room & Area > Room

You can add rooms in the plan view by using the **Room** tool. To do so, invoke this tool from the **Room & Area** panel, as shown in Figure 7-38; the **Modify|Place Room** tab will be displayed. Now, as you move the cursor inside a closed boundary that you need to define as a room in the drawing, a symbol with a cross hair graphics attached to the cursor will appear. Notice that the size of this cross hair graphics will change according to the area of the room

*Figure 7-38 Invoking the **Room** tool*

Using Basic Building Components-II

space of the closed boundary. Before you insert the room, you can select the type of room from the **Type Selector** drop-down list in the **Properties** palette. You can select any of the three options namely, **Room Tag**, **Room Tag With Area**, and **Room Tag With Volume** from the **Type-Selector** drop-down list. You can select the **Room Tag** option to display the inserted room with the tag only. Similarly, you can select the **Room Tag With Area** or **Room Tag With Volume** option from the **Type Selector** drop-down list to attach the room tag to the room to display the information regarding the area or volume of the room. After selecting the required option from the **Type Selector** drop-down list, choose the **Highlight Boundaries** tool from the **Room** panel of the **Modify | Place Room** tab; the **Autodesk Revit Architecture 2015** message box will be displayed, informing that the room bounding elements are highlighted in the drawing. Choose the **Close** button to close the message box.

To add a room with a room tag, choose the **Tag on Placement** tool from the **Tag** panel. You can specify a level up to which the boundary of a room will extend vertically or upward. To do so, select an option from the **Upper Limit** drop-down list in the **Options Bar**. For example, if you have added a room to the floor plan of **Level 1** and you desire to extend the room to **Level 2**, select the **Level 2** option from the **Upper Limit** drop-down list. You can extend the room boundary above the level specified in the **Upper Limit** drop-down list. To do so, click in the **Offset** edit box in the **Options Bar**. The default value displayed in this edit box is **10'**. You can enter a positive value to extend the room boundary above the level that you have selected from the **Upper Limit** drop-down list. Similarly, you can enter a negative value to extend the room boundary below the selected level. You can orient the room tag horizontally or vertically in reference to the current view, or align it with the walls and boundary lines present in the building model. To specify the orientation of the room tag, select an option from the drop-down list displayed next to the **Offset** edit box in the **Options Bar**. You can select the **Leader** check box to place the room tag with a leader.

To add a room, click in an area enclosed by the room-bounding elements such as walls, as shown in Figure 7-39. The room will be added and the area of the room will be equal to the area enclosed by the walls.

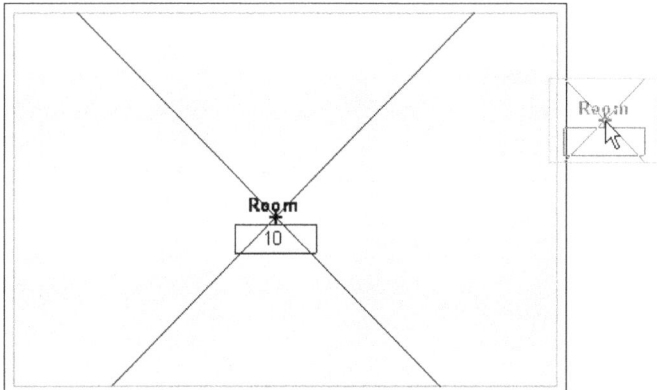

Figure 7-39 The graphical representation of the room

You can also add a room in a free space or in an area that is not enclosed completely, and then add walls or other room bounding elements to the room. In such an instance, the room will be created and the area of the room will be equal to the area enclosed by the walls added later. Figure 7-40 shows a room added to the area that is not enclosed and Figure 7-41 shows the room after enclosing the area by adding a wall segment. On placing a room in a free space or in an area that is not enclosed, Autodesk Revit will display a warning message that the room is not in a properly enclosed region.

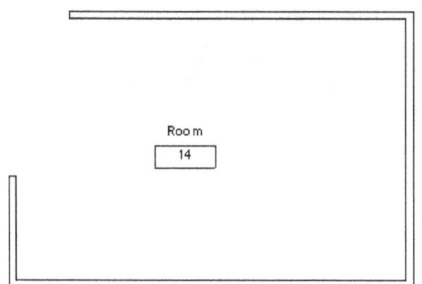

Figure 7-40 Room added in an open boundary

Figure 7-41 Room created after adding the wall segment

Creating Rooms from Room Schedules

Revit Architecture provides you with the flexibility to add rooms from the room schedules. You can add a new room in a room schedule and place the same room in the plan view. To do so, invoke the **Room** tool and select the room type from the **Room** drop-down list in the **Options Bar**. Next, select the room tag from the **Type Selector** drop-down list. The room types will be available in the **Room** drop-down list only when you have added rooms in a room schedule. After selecting the room type from the drop-down list, click in the drawing to place the room; the room will be added with a room tag in the drawing.

Note
*If you do not select the room type from the **Room** drop-down list in the **Options Bar**, a new room will be created and will be numbered after the last number of the room in the schedule.*

Room Bounding Elements

You can use different elements as room bounding elements. These elements define the boundary of the room and help in calculating the area and volume of the room. Walls, roofs, ceilings, curtain systems, floors, columns, and room separation lines can be used as room bounding elements. Autodesk Revit calculates the areas based on the area enclosed by room bounding elements and the room height.

Modifying Room Properties

You can modify the room properties by changing the values of the room parameters in the **Properties** palette. To do so, select the room and click when the crosshair graphics is displayed; the **Properties** palette will be displayed, as shown in Figure 7-42.

Using Basic Building Components-II

*Figure 7-42 The **Properties** palette displaying the properties of a room*

Understanding Room Instance Parameters

The different instance parameters of the room are described in the table given next.

Instance Parameter	Value and Description
Level	Specifies the base level of the room. Level 1 is the default value
Upper Limit	Specifies the upper boundary of the room. The specified level and the value defines the upper limit of the room. The level can be selected from the **Level** drop-down list by clicking on value column of corresponding parameter
Limit Offset	Specifies the value specified to be added in the level to set the total height of the room. This parameter can have negative value. The default value set is 10'. A new value can be entered by clicking in the value field of this parameter
Area	Specifies the total area calculated using the room bounding elements
Perimeter	Defines the perimeter of the room
Unbounded Height	Total height defined by the sum of the room base level, upperlimit and limit offset

Instance Parameter	Value and Description
Volume	Specifies the total volume of the room. The volume is computed only when you select the **Areas and Volumes** radio button in the **Area and Volume Computations** dialog box
Number	Specifies the room number assigned according to the number of rooms added
Name	Specifies the room name. The default name is **Room**. Any name can be assigned to the room
Comments	Some specific comments or description about the room can be entered in this section
Occupancy	Specifies the type of occupancy for structure that can be specified as per the requirement. This parameter can be defined by any name.
Base/Ceiling Finish	A user-defined parameter, defines any type of finish for the base and the ceiling such as GWB
Wall/Floor Finish	Specifies the finish for the walls of the room such as metal paints and coatings of the walls and tiles for the floor
Occupant	Specifies the name of a person, group, or any organization of the occupant
Phase	Specifies the name of the phase in which the room is created

Calculating Room Volumes

To enable the volume computations and calculate room volumes, choose the **Area and Volume Computations** tool from the **Room & Area** panel; the **Area and Volume Computations** dialog box will be displayed. In the **Volume Computations** area of the **Computations** tab, select the **Areas and Volumes** radio button. By default, the **Areas only** radio button is selected in the **Volume Computations** area. Next, choose the **OK** button; the volume computation of room will be enabled and displayed in its instance properties. To view the calculated volume of a room, select it from the drawing; the **Properties** palette will be displayed. In the **Properties** palette, the value in the value column of the **Volume** parameter shows the computed volume of the room.

Note

In Revit, the volume calculations of the room are done considering the finish face of the room-bounding element. When you select a room, the outline and the color fill display the exact periphery and the enclosed area used for calculating the volume of the room.

Using Basic Building Components-II

While computing the room volume, the room volume calculation engine of Autodesk Revit Architecture looks up and down from the measurement height to access the vertical limit of the room-bounding element. You can set the lower and upper limits of the room-bounding elements using the **Properties** palette. The **Base Offset** parameter in the value column in this palette defines the limit of the lower boundary that is used to limit the extent of the room with no floors or prevent floors to leak from floor openings while computing the volume of the room.

The volume is also displayed in the drawing view if the rooms are added in the drawing view with the **Room Tag With Volume** option selected from the **Type Selector** drop-down list.

Cutting Openings in a Wall, Floor, Roof, and Ceiling

In Autodesk Revit Architecture, you can create an opening in the wall, floor, roof, structural floor, ceiling, and structural elements such as beams and braces using any of the tools available in it. To create an opening, invoke any of these tools from the **Opening** panel of the **Architecture** tab, as shown in Figure 7-43. From this panel, you can choose any of these five options, **By Face**, **Wall**, **Vertical**, **Shaft**, or **Dormer** to create an opening.

*Figure 7-43 Various opening tools in the **Opening** panel*

You can use the **By Face** tool to cut openings on the faces of roofs, floors, or ceilings in the building model. This tool is useful in a project when you need to cut an opening in a floor for stairway or skylight opening. You can also use this tool for creating any cut-out in the roof for a chimney. To do so, invoke this tool from the **Opening** panel; you will be prompted to select a planar face of a roof, floor, ceiling, beam, or column. Select the face on which you want to create the opening, as shown in Figure 7-44. Once you select the face, the **Modify | Create Opening Boundary** tab will be displayed. In this tab, you can use various tools to sketch the opening in any view. Now, open the required view and sketch the opening using the reference planes, as shown in Figure 7-45. After sketching the opening boundary on the selected face, choose the **Finish Edit Mode** button from the **Mode** panel to finish the sketch of the opening and then exit the **Modify | Create Opening Boundary** tab. Figure 7-46 shows the resulting opening perpendicular to the selected face.

Figure 7-44 Selecting the face to be cut of the roof

Figure 7-45 Sketching the opening in the ceiling plan using the reference planes

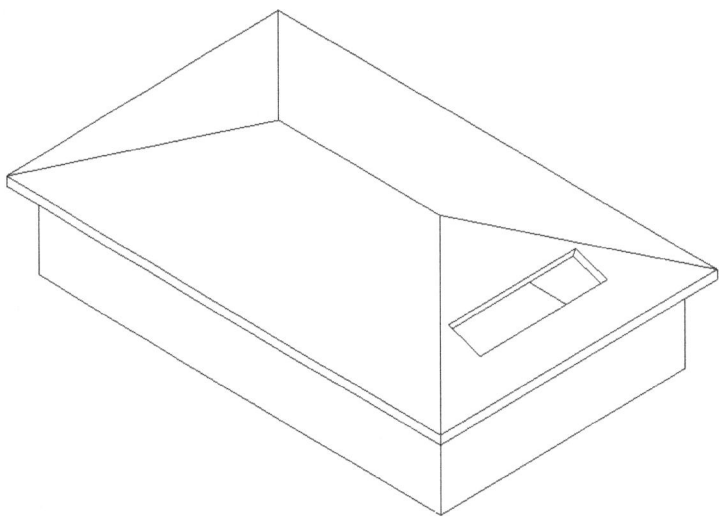

Figure 7-46 Resulting opening perpendicular to the selected face

To cut a vertical opening, choose the **Vertical** tool from the **Opening** panel and select the required ceiling, roof, or floor; the **Modify | Create Opening Boundary** tab will be displayed. You can use various tools from this tab to sketch the boundary of the opening. Sketch the opening in the appropriate view using the sketching tools. After sketching the opening boundary, choose the **Finish Edit Mode** button from the **Mode** panel; a vertical opening will be created in the selected element. You can use the sketching tools to draw a sketch of appropriate size, as shown in Figure 7-47. The opening can also be viewed in the 3D view, as shown in Figure 7-48.

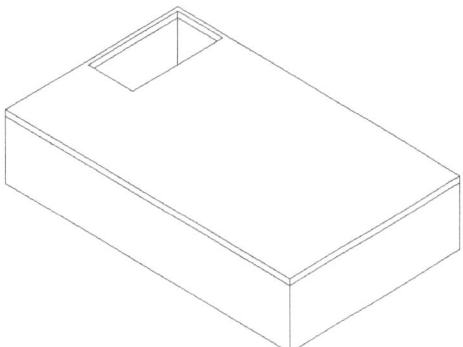

Figure 7-47 Sketching the roof opening in the ceiling plan view

Figure 7-48 Roof opening in the 3D view

To create a rectangular opening in a wall, choose the **Wall** tool from the **Opening** panel in the **Architecture** tab; you will be prompted to select a wall. Select the wall in which you want to cut an opening and then sketch a rectangular opening of the required size by clicking and dragging the cursor.

To create a dormer opening in the dormer roof, choose the **Dormer** tool from the **Opening** panel; you will be prompted to select the roof in which you want to create a dormer opening. Select the roof; the screen will enter the sketch mode. Choose the **Pick Roof/ Wall Edges** tool from the **Pick** panel of the **Modify | Edit Sketch** tab and pick the boundary of the dormer to create the dormer opening. Next, choose the **Finish Edit Mode** button from the **Mode** panel; a dormer opening will be created.

Note
The boundary that you will pick for the dormer opening in a roof should be an edge of the selected roof, wall, or both, and should form a closed loop.

To cut an opening up to the entire height of a building, choose the **Shaft** tool from the **Opening** panel; the **Modify | Create Shaft Opening Sketch** tab will be displayed. Choose a suitable sketching tool from this tab to create an opening of the required shape. Next, choose the **Finish Edit Mode** button from the **Mode** panel; the opening will be created passing through the entire height of the building. Make sure that before sketching the opening, you select the required work plane and the view to sketch the opening.

You can also specify the levels that will be cut by the opening. It will help you to restrict the opening to a particular level. To specify the levels, select the opening; the **Modify | Shaft Openings** tab will be displayed. Select a level for the **Base Constraint** parameter in the **Properties** palette to start the opening. Next, select a level for the **Top Constraint** parameter to end the opening. The opening will be cut through the selected levels.

JOINING WALLS WITH OTHER ELEMENTS

In Autodesk Revit Architecture, walls are not attached to a floor and roof automatically. If needed, they can be attached using the **Attach Top/Base** tool. For example, using the **Attach Top/Base** tool, you can attach the structural layer of a wall to a floor without attaching its finish layer. Similarly, if you need to detach a wall, you can use the **Detach Top/Base** tool.

Using the Attach Top/Base and Detach Top/Base Tools

To attach walls to other elements, first select the walls to be attached; the **Modify | Walls** tab will be displayed. Next, choose the **Attach Top/Base** tool from the **Modify Wall** panel; the **Options Bar** will prompt you to choose whether you want to attach the element to the top or to the bottom of the wall. To attach the floor to the wall, select the **Base** radio button and to attach a roof or a ceiling, select the **Top** radio button. After selecting the required radio button, select the element(s) to be attached to the wall(s); they will be attached to the top/base of the selected wall(s) and the **Options Bar** will return to the previous options, allowing you to attach or detach more elements to the already selected walls.

The wall attachment status can be checked from its instance properties. To do so, select the desired wall; the instance parameters of the selected wall will be displayed in the **Properties** palette. In this palette, the **Top is Attached** and **Base is Attached** instance parameters show the status of attachments for the selected walls, as shown in Figure 7-49. The selection of the check box corresponding to the **Top is Attached** parameter in the value column indicates that the selected wall is attached to an element at its top. Similarly, the selection of the check box displayed in **Value** column of the **Base is Attached** parameter indicates that the selected wall is attached to an element at its base. After you attach walls to other elements, you can detach them. To do so, invoke the **Detach Top/Base** tool from the **Modify** panel of the **Modify | Walls** tab. The usage of this tool is similar to the **Attach Top/Base** tool that has already been discussed.

Figure 7-49 Checking the status of attachments to walls in the **Properties** palette

Using Basic Building Components-II

TUTORIALS

Tutorial 1   Apartment 1

In this tutorial, you will add a floor and a ceiling to the *c06_Apartment1_tut1.rvt* project created in Tutorial 1 of Chapter 6. Also, you will attach walls to the floor. To complete this tutorial, you need to use the following project parameters: **(Expected time: 30 min)**

1. Floor type -
   - For Imperial   **Floor: LW Concrete on Metal Deck**.
   - For Metric   **160mm Concrete With 50mm Metal Deck**
2. Ceiling type-
   - For Imperial   **Compound Ceiling: GWB on Mtl. Stud**,
   - For Metric   **Compound Ceiling: Plain**

   Level- 8'6" from the floor level.

The following steps are required to complete this tutorial:

a. Open the required file.
   - For Imperial   *c06_Apartment1_tut1.rvt*
   - For Metric   *M_c06_Apartment1_tut1.rvt*
b. Hide the annotation tags such as the section line, grids, and the elevation tag.
c. Create the floor using the **Floor** tool, refer to Figures 7-50 through 7-52.
d. Create the ceiling using the **Ceiling** tool, refer to Figures 7-53 and 7-54.
e. Attach walls to the floor.

Opening the Project File and Hiding Annotation Tags

To start with this tutorial, open the specified project file and then hide the annotation symbols and tags such as section line, grids, and elevation tags using the **Visibility/Graphics** tool.

1. Choose **Open > Project** from the **Application Menu** and then open the *c06_Apartment1_tut1.rvt* (*M_c06_Apartment1_tut1.rvt* for Metric) file created in Tutorial 1 of Chapter 6. You can also download this file from *http://www.cadcim.com*. The path of the file is as follows: *Textbooks > Civil/GIS > Revit Architecture > Autodesk Revit Architecture 2015 for Architects and Designers*.

2. Now, to hide the annotation symbols and tags such as section line, grids, and the elevation tags, choose the **Visibility/Graphics** tool from the **Graphics** panel of the **View** tab; the **Visibility/Graphics Overrides for Floor Plan: First Floor** dialog box is displayed.

3. Choose the **Annotation Categories** tab and clear the check boxes under the **Visibility** parameter for **Elevations**, **Grids**, and **Sections**.

4. Now, choose the **Apply** button and then the **OK** button; the specified settings are applied to the plan view and you return to the drawing window.

Creating the Floor

In the following set of steps, you will add floor to the apartment plan using the **Floor** tool.

1. To add a floor to the apartment, choose the **Floor: Architectural** tool from **Architecture > Build > Floor** drop-down; the **Modify | Create Floor Boundary** tab is displayed along with the **Options Bar**. Notice that the drawing area fades when you invoke the **Floor** tool, which indicates that you are in the sketch mode.

2. In the **Options Bar**, select the **Extend into wall (to core)** check box, if it is not selected. Also notice that the **Pick Walls** tool is chosen by default in the **Draw** panel.

3. Move the cursor near the center of the north wall of the apartment plan, and press the TAB key when the wall is highlighted.

4. When the chain of walls is highlighted, click to sketch the floor boundary; the boundary is sketched and appears as a magenta rectangle, as shown in Figure 7-50.

Figure 7-50 The floor boundary sketched using the **Pick Walls** tool

5. Choose the **Finish Edit Mode** button from the **Mode** panel to complete the sketching of the floor.

6. Next, you need to assign the type to the floor. To do so, select the desired option from the **Type Selector** drop-down list in the **Properties** palette, as shown in Figure 7-51.

   For Imperial **Floor : LW Concrete on Metal Deck**
   For Metric   **160mm Concrete With 50mm Metal Deck**

7. Choose the **Modify** button from the **Select** panel of the **Modify | Floor** tab to exit the **Floor: Architectural** tool. The floor is created for the *Apartment 1* project, as shown in Figure 7-52.

Using Basic Building Components-II 7-35

Figure 7-51 Selecting the LW Concrete on Metal Deck floor type

Creating the Ceiling

After creating the floor for the apartment, you need to add a ceiling to it. You will use the **Ceiling** tool to create the ceiling for the apartment in the ceiling plan.

1. To start creating the ceiling, the first thing you need to do is to transform the current view to the ceiling plan view of the first floor. To do so, double-click on **First Floor** from the **Ceiling Plans** head in the **Project Browser**.

   As you open this view, you will notice the appearance of the annotation tags. Repeat steps 2, 3, and 4 given in the **Opening the Project File and Hiding Annotation Tags** section in this tutorial to hide various grids, elevation, window, and section tags from the first floor ceiling plan view.

2. Invoke the **Ceiling** tool from the **Build** panel of the **Architecture** tab; the **Modify | Place Ceiling** tab is displayed.

3. To assign a type to the ceiling, click on the **Type Selector** drop-down list in the **Properties** palette and then select the desired option from it.
   For Imperial   **Compound Ceiling : GWB on Mtl. Stud**
   For Metric   **Compound Ceiling : Plain**
   Next, you need to define the clear height of the ceiling.

*Figure 7-52 The **LW Concrete on Metal Deck** type of the floor created*

4. In the **Properties** palette, click on the value field of the **Height Offset From Level** instance parameter and enter **8'6"(2590 mm)**. Then, choose the **Apply** button; the new height is assigned to the ceiling.

5. Move the cursor inside any room; the room boundary is highlighted. Now, click inside the highlighted boundary area; the ceiling is created. Notice that the created ceiling is not distinctly visible in the ceiling plan because the ceiling type selected has a plain GWB board finish.

6. Repeat step 5 to create individual ceilings for every room in the *Apartment 1* project. After creating all ceilings, press ESC twice to view them in the 3D view of the project.

7. Click on the + symbol for the **3D Views** head in the **Project Browser** and double-click on {**3D**}; the 3D view of the apartment project with the created ceiling is displayed. You can move the cursor over the ceiling of any room to highlight it and display the ceiling type, as shown in Figure 7-53.

Attaching Walls to the Floor

In this section, you will use the **Attach** tool to attach walls to the floor so that you get a clear intersection between the floor and the wall. You need to use the section view to attach the floor.

1. To use the section view, double-click on **Section X** in the **Project Browser**.

2. Now, move the cursor near the external wall that is cut in the section, and when it is highlighted, press TAB to highlight all exterior walls.

Using Basic Building Components-II

Figure 7-53 *Highlighting and displaying the ceiling type for bedroom*

3. Click to select the chain of exterior walls in the section view and then choose the **Attach Top/Base** tool from the **Modify Wall** panel of the **Modify | Walls** tab; the **Options Bar** is displayed.

4. From the **Options Bar**, select the **Base** radio button.

5. Move the cursor near the floor and click when it is highlighted; the floor is attached to walls, as shown in Figure 7-54.

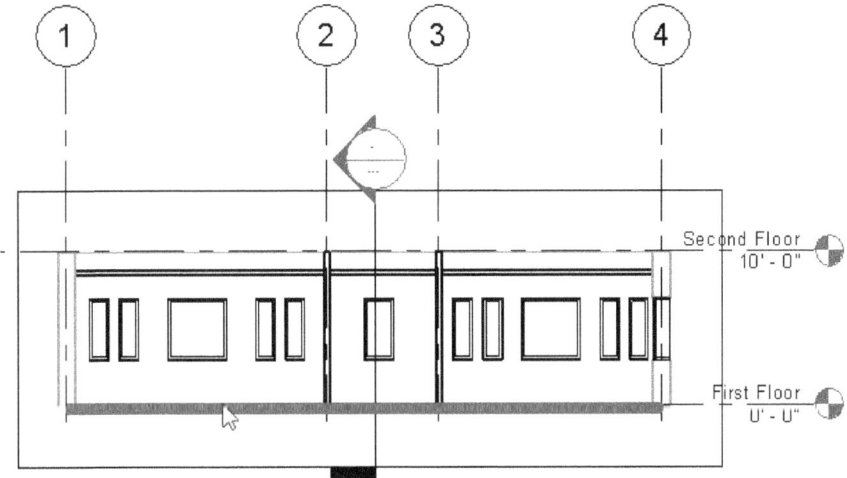

Figure 7-54 *Selecting the floor to attach it with the exterior walls*

This completes the tutorial for adding the floor to the *Apartment 1* project.

6. Double-click on **First Floor** in the **Floor Plans** head in the **Project Browser**; the corresponding floor plan in the drawing window is displayed.

Note
*In this section of the tutorial, as you attach walls with the floor, you may not find any difference in the wall and floor intersections as compared to when they were not attached. To see the difference, attach the wall with the floor and then enter a positive value in the value column corresponding to the **Height Offset From Level** instance parameter in the **Properties** palette.*

7. Choose **Save As > Project** from the **Application Menu**; the **Save As** dialog box is displayed. Enter required name in the **File name** edit box
   - For Imperial   c07_Apartment1_tut1
   - For Metric   M_c07_Apartment1_tut1

   Choose **Save**; the project file is saved.

8. Now, choose **Close** from **the Application Menu** to close the file.

Tutorial 2   Club

In this tutorial, you will add a floor, ceiling, and a roof to the *Club* project created in Tutorial 2 of Chapter 6. In this tutorial, you will also attach floor and ceilings to walls. Figure 7-55 shows the 3D View of the *Club* project after adding roofs and other elements. Use the following project parameters to complete this tutorial: **(Expected time: 30 min)**

1. Floor type -
   - For Imperial   **LW Concrete on Metal Deck**.
   - For Metric   **160mm Concrete With 50mm Metal Deck**
2. Ceiling type-
   - For Imperial   **Compound Ceiling: 2'x 2' ACT System**
   - For Metric   **Compound Ceiling: 600 x 600 mm Grid**

   Level- 11'0" from floor level.
3. Roof type for Hall 1 and Hall 2- Hip roof-
   - For Imperial   **Basic Roof: Insulation on Metal Deck-EPDM**
   - For Metric   **Basic Roof: Steel Bar Joist Steel Deck- EPDM Membrane**

   Roof shape for Hall 1 and Hall 2- Hip roof with Slope as 4"/12" (8.46 mm)
   Roof level for Hall 1 and Hall 2- Roof
   Roof type for Lounge-
   - For Imperial   **Basic Roof: Insulation on Metal Deck - EPDM**
   - For Metric   **Basic Roof: Steel Deck-EPDM Membrane**

   Roof shape for Lounge- Flat
   Roof level for Lounge- **Roof**; Base Offset from level **-1'4"(406 mm)**
   Overhang for all roofs- 4'0" (1220 mm) from the outer face of the exterior walls

Using Basic Building Components-II

The following steps are required to complete this tutorial:

a. Open the required project file.
   For Imperial   c06_Club_tut2.rvt
   For Metric   M_c06_Club_tut2.rvt
b. Hide the annotation tags such as section line, grids, and elevation tag.
c. Create the floor using the **Floor** tool, refer to Figure 7-56.
d. Create the ceiling using the **Ceiling** tool.
e. Create the roof using the **Roof by Footprint** tool, refer to Figures 7-57 through 7-63.
f. Attach all walls to the floor.

Figure 7-55 Sketch view for adding roof to the Club project

Opening the Project File and Hiding Annotation Tags

In this section, you will open the *Club* project that was created in Tutorial 2 of Chapter 6 and then hide annotation symbols and tags before you start creating floor, ceiling, and roof in the next section.

1. Choose **Open > Project** from the **Application Menu** and then open the *c06_Club_tut2.rvt* (*M_c06_Club_tut2.rvt* for Metric) file created in Tutorial 2 of Chapter 6. You can also download this file from *http://www.cadcim.com*. The path of the file is as follows: *Textbooks > Civil/GIS > Revit Architecture > Autodesk Revit Architecture 2015 for Architects and Designers*.

2. After the specified file is opened, ensure that the **First Floor** for the **Floor Plans** is the current view selected and then choose the **Visibility/Graphics** tool from the **Graphics** panel of the **View** tab; the **Visibility/Graphics Overrides for Floor Plan: First Floor** dialog box is displayed.

3. Select the **Annotation Categories** tab to open the list of annotation categories.

4. Clear the check boxes under the **Visibility** parameter for **Elevations**, **Grids**, and **Sections** in the dialog box.

5. Choose **Apply** and then **OK** to apply the settings to the plan view and close the dialog box to return to the drawing window.

Creating the Floor

In the following steps, you will add a floor to the club plan using the **Floor** tool.

1. Invoke the **Floor: Architectural** tool from **Architecture > Build > Floor** drop-down; the **Modify | Create Floor Boundary** tab is displayed.

2. Ensure that the **Pick Walls** tool is chosen in the **Draw** panel. Clear the **Extend into wall (to core)** check box in the **Options Bar**.

3. Move the cursor near any exterior wall of the club building plan until it gets highlighted. When the exterior wall is highlighted, press the TAB key; all exterior walls get highlighted and dashed lines appear in the walls, indicating the extents of the floor.

4. When the chain of walls is highlighted, click to sketch the floor boundary. Ensure that the floor boundary line is sketched on the outer face of the exterior wall, as shown in Figure 7-56. If required, use the flip control to move the floor profile to the outer face

Note
While sketching the floor boundary, make sure it is in a closed loop. Else, a warning message will be displayed and the floor will not be created.

Figure 7-56 The sketched floor boundary

5. Now, finish the sketch of the floor by choosing the **Finish Edit Mode** button from the **Mode** panel.

6. Next, you need to assign a type to the floor. To do so, in the **Properties** palette, select the desired option from the **Type Selector** drop-down list.
    For Imperial   **LW Concrete on Metal Deck**
    For Metric   **160mm Concrete With 50mm Metal Deck**

Using Basic Building Components-II   7-41

To exit from the **Floor: Architectural** tool, choose the **Modify** button from the **Select** panel.

Creating the Ceiling

In this section, you will add ceiling to the *Club* project in the ceiling plan using the **Ceiling** tool.

1. To change the project view to the ceiling plan, double-click on the **First Floor** from the **Ceiling Plans** head of the **Project Browser**; the first floor ceiling plan is displayed in the drawing.

2. Now, assign a type to the ceiling. To do so, invoke the **Ceiling** tool from the **Build** panel of the **Architecture** tab; the properties for the proposed ceiling are displayed in the **Properties** palette.

3. In the **Properties** palette, click on the **Type Selector** drop-down list and select the required option from it.
   For Imperial   **Compound Ceiling: 2' x 2' ACT System**
   For Metric   **Compound Ceiling: 600 x 600mm Grid**

4. Now, you need to assign height to the ceiling. In the **Properties** palette, click in the value field of the **Height Offset From Level** instance parameter and enter **11'0"(3353 mm)**. Then, choose the **Apply** button.

5. Now, move the cursor inside the building profile and notice that each space boundary is highlighted, when you move it inside the boundary.

6. Click inside each room to create the ceiling at the specified height. It appears as a square grid in the first floor ceiling plan.

7. Press ESC to exit from the **Ceiling** tool.

Creating the Roof

In this section, first you will create the hip roof for Hall 1 using the **Roof by Footprint** tool and then similarly create roofs for the Lounge and the Hall 2 areas.

1. First, change the project view to the floor plan of the first floor. To do so, double-click on **First Floor** from the **Floor Plans** head of the **Project Browser**; the floor plan of the first floor is displayed.

2. To create the roof, invoke the **Roof by Footprint** tool from **Architecture > Build > Roof** drop-down.

3. In the **Options Bar**, select the **Defines slope** check box and enter **4'0" (1220 mm)** in the **Overhang** edit box.

4. Choose the **Pick Walls** tool, if it is not chosen, from the **Draw** panel of the **Modify | Create Roof Footprint** tab.

5. Move the cursor near the exterior wall of Hall 1, facing northwest, and click when the dashed line appears on the outer side, as shown in Figure 7-57. The roof boundary line is sketched.

6. Similarly, create boundary lines by using the other three exterior walls of Hall 1 at the same offset distance. The boundary lines are sketched, as shown in Figure 7-58.

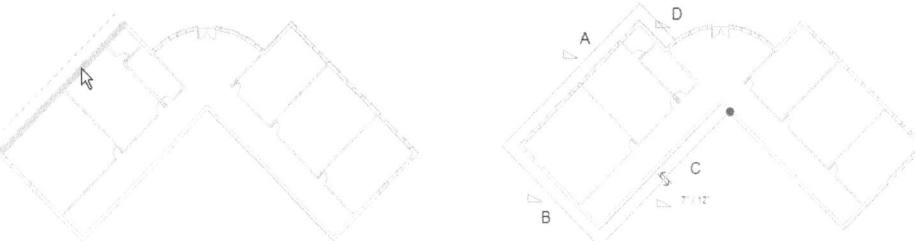

Figure 7-57 Sketching the roof profile   *Figure 7-58* Completing the roof profile of Hall 1

7. Next, you need to join the boundary lines marked as C and D, refer to Figure 7-58. To do so, choose the **Trim/Extend to Corner** tool from the **Modify** panel of the **Modify | Create Roof Footprint** tab and select the two lines marked as C and D to complete the closed rectangular profile of the roof of Hall 1. After completing the profile, press the ESC key to exit the **Trim/Extend to Corner** tool.

8. In the **Properties** palette, click on the value column for the **Base Level** instance parameter and select **Roof** as the base level.

9. Next, click on the value column for the **Base Offset From Level** instance parameter and ensure that **0' 0"(0 mm)** is entered as the base level offset value. Then, choose the **Apply** button.

   To set the appropriate slope for the hip roof, you must select the sketch boundary and then set its slope properties.

10. To select all the four boundary lines, first select one of them and then select the rest by using the CTRL key; the instance properties for the selected boundary lines are displayed in the **Properties** palette.

11. In the **Properties** palette, replace the current value present in the value column of the **Slope** instance parameter by entering **4" / 12"(18.46°)** as the new value of the pitch, as specified in the project parameters, and then choose the **Apply** button.

12. Next, choose the **Finish Edit Mode** button from the **Mode** panel of the **Modify | Create Roof Footprint** tab; the **Revit** message box is displayed.

Using Basic Building Components-II

13. In the message box, choose the **Yes** button to attach the highlighted walls to the roof.

14. Next, to assign a type to the created roof, select the desired option from the **Type Selector** drop-down list in the **Properties** palette.
    For Imperial   **Basic Roof : Insulation on Metal Deck-EPDM**
    For Metric   **Basic Roof : Steel Bar Joist Steel Deck-EPDM Membrane**

15. Double-click on **North** from the **Elevations (Building Elevation)** head in the **Project Browser** to view the roof, refer to Figure 7-59. Make sure the **Shaded** option is chosen in the **View Control Bar**.

Figure 7-59 North elevation of the Club project with the created roof

In the following steps, you will create a flat roof for the **Lounge** area of the Club building.

16. Double-click on **Roof** in the **Floor Plans** head of the **Project Browser**.

17. Invoke the **Roof by Footprint** tool from **Architecture > Build > Roof** drop-down.

18. In the **Options Bar**, clear the **Defines slope** check box.

19. Ensure that the **Overhang** edit box shows **4'0"(1220 mm)** as the overhang value.

20. Choose the **Wireframe** option from the **Visual Style** menu of the **View Control Bar**.

21. Now, move the cursor near the curved wall of the Lounge area. Click when the dashed line appears on the outer face of the wall to sketch the roof boundary curve, as shown in Figure 7-60. To sketch the other two lines for the Lounge roof, you need to use the **Line** tool from the **Draw** panel of the **Modify | Create Roof Footprint** tab.

Figure 7-60 Sketching the curved roof profile

22. Ensure that the **Boundary Line** tool is chosen in the **Draw** panel, and then choose the **Line** tool from the list box.

23. Clear the **Chain** check box in the **Options Bar**.

24. Ensure that the **Defines slope** check box in the **Options Bar** is clear and sketch the two lines to complete the boundary of the Lounge roof, as shown in Figure 7-61.

Figure 7-61 The completed roof profile of the Lounge

25. In the **Properties** palette, click on the value column for the **Base Level** instance parameter and ensure that the **Roof** option is selected from the drop-down list displayed.

26. Enter the value **-1'4"** (**-407 mm**) in the value column for the **Base Offset From Level** parameter as specified in the project parameter.

27. Choose the **Apply** button to apply the specified properties to the roof.

28. Next, choose the **Finish Edit Mode** button from the **Mode** panel of the **Modify | Create Roof Footprint** tab.

Using Basic Building Components-II   7-45

29. Next, to assign a type to the flat roof, select the **Basic Roof : Insulation on Metal Deck-EPDM** option from the **Type Selector** drop-down list in the **Properties** palette. Press ESC to exit from the **Floor: Architectural** tool.

   Now, you need to create roof for Hall 2. Since the roof of Hall 2 is identical to the roof of Hall 1, you can use the **Mirror-Draw Axis** tool to mirror the roof of Hall 1 to create the roof of Hall 2.

30. Double-click on **Roof** in the **Floor Plans** head in the **Project Browser** to display the roof plan of the club building.

31. Before you use the **Mirror-Draw Axis** tool, you need to display the grids in the drawing. To do so, choose the **Visibility/Graphics** tool from the **Graphics** panel; the **Visibility/Graphic Overrides for Floor Plan : Roof Framing** dialog box is displayed.

32. Choose the **Annotation Categories** tab, select the **Grids** check box if it is not selected in the **Visibility** column, and then choose **OK**; the **Visibility/Graphic Overrides for Floor Plan : Roof Framing** dialog box is closed.

33. Now, select the roof of Hall 1; the **Modify | Roofs** tab is displayed.

34. Choose the **Mirror - Draw Axis** tool from the **Modify** panel; you are prompted to pick the start point for the axis of reflection.

35. Click at the point of intersection of the grids A2 and B2 to specify the start point for the axis.

36. Next, click at any point vertically up, as shown in Figure 7-62. Press ESC to exit the modification mode.

37. Double-click on **North** in the **Elevations** node of the **Project Browser** to view the north elevation of the club building, as shown in Figure 7-63.

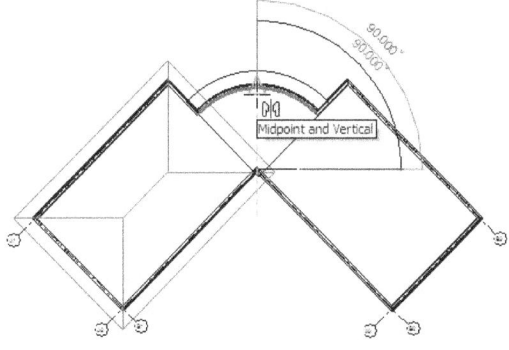

Figure 7-62 Mirroring the roof of Hall 1

Figure 7-63 North elevation of the Club project with the completed roof profile

Attaching Walls to the Floor

While creating the roof, you have already attached the walls to its bottom. Now, you need to attach the walls to the floor using the **Attach** tool.

1. Double-click on **Section X** under the **Sections (Building Section)** head in this **Project Browser** to display the corresponding section view in the drawing window.

2. Move the cursor near the exterior wall, and when it is highlighted, press the TAB key; all exterior walls get highlighted. Now, click to select the chain of exterior walls in the section view.

3. In the **Modify | Walls** tab, choose the **Attach Top/Base** tool from the **Modify Wall** panel; the options for attachment are displayed in the **Options Bar**.

4. Select the **Base** radio button in the **Options Bar**.

5. Next, move the cursor near the floor and click when it is highlighted; the walls are attached to the floor. Now, choose the **Modify** button from the **Select** panel to exit the modification tool.

   This completes the tutorial of creating floor, ceiling, and roof for the *Club* project.

6. Double-click on **First Floor** in the **Floor Plans** head of the **Project Browser** to display the first floor plan in the drawing window.

7. Choose **Save As > Project** from the **Application Menu**; the **Save As** dialog box is displayed. Enter required name in the **File name** edit box
   For Imperial   **c07_Club_tut2**
   For Metric   **M_c07_Club_tut2**
   Choose **Save**; the project file is saved.

8. Choose **Close** from **the Application Menu** to close the file.

Self-Evaluation Test

Answer the following questions and then compare them to those given at the end of this chapter:

1. Floors once created cannot be modified. (T/F)

2. You can sketch a floor in the section view. (T/F)

3. You can use the shape editing tools to modify the horizontal surface of a floor. (T/F)

4. You can use the **Chain** tool to sketch the roof footprint. (T/F)

5. A floor is created even if the sketched profile is not closed. (T/F)

6. When you model a roof, it is automatically associated with a _____.

   a) Level   b) Wall
   c) View   d) Material

7. To define the extents of a room, you must use room bounding elements or room separation_____.

   a) Families   b) Parameters
   c) Lines   d) Tags

8. Using the _____ drop-down list, you can select a ceiling type to be created.

9. The slope of a boundary line can be specified in the value column of the _____ instance parameter.

10. You can use the _____ tool to create a roof profile by sketching its boundaries in a closed loop.

11. You can create an opening in a roof by using the _____ tool.

12. The _____ tool can be used to attach walls to a floor.

Review Questions

Answer the following questions:

1. Which of the following options can be used to convert a sloping roof to a flat roof?

    a) **Opening**
    c) **Join/Unjoin**
    b) **Slope**
    d) **Define Slope**

2. Which of the following options can be used to create a roof overhang?

    a) **Define Slope**
    c) **Overhang**
    b) **Offset**
    d) **Extend to wall core**

3. Which of the following tools can be used to limit the visibility of a datum in a view?

    a) **Visibility/Graphics**
    c) **Scope Box**
    b) **Hidden lines**
    d) **Steering Wheels**

4. When modeling a floor, the floor _____ must be a closed loop.

    a) Type
    c) Slope
    b) Boundary
    d) Function.

5. Which of the following options is used to create sloped roof?

    a) **Defines slope**
    c) **Offset**
    b) **Overhang**
    d) **Scale**

6. A reference plane can be used to provide guides for sketching a roof profile. (T/F)

7. You can modify the slope of a roof after it has been created. (T/F)

8. An automatic ceiling is generated with the center of the room as its center. (T/F)

9. You can create an opening in the ceiling using the **Cut** tool. (T/F)

10. You can select only the sloping side to create an opening perpendicular to its face. (T/F)

11. Walls can be attached to the floors using the **Join Geometry** tool. (T/F)

12. You cannot copy a floor, roof, or ceiling from one project to another. (T/F)

Exercises

Exercise 1 — Apartment 2

Create a floor and a ceiling on the First Floor level of the *c06_Apartment2_ex1.rvt (M_c06_Apartment2_ex1.rvt* for Metric) project created in Exercise 1 of Chapter 6. Attach the walls to the floor. Use the following project parameters:

(Expected time: 30 min)

1. Floor type -
   - For Imperial **Floor: LW Concrete on Metal Deck**
   - For Metric **160mm Concrete With 50mm Metal Deck**

   Extents- to wall core.

2. Ceiling type-
   - For Imperial **Compound Ceiling: GWB on Mtl Stud**
   - **For Metric** **Compound Ceiling: Plain**

   Level- 8'6" (2591 mm) from the First Floor level.

3. Name of the file to be saved-
   - For Imperial **c07_Apartment2_ex1**
   - For Metric **M_c07_Apartment2_ex1**

Exercise 2 — Elevator and Stair Lobby

Create a floor and ceiling on the First Floor level of the *c06_ElevatorandStairLobby_ex2.rvt (M_c06_ElevatorandStairLobby_ex2.rvt* for Metric) project created in Exercise 2 of Chapter 6. Attach the walls to the floor. Also, create openings in the floor and ceiling, based on Figure 7-64. Use the following project parameters. Hide the grids and sections of building and do not create the floor and ceiling in the elevator shafts. **(Expected time: 30 min)**

1. Floor type -
   - For Imperial **LW Concrete on Metal Deck**
   - For Metric **160mm Concrete With 50mm Metal Deck**

   Extents- to wall core.

2. Ceiling type-
   - For Imperial **GWB on Mtl Stud**
   - For Metric **Plain**

   Level- 8'6" (2591 mm) from the floor level.

3. Name of the file to be saved-
   - For Imperial **c07_ElevatorandStairLobby_ex2**
   - For Metric **M_c07_ElevatorandStairLobby_ex2**

Figure 7-64 *Sketch plan for creating an opening for the Elevator and Stair Lobby project*

Answers to Self-Evaluation Test
1. F, **2.** F, **3.** T, **4.** T, **5.** F, **6. Level**, **7. Lines**, **8. Type Selector**, **9. Slope**, **10. Roof by Extrusion**, **11. Opening**, **12. Attach Top/Base**.

Chapter 8

Using Basic Building Components-III

Learning Objectives

After completing this chapter, you will be able to:
• *Add components to a building model.*
• *Create stairs using the Stairs tool.*
• *Add railings to various locations in a project using the Railing tool.*
• *Understand the procedure of adding ramps to a building model.*
• *Add curtain walls with doors and mullions.*
• *Copy elements from one level to another.*

INTRODUCTION

This chapter describes the usage of building elements such as freestanding components, stairs, railings, ramps, and curtain walls. In addition, the chapter discusses how to copy elements to different levels.

USING COMPONENTS IN A PROJECT

Autodesk Revit Architecture provides various freestanding components that can be placed in a project. These include furniture items, plumbing fixtures, electrical fittings, trees, and many other family elements. Unlike other dependent elements, these freestanding components do not have any predefined associativity with other elements. However, it enables you to assign certain restrictions to their placement.

Adding Components

Ribbon: Architecture > Build > Component drop-down > Place a Component
Shortcut Key: CM

You can add components to a building model using the **Place a Component** tool. This tool can be invoked from the **Build** panel. On invoking this tool, the **Modify | Place Component** tab will be displayed. You can use the options in this tab to select the component type and specify the properties of the component to be inserted, load components from the predefined library, or create a new component in the drawing. Alternatively, type **CM** to invoke the **Place a Component** tool.

Revit provides different in-built component types. You can select them from the **Type Selector** drop-down list in the **Properties** palette, as shown in Figure 8-1. You can also load additional component types from the **US Imperial** folder. To do so, choose the **Load Family** tool from the **Mode** panel of the **Modify | Place Component** tab; the **Load Family** dialog box will be displayed. In this dialog box, browse to the **US Imperial** folder and select the required component from the specific sub-folder. After you select the required component and close the **Load Family** dialog box, the selected component will be added in the **Type Selector** drop-down list.

Figure 8-1 The Type Selector drop-down list displaying different component types

After selecting the component from the **Type Selector** drop-down list, select the **Rotate after placement** check box in the **Options Bar**, so that you can rotate the component after placing it. Now, move the cursor to the area where you want to add it. You will notice a component symbol attached to the cursor. Moreover, the temporary dimensions will display the distance of the component from the nearby elements. To place the component, click at the desired location; the temporary dimensions will be highlighted. Click on the appropriate dimension to enter a new value; the component will move to a new distance. As you have selected the **Rotate after placement** check box, the

Using Basic Building Components-III

Rotate tool will be invoked when you add a component in the project. You can then rotate it graphically. To understand the concept of adding components, consider an example. If you need to add a kitchen sink to a kitchen layout plan, choose the **Place a Component** tool from **Architecture > Build > Component** drop-down; the **Modify | Place Component** tab will be displayed. In this tab, choose the **Load Family** tool from the **Model** panel; the **Load Family** dialog box will be displayed. In this dialog box, the **US Imperial** folder with a list of sub-folders will be opened. Select the **Plumbing** sub-folder and choose the **Open** button; the files of different family types of plumbing fixtures will be displayed in the selected sub-folders. Select the desired file and choose the **Open** button; the **Load Family** dialog box will close and the selected family type will be added to the **Type Selector** drop-down list. As you add the component to the **Type Selector** drop-down list, it gets selected automatically. Now, when you move the cursor to the floor plan of the kitchen, an image of the sink will be attached to it and the temporary dimension will appear, as shown in Figure 8-2. Click to add the sink at the appropriate location, as shown in Figure 8-3. Invoke the **Modify** tool from the **Select** panel to exit this tool.

Figure 8-2 Adding a component using the temporary dimension

Figure 8-3 The added component with its controls and temporary dimensions

Now, after you have inserted the desired component in the drawing, you can lock its position with certain elements such as walls. To do so, select the component inserted; the **Options Bar** will be displayed. In **Options Bar**, you can select the **Moves With Nearby Elements** check box to lock the position of the selected component to the nearest element displayed around it. For example, the sink can be locked to its supporting wall by selecting it and then selecting the **Moves With Nearby Elements** check box in the **Options Bar**. The component is locked to the nearby wall. Now, the kitchen sink will move with the wall, as shown in Figure 8-4. Figure 8-5 shows the new location of the sink. The component can, however, be moved freely in its plane of insertion.

You can create components that are specific to a project requirement. For example, while designing the interior of an office space, you may require different shapes and type of workstations to be inserted in your drawing. Therefore, to create and add different types of workstation cubicles, you can use the **Model In-Place** tool. Invoke this tool from **Architecture > Build > Component** drop-down; the **Family Category and Parameters** dialog box will be displayed. Select the desired family category from the list available in the **Family Category** area and then choose the **OK** button. On doing so, the **Name** dialog box will be displayed. In this dialog box, enter a name in the **Name** edit box and then choose **OK**; the dialog box will be closed and the **Family Editor** interface will be opened. You can use various tools from the ribbon in this interface to create in-place models and then specify their datum and in-place properties. After you create the in-place model, choose the **Finish Model** button from the **In-Place Editor** panel in the **Create** tab.

Figure 8-4 Moving the wall with the locked sink   *Figure 8-5* Resulting wall and the moved sink

After you place a component in the drawing, you can modify its instance and type properties. To do so, select a component from the drawing; the **Modify <Family Category>** tab will be displayed and the instance properties for the selected component of a specific family category will be displayed in the **Properties** palette. In this palette, various instance parameters such as level, information about the host, phases created and demolished and so on are displayed with their current values, as shown in Figure 8-6. In this palette, you can modify the current values of various parameters to the desired values. The value of the **Level** parameter indicates the current level on which the component is placed. To change the current value of this parameter, click on its corresponding value field and select the new level from the drop-down list to move the selected component to the new level. Other parameters in the instance parameters table depend on the component selected. Various instance parameters of the components can be modified using this table. In the **Properties** palette, you can also view and modify the type properties of the selected component.

Choose the **Edit Type** button in this palette; the **Type Properties** dialog box will be displayed, as shown in Figure 8-7. In the **Type Parameters** area of this dialog box, you can view the parameters and then modify them. Alternatively, you can display the **Type Properties** dialog box by choosing the **Type Properties** tool from the **Properties** panel of the **Modify < Family Category>** tab.

*Figure 8-6 Instance parameters in the **Properties** palette for the component **Sink Kitchen-Double 42" x 21"***

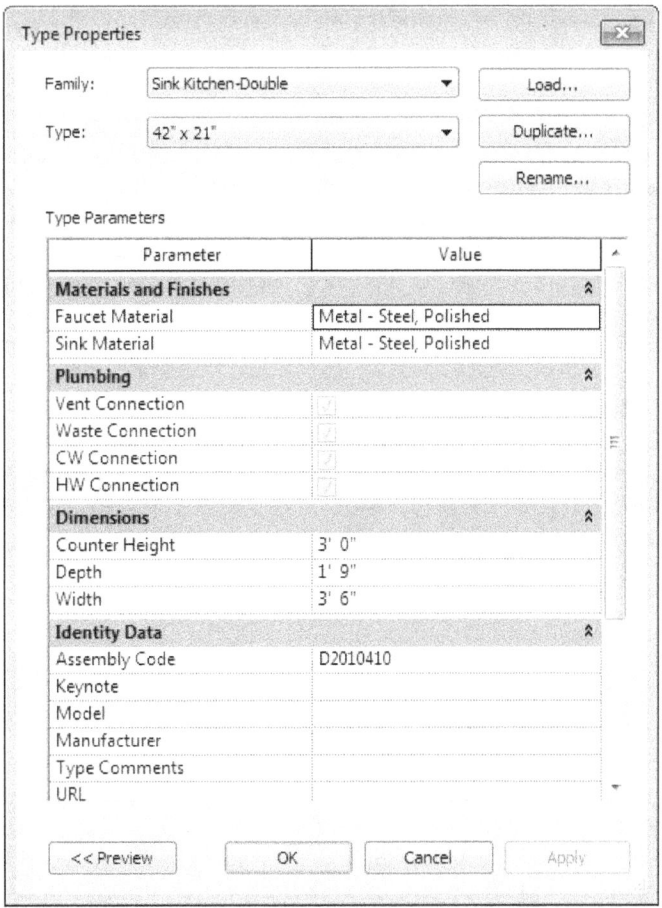

*Figure 8-7 The **Type Properties** dialog box for the component **Sink Kitchen-Double 42" x 21"***

ADDING STAIRS

In Autodesk Revit, you can create a variety of stair shapes such as straight, curved, and spiral stairs with ease. In Revit, stairs are parametric elements; therefore, you can create them by specifying the rules for risers, treads, and stringers. You can create stairs in your building design both in the plan and 3D views.

In Autodesk Revit, you can add stairs to a project in individual components, such as its run, landing, and supports, or by sketching the runs in the required area. To add a stair in components, use the **Stair by Component** tool, and to add stair by sketching, you can use the **Stair by Sketch** tool.

Adding Stair By Component

Ribbon: Architecture > Circulation > Stair drop-down > Stair by Component

In Autodesk Revit, stairs can be added in individual components, such as Run, Landing, and Supports. To do so, invoke the **Stair by Component** tool from the **Build** panel; the **Modify | Create Stair** tab will be displayed. In the **Component** panel of this tab, you can choose the **Run**, **Landing**, or **Support** tool based on the requirement. The usage of some of these tools are discussed next.

Run Tool

You can use the **Run** tool to create a run of a stair. To create the run of stair, invoke the **Stair by Component** tool from the **Circulation** panel; the **Modify | Create Stair** tab will be displayed. In the **Components** panel of this tab, ensure that the **Run** tool is chosen by default. As a result, a list of tools to create the stair run is displayed in the list box displayed in the **Components** panel. The list box contains the **Straight**, **Full-Step Spiral**, **Center-Ends Spiral**, **L-Shape Winder**, **U-Shape Winder**, and **Create Sketch** tool. The usage of some of these tools are discussed next.

Straight Tool

This tool is used to create a stair run with a straight flight. This tool can be invoked from the **Component** panel of the **Modify | Create Stair** tab. As you invoke the **Straight** tool, various options related to the creation of a straight run are displayed in the **Options Bar**. The **Location Line** drop-down list in the **Options Bar** is used to specify the reference line for creating the stairs. You can select the following options from the drop-down list: **Exterior Support: Left**, **Run: Center**, **Run: Left**, **Run: Right**, and **Exterior Support: Right**. The **Run: Center** option is selected by default. To offset the stair run from the specified reference line, you can specify the offset value in the **Offset** edit box. In the **Options Bar**, enter a value in the **Actual Run Width** edit box to specify the run width for stairs. The **Automatic Landing** check box in the **Options Bar** is selected by default. As a result, the landing will be created at the turn between the flight. If you clear this check box, the landing will not be created. You need to specify the instance parameters of the stair run in the **Properties** palette. Select an option from the **Type Selector** drop-down list to specify the type of the stair. Click in the **Value** field corresponding to the **Base Level** parameter and select an option from the displayed drop-down list to assign the level to the base of the stair. You can specify an offset distance by which the base of the stair will

Using Basic Building Components-III

be offseted from the selected level. To specify the offset value, click in the **Value** field corresponding to the **Base Offset** parameter and enter a value. Similarly, you can set the level and offset distance for the top of the stair by selecting a desired option for the **Top Level** parameter and by specifying a desired value to the **Top Offset** parameter. In the **Properties** palette, the other parameters that you can specify for the stair are **Multistory Top Level, Desired Number of Stairs, Actual Tread Depth, Tread/Riser Start Number**, and so on. After specifying the desired parameters, you can start creating the stair in the drawing view. To do so, click in the drawing window to specify the start point of the run. On doing so, a stair run will start from the desired point and the preview of the stair run will be displayed along with the cursor, as shown in Figure 8-8. Next, click again in a desired point to specify the endpoint of the stair run. On specifying the endpoint, the stair run will be created, as shown in Figure 8-9. To finish the stair creation, choose the **Finish Edit Mode** button from the **Mode** panel of the **Modify | Create Stairs** tab. Now, you can view the three-dimensional view of the created stair, refer to Figure 8-10, by choosing the **Default 3D View** tool from the **Create** panel of the **View** tab.

Figure 8-8 Preview of the stair run on specifying the start point

Figure 8-9 The straight stair run created on specifying the endpoint

Figure 8-10 The three-dimensional view of the straight stair

Full-Step Spiral Tool

You can use this tool to create a spiral run by specifying its start point and the center. To create a spiral run, choose this tool from the **Components** panel of the **Modify | Create Stair** tab; you will be prompted to specify the center of the stair. Click at the desired location in the drawing area to specify the center of the spiral stair. On doing so, the preview of the spiral stair will appear with cursor. You can move the cursor away from the specified center of the spiral stair and click at desired point to specify the radius of the stair. On doing so, the spiral stair will be created at the specified center, as shown in Figure 8-11. Choose the **Finish Edit Mode** button from the **Mode** panel of the **Modify | Create Stair** tab to complete the creation of the spiral stair.

Figure 8-11 The three-dimensional view of the spiral stair

Center-Ends Spiral Tool

This tool helps to create a spiral run that is less than 360 degrees, by specifying the center point, start point, endpoint, and the direction of the turn. To create a spiral run by using this tool, choose the **Stair by Component** tool from the **Stair** drop-down in the **Circulation** panel; the **Modify | Create Stair** tab will be displayed. Next, choose the **Center-Ends Spiral** tool from this tab; you will be prompted to specify the center of the stair. Click in the drawing area to specify the center; a preview of the stair will be displayed. Next, click to specify the start point of the stair; you will be prompted to specify the end point. Click in the desired location to complete the stair creation. Note that the turn of the stair can be changed and the end point can be specified on the side where the turn of the stair is be located. The process of creating a Spiral stair by using the **Center-Ends Spiral** tool has been illustrated in Figure 8-12 through 8-15.

L-Shape Winder Tool

This tool in the **Component** panel of the **Modify | Create Stair** tab helps you to create a L-shape stair with a winder. The winder in a stair are steps at the turn that are narrower on one side. These steps are placed to change the direction of landing. The L-shape winder can be created by specifying the start point of the run at the lower end. You can also change the direction of the run by pressing SPACEBAR.

Figure 8-12 Specifying the center of the spiral stair

Figure 8-13 Specifying the start point of the spiral stair

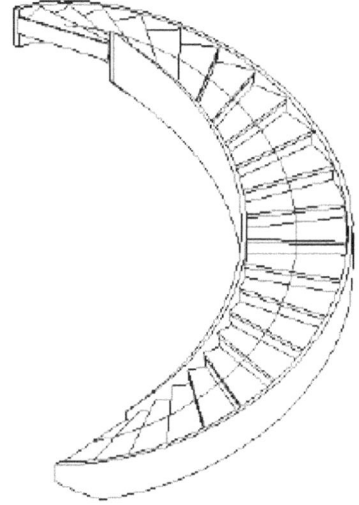

Figure 8-14 Specifying the turn of the spiral stair

*Figure 8-15 Three dimensional view of the spiral stair using the **Center-Ends Spiral** tool*

U-Shape Winder Tool

You can use this tool to create a U-shape stair with winders at turn. To create such stairs, invoke this tool from the **Components** panel of the **Modify | Create Stair** tab, a preview of the U-shape stairs will be displayed in the drawing area. Also, various options and properties of the stairs will be displayed in the **Options Bar** and the **Properties** palette, respectively. In the **Options Bar**, you can select an option from the **Location Line** drop-down list to specify the reference line for the stair. In the **Relative Base Height** edit box, enter a value to specify the height of the base of the stair run relative to its base level. In the **Options Bar**, you can select the **Mirror Preview** check box to flip the start and end of the stair run to be added in the drawing. Figure 8-16 and Figure 8-17 show plans of a U-shape stair created with the **Mirror Preview** check box cleared and selected, respectively.

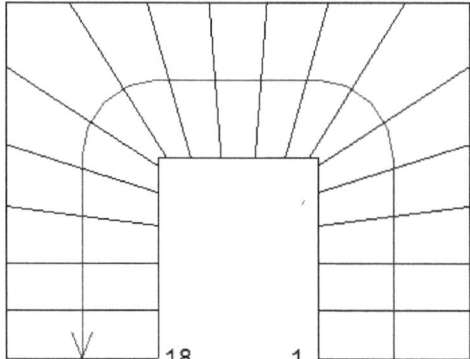

Figure 8-16 *The U shaped winder stair run created with the* **Mirror Preview** *check box cleared*

Figure 8-17 *The U shaped winder stair run created with the* **Mirror Preview** *check box selected*

In the **Properties** palette, you can select a stair type from the **Type Selector** drop-down list. You can also specify the parameters for setting the base level, actual depth of the tread, desired number of risers, start number for tread or riser, and so on. Now, click in the desired point in the drawing area, the U-shape stair with winder will be added in the project view. In the **Mode** panel of the **Modify | Create Stair** tab, choose the **Finish Edit Mode** button to finish the creation of stair run.

Landing Tool

This tool is used to create a landing between two runs. To create landing, choose the **Stair by Component** tool from **Architecture > Circulation > Stair** drop-down; the **Modify| Create Stair** tab will be displayed. From the **Components** panel of this tab choose the **Landing** tool; the **Pick Two Runs** and **Create Sketch** tools are displayed in the list box next to it. You can use the **Pick Two Runs** tool to create a landing by selecting two runs of a stair. On invoking this tool, you will be prompted to select the first run. Click on the first run of the stair; the stair run will be selected and highlighted, as shown in Figure 8-18. Also, you will be prompted to select the second stair run. Click on the second stair run; a landing will be created between the first and second stair runs, as shown in Figure 8-19.

Alternatively, you can use the **Create Sketch** tool in the **Components** panel to create a custom based landing by sketching it in the project view. When sketching a landing using this tool, you need to define the boundary and the stair path. The stair path defines the walk line or the direction of the landing in the stair. Invoke the **Create Sketch** tool from the list box in the **Components** panel; the **Modify | Create Stair > Sketch Landing** tab will be displayed. In the **Draw** panel of this tab, you can use the **Boundary** and **Stairs Path** tools to define the boundary of the landing and path of the stair, respectively. To create the boundary of the landing, choose the **Boundary** tool from the **Draw** panel, if it is not chosen by default. On doing so, various tools to sketch the boundary of the landing will be displayed next to the **Boundary** tool. You can choose a tool or a combination of the tools as per requirement of the project. As you sketch the boundary of the landing, you need to specify options related

Using Basic Building Components-III

to the sketching tool you have chosen in the **Options Bar**. Also, you need to specify various properties of the landing in the **Properties** palette. You can specify the height at which the landing will be created. To do so, enter a desired value in the value field of the **Relative Height** parameter. The value entered for this parameter will be measured in reference to the base of the stair. Now, create the boundary of the landing using the desired sketching tools. Next, choose the **Stairs Path** tool from the **Draw** panel to define the path of the stair run. Figure 8-20 shows a sketched boundary and the stair path of the landing. Now, choose the **Finish Edit Mode** button from the **Mode** panel to finish the sketching of the landing and the stair path; the landing between the runs will be created and the **Modify | Create Stair** tab will be displayed. In this tab you can choose the **Edit Sketch** tool from the **Tools** panel to modify the sketch of the landing. Now, choose the **Finish Edit Mode** button from the **Mode** panel to exit the stair creation mode. Figure 8-21 displays a three-dimensional view of a stair run with a custom sketched landing.

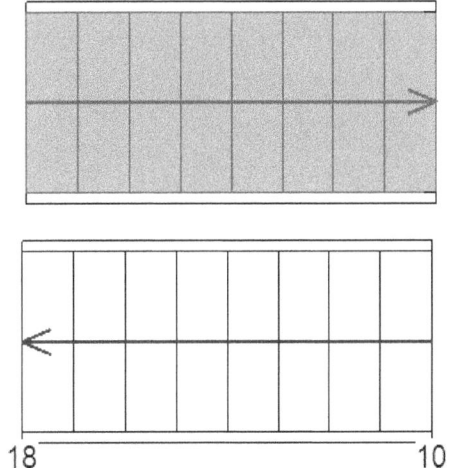

Figure 8-18 The first stair run highlighted

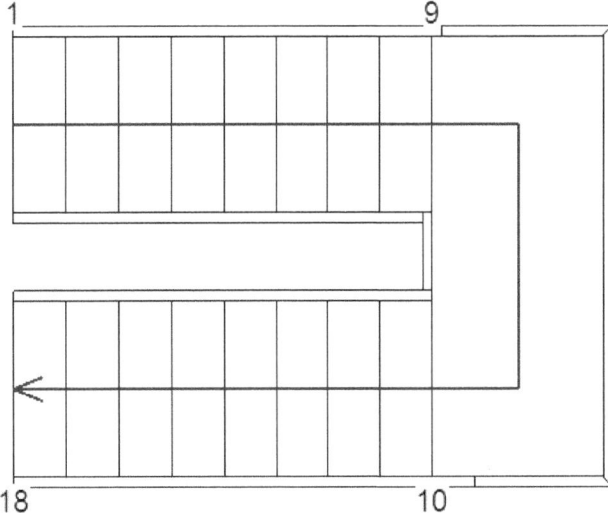

Figure 8-19 Landing created between the first and second stair run

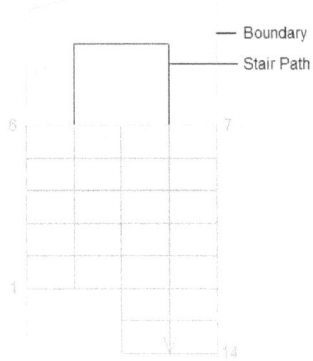

Figure 8-20 Sketched boundary and the stair path of a landing

Figure 8-21 Three-dimensional stair runs with custom based landing

Support Tool

You can use this tool to add a stringer or a carriage by selecting an individual path on a run or landing. Invoke this tool from the **Components** panel of the **Modify | Create Stair** tab; you will be prompted to pick the edge of a stair run or landing to place the support. Choose the **Finish Edit Mode** button from the **Mode** panel; the support will be added to the stairs run, as shown in Figure 8-22.

Using Basic Building Components-III

Figure 8-22 Support added to the stair runs

Converting a Stair Component to a Sketch

In a project, you can convert a stair component into a custom sketch. The custom sketch can then be edited to create a stair of your requirement. To convert a stair component to a custom sketch, select it in the drawing and then choose the **Edit Stairs** button from the **Edit** panel of the **Modify | Stairs** tab; the **Modify | Create Stair** tab will be displayed and the stair component will be created in the editable mode. Now, select the run component from the drawing and then choose the **Convert** tool from the **Tools** panel of the **Modify | Create Stair** tab as shown in Figure 8-23; the **Stair- Convert to Custom** window will be displayed. Choose the **Close** button from this window; the stair component will be converted into a custom sketch. Now, you can edit the shape of the run of the custom stair. To do so, select the stairs and then choose the **Edit Sketch** tool from the **Tools** panel of the **Modify | Create Stair** tab; the **Modify | Create Stair > Sketch Run** contextual tab will be displayed. You can modify the run by using the tools available in the **Draw** panel of this contextual tab.

Figure 8-23 Choosing the **Convert** tool in the **Modify / Create Stair** tab

Adding Stairs by Sketching Runs

You can create a staircase by defining its run. You can use this method to define straight runs, L-shape runs with a landing, U-shape runs, and spiral runs for creating stairs. Although stairs can be created both in the plan and the 3D view for most locations, it is more convenient to sketch them in the plan view.

To define the run for sketching stairs, you need to choose the **Stair by Sketch** tool from **Architecture > Circulation > Stair** drop-down. On doing so, the **Modify | Create Stairs Sketch** tab will be displayed. Choose the **Run** tool from the **Draw** panel, if it is not chosen by default; two tools to sketch the run will be displayed in a list box available next to the **Run** tool. In the list box, the **Line** tool is invoked by default. As a result, you will be prompted to mark the start point. Move the cursor near the location of the start point of the stairs (midpoint of the bottom of the first riser) and click; a rectangular box will be displayed with one end attached to the specified point, as shown in Figure 8-24. Also, the number of risers created and remaining for a particular distance will be displayed. Move the cursor to the desired location and click to specify the endpoint of the first run; the first run of stairs will be sketched, as shown in Figure 8-25. Also, the temporary dimensions and the risers sketched will be displayed. Similarly, create the second run of stairs by clicking the start and endpoint of the stairs based on the risers created and the number of remaining risers displayed in the sketch, refer to Figure 8-26. Choose the **Finish Edit Mode** button from the **Mode** panel of the **Modify | Create Stairs Sketch** tab; the stairs will be created. The stairs created will appear in the plan view with a break line and the **UP** arrow (if specified in the stair properties), as shown in Figure 8-27. You can view the created stairs from a level above it. Similarly, to display a three-dimensional view of the stair created, choose the **Default 3D View** tool from **View > Create > 3D View** drop-down. The view will appear similar to one shown in Figure 8-28.

Figure 8-24 A rectangular box displayed with one end attached to a specified point

Figure 8-25 Sketch of the first run of the stair

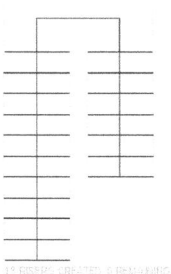

Figure 8-26 Sketch of the second run of the stair along with the first run

Figure 8-27 Plan view of the stair created

Using Basic Building Components-III

Figure 8-28 Three-dimensional view of the stairs created by the **Run** tool

Note
By default, Autodesk Revit creates the railing on both sides of the stair run. The railings can, however, be selected individually and then edited or deleted.

Tip: *Before sketching the stairs by a method, it is advisable to draw reference planes to simplify their sketching process.*

Adding Stairs by Sketching the Boundary and Riser Lines

You can also add stairs by sketching their boundary profile and riser lines. To do so, choose the **Stair by Sketch** tool from the **Architecture > Circulation > Stair** drop-down; the **Modify Create Stairs Sketch** tab will be displayed. Choose the **Boundary** tool from the **Draw** panel of this tab; the sketching tools will be displayed in a list box next to the **Boundary** tool. In this list box, select any tool to start sketching the boundary. After sketching the boundary of the stairs, add risers to it. To add risers, choose the **Riser** tool from the **Draw** panel of the **Modify | Create Stairs Sketch** tab; the sketching tools will be displayed in a list box next to it. Select any tool from the list box and sketch the risers along the boundary lines drawn. After you finish sketching the risers, choose the **Finish Edit Mode** button from the **Mode** panel of the **Modify | Create Stairs Sketch** tab. Figure 8-29 shows an example of the sketched boundary and risers using the reference planes.

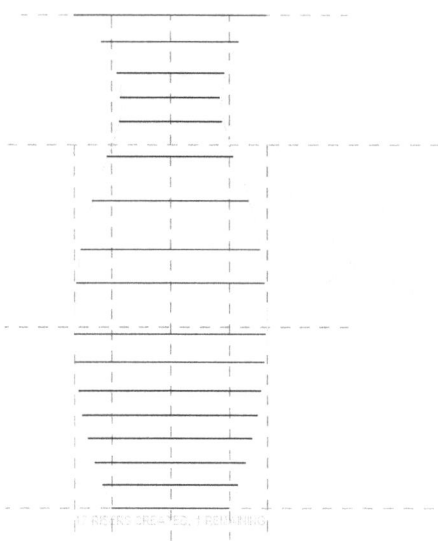

Figure 8-29 Sketched boundary and risers of a stair run using the reference planes

 Note
The start point of the boundary sketch is assumed to be the start of the stairs. However, after creating the stairs, you can use the flip control to change their direction.

The stairs created by sketching the boundary and riser lines can be viewed in the plan view, as shown in Figure 8-30. The 3D view of the stairs created is shown in Figure 8-31.

Figure 8-30 Plan view showing the stair run

Figure 8-31 3D view of the stairs created by using the **Boundary** and **Riser** tools

While sketching the boundary for the stairs with a landing, you may need to break the boundary line at its junctions. This enables Autodesk Revit Architecture to generate the stair railing at the same level as the landing. To split the boundary created, choose the **Split Element** tool

Using Basic Building Components-III

from the **Modify** panel of the **Modify | Create Stairs Sketch** tab; you will be prompted to select an element from the drawing to split the boundary. Select a point along the boundary to specify the start point of the landing of the stairs. As you click over the boundary, it will split into two segments. Similarly, you can use the **Split Element** tool to break the boundary wherever required, as shown in Figure 8-32. Figure 8-33 shows the 3D view of a stair with landing and railing created using the **Boundary**, **Riser**, and **Split Element** tools from the **Modify | Create Stairs Sketch** tab.

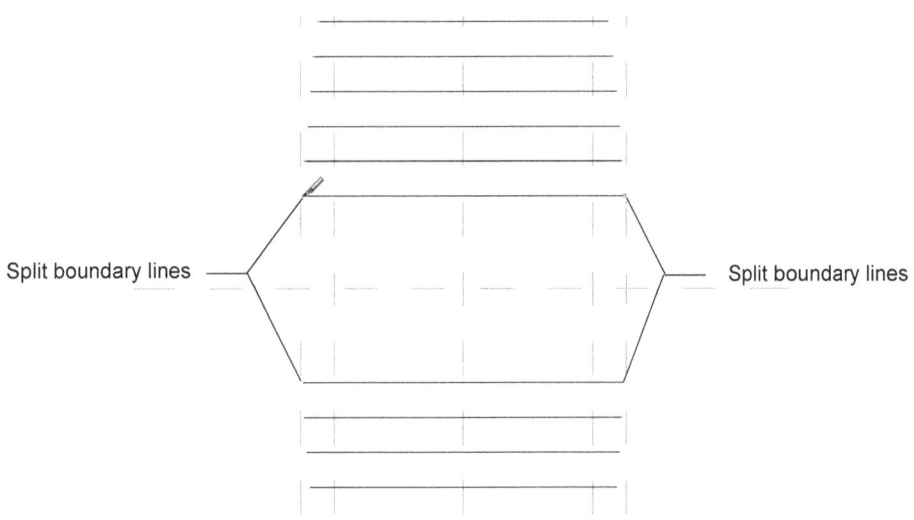

Figure 8-32 Splitting boundary lines

Figure 8-33 The 3D view of the resulting stair railing

Modifying Stairs Properties

You can specify the properties of stairs before creating them and then you can modify its properties. To modify the stairs after you create them, select the stairs; the properties of the stairs will be displayed in the **Properties** palette, as shown in Figure 8-34. In the **Properties** palette, the **Base Level** parameter indicates the level from which the stairs will start, and the **Top Level** parameter indicates the level at which they will end. By default, the current level is set as the base level, and the next story level is set as the top level.

The **Multistory Top Level** parameter can be used to create stairs that continue from the base level to a specified upper level of a multistory building. The level upto which the stairs rise, can be selected from the drop-down list in the value column of the **Multistory Top Level** parameter. The parameters under the **Dimensions** section are used to specify different dimensional parameters for the stairs. The **Width** parameter is used to specify the width of the stair run. You can determine the number of risers in the stairs by specifying a value in the **Value** column of the **Desired Number of Risers** parameter. In the **Value** column for the **Actual Tread Depth** parameter, you can specify a value for the depth of the treads in a stair. Other instance parameters can also be modified in the **Properties** palette. You can choose the **Edit Type** button from the **Properties** palette for viewing and modifying the type properties. On choosing this button, the **Type Properties** dialog box will be displayed, as shown in Figure 8-35. In the **Type Properties** dialog box, you can choose the **Edit** button for specifying the calculation rules. When you choose this button, the **Stair Calculator** dialog box will be displayed. This dialog box can be used to set new rules to calculate the slope of the stairs. In the **Type Properties** dialog box, you can enter the **Minimum Tread Depth** and the **Maximum Riser Height** in their corresponding value columns. Other type parameters that can also be specified in the **Type Properties** dialog box include **Tread Thickness**, **Riser Thickness**, **Nosing Length**, and so on. The **Monolithic Stairs** check box can be selected to create the stairs made up of only a single material.

*Figure 8-34 The **Properties** palette displaying various instance properties of the selected stairs*

Using Basic Building Components-III

*Figure 8-35 The **Type Properties** dialog box for stairs*

Tip: *You can experiment with different type and instance properties to create the required stairs.*

Note
*While creating stairs, you can specify the type of railings that will be attached to it. To do so, choose the **Railings Type** tool from the **Tools** panel of the **Modify / Create Stairs Sketch** tab; the **Railings Type** dialog box will be displayed. Select the railings type from the drop-down list and choose the **OK** button to confirm the selection.*

Tip: *The instance and type parameters depend on the selected component type. Revit Architecture empowers you to modify the appropriate parameter(s) as per the requirement.*

*The rules and calculations set in the **Stair Calculator** dialog box are applicable, if they are set before the creation of the stairs. You cannot modify the rules of the created stairs using this dialog box.*

ADDING RAILINGS

Railings are automatically generated with the stairs but they can also be created by specifying their profile. You can also create them for other locations in the building project such as terraces, passages, and so on. You can select and modify their properties to achieve the desired railing configuration. In Revit, you can add railing by sketching its path or by placing it in a stair or a ramp in the project. The methods of adding a railing by sketching a path and placing it on a host such as stair and ramp is discussed next.

Adding Railings by Sketching the Path

Ribbon: Architecture > Circulation > Railing

Sketch Path   You can add railing in a project by sketching its path. To do so, you can use the **Sketch Path** tool. Invoke this tool from **Architecture > Circulation > Railing** drop-down; the **Modify | Create Railing Path** tab will be displayed. This tab displays various sketching tools to sketch the railing path. You can sketch the railing path with or without a host as per the requirement of the project. The host to the railing can be a floor stairs, ramps and so on. To select a host, choose the **Pick New Host** tool from the **Tools** panel of the **Modify | Create Railing Path** tab; you will be prompted to select an element in the drawing on which the railing is to be created. Select the host if required. In the **Properties** palette, you can select the type of the railing. To assign a type to the railing, select an option from the **Type Selector** drop-down list. In the **Properties** palette, you can also assign various instance parameters such as **Base Level, Base Offset**, **Tread / Stringer Offset**, and so on to the railing. Now, to sketch the railing path, choose any of the drawing tools from the list box that will be displayed in the **Draw** panel of the **Modify | Create Railing Path** tab to sketch. For example, you can use the **Line** tool to define a specific railing path, as shown in Figure 8-36. You can use the **Ref Plane** tool to assist you in sketching the railing boundary, if required. After completing the sketch of the railing path, choose the **Finish Edit Mode** button from the **Mode** panel; the railing will be created, as shown in Figure 8-37.

Modifying Railing Properties

You can modify the properties and parameters of a railing before or after creating it. To specify the properties and parameters of a railing, you can use various instance properties displayed in the **Properties** palette. To specify the type properties of the proposed railing, choose the **Edit Type** button in the **Properties** palette; the **Type Properties** dialog box will be displayed. In this dialog box, the **Edit** buttons in the value column for the **Rail Structure** and **Baluster Placement** type parameters can be chosen to view and modify the parameters of the railing such as rail type, baluster type, baluster spacing, and so on. The **Baluster Offset** parameter indicates the offset distance of the baluster from the sketched rail boundary.

Apart from the preloaded baluster types, you can load additional ones by choosing the **Load Family** tool from the **Load from Library** panel in the **Insert** tab. On choosing the **Load Family** tool, the **Load Family** dialog box will be displayed. In this dialog box, open the **US Imperial > Railings > Balusters (US Imperial > Railings > Balusters** for Metric) and select the desired file(s) for adding baluster type(s) in the project. After selecting the desired file(s), choose the **Open** button in the **Load Family** dialog box; the dialog box will close and the selected baluster type(s) will be loaded into the project.

Using Basic Building Components-III   8-21

*Figure 8-36 Using the **Line** tool to create the boundary for a railing*

Figure 8-37 3D view of the railing created

 Note
Railings are associated with their hosts and are modified with the changes in the host element. For example, if the stairs are deleted, the railing will also be deleted. You can, however, delete the railing independent of its hosts.

Modifying Railing Joints

You can modify the joint type of a joint in a railing. To do so, open the plan or the 3D view in which the railing you wish to edit is visible. Next, select the railing; the **Modify | Railings** tab is displayed. Choose the **Edit Path** tool from the **Mode** panel; the **Modify | Railings > Sketch Path** tab will be displayed and the railing path will be displayed in the sketch mode. In the **Modify | Railings > Sketch Path** tab, choose the **Edit Rail Joins** tool from the **Tools** panel and then move the cursor along the path of the railing. As you move the cursor along the path, you will notice a snap is displayed at the intersection of the railing path or at the point where the two paths join. Click, when the snap is displayed, and then from the **Rail Join** drop-down list in the **Options Bar**, select an option to specify the type of join. Similarly, you can click on other joins in the railing path and change their type as per the project requirement. After you finish assigning the type to the joins, choose the **Finish Edit Mode** button from the **Mode** panel of the **Modify Railings > Edit Path** tab to finish editing the railing joins.

ADDING RAMPS

Ribbon: Architecture > Circulation > Ramp

You can create ramps in Autodesk Revit Architecture in a manner similar to creating stairs. The **Ramp** tool is used to create ramps and can be invoked from the **Circulation** panel. On invoking this tool, the **Modify | Create Ramp Sketch** tab will be displayed. Also, the properties used for creating the ramp will be displayed in the **Properties** palette. You can use various tools and options in this tab to create the sketch of the ramp. In the **Properties** palette, you can assign properties and type to the ramp.

The **Draw** panel of the **Modify | Create Ramp Sketch** tab contains various sketching tools that can be used to create the sketch of the ramp boundary. These tools and their applications are similar to those present in the **Draw** panel of the **Modify | Create Ramp Sketch** tab.

After sketching the ramp boundary for the proposed ramp, you need to view and assign properties to it. To do so, you can use various properties displayed in the **Properties** palette of the ramp. The instance properties of the ramp can be specified in this palette. In the **Properties** palette, the **Width** parameter indicates the width of the ramp, whereas the **Base Level** parameter indicates the level from where the ramp will start, and the **Top Level** parameter indicates the level at which the ramp will end. The slope and width of the ramp can be specified even before it is created. Next, to view and modify the type properties of the proposed ramp, choose the **Edit Type** button in the **Properties** palette; the **Type Properties** dialog box will be displayed. In this dialog box, the value of the **Maximum Incline Length** parameter indicates the maximum length of the ramp before a landing is required. Specify the maximum slope of the ramp in the **Ramp Max Slope (1/x)** parameter value. The **Shape** parameter is used to create a ramp with a solid base or a slab. Figure 8-38 shows an example of sketching a ramp by specifying the start point and the endpoint.

Figure 8-38 Sketching the ramp run

After specifying the instance and type properties of the ramp, you can specify the type of railing to be used for it. To do so, choose the **Railing** tool from the **Tools** panel of the **Modify | Create Ramp Sketch** tab; the **Railings** dialog box will be displayed. In this dialog box, select the railing type from the available drop-down list and choose the **OK** button; the **Railings** dialog box will close and the selected railing type will be assigned to the ramp.

Using Basic Building Components-III

Next, click in the drawing area to specify the start point of the ramp. On doing so, a rectangle shaped geometry will be displayed. This geometry will show the total size required for creating the ramp. The ramp size can be calculated based on the current ramp property settings. The required length of the ramp is also displayed on specifying the first point of the ramp run. Next, specify the endpoint of the ramp and choose the **Finish Edit Mode** button from the **Mode** panel of the **Modify | Create Ramp Sketch** tab. This creates the ramp with the given parameters, as shown in Figure 8-39. If the specified length of the ramp is less or more than the required length, Autodesk Revit Architecture will display a warning message box showing the error and its cause, as shown in Figure 8-40. You can ignore the error, if possible, or rectify the sketch or the properties to create the desired ramp using curtain systems in a project.

Figure 8-39 *3D view of resultant ramp*

Figure 8-40 *The **Warning** message box showing the error type*

USING CURTAIN SYSTEMS IN A PROJECT

In Autodesk Revit Architecture, a typical curtain system comprises the panels, curtain grid, curtain wall, and mullions, as shown in Figure 8-41. Each of these elements can be modified individually. A curtain system can be added by using the **Wall: Architectural** tool or by using the specific curtain system tools. You can also generate the curtain systems of different shapes and configurations. A curtain system created using the **Wall: Architectural** tool is also referred to as a curtain wall. You can create curved, sloping, and store front curtain systems.

Figure 8-41 Typical curtain system elements

Creating a Curtain Wall Using the Wall: Architectural Tool

A curtain wall can be created by using the **Wall** tool. To create a curtain wall, invoke the **Wall** tool and select the required type from the **Type Selector** drop-down list in the **Properties** palette, as shown in Figure 8-42. Note that the **Type Selector** drop-down list displays three different types of curtain wall options such as **Curtain Wall 1**, **Exterior Glazing**, and **Storefront** under the **Curtain Wall** head. After selecting the desired curtain wall type from the **Type Selector** drop-down list, you can start sketching the proposed curtain wall by using the sketching tools available in the **Properties** palette.

*Figure 8-42 Selecting the curtain wall type from the **Type Selector** drop-down list in the **Properties** palette*

Using Basic Building Components-III

Alternatively, select any wall and replace it with the predefined curtain wall using the **Type Selector** drop-down list. If you select the **Curtain Wall** option as a wall type from the **Type Selector** drop-down list, a curtain wall will be created with a single panel. Even a curved curtain wall is first created as a straight curtain wall. You can then use the **Curtain Grid** tool in the **Build** panel of the **Architecture** tab to add curtain grids at a specific distance to give the desired shape, refer to Figure 8-43. The other two curtain wall types available in the **Type Selector** drop-down list have predefined curtain grids. They can, however, be modified to the desired spacing.

Tip: *Autodesk Revit enables you to create elements with minimum faults by warning you about the errors in their creation. The parametric building elements associate with each other and help in creating designs that have the least discrepancies.*

Creating a Curtain Wall by Picking Lines

You can create a curtain wall from existing lines in a drawing. The existing lines can be model lines or edges of elements, such as roofs, curtain panels, and other walls. To create a curtain wall by using the existing lines, choose the **Pick Lines** tool from the **Draw** panel of the **Modify | Place Wall** tab; you will be prompted to select an edge or a line from the drawing. Select the desired edge or line from the drawing; the curtain wall will be created.

For example, you can select the edge of a floor slab or any line in a different level to create the curtain wall. Figure 8-43 shows a flat and a curved curtain system created by using the **Pick Lines** tool. Note that the curved curtain system appears flat when it is created and acquires the actual curved form when the curtain grids are added.

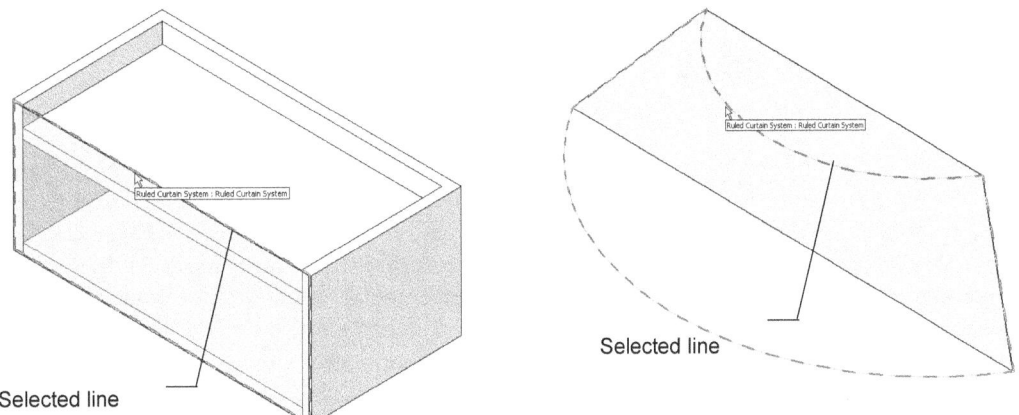

Figure 8-43 A flat and a curved curtain system created using the **Pick Lines** tool

Creating a Curtain System on a Face

Ribbon: Architecture > Build > Curtain System

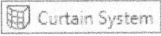

You can create a curtain system on a face by using the **Curtain System** tool. This tool is effective for creating a curtain system on the solids and faces

created by using the massing tools (the use of massing tools is described in Chapter 10). After creating a massing geometry, invoke this tool from the **Curtain Build** panel; the **Modify | Place Curtain System by Face** tab will be displayed and you will be prompted to select a face that will be used to create the curtain system. The selected face can be flat or with a single or double curved faces. After selecting the face, choose the **Create System** tool from the **Multiple Selection** panel in the **Modify | Place Curtain System by Face** tab; a curtain system will be created based on the face selected. The type of the curtain system will be based on the default value selected in the **Type Selector** drop-down list in the **Properties** palette.

You can change the existing type and properties of the curtain system from the **Properties** palette. You can change the existing values in this palette and create a new type.

To create a new type of a curtain system, choose the **Edit Type** button from the **Properties** palette; the **Type Properties** dialog box will be displayed. In this dialog box, choose the **Duplicate** button; the **Name** dialog box will be displayed. Type a name in the **Name** edit box and choose the **OK** button; the **Name** dialog box will close. Now, you can change the values of different parameters of the newly created type in the **Type Properties** dialog box.

In the **Type Properties** dialog box, the parameters in the **Grid 1** Pattern and **Grid 2** Pattern heads specify how the grid lines in the curtain system will be generated. The parameters displayed under the **Grid 1 Pattern** and **Grid 2 Pattern** heads specify the settings for generating vertical grid lines and the horizontal grid lines, respectively.

Now, after changing the values for the new type in the **Type Properties** dialog box, choose **Apply** and then choose **OK**; the changed properties will be applied to the created curtain system and the dialog box will close. Figure 8-44 shows an example of a curtain system created using the **Curtain System** tool.

Adding Curtain Grids

Ribbon: Architecture > Build > Curtain Grid

Curtain grids are added to a curtain system to define its geometry and form a grid for adding mullions. Invoke the **Curtain Grid** tool from the **Build** panel; a preview image of the grid will be displayed on the panels. Also, the **Modify | Place Curtain Grid** tab will be displayed. The **Placement** panel of this tab displays three tools: **All Segments**, **One Segment**, and **All Except Picked**. The **All Segments** tool is invoked by default and lets you place grid segments on all panels where the preview appears. The **One Segment** tool, if invoked, will create a grid segment only in the panel where the preview appears. Similarly, on invoking the **All Except Picked** tool, you can place grid segments on all panels except those you select to exclude.

Using Basic Building Components-III

Figure 8-44 *Example of curtain systems created using the* **Curtain System** *tool*

After you select any tool from the **Placement** panel, move the cursor to a curtain wall or a curtain system where you wish to add the curtain grids. On doing so, a dashed line will appear, indicating the position to place the curtain grid. A horizontal dashed line appears when the cursor is near a vertical edge, and a vertical dashed line will appear when the cursor is close to a horizontal edge. Click at the desired locations to add the curtain grids. The object snap options displayed can also be used for this purpose. Figure 8-45 shows two examples of a curtain grid added to a curtain system by using the **All Segments** and **One Segment** tools.

Figure 8-45 *Adding curtain grids to a curtain system by using the* **All Segments** *and* **One Segment** *tools*

 Tip: *When you create curtain grids individually using the* **Curtain Grids** *tool, you can delete or drag each curtain grid to achieve the appropriate curtain grid pattern.*

Modifying Curtain System Panels

On creating a curtain grid, the curtain system is divided into curtain system panels. Each portion between the curtain grids is treated as a single curtain system panel. By default, each panel is treated as a glazed system panel. However, Autodesk Revit Architecture enables you to modify the properties of each panel. You can create a solid panel or an empty panel. To modify a system panel, select it using the crossing selection method and the **Filter** tool (if required); the **Properties** palette will display the type and properties of the system panel. In the **Properties** palette, the **System Panel : Glazed** option is selected by default in the **Type Selector** drop-down list. In this drop-down list, you can select the **Empty System Panel : Empty** or **System Panel : Solid** option to replace the selected panel(s) with an empty or solid panel, respectively. In this manner, you can create a combination of solid and glazed panels for a curtain system. Figure 8-46 shows the curtain panels of three different types added in a curtain system.

Figure 8-46 Example of different curtain panels added in the curtain system

Adding Doors and Awnings to a Curtain System

The doors and curtain wall awnings can be added to a curtain system by replacing the curtain system panel with them. To add doors and the awning to the curtain wall panel, first you need to load their family types. To do so, choose the **Insert** tab and then choose the **Load Family** tool from the **Load from Library** panel; the **Load Family** dialog box will be displayed. In this dialog box, browse the **US Imperial** folder and load the curtain wall double glass and single glass doors, and awnings from the **Doors** and **Windows** sub-folders, respectively. However, before adding doors, ensure that the curtain panel to be replaced is of the desired door size. This may require you to remove certain curtain grid segments. To remove a grid segment from a grid system, select the grid and choose the **Add/Remove Segments** button in the **Curtain Grid** panel of the **Modify | Curtain Wall Grids** tab. Now, click on the segment to be removed and click anywhere outside the curtain system; the grid segment will be removed. Similarly, you can also add the removed curtain grid segment in a curtain grid system. To do so, select the grid from which a segment has been removed; the removed segment will be highlighted with a dashed line. Now, choose the **Add/Remove Segment** button from the **Curtain Grid** panel of the **Modify | Curtain Wall Grids** and click on the highlighted dashed line; the removed grid will be added. Once the panel of the desired size has been created in the curtain system, select it from the drawing; the **Modify | Curtain Panels** tab will be displayed. From the **Type Selector** drop-down list select any loaded curtain wall doors and awnings. The selected curtain wall doors or awnings will be added to the selected panel.

Adding Mullions

Ribbon: Architecture > Build > Mullion

Once you have created the curtain grid, you can use the **Mullion** tool to add mullions to the segments of curtain grid segments. To use the **Mullion** tool, invoke it from the **Build** panel; the **Modify | Place Mullion** tab will be displayed. Also, the properties of the mullion will be displayed in the **Properties** palette. In this palette, you can select the mullion type from the **Type Selector** drop-down list. Autodesk Revit Architecture provides you with six main types of mullions: **Circular Mullion**, **L Corner Mullion**, **Quad Corner Mullion**, **Rectangular Mullion**, **Trapezoid Corner Mullion**, and **V Corner Mullion**. By default, the **Rectangular Mullion** type is selected in the **Type Selector** drop-down list. After selecting a type from the **Type Selector** drop-down list, you can change the type properties of the mullion you want to place. To do so, choose the **Edit Type** button from the **Properties** palette; the **Type Properties** dialog box will be displayed. In this dialog box change the type parameters, where required, in their corresponding value field and then choose **OK**; the desired change will be applied and the **Type Properties** dialog box will close. Now, you can use the tools from the **Placement** panel in the **Modify | Place Mullion** tab to place the mullions using the curtain grids. The tools available in the **Placement** panel for placing mullions are **Grid Line**, **Grid Line Segment**, and **All Grid Lines**. You can use the **Grid Lines** tool to place a mullion across the entire grid line. Similarly, you can use the **Grid Line Segment** or **All Grid Lines** tool to place a mullion on the individual segment of the grid line or on all grid lines. After you invoke the desired tool, move the cursor near the curtain grid and click when it is highlighted; the mullion will be created on it. This step can be repeated to create mullions for the desired curtain grids, as shown in Figure 8-47. The length of the mullion created for the curtain grid will be equal to the length of the curtain grid. After the mullions are added on a curtain grid, you can control mullion joins. To do so, select the mullion; the **Modify | Curtain Wall Mullions** tab will be displayed. In the **Mullion** panel of this tab, you can choose the **Make Continuous** or **Break at Join** tool to control the mullion joins. You can choose the **Make Continuos** tool to extend the ends of mullions at a join so that they appear as one continuous mullion Alternatively, you can choose the **Break at Join** tool to trim the ends of mullions at a join so that they appear as separate mullions.

COPYING ELEMENTS FROM ONE LEVEL TO ANOTHER

As described earlier, you can copy elements in the same work plane using the **Copy to Clipboard**, **Cut to Clipboard**, and **Paste** tools. For multistory building projects, you need to use the **Paste** tool to copy the elements such as doors, windows, furniture elements, and so on from one level to another level, exactly above or below their original location.

Select the elements to be copied to the other level. The **Filter** tool can be useful in selecting the elements of the same family. After you select the elements, invoke the **Copy to Clipboard** tool from the **Clipboard** panel of the **Modify | (Elements / Components)** tab; the selected elements will be copied to the clipboard.

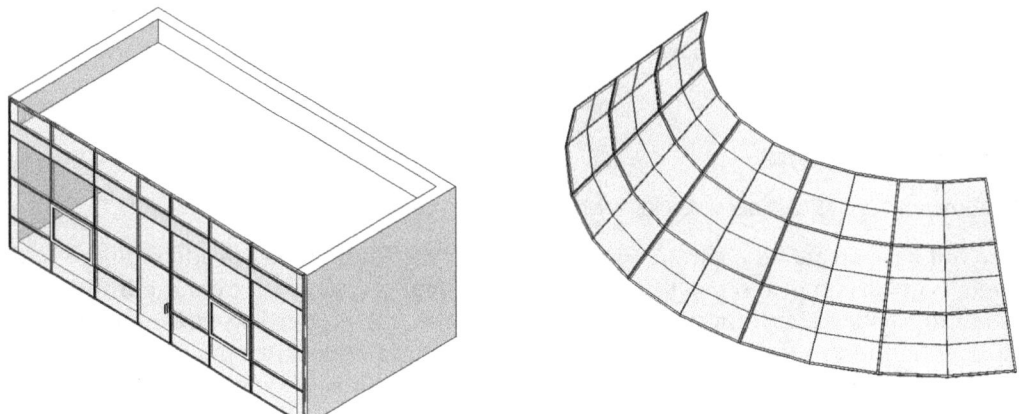

*Figure 8-47 Adding mullions to a curtain system using the **Mullion** tool*

Using the Pasting Tools

After copying the elements to the clipboard, choose the **Paste** drop-down from the **Clipboard** panel; a list of pasting tools will be displayed. Based on the required result, you need to choose the appropriate tool from the list. These tools are discussed below.

The **Paste from Clipboard** tool is used to paste elements from the clipboard into the current view.

The **Aligned to Current View** tool is used to paste elements into the current view, which is different from the view in which the elements were copied. For example, you can copy elements from a plan view to a callout view.

The **Aligned to Same Place** tool is used to copy elements to the same place from they were copied from. This option is useful for developing different design options for the same location.

The **Aligned to Picked Level** tool is used to paste elements into levels by selecting their corresponding level line. You need to be in the elevation view for selecting the level line to paste the elements.

The **Aligned to Selected Levels** tool, the most frequently used tool, enables you to choose the level(s) for pasting the elements. You can choose the desired level(s) from the list of existing levels in the **Select Levels** dialog box.

The **Aligned to Selected Views** tool is useful for copying view specific elements such as dimensions from one level to another.

TUTORIALS

Tutorial 1   Apartment 1

In this tutorial, you will add furniture and sanitary elements to the first floor level of the *c07_Apartment1_tut1.rvt* project created in Tutorial 1 of Chapter 7. The approximate location of components is shown in Figure 8-48. The text has been given for reference and is not to be created. Extend the exterior walls to 3'0" above the top floor level and copy all interior walls, doors, windows, and other elements at the same location on all three upper floors. Also, create a flat roof for the top floor. Use the following parameters for different components to be added:
(Expected time: 30 min)

Alphabets in Figure 8-48 represent the furniture and plumbing components to be used, as given below.

1. Furniture Components

    For Imperial: Furniture components from the **Furniture** folder of the **US Imperial**:
    - A- **Bed-Shaker: Double 56" x 78"**
    - B- **Entertainment Center-72" x 72" x 24"**
    - C- **Dresser-72" x 60" x 18"**
    - D- **Sofa-72"**
    - E- **Table-Dining Oval-36" x 72"**
    - F- **Table-Coffee-36" x 72"**
    - G- **Chair-Corbu**
    - H- **Table-End:24" x 24"** (modify height to 15")

    For Metric: Furniture components from the **Furniture** folder of the **US Metric**:
    - A- **Bed-Shaker: Double 1422 x 1981 mm**
    - B- **Entertainment Center- 1830 x 1830 x 610 mm**
    - C- **Dresser- 1220 x 1525 x 0610 mm**
    - D- **Sofa- 1830 mm**
    - E- **Table-Dining Oval- 0915 x 1830 mm**
    - F- **Table-Coffee- 0915 x 1830 x 0457 mm**
    - G- **Chair-Corbu**
    - H- **Table-End- 0610 x 0610 mm** (modify height to 381 mm)

2. Plumbing Components

    For Imperial: Plumbing components from **Speciality Equipment > Domestic** and **Plumbing** folders of **US Imperial**
    - J- **Kitchenette-Medium**: 8'6" (modified width)
    - K- **Toilet-Domestic-3D**
    - L- **Tub-Rectangular-3D**
    - M- **Sink Vanity-Square**: 20" x 18"

For Metric: Plumbing components from **Speciality Equipment > Domestic** and **Plumbing** folders of **US Metric**
  J- **Kitchenette-Medium**: 2591 mm (modified width)
  K- **Toilet-Domestic-3D**
  L- **Tub-Rectangular-3D**
  M- **Sink Vanity-Square**: 500 x 440 mm

3. Top floor roof type-
   For Imperial   **Basic Roof : Generic 9"** - Flat
   For Metric   **Basic Roof : Generic 400 mm** - Flat

The following steps are required to complete this tutorial:

a. Open the project file, invoke the **Place a Component** tool, and load the components from the additional libraries using the **Load Family** tool.
b. Add and position the components at their desired location in the building model using the **Rotate** and **Move** tools, refer to Figures 8-49 and 8-50.
c. Extend the exterior walls to **3'0"(914 mm)** above the top most level, refer to Figure 8-51.
d. Select the doors, windows, floor, ceiling, and components, and copy them to all upper floors using the **Aligned to Selected Levels** tool, refer to Figure 8-52
e. Create the roof of the topmost floor using the **Roof** tool, refer to Figure 8-53.

Figure 8-48 Sketch plan for adding furniture and plumbing components to the Apartment 1 project

Opening the Project File and Loading Components from Additional Libraries

In this section of the tutorial, you will first open the specified project file and add the components to the first floor plan view by using the **Component** tool. You will use the **Load Family** tool to load the components from the specified additional libraries.

Using Basic Building Components-III   8-33

1. Choose **Open > Project** from **the Application Menu** and open the *c07_Apartment1_tut1.rvt* file created in Tutorial 1 of Chapter 7 and make sure that the first floor plan is displayed. You can also download this file from *http://www.cadcim.com*. The path of the file is as follows: *Textbooks > Civil/GIS > Revit Architecture > Autodesk Revit Architecture 2015 for Architects and Designers*.

2. Next, you need to place the components as specified in the project parameters. To do so, invoke the **Place a Component** tool from **Architecture > Build > Component** drop-down; the **Modify | Place Component** tab is displayed.

3. Next, you need to load additional components to the drawing. To do so, choose the **Load Family** tool from the **Mode** panel; the **Load Family** dialog box is displayed.

4. In the **Load Family** dialog box, select the desired folder to open it.
   For Imperial   **US Imperial > Furniture**
   For Metric   **US Metric > Furniture**

5. In this folder, select the following furniture types from their corresponding folders, by pressing and holding the CTRL key

   For Imperial: **Bed-Shaker** (Folder: Beds), **Chair-Corbu** (Folder: Seating), **Dresser** (Folder: Storage), **Entertainment Center** (Folder: Storage), **Sofa** (Folder: Seating), **Table-Dining Oval** (Folder: Tables), **Table-Coffee** (Folder: Tables), and **Table-End** (Folder: Tables).

   For Metric: **M_Bed-Shaker** (Folder: Beds), **M_Chair-Corbu** (Folder: Seating), **M_Dresser** (Folder: Storage), **M_Entertainment Center** (Folder: Storage), **M_Sofa** (Folder: Seating), **M_Table-Dining Oval** (Folder: Tables), **M_Table-Coffee** (Folder: Tables), and **M_Table-End** (Folder: Tables).

   Note that if in case, these files cannot be loaded simultaneously then load it one by one.

6. After selecting the required families, choose the **Open** button; the **Load Family** dialog box is closed and the selected type becomes available in the **Type Selector** drop-down list in the **Properties** palette. At this stage, it is recommended that you do not click in the drawing area or press ESC.

7. Invoke the **Load Family** dialog box. In this dialog box, choose the **Fixtures** folder from **US Imperial > Plumbing > Architectural** folder (For Metric **US Metric > Plumbing > Architectural** folder). In the **Fixture** folder, load the following fixture types from their corresponding folders:

   For Imperial: **Sink Vanity- Square** (Folder: Sinks), **Toilet-Domestic-3D** (Folder: Water Closets), and **Tub-Rectangular-3D** (Folder: Bathtubs).

   For Metric: **M_Sink Vanity- Square** (Folder: Sinks), **M_Toilet-Domestic-3D** (Folder: Water Closets), and **M_Tub-Rectangular-3D** (Folder: Bathtubs).

8. Repeat step 3 to invoke the **Load Family** dialog box. In this dialog box, access the **Domestic** folder from **US Imperial > Speciality Equipment** (for Metric: **US Imperial > Speciality Equipment**) and load folder from **US Imperial > Speciality Equipment** and load **Kitchenette-Medium** into (for Metric **M_Kitchenette-Medium**) into the project file.

Adding and Positioning Components in the Building Model

You can now select the component type from the **Type Selector** drop-down list and add it to the building model. Different editing tools like **Rotate**, **Copy**, and **Move** can be used to position the components at their desired location and in the required direction. The steps below describe the procedure for a single component, **Bed-Shaker**. The following steps can then be used to add and position other furniture and plumbing components. As mentioned earlier, the exact location of the components is not important for this tutorial.

1. In the **Type Selector** drop-down list of the **Properties** palette, select the **Bed-Shaker : Double 56" x 78"** option, as specified in the parameters for the project.

2. Select the **Rotate after placement** check box in the **Options Bar**.

3. Move the cursor near the west wall of the bedroom and click at the desired location, as shown in Figure 8-49; the component is temporarily placed and the **Rotate** tool is invoked.

4. Move the cursor vertically upward and click when the dashed rectangle (indicating the direction of the bed) is horizontally positioned, as shown in Figure 8-50; the bed is added. Now, press ESC. Depending on the point selected for the placement, you may need to use the **Move** tool to move the component to the desired position.

5. Repeat steps 1 to 4 for adding and positioning the components to the building model at the desired locations based on the given sketch plan, refer to Figure 8-48. These components are listed as they are placed in sketch plan.

    For Imperial:
    Entertainment Center : 72"x 72" x 24"
    Dresser : 72" x 60" x 18"
    Sofa : 72"
    Table-Dining Oval : 36" x 72"
    Table-Coffee : 36" x 72" x 18"
    Chair-Corbu
    Table- End : 24" x 24"
    Kitchenette - Medium : Kitchenette - Medium
    Toilet-Domestic-3D
    Tub-Rectangular-3D
    Sink Vanity-Square : 20" x 18"

Using Basic Building Components-III

For Metric:
Entertainment Center : 1830 x 1830 x 610 mm
Dresser : 1220 x 1525 x 0610 mm
Sofa : 1830 mm
Table-Dining Oval : 0915 x 1830 mm
Table-Coffee : 0915 x 1830 x 0457 mm
Chair-Corbu
Table- End : 0610 x 0610 mm
Kitchenette - Medium : Kitchenette - Medium
Toilet-Domestic-3D
Tub-Rectangular-3D
Sink Vanity-Square : 0500 x 0440 mm

6. After adding all components, press ESC twice.

 Tip: *You can also locate the components from the neighboring elements, based on their dimensions. To do so, select the component to display its temporary dimensions. Select the appropriate temporary dimension and enter the new value. The component is moved to the exact location.*

Figure 8-49 Placing a component temporarily

Figure 8-50 Rotating the component

Modifying the Added Components

The width of the **Kitchenette - Medium** and the height of the **Table- End : 24" x 24"** components can be modified by using the **Type Properties** dialog box.

1. Select the **Kitchenette-Medium : Kitchenette - Medium** component placed in the building model; the **Modify | Specialty Equipment** tab is displayed.

2. Choose the **Type Properties** tool from the **Properties** panel; the **Type Properties** dialog box is displayed.

3. In the **Type Properties** dialog box, choose the **Duplicate** button; the **Name** dialog box is displayed.

4. Enter **8'6" (2591 mm)** in the **Name** edit box and choose the **OK** button to close it.

5. In the **Type Properties** dialog box, enter **8'6" (2591 mm)** as the value for the **Cabinet Width** type parameter.

6. Choose the **OK** button to close this dialog box. The **Kitchenette - Medium** component is modified to the new size. You may need to use the **Move** tool to reposition the component at the desired location.

7. Similarly, select the **Table-End : 24" x 24"** (for Metric **Table- End : 0610 x 0610 mm**) component, access the **Type Properties** dialog box, and then modify the value of the **Height** parameter to **1'3" (381 mm)**. This modifies the height of all instances of the component.

8. Choose the **OK** button; the **Type Properties** dialog box is closed.

The first floor plan, after adding and positioning the components, should appear similar to the sketch plan given for this tutorial.

Extending Walls to the Topmost Level

As described earlier, it is better to extend the exterior walls to the top story, instead of stacking them one above the other. To extend the exterior wall height, you need to set the **Top Constraint** parameter to the topmost level and then use the 3D view to view the changes.

1. To change the current view to a 3D view, double-click on **3D** under the **3D Views** head in the **Project Browser**.

2. Now, move the cursor near the exterior wall and press the TAB key, the chain of exterior walls is highlighted.

3. Click to select the exterior walls; the **Modify | Walls** tab is displayed.

4. In the **Properties** palette for the **Top Constraint** instance parameter, select the option **Up to level: Roof**.

5. Replace the current value of the **Top Offset** parameter with **3'0" (915 mm)**, as specified in the project parameters.

6. Choose the **Apply** button in the **Properties** palette. The exterior walls are extended to 3'0" above the roof level, as shown in Figure 8-51. Press ESC to exit the tool.

Using Basic Building Components-III

Figure 8-51 *Extending the exterior walls to the topmost level*

Note
To exclude the exterior walls, select all elements first and then press the SHIFT key and select the exterior walls.

Copying Elements to Upper Levels

You can now select all elements except the exterior walls and use the **Aligned to Selected Levels** tool to copy them to the upper levels. The following steps describe the general procedure for copying elements to different levels by using the **Aligned to Selected Levels** tool.

1. In the 3D view, select all elements except the exterior walls by creating a selection window from the left to right. All elements, including the interior walls, floor, ceiling, doors, windows, and components need to be selected.

2. Choose the **Copy to Clipboard** tool from the **Clipboard** panel of the **Modify | Multi-Select** tab.

3. Now, choose the **Aligned to Selected Levels** tool from **Modify | Multi-Select > Clipboard > Paste** drop-down; the **Select Levels** dialog box is displayed.

4. In this dialog box, select the **Second Floor**, **Third Floor**, and **Fourth Floor** levels by pressing and holding the CTRL button, as shown in Figure 8-52.

5. Choose the **OK** button to close the **Select Levels** dialog box. The selected elements and components are pasted on the three upper levels.

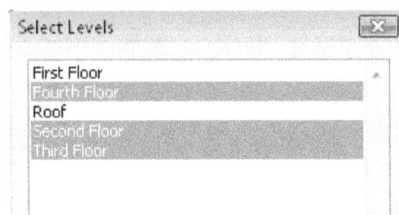

Figure 8-52 Specifying levels to paste the selected elements

Adding Roof to the Top Floor

The top floor is still without a roof. Therefore, you need to use the **Roof** tool to create a flat roof. It is recommended that you create the roof in its corresponding floor plan.

1. Double-click on **Roof** from the **Floor Plans** head in the **Project Browser** to display the roof plan.

2. Choose the **Roof by Footprint** tool from **Architecture > Build > Roof** drop-down; the **Modify | Create Roof Footprint** tab is displayed.

3. Choose the **Pick Walls** tool from the **Draw** panel, if not chosen by default, and then clear the **Defines slope** check box in the **Options Bar**, if selected.

4. Move the cursor near the exterior wall of the plan, and when it is highlighted, press the TAB key to highlight the chain of exterior walls. Click to select them. The roof boundary is displayed. Ensure that it is displayed on the inner face. If it is not displayed on the inner face, click on the flip arrow to flip the selection.

5. Choose the **Finish Edit Mode** button from the **Mode** panel to create the roof boundary at the roof plan level.

6. Next, select the **Basic Roof : Generic - 9"** option (for Metric **Basic Roof : Generic - 400 mm**) from the **Type Selector** drop-down list in the **Properties** palette, as specified in the project parameters.

7. Double-click on **3D** under the **3D Views** head in the **Project Browser** to display the 3D view of the multistory apartment. You can use the **ViewCube** tool from the drawing window to view the other sides of the building model, as shown in Figure 8-53.

8. Double-click on **First Floor** from the **Floor Plans** head in the **Project Browser** to return to the first floor plan.

9. Choose **Save As > Project** from **the Application Menu** and enter the desired name in the **File name** edit box of the **Save As** dialog box.
   For Imperial   c08_Apartment1_tut1
   For Metric   M_c08_Apartment1_tut1
Next, choose **Save**; the project file is saved.

Using Basic Building Components-III   8-39

10. Choose **Close** from **the Application Menu** to close the project file.

Figure 8-53 *Completed multistory apartment*

Tutorial 2   Club

In this tutorial, you will modify the two walls of the *Club* project created in Tutorial 2 of Chapter 7 into curtain walls and add mullions to all curtain grids. Figure 8-54 shows the walls that are to be modified. Use the parameters given next for the different components to be added.   **(Expected time: 30 min)**

1. Curtain wall type - **Curtain Wall: Exterior Glazing**
    Curtain grid spacing:
        For Imperial   Horizontal- **5'0"**, Vertical- **5'0"**
        For Metric   Horizontal- **1524 mm**, Vertical- **1524 mm**

2. Mullion type -
        For Imperial   **Rectangular Mullion: 1.5" x 2.5" Rectangular**,
        For Metric   **Rectangular Mullion: x 2.5" Rectangular**,
    Place mullions at all grid segments.

    The following steps are required to complete this tutorial:

a. Open the *c07_Club_tut2.rvt* project file created in Tutorial 2 of Chapter 7.
b. Select the walls and modify them into curtain walls using the **Type Selector** drop-down list.
c. Modify the vertical and horizontal spacing for curtain grids.
d. Add mullions using the **Mullion** tool, refer to Figures 8-55 and 8-56.

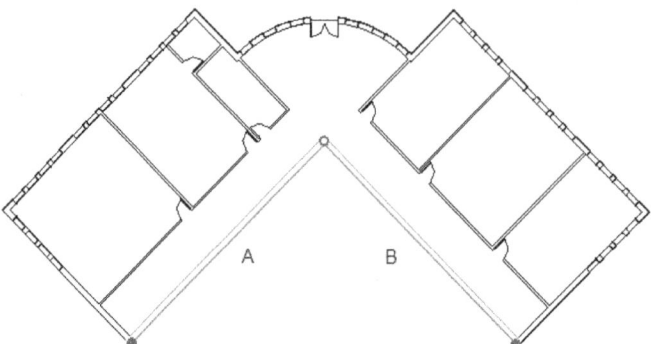

Figure 8-54 Sketch plan for modifying the existing walls into curtain walls for the Club project

Opening the Project File and Modifying the Wall Type

To modify the walls into curtain walls, first you need to open the *c07_Club_tut2.rvt* project file and then make sure that the **First Floor** plan is the current view.

1. Choose **Open > Project** from the **Application Menu** and open the *c07_Club_tut2.rvt* file, created in Tutorial 2 of Chapter 7. Also, open the first floor plan using the **Project Browser**. You can also download this file from *http://www.cadcim.com*. The path of the file is as follows: *Textbooks > Civil/GIS > Revit Architecture > Autodesk Revit Architecture 2015 for Architects and Designers*.

2. Select the two walls marked A and B using the CTRL key, refer to the sketch plan; the **Modify | Walls** tab is displayed.

3. In the **Properties** palette, select the **Curtain Wall: Exterior Glazing** option from the **Type Selector** drop-down list. Autodesk Revit Architecture displays an error message indicating that the curtain wall cannot be joined to the exterior wall. Choose the **Unjoin Elements** button to proceed. The walls are replaced by the selected curtain wall type.

Modifying the Curtain Wall Parameters

Next, you will modify the vertical and horizontal spacing of the curtain grid using the **Type Properties** dialog box based on the given project parameters.

1. Ensure that the curtain walls are still selected. Next, choose the **Edit Type** button from the **Properties** palette; the **Type Properties** dialog box is displayed.

2. In the **Value** columns of the **Spacing** type parameter in the **Vertical Grid** pattern and **Horizontal Grid** pattern heads, enter the value **5'0"(1524 mm)**.

3. Choose the **Apply** and then **OK** button to return to the drawing window. The curtain wall grid is modified to the new spacing.

Using Basic Building Components-III

Modifying Curtain System Panels

Now, you need to replace the top row of the curtain wall panel with solid panels to hide the ceiling.

1. Open the **South** elevation using the **Project Browser**.

2. Select the top row of curtain panels using the crossing window; the **Modify | Curtain Panels** tab or the **Modify | Multi-Select** tab is displayed.

3. If the **Modify | Multi-Select** tab is displayed, choose the **Filter** tool from the **Selection** panel to modify the **Filter** dialog box is displayed.

4. In the **Filter** dialog box, clear all check boxes except the **Curtain Panels** and then choose the **OK** button to close the dialog box; the **Modify | Curtain Panels** tab is displayed.

5. In the **Properties** palette, select **System Panel : Solid** from the **Type Selector** drop-down list to replace the selected panels. Press ESC to exit.

Adding Mullions

Mullions can be added using the **Mullion** tool. You need to choose the **All Grid Lines** option to add mullions to all curtain grids.

1. Choose the **Mullion** tool from the **Build** panel of the **Architecture** tab; the **Modify | Place Mullion** tab is displayed.

2. In the **Properties** palette, select the desired mullion type from the **Type Selector** drop-down list.
   For Imperial   **Rectangular Mullion: 1.5" x 2.5"**
   For Metric   **Rectangular Mullion: 50 x 150 mm**

3. Select the **All Grid Lines** tool from the **Placement** panel.

4. Move the cursor in the left curtain grid area and click when the curtain wall of Hall 1 is highlighted, as shown in Figure 8-55; the mullions are automatically added to all the curtain grids. Similarly, add mullions to the Hall 2 curtain walls.

5. Choose the **Visual Style** button from the **View Control Bar** and choose the **Shaded** option from the flyout displayed, to view the shaded South elevation, as shown in Figure 8-56.

6. Double-click on the **First Floor** in the **Floor Plans** head in the **Project Browser** to return to the first floor plan view.

7. Choose **Save As > Project** from **the Application Menu** and enter the required name in the **File name** edit box of the **Save As** dialog box.
   For Imperial   **c08_Club_tut2**
   For Metric   **M_c08_Club_tut2**
   Next, choose **Save**; the project file is saved.

8. Choose **Close** from the **Application Menu** to close the file.

Figure 8-55 Selecting a curtain wall to add mullions

Figure 8-56 South elevation of the club project showing the curtain wall created with mullions

Tutorial 3   Elevator and Stair Lobby

In this tutorial, you will open the *Elevator and Stair Lobby* project created in Exercise 2 of Chapter 7 and extend the walls to 3'0"(915 mm) above the roof level. You can also download this file from the *www.cadcim.com*. Copy all doors, windows, and components at the same location on all upper floors. Also, create a flat roof for the stairs portion at the roof level. Add stairs to the project based on the project parameters, as shown in Figure 8-57. The texts and dimensions have been given for reference and are not to be created. Use the project parameters given next.   **(Expected time: 45 min)**

1. Stairs: **Width- 5'0"(1524 mm), Minimum Tread Depth- 11"(279 mm), Maximum Riser Height- 7"(178 mm)**

2. Roof type-
   For Imperial   **Basic Roof : Generic 9 " - Flat**
   For Metric   **Basic Roof : Generic 400mm - Flat**

The following steps are required to complete this tutorial:

a. Open the project file and extend the walls using the **Top Constraint** parameter.
b. Copy the elements such as door, windows, floor, ceiling, and openings to the upper floors using the **Paste** tool.
c. Create the flat roof at the top most floor using the **Roof** tool, refer to Figure 8-58.

Using Basic Building Components-III   8-43

d. Add stairs to the project using the **Stairs** tool, refer to Figures 8-59 through 8-63.

e. Create railings for the stairs at the fourth floor, refer to Figures 8-64 and 8-65.

Figure 8-57 Sketch plan for adding stairs to the Elevator and Stair Lobby project

Opening the Project File and Extending the Walls

First, open the *c07_ElevatorandStairLobby_ex2.rvt* project. The walls can be extended by setting the **Top Constraint** parameter to the roof level.

1. Choose **Open > Project** from the **Application Menu** and open the **c07_ElevatorandStairLobby_ex2.rvt** (for Metric **M_c07_ElevatorandStairLobby_ex2.rvt**) file created in Exercise 2 of Chapter 7 and ensure that the first floor plan is opened.

   You can also download this file from *www.cadcim.com*. The path of the file is as follows: *Textbooks > Civil/GIS > Revit Architecture > Autodesk Revit Architecture 2015 for Architects and Designers*.

2. Select all elements using the crossing method and then choose the **Filter** tool from the **Selection** panel in the **Modify | Multi-Select** tab; the **Filter** dialog box is displayed.

3. In the **Filter** dialog box, clear all check boxes except the **Walls** check box and choose **OK**; all walls in the project are selected.

4. In the **Properties** palette, click in the **Value** field corresponding to the **Top Constraint** instance parameter and select the **Up to level: Roof** option from the drop-down list displayed.

5. Enter **3'0"(915 mm)** in the **Value** field for the **Top Offset** parameter and then choose the **Apply** button. Now, press ESC to exit the selection.

Copying Elements to Upper Floors

In this section, you will select elements and components using the **Filter** tool and use the **Paste** tool to copy them to the upper levels.

1. Select all elements using the crossing method and then choose the **Filter** tool from the **Selection** panel of the **Modify | Multi-Select** tab; the **Filter** dialog box is displayed.

2. Clear the check box corresponding to **Walls** in the **Filter** dialog box and then choose the **OK** button; the dialog box is closed.

3. Next, choose the **Copy to Clipboard** tool from the **Clipboard** panel of the **Modify | Multi-Select** tab is displayed.

4. Choose the **Aligned to Selected Levels** tool from **Modify | Multi-Select > Clipboard > Paste** drop-down; the **Select Levels** dialog box is displayed.

5. While holding the CTRL key, select the **Second Floor**, **Third Floor**, and **Fourth Floor** levels and then choose **OK**; the **Select Levels** dialog box closes. The selected elements and components are pasted at the specified levels. Press ESC to exit the selection.

6. To view the multistory building model and exit from the current selection, choose **3D** from the **Project Browser**.

Adding Roof to the Roof Floor

You need to use the **Roof** tool to create a flat roof at the top floor level.

1. Double-click on **Roof** from the **Floor Plans** head in the **Project Browser** to display the roof floor plan.

2. Choose the **Roof by Footprint** tool from **Architecture > Build > Roof** drop-down; the **Modify | Create Roof Footprint** tab is displayed.

3. Ensure that the **Defines slope** check box is cleared in the **Options Bar**. Also, ensure that the **Pick Walls** tool is chosen by default in the **Draw** panel of the **Modify | Create Roof Footprint** tab.

4. Sketch the roof using the **Pick Walls** tool. Ensure that the roof boundary is created on the inner face and is connected end-to-end.

Note

You can also create the roof separately for elevator, lobby, and stairs area.

5. Choose the **Finish Edit Mode** button from the **Mode** panel to create the roof at the roof level.

Using Basic Building Components-III   8-45

6. In the **Properties** palette, click in the **Type Selector** drop-down list and select the required option from it.

   For Imperial **Basic Roof : Generic -9"**
   For Metric   **Basic Roof : Generic -400 mm**

7. Double-click on **3D** under the **3D Views** head in the **Project Browser** to display the 3D view of the multistory apartment.

8. Right-click on the **ViewCube** tool; a shortcut menu is displayed. Choose **Orient to a Direction > Northwest Isometric** from the shortcut menu.

   The northwest view of the building model is displayed in the drawing window, as shown in Figure 8-58.

Figure 8-58 The Northwest view of the Elevator and Stair Lobby project

Adding Stairs

To add stairs to the project, you should first open the appropriate view. For most of the locations, you will find it easier to sketch the stairs in the plan view. Since the stairs start from the first floor, you can open the corresponding floor plan. Use the **Run** tool to sketch the stair run and the **Boundary** tool to create the semicircular landing. Before sketching the stairs, draw reference planes to assist you in sketching the run.

1. Double-click on the **First Floor** from the **Floor Plans** head of the **Project Browser**.

2. Choose the **Stair by Sketch** tool from the **Architecture > Circulation > Stair** drop-down; the **Modify | Create Stairs Sketch** tab is displayed.

3. In the **Properties** palette, click in the value field corresponding to the **Width** instance parameter and type **5'0"(1524 mm)**.

4. Next, click in the value field corresponding to the **Multistory Top Level** parameter and select the **Fourth Floor** option from the drop-down list displayed.

Note
*For metric tutorial, you are required to set the number of risers to 18 against the **Desired Number of Risers** parameter in the **Properties** palette.*

5. After setting the stairs properties, you can draw the reference planes. To do so, invoke the **Ref Plane** tool from the **Work Plane** panel; the **Place Reference Plane** tab is displayed.

6. Draw the reference planes, as shown in Figure 8-59 (Dimensions have been given only for reference).

7. After drawing the reference planes, press ESC. Next, choose the **Modify | Create Stairs Sketch** tab and then choose the **Run** tool from the **Draw** panel.

Figure 8-59 Drawing reference planes to locate the start point and the endpoints of the stair run

8. Move the cursor near the start point of the first run and click when the **Endpoint** object snap appears, refer to Figure 8-60.

9. Move the cursor vertically up until the **Intersection** object snap appears and click to sketch the first end of the run of stairs, as shown in Figure 8-60.

10. Similarly, click to specify the start point of the next run of stairs, as shown in Figure 8-61.

11. Move the cursor vertically downward and click when the intersection object snap appears, refer to Figure 8-61. On doing so, the stairs are sketched with the rectangular mid-landing, as shown in Figure 8-62. You can now edit their boundary and sketch the profile of the landing using the **Boundary** tool.

Using Basic Building Components-III

Figure 8-60 Specifying the start point and the endpoint of the first run of stairs

Figure 8-61 Specifying the start point and the endpoint of the second run of stairs

Figure 8-62 Sketch of the stairs with two runs

12. Choose the **Modify** button from the **Select** panel.

13. Now, select the three boundary lines of the mid-landing and press the DELETE key.

14. Invoke the **Boundary** tool from the **Draw** panel and use the **Pick Lines** tool and other modification tools to draw the semicircular boundary of the landing, as shown in Figure 8-63.

Note
While sketching the semicircular boundary for the landing of the stairs, make sure that its endpoints join with the endpoints of the boundary of the stairs.

15. Choose the **Finish Edit Mode** button from the **Mode** panel to create the stairs. Autodesk Revit Architecture automatically creates the stairs up to the roof level. By default, railings are created on both sides of the stairs. The wall-side railing has not been shown in the sketch plan. You can delete it from the drawing by selecting it and then pressing DELETE.

Creating Railings

The next step is to complete the railing of the stairs at the fourth floor level.

1. Double-click on the **Fourth Floor** from the **Floor Plans** head in the **Project Browser** to display the corresponding floor plan. Next, choose **Visual Style > Wireframe** from the **View Control Bar** to display the view in wireframe.

Using Basic Building Components-III   8-49

Figure 8-63 Sketching a new boundary for the mid-landing

2. Now, choose the **Sketch Path** tool from the **Architecture > Circulation > Railing** drop-down; the **Modify | Create Railing Path** tab is displayed. Also, Autodesk Revit Architecture enters the sketch mode with the **Line** tool invoked from the **Draw** panel of the **Modify | Create Railing Path** tab.

3. Sketch the line defining the railing, as shown in Figure 8-64.

Figure 8-64 Sketching the railing at the roof level

4. Choose the **Finish Edit Mode** button from the **Mode** panel to create the railing.

5. Double-click on **Section V** from the **Sections (Building Section)** head in the **Project Browser** to view the section through the stairs. Increase the size of the section boundary box to display the complete building section. It appears similar to the illustration shown in Figure 8-65.

Figure 8-65 Section through the stairs

6. Return to the first floor plan view using the **Project Browser**.

7. Choose **Save As > Project** from the **Application Menu** and enter **c08_ElevatorandStairLobby_tut3** in the **File name** edit box of the **Save As** dialog box. Next, choose **Save** to save the project file.

8. Choose **Close** from **the Application Menu** to close the project file.

Self-Evaluation Test

Answer the following questions and then compare them to those given at the end of this chapter:

1. Components can be moved from one level to another level by dragging them. (T/F)

2. You cannot modify the properties of in-built components. (T/F)

3. You can add mullions to curtain walls by selecting curtain grids individually. (T/F)

4. You can change the direction of stairs after it has been created. (T/F)

5. The **Paste** tool can be used to copy elements from one level to multiple levels. (T/F)

6. You can lock components with other elements by using the _____ option.

7. After selecting the stairs, you can choose the _____ button from the **Modify | Create Stairs Sketch** tab of the ribbon to modify the sketch and the properties of the selected stairs.

Using Basic Building Components-III

8. You can use the _____ tool to break the boundary line at landings.

9. The _____ tool is used to add mullions to a curtain grid.

10. For curtain grids, you can enter a value for the _____ parameter to set the spacing between the vertical curtain grids.

Review Questions

Answer the following questions:

1. By modifying the **Level** instance parameter, you can move the component from one level to another. (T/F)

2. The rules set in the **Stair Calculator** cannot be modified. (T/F)

3. While sketching stairs, Autodesk Revit Architecture displays the number of treads created as well as the remaining ones. (T/F)

4. You can use the **Cut** tool to break a boundary line at mid-landings. (T/F)

5. For curtain walls, doors can be added by replacing the panels with the curtain wall door. (T/F)

6. You can modify the slope of the ramp after creating it. (T/F)

7. You can use the combination of the **Run** and **Boundary** tools to create stairs. (T/F)

8. Which of the following parameters can be used to create stairs from the lowest to the top level in a multilevel building model?

   a) **Top Level**   b) **Base Level**
   c) **Multistory Top Level**   d) **Stair Rules**

9. Which of the following tools can be used to draw guidelines to sketch the stairs?

   a) **Ref Plane**   b) **Work Plane**
   c) **Lines**   d) **Grid**

10. Which of the following options can be used to add mullions partially along curtain grids?

    a) **All Empty Segments**   b) **Entire Grid Line**
    c) **Curtain Grid**   d) **Grid Line Segment**

Exercise

Exercise 1   Apartment 2

Add furniture and sanitary components to the *c07_Apartment2_ex1.rvt* project created in Exercise 1 of Chapter 7. The approximate location of the components is given in Figure 8-66. The text has been given only for reference and is not to be created. Extend the exterior walls to 3'0" above the roof level and copy all interior walls, interior doors, windows, and components at the same location on all the three upper floors. Also, create a flat roof at the roof level. Use the following parameters for various components to be added. The Northeast 3D view of the completed project should appear similar to the illustration shown in Figure 8-67.

(Expected time: 30 min)

Alphabets in Figure 8-66 represent the furniture and plumbing components to be used, as given below.

1. Furniture Components

    For Imperial: Furniture components from the **Furniture** folder of the **US Imperial**:
    - A- **Bed Shaker: Double 56" x 78"**
    - B- **Entertainment Center: 72" x 72" x 24"**
    - C- **Dresser- 72" x 60" x 18"**
    - D- **Sofa: 72"**
    - E- **Table-Ellipse : 72" x 36"**
    - F- **Table-Coffee : 36" x 72" x 18"**
    - G- **Table-End: 24" x 24"**

    For Metric: Furniture components from the **Furniture** folder of the **US Metric**:
    - A- **Bed Shaker: Double 1422 x 1981 mm**
    - B- **Entertainment Center: 1830 x 1830 x 0610 mm**
    - C- **Dresser- 1220 x 1525 x 0610 mm**
    - D- **Sofa: 1830 mm**
    - E- **Table-Ellipse : 1800 x 0900 mm**
    - F- **Table-Coffee : 0915 x 1830 x 457 mm**
    - G- **Table-End: 0610 x 0610 mm**

Using Basic Building Components-III 8-53

2. Plumbing Components
   For Imperial: Plumbing components from the **Plumbing Fixtures** folder of the **US Imperial**:
   J- **Kitchenette-Medium**: **8'6"** (modified size)
   K- **Toilet-Domestic-3D**
   L- **Tub-Rectangular-3D**
   M- **Sink Vanity- Square: 24" x 19"**

   For Metric: Plumbing components from the **Plumbing Fixtures** folder of the **US Metric**:
   J- **Kitchenette-Medium**: **2591 mm** (modified size)
   K- **Toilet-Domestic-3D**
   L- **Tub-Rectangular-3D**
   M- **Sink Vanity- Square 0610 x 0483 mm**

3. Roof type- **Basic Roof: Generic 400mm** - Flat

4. Name of the file to be saved-
   For Imperial   c08_Apartment2_ex1
   For Metric   M_c08_Apartment2_ex1

Figure 8-66 Sketch plan for adding components to the Apartment 2 project

Figure 8-67 The Northeast 3D view of the Apartment 2 project

Answers to Self-Evaluation Test
1. F, 2. F, 3. T, 4. T, 5. T, 6. Move with Nearby Elements, 7. Modify Sketch 8. Split, 9. Mullion, 10. Spacing

Chapter 9

Adding Site Features

Learning Objectives

After completing this chapter, you will be able to:
- *Create contoured sites using the Toposurface tool.*
- *Modify the site parameters.*
- *Add property lines to the site plan using the Property Line tool.*
- *Add building pads in the site plan using the Building Pad tool.*
- *Add parking components to the site plan.*
- *Add site components and plantations to the site plan.*

INTRODUCTION

In the previous chapters, you learned the usage of different building elements such as walls, doors, windows, stairs, ramps, curtain wall, and so on. Now, in this chapter you will learn to create contoured sites and modify the site parameters. Moreover, you will also learn to add property line, building pad, parking components, and so on to the site plan with the help of various tools available in Revit Architecture.

WORKING WITH SITE FEATURES

Autodesk Revit Architecture provides you with various tools to create site features. These tools can be accessed from the **Model Site** and **Modify Site** panels in the **Massing & Site** tab, refer to Figure 9-1.

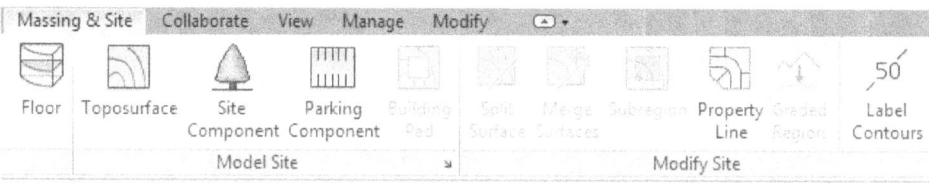

Figure 9-1 Tools in the Massing & Site tab

Note

In the Massing & Site tab, the tools in the Conceptual Mass and Model by Face panels are used for creating building massing and are not useful for creating site features.

The **Model Site** panel in the **Massing & Site** tab consists of various tools that are used for creating site features. These tools are **Toposurface**, **Site Component**, **Parking Component**, and **Building Pad**. In the **Model Site** panel, there is an inclined arrow placed at the lower right corner. On clicking the arrow, the **Site Settings** dialog box will be displayed. You can use this dialog box to change different settings related to the entire site. The options in this dialog box will be discussed later in this chapter. In the **Model Site** panel of the **Massing & Site** tab, the **Building Pad** tool will be inactive by default. To activate this tool, open a 3D view or a site plan view and create a toposurface in the drawing. A toposurface is a contoured site that can be generated using the **Toposurface** tool in the **Model Site** panel. The **Building Pad** tool is used to create a pad for placing a building block. Similarly, you can use the **Site Component** and **Parking Component** tools to insert components like trees, bollards, building signs, planters, parking space, and so on.

The tools in the **Modify Site** panel in the **Massing & Site** tab can be used to modify the site features in your drawing. The tools available in this panel are **Split Surface**, **Subregion**, **Merge Surface**, **Property Line**, and **Graded Region**. You can modify the created surfaces using the **Split Surface** and **Merge Surface** tools. The **Subregion** tool enables you to create smaller regions on a toposurface. The **Property Line** tool demarcates the extent of the site.

The **Graded Region** tool can be used to create a graded region. This graded region is created from an existing toposurface in the current phase. In the graded region, you can add or delete points, change the elevations of points, and also simplify the surface within it.

Adding Site Features

 Tip: *You can also generate a toposurface by picking points at different elevations. To do so, first pick points at one elevation, change the elevation, and then pick points at the new elevation.*

Creating a Toposurface

Ribbon: Massing & Site > Model Site > Toposurface

 A toposurface, also called topograhical surface, is a graphical representation of the terrain of the site of a building project. The topograhical surfaces comprises of a contour lines to represent elevation of the terrain. To create a toposurface for a building project, invoke the **Site** floor plan view or a **{3D}** view from the **Project Browser** and then invoke the **Topographies** tool from the **Model Site** panel. On doing so, the **Modify | Edit Surface** tab will be displayed. The tools displayed in this tab are shown in Figure 9-2. They can be used to sketch and create topographical surfaces, which are defined by picking the elevation points.

*Figure 9-2 Tools displayed in the **Modify / Edit Surface** tab*

In the **Modify | Edit Surface** tab, the **Place Point** tool in the **Tools** panel is chosen by default. This tool can be used to pick elevation points to define the profile of the surface. When this tool is invoked, the **Elevation** edit box and a drop-down list become available in the **Options Bar**. The **Elevation** edit box is used to specify the elevation of the points. You can select the **Absolute Elevation** option from the drop-down list, if it is not selected by default, to pick points at the specified distance (elevation) from the base level. However, if you create the second or the subsequent surfaces, or edit an existing surface by placing more points at the specified elevation, the **Relative to Surface** option will become available in the drop-down list. You can select this option to pick points at the specified distance, above or below a selected surface. After specifying the distance (elevation), move the cursor and pick the points in the site plan view. On picking three points, Revit will generate a triangle, as shown in Figure 9-3. On picking additional points, you will notice that the elevation points join to form a continuous loop, as shown in Figure 9-4.

Figure 9-3 *A triangular surface generated by picking three points*

Figure 9-4 *Picking elevation points to sketch the toposurface*

In Autodesk Revit Architecture, you can generate a toposurface automatically from a 3D contour data that can be imported to your drawing. The file format of the imported data can be DWG, DXF, or DGN. Similarly, you can generate a toposurface automatically from a point file that can be in CSV or TXT format. Note that the points in a point file can be generated by a Civil Engineering software application. In Revit, you can generate a toposurface from a 3D contour data by choosing the tools from the **Create from Import** drop-down in the **Tools** panel of the **Modify | Edit Surface** tab. On doing so, a drop-down menu will be displayed. In this drop-down menu, you can choose any of the following two tools: **Select Import Instance** or **Specify Points File**. Choose the **Select Import Instance** tool to create a toposurface using the 3D contour data that has been imported to your drawing. Similarly, you can choose the **Specify Points File** tool to create a toposurface from a point file. As mentioned above, this

Adding Site Features 9-5

point file will have points that are generated by a Civil Engineering application software and it will provide contour data that is created using a regularized grid of elevation points. Revit will import these points from the specified point file and then generate a toposurface.

Note
*The 3D contour data must be imported to your drawing before you create a toposurface from the contour data. To import the data, you can use the **Import CAD** tool from the **Import** panel of the **Insert** tab of the ribbon. You will learn more about this tool in Chapter 16 of this textbook.*

Before you create a toposurface, you can make specific settings to clean the unwanted spot elevations in a surface for a specified accuracy level. To do so, choose the **Simplify Surface** button from the **Tools** panel in the **Modify | Edit Surface** tab; the **Simplify Surface** dialog box will be displayed. In this dialog box, enter a suitable value in the **Accuracy** edit box and choose the **OK** button; the dialog box will close and the surface accuracy value will be assigned to the proposed surface. Now, you can pick points at different elevations to define the contours of the site. In this way, you can sketch different closed curves with different elevation points defining various levels in the toposurface. Complete the contour and choose the **Finish Surface** button from the **Surface** panel of the **Modify | Edit Surface** tab; the surface will be created. Figure 9-5 shows the sketched concentric contour lines in a toposurface. You can view the newly created toposurfaces in the elevation view, as shown in Figure 9-6. You can also set different properties of toposurfaces before or after creating them. To modify a toposurface, select it from the drawing; the **Modify | Topography** tab will be displayed. You can modify the locations of points in the surface by choosing various tools such as **Move**, **Copy**, **Mirror-Pick Axis**, **Mirror-Draw Axis**, and **Rotate** from the **Modify** panel of the **Modify | Topography** tab.

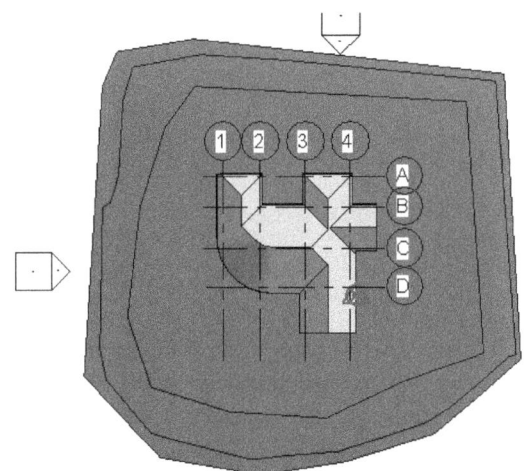

Figure 9-5 Sketched concentric contour lines

Figure 9-6 Toposurfaces in the elevation view

Creating Topographical Subregions

Ribbon: Massing & Site > Modify Site > Subregion

The **Subregion** tool is used to create a region on a toposurface. This tool is available only after a toposurface has been created. In a project, you can use the region created by the **Subregion** tool to represent various site features such as parking lots, pedestrian pavements, and so on. You can also assign different materials to each subregion. This tool can be effectively used to create conceptual site plans. Autodesk Revit Architecture also calculates the area of each subregion for scheduling purposes.

To invoke the **Subregion** tool, choose it from the **Modify Site** panel in the **Massing & Site** tab; the **Modify | Create Subregion Boundary** tab will be displayed. From the **Draw** panel of the **Modify | Create Subregion Boundary** tab, you can invoke the **Line** tool and different sketching tools to sketch the subregion profile. After you have sketched the profile, choose the **Finish Edit Mode** button from the **Mode** panel to create the subregion. Once the subregion has been created, you can modify it. To do so, select the required subregion in the toposurface from the drawing; the **Modify | Topography** tab will be displayed. From this tab, choose the **Edit Boundary** button from the **Subregion** panel; the **Modify | Edit Boundary** tab will be displayed. You can use various tools from this tab to modify the sketch of the selected subregion.

Splitting a Topography

Ribbon: Massing & Site > Modify Site > Split Surface

The **Split Surface** tool can be used to split a toposurface into two surfaces and then different materials can be assigned to them. In the project, you can use this tool to depict water bodies, special site features, and so on. To split a surface, invoke this tool from the **Modify Site** panel; you will be prompted to select the surface that you want to split from the drawing. On selecting the surface, the **Modify | Split Surface** tab will be displayed and Autodesk Revit Architecture will enter the sketch mode. In the **Modify | Split Surface** tab, you can use various sketching tools to draw lines, circles, polygons, and so on to split a selected surface. These tools are displayed in the list box available in the **Draw** panel. In the list box in the **Draw** panel, the **Line** tool is chosen by default. You can choose other tools like **Circle**, **Rectangle**, **Ellipse**, and **Pick Lines** to draw the profile of the boundary that will split the selected surface into two parts.

A split surface can be sketched by using two methods. The first method is to create a closed loop that does not touch the boundaries of a surface, as shown in Figure 9-7. The second method is to create an open line with both ends lying on the boundary. You can assign the new split surface a new material. To do so, select the split surface from the drawing; the instance properties of the surface will be displayed in the **Properties** palette. In this palette, click on the value column for the **Material** instance parameter and choose the new material; the new material will be assigned to the new split surface. Now, you can view the assigned material in the split surface in 3D view with the **Shaded** option enabled. The view will appear similar to the illustration shown in Figure 9-8.

Adding Site Features

*Figure 9-7 Splitting a topographical surface using the **Split Surface** tool*

Figure 9-8 3D view of the split toposurface with assigned materials

Merging Toposurfaces

Ribbon: Massing & Site > Modify Site > Merge Surfaces

You can merge or rejoin the split surfaces when they overlap or share a common edge. To do so, invoke the **Merge Surfaces** tool from the **Modify Site** panel. Next, select the primary surface. The primary surface is the one whose properties are acquired by the resulting merged surface. Now, select the secondary surface, as shown in Figure 9-9; the two selected surfaces will merge, as shown in Figure 9-10.

Figure 9-9 Selecting the two split surfaces to be merged

Figure 9-10 The resulting merged surface

 Tip: To develop a site, you can create pavement patterns, road linkages, or special features for various building blocks and then merge them using the **Merge Surfaces** tool.

Creating a Topography Using Imported Data

Autodesk Revit Architecture provides you with the option of importing data and using it to create a toposurface. Based on the type of the data imported, Revit automatically creates a toposurface. The data imported can be 3D data consisting of contours in the DWG, DXF, or DGN format, or the point files consisting of points.

Creating a Surface Using the Point File Data

As has been discussed already in the previous sections, you can import a point file into the current project and create a toposurface. To do so, choose the **Topographies** tool from the **Model Site** panel in the **Massing & Site** tab; the **Modify | Edit Surface** tab will be displayed. In this tab, choose the **Specify Points File** tool from **Tools > Create from Import** drop-down, refer to Figure 9-11; the **Open** dialog box will be displayed.

Figure 9-11 Choosing the **Specify Points File** tool to import the point data

In the **Files of type** drop-down list, select the required file format to import the data. You can select the **CSV Files** option to import the file in the CSV format or select the **Comma delimited Text** to import the file in the text form. Navigate to the required location using the **Look in** drop-down list and select the required file. Next, choose the **Open** button from the **Open** dialog box; the **Format** dialog box will be displayed. In this dialog box, select an option from the **One unit in the file equals one** drop-down list to assign the drawing units to the imported points. After assigning the units, choose the **OK** button to close the **Format** dialog box. On doing so, the point data will be imported and the toposurface will automatically be created based on the coordinates of points in the imported point file. Next, choose the **Finish Surface** button from the **Surface** panel in the **Modify | Edit Surface** tab; the toposurface will be created.

Another method to create a toposurface is by using the 3D contour data. To do so, you need to import the 3D contour data by using the DWG, DXF or DGN format. You can import the required 3D contour data by choosing the **Import CAD** tool from the **Import** panel of the **Insert** tab. After you have imported the required data, choose the **Select Import Instance** tool from **Modify |Edit Surface > Tools > Create from Import** drop-down and select the imported 3D data from the drawing view; the **Add Points from Selected Layers** dialog box will be displayed. Select the layers to which you want to apply the elevation points and choose the **OK** button; a toposurface based on the elevations points will be placed along the contour lines.

Note
The data imported in the point file must contain the numeric x, y, and z coordinate values in the CSV or the TXT format. The other numeric information about the points should be given after the x, y, and z values in the file.

Tip: *The **Graded Region** tool is used to modify the toposurface. You can modify the toposurface phase assignment, define new elevation points on the contoured toposurface, and demolish the old toposurface by using this tool.*

SETTING THE SITE PROPERTIES

You can change the settings of the toposurface related to the entire site. To do so, choose the **Massing & Site** tab and then choose the **Site Settings** button displayed as an inclined arrow at the lower right corner of the **Model Site** panel; the **Site Settings** dialog box will be displayed, as shown in Figure 9-12. The parameters in the **Contour Line Display** area of the dialog box are used to control the display of contours in the views. The **At Intervals of** edit box is used to specify the intervals at which the contour lines will appear. The **Passing Through Elevation** is the base level at which the contours start. For example, if you set the contour intervals at 10 and pass through elevation value of 5 in the **Passing Through Elevation** edit box, then 5 will be the base level of contour. So, each line will appear at interval of 10, and the contour will appear as -5, 5,15, 25, 35 and so on.

Additional contours can also be generated between the sketches by specifying the parameters in the **Additional Contours** table in the **Site Settings** dialog box. Choose the **Insert** button to add the additional contours. In the **Additional Contours** area, the **Start** column displays the elevation at which the contour lines become visible, and the **Stop** column displays the level at which they are no longer displayed. The **Increment** column value is used to set the interval for each additional contour. The **Range Type** column can be used to insert single or multiple additional contours. On selecting the **Single Value** option, the **Stop** and **Increment** edit boxes will be disabled. The **Subcategory** column is used to assign the subcategory under which the contours will be added. You can assign a material to the site when it is cut in section view. To do so, choose the button on the right of the **Section cut material** edit box in the **Section Graphics** area; the **Materials Browser** dialog box will be displayed. Select the material from the **Materials Browser** dialog box, such as **Grass**, **Earth**, **Water**, and so on. The **Elevation of poche base** edit box is used to set the depth of the cross-section of the topographical elements such as earth. Choose the **OK** button to close the **Site Settings** dialog box.

Figure 9-12 The Site Settings dialog box

ADDING PROPERTY LINES

Ribbon: Massing & Site > Modify Site > Property Line

The **Property Line** tool is used to demarcate and define the extents of the property of a building project based on the survey data. Property lines can be sketched only in the plan views; therefore, these lines can be created only when a plan view, preferably a site plan view, is selected. Property lines can be added by two methods. The first method is by entering distances and bearings and the second method is by sketching. On invoking the **Property Line** tool from the **Massing & Site** tab, the **Create Property Line** window will be displayed, as shown in Figure 9-13. This window displays two options: **Create by entering distances and bearings** and **Create by sketching**. On selecting the first option, you will be using a table of distances and bearings to create a property line. Alternatively, you can choose the second option to create property lines by sketching.

Adding Site Features 9-11

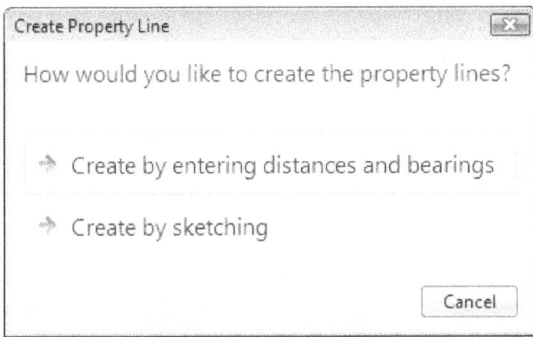

Figure 9-13 The **Create Property Line** *window showing the methods for creating the property line*

Sketching Property Lines

When you choose the **Create by sketching** option from the **Create Property Line** dialog box, the **Modify | Create Property Line Sketch** tab will be displayed. The **Draw** panel of this tab displays various sketching tools that can be used to draw the geometry of a property line. Choose the appropriate sketching tools and then the **Finish Edit Mode** button from the **Mode** panel to exit the sketching option and create the property line. The property line appears as a dashed line in the site plan view. Figure 9-14 shows an example of a property line created for a contoured site (highlighted for illustration).

Figure 9-14 *Sketched property lines (highlighted)*

Creating Property Lines Using Distances and Bearings

You can also create property lines by entering survey data into the project. To do so, choose the **Create by entering distances and bearings** option from the **Create Property Line** window; the **Property Lines** dialog box will be displayed, as shown in Figure 9-15. In the **Deed Data** area of this dialog box, you can view and enter the bearings and distances of the line segments that constitute the property line. The **Deed Data** area contains seven columns, namely **Distance**, **N/S**, **Bearing**, **E/W**, **Type**, **Radius**, and **L/R**. You can view and edit the bearing distance of the line segment in the **Distance** column. The **N/S** and **E/W** columns specify the North/South and East/West directions, respectively. Click on the field of the **N/S** column; a drop-down list will be displayed. Select the **N** or the **S** option from the drop-down list to specify the direction reference. Similarly, you can select the **E** or **W** option from the drop-down list in the **E/W** column. The **Bearing** column in the **Deed Data** area of the **Property Lines** dialog box displays the angle that the line segment of the property line subtend with the directions. To specify angle value of a line segment, click on the corresponding field of the **Bearing** column and enter a value in the edit box displayed. The value displayed in the **Type** column will specify whether a specified line segment will be an arc or a line. Click on the corresponding field of the **Type** column; a drop-down list containing two options, **Line** and **Arc** will be displayed. To assign a type to the property line segment, select any of these options. Notice that on selecting the **Arc** option from the drop-down list, the fields corresponding to the **Radius** and **L/R** columns will be activated. Click on the field corresponding to the **Radius** column and enter a value in the edit box displayed. Similarly, click on the field of the **L/R** column; a drop-down list will be displayed. From this drop-down list, you can select any of the two options: **L** or **R**. You can select **L**, if you want the arc to appear on the left of the line segment and **R**, if you want the arc to appear on the right of the line segment.

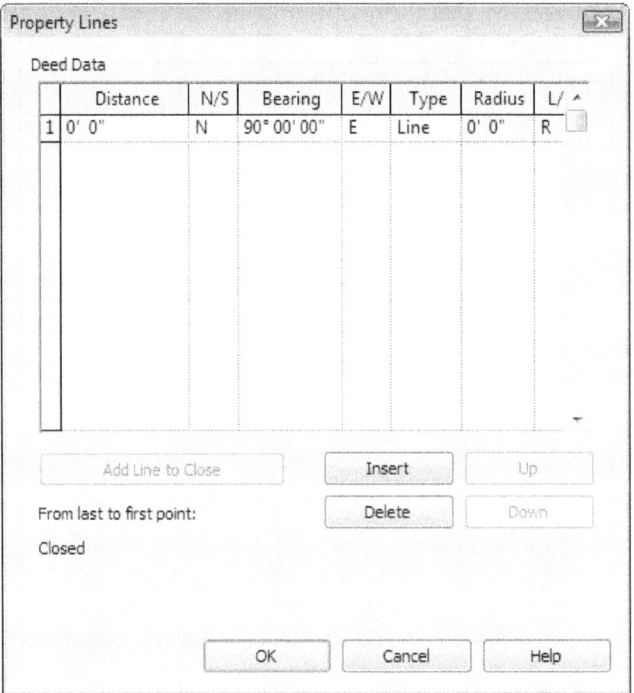

Figure 9-15 The **Property Lines** *dialog box showing the distance and bearing of various property line segments*

You can choose the **Add Line to Close** button in the **Deed Data** area of the **Property Lines** dialog box to add a line segment such that the line connects the first and the previous line segment to close the geometry. This button will remain inactive in its default state, unless a positive value is entered for the first line segment in the **Distance** column.

You can choose the **Insert**, **Delete**, **Up**, or **Down** button in the **Deed Data** area to add, delete or reorder a line segment of the property line. After you specify the line segments of the property line, choose the **OK** button, the **Property Lines** dialog box will close. Now, click in the drawing area; a property line will be created.

In Autodesk Revit Architecture, you can convert a sketched property line to a table-based property line. To do so, select a property line from the drawing and choose the **Edit Table** tool from the **Property Lines** panel in the **Modify | Property Lines** tab. On doing so, Autodesk Revit Architecture displays a warning that the sketched property lines, once converted into the table-based property lines, cannot be converted back. It also warns that the constraints applied while sketching, will be lost during the conversion process. You can choose the **Yes** button to proceed. The sketched property lines are converted into the table-based property lines.

The **Deed Data** table shows the distance and bearing of various line segments constituting the selected property line. These bearings are given with respect to the true north setting for the project. To set the true north for the project, ensure that you are in the **Site** view and then click in the value field corresponding to the **Orientation** parameter in the **Properties** palette and select the **True North** option from the drop-down list displayed. Next, choose the **Rotate True North** tool from **Manage > Project Location > Position** drop-down and rotate the site by clicking and specifying the angle in the drawing area.

Creating Building Pads

Ribbon: Massing & Site > Model Site > Building Pad

In a project, you can develop a level area for your building model in the site. This level area, which provides a minimal slope for a building drainage, is called a building pad. The creation of a building pad provides you more flexibility in the design as you will not be dictated by grade elevations, floor transitions, building shapes or other consideration. In Revit, you can create a building pad by using the **Building Pad** tool. To do so, invoke this tool from the **Model Site** panel of the **Massing & Site** tab; the **Modify | Create Pad Boundary** tab will be displayed.

Note
*The building pad is a toposurface hosted element and can be added only to an existing topographical surface. This **Building Pad** tool will be activated in the **Model Site** panel only if there is an existing toposurface in the drawing.*

On displaying the **Modify | Create Pad Boundary** tab, Revit enters the sketch mode. Before creating the building pad geometry, make sure that the **Boundary Line** button in the **Draw** panel is chosen by default. Now, if the building block has already been placed, choose the **Pick Walls** tool (default) from the **Draw** panel in the **Modify | Create Pad Boundary** tab. Select the desired walls and choose the **Finish Edit Mode** button from the **Mode** panel; the building pad will be created along the periphery of the desired walls that you have picked. Alternatively, you can create the building pad boundary by invoking other sketching tools such as **Line**, **Circle**, **Ellipse**, and so on from the list box in the **Draw** panel of the **Modify | Create Pad Boundary** tab.

You can assign the desired properties to the building pad to be created. To do so, you can use the properties available in the **Properties** palette, as shown in Figure 9-16. The **Level** parameter in this palette can be used to specify the level of the building pad. You can specify the height of the pad from the specified level in the value column of the **Height Offset From Level** instance parameter. You can choose the **Edit Type** button to display the **Type Properties** dialog box, as shown in Figure 9-17. You can modify the structural parameters and also create a new building pad using this dialog box.

Figure 9-16 The **Properties** palette for a building pad

Figure 9-17 The partial view of the **Type Properties** dialog box for a building pad

Based on the level specified in the pad properties, the building pad may not be visible in the site plan view. To view it, you need to generate a section view through the site. Figure 9-18 shows an example of the building pad (highlighted) created on a contoured site.

Autodesk Revit Architecture automatically creates a puncture of the required depth at the location of the building pad. When you generate a transverse section view through the building pad, it appears similar to the illustration shown in Figure 9-19.

Adding Site Features 9-15

Figure 9-18 Building pad created on a contoured site

Figure 9-19 Section view of the resulting building pad

Adding Slope to Building Pads

While creating a building pad, sometimes it is necessary to provide a slope for drainage facilities. Revit allows you to add slopes to the building pads while creating the project. To create a slope in the building pad, sketch the boundary of the building pad and then choose the **Slope Arrow** tool from the **Draw** panel in the **Modify | Create Pad Boundary** tab; the list box next to the **Slope Arrow** tool will display two tools: **Line** and **Pick Lines**. In the list box, the **Line** tool is invoked by default. Now, click on the pad to specify the first point of the slope arrow and then drag the cursor in the required direction; a blue colored dotted line with a pink colored arrow head will follow the cursor. Next, click to specify the endpoint of the slope arrow, the controls of the arrow head and a temporary dimension indicating the length of the slope arrow will be displayed.

Now, in the **Properties** palette, click in the value column corresponding to the **Specify** instance parameter; a drop-down list will be displayed. In this drop-down list, you can select either the **Height at Tail** option or the **Slope** option. In the slope line, the start point is called as tail and the endpoint is called as head. Select the **Height at Tail** option from the drop-down list to set values for various parameters such as **Level at Tail**, **Height Offset at Tail**, **Level at Head**, and **Height Offset at Head**. These parameters will help you create a slope in the building pad based on your requirement. Similarly, select the **Slope** option from the drop-down list for the **Specify** parameter and specify the slope of the building pad in the **Slope** instance parameter. After specifying the desired values in the **Properties** palette, choose the **Apply** button to accept the specified values and close the dialog box.

ADDING SITE COMPONENTS

| **Ribbon:** | Massing & Site > Model Site > Site Component |

You can add different site components such as trees, bollards, building signs, planters, and so on to a site using the **Site Component** tool. The procedure for adding site components is similar to that of adding building components (for more information, refer to the Adding Components section in Chapter 8).

Invoke the **Site Component** tool from the **Model Site** panel in the **Massing & Site** tab; the **Modify | Site Component** tab will be displayed. In the **Properties** palette, select the component to be added from the **Type Selector** drop-down list and insert it into the drawing. You can add other components in your drawing apart from those available in the **Type Selector** drop-down list. To do so, choose the **Load Family** button in the **Mode** panel of the **Modify | Site Component** tab; the **Load Family** dialog box will be displayed. You can use this dialog box to load site components from the libraries available in the **US Imperial > Site** folder location. This folder contains four subfolders: **Accessories**, **Logistics**, **Parking**, and **Utilities**. Each subfolder contains elements related to its title. For example, the **Utilities** subfolder contains elements such as **Fire Hydrant**, **Manhole**, and so on.

After choosing the desired components from the **Load Family** dialog box, choose the **OK** button; the components chosen will be added to the **Type Selector** drop-down list in the **Properties** palette. Now, you can choose the appropriate component type to add it to the site.

To add planting components to the site, load the plantation elements from the **Planting** subfolder in the **US Imperial** folder, using the **Load Family** dialog box. Next, select the tree type from the **Type Selector** drop-down list and add it to the site in the site plan view, as shown in Figure 9-20.

After you add trees to the site, they automatically get attached to the topographical level at the specified point of placement. The added components can be viewed in the section or 3D view of the site. The trees appear as simple lines unless the view is rendered. Figure 9-21 shows a rendered view of the contoured site with trees.

Adding Site Features

Figure 9-20 Adding planting components to a contoured site

Figure 9-21 Rendered view of the contoured sites with trees

ADDING PARKING COMPONENTS

Ribbon: Massing & Site > Model Site > Parking Component

You can add parking components by using the **Parking Component** tool. To add parking components, invoke this tool from the **Model Site** panel; the **Modify | Parking Component** tab will be displayed and the type and properties for the proposed parking components will be displayed in the **Properties** palette. In this palette, select the appropriate type of parking space from the **Type Selector** drop-down list and add it to the site plan. Similar to a building pad, parking components are toposurface hosted components. You can add as many parking spaces as required. The **Rotate after placement** check box can be selected from the **Options Bar** to invoke the **Rotate** tool and rotate the parking component after you have placed it.

ADDING LABELS TO CONTOURS

Ribbon: Massing & Site > Modify Site > Label Contours

The **Label Contours** tool is used to label the elevation levels of toposurfaces or contours. To invoke this tool and add labels to the contours or toposurfaces displayed in the drawing, choose the **Label Contours** tool from the **Modify Site** panel; the **Modify | Label Contours** tab will be displayed. In this tab, choose the **Edit Type** button from the **Properties** panel; the **Type Properties** dialog box will be displayed. In this dialog box, specify the font and size of the text. After this, choose the **OK** button to accept the specified values and close the dialog box.

To add labels, sketch a line that intersects the contour to be labeled. To create labels for multiple contours, sketch a line that intersects all of them. Autodesk Revit Architecture automatically adds labels to each contour based on their respective elevations. Figure 9-22 shows the example of labels added to alternate contours.

Figure 9-22 Labels added to the contours

Adding Site Features

TUTORIAL
Tutorial 1   Site Plan

In this tutorial, you will create a contoured site plan for an apartment complex on the basis of Figure 9-23. The approximate locations and sizes of roads, parking components, building pads and site components are also given. You can assume the missing dimensions. The texts and dimensions have been given only for reference and are not to be created. Given below are the parameters for various components to be added.

(Expected time: 2hr 15 min)

1. Project File Parameters:
   Template File-
       For Imperial   *default.rte*
       For Metric   *DefaultMetric.rte*

   File name to be assigned-
       For Imperial   *c09_SitePlan_tut1.rvt*
       For Metric   *M_c09_SitePlan_tut1.rvt*

2. Property size-
       For Imperial   **600'0" X 500'0"** (Extents of property line)
       For Metric   180000 X 15000 mm

3. Site settings:
   Contours at **1'0"(300 mm)** intervals
   Site material- **Grass**, Road material- **Asphalt**
   Elevation of Poche base-
       For Imperial   **5'0"**
       For Metric   **1500 mm**

4. Building Pads:
   Apartment blocks-3 Nos. building pads- size **106'0" X 151'0" (31800 X 45300 mm)** - placed symmetrically about the center of the design scheme
   Club 1 and Club 2-symmetrical building pads as per the dimensions given in sketch plan
   Building pad level-Level 2

5. Width of the straight pedestrian walkway- **8'(2400 mm)**, circular- **12'(3600 mm)**.

6. Parking Component-
       For Imperial   **Parking Space: 9' X 18': 90 deg**
       For Metric   **Parking Space: 4800 X 2400 mm- 90 deg**

7. Site Component-
       For Imperial   **Tree - Deciduous: Red Ash - 25'** placed on Level 2
       For Metric   **M_RPC Tree - Deciduous: Red Ash - 7.6 meters**

The following steps are required to complete this tutorial:

a. Open a new project file using the default template file and open the **Site Plan** view.
b. Create reference planes to assist in sketching contours.
c. Modify the site setting to create additional contours at **1'0"** interval.
d. Use the **Topographies** tool to sketch the contours, refer to Figures 9-24 through 9-26.
e. Create property line using reference planes and the **Property Line** tool, refer to Figure 9-27.
f. Add building pads using the **Building Pad** tool, refer to Figures 9-28 through 9-30.
g. Use the **Subregion** tool to create roads, refer to Figures 9-31 and 9-32.
h. Add parking components using the **Parking Component** tool, refer to Figures 9-33 through 9-35.
i. Add site components using the **Site Component** tool, refer to Figures 9-36 through 9-39.

Figure 9-23 Sketch plan for creating the site plan with contours, site components, and building pads

Opening a New Project File and Opening the Site Plan View

In this section, you will open a new project file using the **New** tool. As mentioned earlier, the site contours should be created in the **Site** view. Therefore, you will open the **Site** view using the **Project Browser**. You can also hide the elevation tags using the **Visibility/Graphics** tool.

1. To open a new project, choose **New** option under the **Projects** head from the interface screen; the **New Project** dialog box is displayed.

2. Choose the **Browse** button; the **Choose Template** dialog box will be displayed.

3. In the **Choose Template** dialog box, select the *default* template file from the **US Imperial** folder (select the *DefaultMetric* template file from the **US Metric** folder) and choose **Open**; the **New Project** dialog box will be displayed. In this dialog box, ensure that for Imperial *default.rte (DefaultMetric.rte* for Metric) is the selected template file and then choose **OK**; the dialog box closes and a new project file opens in the drawing window.

4. In the **Project Browser**, double-click on **Site** under the head **Floor Plans** to display the site plan view.

5. Select the elevation symbol in the drawing window and right-click; a shortcut menu is displayed.

6. Choose **Hide in View > Category** from the shortcut menu; the elevation symbol get hidden in the site plan view. Similarly, select the project base point and the survey point symbols in the drawing window and then hide them.

Creating Reference Planes

Before creating contours, you need to draw reference planes to provide guidelines for sketching the site periphery and contour profile. In this section, you will draw the reference planes for the contour profile.

1. To draw a reference plane, invoke the **Ref Plane** tool from the **Work Plane** panel in the **Architecture** tab.

2. To start the first reference plane, move the cursor to the drawing window and click on the upper left corner of the screen.

3. Now, move the cursor horizontally to the upper right corner of the screen and click to end the reference plane.

4. Next, to create the second reference plane, move the cursor to the lower left corner of the drawing window in alignment with the first reference plane and then click at an appropriate location; the creation of the second reference plane starts.

5. Now, move the cursor to the lower right corner and click to end the second reference plane. Notice that a temporary dimension appears between the two reference planes.

6. Now, click on the value of the temporary dimension; an edit box is displayed. Enter **650'0"(198120 mm)** in the edit box and press ENTER.

7. Similarly, create two vertical reference planes at a distance of 750'0" (228600 mm).

8. Now, right-click on the open area of the drawing window; a shortcut menu is displayed. Choose the **Zoom To Fit** option from the shortcut menu; the screen view fits to the extent of the sketched reference plane, offering more clarity to the view displayed.

9. Press ESC twice to exit the **Ref Plane** tool.

10. Now, use the dragging method to extend the four reference planes, horizontally and vertically, such that they intersect each other, as shown in the sketch plan in Figure 9-23.

Modifying the Site Settings

Before creating the contours, you need to modify the site settings to achieve the desired contour layout. In this section, you will use the **Site Settings** dialog box to set parameters for creating additional contours. Then, you will create three topographical surfaces to generate all site contours, as shown in the sketch plan.

1. Choose the **Massing & Site** tab and then choose the inclined arrow button placed on the right of the **Model Site** panel; the **Site Settings** dialog box is displayed.

2. Make sure that the check box that is placed before the **At Intervals of** edit box is selected and then enter **1'0"** (304.8) in the **At Intervals of** edit box. Also, ensure that in the **Passing Through Elevation** edit box 0' 0" (0 mm) is entered.

3. Now, in the **Site Settings** dialog box, choose the **Insert** button to insert additional contours.

4. In the **Increment** column of the **Additional Contours** table, ensure that for Imperial **1' 0"** and for Metric **1000** is set as the default value.

5. In the **Section Graphics** area, choose the browse button on the right of the **Section cut material** edit box; the **Material Browser** dialog box is displayed. In this dialog box, enter **Grass** as the material in the **Searches for Material** edit box and press ENTER; the Grass material is displayed in the Autodesk Material Library.

Note
*If the Autodesk Library panel is not displayed, then choose the **Shows/Hides library panel** button from the right side of the **Project Materials: All** pane.*

6. Double-click on Grass in the **Autodesk Material Library**, it is added under the **Project Materials: All** area.

Adding Site Features   9-23

7. Select the material under the **Project Materials: All** area and choose **OK** to accept the other specified values and to close the **Material Browser** dialog box.

8. In the **Section Graphics** area of the **Site Settings** dialog box, enter **-5'0" (-1525 mm)** in the **Elevation of poche base** edit box.

9. Now, choose **OK**; the specified setting is applied and the **Site Settings** dialog box is closed.

Creating Site Contours

In this section, you will use the **Topographies** tool and the **Point** tool and also pick points to generate the desired profile of contours. The contours should be created from the lowest to the highest level to be fully visible. You can first create a topographical surface at the base level and then create two more surfaces at **5'0"(1525 mm)** and **10'0"(3048 mm)** level. Autodesk Revit Architecture automatically generates the intermediate contours at **1'0"** (304.8 mm) level.

1. Choose the **Topographies** tool from the **Model Site** panel in the **Massing & Site** tab; the **Modify | Edit Surface** contextual tab is displayed. Ensure that the **Place Point** tool in the **Tools** panel is invoked; the **Elevation** edit box in the **Options Bar** shows **0'0"** as the elevation, and the **Absolute Elevation** option is selected (default option) in the drop-down list.

2. Move the cursor to the upper left corner and click to start the topographical surface. Ensure that the toposurface is drawn within the sketched reference plane.

   Click on multiple points to form a closed loop, as shown in Figure 9-24. The exact shape of the toposurface profile is not important for this tutorial.

3. Choose the **Finish Surface** button from the **Surface** panel in the **Modify | Edit Surface** tab to complete the lowest topographical surface.

4. Select the toposurface created; the **Modify | Topography** tab is displayed. In this tab, choose the **Edit Surface** tool from the **Surface** panel; the **Modify | Edit Surface** tab is displayed.

5. Choose the **Place Point** tool from the **Tools** panel.

6. In the **Options Bar**, enter **5'0" (1525 mm)** in the **Elevation** edit box and press ENTER.

7. Next, move the cursor to the upper left corner of the toposurface created and click inside it to start the second topographical surface.

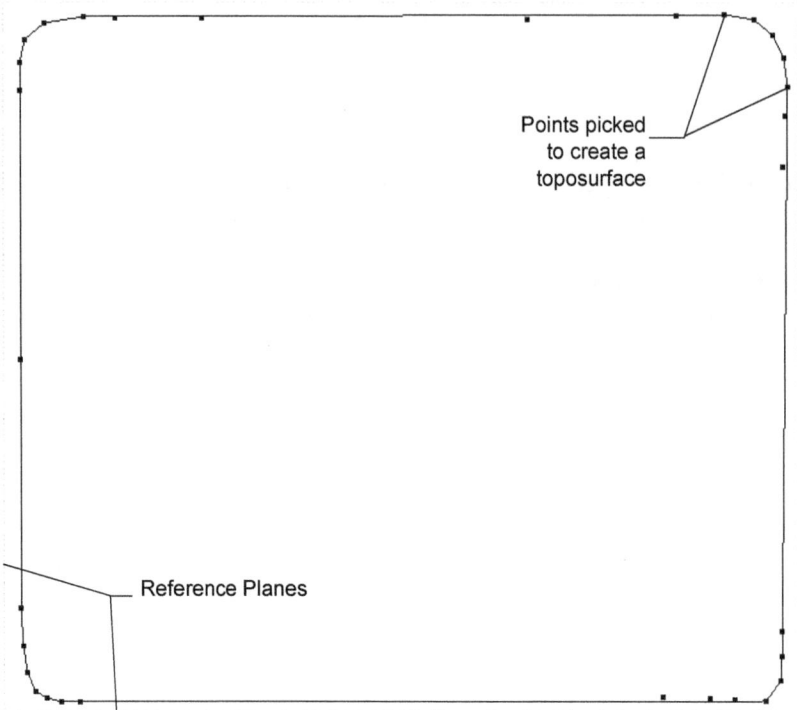

Figure 9-24 Picking points to sketch the lowest topographical surface of the site plan

8. Click on multiple points along the inner surface of the first profile to create the second topographical surface, as shown in Figure 9-25. You will notice that as you pick the points, Autodesk Revit Architecture automatically generates the intermediate contours at **5'0"** level.

Adding Site Features 9-25

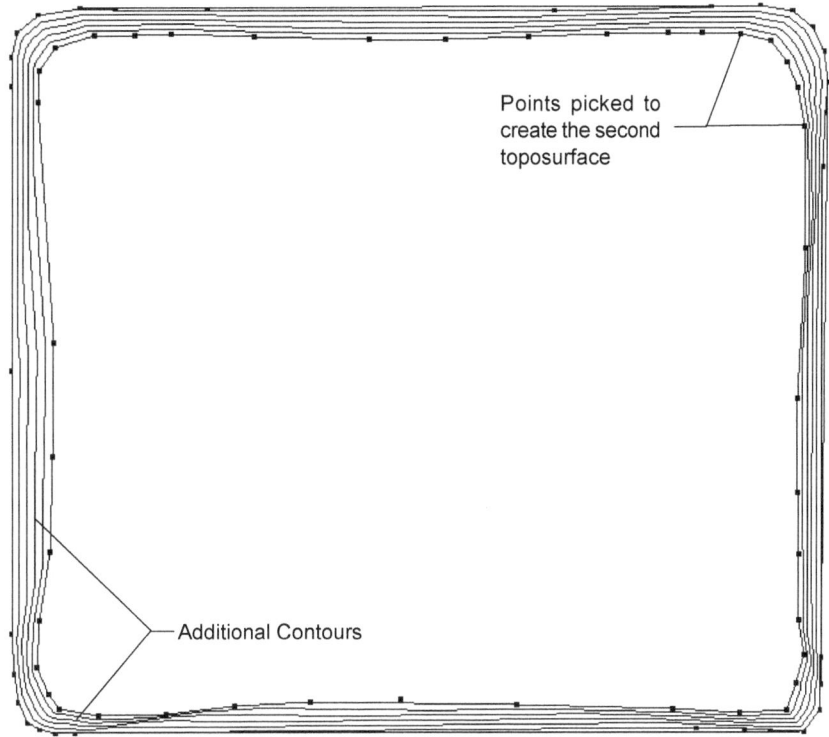

Figure 9-25 *Picking points to sketch the topographical surface at **5'0"** level*

9. Choose the **Finish Surface** button from the **Modify | Edit Surface** tab to create the second topographical surface.

10. Similarly, using the **Edit Surface** tool create the third topographical surface at 10'0" level from the second toposurface, as shown in Figure 9-26.

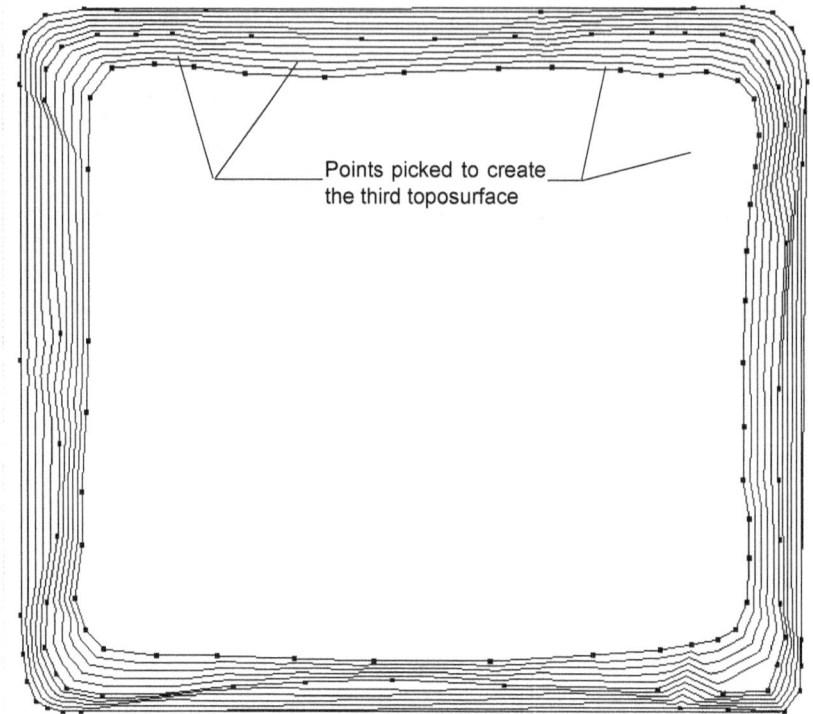

*Figure 9-26 Picking points to sketch the third topographical surface at **10'0"** level*

11. After creating the toposurface, choose the **Finish Surface** tool from the **Surface** panel of the **Modify|Edit Surface** tab.

Adding the Property Line

In this section, you will create a property line of an appropriate length using the **Property Line** tool. You will create reference planes to locate the corner of the property line.

1. Choose the **Architecture** tab, and then invoke the **Ref Plane** tool from the **Work Plane** panel. Now, you can start creating the desired reference planes.

2. Create two horizontal reference planes at a distance of **500' (152400 mm)** and two vertical reference planes at a distance of **600' (182880 mm)**, intersecting at the four corners of the property line, as specified in the sketch plan.

3. Choose the **Massing & Site** tab and then choose the **Property Line** tool from the **Modify Site** panel; the **Create Property Line** window is displayed.

4. In this window, choose the **Create by sketching** option; the **Modify | Create Property Line Sketch** tab is displayed.

Adding Site Features

5. From the **Draw** panel in the **Modify | Create Property Line Sketch** tab, choose the **Rectangle** tool.

6. Now, sketch the rectangular property line by selecting the two diagonal intersections of the reference planes created in step 2. The temporary dimensions displayed can be used to verify the size of the sketched rectangle.

7. Choose the **Finish Edit Mode** button to finish sketching the property line. Figure 9-27 shows the property line created (highlighted for illustration purpose).

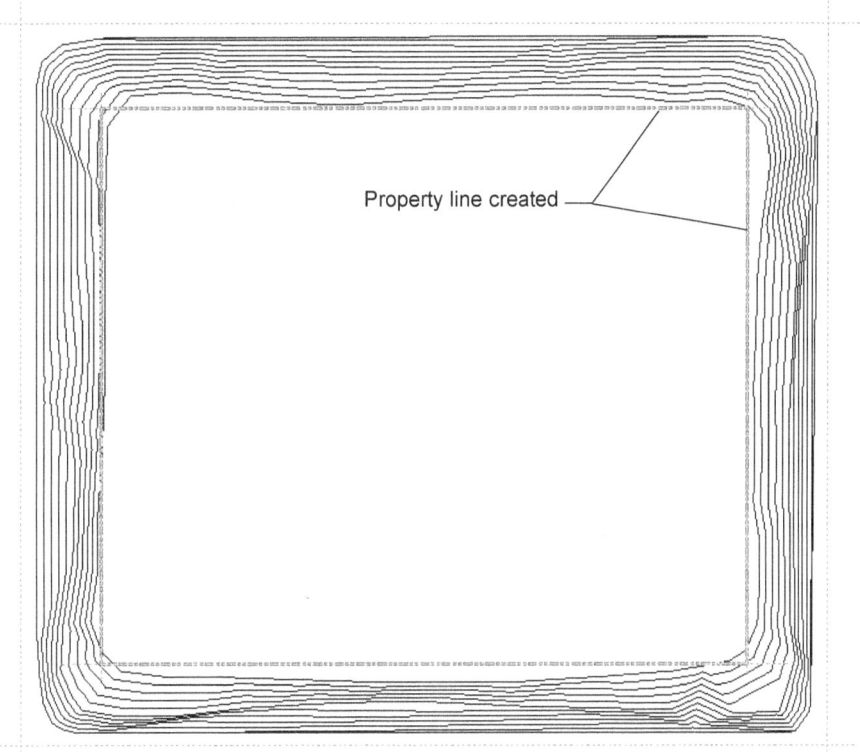

Figure 9-27 Property line created for the site plan

Adding the Building Pads

The next step is to add building pads to the site plan. They are placed symmetrically around the central point of the layout. You will first create a single apartment block building pad and then use the **Radial Array** tool to create multiple copies of the building pad. The club-building pad can be added using the sketching tools. But, first you must locate the center of the design scheme using the reference planes.

1. Choose the **Architecture** tab and then choose the **Ref Plane** tool from the **Work Plane** panel.

2. Create a horizontal reference plane at a distance of 200' (60960 mm) from the lower horizontal property line. Now, create a vertical reference plane between the midpoint of the two horizontal property lines, as given in the sketch plan. Their point of intersection is the center of the design scheme. Similarly, create additional reference planes to locate building pads, which are shown as reference lines in the sketch plan.

3. Choose the **Massing & Site** tab and then choose the **Building Pad** tool from the **Model Site** panel; the **Modify | Create Pad Boundary** tab is displayed.

4. In the **Properties** palette, select the **Level 2** option from the drop-down list displayed in the value field of the **Level** instance parameter.

5. Ensure that the **Boundary Line** button is chosen in the **Draw** panel, and then invoke the **Rectangle** tool from the list box.

6. Sketch the Apartment Block 1 building pad with the dimension **106' X 151' (32308 x 46024 mm)** by clicking on the two diagonal intersection points on the reference planes, refer to Figure 9-28.

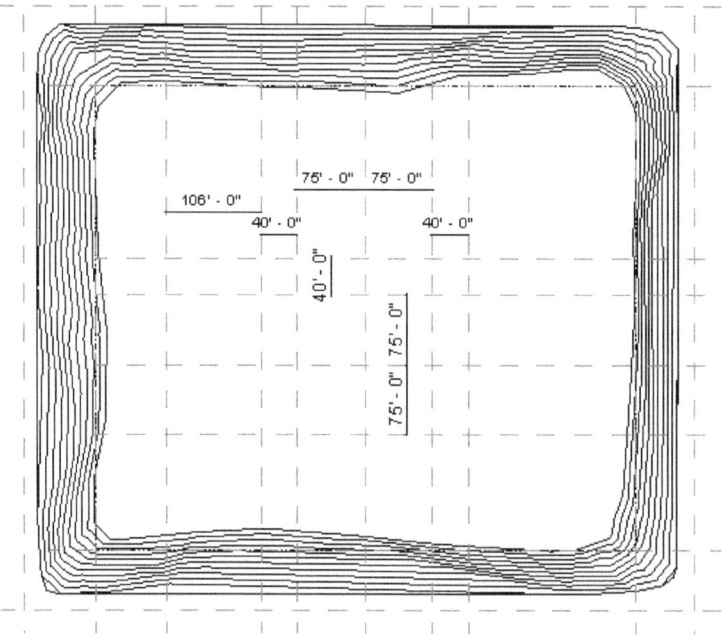

Figure 9-28 Reference Plane dimensions

7. Choose the **Finish Edit Mode** button from the **Mode** panel in the **Modify | Create Pad Boundary** tab to add the building pad, as shown in Figure 9-29; the **Modify | Pads** tab is displayed.

8. Select the created building pad, if not selected, to create its radial array and then choose the **Array** tool from the **Modify** panel in the **Modify | Pads** tab.

Adding Site Features 9-29

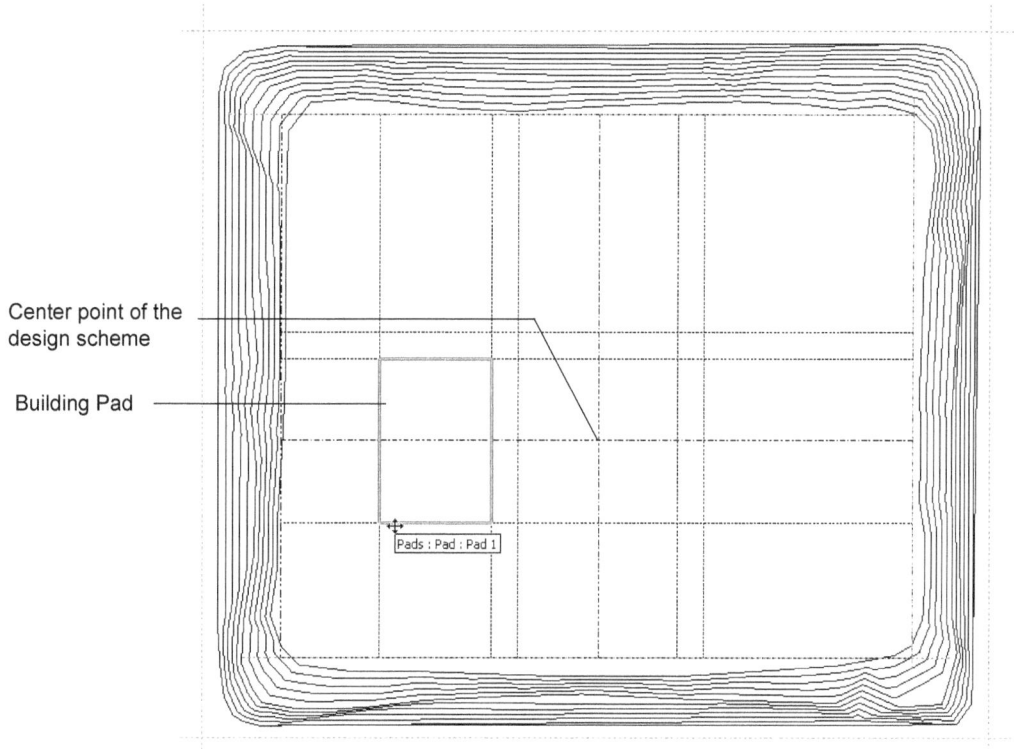

Figure 9-29 *Creating reference planes and adding the building pad (highlighted)*

9. Choose the **Radial** button from the **Options Bar** and then create the two additional building pads by moving the center of the radial array to the center of the design scheme, as shown in Figure 9-30.

10. Similarly, sketch the building pad for the club building based on the dimensions and location refer to Figure 9-31. Use the **Mirror - Pick Axis** tool or the **Mirror-Draw Axis** tool to create a copy of this pad, as shown in Figure 9-31.

Figure 9-30 *Creating a radial array of the building pad*

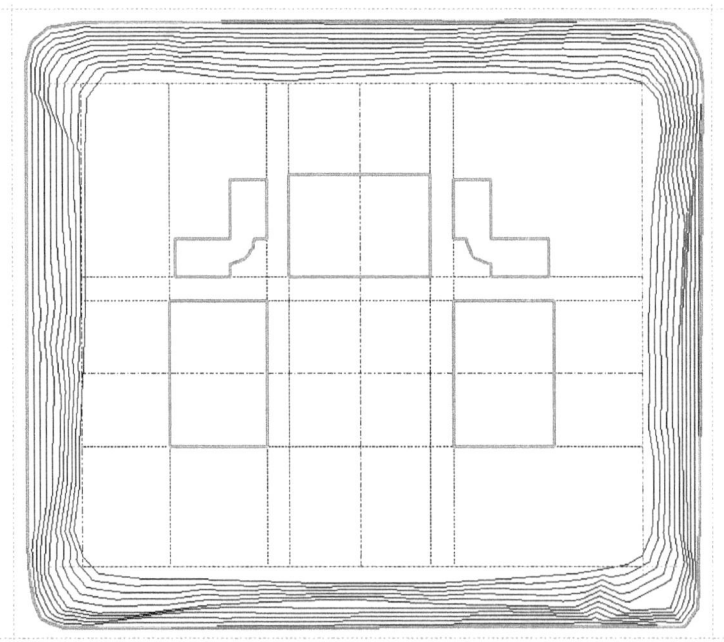

Figure 9-31 *Creating the building pads for the club buildings*

Adding Site Features

Creating Roads Using the Subregion Tool

Now, create roads for the site plan using the **Subregion** tool. You can create a subregion on the topographical surface in such a manner that a separate surface is created for the road. It can then be assigned a different material. You can use the sketching tools to sketch the road profile.

1. Before you create subregions for the road and the pedestrian walkway, the first thing you need to do is sketch the reference planes for them according to the dimensions and locations given in the sketch plan, refer to Figure 9-23. To do so, choose the **Architecture** tab and invoke the **Ref Plane** tool from the **Work Plane** panel to create reference planes to locate all corners of the outer profile of the road and the references for the pedestrian walkway.

2. Now, create a subregion for the road. To do so, choose the **Massing & Site** tab and then choose the **Subregion** tool from the **Modify Site** panel; the **Modify | Create Subregion Boundary** tab is displayed.

3. Next, use the sketching tools in the **Draw** panel to sketch the road profile according to the sketch plan.

4. After you sketch the road profile, choose the **Finish Edit Mode** button from the **Mode** panel; the topographical subregion is created and displayed, as shown in Figure 9-32 (highlighted for illustration purpose).

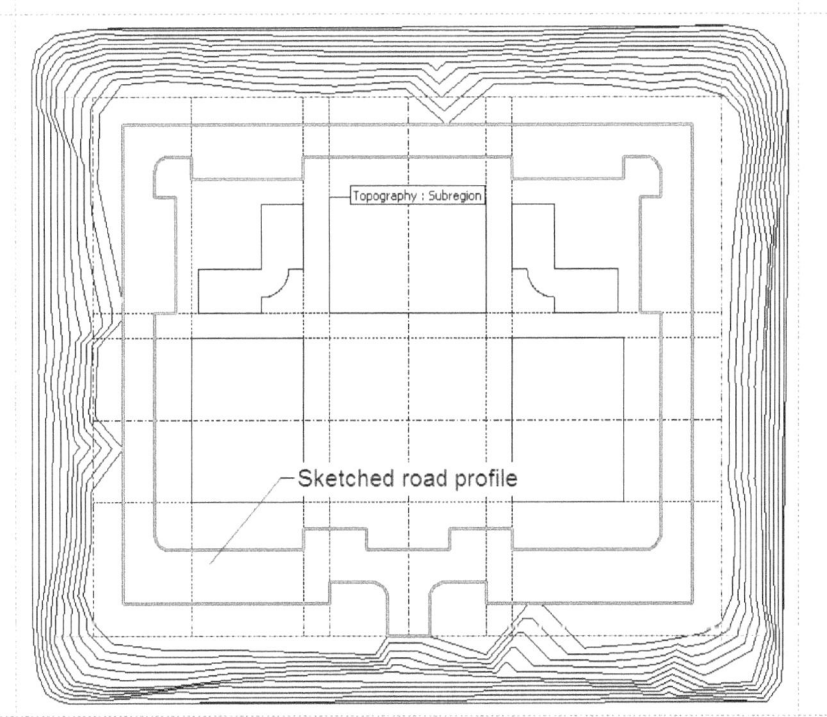

Figure 9-32 Creating the road profile (highlighted) using the **Subregion** tool

5. Similarly, create another subregion for the pedestrian walkway to enter each apartment block, as shown in Figure 9-33, by using the available sketching and editing tools.

After creating contours, building pads, and subregions, you need to assign the appropriate material to their surface. This tutorial introduces you to the concept of applying materials to various elements. You will learn more about using materials in Chapter 15.

Figure 9-33 Pedestrian walkway profile created

6. To apply a material to the road subregion, select it; the instance properties of the selected subregion are displayed in the **Properties** palette.

7. In this palette, click on the value field for the **Material** instance parameter and then choose the **Browse** button on the right of the edit box to display the **Material Browser** dialog box.

8. From the list of names, select **Asphalt Shingle** and then choose the **OK** button; the **Material Browser** dialog box is closed.

9. Similarly, select the site contours toposurface and apply the material **Grass** to it.

Adding Site Features

Adding Parking Components

In this section, you will add the parking components to the site plan using the **Parking Component** tool.

1. Choose the **Massing & Site** tab and then choose the **Parking Component** tool from the **Model Site** panel; the **Modify | Parking Component** tab is displayed.

2. In the **Properties** palette, select the **Parking Space: 9' X 18'-90 deg (4800 X 2400 mm-90 deg)** option from the **Type Selector** drop-down list, as specified in the component parameters for the project.

3. Move the cursor near the entrance of the lower left corner of the site and click near the location shown in Figure 9-34. (You may need to use the **Zoom In Region** tool to enlarge the portion of the site). The selected parking component is added to the site plan. Depending upon the point selected for placement, you may need to use the **Move** or **Flip** tool to orient the component to the desired position.

4. Create multiple copies of the added parking component using the **Array** tool. Choose the **Linear** button from the **Options Bar** and create an array of 7 components placed consecutively, as shown in Figure 9-35.

5. Repeat steps 1 to 4 and add the same parking component to the other seven places in the project. The site plan appears similar to the illustration shown in Figure 9-36.

Figure 9-34 Adding the parking component

Figure 9-35 Creating an array of the parking components

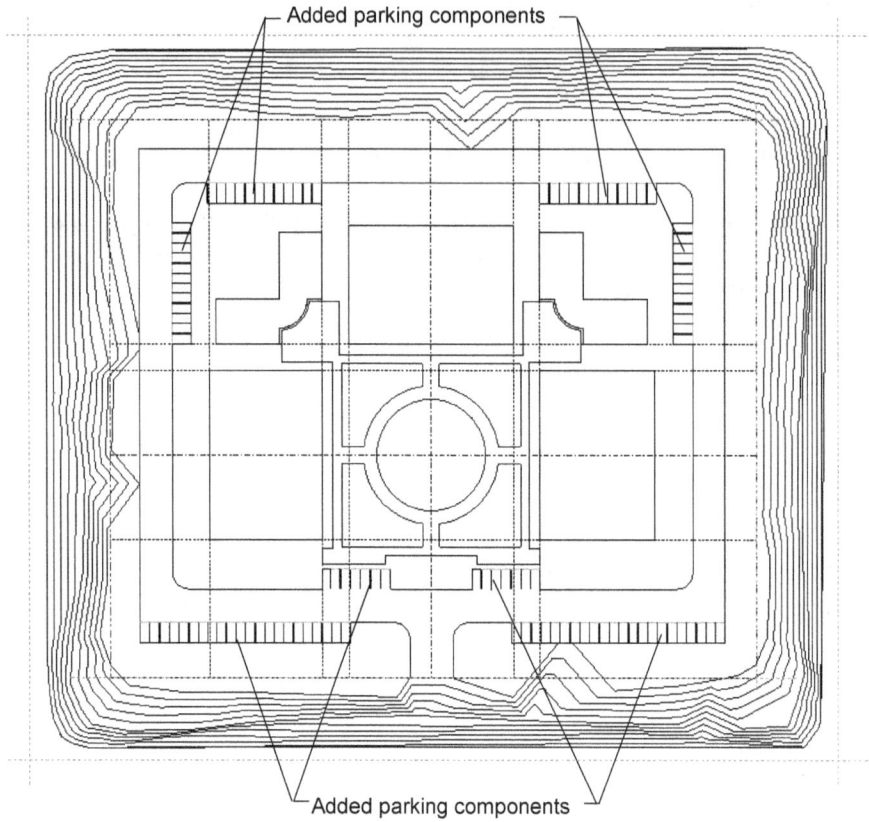

Figure 9-36 *Parking components added*

Adding Site Components

In this section, you will add site components from the in-built library of Autodesk Revit. The procedure is the same as that of adding parking components.

1. Choose the **Site Component** tool from the **Model Site** panel in the **Massing & Site** tab.

2. Next, you need to load the desired site component from the library. To do so, choose the **Load Family** tool from the **Mode** panel; the **Load Family** dialog box is displayed.

3. Now, browse to **US Imperial > Planting** and select **RPC Tree - Deciduous** and then choose **Open**.

4. Next, in the **Properties** palette, select the required option from the **Type Selector** drop-down list, as specified in the site component parameters for the project.
   For Imperial   **RPC Tree - Deciduous : Red Ash-25'**
   For Metric   **RPC Tree - Deciduous : Red Ash- 7.6 Metres**

Adding Site Features

5. Move the cursor to the site plan and click to add the planting component. Add multiple trees by clicking points on the site plan.

   The trees can be placed at an approximate location, as given in the sketch plan.

6. Next, select all trees from the site plan; the instance properties of the selected trees are displayed in the **Properties** palette.

7. Now, select **Level 2** from the drop-down list corresponding to the **Level** parameter.

   The complete site plan with site components appears similar to the illustration given in Figure 9-37.

Figure 9-37 Complete site plan with site components

Creating Sections through the Site

You can use the **Section** tool to create section lines horizontally and vertically through the site.

1. Choose the **View** tab and then invoke the **Section** tool from the **Create** panel.

2. Create horizontal section line from the left to the right across the center of the design scheme.

3. Similarly, create a vertical section line from the bottom to the top across the center. The two section lines are created and their corresponding views are added under the **Sections (Building Section)** head in the **Project Browser**.

4. Using the **Project Browser**, rename the horizontal section **Section1** as **Longitudinal Section** and the vertical section **Section 2** as **Transverse Section**.

5. Double-click on **Longitudinal Section** under the **Sections (Building Section)** head in the **Project Browser** to view the longitudinal section.

6. Double-click on **Transverse Section** under the **Sections (Building Section)** head in the **Project Browser** to view the transverse section.

   You may need to increase the view range box by dragging the section box from the top or the bottom. Also, drag the levels to the sides of the section view. Ensure that the scale of the view shown in the **View Control Bar** is 1"=20'0" (1: 100).

7. Choose **Visual Styles > Shaded** from the **View Control Bar** to display the shaded view of the Longitudinal and Transverse sections, as shown in Figure 9-38 and Figure 9-39.

Figure 9-38 Longitudinal section through the site

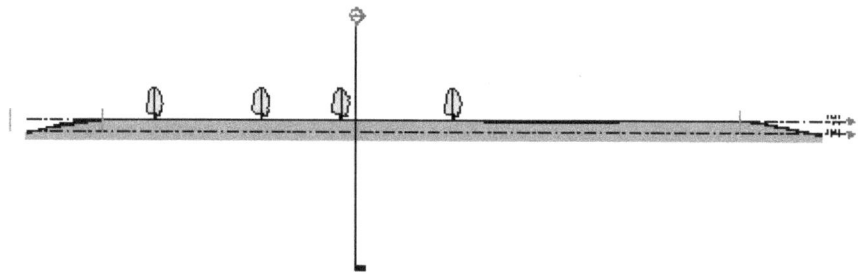

Figure 9-39 Transverse section through the site

8. Similarly, open the site plan and choose **Visual Styles > Shaded** from the **View Control Bar** to display the shaded view of the site plan, as shown in Figure 9-40.

9. Choose **Save As > Project** from the **Application Menu** to save the project. Specify the file name in the **File name** edit box and choose **Save**.
   For Imperial   **c09_SitePlan_tut1**
   For Metric   **M_c09_SitePlan_tut1**
   The project file is saved.

10. Choose **Close** from the **Application Menu** to close the project file.

Tip: *The modified material properties are not visible in the hidden lines view type. You can choose the **Visual Style** button in the **View Control Bar** and then choose **Shaded** option from the menu to graphically view the modified materials.*

Figure 9-40 Complete site plan

Self-Evaluation Test

Answer the following questions and then compare them to those given at the end of this chapter:

1. You can pick points at different elevation levels while creating a toposurface. (T/F)

2. When you pick points to create a toposurface, they automatically join to form a loop. (T/F)

3. A toposurface can be split along a straight line only. (T/F)

4. The specified depth and height offset is automatically cut in the toposurface. (T/F)

5. When you add site components, they get attached at the elevation level of the point picked on the toposurface.

6. The _____ tool is used to join two topographical surfaces that overlap or have a common edge.

7. The depth of the cross-section of the topographical surface can be specified in the _____ edit box of the **Site Settings** dialog box.

8. The _____ tool is used to add a building pad to a topographical surface.

9. The _____ option can be chosen to invoke the **Rotate** tool immediately after placing a parking component.

10. After creating a topographical surface, you can choose the _____ button from the **Modify | Topography** tab to edit it.

11. Which of the following tools helps to insert the entourages in the project ?

    a) **Parking Component**   b) **Topographies**
    c) **Site Component**   d) **Split Surface**

12. Which of the following tools helps to define the extents of the project ?

    a) **Property Line**   b) **Graded Region**
    c) **Subregion**   d) **Building Pad**

Review Questions

Answer the following questions:

1. While creating a topographical surface, the **Relative to Surface** option is used to pick points relative to the base level. (T/F)

2. The properties of a toposurface cannot be modified after its creation. (T/F)

3. The **Split Surface** tool is used to break the created toposurface into two separate surfaces. (T/F)

4. On merging two toposurfaces, the merged toposurface acquires the properties of the toposurface that was selected first. (T/F)

5. The **Work Plane** tool is used to draw multiple guidelines for locating points before creating a property line. (T/F)

6. The thickness of a building pad cannot be specified. (T/F)

7. A property line, once added, cannot be edited. (T/F)

8. Which of the following parameters can be used to specify the distance of a building pad from the base level?

   a) **Level**
   c) **Height Offset from level**
   b) **Structure**
   d) **Thickness**

9. Which of the following tools is used to create a region on a toposurface?

   a) **Topographies**
   c) **Subregion**
   b) **Pad**
   d) **Parking component**

10. Which of the following site setting parameters can be used to create additional contours?

    a) **At Intervals of**
    c) **Passing Through Elevation**
    b) **Additional Contours**
    d) **Elevation of poche base**

Exercises

Exercise 1 — Site Plan

Create the peripheral pedestrian walkway for the *Site Plan* project created in Tutorial 1 of this chapter, as shown in Figure 9-41. The sketch plan shows the pathway in white. You can assume the width of the walkway at various locations. Assign the material **Site - Sand** to the created pathway surface. Save the file as *c09_SitePlan_ex1.rvt (M_c09_SitePlan_ex1.rvt)*.

(Expected time: 30 min)

Figure 9-41 Sketch plan for adding the peripheral pedestrian walkway to the Site Plan project

Exercise 2 — Museum Site Plan

Create the site plan for a new project, a museum, by adding a site toposurface, road subregion, pedestrian walkway subregion, parking components, and trees, based on the illustration given in Figure 9-42. The dimensions and texts have been given only for reference and are not to be added. The site plan is symmetrical along the diagonal axis and you can assume the missing dimensions. **(Expected time: 30 min)**

1. Project File Parameters:
   - For Imperial   Template File- *default.rte*
   - For Metric   Template File- *DefaultMetric.rte*

   File Name to be assigned-
   - For Imperial   *c09_MuseumSitePlan_ex2.rvt*
   - For Metric   *M_c09_MuseumSitePlan_ex2.rvt*

2. Property size-
   - For Imperial   **150'0" X 150'0"** (Extents of property line)
   - For Metric   **45720 X 45720 mm**

3. Site settings:
   Contours at 1'0 (304.8 mm) intervals, top of site level- **5'0" (1525 mm)**
   Site material- **Site - Grass**, Road material- **Asphalt**, Walkway material- **Sand**
   Elevation of poche base- **-5'0" (-1525 mm)**

4. Building Pad: Level - **5'0" (1525 mm)**
   As per the dimensions given in the sketch plan - placed symmetrically along the diagonal axis.
   Building pad base level- **Level 2**

5. Parking Component-
   - For Imperial   **Parking Space: 9' X 18'-90 deg**
   - For Metric   **Parking Space: 4800 X 2400- 90 deg**

6. Site Component-
   - For Imperial   **RPC Tree - Deciduous: Red Ash-25'**
   - For Metric   **RPC Tree - Deciduous: Red Ash-7.6 Metres**

Figure 9-42 Sketch plan for creating the site plan for the Museum project

Answers to Self-Evaluation Test
1. T, 2. T, 3. T, 4. T, 5. T, 6. Merge Surface, 7. Elevation of poche base, 8. Building Pad, 9. Rotate after placement, 10. Edit Surface, 11. Site Component, 12. Property Line.

Chapter 10

Using Massing Tools

Learning Objectives

After completing this chapter, you will be able to:
- *Understand the concept of massing in Autodesk Revit Architecture.*
- *Create massing geometries using the Massing tool.*
- *Cut massing geometries using the Void Form tools.*
- *Convert a massing geometry into building elements.*
- *Add other building elements to a converted geometry.*
- *Create conceptual massing in conceptual design environment.*
- *Create a family and its types.*

INTRODUCTION

In the earlier chapters, you learned to use different building elements and components to create a building model. These building elements are parametrically associated and enable you to generate a building model based on specific design requirements such as wall types, door width, window height, and so on. Each of the elements must be assigned specific properties to achieve the desired element parameters, thereby making a building model accurate. Needless to say, this is a fairly time-consuming procedure. Autodesk Revit Architecture provides you with an alternative and much easier method to create a building model, known as massing.

UNDERSTANDING MASSING CONCEPTS

At the conceptualization stage of a project, you may want to study it in terms of its building volumes and shapes. You may also want to convey the basic idea of the structure of a building in a three-dimensional form without putting in a lot of detailing. This can be achieved by using various tools for creating massing geometries.

The tools for creating massing geometry not only enable you to conceive and create a variety of building shapes and volumes with relative ease but also conveys the potential design in terms of building masses and geometric shapes. You can create and edit geometric shapes and amalgamate them to form a building structure. This process can be compared to the creation of building a model using foam blocks. You have the freedom of choice to add or cut geometric shapes and join different blocks or masses to form an assembly. Figure 10-1 shows a group of volumes that can be created to represent the building volume and mass.

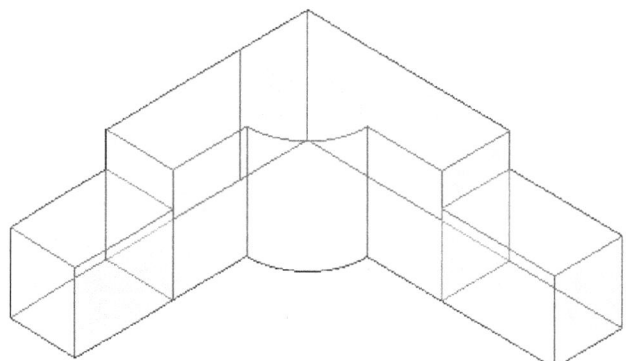

Figure 10-1 Building blocks created using the massing geometry

Autodesk Revit Architecture also enables you to convert a building mass into building elements. Building blocks can be transformed into an assembly of individual building elements such as walls, roof, and floor. The transformation carried out by using the tools provided for replacing massing faces with predefined wall, roof, and floor types, allows you to convert the same building mass into a building model. You can then develop it into a detailed building model by incorporating individual building elements with specified parameters.

Autodesk Revit Architecture provides a much-needed continuity in the design development of a building project by using the same building model from its conceptualization to completion.

Using Massing Tools

It also enables you to control the visibility of geometry between the building volumes (massing) and building elements (shell) during the initial stages of project development. Other project information such as its total area can also be extracted from the building massing.

It is, however, important to understand the limitations of the massing tool. This tool is only meant for conceptual design development using simple geometric shapes. You can place the predefined massing family elements provided in additional libraries. Autodesk Revit Architecture attempts to translate the massing geometry into building elements or shell. So, it is not recommended to be used for the development of a detailed geometry such as columns, cavity walls, footing, and so on.

CREATING THE MASSING GEOMETRY

In Autodesk Revit Architecture, you can create the massing geometry in any of these three environments: Family Editor, Conceptual Design, and Project.

To create the massing geometry in the Family Editor environment choose **New > Family** from the **Application Menu**; the **New Family - Select Template File** dialog box will be displayed. In this dialog box, choose the *Generic Model.rft* file (commonly used) from the **English_I** folder (for Metric the *Metric Generic Model.rft* file (commonly used) from the **English** folder) and then choose the **Open** button; a new file will open in the Family Editor environment. In the new file, create the massing geometry using various tools available in the ribbon.

The Conceptual Design environment is a new environment in Revit Architecture. This environment is a type of Family Editor that provides the advanced modeling tools and techniques for creating massing families. To start creating a mass in this environment, choose **New > Conceptual Mass** from the **Application Menu**; the **New Conceptual Mass - Select Template File** dialog box will be displayed. In this dialog box, select the **Mass** template file from the **Conceptual Mass** folder and then choose **Open**; a new file in the Conceptual Design environment will open. In the new file, you can create the massing geometry using various tools available in the **Create** tab of the ribbon, as shown in Figure 10-2.

*Figure 10-2 Different tools available in the **Create** tab of the ribbon*

The Project environment is the most common environment used in a project design. To start creating a mass in this environment, open a new file or an existing file by choosing **New > Project** or **Open > Project** from the **Application Menu**. After opening a new file or an existing file, choose the **Massing & Site** tab. In this tab, the massing tools can be accessed from the **Conceptual Mass** panel. The **Conceptual Mass** panel contains the following tools for massing: **In-Place Mass**, **Show Mass by View Settings**, and **Place Mass**.

The options in the **Model by Face** panel are used to convert the conceptual mass created into real building elements like walls, floors, roofs, and curtain systems. As such, these tools are also called the Building Maker tools.

When you create shapes in massing, Autodesk Revit Architecture creates its corresponding building elements. It is, therefore, imperative to consider the associativity of the massing and shell elements. The massing elements may need to be transformed into individual building elements simultaneously. Therefore, the massing geometry must be created accordingly.

For example, when you create a complex geometric massing shape and convert faces into building elements, you may find that some planes do not acquire the desired building element characteristics. The inclined planes and the curved surfaces are converted into in-place roofs.

Creating a Massing Geometry in the Family Editor

As discussed earlier, the Family Editor environment provides tools to create massing geometry. To create a new mass, choose **New > Family** from the **Application Menu**; the **New Family - Select Template File** dialog box will be displayed. In this dialog box, select the *Generic Model.rft* file (commonly used) from the **English_I** folder (for Metric the *Metric Generic Model.rft* file (commonly used) from the **English** folder) and choose **Open**; a new file will open using the selected template file.

In the Family Editor environment, the **Create** tab contains tools to create massing geometry. These tools can be used to create massing geometries in solid or in void form.

To create a solid form, invoke the **Extrusion / Blend / Revolve / Sweep / Swept Blend** tool from the **Forms** panel of the **Create** tab. These tools are used to create different solid forms. Similarly, to create a void form, choose the **Extrusion / Blend / Revolve / Sweep / Swept Blend** tool from the **Void Forms** drop-down in the **Forms** panel. You can create a massing geometry using any of these massing tools or a combination of the **Solid** and **Void** tools. The usage of these tools for creating simple massing geometries is described next. However, a designer can select the appropriate tool judiciously depending on the massing geometry to be created. Various tools used to create a solid or a void geometry are explained in the next sections.

Creating an Extrusion

Ribbon: Create > Forms > Extrusion

The **Extrusion** tool is used to create a massing geometry by adding height to a sketched profile. You can invoke this tool from the **Forms** panel in the **Create** tab of the ribbon in the Family Editor. On doing so, the **Modify | Create Extrusion** tab will be displayed. In this tab, you can specify different options to sketch an extrusion profile and create a massing geometry. Figure 10-3 shows different options in the **Modify | Create Extrusion** tab.

*Figure 10-3 Different options in the **Modify / Create Extrusion** tab*

Using Massing Tools

To create an extrusion, first you need to define work plane to sketch a profile. To define the work plane, you can invoke the **Set** tool available in the **Work Plane** panel of the **Modify | Create Extrusion** tab. After specifying the work plane, you can invoke the **Reference Plane** tool in the **Datum** panel of the **Create** tab to draw reference planes for locating exact points to sketch a profile. To sketch the 2D profile to be extruded, you can invoke any of the sketching tools available in the **Draw** panel of the **Modify | Create Extrusion** tab. You can invoke the appropriate tool (s) depending on the shape of the profile that must form a closed loop. In the **Properties** panel, choose the **Properties** tool to display the **Properties** palette, if it is not displayed by default. In this palette, you can specify the start and end levels of extrusion and other properties. The **Extrusion Start** instance parameter in the **Properties** palette indicates the start level of extrusion from the base level. The **Extrusion End** parameter indicates the top level of extrusion. The difference between these two parameters is calculated as the depth of the extrusion. You can also enter its value in the **Depth** edit box of the **Options Bar**. Autodesk Revit Architecture assumes the depth of extrusion from the base level. After sketching the profile, choose the **Finish Edit Mode** button from the **Mode** panel to finish the sketch of the profile for extrusion.

For example, to create a high-rise building, invoke the **Extrusion** tool from the **Forms** panel. In the **Options Bar**, you can specify the height of extrusion in the **Depth** edit box and also if required select the **Chain** check box if it is not selected by default. Next, in the **Draw** panel of this tab, the **Line** tool (invoked by default) can be used to sketch the extrusion profile. You can also use other sketching tools available in the **Draw** panel to sketch the profile. Sketch the base of the specified dimension using temporary dimensions, as shown in Figure 10-4. After the profile is completed, choose the **Finish Edit Mode** button to extrude the sketched profile to the specified depth. The building mass created can be viewed in the 3D view, as shown in Figure 10-5.

Figure 10-4 Sketch of a building profile to be extruded

Figure 10-5 Massing geometry created by using the **Extrusion** tool

Creating a Revolved Geometry

Ribbon: Create > Forms > Revolve

The **Revolve** tool is used to create a solid geometry by revolving a profile about an axis. This tool can also be used to create shapes such as domes, donuts, cylinders, and so on. To create a revolved geometry, invoke this tool from the **Forms** panel; Autodesk Revit Architecture enters the sketch mode and the **Modify | Create Revolve** tab will be displayed, as shown in Figure 10-6.

*Figure 10-6 Options in the **Modify / Create Revolve** tab*

In the **Draw** panel, the **Boundary Lines** tool is chosen by default. As a result, various sketching tools used to sketch the profile of the revolved geometry are displayed in a list box of this panel. Before invoking any of the sketching tools, you need to set the work plane. To do so, choose the **Create** tab, and then choose the **Set** tool from the **Work Plane** panel; the **Work Plane** dialog box will be displayed. In this dialog box, you can use various options to specify the required work plane for sketching the profile of the revolved geometry. After selecting the required plane, you can sketch the profile of the revolved geometry.

To sketch this profile, choose the **Modify | Create Revolve** tab. Next, you can use various sketching tools from the list box in the **Draw** panel. The sketched profile must be a single closed loop or multiple closed loops that do not intersect. After defining the profile, you need to define the axis about which the profile will revolve. To do so, invoke the **Axis Line** tool from the **Draw** panel; two tools, **Line** and **Pick Lines**, will be displayed in the list. The **Line** tool is used to draw a line that can be used as an axis and the **Pick Lines** tool is used to pick a line or an edge to define the axis of revolution. After completing the sketch and defining the axis of revolution, choose the **Finish Edit Mode** button from the **Modify | Create Revolve** tab; the **Modify | Revolve** tab will be displayed and the revolved geometry will be created.

In the **Modify | Revolve** tab, you can change the instance property of a revolved geometry in the **Properties** palette. In this palette, you can set the start and end angles of revolution. The default values for these two parameters are 0-degree and 360-degree, respectively.

For example, to create a dome, you can sketch the profile and define the axis for the profile, as shown in Figure 10-7. Before you start the sketch, you need to set the work plane that is perpendicular to the horizontal plane. The resultant revolved massing geometry is shown in Figure 10-8. Figure 10-9 shows an example of the revolved geometry in which the **End Angle** and **Start Angle** parameters in the **Properties** palette have been assigned the values 180.000° and 0.000°, respectively.

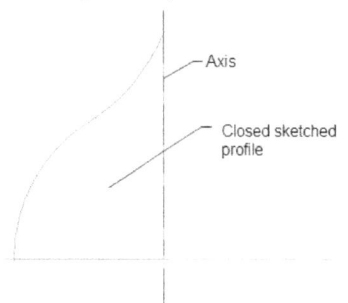

Figure 10-7 Sketching a close profile for a revolved geometry

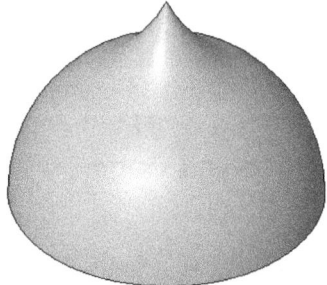

Figure 10-8 Massing geometry created by using the **Revolve** tool

Using Massing Tools

Figure 10-9 *Revolved geometry created by revolving the profile at an angle of 180 degrees*

 Tip: *In Autodesk Revit Architecture, you can quickly edit the revolve angle of a revolved geometry by selecting the geometry from the drawing and then changing the temporary angular dimension displayed in the geometry.*

Creating a Sweep

Ribbon: Create > Forms > Sweep

The **Sweep** tool is used to create a massing feature by selecting a profile along a sketched path. To create a massing feature by sweeping a profile, invoke the **Sweep** tool from the **Forms** panel; the sketch mode will be invoked and the **Modify | Sweep** tab with its related tools will be displayed, as shown in Figure 10-10. The **Sketch Path** tool in the **Sweep** panel of the **Modify | Sweep** tab is used to sketch the path to be used for extrusion. On invoking this tool, the **Modify | Sweep** tab will be replaced by the **Modify | Sweep > Sketch Path** tab, which contains tools to draw path. Using the tools from the **Draw** panel, you can sketch the desired shape of the path, which can be an open or closed profile. After sketching the path, choose the **Finish Edit Mode** button from the **Mode** panel; the **Modify | Sweep** tab will be displayed. In this tab, you can sketch a profile or load a profile for the sweep geometry. To sketch a profile, choose the **Edit Profile** tool from the **Sweep** panel in the **Modify | Sweep** tab; the **Go To View** dialog box will be displayed. In this dialog box, select an appropriate view and sketch the profile using different sketching tools. After sketching the profile, choose the **Finish Edit Mode** button from the **Mode** panel; the **Modify | Sweep > Edit Profile** tab will be displayed. In this tab, choose the **Finish Edit Mode** button from the **Mode** panel; a sweep geometry will be created. Figure 10-11 shows the example of a 2D path with a sketched profile and Figure 10-12 shows the resulting massing shape.

Figure 10-10 *Options in the **Modify / Sweep** tab with its related tools*

Autodesk Revit Architecture also provides in-built profiles that can be used in projects. These profiles are available in the **Profile** drop-down list in the **Sweep** panel of the **Modify | Sweep** tab. You can also choose the **Load Profile** button from the **Sweep** panel and access additional profiles in the **Profiles** subfolder in the **US Imperial** folder (for Metric **US Metric** folder). You can modify the properties of the sweep profile such as its **Structural**, **Mechanical**, and **Others**. To do so, select the massing created by the **Sweep** tool; the **Modify | Sweep** tab will be displayed. In this tab choose the **Edit Sweep** tool from the **Mode** panel; the properties of the sweep model will be displayed in the **Properties** palette. In this palette, click on the value field corresponding to the **Part Type** parameter under the **Mechanical** head; a drop-down list will be displayed. You can select an option from the displayed drop-down list to specify a part type to the sweep model. In the **Properties** palette, select the check box corresponding to the **Can host rebar** parameter to allow the sweep mass to host rebar for structural detailing.

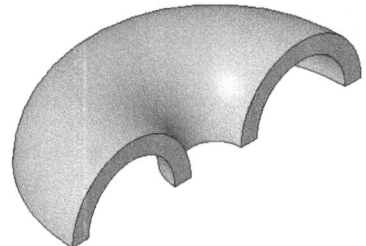

Figure 10-11 Sketching the profile and the 2D path for creating a sweep

Figure 10-12 Massing geometry created by using the **Sweep** tool

Creating a Blend

Ribbon: Create > Forms > Blend

Using the **Blend** tool, you can create a massing geometry by blending or linking two profiles. To create a massing geometry using this tool, invoke it from the **Forms** panel; the **Modify | Create Blend Base Boundary** tab will be displayed. The tools in this tab are used to create and edit a blend. Figure 10-13 shows various tools in the **Modify | Create Blend Base Boundary** tab.

Figure 10-13 Different tools in the **Modify / Create Blend Base Boundary** tab

After setting the work plane, you can sketch the base profile using different sketching tools available in the **Draw** panel. In the **Properties** palette, you can specify values in the value fields of the **First End** and **Second End** instance parameters to set the height of the blend geometry. After completing the base profile, you can choose the **Edit Top** option from the **Mode** panel in the **Modify | Create Blend Base Boundary** tab to display the **Modify | Create Blend Top Boundary** tab. In this tab, you can sketch the profile of the top of the blend geometry in any work plane. The depth of the blend geometry can be specified in the **Depth** edit box available in the **Options Bar**.

The **Edit Vertices** tool in the **Mode** panel of the **Modify | Create Blend Top Boundary** tab will be available only after both the base and top profiles are sketched. This tool enables

Using Massing Tools

you to specify the connectivity between the vertices of their profiles. After sketching both the profiles, choose the **Finish Edit Mode** button from the **Mode** panel to create the blend geometry. Figure 10-14 shows two circular profiles being sketched as the base and top profiles. The resulting geometry is shown in Figure 10-15.

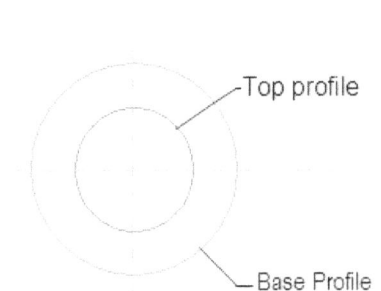

Figure 10-14 Sketching the base and top profiles to create a blend massing

Figure 10-15 Resulting shape after blending the base and top profiles

Creating a Swept Blend

Ribbon: Create > Forms > Swept Blend

 The solid swept blend geometries are created by using the **Swept Blend** tool. This tool has combined features of the **Sweep** and **Blend** tools. A geometry created using the **Swept Blend** tool consists of a path and two different profiles drawn at the either end of the path.

To create a swept blend geometry, choose the **Swept Blend** tool from the **Forms** panel; the screen will enter into the sketch mode and the **Modify | Swept Blend** tab will be displayed, as shown in Figure 10-16.

Figure 10-16 Different options in the **Modify / Swept Blend** tab

The **Modify | Swept Blend** tab contains various tools to sketch and edit the path and profiles of a solid swept blend geometry. Figure 10-17 shows the graphical representation of the solid swept blend geometry.

To create the geometry, first you need to sketch the 2D path. To do so, choose the **Sketch Path** tool from the **Swept Blend** panel; the sketch mode will be invoked. You can use various sketching tools in the **Draw** panel to sketch the 2D path. Next, choose the **Finish Edit Mode** button from the **Mode** panel of the **Modify | Swept Blend > Sketch Path** tab. Alternatively, you can define the 2D path for the solid swept blend geometry by choosing the **Pick Path** tool from the **Swept Blend** panel and then selecting an existing open curve or the edges of elements. The desired 2D path is always an open geometry composed of single segment. Once you have sketched or picked the 2D path, you need to define a profile at either end.

Choose the **Select Profile 1** tool from the **Swept Blend** panel and then choose the **Edit Profile** tool from the **Edit** panel; the **Go To View** dialog box will be displayed. Choose the required option from this dialog box and then choose the **Open View** button; the view will change based on the option chosen and the **Modify | Swept Blend > Edit Profile** tab will be displayed. Sketch the first profile at the end of the 2D path where you can see the reference plane with a red dot prominently displayed by using the appropriate sketching tools from the **Draw** panel. Next, to finish the sketching of the first profile, choose the **Finish Edit Mode** button from the **Mode** panel of the **Modify | Swept Blend > Edit Profile** tab. Similarly, you can define the second profile. To do so, choose the **Select Profile 2** option from the **Swept Blend** panel and then choose the **Edit Profile** option from the **Mode** panel in the **Modify | Swept Blend** tab; the **Modify | Swept Blend > Edit Profile** tab will be displayed. Sketch the second profile and then choose the **Finish Edit Mode** button from the **Mode** panel; the **Modify | Swept Blend** tab will be displayed. Now, choose the **Finish Edit Mode** button from the **Mode** panel; the solid swept blend geometry will be created, as shown in Figure 10-18.

Figure 10-17 The profiles and the 2D path for creating a Swept Blend geometry

Figure 10-18 Massing geometry created by using the **Swept Blend** tool

Editing a Massing Geometry in the Family Editor
In Autodesk Revit Architecture, you can easily edit a massing geometry. It can be edited using drag controls or by editing massing parameters.

Resizing a Massing Geometry by Using Drag Controls
On selecting a massing geometry, a number of drag controls will be displayed as arrows. You can use the drag control to drag the desired face. The entire massing geometry is automatically updated based on the dragged face. For example, Figure 10-19 shows a cuboid with drag controls displayed on all its faces. When you drag a plane of the cuboid using drag controls, Autodesk Revit Architecture immediately updates the geometry, as shown in Figure 10-20.

Using Massing Tools

 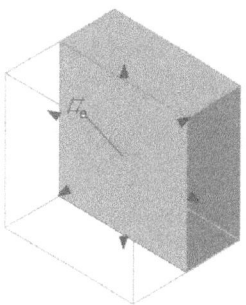

Figure 10-19 The geometry with the drag controls

Figure 10-20 The massing geometry resized using the drag controls

Editing a Massing Geometry

The parameters of a massing geometry can be modified in the Family Editor, when selected. For example, select a massing geometry created by using the **Extrusion** tool; the **Modify | Extrusion** tab will be displayed. In this tab, choose the **Edit Extrusion** tool from the **Mode** panel; the **Modify | Extrusion > Edit Extrusion** tab will be displayed. From the **Draw** panel of this tab, you can use various sketching tools to alter the sketch of the extrusion profile. You can also change the properties of extrusion like height, material, and visibility from the **Properties** palette . In this palette, you can change the height of extrusion by changing the values of the **Extrusion End** and **Extrusion Start** parameters. Similarly, you can change other parameters. Next, in the **Modify | Extrusion > Edit Extrusion** tab, choose the **Finish Edit Mode** button from the **Mode** panel; the editing of the selected extruded mass will be finished.

Similar to the example discussed earlier, you can also edit other massing geometries such as Sweep, Swept Blend, Revolve, and Blend.

To a certain extent, massing features can also be modified like other building elements. You can use the editing tools such as Mirror, Copy, Group, Array, and so on along with the massing tools.

Creating Cuts in a Massing Geometry Using the Family Editor

You can cut a massing geometry by creating a void form in it. This void form is cut or subtracted from the massing geometry it intersects. You can create void forms by using the tools displayed in the **Void Forms** drop-down in the **Forms** panel of the **Create** tab. The **Void Forms** drop-down displays five tools: **Void Extrusion**, **Void Blend**, **Void Revolve**, **Void Swept Blend**, and **Void Sweep**. You can choose an appropriate tool to generate the shape and volume of the void form. The method of creating a void form using these tools is similar to that of creating a solid form.

When any of the tools from the **Void Forms** drop-down is invoked, a contextual tab is displayed. For example, if you invoke the **Void Extrusion** tool, the **Modify | Create Void Extrusion** tab will be displayed. You can use the options in this tab to sketch the profile for the extruded void geometry. After sketching the profile of the extruded void geometry, choose the **Finish Edit Mode** button from the **Mode** panel of the **Modify | Create Void Extrusion** tab; the **Modify | Void Extrusion** tab will be displayed. From this tab, you can use various editing options to modify the extruded void geometry. Next, click in the drawing area or press ESC; the void form will automatically cut its shape and volume from the intersecting massing geometry.

For example, Figure 10-21 shows the profile of an arcade sketched using the **Void Extrusion** tool. Now, when you choose the **Finish Edit Mode** button from the **Modify | Create Void Extrusion** tab, the cutting geometry, an arcade in this case, is generated and automatically cut from the larger massing geometry. Figure 10-22 shows the resulting massing geometry.

 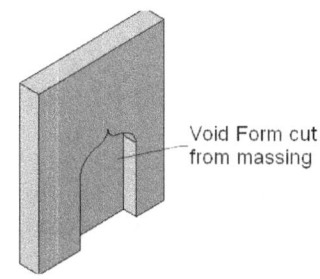

Figure 10-21 The profile for creating a void form using the **Void Extrusion** tool

Figure 10-22 The generated void form and the resulting massing geometry

Similarly, you can also use the **Void Revolve**, **Void Sweep**, **Void Blend**, and **Void Swept Blend** tools from the **Void Forms** drop-down to create the void form. For example, to create a tunnel through a building block, you can use the **Void Sweep** tool to sketch a semicircular profile and to specify its path, as shown in Figure 10-23. The resulting void form will be cut from the cuboid to create an arched opening through the building block, as shown in Figure 10-24.

 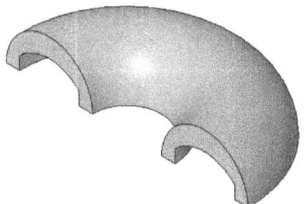

Figure 10-23 Sketching the profile for creating a void form

Figure 10-24 The generated void form and the resulting massing geometry

You can also use various editing tools such as **Copy**, **Mirror**, **Array**, and so on to create multiple copies of the void form profile for a single massing geometry. For example, a commercial building block has a semicircular vertical cut as the void form on one of its sides, you can select the 2D profile of the void form and use the **Copy** tool to create its duplicate.

Loading Massing Geometry into the Project

After creating massing geometries in the Family Editor, you can load them into the Project environment. To do so, choose the **Load into Project** tool from the **Family Editor** panel of the **Modify** tab; the current project file will appear if one project file is opened on the screen. Note that if more than one project file is opened in the current session, the **Load into Projects** dialog box will be displayed, as shown in Figure 10-25. In this dialog box, you can select the check box(es) to select the project(s) in which the created mass will be loaded. After selecting the required check box(es), choose **OK**; the mass will be loaded into the selected project file(s) corresponding to the check boxes selected. In this project file, the **Modify | Place Component** tab is chosen and you will notice that the mass created in the Family Editor appears in the drawing area along with the cursor.

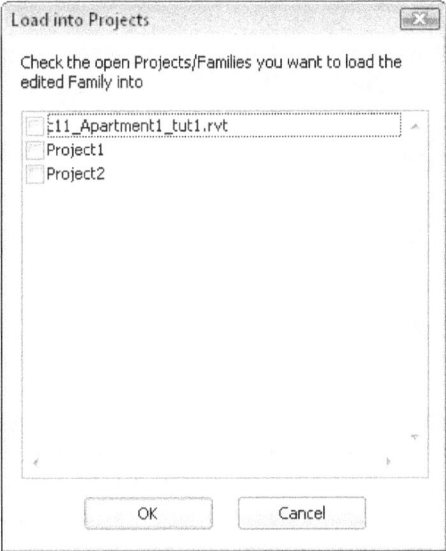

*Figure 10-25 The **Load into Projects** dialog box*

Placing the Massing Geometry in a Project

In the Project environment of Autodesk Revit Architecture, you have the option to add a predefined massing geometry to the project using the **Place Mass** tool. To add a predefined geometry, invoke this tool from the **Conceptual Mass** panel of the **Massing & Site** tab; the **Massing - Show Mass Enabled** window will be displayed. Choose the **Close** button from the window; the **Revit** message box will be displayed. Choose the **Yes** button from this message box; the **Load Family** dialog box will be displayed. In this dialog box, browse to the **Mass** subfolder in the **US Imperial** folder and then select a massing family. After selecting the massing family, choose the **Open** button; the **Load Family** dialog box will be closed. Also, the **Modify | Place Mass** tab will be displayed and the selected family will be loaded into the project. Now, click in the drawing area to place the loaded massing geometry.

In Revit Architecture, you can either align a mass geometry with the selected faces of the components created or place it on the defined work plane based on your requirement. To place a mass geometry on a selected face, choose the **Place on Face** tool from the **Placement** panel of the **Modify | Place Mass** tab and then place the cursor on the face of the component with which you want to align the massing geometry. You will notice that the mass geometry is aligned with the face on which the cursor is placed. Now, you can click to place the mass on the plane. Similarly, while placing a mass in a drawing, you can place it at a desired level. To do so, choose the **Place on Work Plane** tool from the **Placement** panel of the **Modify | Place Mass** tab; the options for placing the mass will be displayed in the **Options Bar**. In the **Options Bar**, select the required level from the **Placement Plane** drop-down list and click in the drawing area; a mass will be created in the selected level. Before aligning the mass geometry to a desired face or in a work plane, you can also rotate it about an axis. To do so, select the **Rotate after placement** check box from the **Options Bar**. After placing the mass geometry in the drawing, you can edit its geometrical properties such as height, width, radius, and so on, depending upon the type of geometry created. To do so, modify the instance parameters displayed in the **Properties** palette. In the **Dimensions** category of the **Properties** palette, you can select the desired dimension instance parameter and change its value in its respective value field.

Creating the In-Place Mass in a Project

In the Project environment, you have the option to create an in-place massing geometry by using the **In-Place Mass** tool. Invoke this tool from the **Conceptual Mass** panel of the **Massing & Site** tab; the **Name** dialog box will be displayed. In this dialog box, enter the name of the mass in the **Name** edit box and choose **OK**; the **Create** tab will be displayed. You can use the options in this tab to sketch the massing profile and convert it into a solid or void form. To sketch the profile for the mass, choose the **Model** tool from the **Draw** panel; the **Modify | Place Lines** tab will be displayed. You can use various sketching tools available in the **Draw** panel of this tab. While sketching, you can also use the **Reference Plane** tool from the **Draw** panel to draw references for the sketch. After sketching the profile, you can use any of the tools displayed in the **Create Form** drop-down in the **Form** panel. The **Create Form** drop-down displays two tools: **Solid Form** and **Void Form**. You can use the **Solid Form** tool to create a solid form and the **Void Form** tool to create a void form. To use any of the tools from the **Create Form** drop-down, you can need to select the sketched profile from the drawing and then invoke the **Solid Form** or **Void Form** tool. After invoking any of these tools; the **Modify | Form** tab will be displayed. In this tab, you specify the settings to change the instance property of the mass created, divide the surfaces of the mass, and modify geometrical elements of the mass.

You can change the instance properties of the massing geometry like material and visibility from the **Properties** palette. After changing the instance properties of the selected massing geometry, you can change the geometrical property of the surface by adding edges and profiles. The tools for changing the geometrical properties are: **X-Ray**, **Add Edge**, and **Add Profile**. You can invoke these tools from the **From Element** panel of the **Modify | Form** (solid form) tab.

The **X-Ray** tool in the **Element** panel of the **Modify | Form** tab is used to display the geometry skeleton like vertices and edges of the mass. The **Add Edge** tool can be used to add edges to the form of the mass and the **Add Profile** tool is used to add profile to the surface of the mass. Figure 10-26 shows the added edge and profile in the **X-Ray** mode.

Using Massing Tools

Figure 10-26 Massing geometry with added edge and profile in the **X-Ray** mode

Dividing Edges or Paths

You can divide a line or edge of a form to define the nodes on which the components can be placed. On dividing a line or edge, nodes are applied to the division points that denote the position of the points of placement for components. You can divide a line or an edge of a form by using any of the following methods: Specifying number of divisions, Specifying distance between divisions, or by using the point of intersection between the line or edge with the levels, reference planes, or divided paths. To divide a path on an edge, select a form from the project view; the **Modify | Mass** tab will be displayed. In this tab, choose the **Edit In-Place** tab; the form will be displayed in the editable mode. Select an edge of the form; the **Modify | Form** tab will be displayed. In this tab, choose the **Divide Path** tool from the **Divide** panel; the properties of the path division will be displayed in the **Properties** palette. Also the selected edges will display 6 nodes in equal division along its edge. You will also notice the number **6** displayed above the edge. You can click on the number and enter a different numerical value in the edit box displayed to increase the number of nodal divisions along the edge.

MASSING IN CONCEPTUAL DESIGN ENVIRONMENT

Conceptual design is the very first phase of a design process. The primary objective of a conceptual design is to create a representation of the idea generated for creating the building mass of a project. For creating a building project, conceptual design is very important for architects, engineers, and designers as it helps in finding out the final representation of the design intent. It thus enables them to create a more specific sets of plans.

In Revit Architecture, you can create conceptual designs in any of the following environments: Conceptual Design Environment and Revit Project Environment. The Conceptual Design Environment is used to create massing families as conceptual designs that reside outside the Project Environment. These families can be loaded in the Revit Project Environment that forms the basis to create detail design by applying walls, roofs, floors, and curtain systems to them. In the Revit Project Environment, you can create conceptual designs by using the **In-Place Mass** or **Place Mass** tool from the **Conceptual Mass** panel in the **Massing & Site** tab. In this environment, you cannot create 3D reference planes and view 3D levels.

Interface of the Conceptual Design Environment

To open the interface of the Conceptual Design Environment, choose the Application button and then choose **New > Conceptual Mass** from the **Application Menu**. On doing so, the **New Conceptual Mass-Select Template File** dialog box will be displayed. In this dialog box, select the **Mass.rft** file from the **Conceptual Mass** folder in the English_I folder (for Metric the **Metric Mass.rft** file from the **Conceptual Mass** folder in the **English** folder) and then choose the **Open** button; the interface of the Conceptual Design Environment along with the settings of the selected template file will be displayed, as shown in Figure 10-27. From the interface of the **Conceptual Design Environment**, you can use various tools in the ribbon to create the conceptual mass.

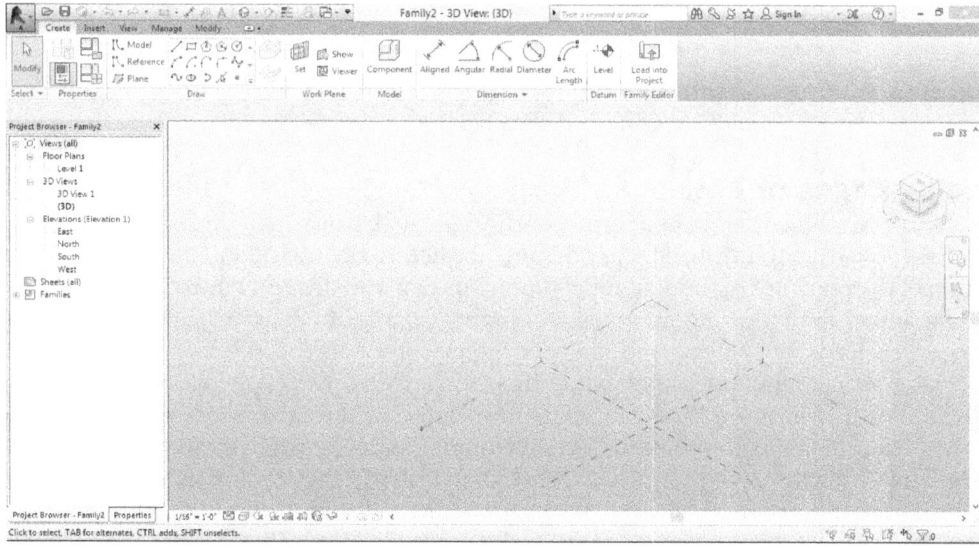

Figure 10-27 The Conceptual Design Environment interface

Creating Masses in Conceptual Design Environment

In the Conceptual Design Environment, you can create the conceptual mass by using various tools from the ribbon. The ribbon of the Conceptual Design Environment, as shown in Figure 10-28, consists of the following tabs: **Create**, **Insert**, **Views**, **Manage**, and **Modify**. The **Create** tab is chosen by default. From the **Create** tab, you can access the tools required to create the Conceptual Mass. From the **Workplane** panel of the **Create** tab, you can choose any of the tools such as **Set**, **Show**, and **Viewer** that can be used for setting, showing, and viewing workplane to be used to create the conceptual mass. You can choose the **Level** tool in the **Datum** panel to add levels that will assist in the creation of its conceptual mass. You can add levels in 3D and elevation views in the Conceptual Design Environment. The **Draw** panel of the **Create** tab contains tools that can be used to sketch conceptual mass. In this panel, you can use the **Model**, **Reference**, and **Plane** tool to sketch the model lines, reference lines and reference planes to create the conceptual mass. When you choose the **Model** or **Reference** tool from the **Draw** panel, the **Draw on Face** and the **Draw on Work Plane** will be activated. You can use any of these tools to specify the plane in which conceptual mass will be created. Also, on choosing the **Model** or **Reference** tool from the **Draw** panel, a contextual tab will be displayed along with various options in the **Options Bar**. This tab contains options that help in sketching the model or reference line. In the **Family Editor** panel of the **Create** tab, you can choose the **Load into Project** tool to load the conceptual mass into the project file. From the **Dimension** panel of the **Create** tab, you can choose various tools to dimension the sketch of the conceptual mass. In the ribbon of the Conceptual Design Environment, the tools in the other tabs such as **Insert**, **View**, **Manage**, and **Modify** are same as those in the Project Environment. In the next sections, the method and the tools involved in the process of drawing and creating the conceptual mass are discussed.

Using Massing Tools 10-17

Figure 10-28 The ribbon of the Conceptual Design Environment

Sketching the Conceptual Design Environment

To sketch a profile of the conceptual mass in the Conceptual Design Environment, you can use the floor plan views or the 3D views depending upon the project requirement. You can draw a profile of the conceptual mass with or without using references. You can use the references to create constraints and reference for the conceptual mass. To draw references for the profile conceptual mass, you can invoke the **Reference** tool from the **Draw** panel of the **Create** tab. After invoking the **Reference** tool, you can draw the reference by using various sketching tools such as **Line**, **Rectangle**, **Circle**, **Pick Lines**, and **Point Elements** from the list box displayed next to it.

After sketching the reference, you will sketch the model lines for the profile of the conceptual mass. To do so, choose the **Model** tool from the **Draw** panel; the **Modify | Place Lines** tab will be displayed. In the **Draw** panel of this tab, you can use the sketching tools such as **Line**, **Rectangle**, and others to sketch the conceptual mass. When you invoke a sketching tool, its corresponding options are displayed in the **Options Bar**. These options assist in sketching the profile. After you sketch the conceptual mass, you can also use various editing tools such as **Offset**, **Move**, **Copy**, and others from the **Modify** panel of the **Modify | Place Lines** tab to edit the sketch. Figure 10-29 displays a sketched profile of a conceptual mass. After sketching the conceptual mass, select it; the **Modify | Line** tab will be displayed. In the **Form** panel of this tab, you can click on the **Create Form** drop-down and choose the **Solid Form** or the **Void Form** tool from the drop-down menu. You can choose the **Solid Form** tool to create a solid from the sketched lines. Alternatively, choose the **Void Form** tool to create a void or cavity in an existing solid. On choosing the **Solid Form** tool from the **Create Form** drop-down, the **Modify | Form** tab will be displayed. Also, the selected sketch line will extrude to a certain height and will appear along with its temporary dimensions. Figure 10-30 displays a solid extruded from the sketched lines.

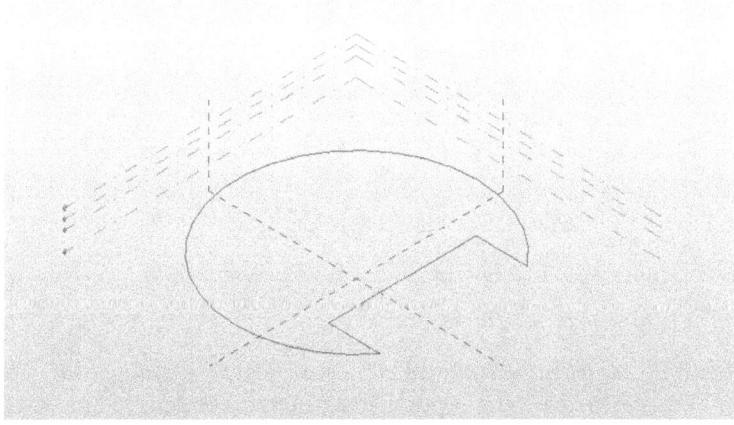

Figure 10-29 Sketched profile of a conceptual mass

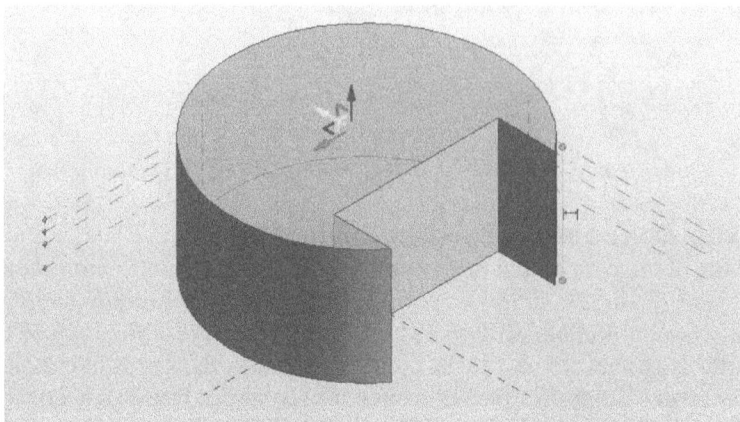

Figure 10-30 Solid extruded from the sketched lines

After creating a solid, you can edit its profile. To do so, select the extruded face of the solid profile and then choose the **Edit Profile** tool from the **Mode** panel of the **Modify | Form** tab. On doing so, the profile of the selected face will enter the sketch mode, as shown in Figure 10-31. You can edit the sketch using various tools in the **Modify Form > Edit Profile** tab. After editing the sketched profile, choose the **Finish Edit Mode** button from the **Mode** panel to return to the **Modify | Form** tab.

You can divide the surfaces of a conceptual mass, add profile and edge to its form, display the geometric skeleton of its form, and dissolve the surfaces of its form. The various tools that you can use to perform these functions are **Divide Surface**, **X-Ray**, **Add Profile**, **Add Edge**, and **Dissolve**, which are discussed next.

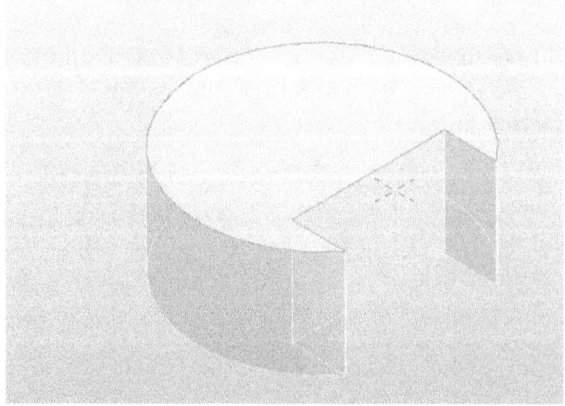

Figure 10-31 Profile of the selected face in the editing mode

Using X-Ray

The **X-Ray** tool can be used to display the underlying geometric skeleton of a selected form. The mode in which the geometric skeleton of the selected form will be displayed is called the X-Ray mode. In this mode, as the surfaces become transparent this allows you to directly interact with the individual elements. It is to be noted that at a time

Using Massing Tools

only one form in all the model will be visible in the X-Ray mode. To switch the display of a form to the X-Ray mode, select it and then choose the **X-Ray** tool from the **Form Element** panel of the **Modify | Form** tab. Once you switch the form to the X-Ray mode, you can select the element again and choose the **X- Ray** tool to restore its visibility to its previous mode.

Adding Profiles

After you create a conceptual mass, you can add cross-section profiles to it. An edge is a profile that may be a single line, chain of connected lines, or a closed loop, depending upon the geometry of the form. The added profile can be used to generate a form or edit the geometry of the existing form. To add a profile to a form, select it and then choose the **Add Profile** tool from the **Form Element** panel of the **Modify | Form** tab. On doing so, the cursor changes to a cross mark and at the **Status Bar**, you will be prompted to insert a new profile at the cross-section of the form element. Move the cursor on the surface of the form, the surface of the form will be highlighted in a blue border and a probable profile will be displayed at the position of the cursor. Click at a desired point on the surface of the form to add the profile. Note that the added profile in the form will only be visible in the X-Ray mode. Figure 10-32 displays a form with added profiles.

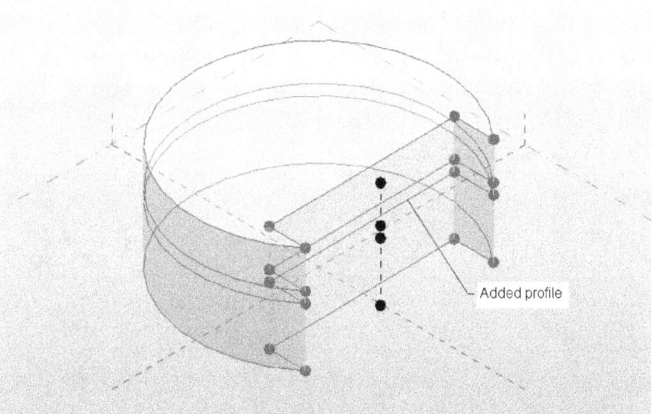

Figure 10-32 Profiles added in the form

Adding Edges

After you create a conceptual mass, you can add edges to it. To add an edge select the form and then choose the **Add Edge** tool from the **Form Element** panel of the **Modify | Form** tab. On doing so, the cursor will change into a cross mark. Place the cursor on the surface of the form; an edge will appear at the point of the cursor. Click at the desired point on the surface and add the edge to the surface of the form, as shown in Figure 10-33.

Figure 10-33 Edge added to the form

Dissolve

 You can delete the surface of the form and retain its profile. You can also edit the retained profiles and recreate a form. To delete the surface of a form, select the form and choose the **Dissolve** tool from the **Form Element** panel of the **Modify | Form** tab. On doing so, the surface(s) will be deleted from the form. Figure 10-34 displays a form with its surfaces removed on applying the **Dissolve** tool.

Figure 10-34 Surfaces removed from the form

Tip: *You can divide the surface of the form. To do so, select the surface of the form and then choose the **Divide Surface** tool from the **Form Element** panel of the **Modify / Form** tab. On doing so, the **Modify / Divided Surface** tab will be displayed. You can use various tools from the displayed tab and options from the **Options Bar** to divide the selected surface.*

CREATING BUILDING ELEMENTS FROM THE MASSING GEOMETRY USING BUILDING MAKER TOOLS

After generating the shape and volume of massing forms, you can convert them into building elements such as walls, floors, roofs, and curtain systems. You can select the faces of the generated massing geometry and replace them with the desired building element. To convert faces into building elements, you can use various tools from the **Model by Face** panel of the **Massing & Site** tab in the ribbon.

Creating Walls by Selecting Faces

Ribbon: Massing & Site > Model by Face > Curtain System

You can convert the faces of the placed mass into walls. To do so, choose the **Wall** tool from the **Model by Face** panel of the **Massing & Site** tab; the **Modify | Place Wall** tab will be displayed. In this tab, select the wall type to be used for conversion from the **Type Selector** drop-down list. In the **Draw** panel of this tab, make sure that the **Pick Faces** option is chosen. In **Options Bar**, select the appropriate values of the **Level**, **Height**, and **Location Line** from their respective drop-down lists.

Now, to convert the faces into walls, move the cursor over the massing geometry. You will notice that the faces that can be converted are highlighted. Next, click on the desired face to make the conversion. You can use the TAB key to select all the faces of the massing geometry that can be converted into walls. Figure 10-35 shows the selected faces of the massing geometry and Figure 10-36 shows the walls created.

Figure 10-35 Selected wall face

Figure 10-36 Massing face converted into walls

Creating Floors by Selecting Faces

Ribbon: Massing & Site > Model by Face > Floor

To create a floor in a massing geometry, first you need to define the floor area faces by selecting the massing geometry and then choosing the **Mass Floors** tool from the **Model** panel of the **Modify | Mass** tab. On doing so, the **Mass Floors** dialog box will be displayed. Select the levels at which the floor area faces are required and choose the **OK** button. Autodesk Revit Architecture will automatically generate the floor area faces based on the massing geometry and the defined levels.

Next, to add the floor to the floor area faces, you need to invoke the **Floor by Face** tool from the **Conceptual Mass** panel; the **Modify | Place Floor by Face** tab will be displayed. You can select a floor type from the **Type Selector** drop-down list. Next, move the cursor over the massing geometry; the floor area faces will be highlighted. Now, you can choose the **Select Multiple** tool from the **Multiple Selection** panel and use the crossing options to create a selection of multiple floor area faces. Next, choose the **Create Floors** button in the **Multiple Selection** panel of the **Modify | Place Floor by Face** tab to create floors. Autodesk Revit Architecture will convert all the selected floor area faces into the selected floor type. Figure 10-37 shows the floor area faces generated for a multistory building. The floors created are shown in Figure 10-38.

Figure 10-37 Generated floor area faces

Figure 10-38 Floor area faces converted into floors

Creating Roofs by Selecting Faces

Ribbon: Massing & Site > Model by Face > Roof

You can use the **Roof** tool in the **Massing & Site** tab to convert the massing faces into roofs. Faces can be horizontal planes of any shape or those created by using the **Extrusion**, **Revolve**, **Blend**, **Sweep**, or **Swept Blend** tool.

Invoke the **Roof** tool from the **Model by Face** panel; the **Modify | Place Roof by Face** tab will be displayed. From this tab, select the roof type to be used from the **Type Selector** drop-down list. Next, move the cursor over the massing geometry and click to select the highlighted face. Next, choose the **Create Roof** button in the **Multiple Selection** panel to convert it into a roof. Figures 10-39 and 10-40 show the top face of a multistory building converted into a roof.

Using Massing Tools

Figure 10-39 The top face selected for conversion into a roof

Figure 10-40 The top face of the massing geometry converted into a roof

Creating Curtain Systems by Selecting Faces

Autodesk Revit Architecture provides you with the **Curtain System** tool to convert the planar and non-planar faces into curtain systems. Invoke this tool from the **Model by Face** panel; the **Modify | Place Curtain System by Face** tab will be displayed. In this tab, select the curtain system type from the **Type Selector** drop-down list. In the **Properties** palette, you can modify the instance and type properties of the curtain system before creating it. Next, move the cursor over the face that needs to be converted into the curtain system and click to select it. Choose the **Create System** tool from the **Multiple Selection** panel to create the curtain system. Figure 10-41 shows the example of a curtain system of a dome. You can then add mullions to the curtain system using the **Mullions** tool, as shown in Figure 10-42. Figure 10-43 shows another example of using the **Curtain System** tool to convert non-planar massing faces into curtain systems.

Figure 10-41 Creating a curtain system using the **Curtain System** tool

Figure 10-42 Mullions added to the curtain system using the **Mullions** tool

Figure 10-43 Converting non-planar massing faces into curtain systems with mullions

Controlling the Visibility of a Massing Geometry

To hide or display a massing geometry, choose the **Show Mass by View Settings** tool from **Massing & Site > Conceptual Mass > Show Mass by View Settings** drop-down. However, the use of this tool has a temporary effect on the visibility of the massing forms. When a project file is closed, the show mass settings are not saved in it. Therefore, next time when you will open the project file, the massing forms will not be visible.

To display massing form permanently in a project file, invoke the **Visibility/Graphics** tool from the **Visibility/Graphics** panel of the **View** tab; the **Visibility/Graphics Overrides** dialog box for the current view will be displayed. In this dialog box, select the check box for the **Visibility** parameter of the **Mass** model category.

Adding other Building Elements

After converting the massing geometry into basic building elements, you can add other building elements such as doors, windows, roofs, and so on to the basic building elements. You can also use various editing tools to copy, edit, and delete the converted building elements.

Figure 10-44 shows the example of a building model in the plan view with modified wall type and added windows. You can use the editing tools such as **Mirror**, **Array**, and **Paste Aligned** to copy elements and create a building model of desired shape with specified parameters, as shown in Figure 10-45.

Like other building models, you can also create the standard building views of the converted massing model. Autodesk Revit Architecture also provides the facility to extract the areas and other statistical figures of the created massing geometry.

Figure 10-44 Plan view showing the modified wall type and added windows

Figure 10-45 A multistory building with building components

Using Massing Tools

Tip: *With the **Massing** tool, Autodesk Revit Architecture enables you to create a variety of shapes and volumes. Based on the desired geometry, you can use a combination of tools. The massing geometry can also be used to generate the rendered views of conceptual building volumes. This can prove to be an effective tool for communicating the design intent to the entire project team before starting the detailed project plans.*

CREATING FAMILIES

Revit family is defined as a collection of parametric components or elements having similar graphical representation, utility, and common parameters. By nature, all the elements used in Revit Architecture are family-based. A Revit family has a wide range of collections starting from a wall to a window and extended up to two-dimensional annotations or symbols required for your project. In Autodesk Revit Architecture, each family inherits the character of some specific type. Each type is a member of Revit family that consists of certain parameters known as **Type Parameters**. These parameters are constant for identical types. For example, a **Single-Flush** door family can have different types such as **Single-Flush : 36" x 84"** in Imperial **(Single-Flush : 0915 x 2134 mm** in Metric), **Single-Flush : 30" x 84" (Single-Flush : 0915 x 2032 mm** in Metric), and others. You can access these types from the **Type Selector** drop-down list.

In Autodesk Revit Architecture, families are useful tools as they are driven by the Revit parametric change engine. This engine helps to reflect the changes made in a family throughout the project. You can edit the parameters of a family after you have created it in a project using the **Revit Family Editor**. The **Revit Family Editor** is an interface that allows you to create or make changes in a family. At the same time, it helps you add or modify specific parameters of your model while defining it as a family type.

While creating a project, you may need to define a family inside another family. This type of family is called nested family. For example, if you are creating a window family, you can create another family inside it for hardware items such as knobs, bolts, and so on. The use of nested family adds details to the family you have created.

In Autodesk Revit Architecture, there are three types of families: System families, In-place families, and Standard component families. These families are differentiated on the basis of their creations and utilities in a project.

The System families includes the most common building components that are frequently used in a project such as walls, floors, roofs, and ceilings. You cannot create a new system family of your own, but you can create duplicate families and modify their properties as per your need. The In-place families are project-specific, therefore, you can use them when you need to create a unique component for a specific project. For example, you may need to design a unique table, featuring curved edges and material finishes, specific to the flooring of a dining area. In such a case, you can use the In-place families for creating the table. Also, you can save this table for further use. In Revit Architecture, the Standard component families are the basic components that are commonly used in a building design. These families are not project-specific. Whenever a need arises, you can download these families from common libraries. You can place the Standard component families in a project template so that they can be used whenever you start a new project. Revit Architecture allows you to load the required family of door, window, and so on from the in-built Revit library. To do so, choose the **Load Family** tool from the **Load from Library** panel in the **Insert** tab; the **Load Family** dialog box will be displayed. Select the required file for the family from the appropriate folder and then choose **Open**; the family will be loaded into the project.

In Autodesk Revit Architecture, you can save a selected family or all the families loaded in the current project or template to a location on your system or to a network location. To save a family loaded in the current project choose **Save As > Library > Family** from the **Application Menu**; the **Save Family** dialog box will be displayed. In this dialog box, browse to a folder location to save the family file. Next, in the **File name** edit box, enter the name of the file and then select an option from the **Family to save** drop-down list to specify a family or all families loaded in the project. Next, choose the **Save** button; the selected family will be saved at the specified location. Note that in-place families and system families, such as walls, and patterns cannot be saved. Revit Architecture also enables you to create your own customized families and then use them in a project. There are two methods that you can use to create a family. These methods are discussed next.

Creating In-Place Families

This method is used to create custom families such as the furniture for reception and workstations in a building model. You can create a family while working on a project. The family created is saved within the project and gets updated according to the changes made in the project.

To create an In-Place family, choose the **Model In-Place** tool from **Architecture > Build > Component** drop-down; the **Family Category and Parameters** dialog box will be displayed. In the **Family Category** area, select an option from the **Filter list** drop-down list to filter the list of categories that will be displayed in the list box displayed below it. Double-click on the required category from the list box; the **Name** dialog box will be displayed. In this dialog box, enter a name for the family in the **Name** edit box and then choose the **OK** button; the sketch mode will be invoked and the options in the **Create** tab will be displayed. Sketch the reference planes and set the work plane to help you sketch the geometry for the family using the required sketching tools from the **Model** panel and the **Forms** panel. After creating the massing geometry, choose the **Finish Model** button from the **In-Place Editor** panel; a family will be created. After creating the geometry of a family, you can assign materials to the family and create family types with different dimensions.

Creating Families Using Standard Family Templates

In this method, you can create a new family by using certain standard in-built family templates as platform. These templates provide you with some parameters, reference planes, and dimensions in different views that are already saved in templates. You have to create the geometry for a family in the required view. To do so, you need to sketch reference planes, dimension reference planes, label dimensions, and then sketch the profile for the family using the required sketching tools. Once you have created the profile, apply materials to it and create family types by assigning different dimensions to the geometry. At the end, give a name to the template, save it, and load the family into the project to use it in your drawing.

Using Massive Tools

The steps to create a family are explained next with an example of an arch-shaped panel window, as shown in Figure 10-46. The window is created using a standard template.

Figure 10-46 An arch-shaped window with panels

Selecting a Template

The first step to create a family using standard template is to select a suitable template to be used as a platform. To do so, choose **New > Family** from the **Application Menu**; the **New Family - Select Template File** dialog box will be displayed. In this dialog box, select the required template for Imperial from the **Family Templates > English_I** folder and then select the **Generic Model.rft** file (for Metric from the **Family Templates > English** folder and then select the **Metric Generic Model.rft** file). For creating an arch-shaped window with panels, select the **Generic Model wall based** template and choose the **Open** button; the template with a geometry and a reference plane will be displayed in the drawing area. Choose the **Tile Windows** tool from the **Windows** panel of the **View** tab to view all the views saved in the template, as shown in Figure 10-47.

Figure 10-47 Different views saved in the template

Adding Reference Planes

Once you have selected the template, the next step is to add reference planes to the required view. You can do so by using the **Reference Plane** tool. To add reference planes, open the **Elevations : Placement Side** view and then invoke the **Reference Plane** tool from the **Datum** panel of the **Create** tab; the **Modify | Place Reference Plane** tab will be displayed. Invoke the **Line** tool from the **Draw** panel of this tab and sketch reference planes based on the dimensions of the geometry. Sketching the reference planes helps you sketch the geometry of the plane easily. Figure 10-48 shows the reference planes sketched for the arch-shaped window.

Dimensioning

To use the tools for dimensioning, choose the **Annotate** tab and then choose any of the dimensioning tools from the **Dimension** panel, and dimension the reference planes. Dimensioning the sketched reference planes helps you control the parametric geometry, refer to Figure 10-48.

Figure 10-48 Dimensioning the sketched reference planes

Labeling the Dimensions

After dimensioning the reference planes, you need to label dimensions. The dimensions that are labeled become the type and instance parameters for a family. To label dimensions, select the dimension and right-click; a shortcut menu will be displayed. Choose **Label** from the shortcut menu; a drop-down list will be displayed. Select **Add Parameter** from the drop-down list, as shown in Figure 10-49; the **Parameter Properties** dialog box will be displayed. In this dialog box, enter labels for sill height, height, width, and rise, as shown in Figure 10-50.

Using Massing Tools

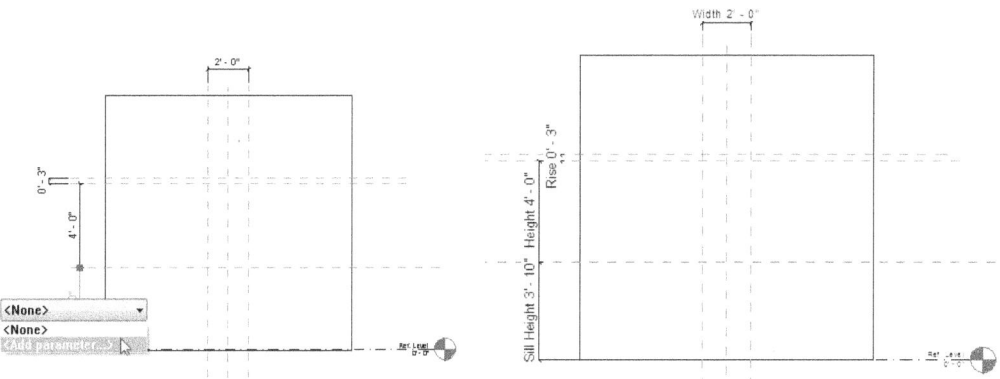

Figure 10-49 The drop-down list displayed after choosing the **Label** option from the shortcut menu

Figure 10-50 The reference planes after being labeled

Creating an Opening

After dimensioning and labeling the dimensions, the next step is to create an opening in the window. The shape of the opening depends upon the shape of the window. To create an opening, invoke the **Opening** tool from the **Model** panel of the **Create** tab; the sketch mode will be invoked. Next, use the required sketching tools and sketch the opening for the window. You can sketch the opening of any shape based on the shape of the window. Next, choose the **Finish Edit Mode** button from the **Mode** panel of the **Modify | Create Opening Boundary** tab to finish the sketch of the opening. Figure 10-51 shows an arch-shaped opening created using the **Line** and **Start-End-Radius Arc** tools. Now, you can view the opening in a 3D view.

Figure 10-51 Sketching the arch-shaped opening for the window

Adding Reference Planes for Sash and Glass

You need to add reference planes to place the window frame, sash, and glass. These planes can be added on the right or left elevation view. Figure 10-52 shows three planes added to the right elevation view at a distance of 0' 1"(25 mm) and 0' 1.5"(38 mm) from the center reference plane and at the exterior edge of the wall. You can also give names to the reference planes. To do so, select the required plane and in the **Properties** palette, enter a name in the value column for the **Name** parameter. The reference planes can be named as Sash, Glazing, and Exterior.

Figure 10-52 *The right elevation view with three reference planes*

Creating a Solid Sweep

The next step is to create a solid sweep for the window frame using the **Sweep** tool in the required view. To use this tool, you need a profile and a path. To sketch a path, change the current view to the **Placement Side** view and then choose the **Sweep** tool from the **Forms** panel of the **Create** tab; the screen will enter into the sketch mode. Invoke the **Sketch Path** tool from the **Sweep** panel of the **Modify | Sweep** tab, and sketch the path similar to the shape of the opening. Make sure that the path and the opening overlap each other. After sketching the 2D path, choose the **Finish Edit Mode** button from the **Mode** panel of the **Modify | Sweep > Sketch Path** tab; the path will be sketched and the **Modify| Sweep** tab will be displayed.

Next, you need to sketch the profile for creating the solid sweep feature. To do so, choose the **Select Profile** tool and then the **Edit Profile** tool from the **Sweep** panel of the **Modify | Sweep** tab; the **Go To View** dialog box will be displayed. Select the required view from the dialog box and choose the **Open View** button; the corresponding view will open with a wall and a red circular symbol. This symbol represents the point of intersection of the path and the profile. Sketch the profile using the sketching tool from the **Draw** panel of the **Modify | Sweep > Edit Profile** tab and then choose the **Finish Edit Mode** button from the **Mode** panel. Next, choose the **Finish Edit Mode** button from the **Mode** panel of the **Modify | Sweep** tab to create the sweep geometry. Figure 10-53 shows a circular profile sketched on the right elevation view with the red symbol at the center. Open the 3D view and choose **Visual Style > Shaded** from **View Control Bar**. Figure 10-54 shows the 3D view of the sweep. This completes the geometry of the window frame.

Using Massing Tools

Figure 10-53 A circular profile sketched in the right elevation view

Figure 10-54 The 3D view of the sweep created

Adding the Sash to the Window

After creating the geometry for the window, you need to add sash or frame to the window using the **Extrusion** tool. Before you invoke the **Extrusion** tool, you need to change the current view to the **Placement Side** view and then set the work plane. To do so, first double- click on **Placement Side** under the **Elevations** head in the **Project Browser** and then invoke the **Set** tool from the **Work Plane** panel of the **Create** tab; the **Work Plane** dialog box will be displayed. In this dialog box, ensure that the **Name** radio button is selected, and then select **Reference Plane : Sash** from the drop-down list displayed next to the **Name** radio button. Now, choose **OK**; the current work plane will be set. Now, invoke the **Extrusion** tool from the **Forms** panel of the **Create** tab; the **Modify | Create Extrusion** tab will be displayed. In the **Options Bar**, enter values for the depth and the offset for extrusion in the **Depth** and **Offset** edit boxes. Next, invoke the **Pick Lines** tool from the **Draw** panel and click to pick the inner lines and arc by using the TAB key. Again, pick the lines and arc that you just added to create an offset. Next, to create an extrusion geometry, choose the **Finish Edit Mode** button from the **Mode** panel. Figure 10-55 shows the offset created for sash in the **Placement Side** view after selecting it. The depth and offset values of extrusion are set to **0'3"(76 mm)**.

Figure 10-55 Offset created for the solid extrusion of the sash in the **Placement Side** view

Creating Panels

After adding sash, you need to add wooden panels using the **Extrusion** tool. To do so, choose the **Extrusion** tool from the **Forms** panel. Next, sketch the panel in any pattern using the appropriate sketching tool and then extrude the sketch. Figure 10-56 shows a vertical panel and a horizontal panel created using the **Rectangle** sketch tool. Next, to create an extrusion geometry, choose the **Finish Edit Mode** button from the **Mode** panel. Figure 10-57 shows the 3D view of the window with sash and panels.

Figure 10-56 *The vertical and horizontal panels created using the **Rectangle** sketch tool*

Figure 10-57 *3D view of the window with sash and panels*

Adding the Glass

The next step after creating panels is to add glass to the window using the **Extrusion** tool. To add the glass, invoke the **Set** tool from the **Work Plane** panel; the **Work Plane** dialog box will be displayed. From the **Name** drop-down list, select the reference plane sketched earlier to place the glass. Open the required view and invoke the **Extrusion** tool. Enter the required values for depth and offset in the **Depth** and **Offset** edit boxes in **Options Bar**. Using the **Pick Lines** tool from the **Draw** panel, pick the inner sides of sash and lock them. Locking the sides will enable them to change according to the geometry. Figure 10-58 shows the locked lines for creating the glass. Choose the **Finish Edit Mode** button to complete the sketch.

Figure 10-58 *Lines picked and locked to add the glass*

Using Massing Tools

Assigning Materials

Once you have created the arch-shaped window with frame and panels, the next step is to assign materials to different components of the arch-shaped window. To do so, choose the **Materials** tool from the **Settings** panel of the **Manage** tab; the **Material Browser** dialog box will be displayed. In this dialog box, double-click on the name of the desired material in the **Autodesk Materials** area; the material will be displayed in the **Project Materials: All** area. Next, select the **Duplicate Selected Material** option from the **Creates or duplicates a material** drop-down list located at the lower left corner of the **Material Browser** dialog box; the material will be duplicated and displayed in the **Project Materials: All** area. Select the duplicated material, if it is not selected, and right-click; a shortcut menu will be displayed. Choose the **Rename** option from this menu and rename the material.

Now to apply this material, you need to select the required category and then apply the material to that category. To do so, invoke the **Family Category and Parameters** tool from the **Properties** panel of the **Create** tab; the **Family Category and Parameters** dialog box will be displayed. Ensure that the **Architecture** check box is selected in the **Filter list** drop-down list. Select the **Windows** category from the **Family Category** area and choose the **OK** button. Now, you need to assign this material to the required components of the window such as solid sweep and sash.

To assign the materials, select the sweep geometry in the **Placement Side** view or the 3D view and in the **Properties** palette, set the value for the **Subcategory** parameter to **Frame/Mullion**. In the **Material** parameter, click in the value column; a browse button will be displayed on the right. Choose the Browse button; the **Materials Browser** dialog box will be displayed. In the **Project Materials: All** area of this dialog box, select the material that you have duplicated or renamed and choose the **OK** button to apply it. You can also edit the visibility/graphics overrides by choosing the **Edit** button in the **Value** column for the **Visibility/Graphics Overrides** parameter. Choose the **Apply** button in the **Properties** palette. Open the 3D view and choose **Visual Style > Shaded** from **View Control Bar** to view the assigned material in the shade mode. Similarly, select the solid extrusion created for the sash and panels and assign the material as explained above. You can assign the same material or select any other material from the **Material Browser** dialog box. To apply a glass material to the solid extrusion of glass, select the extrusion and then set the value for the **Subcategory** and **Material** parameters to **Glass** in the **Properties** palette. Next, choose the **Apply** button. Open the 3D view and then view the family in the shade mode. Figure 10-59 shows 3D view of an arch-shaped window with panels after assigning the Wood/Oak, Red, Stained, and Dark Polished material to the frame. The procedure for assigning materials is discussed in detail in Chapter 15.

Figure 10-59 The final 3D view of the arch-shaped window with panels

Creating Family Types

After creating family, you need to create family types by assigning different dimensions to geometry. To create family types, invoke the **Family Types** tool from the **Properties** panel in the **Create** tab; the **Family Types** dialog box will be displayed, as shown in Figure 10-60. Choose the **New** button from the **Family Types** area; the **Name** dialog box will be displayed. Enter a name in the **Name** dialog box and choose the **OK** button to save the settings by this name. Change the value of the **Height** and **Width** parameters and choose the **OK** button. You have finished creating one of the family types of the window. Similarly, assign different values to the **Height** and **Width** parameters and name the types accordingly. Figure 10-61 shows the family types created for the arch-shaped window family in the **Name** drop-down list. Select the window and then select the types from the **Name** drop-down list to check whether the window changes according to the type selected.

*Figure 10-60 The **Family Types** dialog box*

Using Massing Tools

*Figure 10-61 The **Name** drop-down list displaying different window types*

Loading the Family

Once you have created the family, you need to save it and then load it into the required project. Save the family at the required location and choose the **Load into Project** option from the **Family Editor** panel in the **Modify** tab, to load it into the current project. Once you have loaded the family, you will notice that the family types will be added to the **Type Selector** drop-down list after invoking the **Place Component** tool. Figure 10-62 shows the family types of the arch-shaped window added to the **Type Selector** drop-down list. Select the window loaded and verify if the window changes based on the types selected from the **Type Selector** drop-down list. If the family types are not responding, select and edit that particular type. This happens mostly when the elements are not locked.

*Figure 10-62 The **Type Selector** drop-down list*

TUTORIAL
Tutorial 1   Office Building 2

In this tutorial, you will create massing geometry for a five-story office building based on the shape shown in Figure 10-63. It consists of a 50'0" X 50'0" (15240 X 15240 mm) central hall that is 60'0" (18288 mm) high. It has a 30'0"(9144 mm) diameter cylindrical atrium with a hemispherical dome at the top level. The central hall is flanked by the right and left wings that are 40'0"(12192 mm) high. The entrance area is 30'0"(9144 mm) high. Use the dimensions of the building given in the floor plan shown in Figure 10-64 and the dimensions of the elevation shown in Figure 10-65. The dimensions and the text have been given for reference and are not to be created. After creating the massing geometry, convert it into building elements with the parameters given next. **(Expected time: 1 hr 15 min)**

Figure 10-63   *3D sketch view of the office building*

1. Project parameters:
   For Imperial   Template File- *default.rte*,
                               File name to be assigned- *c10_Office-2_tut1.rvt*
                               Floor to floor height of the building - **10'0"**

   For Metric   Template File- *DefaultMetric.rte*,
                               File name to be assigned- M_*c10_Office-2_tut1.rvt*
                               Floor to floor height of the building - **3048 mm**

2. Building Element types for the converted shell elements:
   For Imperial   Floor: **Floor : LW Concrete on Metal Deck**
                             Walls: Central Hall- **Basic Wall: Exterior - Brick on CMU**

Using Massing Tools 10-37

Left and Right Wing, and Entrance- **Curtain Wall: Exterior Glazing** (Spacing 5'0" horizontal, 10'0" vertical)
Flat Roof: **Roof : Generic 9"**
Curtain system for dome: Spacing **3'6"** horizontal, **7'0"** vertical; Mullion type

For Metric   Floor: **Floor : LW Concrete on Metal Deck**
Walls: Central Hall- **Basic Wall: Exterior - Brick on CMU**
Left and Right Wing, and Entrance- **Curtain Wall: Exterior Glazing** (Spacing 1524 mm horizontal, 3048 mm vertical)
Flat Roof: **Roof : Generic 400 mm**
Curtain system for dome: Spacing **1067 mm** horizontal, **2134 mm** vertical; Mullion type

The following steps are required to complete this tutorial:

a. Open a new project file, using the default template file.
b. Add levels using the **Level** tool.
c. Create a massing geometry using the **Form** tool, refer to Figures 10-66 through 10-69.
d. Cut the geometry based on the sketch plan to create the atrium and the entrance using the **Void Form** tool, refer to Figures 10-70 through 10-73.
e. Use the **Solid Form** tool to generate the atrium dome, refer to Figures 10-74 through 10-76.
f. Convert the massing geometry into the specified building elements, refer to Figures 10-77 through 10-81.

Figure 10-64 Sketch plan for the office building

Figure 10-65 Elevation for the office building

Opening the Project File and Adding Levels

You need to first open a new project file using the **New** tool. As the building is five-story high, you need to create four additional levels and rename them according to the floor levels.

1. Choose **New > Project** from the **Application Menu**; the **New Project** dialog box is displayed.

2. Select the **Architectural Template** option from the drop-down list in the **Template file** area, if it is not selected by default.

3. Choose the **OK** button to close the **New Project** dialog box; the new project file is opened in the drawing window.

4. In the **Project Browser**, double-click on **South** in the **Elevations (Building Elevation)** head to display the corresponding view.

5. Choose the **Level** tool from the **Datum** panel in the **Architecture** tab.

6. Add four levels above level 2 at an elevation of 10'0" (3048 mm) each. (For more information on adding levels, refer to Adding Levels section in Chapter 6)

7. Rename the levels as follows:
   Level 1- First Floor
   Level 2- Second Floor
   Level 3- Third Floor
   Level 4- Fourth Floor
   Level 5- Fifth Floor
   Level 6- Roof

   While renaming the levels, choose the **Yes** button in the **Revit** conformation box to rename the corresponding views.

Creating the Massing Geometry

Now, you can start creating the massing geometry using the tools for massing. The central hall and the two wings can be generated using the **Form** tool.

Note
The massing geometry can be created using different methods and tools. The steps given below describe a general procedure to create massing geometry. The steps and methods may vary depending on the design intent.

1. Double-click on the **First Floor** under the **Floor Plans** head in the **Project Browser** to display the corresponding plan.

2. Choose the **In-Place Mass** tool from the **Conceptual Mass** panel of the **Massing & Site** tab; the **Massing - Show Mass Enabled** message box is displayed.

3. Choose **Close** from this message box; the **Name** dialog box is displayed.

4. In the **Name** edit box of the **Name** dialog box, enter the name **Central Hall** and then choose the **OK** button.

Using Massing Tools   10-39

5. Invoke the **Rectangle** sketching tool from the **Draw** panel of the **Create** tab.

6. Move the cursor in the area lying in the mid of the four elevation tags and sketch a square with 50'0"(15240 mm) side. After sketching the square, choose the **Modify** button.

7. Now, select the created square and choose the **Solid Form** tool from **Modify|Lines > Form > Create Form** drop-down; the **Modify |Form** tab is displayed.

8. Next, choose the **Default 3D** tool from the **Create** panel of the **View** tab; the 3D view of the mass created is displayed.

9. Now, move the cursor over the top face of the box created, refer to Figure 10-66, and click when the edges of the faces are highlighted. On doing so, two temporary dimensions are highlighted.

10. Click on the dimension value of the lower dimension (dimension that specifies the height of the box) and enter **60' (18288 mm)** in the edit box. Now, press ENTER; the box is resized to the height 60' (18288 mm).

11. Choose the **Modify** button and then right-click in the drawing area; a shortcut menu is displayed. Choose **Zoom To Fit** from the shortcut menu; the box created can now be viewed completely.

12. Now, choose the **Finish Mass** button from the **In-Place Editor** panel of the **Modify** tab; the Central Hall massing is created.

   Similarly, you need to create the left and right wings of the building using the **Form** tool. You will sketch the profile in the first floor plan view and extrude it to a height of 40'0" (12192 mm), as specified in the sketch plan.

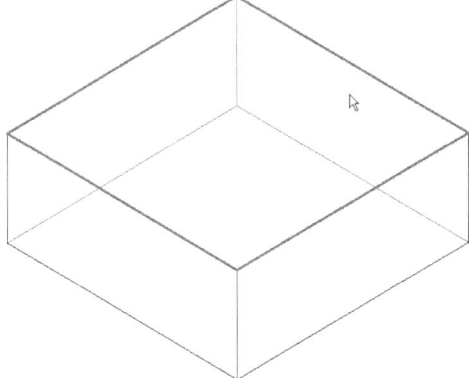

Figure 10-66 Selecting the top face of the central hall

13. You will create the mass for left and right wings of the building, double-click on **First Floor** under the **Floor Plans** head in the **Project Browser** to display the corresponding plan.

14. Now, choose the **In-Place Mass** tool from the **Conceptual Mass** panel of the **Massing & Site** tab; the **Name** dialog box is displayed.

15. In the **Name** dialog box, enter the name **Wings** and choose the **OK** button.

16. Invoke the **Line** tool from the **Draw** panel of the **Create** tab and ensure that the **Chain** check box is selected in the **Options Bar**.

17. Move the cursor near the lower right corner of the square and sketch the profile based on the dimensions given in the sketch plan, refer to Figure 10-64. The profile for the right wing is sketched, as shown in Figure 10-67.

    Note that the sketch for the wings should be a closed sketch.

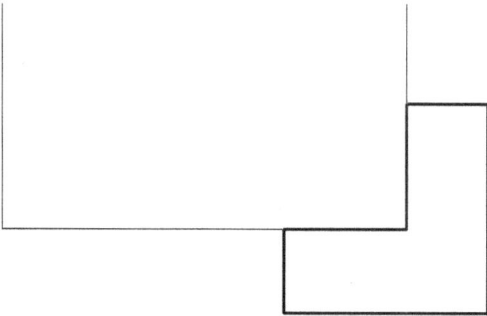

Figure 10-67 Sketched profile for the right wing

18. Choose the **Modify** button from the **Select** panel to clear the current selection.

19. Now, select the sketched profile for the right wing and choose the **Mirror - Draw Axis** tool from the **Modify** panel of the **Modify | Lines** tab.

20. Draw a line from the top right corner to the bottom left corner of the central square to define the mirror axis line. The profile is mirrored at the diagonally opposite corner of the square, as shown in Figure 10-68.

21. Now, ensure that the mirrored profile is selected and the **Modify | Lines** tab is chosen.

22. Choose the **Solid Form** tool from the **Modify | Lines > Form > Create Form** drop-down.

23. Next, select the other profile at the lower right corner and repeat Step 22.

24. Choose the **Modify** button from the **Select** panel and then choose the **Default 3D** tool from the **Create** panel of the **View** tab; the 3D view of the mass created is displayed.

25. Now move the cursor over the top face of the created mass marked as A (refer to Figure 10-68) and then click on the face when it is highlighted. On doing so, two temporary dimensions are displayed.

Using Massing Tools   10-41

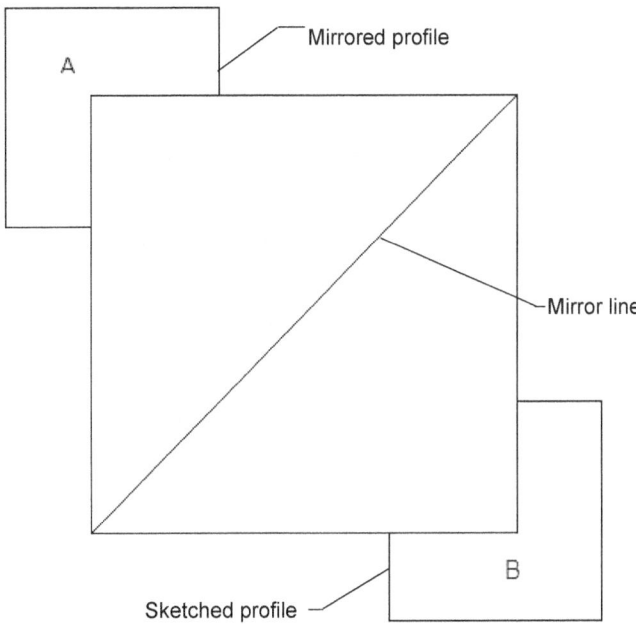

Figure 10-68 *Creating a mirror copy of the sketched profile*

26. Click on the dimension value of the lower displayed dimension and enter **40'** in the edit box.

27. After entering the value in the edit box, press ENTER; the selected face of the mass will be extended to a height of 40' from the First Floor level and mass corresponding to it is resized.

28. Next, select the top face of the other mass marked B and repeat step 25 to 27.

29. Now, after you create the masses for the wings, choose the **Modify** button in the **Select** panel; the current selection is cleared.

30. Now, choose the **Finish Mass** button from the **In-Place Editor** panel of the **Modify** tab; the masses for the wings are created.

31. Now, move the cursor over the **ViewCube** tool and right-click; a shortcut menu is displayed. Choose **Orient to a Direction > Northeast Isometric** from the shortcut menu; the 3D view of the created mass geometry is displayed, as shown in Figure 10-69.

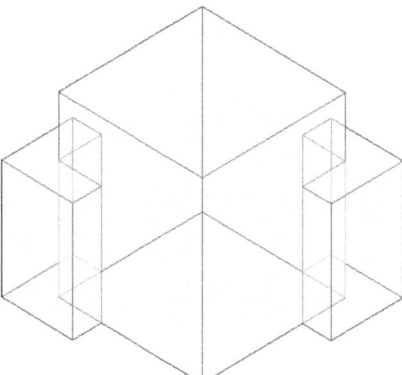

*Figure 10-69 The **Northeast Isometric** view of the central hall and the two wings*

Cutting the Massing Geometry

After creating the desired building block, you can now cut them to create the atrium and the entrance. The **Void Form** tool can be used to create the desired void geometry.

1. Double-click on **First Floor** under the **Floor Plans** head in the **Project Browser** to display the first floor plan view.

2. Choose the **Central Square** hall; the **Modify | Mass** tab is displayed.

3. Choose the **Edit In-Place** tool from the **Model** panel of the **Modify | Mass** tab; the **Modify** tab is displayed.

4. Next, choose **Visual Style > Wireframe** from **View Control Bar**.

5. Draw reference planes diagonally to locate the center of the square by using the **Plane** tool from the **Draw** panel of the **Modify** tab. After creating the reference planes, choose the **Modify** button from the **Select** panel to clear the current selection.

6. Now, invoke the **Circle** tool from the **Draw** panel of the **Modify** tab.

7. Move the cursor at the center of the square. Use the reference planes to locate the center and click to specify it.

8. Move the cursor to the right and enter the value **15'0"**. Next, press ENTER; the circle of **30'0"** diameter is created. Now, press ESC twice to exit and then select the circle created.

9. Choose the **Void Form** tool from **Modify | Lines > Form > Create Form** drop-down; two circular images are displayed.

10. Choose the left image and then choose the **View** tab. Next, choose the **Default 3D** tool from the **Create** panel; the 3D view of the mass created is displayed.

Using Massing Tools

11. Now, select the two segments of the circle profile of the void created by using the CTRL key, as shown in Figure 10-70. On selecting the segments, the corresponding pivot points are displayed. Hold and drag the blue segments till they cross the upper face of the central hall. Choose the **Modify** button.

Figure 10-70 *The segments selected for the circular void*

12. Now, double-click on **First Floor** under the **Floor Plans** head in the **Project Browser** to display the corresponding plan.

13. Next, choose the **Modify** tab and invoke the **Center-ends Arc** tool from the **Draw** panel.

14. Move the cursor to the center of the atrium circle and then click. Next, move the cursor horizontally toward the left and enter the value **20'0"** to specify the radius. Now, press ENTER.

15. Move the cursor counterclockwise and click to create a quarter arc, as shown in Figure 10-71.

Figure 10-71 *Sketching an arc to create a cutting geometry*

16. Choose the **Line** sketching tool and ensure that the **Chain** check box is selected.

17. Sketch the profile of the cutting geometry, as shown in Figure 10-72.

Figure 10-72 *Profile of the cutting geometry*

18. Choose the **Modify** button from the **Select** panel and then select the profile that was created recently.

19. Choose the **Void Form** tool from **Modify | Lines > Form > Create Form** drop-down; the void mass will be created.

20. Next, choose the **View** tab and then choose the **Default 3D** tool from the **Create** panel; the 3D view of the created mass is displayed.

21. Now, move and place the cursor over the **ViewCube** tool and right-click; a shortcut menu is displayed.

22. Choose **Orient to a Direction > Front Left Isometric** from the shortcut menu.

23. Next, select the top face of the void geometry created, as shown in Figure 10-73.

24. After selecting the top face, click on the dimension value of the temporary dimension that is displayed at the bottom. Enter **30'** in the displayed edit box and press ENTER.

25. Now, choose the **Modify** button from the **Select** panel and then choose the **Finish Mass** button from the **In-Place Editor** panel of the **Modify** tab.

26. Next, right-click on the drawing area and choose **Zoom To Fit** from the shortcut menu.

Using Massing Tools

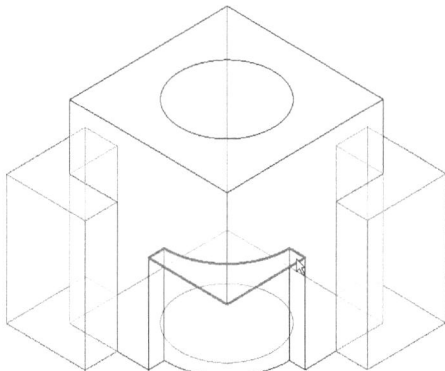

Figure 10-73 Selecting the face of the void geometry to edit the height

27. Choose the **Finish Mass tool** from the **In-Place Editor** panel of the **Modify** tab.

Creating the Atrium Dome

The atrium dome can be added using the **Form** tool. It is a hemispherical dome having a radius of 20'0"(6096 mm) same as the radius of the atrium.

1. Choose the **In-Place Mass** tool from the **Conceptual Mass** panel of the **Massing & Site** tab; the **Name** dialog box is displayed.

2. In this dialog box, enter **Dome** in the **Name** edit box and choose the **OK** button.

3. Choose the **Set** tool from the **Work Plane** panel of the **Create** tab; you are prompted to pick a plane.

4. Select the right side entrance wall as the work plane, as shown in Figure 10-74. Note that to confirm that the selected face has been assigned the current work plane, choose the **Show** button from the **Work Plane** panel of the **Create** tab; the selected plane is highlighted.

5. Now, choose the **Reference** tool from the **Draw** panel of the **Create** tab and invoke the **Line** tool.

Figure 10-74 Selecting the right side entrance wall as the work plane

6. Sketch the reference lines for the dome, as shown in Figure 10-75.

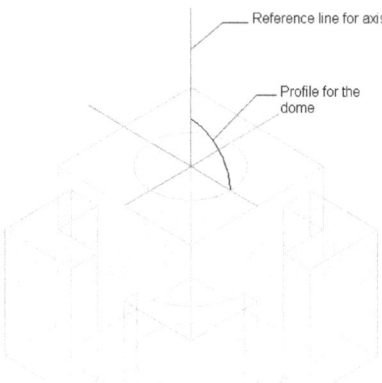

Figure 10-75 *The reference line and the profile for the dome*

7. Now, choose the **Model** tool from the **Draw** panel of the **Modify** tab and then invoke the **Center-ends Arc** sketching tool from the **Draw** panel.

8. Using the center of the atrium roof as the center of the curve, sketch a quarter arc, refer to Figure 10-75. Next, choose the **Modify** button to clear the current selection.

9. Select the reference line that defines the vertical axis and then select the arc using the CTRL Key, refer to Figure 10-75.

10. Now, choose the **Solid Form** tool from the **Form** panel; the dome will be created, as shown in Figure 10-76.

11. Choose the **Finish Mass** button from the **In-Place Editor** panel of the **Modify** tab to finish the creation of the dome geometry. Ignore the warning message displayed, if any. Now, choose the **Modify** button from the **Select** panel.

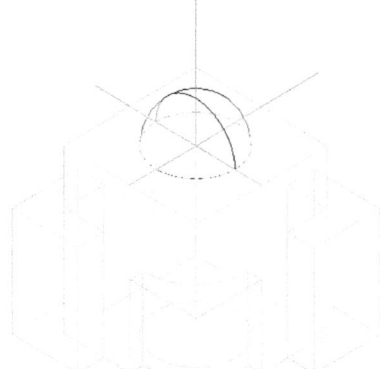

Figure 10-76 *The dome created for the Atrium*

Using Massing Tools

Converting Massing Geometry into Building Elements

You can now convert the massing geometry into building elements using the **Floor**, **Wall**, and **Roof** tools. In order to create floors, you must first create different floor area faces.

1. Select the **Central Hall** and **Wings** massing geometries by holding the CTRL key; the **Modify | Mass** tab is displayed.

2. Choose the **Mass Floors** tool from the **Model** panel; the **Mass Floors** dialog box is displayed.

3. In the **Mass Floors** dialog box, select the check boxes for all the floors and choose the **OK** button; the floor area faces are created for the selected floors. Now, choose the **Modify** button.

4. Next, choose the **Floor** tool from the **Model by Face** panel of the **Massing & Site** tab; the **Modify | Place Floor by Face** tab is displayed.

5. In the **Properties** palette, select **Floor: LW Concrete on Metal Deck** from the **Type Selector** drop-down list.

6. Using the crossing window, select all the floor faces and then choose the **Create Floor** tool from the **Multiple Selection** panel; Autodesk Revit Architecture creates floors at the floor area faces. Now, choose **Visual Style > Shaded** from the **View Control Bar**. The shaded view of the model is shown in Figure 10-77.

7. Now, choose the **Wall** tool from the **Model by Face** panel of the **Massing & Site** tab; the **Modify | Place Wall** tab is displayed.

8. In the **Properties** palette, select the **Basic Wall : Exterior - Brick on CMU** wall type from the **Type Selector** drop-down list.

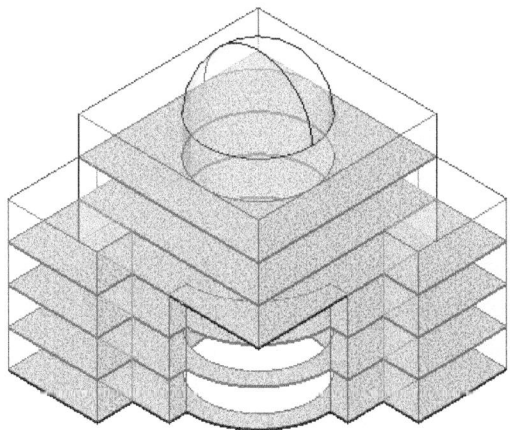

Figure 10-77 Floor areas of the massing converted into floors

9. Now, move the cursor over the central hall massing geometry and when an exterior wall is highlighted, click to convert the wall face into the selected wall type.

10. Similarly, click on the other exterior walls of the central hall including the two side walls of the entrance. The resultant 3D view is shown in Figure 10-78.

Figure 10-78 Converting the massing into walls

11. Next, in the **Properties** palette, select the **Curtain Wall : Exterior Glazing** wall type from the **Type Selector** drop-down list.

12. Choose the **Edit Type** button in the **Properties** palette ; the **Type Properties** dialog box is displayed.

13. In the **Type Properties** dialog box, enter **5'0"(1524 mm)** in the **Value** field of the **Spacing** parameter in the **Vertical Grid** category and **10'0"(3048 mm)** for the **Spacing** parameter in the **Horizontal Grid** category.

14. Now, choose **Apply** and **OK**; the **Type Properties** dialog box is closed and the specified parameters are applied to the selected type.

15. Next, highlight and click on the exterior walls of the right and left wings to convert them into the selected exterior glazing walls.

16. Similarly, convert the curved entrance wall into the exterior glazing wall type. The 3D view now appears similar to the illustration shown in Figure 10-79. Now, choose the **Modify** button.

Using Massing Tools 10-49

Figure 10-79 Converting the entrance wall massing into walls

17. Next, choose the **Roof** tool from the **Model by Face** panel of the **Massing & Site** tab; the **Modify | Place Roof by Face** tab is displayed.

18. In the **Type Selector** drop-down list, select the specified roof type.
    For Imperial   **Basic Roof : Generic - 9"**
    For Metric   **Basic Roof : Generic - 400 mm**

19. Highlight the roof face of the central hall and click.

20. Now, choose the **Create Roof** tool from the **Multiple Selection** panel of the **Modify | Place Roof by Face** tab; the roof is created on the selected face.

21. Similarly, create the roof of the same type for the two wings. After creating the roofs, the 3D view appears similar to the one shown in Figure 10-80. Next, you will create the curtain wall system for the dome.

22. To create a curtain system for the dome, choose the **Curtain System** tool from the **Model by face** panel of the **Massing & Site** tab; the **Modify | Place Curtain System by Face** tab is displayed.

23. Choose the **Type Properties** tool from the **Properties** panel; the **Type Properties** dialog box is displayed.

Figure 10-80 Converting the massing into roof

24. Choose the **Duplicate** button; the **Name** dialog box is displayed. Enter **3'6" X 7'0"** (**1067 x 2134 mm**) in the edit box and then choose the **OK** button.

25. Enter the values **7'0"** (**2134 mm**) and **3'6"**(**1067 mm**) in the **Value** fields of the **Spacing** parameters under the **Grid 1 Pattern** and **Grid 2 Pattern** categories, respectively.

26. Choose the **OK** button; the **Type Properties** dialog box is closed.

27. Now, select both the curved faces of the dome and then choose the **Create System** tool from the **Multiple Selection** panel of the **Modify | Place Curtain System by Face** tab. The curved surfaces of the dome are converted into curtain systems. Now, choose the **Modify** button.

28. Next, you need to add a door to the entrance. To start with, choose the **Insert** tab and then choose the **Load Family** tool from the **Load from Library** panel; the **Load Family** dialog box is displayed.

29. In this dialog box, browse to the **US Imperial > Doors** folder and then choose the **Curtain Wall Dbl Glass** family file. After choosing the file, choose **Open**; the selected file is loaded in the drawing.

30. Choose the **Modify** button and then select the two curtain panels of the exterior glazing by the window selection process.

31. Invoke the **Filter** tool from the right end of the **Status Bar**; the **Filter** dialog box is displayed.

32. In the **Filter** dialog box clear all the check boxes except the **Curtain Panel** check box and then choose the **OK** button; the **Filter** dialog box is closed and selection is done, as shown in Figure 10-81.

Using Massing Tools

Figure 10-81 *Selecting panels from the glazing*

33. From the **Type Selector** drop-down list, select the **Curtain Wall Dbl Glass** option. Next, choose the **Modify** button.

34. To add mullions to the exterior glazing, choose the **Mullion** tool from the **Build** panel of the **Architecture** tab; the **Modify | Place Mullion** tab is displayed.

35. In the **Type Selector** drop-down list, select the desired mullion type
    For Imperial   **Rectangular Mullion : 1" Square**
    For Metric   **Rectangular Mullion : 30 mm Square**.

36. Next, choose the **All Grid Lines** tool from the **Placement** panel and move the cursor over the exterior glazings. Click on each face of the glazing when it is highlighted. Add all the curtain systems to the project, including the exterior wing walls, the curved entrance wall, and the dome. Use the **Grid Line Segment** tool from the **Placement** panel to add grids, if required.

    The completed 3D view of the project appears similar to the one shown in Figure 10-63.

37. Choose **Save As > Project** from the **Application Menu**; the **Save As** dialog box is displayed.

38. Enter **c10_Office-2_tut1** in the **File name** edit box and choose **Save**; the file is saved.

39. Now, choose **Close** from the **Application Menu** to close the Autodesk Revit Architecture session.

Tutorial 2   Architectural Column

In this tutorial, you will create an architectural column as shown in Figure 10-82. Some of the dimensions are given and some are to be assumed. After creating the massing geometry, load it into the project to apply in a building model, refer to Figure 10-83.

(Expected Time: 50 min)

1. Project parameters:
   For Imperial   Template File- *Generic Model.rfa*,
                    File name to be assigned- *c10_archicolumn_tut2.rvt*
                    Floor to floor height of the column - **10'0"**

   For Metric   Template File- *Metric Generic Model.rfa*,
                    File name to be assigned- *M_c10_archicolumn_tut2.rvt*
                    Floor to floor height of the column - **3048 mm**

Figure 10-82 An architectural column

Figure 10-83 An architectural column in a building Model

Using Massing Tools

The following steps are required to complete this tutorial:

a. Open a new family using the default template file.
b. Create reference planes using the **Reference Planes** tool, refer to Figures 10-84 through 10-90.
c. Create the architectural column using the **Forms** tool, refer to Figures 10-91 through 10-98.
d. Cut the geometry based on the sketch plan using the **Void Form** tool, refer to Figures 10-100 through 10-104.
e. Modify the column by assigning material.
f. Download and open the project file.
g. Use the Family and load it into the project, refer to Figures 10-107 through 10-109.

Opening the Family and Creating Reference Planes

In this section, you will create reference planes to form the architectural column.

1. Choose **New > Family** from the **Application Menu**; the **New Family - Select Template File** dialog box is displayed.

2. In this dialog box, browse to the *English_I folder* (*English folder* for Metric) and select the **Generic Model.rft (Metric Generic Model.rft)** template file. Now, choose the **Open** button; the selected template file is opened.

3. In the **Project Browser**, double-click on **Back** under the **Elevations (Elevation 1)** head; the corresponding view is displayed.

4. Choose the **Reference Plane** tool from the **Datum** panel in the **Create** tab; the **Modify |Place Reference Plane** contextual tab is displayed.

5. Choose the **Line** tool from the **Draw** panel, if it is not selected by default.

   Now, you will create reference planes.

6. Move the cursor to the left end of the **Reference level** and then move the cursor upwards till the alignment line appears.

7. Enter 8" in the edit box displayed, as shown in Figure 10-84 and press ENTER; the cursor snap appears. Now, draw the reference plane by dragging the cursor in the horizontal direction as shown in Figure 10-85.

Figure 10-84 Entering value 8" on the appearance of alignment line

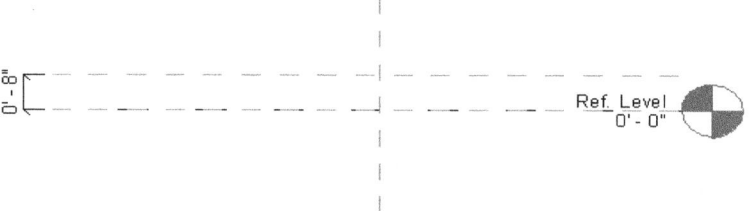

Figure 10-85 Reference plane drawn at a height of 8"

8. Similarly, sketch other reference planes at heights 6"(152 mm), 6"(152 mm), 9'(2743 mm), 6"(152 mm), 1'(305 mm), and 8"(203 mm), as shown in Figure 10-86. Choose the **Modify** tool from the **Select** panel to clear the selection.

9. Select the **Center(Left/Right)** reference plane; a pinned symbol is displayed. Click on this symbol to unpin it. Next, drag the vertical reference line so that it crosses the topmost reference line, as shown in Figure 10-87.

10. Click anywhere in the drawing area; the selection is cleared.

Using Massing Tools

Figure 10-86 Reference planes drawn at specified heights

Figure 10-87 The **Center(Left/Right)** reference plane stretched to the top

Next, you will sketch vertical reference plane.

11. Invoke the **Reference Plane** tool from the **Datum** panel of the **Create** tab; the **Modify | Place Reference Plane** contextual tab is displayed.

12. In this tab, the **Line** tool is chosen by default. Now, place the cursor at the bottom of the **Center(Left/Right)** reference plane and then move the cursor toward left; an alignment line appears. Enter 6"(152 mm) in the edit box displayed, as shown in Figure 10-88 and press ENTER. Move the cursor in vertical direction and draw a line parallel to the **Center(Left/Right)** reference plane, as shown in Figure 10-89.

Figure 10-88 Drawing 6" reference plane to the left of the **Center(Left/Right)** reference plane

13. Similarly, sketch other reference planes each at a distance of 6"(152 mm), 2"(51 mm), and 4"(102 mm) from the respective drawn reference planes, as shown in Figure 10-90.

*Figure 10-89 Vertical reference plane drawn to the left of the **Center(Left/Right)** reference plane*

*Figure 10-90 Vertical reference planes drawn to the left of the **Center(Left/Right)** reference plane at specified distances*

14. Repeat the procedure followed in steps 11 through 13 to sketch the vertical reference planes at the other side of the **Center(Left/Right)** reference plane.

15. Press the ESC button to clear the selection.

Creating the Architectural column

Now, you will create an architectural column using the **Extrusion** and **Void Extrusion** tools.

1. In the **Project Browser**, double-click on **Front** in the **Elevation (Elevation 1)** head; the front view is displayed in the drawing.

2. Right-click on the drawing area; a shortcut menu is displayed. Choose the **Zoom to Fit** tool to fit the drawing.

3. Choose the **Extrusion** tool from the **Forms** panel of the **Create** tab; the **Modify|Create Extrusion** contextual tab is displayed.

4. Invoke the **Rectangle** sketching tool in the **Draw** panel of the **Modify|Create Extrusion** tab.

5. Move the cursor in the drawing and draw a rectangle of 10' x 2' (3048 x 610 mm) starting at a point where the third reference plane from the top intersects the second reference

Using Massing Tools

plane at the left of the **Center(Left/Right)** reference plane. The rectangle ends at the point where sixth reference plane from the top intersects the second reference plane to the right of the **Center(Left/ Right)** reference plane, refer to Figures 10-91 and 10-92.

Figure 10-91 Starting Point to draw a rectangle   *Figure 10-92* End point of a rectangle

5. Choose the **Finish Edit Mode** button from the **Mode** panel of the **Modify|Create Extrusion** contextual tab; the **Modify | Extrusion** contextual is displayed.

6. In the **Properties** palette, enter **7'10" (2388 mm)** in the **Extrusion Start** value field. Similarly, enter **10' (3048 mm)** in the **Extrusion End** value field. Choose the **Apply** button to apply the changes and then press ESC; the selection is cleared.

   Now, you will create the base of the column.

7. Choose the **Extrusion** tool from the **Forms** panel of the **Create** tab; the **Modify | Create Extrusion** tab is displayed.

8. Invoke the **Rectangle** tool from the **Draw** panel of this tab.

9. Place the cursor at the intersection of the reference planes, which is next to the left corner of the column at the base. Now, click to draw a rectangle starting from point P1, and ending rectangle at point P2, as shown in Figure 10-93 and Figure 10-94.

10. In the **Properties** palette, enter **7'10"(2388 mm)** in the **Extrusion Start** parameter value field and enter **10'(3048 mm)** in the **Extrusion End** value field. Choose the **Apply** button to apply the changes.

11. Choose the **Finish Edit Mode** button and then press ESC.

Figure 10-93 Starting point of rectangle drawn at the base

Figure 10-94 Ending point of rectangle drawn at the base

12. Similarly, draw another rectangular base exactly below the drawn rectangle using the **Extrusion** tool, starting from the point P3 and ending at point P4, as shown in Figure 10-95. Next, enter values for the **Extrusion End** and **Extrusion Start** parameters as stated earlier.

Figure 10-95 Rectangle drawn below to form the base of an architectural column

Using Massing Tools

13. Choose the **Finish Edit Mode** button to complete the rectangle and press ESC.

    Now, you will create the crown of the column.

14. Choose the **Extrusion** tool from the **Forms** panel of the **Create** tab; the **Modify | Create Extrusion** tab is displayed.

15. Invoke the **Rectangle** tool from the **Draw** panel of the contextual tab.

16. Now place the cursor at the intersection of the reference planes lying next to the left corner of the column at the top. Now, click on the point which is specified as point P5, draw a rectangle from point P5 ending at point P6, as shown in Figure 10-96.

17. Choose the **Finish Edit Mode** button from the **Mode** panel of this contextual tab.

18. In the **Properties** palette, enter **7'10" (2388 mm)** in the **Extrusion Start** parameter value field and enter **10'(3048 mm)** in the **Extrusion End** parameter, if the values are not entered. Now, choose the **Apply** button to apply the changes.

19. Now, to create the main crown of an architectural column, follow steps 14 and 16. Start drawing the rectangle at point P7 ending at point P8, as shown in Figure 10-97. In the **Properties** palette, enter values for the **Extrusion Start** and **Extrusion End** parameters as stated earlier.

20. Choose the **Finish Edit Mode** button from the **Mode** panel of the contextual tab. Figure 10-98 shows the crowns created in an architectural column.

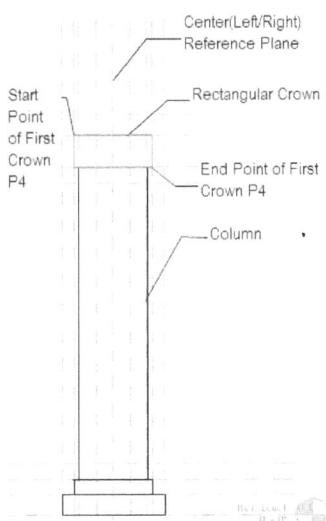

Figure 10-96 Rectangular crown of an architectural column

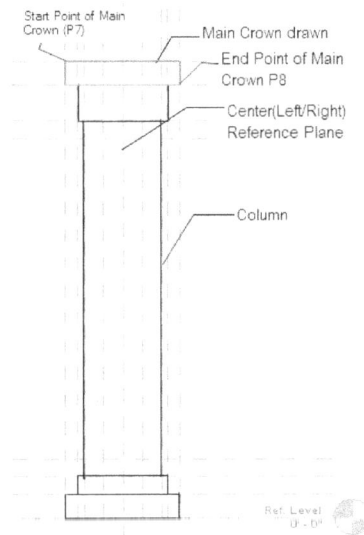

Figure 10-97 Main rectangular crown of an architectural column

Figure 10-98 Crown created in an architectural column

Cutting the Geometry

After creating the desired column mass in a family, you can cut the geometry using the **Void Forms** tool.

1. To create void in geometry, choose the **Void Extrusion** tool from **Create > Forms >Void Forms** drop-down, as shown in Figure 10-99; the **Modify | Create Void Extrusion** contextual tab is displayed.

*Figure 10-99 Invoking the **Void Exrusion** tool from the **Voids** drop-down*

2. Invoke the **Line** tool from the **Draw** panel of this tab and ensure that the **Chain** check box is selected. Draw void extrusion in the column at three reference planes inside the flange.

3. Now, move the cursor over the base of the column at the reference plane R1 inside the flange of the column and then draw a horizontal line moving in the left direction. Enter **1"** (25.4 mm) in the edit box displayed and press ENTER, as shown in Figure 10-100.

4. Move the cursor upward and enter **9' (2743 mm)** in the edit box displayed. Press ENTER and then move the cursor in the horizontal direction towards right. Enter **2"(51 mm)** in the edit box and press ENTER. Now, move the cursor downward, enter **9'** in the edit box and press ENTER. Next, move the cursor inward to complete a rectangle, as shown in Figure 10-101 through Figure 10-103. Choose the **Finish Edit Mode** button to form extrusion.

Using Massing Tools

5. In the **Properties** palette, enter **9'6" (2896 mm)** in the **Extrusion Start** parameter and enter **10'(3048 mm)** in the **Extrusion End** parameter. Choose the **Apply** button to apply the changes.

Figure 10-100 Line of 1" is drawn on the reference line inside the flange of column

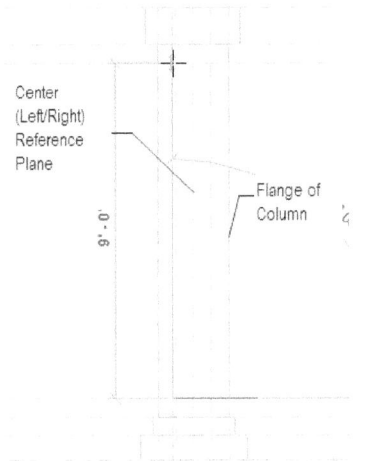

Figure 10-101 Vertical line of 9' is drawn

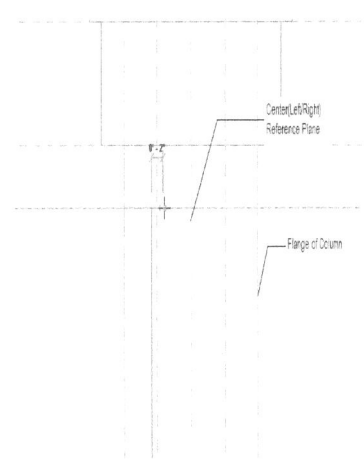

Figure 10-102 Horizontal line of 2" drawn moving towards east

Figure 10-103 Resultant Void Extrusion

6. Similarly, draw two more two void extrusions at reference planes R2, and R3, as shown in Figure 10-104 and enter values as specified for the first void extrusion in the **Properties** palette .

7. Choose the **Finish Edit Mode** button from the **Mode** panel of the **Modify|Create Void Extrusion** tab.

8. Now, select the **Default 3D** tool from the **Create** panel of the **View** tab to view the column in three dimensions. Choose the **Visual Style > Shaded** from the **View Control Bar,** the shaded view in three dimensions is displayed, as shown in Figure 10-105.

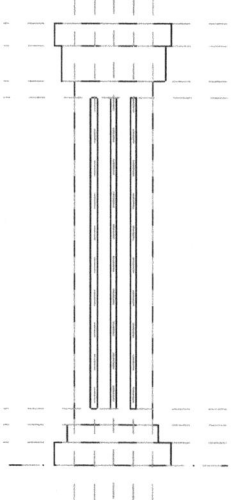

Figure 10-104 Void Extrusion formed at the three reference planes

Using Massing Tools 10-63

Figure 10-105 Three Dimensional View of an architectural column with the **Shaded** Style

Assigning Material to Column

In this section, you will assign material and then apply that material over the column.

1. Select the complete element by using the CTRL key; the **Modify|Extrusion** contextual tab is displayed.

2. In the **Properties** palette, click on the value field corresponding to the **Material** parameter under the **Material and Finishes** head; a browse button is displayed. Choose the browse button; the **Material Browser** dialog box with the **Material Editor** pane is displayed.

3. In the **Material Browser** dialog box, click on **Default** in the **Project Materials: All** area; the **Material Editor** pane displays the properties of this material.

4. In this dialog box, select the **Duplicate Selected Material** option from the **Creates or Duplicate Material** drop-down list; the material is duplicated and is displayed in the **Project Materials: All** area.

5. Select the duplicate material and right-click on it; a shortcut menu is displayed. Choose the **Rename** option from the shortcut menu and rename the material as **Concrete**.

6. Choose the **Appearance** tab in the **Material Editor** pane; the **Material Editor** pane will display the appearance properties of the selected material. Choose the **Replaces this asset** button in this tab; the **Asset Browser** dialog box is displayed.

7. In this dialog box, click on the **Appearance Library** arrow; a list of material is displayed. Select the **Concrete/Cast-In-Place** option from the list.

8. Next, select the **Flat - Broom Gray** material from the material list in the right pane in the **Asset Browser** dialog box and click on the double-arrow button; the material is assigned to the column.

9. Choose the **Close** button from the **Asset Browser** dialog box; the dialog box is closed and you can see the updated preview in the **Material Editor** pane.

10. In the **Appearance** tab, select the **Transparency** check box and set the value of the **Amount** spinner to 0 and then choose the **Apply** button to apply the changes.

11. Next, choose the **Graphics** tab in the **Material Editor** pane and select the **Use Render Appearance** check box. Choose the **Apply** button to apply the changes and then choose the **OK** button; the **Material Browser** dialog box is closed.

12. Choose **Save As > Family** from the **Application Menu**; the **Save As** dialog box is displayed. Enter **architecture_column.rfa** in the **File name** edit box, as shown in Figure 10-106. Choose the **Save** button from this dialog box; the family is saved.

Figure 10-106 The **Save As** *dialog box*

Using Massing Tools

Downloading and Opening the File

Before loading the family, you need to download the tutorial data to your computer.

1. Log on to *www.cadcim.com* and browse to the *Textbooks > Civil/GIS > Revit Architecture > Autodesk Revit Architecture 2015 for Architects and Designers*. Next, select *c14_RevitArchi2015.zip* file from the **Tutorial Files** drop-down list and then choose the corresponding **Download** button to download the data file.

2. Extract the contents of the zip folder to the following location:
    C:\RevitArchi_2015

    Notice that the *c14_RevitArchi2015* folder is created within the *RevitArchi_2015* folder.

3. Choose **Open > Project** from the **Application Menu**; the **Open** dialog box is displayed. Now, browse to *C:\Revit_Archi_2015 \ c14_RevitArchi2015 \ Tutorial \ c14_club_tut2.rvt* and choose the **Open** button.

Loading an Architectural Column in Project

In this section, you will load the architectural column in the project.

1. In the Club project, double-click on **Site Plan** in the **Floor Plans** head in the **Project Browser**; the plan will be opened in the drawing window.

2. Now, select the **architectural column-3D View{3D}** from the **Switch Windows** drop-down list in the **Windows** panel of the **View** tab; the family is displayed.

3. Choose the **Load into Project** tool from the **Family Editor** panel in the **Modify** tab; you will be prompted to place that column.

    Note
    *If more than one project is opened in Revit Architecture, then on choosing the **Load into Project** tool; the **Load into Projects** dialog box is displayed. Select the check box corresponding to the project in which you want to load the family.*

4. Now, using the **Rotate** and **Move** tools, place the column at corners C1 and C2, as shown in Figure 10-107.

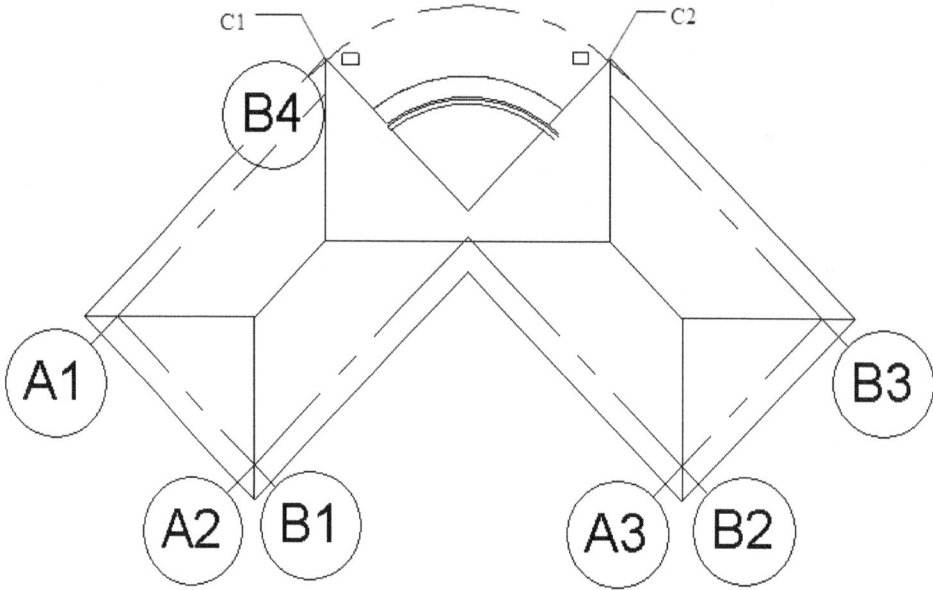

*Figure 10-107 Placing the Column at the corner using the **Rotate** and **Move** tools*

5. After placing the column, invoke the **Roof by Footprint** tool from the **Architecture > Build > Roof** drop-down; the **Modify | Create Roof Footprint** tab is displayed.

6. Sketch the roof in the arc form using the **Line** and **Start-End-Radius Arc** tools from this tab, as shown in Figure 10-108. Now, choose the **Finish Edit Mode** button from the **Mode** panel.

7. In the **Properties** palette, click on the value field corresponding to the **Base Level** parameter and select the **Roof** option from the drop-down list displayed. Similarly, click in the value field of the **Base Offset From Level** edit box and enter **-2'2"(660 mm)**. Choose the **Apply** button; the desired changes are applied to the drawing.

8. Choose the **Modify** button from the **Select** panel to clear the selection; the architectural column is loaded to the project as shown in Figure 10-109.

9. Choose **Save As > Project** from the **Application Menu**; The **Save As** dialog box is displayed. Enter required name in the **File name** edit box and choose **Save**; the project file is saved.
   For Imperial   **c10_clubarchicolumn_tut2**
   For Metric   **M_c10_clubarchicolumn_tut2**

10. Now, choose **Close** from the **Application Menu**; the file is closed.

Using Massing Tools 10-67

*Figure 10-108 Roof sketched using the **Line** and **Start-End-Radius Arc** tool*

Figure 10-109 The architectural column loaded in the project

Self-Evaluation Test

Answer the following questions and then compare them to those given at the end of this chapter:

1. The **Extrusion** tool is used to create the massing perpendicular to the sketched profile. (T/F)

2. Using the **Blend** tool, you can link two profiles at different levels. (T/F)

3. You cannot specify a negative value in the **Depth** edit box. (T/F)

4. A massing geometry once created cannot be resized. (T/F)

5. The **Void form** option is used to create a cut in a massing geometry. (T/F)

6. Which of the following dialog boxes is displayed on choosing the **Model-In Place** tool from the **Component** drop-down.

   a) **Family Category and Parameters**
   b) **Load Family**
   c) **Massing- Show Mass Enabled**
   d) **Revit**

7. Which of the following tool in the **Element** panel of the **Modify | Form** tab is used to display the geometry skeleton like vertices and edges of the mass.

   a) **Add Edge**
   b) **Add Profile**
   c) **X-Ray**
   d) **Divide Edges**

8. The _____ tool is used to add massing by sketching a profile and defining an axis.

9. The _____ tool is used to specify the connection of vertices while using the **Blend** tool.

10. Using the _____ tool, you can display or hide a massing geometry.

11. The start point and endpoint of a solid extrusion can be specified in the _____ dialog box.

12. To modify a massing geometry, select it and choose the _____ button from the **Options Bar** to modify its profile and properties.

Review Questions

Answer the following questions:

1. The drag controls can be used to resize a massing geometry. (T/F)

2. You can use the editing tools such as **Move**, **Mirror**, **Copy**, and so on while sketching a massing geometry. (T/F)

3. The **Blend** tool extrudes a profile along a defined path. (T/F)

4. You can extrude multiple closed profiles using the **Extrude** tool. (T/F)

5. The **Work Plane** tool can be used to define a plane in which the profile is to be sketched. (T/F)

6. You can load additional profiles while using the **Sweep** tool. (T/F)

7. Once a massing geometry has been converted into building elements, it cannot be viewed as a massing geometry. (T/F)

8. Mullions are added to a curtain wall without the presence of grids. (T/F)

Using Massing Tools

9. Which of the following parameters in the **Properties** palette can be used to specify the extrusion from the base level?

   a) **Level**
   b) **Extrusion End**
   c) **Depth**
   d) **Extrusion Start**

10. Which of the following tools is used to create a curved tube?

    a) **Blend**
    b) **Revolve**
    c) **Extrude**
    d) **Sweep**

11. Which of the following tools can be used to create a sphere?

    a) **Sweep**
    b) **Revolve**
    c) **Extrude**
    d) **Blend**

12. From which of the following panels, the **Curtain System** tool is invoked ?

    a) **Circulation**
    b) **Model by Face**
    c) **Model Site**
    d) **Conceptual Mass**

Exercises

Exercise 1 — Office Towers

Create a massing geometry for an office building that consists of two identical 400'0" high towers with a connecting passage at 200'0" height. Each tower has a 50'0" X 50'0" base with an offset of 5'0" at 200'0" and 300'0" levels. There are two masts on each tower with a base radius of 2'6" and the top radius of 0'6" The connecting passage is 150'0" long and has a width and height of 25'0" with a vault roof. The plan view of the building is shown in Figure 10-110. The 3D, elevation, and shaded views of the building are shown in Figures 10-111, 10-112, and 10-113, respectively. The dimensions and text have been given for reference and are not to be created. Assume the missing dimensions proportionate to the building design. After creating the massing, convert it into the building elements with the parameters given next. **(Expected time: 45 min)**

1. Project File Parameters:
   Template File- **Architectural Template**,
   File Name to be assigned- *c10_OfficeTowers_ex1.rvt*

2. Building Element types for the converted shell elements:
   Floor: **Floor : LW Concrete on Metal Deck**
   Walls: Towers- **Curtain Wall: Exterior Glazing**
             (horizontal and vertical spacing- 10'0")
             Connecting Passage- **Curtain Wall: Curtain Wall 1**
   Roof: **Basic Roof : Generic 9"**

After completion, the building model will appear similar to the illustration given in Figure 10-113.

Figure 10-110 Sketch plan for a multistory office building

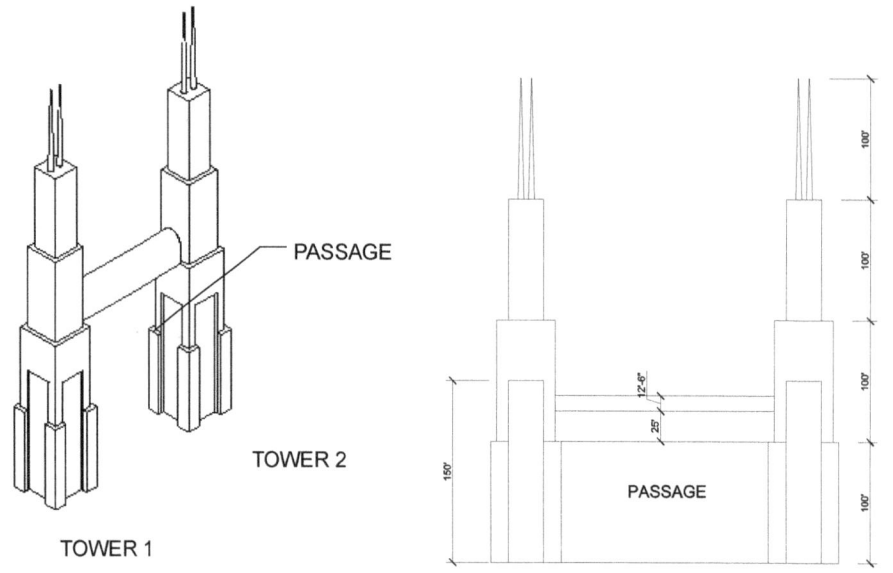

Figure 10-111 3D view of the building   *Figure 10-112* Elevation view of the building

Figure 10-113 Shaded 3D view of the building

Using Massing Tools   10-71

Exercise 2   Stadium

Create a massing geometry for a Stadium. Its plan view is shown in Figure 10-114. It consists of the field area and stands. In the stands, the tread of the lower tier is 3'0" and the riser is 1'0". Similarly, the tread of the lower-tier is 3'0" and the riser is 1'6". The cross-section view of stands is shown in Figure 10-115. Assume the missing dimensions proportionate to the sketch plan. Use the following building parameters.

(Expected time: 30 min)

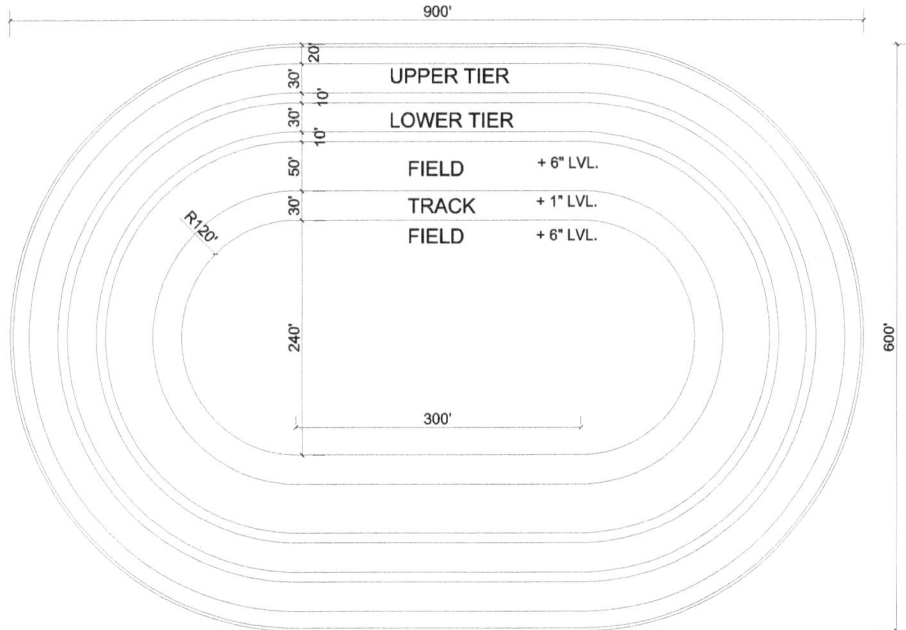

Figure 10-114 Sketch plan of the Stadium

1. Project File Parameters:
   Template File- **Architectural Template**,
   File Name to be assigned- *c10_Stadium_ex2.rvt*

   After completion, the building model will appear similar to the illustration given in Figure 10-116.

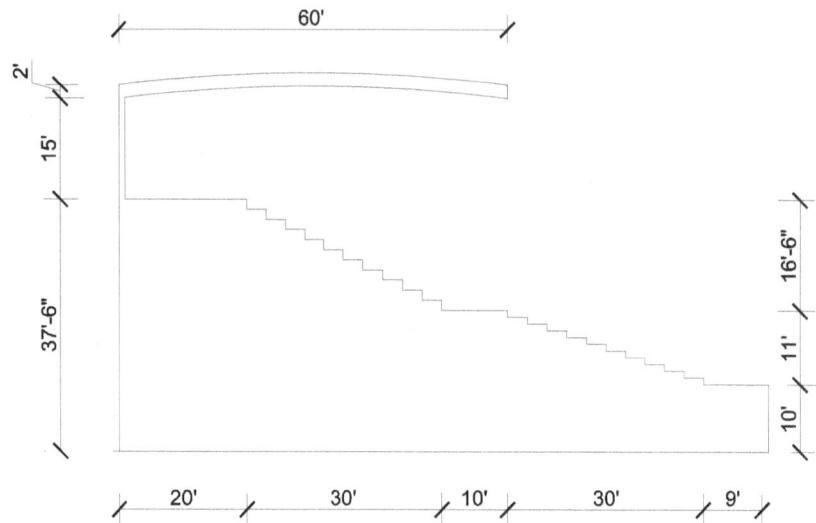

Figure 10-115 Cross-section view of the stands

Figure 10-116 3D view of the stadium

Answers to Self-Evaluation Test
1. T, 2. T, 3. F, 4. F, 5. T, 6. Massing- Show Mass Enabled, 7. X-Ray, 8. Revolve, 9. Edit Vertices, 10. Show Mass, 11. Properties, 12. Edit

Chapter 11

Adding Annotations and Dimensions

Learning Objectives

After completing this chapter, you will be able to:
- *Add tags to building elements using the Tag tool.*
- *Add room tags to the interior spaces using the Room Tag tool.*
- *Add symbols to project view using the Symbol tool.*
- *Create dimensions using various dimensioning tools.*
- *Modify dimensions based on the given parameters.*
- *Add spot elevation to a building model using the Spot Elevation tool.*

INTRODUCTION

In the previous chapters, you have learned to create and add different building elements to a project. This will help you to convey the design intent of the project, graphically. However, in order to execute a building or an interior project from drawings into reality, you need to add documentation to the drawing. In this chapter, you will learn to add tags to elements and spaces, create dimensions, use annotations, create schedules and details, and add dimensions to the elements. In later chapters of this book, you will learn about the tools that are used to document an Autodesk Revit Architecture project and add content to it. You will also learn to compose and plot sheets in later chapters.

ADDING TAGS

You can easily tag various elements in a building model. A tag is a useful annotation that assists in identifying the tagged building element. When you design complex building models using Autodesk Revit Architecture, tags play an important role in arranging various elements in schedules. You can then add necessary description for each tagged element in tabulated form. Figure 11-1 shows the usage of various tags in an interior layout.

Figure 11-1 *Various tags in an interior layout*

Autodesk Revit Architecture provides various tools that are used to add and edit tags. When you open the default template file, tags of a certain category of elements are preloaded. Therefore, when you add the elements such as doors and windows, Autodesk Revit Architecture automatically tags them. For the other elements, you need to load their respective tags from the Autodesk Revit Architecture library. Like other annotations, tags are also view-specific and they appear only in the view they have been created in. You can control the visibility of tags by choosing the **Visibility/Graphics** tool from the **Graphics** panel of the **View** tab. On doing so, the **Visibility/Graphics Overrides for <current view >** dialog box will be displayed. The **Annotation Categories** tab of this dialog box contains the list of tag categories such as **Door Tags**, **Window Tags**, **Furniture Tags**, **Electrical Fixture Tags**, and so on. You can select the appropriate check boxes to control the visibility of each category of tags. The methods used for tagging the elements are described next.

Tagging Elements by Category

Ribbon: Annotate > Tag > Tag by Category

To attach a tag to an element based on the element category, choose the **Tag by Category** tool from the **Tag** panel of the **Annotate** tab, as shown in Figure 11-2. On doing so, the **Modify |Tag** contextual tab will be displayed and the parameters related to placing and orienting will be displayed in the **Options Bar**. In the **Options Bar**, you can select the **Horizontal** or **Vertical** option from the drop-down list displayed on the left, based on the desired direction of the text in the tag, refer to Figure 11-1. The **Leader** check box is selected by default in the **Options Bar**. As a result, a leader will be displayed with the tag. You can clear this check box, if you do not require a leader to be displayed with the tag. As the **Leader** check box is selected, the options in the drop-down list displayed on the right of it will be enabled. From this drop-down list, you can select two options: **Attached End** and **Free End**. On selecting the **Attached End** option from the drop-down list, you will not be able to move the end of the leader with the tag away from the element category it is attached to. As you select the **Attached End** option from the drop-down list, the edit box on its right gets enabled. In this edit box, you can specify the length of the leader or the distance of the tag from the attached element. Alternatively, if you select the **Free End** option from the drop-down list, the end of the leader can be moved away from the element it is attached to.

*Figure 11-2 Choosing the **Tag by Category** tool from the **Annotate** tab*

Loading Tags and Symbols

By default, Autodesk Revit Architecture loads tags and symbols for certain categories of elements such as areas, drawing sheets, walls, and so on. To insert tags in the drawing area, you can choose the **Loaded Tags And Symbols** tool from the **Tag** drop-down of the **Annotate** tab; the **Loaded Tags And Symbols** dialog box will be displayed. This dialog box displays the category-wise list of the loaded tags with their loaded symbols, as shown in Figure 11-3. In this dialog box, you can control the display of the categories in the categories list by clicking on the **Filter list** drop-down list and selecting the check box(es) of the catagory(ies) that you want to display in the list.

In case, the category of elements to be tagged does not have its corresponding tag or symbols already loaded, choose the **Load Family** button from the **Loaded Tags And Symbols** dialog box; the **Load Family** dialog box will be displayed.

You can select various categories of tags from the **Library > US Imperial > Annotations** folder path as required. The **Preview** area of the **Load Family** dialog box displays the preview image of the selected tag, as shown in Figure 11-4. You can select the appropriate tag from the list and choose the **Open** button to load it into the project. On doing so, the desired tag will be added to the list of loaded tags for the corresponding element category in the **Loaded Tags And Symbols** dialog box.

Figure 11-3 The **Loaded Tags** dialog box displaying the list of loaded tags

Another method of loading the tags is to invoke the **Tag by Category** tool and select the element to be tagged. In case, you select an element that does not have a corresponding tag already loaded, the **No Tag Loaded** message box will be displayed, as shown in Figure 11-5. This message box will inform that you have not loaded a tag for the selected object type. Choose the **Yes** button; the **Load Family** dialog box will be displayed. From this dialog box, select the desired file and choose the **Open** button; the tag will be loaded. After loading, when you move the cursor near the element, a preview image of the tag will be displayed along with it. Move the cursor to the desired position and click when the tag appears to place it. Next, select different elements of the same category and tag them individually. The added tag appears similar to the illustration shown in Figure 11-6. When you select a tag, its controls will be displayed, as shown in Figure 11-7.

Adding Annotations and Dimensions

Figure 11-4 The **Load Family** dialog box

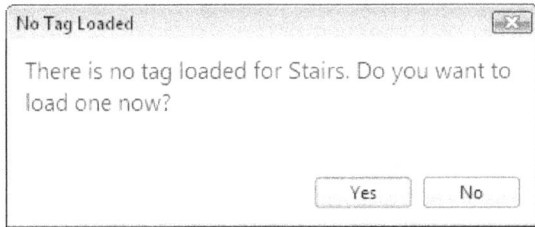

Figure 11-5 The **No Tag Loaded** message box for loading tags

Figure 11-6 An example showing the element and the added furniture tag

Figure 11-7 The selected tag with its controls

The move control displayed with the tag can be used to move the tag to the desired location. The leader elbow control can be used to adjust the leader. The ? control can be used to enter text for the label of the tag. When you add a label, Autodesk Revit Architecture displays the message box informing you that you are changing a type parameter of the tag and that it could affect many elements. Choose **Yes** to continue; the entered value appears as the label in the tag.

Editing Tags

You can also edit an added tag easily. You can edit not only the tag label but also the tag type. To edit a tag, select the added tag and then select the desired tag type from the **Type Selector** drop-down list in the **Properties** palette to replace it with the existing tag type. The options available in the **Options Bar** can be used to convert a horizontal tag into a vertical one and vice versa. You can also add or remove the leader for an added tag using the **Leader** check box. You can modify the instance properties of the selected tag in the **Properties** palette. In this palette, you can modify the visibility of the leader using the check box for the **Leader Line** parameter. The direction of the tag label can also be modified using the **Orientation** parameter.

To modify the type parameter of the selected tag, choose the **Edit Type** button from the **Properties** palette; the **Type Properties** dialog box will be displayed. In this dialog box, you can select the arrowhead type for the leader from the drop-down list in the **Value** column of the **Leader Arrowhead** type parameter. Alternatively, you can invoke the **Type Properties** dialog box of the selected tag by choosing the **Type Properties** tool from the **Properties** panel of the contextual tab to modify the type properties.

> **Tip:** *It is easier to first add tags to all elements and then add the labels, or edit them individually. Autodesk Revit displays the alignment line to facilitate the placement of multiple tags at desired locations.*

> **Note**
> *The contextual tab contains a set of tools that relate only to the context of that tool or element. For example, for a selected door tag, the name of the contextual tab will be **Modify / Door Tags**.*

Tagging All Elements in a View

Ribbon: Annotate > Tag > Tag All

The **Tag All** tool is used to tag all elements that are visible in the current view. On choosing this tool, the **Tag All Not Tagged** dialog box will be displayed, as shown in Figure 11-8. In this dialog box, there are two radio buttons: **All objects in current view** and **Only selected objects in current view**. By default, the **All objects in current view** radio button will be selected. The **Only selected objects in current view** radio button will be active and ready for selection only when objects to be tagged are selected prior to invoking the **Tag All Not Tagged** dialog box. The selection of the **All objects in current view** radio button ensures that all objects present in the current view will be tagged, provided their categories are selected from the **Category** column of the **Tag All Not Tagged** dialog box. The table below the radio buttons displays the list of category tags of all elements present in the current view and their corresponding loaded tags.

Note
*If the category of element you wish to tag does not appear in this list, you need to load the corresponding tag family and then use the **Tag All** tool.*

You can select only one category at a time. Select the category of elements to be tagged and the tag type to be used from the **Tag All Not Tagged** dialog box, as shown in Figure 11-8. You can select the **Leader** check box to add a leader to the elements. You can also modify the length and orientation of the leader in the dialog box by entering a value in the **Leader Length** edit box and selecting an option from the **Tag Orientation** drop-down list, respectively. Next, choose the **Apply** button to apply the setting to the current view. For example, you can tag all furniture elements in a layout plan view by using the **Tag All** tool, as shown in Figure 11-9.

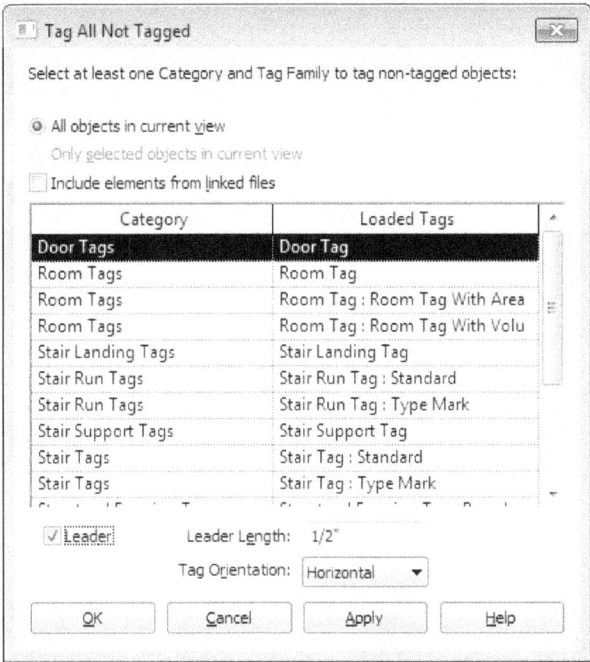

*Figure 11-8 Selecting the category of elements to be tagged from the **Tag All Not Tagged** dialog box*

In Revit Architecture, you can use the **Tag All** tool to tag rooms or areas. If you tag the elements whose visibility has been turned off, the **Tag Visibility Enabled** message box will be displayed. This message box displays a message informing that the visibility of all elements, whose visibility is turned off, will be turned on while adding tags. Choose **Yes** to continue; the tags will be added to all elements belonging to the selected category. You can then edit them individually. This process needs to be repeated for tagging elements category-wise.

Figure 11-9 *The furniture elements tagged using the* **Tag All** *tool*

Tagging Treads or Risers

In a project view, you can display the numbering of treads or risers for a run in a component based stair. The numbering for the run can be displayed in a plan, elevation, or in a section view. Like any other annotation, the numbering in the treads or risers is view-specific. To add the numbers of tread or risers in a plan view, choose the **Tread Number** tool from the **Tag** panel of the **Annotate** tab; you will be prompted to pick a reference line of a stair to place the Stair or Tread number. Move the cursor and place it over the stair at a location where you desire to place the numbers. You can place the numbers in any of the following locations of the stair run: Left, Right, Center, Left Quarter, and Right Quarter. Click on the desired reference line on the stair run; the riser or tread will be numbered along the stair path, as shown in Figure 11-10.

Figure 11-10 *Stairs with tread numbers*

Note
You cannot annotate the treads or risers in the sketch mode.

ROOM TAGS

Room tags are useful annotation tools for your drawing and they help you set information about the type of occupancy and define the enclosed area and volume. Autodesk Revit Architecture enables you to define and add a nomenclature to various interior and exterior spaces in a building project. This is important not only for identifying each space, but also for creating a room-wise project schedule. In Autodesk Revit Architecture, a room is also treated as an element of the project, similar to the other elements such as a wall, door, or window.

In a building model, rooms and their tags are interrelated to each other. You can add a room with a tag. To do so, choose the **Room** tool from the **Room & Area** panel of the **Architecture** tab; the **Modify | Place Room** tab will be displayed. In the **Tag** panel of this tab, the **Tag on Placement** option is selected by default. As a result, the room added will have a tag. If you want to add a room without a tag, invoke the **Room** tool, deselect the **Tag on Placement** option from the **Tag** panel, and click at the desired place. You can add the room tag later by using the **Room Tag** tool from the **Tag** panel of the **Annotate** tab.

Autodesk Revit Architecture provides you with the option to keep the tag either in its original position or inside the room that has been moved. When you move a room that has a tag attached to it, an alert message will be displayed in the **Autodesk Revit Architecture 2015** dialog box, informing that the room tag is outside of its room. To enable the room tag such that it adjusts itself within the room at the new position, choose the **Move to Room** button from the displayed dialog box; the room tag will automatically move inside the room. Next, choose the **OK** button; a leader will be added to the room tag and the room tag will be placed outside the room that has been moved.

Room Separation

Ribbon: Architecture > Room & Area > Room Separator

Rooms are the defined spaces in a building and are used for specific utilities in a building project. They are divided into different parts to define the purpose of their utilization. They can be separated by a wall or without a wall depending upon the need of the project and the nature of the space. Revit defines a room by assessing the interior edges of the walls bounding the space. While working on large projects, you may need to define rooms by specifying the room boundary by using the **Room Separator** tool. This tool helps you add room-bounding lines to separate and adjust the room boundaries and create separate boundary enclosures without the intervention of a wall.

Invoke the **Room Separator** tool from the **Room & Area** panel; the **Modify | Place Room Separation** tab will be displayed. In this tab, the **Draw** panel displays various sketching tools that can be used to sketch the lines defining the separation boundary of the room. You can also use the **Pick Lines** tool from the **Draw** panel to pick the elements that define the room separation lines. To control the visibility of the separation lines, choose the **Visibility/Graphics** tool from the **Graphics** panel of the **View** tab; the **Visibility/Graphics Overrides for <contextual view>** dialog box will be displayed. From this dialog box, choose the **Model Categories** tab and expand the **Lines** group by clicking on the (**+**) sign in the **Visibility** column of the **Model Categories** tab. Now, if you select the check box beside the **Room Separation** option, the separation lines will be visible in the plan view and can be printed. If you clear the check box, the separation lines will be hidden in the plan view but the room boundaries will be retained. There may be instances when you do not want to use a particular wall as a room-defining wall. In this case, set the property of that wall as non-room bounding by clearing the check box for the **Room Bounding** instance parameter. On doing so, the selected wall will not be considered while defining the room.

For example, Figure 11-11 shows the 3D view of a room that has an intermediate wall with an arched opening. Assume that you want to ignore it while defining the entire room. To do so, clear the check box corresponding to the **Room Bounding** instance parameter in the **Properties** palette. Autodesk Revit Architecture will ignore the intermediate wall and the room boundaries will be extended to the exteriors walls, refer to Figure 11-12. In this manner, you can add identification to each space and later create a schedule of areas. You will learn more about creating schedules in Chapter 12 of this textbook.

Figure 11-11 An intermediate room with a wall having an arched opening

Figure 11-12 Defining a room by changing the **Room Bounding** parameter of the intermediate wall

Adding Annotations and Dimensions

Tagging Rooms

Ribbon: Architecture > Room & Area > Tag Room drop-down > Tag Room
Shortcut Key: RT

To add room tags, choose the **Tag Room** tool from the **Room & Area** panel; the **Modify | Place Room Tag** tab will be displayed. From the **Type Selector** drop-down list of the **Properties** palette, you can select any of these three options, **Room Tag**, **Room Tag With Area**, and **Room Tag With Volume**. To display the room tag along with its area, select the **Room Tag With Area** option in the **Type Selector** drop-down list. Similarly, you can display the volume of the room along with its tag by selecting the **Room Tag With Volume** option from the **Type Selector** drop-down list. By default, the **Room Tag** option is selected from the **Type Selector** drop-down list. As a result, the room tag is displayed without its area and volume. Now, after you select a specific type for the Room tag to be inserted, you can specify its instance and type properties from the **Properties** palette.

In **Options Bar** of the **Modify | Place Room Tag** tab, various options are displayed. These options work similar to the options described for the tags earlier in this chapter. When you move the cursor inside the room to be tagged, its boundaries will be highlighted. This indicates that the room is enclosed.

Note
If the room is not enclosed by bounding walls, the room tag will still be displayed. This means the room tags can also be added to the spaces that are not enclosed. However, the parameters such as area, perimeter, and so on will not be generated for these spaces in the schedule.

When selected each room tag displays its controls. You can click on the text control to add a label to the room tag. Figure 11-13 shows an example of an interior layout plan with various room tags.

Tip: *By default, the room tags are visible in the floor plan in which they are created. Autodesk Revit Architecture automatically numbers them sequentially.*

KEYNOTES

Keynote is a type of tag family. It is available for all model elements, detail components, and materials. Although you can add annotations to detail views using the **Text** tool, when it comes to labeling the components in detail, it is preferable to use keynotes. In keynoting, pre-defined list of notes is used. The notes are organized in a keyed list defined in a separate text file.

The keynoting data provided in Revit Architecture is based on a separate text file containing the list of different keynotes. In Autodesk Revit Architecture, keynoting can be done by following any of the two systems, the 1995 CSI (Construction Specifications Institute) Master Format system, and the revised version of the 1995 CSI Master Format system, which was introduced in the year 2004.

Figure 11-13 An interior layout plan with various room tags

The 1995 CSI (Construction Specifications Institute) Master Format system is widely used in the United States. This format system follows 16 divisions to organize construction processes and materials and uses a tab-delimited series of keys matching the descriptive labels. In this system, you do not need to actually utilize the keys in order to use the keynoting functionality to label your drawings. Revit Architecture can add either the keys or the descriptive labels.

The revised version of the 1995 CSI Master Format system, introduced in the year 2004, has not yet seen widespread acceptability amongst the AEC professionals. This revised version is based upon 50 divisions to organize construction processes and materials.

Revit's keynote files (*RevitKeynotes_Imperial.txt*, *RevitKeynotes_Imperial2004.txt*, and *RevitKeynotes_Metric.txt*) are stored as an ASCII text file format in the **US Imperial** folder. These files can be opened in a notepad and can be modified according to the company's keynoting system.

Loading Keynote File

Before you can use keynoting in a project, you must first load a keynote file. To do so, choose the **Keynoting Settings** tool from the **Annotate > Tag > Keynote** drop-down; the **Keynoting Settings** dialog box will be displayed, as shown in Figure 11-14. The **File locations** edit box in the **Keynote Table** area of this dialog box displays the path of the keynote file. To change the file path or to select a different keynote file, choose the **Browse** button next to the **File Location** edit box; the **Browse for Keynote File** dialog box will be displayed. Choose the desired keynote file from this dialog box and choose the **Open** button; the desired file will now replace the previous file and its path will be displayed in the **File Location** edit box.

*Figure 11-14 The **Keynoting Settings** dialog box*

After you specify the desired file, choose the **View** button next to the **Keynote Table** area to display the **Keynotes** dialog box. This dialog box displays the keynotes but does not allow you to edit them. Next, choose the **OK** button to close it. Again in the **Keynoting Settings** dialog box, use other options and choose the **OK** button; the dialog box will close and the specified standards in the file will now be assigned to all keynotes to be placed after the new settings.

Placing Keynotes

In Autodesk Revit Architecture, there are three types of keynotes that you can use to detail your drawing. The three types of keynotes are: Element, Material, and User.

The Element keynote annotates building elements. The tag reads the keynote assigned to the element in the model such as the keynote assigned to a wall or door, not to the individual layers or components of the wall or door. To add the Element keynotes in the detail view of your drawing, choose the **Element Keynote** tool from **Annotate > Tag > Keynote** drop-down; the **Modify | Place Element Keynote** tab will be displayed. Now, in the **Properties** palette, click on the **Type Selector** drop-down list and select the desired type from the list displayed. From the **Type Selector** drop-down list, you can select any of these four options of Keynote Tags: for Imperial **Keynote Tag Keynote Number**, **Keynote Tag Keynote Number-Boxed-Large**, **Keynote Tag Keynote Number-Boxed-Small**, or **Keynote Tag Keynote Text** (for Metric **M_Keynote Tag Keynote Number**, **M_Keynote Tag Keynote Number-Boxed-Large**, **M_Keynote Tag Keynote Number-Boxed-Small**, or **M_Keynote Tag Keynote Text**). If you select the **Keynote Number** option from the drop-down list, the added keynote will only display the keynote number in your drawing.

However, if you select the **Keynote Number-Boxed-Large** or **Keynote Number-Boxed-Small** option, keynote will be displayed with a number inside a large or a small box, respectively. If you select the **Keynote Text** option from the **Type Selector** drop-down list, the keynote will be displayed only with the keynote text in the drawing.

After you select a type from the **Type Selector** drop-down list, you can use the options in the **Options Bar** of the **Modify | Place Element Keynote** tab to select the keynote tag orientation (horizontal or vertical) from the drop-down list, and select or clear the **Leader** check box to show or hide the keynote tag leader.

After using the options from the **Options Bar**, move the cursor in the drawing area and click over the relevant element that you want to tag; an arrowhead will appear at this location. Next, click for the second point of the first segment for the leader. Now, click again to specify the final point for the end of the second segment of the leader and the location of the keynote tag. If the element already has a value assigned for the keynote, it will automatically appear in the tag. If the keynote is not yet assigned, the **Keynotes - <path of the keynote file>** dialog box will be displayed, as shown in Figure 11-15. Select any of the keynote values from the hierarchies in the **Key Value** column. Next, choose the **OK** button; the **Keynotes** dialog box will be closed and a keynote value will be assigned to the desired element and it will be displayed in the drawing.

Figure 11-15 The **Keynotes** *dialog box*

The Material keynote annotates building materials. The text in the tag reads the keynote assigned to the material, such as the layers of a wall or the components of a door. The User keynote annotates the user-defined components. This type of keynote, when used always displays the **Keynotes** dialog box on clicking the relevant element so that you can select the keynote that you want to assign, thus overriding any predefined keynote. Since it is an override, it will not update if you later modify the type or material of the selected element. To add the Material or User keynote to your drawing, choose the **Material Keynote** or **User Keynote** tool from **Annotate > Tag > Keynote** drop-down. The method of placing any of these two keynotes is the same as that of placing the Element keynote.

Adding Annotations and Dimensions

The **Type Properties** and the **Material Browser** dialog box can be used to assign the keynote values to different elements. To assign a keynote value in the **Type Properties** dialog box, select the desired element from the drawing and then choose the **Edit Type** button in the **Properties** palette; the **Type Properties** dialog box will be displayed. Click in the value column of the **Keynote** parameter; a **Browse** button will be displayed on the right. Choose this button; the **Keynotes** dialog box will be displayed. Choose the required keynote division and then choose the **OK** button; the **Keynotes** dialog box will be closed and the keynote number will be displayed in the **Value** column of the **Type Properties** dialog box. Again, choose the **OK** button to close the **Type Properties** dialog box; the selected elements and the other elements of the same type, and the element particular to the materials will automatically take the assigned keynote values.

Similarly, to assign a keynote value in the **Material Browser** dialog box, first invoke the **Type Properties** dialog box and then choose the **Edit** button in the **Value** column corresponding to the **Structure** parameter. On doing so, the **Edit Assembly** dialog box will be displayed. In this dialog box, click on the field under the **Material** column corresponding to the **Structure** function; a browse button will be displayed on the right. Choose this button; the **Material Browser** dialog box will be displayed. In this dialog box, choose the **Identity** tab; the information about the material will be displayed. In the **Revit Annotation Information** area, enter the desired keynote value in the **Keynote** edit box. Alternatively, you can choose the browse button next to the **Keynote** edit box; the **Keynotes** dialog box will be displayed. Choose the required keynote division and then choose the **OK** button; the keynote number will be displayed in the **Keynote** edit box. Now, choose the **OK** button; the **Keynote** dialog box and the **Material Browser** dialog box will be closed.

Note
*The **Edit Assembly** dialog box will be displayed only for **Wall** types.*

Adding Keynote Legends

Ribbon: View > Create > Legends drop-down > Keynote Legend

A keynote legend defines the keynote along with its property and functional description in tabulated format.

To create a new keynote legend, choose the **Keynote Legend** tool from the **Create** panel; the **New Keynote Legend** dialog box will be displayed. Specify a legend name in the **Name** edit box of the dialog box and choose the **OK** button; the **Keynote Legend Properties** dialog box will be displayed. To assign properties and parameters to the keynote legend, you can choose various tabs such as **Fields**, **Filter**, **Sorting/Grouping**, **Formatting**, and **Appearance** from the **Keynote Legend Properties** dialog box. Next, choose the **OK** button to exit the **Keynote Legend Properties** dialog box; a keynote legend will be added in the drawing. A keynote legend has two columns: **Key Value** and **Keynote Text**. **Key Value** in the legend lists all keynotes of the elements in the project that are tagged with a keynotes and the **Keynote Text** column lists the description of the associated **Key Value** in the **Keynote Legend**.

A keynote legend only gives information about the elements that are tagged with a keynote. To view the keynote legend created by you, expand the **Legends** group in the **Project Browser**; the **Keynote Legend** will be displayed under the **Legends** node.

ADDING SYMBOLS

Ribbon: Annotate > Symbol > Symbol

The **Symbol** tool is used to add the 2D annotation drawing symbols to a project view to make it more informative. For example, you can use the **Symbol** tool to insert a north symbol, graphical scale, centerline symbol, and so on into a specific project view. Like other annotations, symbols are also view-specific in character.

When you choose the **Symbol** tool from the **Symbol** panel, the **Modify | Place Symbol** tab will be displayed. Now, from the **Type Selector** drop-down list which shows the loaded symbols in the project, select the required symbol. The instance and type properties depend on the selected symbol. You can modify the instance and type properties of a symbol from the **Properties** palette. The **Number of Leaders** spinner available in the **Options Bar** enables you to add multiple leaders to a single symbol. If the **Rotate after placement** check box is selected, the **Rotate** tool will be invoked as soon as you place the symbol. As a result, you can reorient the symbol after placing it.

The selected symbol can be added to the project view by clicking at the desired location. Figure 11-16 shows an example of the centerline symbol added to a plan view. Multiple instances of the symbol can then be placed by clicking on the locations of other instances.

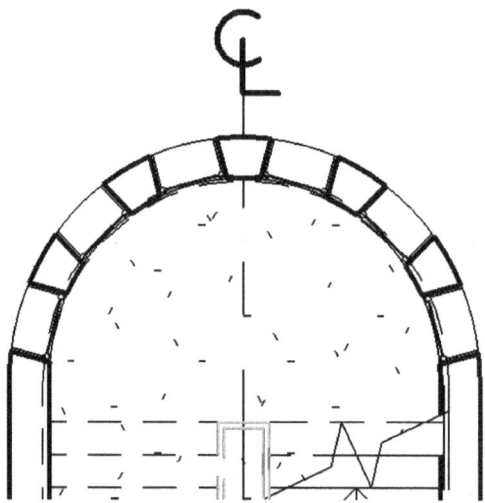

Figure 11-16 Adding the centerline symbol to the plan view

ADDING DIMENSIONS

Dimensions play a crucial role in the presentation of a project. Although the building model conveys the graphical image of the design, yet to materialize it at the site, the building view must provide information and statistics regarding each element. Since the design drawing is used for the actual construction of a project, it is essential to describe the building parts in terms of actual measurement parameters such as length, width, height, angle, radius, diameter, and so on. All these information can be added into the project using dimensions. The information conveyed through dimensions is, in most cases, as important as the project view itself. It ensures that the project drawings are read and interpreted in appropriate way. Adding dimensions also ensures that there are no discrepancies between various elements used in the generation of the building drawings.

In an Autodesk Revit Architecture project, you can add dimensions based on the actual dimensions of the created elements. In other words, they are as truthful as the project elements themselves. The units play an important role in describing the detailing with which the project is required to be constructed. For example, the use of fractional inches indicates the amount of detailing that has been considered while generating the design. It also reflects the extent of detailing and the precision required for the accomplishment of the project. Therefore, the dimensions are used, not only to specify the sizes of elements, but also as the instructions to the persons involved in the project such as cost estimators, project managers, site engineers, contractors, supervisors, and so on.

You can dimension straight lines and arcs as well. There are two types of dimensions that can be created for an element: temporary dimensions and permanent dimensions. The temporary dimensions appear while creating or selecting the element, but they are not displayed in project views. On the other hand, the permanent dimensions appear in the views in which they are created and describe a particular size or distance.

In Revit Architecture, you can create linear dimensions, referencing circle, ellipse, or arc centers as well as dimensions from the intersection of lines, walls and references. The size of dimensions is based on the selected scale for the project. However, you can modify various parameters of the dimension. Autodesk Revit Architecture automatically calculates the dimensions of the selected element from the nearby elements.

You can also format the dimension texts as you do for the normal texts and can also adjust the width factor of the dimension text. You can set the dimension text as underlined, italicized, and bold by using the **Type Properties** dialog box.

The dimensioning options provided in Autodesk Revit Architecture enable you to dimension elements in a variety of ways. You can choose the option that is most suitable for the dimensioning of a particular element type. Remember that the dimensioning conventions and standards followed in the industry should also be considered while dimensioning a project.

Types of Dimensions

In Autodesk Revit Architecture, you can use two types of dimensions: temporary and permanent. By default, the temporary and permanent dimensions use the units settings specified in the initial start-up of the project. The temporary dimensions are not view-specific, whereas the permanent dimensions are view-specific. It means that if you change the view, the permanent dimensions will not be visible. These two types of dimensions are discussed in detail in the next section.

Temporary Dimensions

Autodesk Revit Architecture displays a dimension when you draw an element or place a component in a view. The dimension that appears dynamically to assist you in drawing and placing elements for your project is called temporary dimension. This type of dimension is not view-specific and can be seen in any view when you draw or select an element. The temporary dimensions help you in positioning the elements at the desired location and references. While sketching the lines instantly of a desired length and angle, the temporary dimensions can also help you speed up your drafting work.

Temporary dimension appears only in three instances. First, when you draw any element; second, when you select any element; and third, when you place any component in your project. In Autodesk Revit Architecture, temporary dimensions are displayed in blue color.

When you place a component in your project, the temporary dimension becomes a useful tool to guide the exact placing of the component with respect to a fixed element or a component. While placing a component, the temporary dimensions are created to the nearest perpendicular element or component with a predefined snap increment setting to assist in the proper placement of the component, as shown in Figure 11-17.

While using the temporary dimension, you can set the point of reference of the element you are placing or considering for reference. To change the setting of the temporary dimension, choose the **Temporary Dimensions** tool from **Manage > Settings > Additional Settings** drop-down; the **Temporary Dimension Properties** dialog box will be displayed, as shown in Figure 11-18. This dialog box contains two areas: **Walls** and **Doors and Windows**. You can change the measurement reference of the temporary dimension for walls by selecting any one of the four radio buttons namely, **Centerlines**, **Center of Core**, **Faces**, and **Faces of Core** in the **Walls** area of the **Temporary Dimension Properties** dialog box. To change the point of references for placing and referring doors and windows, you can select any of the two options namely: **Centerlines** and **Openings** from the **Doors and Windows** area of the **Temporary Dimension Properties** dialog box.

Adding Annotations and Dimensions   11-19

Figure 11-17 Temporary dimensions displayed while placing a component

These settings will help you set the references of walls, doors, and windows for temporary dimensions while creating or placing the elements or components in your model.

*Figure 11-18 The **Temporary Dimension Properties** dialog box*

Permanent Dimensions

Permanent dimensions are the dimensions that are placed during the documentation of the drawing. These dimensions occur in two states, modifiable and non-modifiable. After you have placed the permanent dimension using the appropriate dimension tools, you can adjust it according to your requirement. To do so, select the reference object of the required dimension; the state of the permanent dimension will change from non-modifiable to modifiable. A permanent dimension in its modifiable state allows you to change the current dimension provided that the dimension is not locked. The non-modifiable state of permanent dimensions refers to a state in which the size of the text and other related components appear in its true size.

Dimensioning Terminology

Before using the dimensioning tools, it is important to understand the dimensioning terms that are used in Autodesk Revit Architecture. Figure 11-19 shows common dimensioning terminologies that are discussed next.

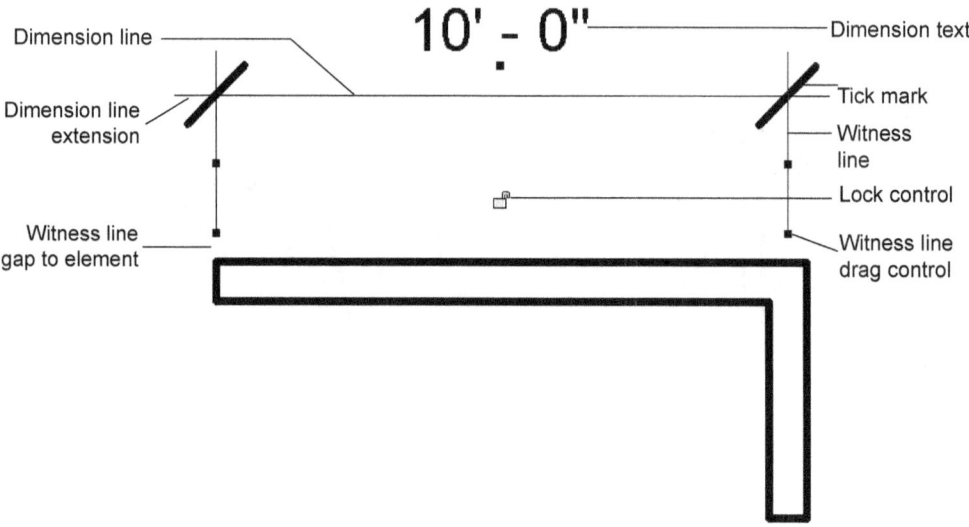

Figure 11-19 Various dimensioning terms

Dimension Line

The dimension line indicates the distance or angle that is being measured. By default, this line has tick marks at both the ends and the dimension text is placed along the dimension line. For angular or radial dimensions, this line is an arc.

Dimension Text

The dimension text represents the actual measurement (dimension value) between the selected points, as calculated by Autodesk Revit Architecture. This value cannot be modified manually, but you can add prefixes or suffixes to it. Note that the dimension text value is automatically updated when the size of the element is modified.

Tick Marks

Tick marks are added at the intersection of the dimension line with the witness line. As the drafting standards differ from company to company, Autodesk Revit Architecture allows you to select the tick marks from a range of in-built symbols. You can also modify its parameters.

Witness Lines

Witness lines are generated from the selected element and extend toward the dimension line. Generally, they are generated perpendicular to the dimension line. You can use the witness line drag controls to move them to the desired location. Another method of moving them is to select them and then choose the **Edit Witness Lines** button from the ribbon, or right-click and then choose the **Edit Witness Lines** option from the shortcut menu displayed. The dimension value automatically changes to the new distance between the witness lines. You can also control the parameters of the witness lines such as the gap to the element, extension beyond the dimension line, type, and so on.

Adding Permanent Dimensions

Permanent dimensions are added specifically for a particular measurement. In Autodesk Revit Architecture, you can access various dimensioning tools from the **Dimension** panel in the **Annotate** tab, as shown in Figure 11-20. You can choose the appropriate dimension type and the dimension tool to add dimensions to the element. The usage of these dimensioning tools is described next.

Figure 11-20 Dimensioning tools in the **Dimension** panel of the **Annotate** tab

Aligned Dimensions

Ribbon: Annotate > Dimension > Aligned

The **Aligned** tool is used to dimension two orthogonal references or points such as the wall ends. To dimension two orthogonal references, invoke the **Aligned** tool from the **Dimension** panel; the **Modify | Place Dimensions** tab will be displayed. To change the type for the aligned dimension, select an option from the **Type Selector** drop-down list in the **Properties** palette. Next, to set the snap point for the cursor, select an option from the first drop-down list in the **Options Bar**. For example, if you select the **Wall centerlines** option from the drop-down list, the cursor will snap to the centerline of the wall when placed above the wall. Next, select **Individual References** from the **Pick** drop-down list. Now, place the cursor at a reference point on an element; the reference point will be highlighted when the system allows you to place the dimension. Now, left-click to specify the reference and then place the cursor at the location you want to place the next reference point and click. As you move the cursor upward, a dimension line will appear. Move the cursor away from the component and left-click again; a permanent aligned dimension will appear, as shown in Figure 11-21. This tool can also be used to dimension between the center of the arc wall and other walls or lines.

Figure 11-21 Dimension created using the **Aligned** dimension tool

If you select **Entire Walls** from the drop-down list in the **Options Bar**, the **Options** button will be activated. Choose the **Options** button; the **Auto Dimension Options** dialog box will be displayed. Select the check boxes in the dialog box. You can now dimension the openings, doors, windows, and the intersecting walls simultaneously. You can also define the references for dimensioning by selecting the **Centers** or **Widths** radio buttons in the **Select references** area. After selecting various options in the **Auto Dimension Options** dialog box, choose the **OK** button; the dialog box will close. Now, click on the wall that you want to dimension and then move the cursor away from the wall. Click again in the drawing. You will see that the walls, doors, and openings are dimensioned separately according to the references defined in the **Auto Dimension Options** dialog box.

Linear Dimensions

Ribbon: Annotate > Dimension > Linear

The **Linear** tool is used to dimension straight elements and distances. It measures the shortest distance between the two specified points. To dimension straight elements, invoke this tool from the **Dimension** panel; the **Modify | Place Dimensions** tab will be displayed. From the **Type Selector** drop-down list in the **Properties** palette, select an option to assign a type to the linear dimension that you want to create. After selecting this option, select the first point by clicking at the appropriate location. After selecting the first point, select the second point of reference for the dimension; the dimension line appears. You can now move the cursor to the desired location and click to place the dimension. The created dimension displays various parameters controls. You can invoke any other tool or press ESC to exit the **Linear** tool. The linear dimension will be created, as shown in Figure 11-22.

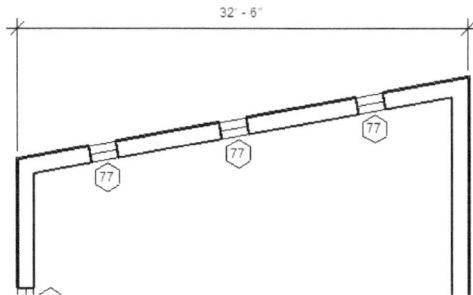

*Figure 11-22 Dimension created using the **Linear** dimension tool*

Angular Dimensions

Ribbon: Annotate > Dimension > Angular

The **Angular** tool is used to dimension an angle. This tool creates a dimension arc (dimension line in the shape of an arc with tick marks at both ends) to indicate the angle between two non-parallel elements, as shown in Figure 11-23. To dimension or measure an angle, invoke the **Angular** tool from the **Dimension** panel; the **Modify | Place Dimension** tab will be displayed. From the **Type Selector** drop-down list in the **Properties** palette, select an option from the list of types displayed. After selecting an option from the drop-down list, move the cursor and then click to place the dimension. This option can also be used to dimension when the angular dimension appears on the desired angle, as shown in Figure 11-24.

Adding Annotations and Dimensions

Radial Dimensions

Ribbon: Annotate > Dimension > Radial

The **Radial** tool is used to dimension the radius of a circular or an arc profile, as shown in Figure11-25. The dimension text generated by Autodesk Revit Architecture has a prefix **R**, which indicates a radial dimension. To create a radial dimension, invoke this tool from the **Dimension** panel; the **Modify | Place Dimensions** tab will be displayed.

Figure 11-23 Dimension created between two walls using the **Angular** tool

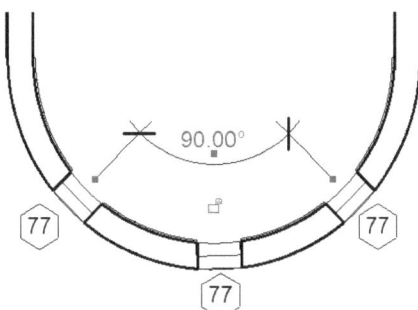

Figure 11-24 Angular dimension created for an arc wall using the **Angular** tool

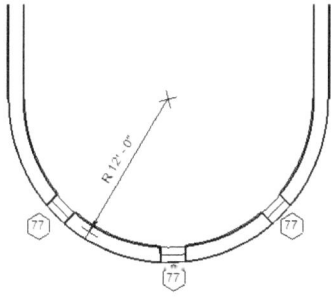

Figure 11-25 Radial dimension created for an arc wall using the **Radial** tool

From the **Type Selector** drop-down list, select an option from the list of types displayed. After selecting this option, move the cursor near the profile and click when the appropriate snap option appears; a center mark for the radial dimension will automatically be generated. Move the cursor and place the dimension.

Diametric Dimensions

Ribbon: Annotate > Dimension > Diameter

 The **Diameter** tool is used to dimension the diameter of a circular or an arc profile. The dimension text generated by Autodesk Revit Architecture has a prefix ø, which indicates a diametric dimension. To create a diametric dimension, invoke this tool from the **Dimension** panel; the **Modify | Place Dimensions** tab will be displayed. Place the cursor on the curve of a circle or arc, and then click; a temporary dimension displaying the diameter of the curve will be displayed. Move the cursor along the dimension line, and click to place the diametric dimension.

> **Tip:** *You can press the TAB key to switch the reference point for the dimension between a wall face and a wall centerline.*

Arc Length Dimensions

Ribbon: Annotate > Dimension > Arc Length

The **Arc Length** tool can be used to dimension an arc wall, based on its overall length. Invoke this tool from the **Dimension** panel; the **Modify | Place Dimensions** tab will be displayed. Now, select the dimension type from the **Type Selector** drop-down list. Now, move the cursor near the arc wall and click to specify the radial point. Select the start and end references that will define the points between which the arc length is to be measured. Move the cursor away from the arc wall and click to place the arc length dimension; the arc length dimension will be created, as shown in Figure 11-26.

Figure 11-26 Dimension created for an arc wall using the
Arc Length *tool*

Adding Alternate Dimension Units

In a project, besides the main dimensions, you can also display alternate dimensions in your model. These alternate dimensions can be both permanent and spot dimension types. The alternate dimension units display both imperial and metric units simultaneously in drawings. To add an alternate dimension to the main dimension in a project select any of the dimension tool from the **Dimension** panel of the **Annotate** tab; the **Modify | Place Dimension** contextual tab and various related instance properties in the **Properties** palette will be displayed. Now, in the **Properties** palette, choose the **Edit Type** button; the **Type Properties** dialog box will be displayed. In this dialog box, choose the **Duplicate** button; the **Name** dialog box will be displayed. Enter the name **Alternate Units** in the **Name** edit box and choose the **OK** button to return to the **Type Properties** dialog box. Now, in the **Type Properties** dialog box, click on the **Value** field corresponding to the **Alternate Units** parameter; a drop-down list with the **None**, **Right**, and **Below** options will be displayed. You can select an option as per your requirement. On selecting the **Right** option, the alternate units will be displayed in-line to the primary units, and on selecting the **Below** option, the alternate units will be displayed below the primary units. Now, click on the **Value** field corresponding to the **Alternate Units Format** parameter; the **Format** dialog box will be displayed. In this dialog box, select the **Meters** option from the **Units** drop-down list, select the **'m'** option from the **Units Symbol** drop-down list and then choose the **OK** button; the **Format** dialog box will be closed. You can also assign square brackets '[]' to the **Alternate Prefix** and **Alternate Suffix** value fields. Now, choose the **OK** button; the **Type Properties** dialog box will be closed and the drawing window will be displayed.

To assign alternate units to a building model in the drawing, select the **Linear Dimension Style Alternate Units** option from the **Type Selector** drop-down list. Now, the cursor will change and the witness line of the selected dimension is subjected to change, as shown in Figure 11-27. You can select one of the options such as **Wall Centerline**, **Wall Faces**, **Center of core**, **Faces of core** from the drop-down list available in the **Options Bar** of the **Modify | Place Dimension** tab. Next, place the cursor at the face of the wall; primary units along with alternate dimension units will be displayed, as shown in Figure 11-28.

Figure 11-27 The witness line is subjected to change

Figure 11-28 The primary units along with alternate units

Baseline and Ordinate Dimensions

You can dimension a series of elements and components simultaneously. This can be done by using the baseline and ordinate dimensioning techniques.

A baseline dimension is a stacked dimension that originates from a common baseline. It creates a referenced dimension from the first witness line, which acts as a base for adding dimension, as shown in Figure 11-29. An ordinate dimension is generated to show the level of a particular point measured from a fixed point, called datum, as shown in Figure 11-30. The ordinate dimension of a point shows the measurement of its perpendicular distance from the datum or the origin point. Note that you can use the baseline and ordinate dimensioning techniques only for linear and aligned dimensions.

Figure 11-29 The selected baseline dimension and its components

Figure 11-30 The selected ordinate dimensions and their components

Methods of Creating and Placing Baseline and Ordinate Dimensions

To create a baseline dimension or an ordinate dimension, choose the **Aligned** or **Linear** dimension tool from the **Dimension** panel in the **Annotate** tab; the **Modify | Place Dimensions** tab will be displayed. To create a new dimension style by using the baseline or

Adding Annotations and Dimensions

ordinate dimension technique, choose the **Type Properties** tool from the **Properties** panel; the **Type Properties** dialog box will be invoked. Choose the **Duplicate** button from this dialog box and name the new dimension style in the **Name** dialog box as per the standard nomenclature system followed for the baseline or ordinate dimension.

To create a baseline dimension, in the **Type Properties** dialog box, click on the **Value** field corresponding to the **Dimension String Type** parameter and select the **Baseline** for creating a baseline dimension. Similarly, you can also set the value of the **Dimension String Type** parameter to **Ordinate** for creating an ordinate dimension. You can also invoke the **Type Properties** dialog box for the linear or aligned dimension type by choosing the **Linear Dimension Types** tool from the **Dimension** panel in the **Annotate** tab.

After creating the style for the baseline or ordinate dimension, you can use it in your project. To start dimensioning, use the same method as discussed earlier. After invoking any of the dimension tools (**Linear** or **Aligned**), select the desired type from the **Type Selector** drop-down list. To create a baseline dimension, select the first point for the dimension in the drawing area. This is the origin of the baseline dimension. Next, continue to select the necessary reference points and when you have reached the last reference point, move the cursor away from the last element, and click; the baseline dimension will be displayed.

You can control the distance between the consecutive baseline dimension lines before or after placing the dimensions in the drawing. To do so, enter the **Baseline Offset** value in the **Options Bar** to adjust the distance between the dimension lines. Similarly, to create an ordinate dimension, select the desired dimension style. Next, select a fixed point called datum (00) and then select other points in a series to get the perpendicular distance of these points with respect to the datum.

Editing Dimensions

You can edit various properties of a dimension before or after creating it. To modify any dimension in the drawing, select it; the **Modify | Dimensions** tab will be displayed. From this tab, you can use various options to modify and edit the dimension selected. The **Type Selector** drop-down list displays various in-built dimension types available in Autodesk Revit Architecture. You can select the appropriate dimension type from the drop-down list to assign it to the selected dimension.

Modifying Dimension Parameters

You can modify various parameters of a dimension such as the dimension text font, gap of the witness line from the element, and so on, to achieve the desired dimension style. To do so, select the dimension created and then you can use various parameters in the **Properties** palette. You can add a leader to the dimension by selecting the check box corresponding to the **Leader** instance parameter. To access and modify the type parameters, choose the **Edit Type** button in the **Properties** palette; the **Type Properties** dialog box will be displayed, as shown in Figure 11-31. You can create a new dimension style with the parameters most suitable to the project by using the **Duplicate** button. Various type parameters and their usage are described next.

Tip: *You can invoke the **Type Properties** dialog box for individual type directly by choosing the corresponding tool from the **Dimension** panel.*

Using the **Leader** parameter, you can specify the type of line to draw for the leader. You can select the **Arc** or **Line** option from the drop-down list corresponding to its **Value** column. You can specify the type of tick mark for the leader by selecting an option from the **Value** column corresponding to the **Leader Tick Mark** parameter. You can specify the condition for the display of the leader. To do so, select an option from the drop-down list in the **Value** column corresponding to the **Show Leader When Text Moves** parameter. For the **Tick Mark** parameter, you can select the mark type to be used as the tick mark. Select the desired mark from the drop-down list in the **Value** column. The **Line Weight** parameter sets the line weight or thickness for the dimension line. You can select the value ranging from 1 to 16, depending on the desired thickness. The **Tick Mark Line Weight** parameter sets the thickness of the tick mark line. The **Dimension Line Extension** parameter sets the distance of the extension of the dimension line beyond its intersection with the witness line.

In an equality dimension you can change the default label from **EQ** to a different text description for the dimension type. To do so, you can use the **Equality Text** parameter under the **Other** head. Also, you can assign an equality formula that is used to display equality dimension labels. An equality formula can be used for aligned, linear, or arc dimension types. This formula will allow you to display a single label for equality dimensions applied for more than two segments. For example, if an equality dimension includes three consecutive segments of length 5' (1524 mm), and you desire to display a single label displaying 3' x 5' (914 x 1524 mm) text, then you can use the equality formula.

To define the equality formula, choose the button displayed in the **Value** field corresponding to the **Equality Formula** parameter; the **Dimension Equality Formula** dialog box will be displayed. You can use this dialog box to define the way the single label will be displayed in the dimension. In the **Type Properties** dialog box, apart from various dimension settings, you can also set various parameters for the dimension texts such as **Text Size**, **Text Offset**, and so on. After modifying the parameter(s), choose the **Apply** button to apply the changes.

Adding Annotations and Dimensions

Figure 11-31 The partial view of the **Type Properties** dialog box for dimensions

Controlling the Display of Tick Marks and Dimension Arrows

Revit Architecture provides you the flexibility to control the display of tick marks and dimension arrows while dimensioning small segments. When the dimensioning segments are too small to accommodate the dimension arrow, Revit Architecture flips the dimension arrows on the exterior side and displays diagonal tick marks, as shown in Figures 11-32 through 11-34.

To control the display of the tick marks and the arrow of a dimension, you need to select the dimension and invoke the **Type Properties** dialog box by choosing the **Type Properties** tool from the **Properties** panel. In the **Type Properties** dialog box of the dimension, there are two parameters: **Flipped Dimension Line Extension** and **Interior Tick Mark**. These parameters are enabled only when the **Tick Mark** parameter is set to **Arrow** type. The **Flipped Dimension Line Extension** parameter controls the length of the dimension line beyond the arrows, after the arrows are flipped. The **Interior Tick Mark** parameter displays the type of tick marks to be displayed in case the small multiple segments need to be dimensioned. You can lock the permanent dimensions once you have finished adding them to the project and add linear dimensions automatically to linear walls.

Figure 11-32 Dimension arrows replaced by the tick marks

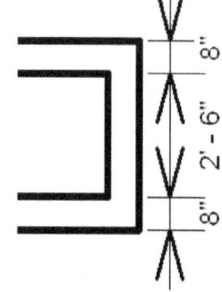

Figure 11-33 Dimension arrows on the interior side of the witness lines

Figure 11-34 The flipping of arrows on the exterior side in case of small segments

Locking Dimensions

On adding a permanent dimension, a lock control symbol is displayed. It also appears when you select a permanent dimension. This symbol can be used to lock or unlock the dimension for the element. When the symbol is unlocked, you can modify the element that the dimension refers to. In such cases, the dimension is also modified with the element. When you lock a dimension, the element that it refers to is also locked with it. This means that you cannot modify the element or the distance between the points to which it refers to. You can, however, move the element along with the dimension. Once the dimension is locked, you must unlock it to change its value.

Creating Linear Wall Dimensions Automatically

Autodesk Revit Architecture provides the option to create dimensions automatically for linear walls. To do so, invoke the **Aligned** tool from the **Dimension** panel of the **Modify | Place Dimensions** tab and then select the **Entire Walls** option from the **Pick** drop-down list in **Options Bar**. This option enables you to pick a linear wall and create the dimensions associated with it. Next, choose the **Options** button from the **Options Bar**; the **Auto Dimension Options** dialog box will be displayed. In this dialog box, you can select the required references to create the dimensions. You can add dimensions to openings or to the walls intersecting with the selected wall. You can also specify whether to use the center of openings or their widths for giving reference. After selecting the appropriate option, select the linear wall to add the dimensions. When the **Openings** option is selected from the **Auto Dimension Options** dialog box, Autodesk Revit Architecture will create the dimensions that refer to the center or widths of openings. When you select the **Intersecting Walls** option, the automatic dimensions refer to all perpendicular walls intersecting the selected wall.

ADDING SPOT DIMENSIONS

Besides adding spot elevations, Revit Architecture also allows you to add coordinates. The spot dimensions are the dimensions that display the elevation level and the coordinates of a point with respect to the base level. They can be placed in the plan, elevation or 3D views. You can add spot dimensions on non-horizontal and non-planar surfaces. You can use the spot elevation to specify the elevation level of points on a ramp, road, topographical surface, stairs, and other features. The properties of the spot elevation are similar to the properties of dimensions.

Placing a Spot Dimension

To place a spot dimension, choose the **Spot Elevation**, **Spot Coordinate** or **Spot Slope** tool from the **Dimension** panel of the **Annotate** tab; the **Modify | Place Dimensions** tab will be displayed. From this tab, select the type of spot dimension symbol to be used from the **Type Selector** drop-down list. Move the cursor near the edge of the element and click to select the point of reference when the edge of the element is highlighted. If you have selected the spot dimension without a leader, it will be placed at the selected point. If the type of spot dimension selected is with a leader, an arrow will start from the specified point. Move the cursor and click to locate the elbow of the leader. Now, move the cursor to the desired location and click again to place the spot dimension; the spot dimension will be created. Figure 11-35 show the spot elevations added in the plan view and Figure 11-36 shows the spot elevations and spot coordinates added to a 3D view.

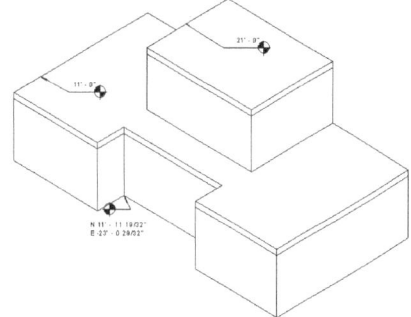

Figure 11-35 Placing the spot elevation in the plan view

Figure 11-36 Placing the spot elevation in the 3D view

You can dimension the elevation of the top and bottom edges of elements or masses with thickness using the **Spot Elevation** dimensioning tool. When you place a spot elevation in your drawing, you can place it with a leader or without a leader. You can also add supplementary text along with the spot elevation and spot coordinates. You can maintain the relative location of the spot elevation and spot coordinates with respect to the referenced element when the elements are rotated. To do so, select the **Rotate with Component** check box in the **Type Properties** dialog box for the spot elevation and spot coordinates. You can display both the spot elevation and the spot coordinates in your project by using the **Spot Coordinate** tool.

Note

On choosing the spot elevation/coordinate, you will notice that Autodesk Revit Architecture displays the temporary spot elevation/coordinates on moving the cursor to the required points, similar to a temporary dimension.

Modifying Spot Dimension Properties

Similar to other dimensions, you can also modify various properties of spot dimensions before or after creating them. To modify the instance parameters of a spot dimension, select it; the instance properties of the selected spot dimension will be displayed in the **Properties** palette. In this palette, you can select the check box in the value field corresponding to the **Leader** parameter to display the leader with the spot dimension. In the **Properties** palette, you can specify other instance parameters to specify the setting of the text and the leader. You can modify the type properties of the spot dimension. To do so, select a spot dimension and choose the **Type Properties** tool from the **Properties** panel; the **Type Properties** dialog box will be displayed, as shown in Figure 11-37. An important property of the spot dimension is the elevation origin. By default, Autodesk Revit Architecture assumes the project origin as the base level. It then calculates the distance or the elevation of the spot level from this origin. You can use the default setting or specify a different elevation origin to calculate the spot elevations. This can be done by setting the value of the **Elevation Origin** type parameter to **Relative**. You can also select a placed spot level and modify its relative base level.

The **Type Properties** dialog box is used to modify the properties that affect the appearance of the spot level dimensions. The **Symbol** type parameter in this dialog box is used to specify the symbol for representing the spot dimension. Click in the corresponding **Value** column and select the symbol from the drop-down list. If you need the dimensions with a leader line, select the **Leader** check box in the **Options Bar**. The line weight and arrow type of the leader line is specified in the **Leader Line Weight** and **Leader Arrowhead** parameters, respectively.

The parameters such as **Text Size**, **Text Offset from Leader**, **Text Location**, **Text Font**, and so on can be set for the text used for representing the spot elevation. If required, you can also add suffix or prefix to the spot elevation using the **Suffix** and **Prefix** instance parameters.

Converting Temporary Dimensions to Permanent Dimensions

As described in the earlier chapters, temporary dimensions appear while you create various elements such as walls, doors, windows, and so on. They can be used to specify the size and location of the elements in the building model refer to Chapter 3, Creating Walls. You can move or resize an element by clicking on the temporary dimension and entering a new value. When you create an element, a conversion control symbol will also be displayed along with the temporary dimension, as shown in Figure 11-38. When you click on this symbol, the temporary dimension will be converted into a permanent dimension, as shown in Figure 11-39.

Adding Annotations and Dimensions

*Figure 11-37 The **Type Properties** dialog box for spot dimension*

Figure 11-38 A temporary dimension with the conversion control

Figure 11-39 Converted permanent dimension

Tip: *As described earlier, the temporary dimensions can be used to move or copy the elements to the desired locations. For example, when you modify the temporary dimension of a selected wall segment, it is modified as per the value of the length. Thus, in Autodesk Revit Architecture, building elements and their dimensions are parametrically associated with each other.*

TUTORIAL

Tutorial 1 — Apartment 1

In this tutorial, you will first add rooms to the enclosed spaces of the *Apartment 1* project created in Tutorial 1 of Chapter 8, and then name the rooms by using the **Room Tag** tool. You will also tag the furniture and then dimension the ground floor plan view, based on the sketch plan shown in Figure 11-40. The dimensions shown on the top and right sides of the plan are referenced to the wall centerlines, whereas the dimensions on the bottom and left side are referenced to the wall faces. The exact location of the tags and dimensions is not important in this tutorial. Use the parameters given below for creating the dimensions.

(Expected time: 45 min)

1. Room tag- **Room Tag: Boxed**

2. Furniture tag- **Furniture Tag: Standard** with leader arrowhead- **Arrow 30 Degree**

3. Dimension Parameters:
   Dimension type to be based on the following options:
   For Imperial   **Linear w Center - 3/32" Arial** and **Linear - 3/32" Arial**
   For Metric   **Diagonal Center - 2.5 mm Arial** and **Linear - 3/32" Arial**

   New dimension type names- **Linear Dimension - CL** and **Linear Dimension - Faces**
   Tick Mark-   For Imperial   **Dot Filled 1/16"**
                 For Metric   **Filled Dot 3mm**
   Witness Line Gap to Element-   For Imperial   **1/4"**
                                   For Metric   **6.35mm**

The following steps are required to complete this tutorial:

a. Open the specified project file and the first floor plan view.
b. Use the **Room** and **Room Tag** tools and add rooms and room tags, refer to Figures 11-41 through 11-45.
c. Invoke the **Tag** tool and then load and add the furniture tags, refer to Figures 11-46 through 11-49.
d. Invoke the **Dimension** tool and set the type parameters.
e. Add dimensions to the project plan view using the wall centerlines as the reference, refer to Figures 11-50 through 11-52.
f. Add dimensions using automatic dimensioning with wall faces as the reference, refer to Figure 11-54.

Adding Annotations and Dimensions

11-35

Figure 11-40 Sketch plan for adding room tags, furniture tags, and dimensions to the Apartment 1 project

Opening the Project File

1. To begin this tutorial, open the file that you have created in Tutorial 1 of Chapter 8 for the *Apartment 1* project. To do so, choose **Open > Project** from the **Application Menu** and open *c08_Apartment1_tut1.rvt*. You can also download this file from *http://www.cadcim.com*. The path of the file is as follows: *Textbooks > Civil/GIS > Revit Architecture > Autodesk Revit Architecture 2015 for Architects and Designers*.

2. After you open the file, double-click on **First Floor** in the **Floor Plans** head from the **Project Browser**; the first floor plan is displayed.

Adding Room and Room Tags

In this section of the tutorial, you will first add rooms (without a tag) to the enclosed space. To add room tags to the interior spaces, you need to invoke the **Room Tag** tool. The room tag is preloaded in the default template file. As this template will be used in this tutorial, you do not need to load it. Next, you need to move the cursor inside the enclosed space and click to add the room tag. You can then click on the tag and rename it. Autodesk Revit Architecture sequentially numbers the room tags. Therefore, you need to add them based on the sequence given in the sketch plan.

Note
*In a building project, you can add rooms with tags attached to them and then rename the tags according to the space functionality. In this section of the tutorial, the rooms are added without tags and then the tags are added to make you understand the use of the **Room** tool and the **Room Tag** tool separately.*

1. To insert rooms to the closed spaces of the *Apartment 1*, invoke the **Room** tool from the **Room & Area** panel in the **Architecture** tab; the **Modify | Place Room** tab is displayed. Now, as you move the cursor in the drawing area, you will notice a blue rectangle along with the default text **Room** attached to it. Next, you need to ensure that while adding rooms, the tags should not appear.

   Note that the **Tag on Placement** button is not chosen in the **Tag** panel.

2. Move the cursor inside the living room (for location refer to Figure 11-40), and click in the enclosed space. Notice that when you click inside the enclosed space, it is shaded with blue color and the shading becomes transparent. Also, notice that the room is marked by two diagonal lines and a rectangle, showing the extent of the enclosed space.

3. Without exiting the **Room** tool, repeat step 3 to add room to the kitchen, toilet, bed room, dress, and lobby, refer to Figure 11-40. Note that after adding the last room, you need to add press ESC to exit.

4. After adding the rooms to the spaces, you need to tag them. To do so, choose the **Room Tag** tool from the **Tag** panel of the **Annotate** tab; the **Modify | Place Room Tag** tab is displayed. Notice that when you invoke the **Room Tag** tool, all rooms in the drawing are displayed in a blue transparent shade with the diagonal lines showing their extents.

5. Move the cursor inside the living room; a Room tag attached to the cursor is displayed, as shown in Figure 11-41. Click to add the tag, as shown in Figure 11-42. Now, press ESC to exit from the **Room Tag** tool.

Figure 11-41 Preview of the room tag and the highlighted room boundary

Figure 11-42 The room tag added

6. Select the room tag marked **1**(in the living room) and click on the text **Room**; an edit box is displayed.

Adding Annotations and Dimensions

7. Type **Living Room** in the edit box, as shown in Figure 11-43. Now, press ENTER and then ESC. The room tag is renamed, as shown in Figure 11-44.

Figure 11-43 Renaming the room tag   *Figure 11-44* The renamed room tag

8. Repeat steps 5 to 7 to add and rename the room tags of the other rooms in the first floor plan in the sequence of the room tag numbers shown in the sketch plan. Also, refer to the sketch, as shown in Figure 11-40, to name the respective rooms.

Note
Depending on the view scale, the text height and other parameters of the room tag are automatically calculated by Autodesk Revit Architecture.

9. Click on each room tag and rename it based on the given sketch plan. Rename the tags for the bed room, kitchen, toilet, lobby, and dress. The completed room tags on the first floor level are shown in Figure 11-45.

Adding Furniture Tags

In this section of the tutorial, you will use the **Tag** tool to add tags to the furniture items. The furniture tags were not loaded into this project file initially. Therefore, when you select a furniture item, Autodesk Revit Architecture prompts you to load the furniture tag from its library. You can load the furniture tag and then add tags to the items. You can also set the properties of the leader, as specified in the project parameters. The added tags can then be suitably renamed.

1. Choose the **Annotate** tab and then choose the **Tag by Category** tool from the **Tag** panel.

2. Move the cursor over the bed in the bedroom and click when it is highlighted.

On doing so, Autodesk Revit Architecture displays a message box informing that no tag is loaded for the element type selected and prompts you to load the tag.

Figure 11-45 The room tags added to all rooms in the first floor plan view

3. In the message box, choose the **Yes** button; the **Open** dialog box is displayed.

4. Browse to the **Annotations > Architectural** folder and select **Furniture Tag** from the list of family files.

5. Choose the **Open** button to load the furniture tag.

6. Move the cursor over the bed and click when the furniture tag is displayed at an appropriate location; the furniture tag is added without a name and a "?" symbol, as shown in Figure 11-46.

7. Press ESC and select the furniture tag added in the previous step. On doing so, the **Modify | Furniture Tags** tab is displayed.

8. From the **Type Selector** drop-down list, select **Furniture Tag: Standard** to replace the boxed tag with a standard furniture tag without a box, as given in the project parameters.

9. Next, click on the tag name marked **?** to display the edit box and enter the name **Double Bed** in it, as specified in the sketch plan shown in Figure 11-47. Next, press ENTER; Autodesk Revit Architecture displays a message box informing that you are changing a type parameter and it could affect many elements.

10. Choose **Yes** in the message box; the furniture tag is renamed.

Next, you need to add an arrowhead to the furniture tag leader, as per the parameters given.

Adding Annotations and Dimensions

11. Choose the **Type Properties** tool from the **Properties** panel; the **Type Properties** dialog box is displayed.

Figure 11-46 Using the Tag tool to add a furniture tag

Figure 11-47 Renaming the furniture tag

12. Click in the **Value** column for the **Leader Arrowhead** parameter and select **Arrow 30 Degree** from the drop-down list.

13. Choose **Apply** and then **OK**; the **Type Properties** dialog box closes and the arrowhead is added to the furniture tag leader.

14. Drag the furniture tag upward to the new location using the move control, as shown in Figure 11-48.

15. Drag the leader elbow control, represented by the blue dot, upward in such a way that the leader appears similar to that shown in Figure 11-49.

16. Similarly, add other furniture tags to various furniture items in the **First Floor** plan view based on the given sketch plan.

Invoking the Dimension Tool and Setting the Dimension Parameters

In this section of the tutorial, you will add dimensions to the project view. Note that the sketch plan shows two types of linear dimensions, centerline and wall faces. You will select the appropriate dimension type from the **Type Selector** drop-down list. Further, you will use the **Type Properties** dialog box to create a new dimension style and set the parameters for the new dimension type, as specified in the project parameters.

1. To start dimensioning the project view, invoke the **Aligned** tool from the **Dimension** panel of the **Annotate** tab; the **Modify | Place Dimensions** tab is displayed.

Figure 11-48 Dragging the furniture tag to a new location

Figure 11-49 Adjusting the tag leader at the new tag location

2. Select the required dimension style from the **Type Selector** drop-down list.
   For Imperial   **Linear Dimension Style: Linear w Center - 3/32" Arial**
   For Metric   **Linear Dimension Style: Diagonal Center - 2.5mm Arial**

3. Choose the **Edit Type** button from the **Properties** palette; the **Type Properties** dialog box is displayed.

4. Choose the **Duplicate** button to display the **Name** dialog box.

5. Enter **Linear Dimension - CL** in the **Name** edit box and choose the **OK** button.

6. Click in the **Value** column corresponding to the **Tick Mark** type parameter and select **Dot Filled 1/16" (Filled Dot 3mm)** from the drop-down list, as specified in the project parameters.

7. Click in the **Value** column corresponding to the **Witness Line Gap to Element** type parameter and enter the value **1/4"(6 mm)**.

8. Choose the **Apply** button and then the **OK** button to close the **Type Properties** dialog box.

9. Repeat steps 2 to 5 to create another dimension style using the **Linear Dimension Style: Linear - 3/32" Arial** and rename it to **Linear Dimension - Wall Faces**. Modify the **Tick Mark** and **Witness Line Gap to Element** parameters to the values used for the **Linear Dimension - CL** dimension style.

Adding Annotations and Dimensions   11-41

Adding Dimensions to the Project View

Now, add the dimensions to the project plan. As all the dimensions to be added are linear dimensions, use the **Linear** option to create them. In the following steps, you will add dimensions to the project plan using different methods. First, you will create centerline dimensions on the right and topsides of the plan view, using the **wall centerlines** and **Individual References** options. Next, you will use the **wall faces** and **Entire Walls** options to create the interior dimensions of various rooms placed on the left and bottom of the plan view.

1. Select **Linear Dimension - CL** from the **Type Selector** drop-down list.

2. Ensure that the **Wall centerlines** option is selected from the drop-down list displayed in the **Options Bar**, and **Individual References** is selected in the **Pick** drop-down list.

3. Move the cursor over the south wall near the right corner of the plan view until the object snap for the wall centerline is highlighted, as shown in Figure 11-50. Click to start the dimension.

4. Move the cursor vertically upward until the object snap for the centerline of the north wall is displayed. Now, click to specify the endpoint of the dimension distance; the dimension line is displayed and the dimension moves with the cursor, as shown in Figure 11-51.

Figure 11-50 Selecting the wall centerline reference to start a dimension

Figure 11-51 Selecting the second wall centerline reference

5. Move the cursor toward the right until it crosses the exterior wall and click to specify the location of the dimension. The dimension is created and its controls are highlighted, as shown in Figure 11-52.

Figure 11-52 The dimension with its controls

6. To add dimensions to the north wall, choose the **Entire Walls** option from the **Pick** drop-down list in the **Options Bar**.

7. Move the cursor over the north wall and click when it is highlighted.

    Autodesk Revit Architecture automatically selects the centerlines of the end walls and displays the dimension.

8. Move the cursor such that the dimension appears above the north wall, as shown in Figure 11-53, and click to place the dimension.

Figure 11-53 Adding dimensions to the north wall

9. Select the **Wall faces** option from the drop-down list on the left of the **Options Bar**.

10. Choose the **Options** button in the **Options Bar** to display the **Auto Dimension Options** dialog box.

Adding Annotations and Dimensions 11-43

11. Select the **Intersecting Walls** check box and choose the **OK** button.

12. Move the cursor over the west wall and click when it is highlighted; the dimensions are displayed.

13. Move the cursor such that the dimensions appear on the left side of the west wall and click to add them, as shown in Figure 11-54.

Figure 11-54 Dimensions added to the west wall

14. Using the above settings, add dimensions to the south wall.

15. Choose **Save As > Project** from the **Application Menu**; the **Save As** dialog box is displayed. Enter **c11_Apartment1_tut1 (M_c11_Apartment1_tut1)** in the **File name** edit box and then choose **Save**.

16. Choose **Close** from the **Application Menu** to close the project file.

The completed *Apartment 1* plan view appears similar to the sketch plan given for this tutorial.

Self-Evaluation Test

Answer the following questions and then compare them to those given at the end of this chapter:

1. When you drag a room tag, the leader is set automatically. (T/F)

2. You cannot control the visibility of tags in a project view. (T/F)

3. You can edit the tags added to a project view after adding them. (T/F)

4. Autodesk Revit Architecture automatically detects the boundary of a room while adding a room tag. (T/F)

5. Radial dimensions are used to dimension the angle between two inclined walls. (T/F)

6. The **Tag** tool is available in the _____ tab.

7. The _____ tool is used to tag all elements in the view that are not tagged.

8. Using the _____ tool, you can sketch the room separation boundary, while adding a room tag.

9. The distance of the witness line from the selected element can be set in the **Value** column for the _____ type parameter.

10. The _____ tool is used to create a radius dimension.

Review Questions

Answer the following questions:

1. If an element whose tag is not loaded is selected for tagging, Autodesk Revit Architecture will prompt you to load the corresponding tag. (T/F)

2. You can add a leader to a room tag even after the tag is added. (T/F)

3. A permanent dimension can be converted into a temporary dimension. (T/F)

4. Temporary dimensions can be used to resize walls. (T/F)

5. When you select more than one element, the temporary dimensions can be made visible using the **Activate Dimensions** button. (T/F)

6. You cannot change the room tag type after adding it. (T/F)

7. The **Load from Library** tool can be used to load tags. (T/F)

Adding Annotations and Dimensions

8. Which of the following parameters can be modified to convert a room-bounding wall into a non-room bounding wall?

   a) **Unconnected Height**
   c) **Room Bounding**
   b) **Base Constraint**
   d) **Top Constraint**

9. Which of the following options of the **Dimension** tool is used to create a dimension at an angle between the two points on an arc?

   a) **Linear**
   c) **Angular**
   b) **Radial**
   d) **Arc Length**

10. Which of the following type parameters is used to modify the distance between the dimension text and the dimension line?

    a) **Witness Line Length**
    c) **Text Offset**
    b) **Witness Line Extension**
    d) **Witness Line Gap to Element**

Exercises

Exercise 1   Club

Add rooms (without tags), room tags, and dimensions (linear, radial, and angular) to the first floor plan view of the *Club* project created in Tutorial 2 of Chapter 8, based on the sketch plan shown in Figure 11-55. Use the **Room Separator** tool to demarcate and tag the entrance lounge and passages. Note that dimensions for the east side hall are referenced to the wall centerlines, while those for the west hall are referenced to the wall faces. You can provide suitable names to the modified dimension styles. Ensure that the scale for the first floor plan view is set to 1/16"=1'0" (1: 200). The exact location of the room tags and dimensions is not important for this exercise. Use the following parameters for creating room tags and dimensions.

(Expected time: 30 min)

1. Room Tags:
   Room Tag with Area

2. Dimension Parameters:
   For Imperial   Tick Mark- **Arrow Filled 30 Degree**
                          Witness Line Gap to Element- **1/8"**
                          Text Size- **1/8"**
                          Text Offset- **1/16"**
   For Metric   Tick Mark- **Arrow Filled 30 Degree**
                          Witness Line Gap to Element- **3mm**
                          Text Size- **3mm**
                          Text Offset- **6mm**

3. Name of the file to be saved-
   For Imperial   **c11_Club_ex1**
   For Metric   **M_c11_Club_ex1**

Note
Dimensions and area values may deviate slightly from that shown in the sketch plan.

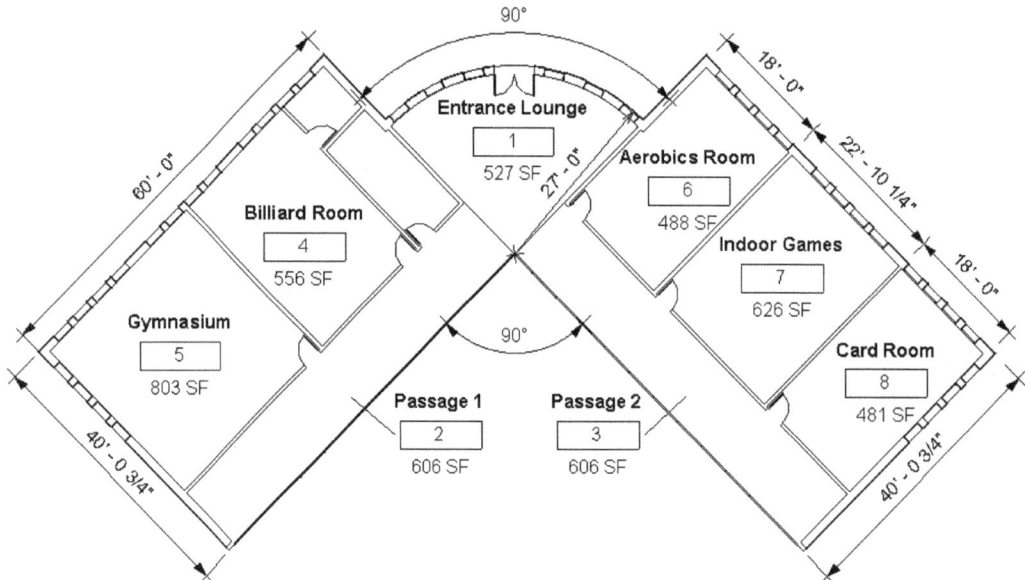

Figure 11-55 Sketch plan for adding room tags and dimensions to the Club project

Exercise 2   Elevator and Stair Lobby

Add text and dimensions to the first floor plan view of the *Elevator and Stairs Lobby* project created in Tutorial 3 of Chapter 8. Figure 11-56 shows the partial first floor sketch plan of the project. The dimensions are to be added symmetrically on both sides of the vertical axis. Ensure that the view plan scale is set to 1/8"=1'0" (1: 400). All dimensions have wall centerlines as the reference. The exact location of the tags and dimensions is not important for this exercise. Use the following parameters for creating the dimensions.   **(Expected time: 30 min)**

1. Dimension Parameters:
   For Imperial   Dimension type to be based on: **Linear w Center 3/32" Arial**
                   New dimension type name- **Linear 3/32" Arial-Stairs**
                   Tick Mark- **Diagonal 1/8"**
                   Witness Line Gap to Element- **1/8"**
   For Metric   Dimension type to be based on: **Diagonal Center 2.5 mm Arial**
                   New dimension type name- **Linear 2.5 mm Arial-Stairs**
                   Tick Mark- **Diagonal 3mm**
                   Witness Line Gap to Element- **3mm**

Adding Annotations and Dimensions 11-47

2. Name of the file to be saved-
   For Imperial   **c11_ElevatorandStairLobby_ex2**
   For Metric   **M_c11_ElevatorandStairLobby_ex2**

Figure 11-56 Partial sketch plan for adding text and dimensions to the Elevator and Stair Lobby project

Exercise 3   Building 1

Create the wall profile shown in Figure 11-57 using the wall centerline dimensions given in the plan. Also, create the dimensions for the profile. You can assume various dimension parameters for this exercise. Save the project file as *c11_Building1_ex3.rvt(M_c11_ Building1_ex3.rvt).*   **(Expected time: 15 min)**

Figure 11-57 *Sketch plan for creating the wall profile and dimensions*

Answers to Self-Evaluation Test
1. T, 2. F, 3. T, 4. T, 5. F, 6. Annotate, 7. Tag All, 8. Room Separator, 9. Witness Line Gap to Element, 10. Radial

Chapter 12

Creating Project Details and Schedules

Learning Objectives

After completing this chapter, you will be able to:
- *Create a callout view using the Callout tool.*
- *Create project details using the Detail Lines and Detail Component tools.*
- *Create a drafting detail using the Drafting View tool.*
- *Add text notes to the project detail using the Text tool.*
- *Add 3D text to a building model using the Model Text tool.*
- *Add revision cloud and revision tag to a project detail.*
- *Create project schedules using the Schedule/Quantities tool.*

PROJECT DETAILING IN Autodesk Revit Architecture

For a building or an interior project, details are as important as the building design. Apart from enabling architects and building industry professionals to convey their ideas about materializing a project on site, details describe the materials to be used for construction and their usage. The interconnection of various materials used in a project can be explained graphically using the enlarged views of specific locations. The extent of detailing provided for a project also describes the precision desired while using materials. It can also be used to describe the procedure to be followed for achieving the design intent. For example, you may want to describe the procedure for fabricating a furniture item or explain the interconnection of various materials on the floor or roof joint. The information provided through details helps the fabricator, builder, or contractor understand the architect's concept of achieving the desired design intent. The executing agency can then construct the project, based on these details.

Autodesk Revit Architecture empowers architects and other building industry professionals to create details with relative ease. This chapter describes the general procedure of adding details to an Autodesk Revit Architecture project. There are two basic methods of creating details:

1. **Using the building model**: This method is used to create details based on project views. This means you can enlarge the desired portion of a project view using the callout view, and then sketch the detail over it.

2. **Creating a drafted detail**: The second method is to sketch the details that do not use a project view. This can be done by using drafting view. The drafting details are not parametrically associated with a building model.

Based on the detailing required, you can select the method that is more suitable to the project requirement.

CREATING DETAILS USING A BUILDING MODEL

This method uses an enlarged portion of a building model view to create the project detailing. You can create a callout view by using plan, section, elevation, or detail view as its parent view. A new view is added to the **Project Browser** and is displayed under the same head as the parent view. The callout view is dependent on its parent view and is deleted if the parent view is deleted.

You can then sketch detail lines over the callout view to create the detail. Autodesk Revit Architecture provides various in-built detail components that can also be added to the detail view. In addition to this, while detailing you can crop views, sketch boundaries, and fill the sketched boundary with a required filling material. Also, you can add break lines, dimensions, and annotations to the detailed views. The various tools and methods to create detailed views are discussed next.

Callout View

A callout view is used to display an enlarged view of a part of a building model. This view is important for detailing. Creating callout view is a common practice amongst engineers as it helps them to view the project more precisely and with a higher detail. In an architectural project, callout is used to show details of the basic building elements in a model. You can create callout in plan view or in elevation view. Note that, the callout tag added to these views will be linked to the callout view.

A callout tag consists of the following parts: callout bubble, callout head, leader line, as shown in Figure 12-1. The callout bubble is the line drawn around that part of the model that you want to enlarge. The callout head is the symbol that represents the callout displaying detail number and sheet number of a model. The line connecting the callout bubble to the callout head is called the leader line.

You can create callout views either by sketching or by creating a rectangle. The methods of creating and displaying callout view, modifying callout view properties, and adding detail lines to a callout view are discussed in the next section.

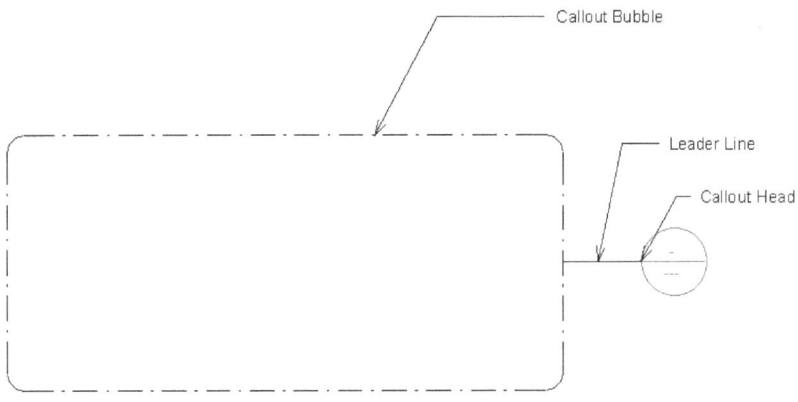

Figure 12-1 A callout tag

Creating a Callout View Using the Rectangle Tool

Ribbon: View > Create > Callout drop-down > Rectangle

As mentioned above, a callout view is used to give a detailed description about some specific section of a model around which it is drawn. To create a callout view, invoke the **Rectangle** tool from the **Callout** drop-down in the **Create** panel; the **Modify | Callout** tab will be displayed. In the **Properties** palette, the **Type Selector** drop-down list displays the type of callout view to be generated. There are two options in this drop-down list: **Detail View : Detail** and **Floor Plan : Floor Plan** (for current view). Note that **Detail View : Detail** option in the **Type-Selector** drop-down list will only be visible whenever there is any detail view in the project. You can select the **Detail View : Detail** option for providing the detailed information about a specific part in a building model. Similarly, you can select the **Floor Plan : Floor Plan** (for current view) option to provide more information about a part of the current view. The check box on the left of the **Reference other view** drop-down list is cleared by default. You can select this check box to create a reference callout. When you select the check box, the **Reference other view** drop-down list will be activated. From this drop-down list, you can select an option to specify the existing view that the callout will refer to. After selecting the desired type and option, move the cursor to the top left corner of the area that you want to enlarge and then drag it toward the lower right corner of the area to create a callout bubble, as shown in Figure 12-2. Release the left mouse button when the required area is enclosed in it.

Figure 12-2 A callout bubble showing the first and second points

Creating a Callout View Using the Sketch Tool

Ribbon: View > Create > Callout drop-down > Sketch

In Autodesk Revit, you can create a customized callout view by using the draw tools. To do so, invoke the **Sketch Path** tool from the **Create** panel of the **View** tab; the **Modify | Edit Profile** tab will be displayed. In the **Draw** panel of this tab, the **Line** tool is selected by default. You can also select other sketching tools to create a callout of desired type. Next, choose the **Finish Edit Mode** button to exit the **Modify | Edit Profile** tab. In the **Properties** palette, the **Type Selector** drop-down list displays the type of callout view to be generated. There are two options in this drop-down list: **Detail View : Detail** and **Floor Plan : Floor Plan** (for current view). You can select the **Detail View : Detail** option for providing detailed information of a specific part in a building model. Similarly, you can select the **Floor Plan : Floor Plan** (for current view) option to provide more information about a part of the current view.

Creating Project Details and Schedules

Displaying a Callout View

After you create a callout in the existing view, a new callout view is added to the **Project Browser** under the parent category. The parent category is the category in which the callout view is created. Therefore, if you create a callout view in the section view, the callout view will be added under the **Sections** heading in the **Project Browser**. Double-click on its name in the **Project Browser** under the **Sections** heading to display the corresponding callout view in the drawing window. Figure 12-3 shows an example of a callout view.

Figure 12-3 A callout view displayed

Alternatively, highlight the callout bubble and right-click to display the shortcut menu. Choose **Go To View** from the shortcut menu to display the callout view.

Modifying Callout View Properties

You can modify the appearance of a callout bubble in the parent view by using the bubble controls. These controls are displayed when the callout view is selected. The drag controls can be used to modify the extent of a callout view. The rotation control is used to rotate a callout bubble along with its leader and tag. The leader elbow control can be dragged to some desired location.

The instance properties of the callout view are different for different type of callouts. To modify the instance properties of a callout view, select it from the drawing; the instance properties of the selected callout view will be displayed in the **Properties** palette. In the **Properties** palette shown in Figure 12-4, the **View Name** instance parameter under the **Identity Data** head is used to specify a name for a Callout view. The title for the sheet can be entered in the **Title on Sheet** parameter. The **Display Model** parameter under the **Graphics** head is used to set the display type for the view of a building model. By default, this parameter is set to **Normal**. You can set the value of the **Display Model** parameter to **Halftone** from its corresponding drop-down list to display the model element in the current view as a faded image. You can select the **Do not display** option from the drop-down list corresponding to the **Display Model** parameter to hide the model element in the current view. The **Underlay** parameter under the **Graphics** head can be used to set the display of model elements that are displayed in other levels and are not visible in the current view. By default, the **Underlay** parameter is set to **None**. You can select a level from the drop-down list corresponding to this parameter to make the elements of the selected level visible in the current view. The elements that are displayed as underlay appear dimmed. The **View Template** parameter under the **Identity** head can be used to assign a view template to each view in a project. By default, the **None** option is selected in this parameter. To assign an existing view template or to create a new template and assign it to the current view, choose the **<None>** button displayed corresponding to the **View Template** parameter; the **Apply View Template** dialog box will be displayed, as shown in Figure 12-5. In the **View Templates** area of this dialog box, you can select the desired options from the **Discipline filter** and **View type** drop-down lists to limit the view templates that will be displayed in the **Names** list box. In the **Names** list box you can select the desired template to be assigned to the view. On selecting a template from the **Names** list box, its corresponding parameters will be displayed in the **View Properties** area. You can modify the parameter as per the requirement of the project. In the **View Templates** area, you can select an existing view template and choose the **Rename** button; the **Rename** dialog box will be displayed. In the **New** edit box, enter the desired name and choose the **OK** button; the selected template is renamed and will be displayed in the **Names** list box. In the **View templates** area, you can choose the **Delete** and **Duplicate** buttons to delete an existing view template and create a copy of an existing view template, respectively. To apply a view template to the current view, select the view template from the **Names** list box and choose the **Apply** button. To close the **Apply View Template** dialog box, choose the **OK** button.

Figure 12-4 The partial view of the **Properties** palette displaying the instance properties of a callout view

Creating Project Details and Schedules

The amount of details to be displayed in the callout view can be controlled by using the **Detail Level** parameter under the **Graphics** head. From the drop-down list corresponding to this parameter, you can select any of the three options: **Coarse**, **Medium**, and **Fine**. The **Coarse** option is selected by default in the drop-down list. As a result, model elements are displayed with less details in the current view. You can select the **Fine** option from this drop-down list to display the layers of various materials used in a building model. On selecting the **Fine** option, additional lines are displayed in the callout view. These lines describe composite materials. The **Edit** button in the value column for the **Visibility /Graphics Overrides** parameter can be used to control the visibility of different models and annotation elements in the callout view. The **View Scale** instance parameter is used to set the scale for the callout view. You can use the drop-down list in the value column to select a scale for the callout view.

Figure 12-5 The **Apply View Template** *dialog box*

Adding Details to the Callout View

Autodesk Revit Architecture provides various tools to add details to a callout view. In the callout view, you can sketch lines using the **Detail Line** tool and add the detail components provided in the Autodesk Revit Architecture's library.

Adding Detail Lines

Ribbon: Annotate > Detail > Detail Line
Shortcut Key: DL

The **Detail Line** tool is used to create lines for a detail view. Detail lines are view-specific and appear only in the view in which they are created. You can use the callout view of a building model and trace detail lines over the image using their varying thicknesses.

You can invoke the **Detail Line** tool from the **Detail** panel of the **Annotate** tab. On doing so, the **Modify | Place Detail Lines** tab will be displayed. In the **Line Style** panel of this tab, you can select the type of detail line from the **Line Style** drop-down list. You can select appropriate detail line based on its usage. Alternatively, you can select a type by clicking in the value field corresponding to the **Line Style** parameter in the **Properties** palette and then selecting an option from the drop-down list displayed. For example, wide lines can be used to show masonry elements whereas thin lines can be selected to represent lighter materials such as glass and aluminium. The **Draw** panel of the **Modify | Place Detail Lines** tab displays the sketching tools to draw these lines. To add detail lines, you can trace over the underlay elements. On doing so, you will notice that the cursor snaps at various elements on the underlay lines. The entire detail can be sketched using a variety of line thicknesses to achieve the desired graphical representation. You can also add dimensions and symbols to details. Figure 12-6 shows an example of a detail view created over a callout view (shown as underlay) using lines, dimensions, and symbol. However, after completing a detail, you can hide the underlay callout view using the **Display Model** parameter.

Figure 12-6 Adding detail lines in the callout view

Tip: *You can use the TAB key to cycle between various reference snap options such as the wall centerline, wall faces, wall cores, and so on. Left-click when the appropriate snap option is highlighted.*

CROP REGIONS

Crop regions help to crop views to exclude the unwanted content thereby reducing the view size. Revit Architecture has two types of crop regions that allow you to crop views for the model and annotation categories. You can control the visibility of the crop region from **View Control Bar**. The two types of crop regions are discussed next.

Creating Project Details and Schedules

Model Crop Region

You can use the model crop region to crop all model elements such as doors, windows, walls, and so on.

Annotation Crop Region

The annotation crop region crops all the annotation elements such as tags, dimensions, keynotes, and so on. All the elements that are touched partially by the annotation crop region boundary are cropped fully to avoid the partial display of annotations. Figure 12-7 shows both the annotation and model crop regions with drag controls.

Figure 12-7 The model crop and annotation crop regions with drag controls

Note
By default, the annotation crop region is displayed in the callout and duplicate dependent views but this region is not visible in the primary view. Annotations such as door and window tags will not be visible in the annotation crop region if they are a part of the hidden elements or the model crop region.

To view the crop region boundary, choose the **Show Crop Region** button from the **View Control Bar**; the crop region boundary will be displayed with drag controls. You can resize the crop region using the drag controls. Next, choose the **Crop View** button from the **View Control Bar**; the resized crop region boundary will be displayed.

To hide or show the crop regions, choose the **Show Crop Region** or **Hide Crop Region** button from the **View Control Bar**. To show or hide the annotation crop region in the drawing, you can use various options in the **Properties** palette. In this palette, you can select or clear the check box displayed in the Value field corresponding to the **Annotation Crop** parameter. Next, hover the cursor over the drawing and place the cursor over the crop boundary; a colored annotation boundary will be displayed. Click in the drawing to display the annotation crop region boundary along with the drag controls.

Creating the Filled Region

Ribbon: Annotate > Detail > Region drop-down > Filled Region

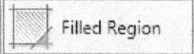

The **Filled Region** tool is used to create a two-dimensional, view-specific fill pattern within a closed boundary. You can invoke the **Filled Region** tool from the **Detail** panel. On doing so, the **Modify | Create Filled Region Boundary** tab will be displayed and the sketch mode will be activated. In this tab, you can select an option from the **Line Style** drop-down list in the **Line Style** panel to select the desired line type. The sketching tools in the **Draw** panel can be used to sketch the boundary of various shapes and sizes. You can change the region properties of the fill pattern within the closed boundary. To do so, choose the **Edit Type** button from the **Properties** palette to display the **Type Properties** dialog box. Next, click in the value field for the **Fill Pattern** parameter type; a button on the right of the field will be displayed. Choose the button; the **Fill Patterns** dialog box will be displayed, as shown in Figure 12-8.

Figure 12-8 The **Fill Patterns** dialog box displaying fill patterns

You can create two types of patterns: Model and Drafting. The Model patterns represent model elements such as brick, sand, carpet, and so on. They are fixed with respect to the model element and are scaled with it. On the other hand, the Drafting patterns are surface patterns that represent materials in a symbolic form. For example, a masonry-concrete block is represented by a diagonal cross-hatch pattern. The density of the drafting patterns is fixed with respect to the drawing sheet.

 Tip: *To create a custom pattern, choose the **New** button from the **Fill Patterns** dialog box; the **New Pattern** dialog box will be displayed. From this dialog box, you can use various options to create a custom pattern for the filled region.*

To create the Model or Drafting pattern, select the **Model** or the **Drafting** radio button in the **Pattern Type** area of the **Fill Patterns** dialog box.

Creating Project Details and Schedules

Note
You can use both model and drafting patterns for the elements in your project. However, on the cut element surfaces in the plan or section view, you can only create drafting patterns.

After selecting the type of pattern from the **Pattern Type** area, select the fill pattern from the display box. Next, choose the **OK** button from the **Fill Patterns** dialog box; this dialog box will close and the selected pattern will be assigned to the **Fill Pattern** parameter in the **Type Properties** dialog box. Choose the **OK** button to close the **Type Properties** dialog box. Next, from the **Draw** panel of the **Modify | Create Filled Region Boundary** tab, you can use various sketching tools to sketch the boundary for the filled region. Next, choose the **Finish Edit Mode** button from the **Mode** panel; the filled pattern will be created within the sketched boundary.

In this way, you can use the **Region** tool to create a pattern by sketching an enclosed boundary. In the detailed view, you can use various patterns to represent different materials with respect to their usage.

Viewing the Area of Filled Region

Revit Architecture allows you to view the surface area of the filled region. To do so, select the filled region; the instance properties will be displayed in the **Properties** palette. In this palette, the value of the **Area** parameter in the value column displays the area of the filled region. The area is defined by project units like square meters or square feet.

Adding Detail Components

Ribbon: Annotate > Detail > Component > Detail Component

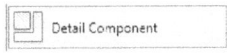

Autodesk Revit Architecture provides various in-built components that can be added to the detail using the **Detail Component** tool. To add components, invoke this tool from the **Detail** panel; the **Modify | Place Detail Component** tab will be displayed. In the **Properties** palette, you can select different types of detail components from the **Type Selector** drop-down list. To select additional types of detail components, choose the **Load Family** tool from the **Mode** panel; the **Load Family** dialog box will be displayed. In this dialog box, choose **US Imperial > Detail Items (Detail Components)**; the **Detail Items** folder will open. This folder contains several subfolders containing various element family files that can be loaded into a project. For example, you can load typical details for a window jamb in metal or wood and use them in the callout detail. The **Structural** folder contains subfolders with a variety of detail components in concrete and wood. After selecting the detail component, move the cursor in the drawing area and click to place it. Thus, you can create details by adding different detail components such as wooden members, steel elements, and so on. Figure 12-9 shows the cross-section of a typical steel column encasement detail. This detail has been created using metal studs and GW board that have been loaded from Autodesk Revit Architecture's library of detail components.

Figure 12-9 Creating a detail view using detail components

Adding an Insulation Barrier

Ribbon: Annotate > Detail > Insulation

The **Insulation** tool is used to add the insulation barrier to a detail view. To add a barrier, invoke this tool from the **Detail** panel; the **Modify | Place Insulation** tab will be displayed. In the **Draw** panel of this tab, you can select any of the two tools: **Lines** and **Pick Lines** to draw the insulation barrier in a detail view. The **Width** edit box in the **Options Bar** is used to enter the value of thickness of insulation barrier. The selection of the **Chain** check box enables you to create a continuous graphical representation. You can enter a value in the **Offset** edit box to create the insulation barrier at an offset distance from a reference. The drop-down list next to the **Offset** edit box shows three options : **to center, to near side**, and **to far side**. These options can be used to select an option to specify the reference of the offset or location for the insulation barrier. After specifying the options in the **Options Bar**, click in the drawing area to start insulation and move the cursor in the desired direction. As you move the cursor, the preview image of insulation graphics will be displayed. Click to specify the endpoint of the insulation barrier. After creating the insulation barrier, you can modify its properties. To do so, select the created insulation barrier from the drawing; the instance properties will be displayed in the **Properties** palette. In this palette, the **Insulation Bulge to Width Ratio (1/x)** instance parameter can be used to change the bulge of the insulation graphic. Figure 12-10 shows an example of an insulation barrier added to the detail view.

Creating Project Details and Schedules

Figure 12-10 An insulation barrier added to the detail view

Adding a Break Line

A break line is added to a detail view as a detail component. To add a break line to a detail view, invoke the **Detail Component** tool from the **Annotate > Detail > Component** drop-down; the **Modify | Place Detail Component** tab will be displayed. If the required break line is not loaded in the drawing, choose the **Load Family** tool from the **Mode** panel and load the *Break Line.rfa* family file by browsing **US Imperial > Detail Items** (for Metric **US Metric > Detail Items**) and choosing the **Div 01-General** folder in the **Load Family** dialog box. After you have selected the file, choose the **Open** button; the **Load Family** dialog box will close and the selected family type will be added to the **Type Selector** drop-down list. Click in the **Type Selector** drop-down list, select the **Break Line : Break Line** option from it, and then move the cursor to the required location and click to add the break line. After placing the break line, you can choose the **Rotate** tool from the **Modify** panel, if required, to orient the break line perpendicular to the element to be discontinued. On doing so, Autodesk Revit Architecture will automatically break the element at the specified location. In this manner, you can add as many break lines as you want to the detail, as shown in Figure 12-11. The two ends of the break line must intersect the edges of the component(s), in order to discontinue their visibility. You can also use the grips to extend the limit of the break line. The grips will be displayed on selecting the break line.

Figure 12-11 Break lines added to the detail view

Adding Text Notes

Text notes can be added to a detail view by using the **Text** tool. To do so, invoke this tool from the **Text** panel of the **Annotate** tab; the **Modify | Place Text** tab will be displayed. Now, from the **Type Selector** drop-down list in the **Properties** palette, select the desired text type. You can also create a new text type or change the existing instance and type properties. To create a new text type or modify the existing type, choose the **Type Properties** tool from the **Properties** panel of the **Modify | Place Text** tab; the **Type Properties** dialog box will be displayed. In this dialog box, you can specify various type parameters such as color, line weight, text font, text size, width factor, and so on. These parameters can be specified in their respective value columns. After specifying the type parameters, choose **Apply** and then the **OK** button to close the **Type Properties** dialog box. In the **Format** panel of the **Modify | Place Text** tab, you can choose the **Align Left**, **Align Center**, or **Align Right** button to set the horizontal alignment of the text to be inserted.

In Autodesk Revit Architecture, you can insert a text with or without a leader. To do so, choose any of the four buttons namely, **No Leader**, **One Segment**, **Two Segments**, and **Curved** from the **Format** panel of the **Modify | Place Text** tab. By default, the **No Leader** button is chosen. As a result, the text will be inserted without a leader. To attach a leader to the text, choose the **One Segment**, **Two Segments**, or **Curved** button from the **Format** panel to display the text with a single segment, double segments, or a curved segment leader. After selecting the required option from the **Modify | Place Text** tab, click in the drawing area. Depending upon the option selected from the **Format** panel, you need to click once or twice in the drawing area. On doing so, a text box will be displayed. Enter the text note in the text box and click in the drawing area again to finish the writing of the text. Figure 12-12 shows the added text and the leader in the detail view. The detailed description of adding text to a project view is described later in this chapter.

Creating Project Details and Schedules

Figure 12-12 Text notes added to the detail view

CREATING DRAFTED DETAILS

Drafted details are created for the details that are not referenced to the existing project views. These details are not linked to a building model, therefore, they do not get updated with it. To create a drafted detail, first create a drafting view and then use the drafting tools provided in Autodesk Revit Architecture to sketch the detail. You can also import in-built details from Autodesk Revit Architecture's detail library and use them. The created drafted detail can then be used as a reference detail.

Creating a Drafting View

To create a drafting view, invoke the **Drafting View** tool from the **Create** panel of the **View** tab; the **New Drafting View** dialog box will be displayed as shown in Figure 12-13. This dialog box is used to set the name and scale for the drafting view.

Figure 12-13 The New Drafting View dialog box

Enter a name for the drafting view in the **Name** edit box. Select the scale for the detailing from the **Scale** drop-down list. If the required scale is not available in the drop-down list, the **Custom** option can be selected to specify the scale of the drafting view. The created drafting view is added under the **Drafting Views** subhead in the **Project Browser**.

Note
The drafting views do not use project views. As a result, when you create drafting views, project views are not displayed in the drawing window.

Drafting a Detail

The method of drafting a detail in the drafting view is similar to the one used in the callout view. In a callout view, lines are traced over the enlarged project view whereas in a drafting view, the project view is not available and a new detail is drafted as if you were drafting on a blank sheet.

You can use the tools in the **Annotate** tab of the ribbon to draft a detail. The **Detail Lines** tool enables you to draw lines with varying thickness. The **Place a Component** tool is used to add in-built detail components from Autodesk Revit Architecture's detail library. The **Insulation** tool enables you to add a graphical insulation symbol to the drafted detail. You can create graphical patterns to represent various building materials using the **Region** tool. The usage of these tools is similar to their usage in a callout view. You can also add dimensions, text notes, and break lines to complete the drafted detail.

Line Style Settings

Ribbon: Manage > Settings > Additional Settings drop-down > Line Styles

Autodesk Revit Architecture provides a variety of line styles that can be used not only in detail views but also in a building model. To view these line styles, choose the **Line Styles** tool from the **Settings** panel; the **Line Styles** dialog box will be displayed. This dialog box displays list of predefined line styles, as shown in Figure 12-14.

Each line style is listed with its parameters such as weight, color, pattern and material. You have the option to change any or all of these parameters. The column for the **Line Weight** parameter displays a drop-down list of the available line weights. Click twice in the **Line Color** column to display the **Color** dialog box and then select the color to be assigned to the corresponding line style from the dialog box. The **Line Pattern** column displays a drop-down list showing the available line patterns. By default, Autodesk Revit Architecture uses **Center 1/4"** as the line pattern for **Centerline**. The column for the **Material** parameter displays the Browse button. On choosing the Browse button, the **Material Browser** dialog box will be displayed. In this dialog box, choose the material to be applied on the line style. Choose the **OK** button; the dialog box will be closed.

Creating a New Line Style

Apart from using these predefined line styles, you can also create a new line style. To do so, choose the **New** button from the **Modify Subcategories** area in the **Line Styles** dialog box; the **New Subcategory** dialog box will be displayed, as shown in Figure 12-15. In this dialog box, specify a new line style name in the **Name** edit box, select an option from the **Subcategory of** drop-down list, and then choose the **OK** button; the new line style will be added to the list of existing line styles. Now, you can set its parameters such as **Line Weight**, **Line Color**, **Line Pattern**, and **Material** to create a new line style. The new line style will be stored only in the project in which it is created.

The **Delete** and **Rename** buttons in the **Line Styles** dialog box can be used to delete or rename the new line styles. Other buttons such as **Select All**, **Select None**, and **Invert** can be used to create a selection of the listed line styles. Note that by default some of these buttons will be inactive.

Creating Project Details and Schedules

*Figure 12-14 The **Line Styles** dialog box displaying the list of in-built lines styles*

*Figure 12-15 The **New Subcategory** dialog box*

Using Line Weights

Ribbon: Manage > Settings > Additional Settings > Line Weights

The **Line Weights** tool is used to control the display of line widths in various scales of a project view. To do so, invoke this tool from the **Settings** panel of the **Manage** tab; the **Line Weights** dialog box will be displayed. This dialog box has three tabs: **Model Line Weights**, **Perspective Line Weights**, and **Annotation Line Weights**, as shown in Figure 12-16.

The **Model Line Weights** tab displays line weights for modeling elements such as walls, doors, windows, and so on. Line weights depend on view scale. This means when elements are displayed at an enlarged scale, model lines are displayed with a greater thickness or weight. The table in the **Line Weights** dialog box shows the width of each defined line weight for the corresponding scale. In this dialog box, sixteen different line weights have been defined for six different view scales. To modify a line weight, click in the appropriate cell of the table and enter a new value. The **Add** button is used to add a new scale. On choosing this button, the **Add Scale** dialog box will be displayed. The new scale can be set by selecting it from the drop-down list in the **Add Scale** dialog box. After setting the scale of the line style, choose the **Line Weights** dialog box. The **Delete** button can be used to delete an added or a predefined view scale.

The **Perspective Line Weights** tab controls line widths for various elements in the perspective view. It contains a list of sixteen model line weights. You can enter a new model line weight in the corresponding cell.

*Figure 12-16 The **Line Weights** dialog box*

The **Annotation Line Weights** tab controls line weights for various annotations such as dimension lines, section lines, and so on. The line weights for annotation symbols are independent of the scale at which they are viewed. This means a dimension line is displayed at the same thickness value irrespective of the view scale. There are sixteen predefined annotation line weights that can be selected from different tabs in the **Line Weights** dialog box. You can click and change their values.

Using Line Patterns

Ribbon: Manage > Settings > Additional Settings > Line Patterns

The **Line Patterns** tool is used to control line patterns. Invoke this tool from the **Settings** panel; the **Line Patterns** dialog box will be displayed, as shown in Figure 12-17. This dialog box displays the names of the predefined lines along with their corresponding patterns. Line patterns are a series of dashes, dots, and spaces. You can modify the properties of the predefined line patterns. To do so, select a line pattern and

Creating Project Details and Schedules

choose the **Edit** button; the **Line Pattern Properties** dialog box will be displayed, refer to Figure 12-18.

To create a new line pattern, choose the **New** button from the **Line Pattern** dialog box; the **Line Pattern Properties** dialog box will be displayed. In this dialog box, enter a name for the line pattern in the **Name** edit box. In the **Type** column of this dialog box, you can specify the type of the line pattern and in the **Value** column, you can specify a value for the specified line pattern.

Figure 12-17 The **Line Patterns** dialog box

Figure 12-18 The partial view of the **Line Pattern Properties** dialog box for the **Dash dot** line pattern

ADDING TEXT NOTES

Text notes form an important part of a project detail. They not only help in adding the specification for various building elements but also help in conveying the specific design intent. Autodesk Revit Architecture provides a variety of options to add text notes to a building model detail view by using the **Text** tool.

Creating Text Notes

Ribbon: Annotate > Text > Text
Shortcut Key: TX

Invoke the **Text** tool from the **Text** panel; the **Modify | Place Text** tab will be displayed, as shown in Figure 12-19. The buttons in the **Format** panel of this tab are used to align text. You can align text to the left, center, or right of the text box. Autodesk Revit Architecture enables you to create text notes with or without a leader. A leader is a line that connects the text note to the referred portion of a project view. To attach a leader to a text note, use any of these four tools: **No Leader**, **One Segment**, **Two Segments**, and **Curved** from the **Format** panel. The **No Leader** tool is chosen by default in this panel and is used to create a text without a leader line. The **One Segment**, **Two Segments**, or **Curved** tool can be used to create a textnote with a single segment, two segments, or a curved leader, respectively, as shown in Figure 12-20. To create a text note, invoke the **Text** tool and choose the appropriate alignment and leader options from the **Modify | Place Text** tab. As you move the cursor in the drawing window, the cursor will change into a text note symbol. If the **No Leader** button is chosen, click near the desired location to add the text note; a text box will be displayed in which you can enter the text note for the location. As you enter the text notes in the text box, more text will appear in it. Click anywhere outside the text box to complete the text note. The text note will be highlighted for editing its parameters. Invoke any other tool or press the ESC key to exit the **Text** tool.

*Figure 12-19 Text options available in the **Modify / Place Text** tab*

To use the **One Segment** tool, click at the location of the start point of the leader or the arrow. As you move the cursor, the leader extends with it. Next, click at the required location to place the text note and then type its content. If you choose the **Two Segments** tool, you need to specify one more point for the elbow of the leader. If you choose the **Curved** tool, you need to specify two points: one for the start point and the other for the endpoint of the arc leader.

Creating Project Details and Schedules

*Figure 12-20 Leaders created using the **One Segment**, **Two Segments**, and **Curved** options*

Editing Text Notes

You can either set the text note properties before creating the text note or can edit its properties afterwards. When you select a text note after it is created, its controls are displayed, as shown in Figure 12-21. You can use them to edit the parameters of a text note. In the selected text note, one blue dot on each side represents the stretch controls that can be used to modify its size. The rotation control placed at the top right corner of the text note is used to rotate it. The location of the leader arrow head remains in its original position and only the text note is rotated. The leader tail automatically adjusts to the rotated text note. You can also drag the location of the leader elbow and the leader head by using the drag control dots. The drag control is used to change the location of the text note.

Figure 12-21 Editing the text note using its controls

As you select the created text note, the **Modify | Text Notes** tab will be chosen. In this tab, you can use various editing tools such as **Copy**, **Mirror**, **Rotate**, **Array**, and so on to edit and arrange the text note. Figure 12-22 shows various options in the **Modify | Text Notes** tab for editing and modifying the selected text. The alignment of the text note can be modified by choosing the appropriate alignment option from the **Format** panel. You can use the appropriate add leader options such as **Add Right Side Straight Leader**, **Add Left Side Straight Leader**, **Add**

Left Side Arc Leader, and **Add Right Side Arc Leader** from the **Format** panel to add a leader to a text note created without a leader. You can also use any of these options to add multiple leaders. The **Remove Last Leader** button in the **Format** panel is used to remove the most recently added leader to a text note. To modify a text note, select the text inside the text box displayed with it, click inside the text box, and then enter the new note. You can also modify the instance properties of the text note such as font style and text size in the **Properties** palette. In this palette, the value assigned to the **Horizontal Align** parameter specifies the horizontal text alignment of the selected text. To change this value, click on the value column and select the desired alignment option from the drop-down list displayed. The **Arc Leaders** instance parameter specifies whether or not an arc leader will be attached to a text. The value column of this parameter displays a check box. By default, this check box is cleared. You can select this check box to attach an arc leader to the text note.

Figure 12-22 Text note editing options in the **Modify / Text Notes** tab

You can also edit the type properties of a text using the **Properties** palette. To do so, choose the **Edit Type** button from the **Properties** palette; the **Type Properties** dialog box will be displayed, as shown in Figure 12-23. In this dialog box, you can edit the type parameters. The font of a text note can be selected from the list of the true type fonts available in Autodesk Revit Architecture. To do so, click on the **Value** column for the **Text Font** parameter and select the required text font from the drop-down list. The **Text Size** parameter indicates the size of the text note. The **Tab Size** parameter sets the tab spacing used in the text notes. The tab spacing can be inserted by pressing the TAB key. You can also select the check boxes for the **Bold**, **Italic**, and **Underline** parameters to set the format of a text note.

The **Type Selector** drop-down list in the **Properties** palette displays the available text types. You have the option to select the appropriate type before creating a text. Alternatively, you can select a created text note and then select a new text type from the **Type Selector** drop-down list to replace the old text type. You can also use the **Copy to Clipboard** and **Paste** tools from the **Modify | Text Notes** tab to copy text notes from one level to multiple levels.

Creating Project Details and Schedules

*Figure 12-23 The **Type Properties** dialog box for text notes*

Creating a Model Text

Ribbon: Architecture > Model > Model Text

The **Model Text** tool enables you to create a text that acts as a 3D building element. The added texts are visible in all related views. They are rendered as a part of a building model and not as annotation symbols. The model text can be added to a selected level or a plane.

To add the model text to a building model, invoke the **Model Text** tool from the **Model** panel. On doing so, the **Edit Text** dialog box will be displayed and you will be prompted to enter the model text notes. After entering the text notes, choose the **OK** button to close the dialog box. The preview image of the text note entered will be displayed in the drawing window attached to the cursor. Click to place the model text at the desired location. Now, you can select the model text and modify its properties. Figure 12-24 shows an example of a model text added to the facade of a building.

Figure 12-24 Model text added to a building model

 Tip: *You should set the work plane before invoking the **Model Text** tool because model text can be placed only in the current work plane.*

Modifying Model Text Properties

You can modify the properties of the model text before or after creating it. To edit the model text, select it from the drawing; the **Modify | Generic Models** tab will be displayed. You can use options in this tab to modify the content of the text, properties (instance and type) of the text, existing work plane of the text, and so on. In the **Modify | Generic Models** tab for the selected text, modification options are available in specific panels. To edit contents in the selected text, choose the **Edit Text** tool from the **Text** panel of the **Modify | Generic Models** tab; the **Edit Text** dialog box will be displayed. Enter suitable content in the dialog box and choose **OK**; the dialog box will be closed and the modified content will be displayed in the model text.

To change the instance and type properties of the selected text, you can use various parameters in the **Properties** palette. In this palette, choose the **Edit** button in the value column of the **Text** instance parameter to enter new text. The **Horizontal Align** parameter can be used to set the alignment or justification of the text to left, center, or right. The **Depth** instance parameter can be used to set the depth or extrusion height of text characters. You can also select and assign materials to the model text using the **Material** parameter. You can access the type parameters of the model text. To do so, choose the **Edit Type** button from the **Properties** palette; the **Type Properties** dialog box will be displayed. This dialog box displays the type parameters for the model text. The function of parameters such as **Text Font**, **Text Size**, **Bold**, **Italic**,

Creating Project Details and Schedules

and so on is similar to those described for text notes. Figure 12-25 shows another example of model text added to a building model.

Figure 12-25 An example showing the model text added to a building model

Note
If a project view intersects the model text, it will be shown as a cut. You can however set the view range parameter to make it appear complete.

Tip: *You can also use the editing tools such as **Copy**, **Move**, **Rotate**, **Array**, **Mirror** and so on for editing the model text.*

REVISION CLOUDS

While creating project plans, you may need to revise a portion of a project view and issue the revised drawings to the concerned authorities. The revision cloud is added to refer and to indicate the revised portion. Except 3D views, you can add the revision cloud to any project view such as floor plans, elevations, sections, and so on. Autodesk Revit Architecture enables you to create the revision clouds of the desired shape and size. You can also add a revision tag to the revision cloud for referring to the revisions made to a specified area.

Creating the Revision Cloud

Ribbon: Annotate > Detail > Revision Cloud

To create a revision cloud, invoke the **Revision Cloud** tool from the **Detail** panel; the **Modify | Create Revision Cloud Sketch** tab will be displayed. You can use various sketching tools in the tab to sketch, edit a sketch, and assign properties to the revision cloud. To sketch the revision cloud, choose the any of the drawing tool from the

Draw panel, move the cursor near the revised area, and click at the desired location to start creating the revision cloud. On moving the cursor, you will notice that a curved bubble-shaped line is displayed. Click to specify the next point of the cloud outline. In this way, you can click at multiple points to sketch the revision cloud of desired size and shape enclosing the portion of the view that needs to be referred for revision. You can choose other standard tools to create revision cloud such as line, rectangle, and so on. You can use SPACEBAR to flip the direction of the cloud. Next, choose the **Finish Edit Mode** button from the **Mode** panel of the **Modify | Create Revision Cloud Sketch** tab to create the revision cloud, as shown in Figure 12-26.

Figure 12-26 The revision cloud created around the portion to be referred for revision

Revit Architecture allows you to hide revision clouds in a view. To hide a revision cloud, select the required revision cloud and right-click; a shortcut menu will be displayed. Then, choose **Hide in view > Category** from the shortcut menu. Hiding clouds in a view does not have any effect on revision tables and schedules.

 Note
If you have tagged the revision cloud, hiding the revision cloud will also hide the tag associated with it.

Adding a Revision Tag

While working on projects, you may need to use multiple revision clouds in a project view. To identify and mark each revision cloud, you can add revision tags to it.

A revision tag can be added using the **Tag by Category** tool. To add a revision tag, invoke the **Tag by Category** tool from the **Tag** panel of the **Annotate** tab and then move the cursor near the revision cloud. Click in the drawing area when the cloud is highlighted; the revision tag will be

Creating Project Details and Schedules

placed. In case it is not loaded in the project file, Autodesk Revit Architecture will prompt you to load it. You can load the *Revision Tag.rfa* family file from the **US Imperial > Annotations** folder. Now, you can move the cursor over the revision cloud and click to place the revision tag. A leader will automatically be added to the revision tag because the **Leader** check box in the **Options Bar** is selected by default. You can then use the drag controls to direct the leader toward the revision cloud, as shown in Figure 12-27. However, you can remove the leader from the revision tag by selecting it and then clearing the **Leader** check box in **Options Bar**. Once you have added the revision tags, Autodesk Revit Architecture will enable you to create revision schedules to be placed on the drawing sheet. You will learn more about creating schedules in the next section.

Figure 12-27 A revision tag added to the revision cloud

Controlling the Visibility of the Revision Tag

Revit Architecture allows you to control the visibility of revision tags before adding revision clouds to a drawing. To specify the visibility settings, choose the **Sheet Issues/Revisions** tool from **Manage > Settings > Additional Settings** drop-down; the **Sheet Issues/Revisions** dialog box will be displayed. In the **Show** column of the dialog box, the **Cloud and Tag** option is selected by default. Click in the **Show** column cell and select any of the following visibility options:

None
This option will turn off the display of both the revision cloud and the tag in the drawing.

Tag
This option will display the tag, but not the revision cloud. You can hover the cursor in the drawing and select the revision cloud when it gets highlighted.

Cloud and Tag

This is the default option and displays both the revision cloud and the tag, if loaded in the drawing.

USING SCHEDULES IN A PROJECT

Schedule is another format for providing project information. In a building project, there may be different items that can be used a number of times at different locations. Schedules are primarily used to provide information regarding these items in a tabulated form. For each item, the schedule tables provide information regarding its size, material, cost, finish, level, and so on. These schedules can then be used by associated agencies for various purposes. They can assist the fabricating agency to manufacture all similar items. The quantity surveyors and estimators can calculate the quantity and cost of the grouped items.

For example, in a building model, a particular window type may be used a number of times in the same layout plan on different floors. Using schedules, you can group these windows in different ways based on their parameters such as location in a project, floor, size of the window, material of construction, and so on.

Schedules are created by extracting information from a building model. In Autodesk Revit Architecture, all elements are parametric. This means that they have several properties associated with them. When you use these elements, the associated information is automatically added to the building model. This information can be then extracted for the creation of schedules.

The power of Autodesk Revit Architecture's parametric change engine enables you to modify elements in a building model at any stage of the project development. The changes are reflected immediately in all project views. As elements are bidirectionally associated, the entire project information is updated immediately and the necessary changes in schedules are reflected automatically. Conversely, when you modify an element in a schedule, all its instances are immediately updated in all project views. Autodesk Revit Architecture also enables you to create schedules based on common group properties of different categories of items. For example, you can create a schedule of all rooms in a project that have the same floor, ceiling, and wall finish. These are termed as Key Schedules.

Note
Some of the parameters of wall such as Base Constraint, Base Offset, Top Constraint, Top Offset, and Unconnected Height are now included in the Wall Schedule and Material Takeoff.

Generating a Schedule

Ribbon: View > Create > Schedules drop-down > Schedule/Quantities

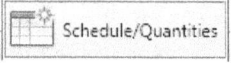

In Autodesk Revit Architecture, you can create a schedule by using the **Schedule/Quantities** tool. You can invoke this tool from the **Create** panel. On doing so, the **New Schedule** dialog box will be displayed, as shown in Figure 12-28.

Creating Project Details and Schedules

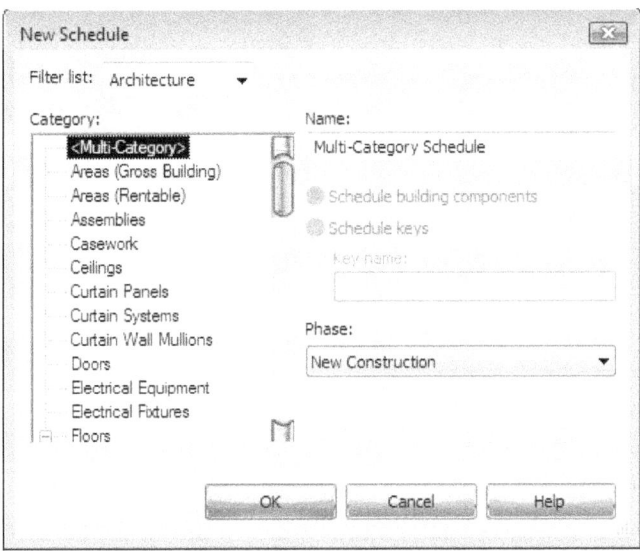

*Figure 12-28 The **New Schedule** dialog box*

In the **New Schedule** dialog box, various categories of building elements are listed in the **Category** list. By default, all the checkboxes are selected in the **Filter List** drop-down. You can select one or more discipline from the **Filter List** drop-down list. Then, you can select the required category from the **Category** list to create a schedule. For example, to generate a door schedule, you can select **Doors** from the **Category** list. The **Wall Sweeps** category in the **Category** list is used to create a schedule for wall sweeps. The category selected for creating a schedule is displayed in the **Name** edit box. The **Schedule building components** radio button is used to create a schedule of building elements. The **Filter List** drop-down list is used to display all the discipline categories. In this drop-down list, you can select the check box of the discipline you want to display. When you choose the **OK** button, the **Schedule Properties** dialog box will be displayed, as shown in Figure 12-29.

The **Schedule Properties** dialog box has options to set the properties of the elements, its formatting, and appearance in a schedule. It contains five tabs: **Fields**, **Filter**, **Sorting/Grouping**, **Formatting**, and **Appearance**. The options in the **Fields** tab can be used to select the headings of a schedule. Select the required headings from the **Available fields** list and choose the **Add** button to add fields to the **Scheduled fields** area. Choose the **Remove** button to remove the selected scheduled fields. You can use the **Move Up** and **Move Down** buttons to move and arrange the fields in the desired order. By choosing the **Add Parameter** button, you can add your own custom field. You can choose the **Calculate Value** button to create a field that is a percentage of another field. The **Include elements in links** check box can be selected to include elements from the linked Revit files into the schedules and drawing files of model elements such as doors, walls, rooms, and so on.

*Figure 12-29 The **Schedule Properties** dialog box*

The options in the **Filter** tab enable you to restrict the display of elements based on certain rules. Based on their parameters and values, you can use maximum four filters for a schedule. For example, to display doors on Level1, you can use the **Level** parameter as one filter and the number **1** as the other filter. The options in the **Sorting/Grouping** tab can be used to sort and group rows in a schedule. The parameter for sorting a schedule can be selected from the **Sort by** drop-down list. You can sort it in the ascending or descending order by selecting appropriate radio button. For example, to arrange doors types in the ascending order of their width, choose **Width** as the **Sort by** parameter and the **Ascending** button.

The **Grand totals** check box can be selected to display the sum total of all the elements. On selecting the **Grand Totals** checkbox the **Custom grand total title** edit box will be enabled. In this edit box, you can enter to assign the title for the **Grand Total** in the schedule. The **Formatting** tab enables you to set the parameters related to the appearance of headings. You can select a heading from the **Fields** list and enter a new heading name in the **Heading** edit box. The orientation and the alignment of the heading can be specified by selecting the desired options from the **Heading orientation** and **Alignment** drop-down lists, respectively. The **Field Format** button is used to format the appearance of fields with numerical values. For such fields, select the **Calculate totals** check box to display their sum totals. You can select the **Hidden field** check box to hide a field in a schedule. On doing so, you can sort out or filter a schedule by using the selected field without actually displaying it in the schedule. The options in the **Appearance** tab can be used to change the appearance of the schedule view. You can use various parameters such as **Header text**, **Body text**, and so on to modify the appearance of a schedule.

Creating Project Details and Schedules

When you choose the **OK** button from the **Schedule Properties** dialog box, Autodesk Revit Architecture scans the building model for the category of elements and displays the schedule based on the parameters specified. Figure 12-30 shows an example of a window schedule with the scheduled fields.

\multicolumn{6}{c}{Window Schedule}
Type Mark	Width	Height	Level	Count	Comments
1	3' - 0"	4' - 0"	Ground Floor	1	
1	3' - 0"	4' - 0"	Ground Floor	1	
2	4' - 0"	4' - 0"	Ground Floor	1	
2	4' - 0"	4' - 0"	Ground Floor	1	
2	4' - 0"	4' - 0"	Ground Floor	1	
3	1' - 4"	4' - 0"	Ground Floor	1	
3	1' - 4"	4' - 0"	Ground Floor	1	
3	1' - 4"	4' - 0"	Ground Floor	1	
3	1' - 4"	4' - 0"	Ground Floor	1	
3	1' - 4"	4' - 0"	Ground Floor	1	
3	1' - 4"	4' - 0"	Ground Floor	1	
3	1' - 4"	4' - 0"	Ground Floor	1	
3	1' - 4"	4' - 0"	Ground Floor	1	
3	1' - 4"	4' - 0"	Ground Floor	1	
3	1' - 4"	4' - 0"	Ground Floor	1	
3	1' - 4"	4' - 0"	Ground Floor	1	
3	1' - 4"	4' - 0"	Ground Floor	1	
1	3' - 0"	4' - 0"	First Floor	1	
1	3' - 0"	4' - 0"	First Floor	1	
2	4' - 0"	4' - 0"	First Floor	1	

Figure 12-30 A window schedule

You can modify the properties of a schedule even after creating it. To do so, click on the schedule name in the **Project Browser**, and from the **Properties** palette, choose the **Edit** button in the **Value** column for the **Fields**, **Filter**, **Sorting/Grouping**, **Formatting**, and **Appearance** instance parameters to access their respective tabs in the **Schedule Properties** dialog box.

For example, the schedule shown in Figure 12-30 can be edited to create a simplified schedule in which the doors with a particular type mark are grouped together. You can access the options in the **Sorting/Grouping** tab, select the **Grand totals** check box and clear the **Itemize every instance** check box to summarize the schedule. On doing so, the modified schedule will be displayed, as shown in Figure 12-31.

\multicolumn{6}{c}{Window Schedule}
Type Mark	Width	Height	Level	Count	Comments
1	3' - 0"	4' - 0"		8	
2	4' - 0"	4' - 0"		12	
3	1' - 4"	4' - 0"		48	

Figure 12-31 The modified window schedule

Tip: *You can modify the appearance of a schedule by dragging the columns to the desired width.*

After calculating the required material quantity, you can use the cost per unit to calculate the total estimated cost for that item. For example, to calculate the total cost of walls for a project, first create a wall schedule showing the area of each wall type. Next, enter the value of the cost per square feet for each wall type directly in the created schedule. Autodesk Revit Architecture automatically assigns the cost to all instances of the same wall type. In the **Fields** tab of the **Schedule Properties** dialog box, you can then use the **Add Parameter** button in the **Schedule Properties** dialog box to add a new column for **Total Cost** for each type of wall. Use the **Calculate Value** button and assign the formula **Cost*Area/1'^2** to calculate the total cost of each type of wall (the factor 1'^2 is used to suppress the units). In the **Formatting** tab, select the **Calculate total** check box for the **Total Cost** column and generate the total cost of the walls in the building project. This procedure can be adopted for each category of elements such as windows, doors, floor, roof, furniture, and so on. The gross total cost of all building elements can then be calculated.

Tip: *The Schedule/Quantities tool can be used to create schedules of the elements related to a building model. For example, you can create wall schedules showing values of wall parameters such as length, height, volume, area, and so on. The values of these parameters can then be used to calculate the required quantity of materials such as brick, plaster, paint, and so on. Similarly, you can create furniture schedule, room schedule, structural schedule, and so on to create an inventory of the dependent and stand-alone elements used in a project. These schedules help you arrange the elements in a tabular form.*

Exporting Schedule to Excel Sheet

In Autodesk Revit Architecture, you can export a schedule to MS Office Excel to generate a spreadsheet. To do so, choose the **Application** button; the **Application Menu** will be displayed. From the **Application Menu**, choose **Export > Reports > Schedule**; the **Export Schedule** dialog box will be displayed as shown in Figure 12-32. Enter the name of file in the **File Name** edit box and select the **Delimited text (*.txt)** from the **File of type** drop-down list. Next, choose the **Save** button; the modified **Export Schedule** dialog box will be displayed, refer to Figure 12-33.

The **Export Schedule** dialog box consists of the **Schedule Appearance** and **Output options** areas.

In the **Schedule Appearance** area, the **Export title** check box is selected by default. As a result, the title of the schedule will be exported to the spreadsheet. On clearing this check box the title of the schedule will not be exported to the spreadsheet. The **Export column header** check box is also selected by default in the **Schedule Appearance** area. As a result, the **Include grouped column header** check box will be activated and selected. Therefore, the columns and the grouped columns will be exported to the spreadsheet. On clearing these check boxes the column and the grouped columns will not be exported to the spreadsheet.

The **Export group headers, footers, and blank lines** check box is selected by default. As a result, the header and footer of the schedule will be exported to the spreadsheet. On clearing this check box, the header and footer will not be exported.

Creating Project Details and Schedules 12-33

The **Output options** area specifies how you want to display the data in the output file. The fields in the output file can be separated by tabs, spaces, commas, or semi-colons. You can select one of these option from the **Field delimiter** drop-down list to separate the text in the field. Select the desired options from the **Text qualifier** drop-down list to specify the text in each field of the file. Next, choose the **OK** button to close the dialog box; the schedule file will be saved at the desired location. To open the saved schedule file in an excel sheet, you need to choose **Start > All Programs > MS Office > Excel 2013**. On doing so, the program will be loaded and the user interface screen will be displayed. Now, choose the **File** button; the **Application Menu** will be displayed. From the **Application Menu**, choose **Open** and select the desired file; the file will be displayed in an excel sheet. If required, you can edit Schedule/Quantities in this sheet.

*Figure 12-32 The **Export Schedule** dialog box*

*Figure 12-33 The **Export Schedule** dialog box with schedule appearance and output parameters*

Creating a Legend View

Ribbon: View > Create > Legends drop-down > Legend

Legends are created to list the symbols and annotations used in project views. You can create them for various elements used in a project such as wall types, tag type, symbols, and so on. A legend is created as a view.

To create a legend, choose the **Legend** tool from the **Create** panel; the **New Legend View** dialog box will be displayed, as shown in Figure 12-34.

Enter a name for the legend in the **Name** edit box. You can set the scale for the legend by selecting the scale from the **Scale** drop-down list. To set a scale other than the options available in the drop-down list, select the **Custom** option and specify the scale in the **Scale value 1:** edit box. Once you choose the **OK** button in the **New Legend View** dialog box, a new view will open in the drawing window and will be added under the **Legends** head in the **Project Browser**. You can then use various tools to create the desired legend type. Next, you will add legend components to the opened legend view. To do so, choose the **Legend Component** tool from **Annotate > Detail > Component** drop-down; the

*Figure 12-34 The **New Legend View** dialog box*

Options Bar will display the associated tools and options. The **Family** drop-down list displays family elements. The required view for the legend can be selected from the **View** drop-down list. The **Host Length** edit box can be used to specify the length of the legend symbol for the selected family type. You can select the desired family element and create a legend. You can use the **Text** tool in the **Text** panel of the **Annotate** tab to add text notes to the legend view. The **Detail Lines** tool can be used to create a tabulated legend with lines.

Similarly, the **Symbol** tool can be used to create a legend of the symbols used in a project. For example, you can create a legend for all the tags used in the project documentation using the **Symbol** tool, as shown in Figure 12-35.

Creating Project Details and Schedules

Figure 12-35 A tag legend

TUTORIALS
Tutorial 1   Apartment 1 - Callout View

In this tutorial, you will create a callout view of the kitchen door jamb in the *Apartment 1* project represented by a highlighted rectangle with a cursor, as shown in Figure 12-36. You will use the *c11_Apartment1_tut1.rvt* file created in Tutorial 1 of Chapter 11. You need to add the detail lines, detail components, text notes, and break lines to complete the door jamb detail, as shown in Figure 12-37. Use the parameters given in the detail and those given below to create it. **(Expected time: 1hr)**

1. Callout view parameters:
   Callout view name to be assigned- **Door Jamb Detail**
   View Scale- **1 1/2" = 1'-0"**   View Scale- **1:10**
   Detail Level- **Fine**

2. Detail component to be loaded from the **US Imperial > Detail Items > Div 06-Wood and Plastic > 061100-Wood Framing** (for Metric **US Metric > Detail Items > Div 06-Wood and Plastic > 06100- Rough Carpentry > 061100-Wood Framing**) and **US Metric > Detail Items >Div 08-Openings > 081400-Wood Doors** folder locations (for Metric **US Metric > Detail Items >Div 08-Doors and Windows > 08200- Wood and Plastic Doors > 08210-Wood Doors**).

Figure 12-36 Sketch plan for adding a callout view to the Apartment 1 project plan

Figure 12-37 The callout view of the Apartment 1 project

Creating Project Details and Schedules   12-37

3. Insulation instance parameters:
   Insulation Width: **2 1/2" (64 mm)**
   Insulation Bulge to Width Ratio: **3**

4. Text note parameters:
   Text Size: **3/32" (2.4 mm)**
   Leader Arrowhead: **Arrow Filled 15 - Degree**

5. Load the break line from **US Imperial > Detail Items** folder (For Metric **US Metric > Detail Items** folder) with the following modified parameters:

   Values for the **Right** and **Left** instance parameter: **0' 4" (102 mm)**
   Values for **Jag Depth**, **Jag Width**, and **Masking depth** parameters: **0' 2" (51 mm)**

   The following steps are required to complete this tutorial:

a. Open the specified project file and then create the callout view using the **Callout** tool, refer to Figure 12-37.
b. Display the view and set its parameters, refer to Figure 12-38.
c. Use the callout view as an underlay and add detail components using the **Detail Component** tool, refer to Figures 12-39 through 12-41.
d. Add detail lines to the callout view using the **Detail Lines** tool, refer to Figures 12-42 through 12-43.
e. Use the **Insulation** tool to add insulation to the detail, refer to Figures 12-45 and 12-46.
f. Invoke the **Text** tool and add the text notes after setting the parameters, refer to Figures 12-47 through 12-49.
g. Add break lines to complete the detail callout view.

Opening the Project File and Creating the Callout View

1. To start a project, choose **Open > Project** from the **Application Menu** and open the *c11_Apartment_tut1.rvt* file created in Tutorial 1 of Chapter 11. The first floor plan is displayed. You can also download this file from *http://www.cadcim.com*. The path of the file is as follows: *Textbooks > Civil/GIS > Revit Architecture > Autodesk Revit Architecture 2015 for Architects and Designers.*

2. Choose the **Zoom in Region** tool from the **Navigation Bar** and zoom near the area inside the rectangle, refer to Figure 12-36.

3. Next, choose the **Rectangle** tool from the **View > Create > Callout** drop-down; the **Modify | Callout** tab is displayed.

4. Click at the two points to define the callout view rectangle, as shown in Figure 12-38.

   The callout view created is displayed as **First Floor- Callout 1** under the **Floor Plans** head in the **Project Browser**.

Figure 12-38 Defining the rectangle to create a callout view

Displaying the Callout View and Setting View Parameters

1. To display the callout view, double-click on the callout view name **First Floor- Callout 1** under the **Floor Plans** head in the **Project Browser**.

   Now, select the door element in the callout view and right-click; a shortcut menu is displayed. Choose **Hide in view > Category** from the shortcut menu; the doors in this view are now hidden, as shown in Figure 12-39.

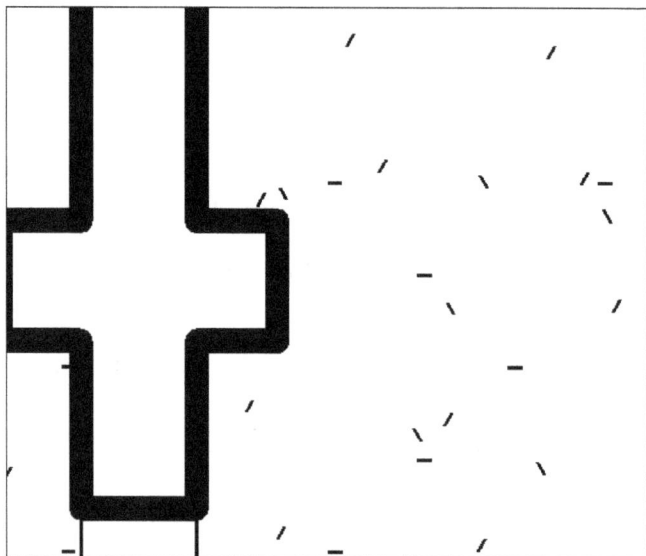

Figure 12-39 Callout view displayed in the viewing area

2. In the **Properties** palette, click in the **Value** field for the **View Name** instance parameter and enter **Door Jamb Detail**.

Creating Project Details and Schedules

3. For the **View Scale** parameter, click in its value field and select the desired option from the corresponding drop-down list.
   For Imperial   **1 1/2" = 1'- 0"**
   For Metric   **1 : 10**

4. Similarly, click in the value fields for the **Display Model** and **Detail Level** parameters and then select **Halftone** and **Fine** from the corresponding drop-down lists.

5. Now, click in the value field of the **Underlay** parameter and select the **First Floor** option from the corresponding drop-down list. Notice that callout view is displayed as an underlay in gray half-tone. Also, notice that some more lines are displayed indicating the material composition of the building elements.

Adding Detail Components

In this section of the tutorial, you will add detail components by using the callout view as an underlay. Further, you will load the desired components, place them at the required location, and then modify their sizes.

1. Choose the **Annotate** tab and then choose the **Detail Component** tool from the **Component** drop-down of the **Detail** panel; the **Modify | Place Detail Component** tab is displayed.

   Next, you need to load the components according to the project parameters.

2. Choose the **Load Family** tool from the **Mode** panel; the **Load Family** dialog box is displayed.

3. Navigate to **US Imperial > Detail Items >Div 08-Openings > 081400-Wood Doors** (for Metric **US Metric > Detail Items >Div 08-Doors and Windows > 08200- Wood and Plastic Doors > 08210-Wood Doors**) and select the **Wood Door Frame-Double Rabbet-Section** file. Now, choose **Open**; the selected file is loaded and it will be available in the **Type Selector** drop-down list.

4. Choose the **Type Properties** tool from the **Properties** panel; the **Type Properties** dialog box is displayed.

5. Choose **Duplicate**; the **Name** dialog box is displayed. Enter **6 1/2" (165 mm)** in the **Name** edit box and choose **OK**. Now, in the **Value** fields for the **Width** and **Stop** parameters, enter **0' 6 1/2" (165 mm)** and **0' 3" (76 mm)**, respectively.

6. Now, choose **OK**; the **Type Properties** dialog box will close.

7. Choose the **Load Family** tool from the **Mode** panel; the **Load Family** dialog box is displayed. In this dialog box, navigate to **US Imperial > Detail Items > Div 06-Wood and Plastic > 061100-Wood Framing** (for Metric **US Metric > Detail Items > Div 06-Wood and Plastic > 06100- Rough Carpentry > 061100-Wood Framing**) and select the **Rough Cut Lumber-Section** file. Next, choose **Open**; the **Specify Types** dialog box is displayed.

8. Choose **1x4R** (for Metric **25 x 100mm**) and **1x6R** (for Metric **25 x 150 mm**) in the **Type** column using the CTRL key and then choose **OK**; the **Specify Types** dialog box will close and the selected types will now be available in the **Type Selector** drop-down list in the **Properties** palette.

9. From the **Type Selector** drop-down list, select **Wood Door Frame-Double Rabbet-Section: 6 1/2" (165 mm)**.

10. Select the **Rotate after placement** check box available in the **Options Bar**.

11. Move the cursor to the viewing area and click near the door jamb location to place the door frame. Rotate it 90 degrees in counterclockwise direction to achieve the correct orientation and then click again. Next, choose the **Modify** button from the **Select** panel. Then, select the placed door frame and use the **Move** tool and the **Midpoint** snap option to move the door frame to the location shown in Figure 12-40. Choose the **Modify** button from the **Select** panel.

Figure 12-40 Adding the door frame as a detail component

12. Similarly, using the **Detail Component** tool and the editing tools, place the **Rough Cut Lumber-Section : 1x4R** (for Metric **Rough Cut Lumber-Section : 1x4R**) component at the locations shown in Figure 12-41.

You need to place another wood board of **6 1/2"** (165 mm) length. You can select and modify the properties of a similar component to create the new one.

Creating Project Details and Schedules

Figure 12-41 Adding the wood board as a detail component

13. Next, invoke the **Detail Component** tool and select the **Rough Cut Lumber-Section : 1x6R** option from the **Type Selector** drop-down list.

14. Choose the **Edit Type** button from the **Properties** palette; the **Type Properties** dialog box is displayed.

15. Choose the **Duplicate** button; the **Name** dialog box is displayed. Enter **1x 6.5R** (for Metric **25 x 165 mm**) in the **Name** edit box.

16. In the **Type Properties** dialog box, enter the value **0' 6 1/2" (165 mm)** in the **Value** column for the **Depth** dimension parameter.

17. Choose **OK**; the **Type Properties** dialog box is closed.

18. Ensure that the detail component **Rough Cut Lumber-Section : 1x6.5R** (**M_Rough Cut Lumber-Section : 25 x 165mm**) is selected in the **Type Selector** drop-down list and place it at the required location, as shown in Figure 12-42.

Figure 12-42 The modified wood board added as a detail component

Adding Detail Lines to the Project Detail

1. Choose the **Detail Line** tool from the **Detail** panel of the **Annotate** tab; the **Modify | Place Detail Lines** tab is displayed.

2. Ensure that the **Thin Lines** option is selected in the **Line Style** drop-down list in the **Line Style** panel. Now, use the snap options to sketch thin lines at 5/8" distance, depicting the double layer gypsum wall board in the callout view. You can also use the **Mirror**, **Offset**, and **Copy** tools to create detail lines. After adding the thin lines, the detail view will appear similar to the graphic shown in Figure 12-43.

Figure 12-43 The detail lines added to the callout view

Creating Project Details and Schedules

3. After you create the details lines, you will add metal studs to support the gypsum boards. To do so, choose the **Detail Component** tool from **Annotate > Detail > Component** drop-down; the **Modify | Place Detail Component** tab is displayed.

4. Choose the **Load Family** tool from the **Mode** panel; the **Load Family** dialog box is displayed. Now, browse to the **US Imperial > Detail Items > Div 05-Metals > 054200- Cold-Formed Metal Joist Framing** folder (**US Metric > Detail Items > Div 05-Metals > 05400-Cold-Formed Metal Joist Framing > 05420- Cold Formed Metal Joist**) and select the **C Joist-Section** (for Metric **M_C Joist-Section**) file. Now, choose **Open**; the selected file will now be loaded and can be selected from the **Type Selector** drop-down list.

5 Ensure that the **C Joist-Section : 5 1/2"** (for Metric **M_C Joist-Section : 64mm**) is selected in the **Type Selector** drop-down list and then choose the **Edit Type** button from the **Properties** palette; the **Type Properties** dialog box is displayed.

6. Choose **Duplicate**; the **Name** dialog box is displayed. Enter **2 1/2" (64 mm)** in the **Name** edit box and then choose **OK** to close the **Name** dialog box.

7. Now, in the **Type Properties** dialog box, click in the **Value** fields of the **Width** and **Depth** parameters and enter **2 1/2" (64 mm)** and **1 1/2" (38 mm)**, respectively.

8. Choose **OK**; the **Type Properties** dialog box closes and the new type of joist section is selected in the **Type Selector** drop-down list.

9. Move the cursor in the drawing area and then use the editing tools to add the selected type of joist to the detail view, as shown in Figure 12-44.

Figure 12-44 The medium detail lines added to the detail view

Adding an Insulation to the Detail

After you have added detail components and detail lines, you will add the insulation between the metal joist framing members by using the **Insulation** tool.

1. To add insulation, choose the **Insulation** tool from the **Detail** panel of the **Annotate** tab; the **Modify | Place Insulation** tab is displayed.

2. Ensure that the **Line** tool is chosen in the **Draw** panel. Next, enter **0' 2 1/2" (64 mm)** in the **Width** edit box in the **Options Bar**.

3. Move the cursor to the drawing window and click to specify the location of the start point and end point of the insulation, as shown in Figure 12-45. Now press ESC twice; the insulation is created.

4. Next, select the insulation that you have recently created; the **Modify | Insulation Batting Lines** tab is displayed.

5. In the **Properties** palette, click in the value column of the **Insulation Bulge to Width Ratio (1/x)** parameter and enter **3**. Now, choose **Apply**; the type property of the selected component gets modified.

6. Similarly, to add other insulations, repeat steps 1 to 3 of this section. Refer to Figure 12-46 for location.

Figure 12-45 Sketching the insulation

Figure 12-46 The insulations added to the detail view

Adding Text Notes to the Detail

You need to add text notes to the detail. Use an existing text note style as a template and create a new text type by modifying its parameters, as given in the project parameters.

1. Choose the **Text** tool from the **Text** panel of the **Annotate** tab; the **Modify | Place Text** tab is displayed.

2. From the **Type Selector** drop-down list, select **Text: 3/32" Arial** (for Metric **Text: 3/32" Arial**)

Creating Project Details and Schedules

3. In the **Properties** palette, choose the **Edit Type** button; the **Type Properties** dialog box is displayed.

4. Choose **Duplicate** from the dialog box; the **Name** edit box is displayed.

5. Enter the name **Text Notes** in the **Name** edit box and choose **OK**.

6. In the **Type Properties** dialog box, ensure that the value for the **Text Size** type parameter is **3/32" (2.4 mm)**.

7. For the **Leader Arrowhead** parameter, select **Arrow Filled 15 Degree** from the drop-down list.

8. Choose **Apply** and **OK**; the settings are applied to the text notes and the **Type Properties** dialog box closes.

9. To add the text note with two segment leaders, choose the **Two Segments** tool from the **Format** panel of the **Modify | Place Text** tab. If you want to create a text note with two segment leaders, you need to specify three points. The first point specifies the location of the leader head, the second point specifies the leader elbow, and the third point specifies the start point of the text.

10. Click on the door panel, refer to Figure 12-47, to specify the first point and move the cursor upward in the right direction and then click to specify the elbow point. Next, move the cursor horizontally toward right and click to specify the endpoint of the leader (start point of the text), as shown in Figure 12-47.

11. Enter the text **Wood Door Frame - Double Rabbet-Section**: **6 1/2 "** (for Metric **M_Wood Door Frame - Double Rabbet-Section**: **165mm**) in the edit box, as shown in Figure 12-48. Click outside the text box to complete the text note.

12. Similarly, add other text notes at appropriate locations, as shown in Figure 12-49, and press ESC when you have completed entering the text.

Figure 12-47 Specifying three points for creating the text note with two segment leaders

Figure 12-48 Writing the text of the text note

Adding Break Lines

In this section of the tutorial, you will add break line symbols to the continuing walls at the left and right by using the **Detail Component** tool.

1. Choose the **Detail Component** tool from **Annotate > Detail > Component** drop-down; the **Modify | Place Detail Component** tab is displayed.

2. Choose the **Load Family** tool from the **Mode** panel; the **Load Family** dialog box is displayed. Now, browse to **US Imperial > Detail Items > Div 01 - General** folder (for Metric **US Metric > Detail Items > Div 01 - General** folder) and select the **Break Line** file. Choose **Open**; the **Load Family** dialog box closes, and the **Break Line** option gets selected in the **Type Selector** drop-down list.

3. Move the cursor in the drawing view and add the first break line horizontally at the top of the callout view, refer to Figure 12-37.

4. After you add the first break line, choose the **Modify** button from the **Select** panel and then select the break line you have recently added; the **Modify | Detail Items** tab is displayed.

5. In the **Properties** palette, click in the value fields of the **Right** and **Left** instance parameters and enter **0' 4" (102 mm)**.

6. Similarly, click in the value fields of the **Jag Depth**, **Jag Width**, and **Masking depth** parameters and enter **0' 2" (51 mm)**. Now, choose **Apply** so that the specified instance parameters are assigned to the selected break line.

   Next, you need to add a vertically aligned break line on the left of the callout view, refer to Figure 12-37.

7. Copy the first break line, place it at the specified location, and then rotate it. Use the **Copy** and **Rotate** tools to add this line.

8. In the **Project Browser**, click on the **Door Jamb Detail** sub-head under the **Floor Plans** head; the instance properties of the callout view are displayed in the **Properties** palette.

9. In the **Properties** palette, click in the value field of the **Display Model** instance parameter and select the **Do not display** option from the drop-down list to restrict the display of the building model. Next, choose the **Apply** button.

   The completed tutorial resembles the detail sketch plan, as shown in Figure 12-49.

10. Now, choose **Save As > Project** from the **Application Menu**; the **Save As** dialog box is displayed. Enter **c12_Apartment1_tut1** (for Metric **M_c12_Apartment1_tut1**) and choose **Save**; the project file is now saved.

Creating Project Details and Schedules

11. Now, close the project file by choosing **Close** from the **Application Menu**.

Figure 12-49 Text added to the callout detail

Tutorial 2 — Apartment 1 - Schedules

In this tutorial, you will create the door, room, and wall schedule for the *Apartment 1* project, based on the schedule given in Figures 12-50, 12-51, and 12-52. **(Expected time: 30 min)**

The following steps are required to complete this tutorial:

a. Open the project file and then invoke the **Schedule/Quantities** tool.
b. Set the schedule properties for creating a door schedule using the **Schedule Properties** dialog box, based on the schedules given.
c. Create the door schedule.
d. Set the schedule properties for creating the room schedule using the **Schedule Properties** dialog box based on the schedules given.
e. Create the room schedule.
f. Create the wall schedule.

Opening the Project File and Invoking the Schedule/Quantities Tool

1. Choose **Open > Project** from the **Application Menu** to open the *Apartment 1* project created in the previous tutorial. You can also download this file from *http://www.cadcim.com*. The path of the file is as follows: *Textbooks > Civil/GIS > Revit Architecture > Autodesk Revit Architecture 2015 for Architects and Designers*.

2. Double-click on the **First Floor** under the **Floor Plans** head in the **Project Browser** to open the first floor plan.

3. Invoke the **Schedule/Quantities** tool from **View > Create > Schedules** drop-down; the **New Schedule** dialog box is displayed.

Setting the Parameters for the Door Schedule

1. In the **New Schedule** dialog box, choose **Doors** from the **Category** list and ensure that

the **Schedule building components** radio button is selected. Choose the **OK** button; the **Schedule Properties** dialog box is displayed. You can now set the desired parameters based on the door schedule given in Figure 12-50.

2. In the **Fields** tab, use the CTRL key and select **Count**, **Height**, **Level**, **Type Mark** and **Width** from the **Available fields** list.

3. Choose the **Add** button to add these fields to the **Scheduled fields** list.

   The fields in the **Scheduled fields** list need to be arranged in the same order as they appear in the schedule. To do so, use the **Move Up** and **Move Down** buttons.

Door Schedule				
Type Mark	Level	Width	Height	Count
4	First Floor	2' - 6"	7' - 0"	1
4	Fourth Floor	2' - 6"	7' - 0"	1
4	Second Floor	2' - 6"	7' - 0"	1
4	Third Floor	2' - 6"	7' - 0"	1
8	First Floor	3' - 0"	7' - 0"	1
8	First Floor	3' - 0"	7' - 0"	1
8	Fourth Floor	3' - 0"	7' - 0"	1
8	Fourth Floor	3' - 0"	7' - 0"	1
8	Second Floor	3' - 0"	7' - 0"	1
8	Second Floor	3' - 0"	7' - 0"	1
8	Third Floor	3' - 0"	7' - 0"	1
8	Third Floor	3' - 0"	7' - 0"	1
15	First Floor	3' - 0"	7' - 0"	1
15	Fourth Floor	3' - 0"	7' - 0"	1
15	Second Floor	3' - 0"	7' - 0"	1
15	Third Floor	3' - 0"	7' - 0"	1
Grand total: 16				

   Figure 12-50 Door schedule for the Apartment 1 project

4. Select the **Type Mark** option in the **Scheduled fields** list and choose the **Move Up** button thrice to move this field to the top of the list.

5. Similarly, using the **Move Up** and **Move Down** buttons, arrange the other fields in the following order: **Level**, **Width**, **Height**, and **Count** after the **Type Mark** field.

   Notice that the door schedule to be created is arranged according to the type marks. For this reason, you need to use the **Sorting/Grouping** tab to create this sorting.

6. In the **Schedule Properties** dialog box, choose the **Sorting/Grouping** tab to display its contents.

7. Select the **Type Mark** option from the **Sort by** drop-down list.

Creating Project Details and Schedules 12-49

8. Select the **Grand totals** check box to generate the total count.

9. Choose the **OK** button to close the **Schedule Properties** dialog box.

   Autodesk Revit Architecture displays the created schedule in the drawing window, refer to Figure 12-50. The door schedule is added under the **Schedules/Quantities** head in the **Project Browser**.

Setting the Parameters for the Room Schedule

1. Choose the **View** tab and then invoke the **Schedule/Quantities** tool from the **Schedules** drop-down in the **Create** panel; the **New Schedule** dialog box is displayed.

2. Choose **Rooms** from the **Category** list and choose the **OK** button; the **Schedule Properties** dialog box is displayed. You will use this dialog box to set the desired room schedule parameters.

3. Hold the CTRL key and select **Area**, **Level**, **Name**, **Number**, and **Perimeter** from the **Available fields** list in the **Fields** tab.

4. Choose the **Add** button to add these fields to the **Scheduled fields** list.

5. Using the **Move Up** and **Move Down** buttons, arrange the fields in the following order: **Name**, **Number**, **Level**, **Area**, and **Perimeter**.

6. Choose the **Sorting/Grouping** tab to display its contents.

7. Select the **Number** option from the **Sort by** drop-down list and select the **Grand totals** check box.

   Note
   *The total area of the room is shown in Figure 12-51. Now, use the **Formatting** tab to calculate the total area.*

8. Choose the **Formatting** tab to display its contents.

9. Select **Area** from the **Fields** list and then select the **Calculate totals** check box.

10. Choose the **OK** button to close the **Schedule Properties** dialog box.

    Autodesk Revit Architecture displays the room schedule in the drawing window, refer to Figure 12-51. Its name is added under the **Schedules/Quantities** head in the **Project**

Browser.

Room Schedule				
Name	Number	Level	Area	Perimeter
Living Room	1	First Floor	268 SF	66' - 1 1/2"
Bed Room	2	First Floor	191 SF	56' - 3 1/2"
Kitchen	3	First Floor	81 SF	37' - 0 1/2"
Lobby	4	First Floor	50 SF	28' - 2"
Dress	5	First Floor	44 SF	26' - 7"
Toilet	6	First Floor	70 SF	34' - 0"
Grand total: 6			703 SF	

Figure 12-51 Room schedule for the Apartment 1 project

Setting the Parameters for the Wall Schedule

1. Choose the **View** tab and then invoke the **Schedule/Quantities** tool from the **Schedules** drop-down in the **Create** panel; the **New Schedule** dialog box is displayed.

2. Now, choose **Walls** from the **Category** list and choose the **OK** button; the **Schedule Properties** dialog box is displayed.

3. In the **Fields** tab, press and hold the CTRL key and select **Area, Family, Length, Type,** and **Volume** from the **Available fields** list.

4. Choose the **Add** button to add these fields to the **Scheduled fields** list.

5. Arrange the other fields in the following order: **Family, Type, Length, Volume,** and **Area** using the **Move Up** and **Move Down** buttons.

6. In the **Sorting/Grouping** tab, select the **Type** option from the **Sort by** drop-down list and then select the **Grand totals** check box. Clear the **Itemize every instance** check box.

7. Choose the **Formatting** tab to display its contents.

8. Select **Area** from the **Fields** list and select the **Calculate totals** check box.

9. Similarly, select the **Calculate totals** check box for the **Length** and **Volume** fields.

10. Choose the **OK** button to close the **Schedule Properties** dialog box.

    Autodesk Revit Architecture displays the wall schedule in the drawing window and its name is added under the **Schedules/Quantities** head in the **Project Browser**.

11. You can adjust the column width of the schedule to accommodate the text in the **Type** column using the dragging tool. The created wall schedule appears similar to the

Creating Project Details and Schedules

schedule given in Figure 12-52.

This completes the tutorial for creating the schedules for the *Apartment 1* project.

12. Double-click on **First Floor** in the **Floor Plans** head in the **Project Browser**.

13. Choose **Save As > Project** from the **Application Menu**; the **Save As** dialog box is displayed. Enter **c12_Apartment1_tut2** (for Metric **M_c12_Apartment1_tut2**) in the **File name** edit box and choose **Save**; the project file is saved.

14. Choose **Close** from the **Application Menu** to close the project file.

Wall Schedule				
Family	Type	Length	Volume	Area
Basic Wall	Exterior - Brick on Mtl. Stud	120' - 0"	5196.19 CF	4494 SF
Basic Wall	Interior - 5" Partition (2-hr)	291' - 2"	948.91 CF	2277 SF
Grand total: 24		411' - 2"	6145.09 CF	6771 SF

Figure 12-52 Wall schedule for the Apartment 1 project

Tutorial 3   Road Section Detail

In this tutorial, you will create a new drafting detail of road section, as shown in Figure 12-53. Also, you will use the **Filled Region** tool to sketch the detail elements and the fill region. Use the parameters given below to create the section.   **(Expected time: 30 min)**

1. Drafting view parameters:
    Drafting view name to be assigned- **Road Section Detail**
    View Scale- **1" = 1'-0"**   View Scale- **1:10**
    Detail Level- **Fine**

2. Dimension parameters:
    For Imperial   Dimension style: **Linear Dimension Style: Linear 3/32" Arial**
    For Metric   Dimension style: **Linear Dimension Style: Linear 3/32" Arial**

3. Filled Region parameters:
    Hidden for the earth fill and **Medium** for the other lines
    Fill patterns to be used- **Concrete** and **Earth**

4. Text note parameters:
    For Imperial   Text type- **Text: 3/32" Arial**
                        Leader Arrowhead: **Arrow Filled 30 Degree**

    For Metric   Text type- **Text: 3/32" Arial**
                        Leader Arrowhead: **Arrow Filled 30 Degree**

5. Break line to be loaded from the **US Imperial > Detail Items** folder (for Metric **US Metric > Detail Items**) and the parameters to be adjusted as per the given sketch.

The following steps are required to complete this tutorial:

a. Open a new project file and create a drafting view using the **Drafting View** tool.
b. Set the drafting view parameters.
c. Use the **Filled Region** tool to create elements with fill patterns.
d. Add the text notes.
e. Add the break lines to complete the detail.

Figure 12-53 Sketch for creating the drafting detail of a road section

Opening a New Project File and Creating the Drafting View

1. Choose **New > Project** from the **Application Menu** and open a new project using the default template file.

2. Choose the **View** tab and choose the **Drafting View** tool from the **Create** panel; the **New Drafting View** dialog box is displayed.

3. In the **New Drafting View** dialog box, enter the name **Road Section Detail** in the **Name** edit box.

Creating Project Details and Schedules

4. Select **1"=1'-0"** (for Metric **1:10**) from the **Scale** drop-down list and choose the **OK** button to return to the drawing window. The drafting view created is displayed under the **Drafting Views (Detail)** head in the **Project Browser**.

Creating Detail Elements Using the Fill Patterns

1. Choose the **Annotate** tab and then invoke the **Filled Region** tool from the **Region** drop-down in the **Detail** panel; the **Modify | Create Filled Region Boundary** tab is displayed.

2. Now, from the **Line Style** drop-down list in the **Line Style** panel, select **Medium Lines**.

3. In the **Draw** panel, choose the **Rectangle** sketch tool.

4. Sketch a rectangle, which is **3'0"** (**914 mm**) in length and **0'4"** (**102 mm**) in height.

5. Use the **Zoom in Region** tool to zoom in the rectangle created.

6. Choose the **Edit Type** button from the **Properties** palette; the **Type Properties** dialog box is displayed.

7. Choose **Duplicate**; the **Name** dialog box is displayed. Enter **Concrete** in the **Name** edit box and choose **OK**. Notice that the **Concrete** option is selected from the **Type** drop-down list in the **Type Properties** dialog box.

8. Click in the **Value** column of the **Fill Pattern** parameter and then click on the **Browse** button to display the **Fill Patterns** dialog box.

9. Choose **Concrete** from the list of patterns and choose the **OK** button to return to the **Type Properties** dialog box.

10. Choose the **OK** button to close the **Type Properties** dialog box.

11. Choose the **Finish Edit Mode** button from the **Mode** panel in the **Modify | Create Filled Region Boundary** tab; the sketched rectangle is filled with the selected fill pattern, as shown in Figure 12-54. Press ESC to exit.

Figure 12-54 Sketched rectangle with the fill pattern

12. Similarly, use the **Filled Region** tool to sketch another rectangle measuring **3'0"** (**914 mm**) in length and **0'3"** (**75 mm**) in height above the filled region that has already been created, refer to Figure 12-53.

13. Sketch the profile of the kerb stone at the top right corner of the upper rectangle, refer to Figure 12-53, by using the **Filled Region** tool and then the **Line** tool from the **Draw** panel of the **Modify | Create Filled Region Boundary** tab. The kerb stone is created along with the concrete fill pattern.

Tip: *While sketching the kerb stone or paver block, ensure that the lines drawn in the sketch should be continuous without overlapping each other.*

14. Use the **Filled Region** tool to sketch one paver block measuring **4"** (**102 mm**) in length and **3" (75 mm)** in height at a distance of **1/4" (6.35 mm)** from the kerb stone. Use the **Offset** tool for placing the block at the specified distance. Use **Thin Lines** option as the linetype and **Concrete** option as the fill pattern.

15. Use the **Array** tool to create 7 copies at a distance of **4 1/4" (108 mm)** (center to center), as shown in Figure 12-55.

Figure 12-55 Sketched road section with pavers

16. Invoke the **Filled Region** tool again and select **Invisible lines** from the **Line Style** drop-down list.

17. Sketch the outer profile of the earth, as given in the sketch detail.

18. Choose the **Edit Type** button from the **Properties** palette; the **Type Properties** dialog box is displayed.

19. Choose **Duplicate**; the **Name** dialog box is displayed. Enter **Earth** in the **Name** edit box and choose **OK**.

20. In the **Type Properties** dialog box, click in the **Value** field of the **Fill Pattern** instance parameter and choose the **Browse** button; the **Fill Patterns** dialog box is displayed. Choose the **Earth** pattern name and then choose **OK**; the **Fill Patterns** dialog box closes. Next, choose **OK** to close the **Type Properties** dialog box.

21. Choose the **Finish Edit Mode** button from the **Mode** panel; the earth fill pattern is

Creating Project Details and Schedules 12-55

displayed in the drawing, as shown in Figure 12-56.

Figure 12-56 Sketched earth with the fill pattern

Adding Dimensions to the Detail View

1. Choose the **Aligned** tool from the **Dimension** panel of the **Annotate** tab; the **Modify | Place Dimensions** tab is displayed.

2. In the **Properties** palette, ensure that the **Linear Dimension Style: Linear 3/32" Arial** option (for Metric **Linear Dimension Style: Linear 2.5mm Arial**) is selected from the **Type Selector** drop-down list.

3. Now, move the cursor near the top left corner of the sketch and create a vertical dimension of **0' 3"** (**75 mm**) representing the thickness of the paver.

4. Similarly, add other dimensions to the detail view, as shown in Figure 12-57. Press ESC to exit.

Figure 12-57 Dimensions added to the detail view

Adding Text Notes

1. Choose the **Text** tool from the **Text** panel of the **Annotate** tab; the **Modify | Place Text** tab is displayed.

2. Choose the **Two Segments** tool from the **Format** panel.

3. From the **Type Selector** drop-down list, select **Text : 3/32" Arial** (for Metric **Text : 2.5 mm Arial**).

4. Now, choose the **Type Properties** tool from the **Properties** panel; the **Type Properties** dialog box is displayed.

5. Click on the **Value** field of the **Leader Arrowhead** type parameter and select the **Arrow Filled 30 Degree** option. Then, choose **OK** to exit the dialog box.

6. Click at the top of the paver to specify the first point and subsequently specify two more points to indicate the location of the elbow and text note. Add the text note **8"X6" concrete kerb stone**, as shown in Figure 12-58.

7. Add text notes based on the given sketch section. Press ESC twice.

Figure 12-58 Text notes added to the detail view

Adding Break Lines

In this section of the tutorial, you will add break lines at the left and right sides in the drafting detail view using the **Detail Component** tool.

1. Choose the **Detail Component** tool from **Annotate > Detail > Component** drop-down; the **Modify | Place Detail Component** tab is displayed.

2. Now, choose the **Load Family** tool from the **Mode** panel; the **Load Family** dialog box is displayed.

3. Now, browse to **US Imperial > Detail Items > Div 01-General** folder (For Metric **US Imperial > Detail Items > Div 01-General**) and then select the **Break Line** file.

4. Now, choose **Open**; the selected break line type is displayed in the **Type Selector** drop-down list.

5. Select the **Rotate after placement** check box from **Options Bar**.

6. Now, add two instances of the break line, refer to Figure 12-53.

7. Use the drag controls to modify the size of the break line based on the given sketch.

    The detail view is now complete.

8. Choose **Save As > Project** from the **Application Menu**; the **Save As** dialog box is displayed. Enter **c12_RoadSectionDetail_tut3** (for Metric **M_c12_RoadSectionDetail_tut3**) in the **File name** edit box and choose **Save**; the project file is saved.

9. Now, choose **Close** from the **Application Menu**; the *c12_RoadSectionDetail_tut3.rvt* (for Metric *M_c12_RoadSectionDetail_tut3.rvt*) file closes.

Self-Evaluation Test

Answer the following questions and then compare them to those given at the end of this chapter:

1. You can create a text note without a leader. (T/F)

2. A text note cannot be moved without moving a leader. (T/F)

3. A drafted detail uses an enlarged portion of a project view as an underlay. (T/F)

4. The **Add Right Side Arc Leader** tool can be used to add a curved leader to the right side of the text note. (T/F)

5. Detail Items can be loaded from Autodesk Revit Architecture's library. (T/F)

6. Which of the following is a type of keynote?

    a) Element b) Structure
    c) Material User d) Keynoting

7. Which of the following schedule types helps you show the details regarding the assembly of a component?

    a) Note block c) Drawing list
    b) View list d) Material takeoff

8. The _____ tag can be added to indicate the revisions made to some portion of a project view.

9. The _____ tool is used to create schedules in a project.

10. The _____ parameter is used to set the display of a project view as an underlay.

11. The _____ tool is used to add a graphical representation of an insulation barrier to a detail view.

12. The _____ type of detail view does not use an existing project view.

Review Questions

Answer the following questions:

1. Drag controls can be used to resize a text note. (T/F)

2. A model text is visible only in the view in which it is created. (T/F)

3. You can use various editing tools such as **Move**, **Copy**, **Rotate**, and so on to edit a model text created. (T/F)

4. You can resize the extents of a callout view by using drag controls. (T/F)

5. A text note can be assigned multiple leaders. (T/F)

6. When a text note is dragged to a new location, the leader adjusts automatically. (T/F)

7. The **Region** tool is used to create detail elements by defining a boundary and assigning a fill pattern. (T/F)

8. Which of the following tools can be used to add a 3D text to a building model?

    a) **Text**   b) **Detail Component**
    c) **Level**   d) **Model Text**

9. Which of the following parameters can be modified to control the extent of details shown in a project view?

    a) **View Scale**   b) **Display Model**
    c) **Detail Level**   d) **Referencing Detail**

10. Which of the following instance parameters is used to set the alignment of text notes?

    a) **Horizontal Align**   b) **Text Size**
    c) **Tab Size**   d) **Background**

11. Which of the following option is used to change the fill pattern display for wall cuts in plan?

    a) Projection/surface pattern   b) Cut pattern
    c) Line styles   d) Cut line styles

Exercises

Exercise 1   Club - Drafted Detail

In the *Club* project created in Exercise 1 of Chapter 11, create a drafted detail based on the sketch given in Figure 12-59. Load the required detail items (detail components). Use wide and thin lines to sketch the detail lines. Assume the parameters for adding text notes, dimensions, and break lines. The exact placement of the elements is not important for this exercise. Save the project file as *c12_Club_ex1.rvt* (for Metric *M_c12_Club_ex1.rvt*).

(Expected time: 30 min)

To add the Window jamb detail component in the Project, you need to download the *Window Jamb - Metal Fixed Flush.rfa* file from the website: *www.cadcim.com*

Figure 12-59 Sketch plan for creating a drafted detail for the Club project

Exercise 2   General- Sketch Detail

Create the drafted detail based on the sketch detail shown in Figure 12-60. Use the **Fill Region** tool to create elements and fill patterns. Assume the parameters for adding text notes and dimensions. The exact placement of the elements is not important for this exercise. Save the project file as *c12_sketchdetail_ex2.rvt* (for Metric *M_c12_sketchdetail_ex2.rvt*)

(Expected time: 30 min)

Creating Project Details and Schedules

Figure 12-60 Sketch detail for creating a drafted detail

Exercise 3   Club - Schedules

Create the room and wall schedules for the *Club* project created in Exercise 1 of Chapter 11, based on the schedules shown in Figures 12-61 and 12-62. Use the predefined room schedule available in the **Project Browser** and edit it as per the given fields. Save the project file as *c12_clubschedule_ex3.rvt* (for Metric *M_c12_clubschedule_ex3.rvt*)

(Expected time: 30 min)

Room Schedule				
Name	Number	Level	Area	Perimeter
Entrance	1	First Floor	527 SF	93' - 2 1/4"
Passage 1	2	First Floor	606 SF	138' - 1 1/4"
Passage 2	3	First Floor	606 SF	138' - 0"
Billiard Ro	4	First Floor	556 SF	95' - 8 1/4"
Gymnasiu	5	First Floor	803 SF	113' - 4 1/4"
Aerobics	6	First Floor	488 SF	90' - 10"
Indoor Ga	7	First Floor	626 SF	100' - 8 1/4"
Card Roo	8	First Floor	481 SF	90' - 4 1/4"
Grand total: 8			4692 SF	860' - 2 1/2"

Figure 12-61 Room schedule for the Club project

Wall Schedule				
Family	Type	Length	Area	Volume
Basic Wall	Exterior - Split F	13' - 1 1/2"	200 SF	236 CF
Basic Wall	Exterior - Split F	58' - 10 1/4"	709 SF	836 CF
Basic Wall	Exterior - Split F	38' - 10 1/4"	501 SF	593 CF
Basic Wall	Exterior - Split F	38' - 10 1/4"	521 SF	614 CF
Basic Wall	Exterior - Split F	58' - 10 1/4"	713 SF	837 CF
Basic Wall	Exterior - Split F	13' - 1 1/2"	189 SF	222 CF
Basic Wall	Exterior - Split F	42' - 5 1/4"	480 SF	567 CF
Basic Wall	Interior - 6 1/8"	59' - 0"	635 SF	324 CF
Basic Wall	Interior - 6 1/8"	28' - 10 1/4"	315 SF	161 CF
Basic Wall	Interior - 6 1/8"	15' - 8 3/4"	185 SF	94 CF
Basic Wall	Interior - 6 1/8"	9' - 0"	98 SF	50 CF
Basic Wall	Interior - 6 1/8"	28' - 10 1/4"	336 SF	172 CF
Basic Wall	Interior - 6 1/8"	59' - 0"	635 SF	324 CF
Basic Wall	Interior - 6 1/8"	15' - 8 3/4"	185 SF	94 CF
Basic Wall	Interior - 6 1/8"	28' - 10 1/4"	336 SF	172 CF
Basic Wall	Interior - 6 1/8"	28' - 10 1/4"	336 SF	172 CF
Curtain Wall	Exterior Glazing	58' - 10 1/4"	880 SF	
Curtain Wall	Exterior Glazing	58' - 10 1/4"	883 SF	

Figure 12-62 Wall schedule for the Club project

Answers to Self-Evaluation Test
1. T, **2.** F, **3.** F, **4.** T, **5.** T, **6.** Material User, **7.** Material Takeoff, **8.** Revision, **9.** Schedule/Quantities, **10.** Display Model, **11.** Insulation, **12.** Drafting view.

Chapter 13

Creating Drawing Sheets, and Plotting

Learning Objectives

After completing this chapter, you will be able to:
• *Add drawing sheets to a project using the Sheet tool.*
• *Add views to a drawing sheet.*
• *Modify view properties of a drawing sheet.*
• *Add schedules to a drawing sheet.*
• *Modify a building model on a drawing sheet.*
• *Create duplicate dependent views.*
• *Print drawing sheets and project view.*

INTRODUCTION

In the previous chapters, you learned to create views of a building model. You also learned to add information to the views and create additional detail views. The views should be organized in proper format and sequence, and should also be stored on paper. The organized drawing sheets can be issued to the concerned agencies during progressive stages of the project. The printed drawing sheets enable a better understanding of the project and also results in smooth coordination between the associated agencies. They also form a printed reference for the modifications and detailing that are carried out during the project development and execution.

Using Autodesk Revit Architecture, you can easily compose the building views on a drawing sheet. You can first choose the appropriate title block for the drawing sheet and then add the desired views to it. You can control the visibility of various categories and set the scale for the printing of each view. You can also modify the building model and create new views. Having composed the drawing sheets, you can print them on the desired print media using various settings. This chapter explains the general procedure for creating, composing, and printing drawing sheets.

CREATING DRAWING SHEETS

In Autodesk Revit Architecture, drawing sheets are treated like views in a project. They are defined by a border and a title block. Therefore, to create a drawing sheet, you first need to add a sheet view to the project.

Adding a Drawing Sheet to a Project

Ribbon: View > Sheet Composition > Sheet

To add a drawing sheet to a project, choose the **Sheet** tool from the **Sheet Composition** panel; the **New Sheet** dialog box will be displayed. This dialog box has two areas: **Select titleblocks** and **Select placeholder sheets**. Select the required title block for the drawing sheet from the list of title blocks. To load drawing sheets other than the ones in the list of title blocks in the **Select titleblocks** area, choose the **Load** button from the **New Sheet** dialog box; the **Load Family** dialog box will be displayed. Next, choose **US Imperial> Titleblocks** (for Metric **US Metric > Titleblocks**); the list of titleblocks family files will be displayed, as shown in Figure 13-1. Select the desired family file from the list to load it into your project and choose the **Open** button; the title block corresponding to the selected family file will be added to the list of title blocks in the **Select titleblocks** area. Select a titleblock from the list and choose the **OK** button; a titleblock of the selected family will be displayed in the drawing window, as shown in Figure 13-2.

A titleblock is used to convey the project information and the drawing sheet title. The project information includes client, project name, project title, project number, date of issue of drawing, drawing sheet number, scale, and so on.

Creating Drawing Sheets and Plotting 13-3

Figure 13-1 The **Load Family** dialog box displaying the list of titleblocks family

Figure 13-2 Sheet view with the selected title block

The project information can be added to a project using the **Project Information** tool. Invoke this tool from the **Settings** panel of the **Manage** tab; the **Project Properties** dialog box will be displayed. In this dialog box, you can add the project information such as the **Author**, **Project Issue Date**, **Project Status**, and **Client Name** in the **Value** field of their respective parameters. Figure 13-3 shows the partial view of the **Project Properties** dialog box displaying the instance parameters of the **Project Information** tool. Other project related information such as the name of the client or owner, the address of the project, its name and number can also be entered in the corresponding **Value** fields. The information entered in this dialog box is automatically entered in the title block. The other information provided in the sheet such as sheet name, sheet number, drawn by, scale, and so on may vary from sheet to sheet, and these are treated as instance parameters for the title block. To enter these information, select the title block; the instance parameters will be displayed in the **Properties** palette. Add relevant information in the palette and choose **Apply**; the added information will be updated in the selected title block.

Figure 13-3 The partial view of the **Project Properties** dialog box with the project related information

You can enter the project related information directly by selecting the title block, clicking on the appropriate parameter, and then entering a value in the displayed edit box. The entered values are saved as project information for the other sheet views. As you add sheets to a project, their names and numbers are displayed in the **Sheets** head of the **Project Browser**.

Note
*In the new drawing sheets, only that information will be displayed which will be entered in the **Project Properties** dialog box. Also, as you add a new sheet, the sheet number will increment automatically in a sequence.*

Tip: *In a project, there may be large number of drawing sheets. The information provided in the title block plays an important role in identifying the drawing sheet.*

Adding Views to a Drawing Sheet

Ribbon: View > Sheet Composition > Place View

To add views to a drawing sheet, choose the **Place View** tool from the **Sheet Composition** panel; the **Views** dialog box will be displayed with a list of views to be added to the drawing sheet, as shown in Figure 13-4. Select the required view and choose the **Add View to Sheet** button. On doing so, the selected view will appear as a viewport represented by a rectangle attached to the cursor. Move this cursor to the drawing area in the sheet and click in the preferred location to add the selected view. Next, in the **Properties** palette, change the **View Scale** parameter by selecting a suitable scale from the drop-down list in its Value field and choose **Apply**. The added view will adjust to the specified scale and appear in the sheet, as shown in Figure 13-5.

Figure 13-4 The list of views to be added to the drawing sheet in the **Views** dialog box

The viewport of the inserted view displays a label line at the bottom left corner. The label line shows the view name, view scale, and view number, as shown in Figure 13-6. In this manner, you can add a number of views to the same drawing sheet and create a complete set of drawing sheets for a project. You can modify various properties associated with the viewport in the **Properties** palette.

Figure 13-5 The added view in the title block

Modifying View Properties

To modify the properties associated with a view in a sheet, select the viewport corresponding to it; the **Properties** palette and the **Options Bar** will be displayed. The **Properties** palette for the viewport displays various instance parameters associated with the viewport, as shown in Figure 13-7. Based on the requirement, you can modify these values. In the **Properties** palette, click on the value column corresponding to the **View Scale** parameter and select an option from the drop-down list displayed to modify the scale of the view. In the palette, you can select the **Coarse**, **Medium**, or **Fine** option from the drop-down list corresponding to the value column of the **Detail Level** instance parameter to define the level of details to be displayed in a view. To control the visibility of different categories of elements in each viewport, choose the **Edit** button for the **Visibility/Graphics Overrides** parameter; the **Visibility/Graphics Overrides for Elevation (current view)** dialog box will be displayed for the corresponding view. In this dialog box, you can control the visibility of various model and annotation elements. In the **Properties** palette, you can rename the corresponding view of the selected viewport by entering a name in the value column corresponding to the **View Name** parameter. In the **Properties** palette, you can click on the value column corresponding to the **Rotation on Sheet** instance parameter to rotate the view clockwise or counterclockwise. Alternatively, you can rotate the view by selecting an option from the **Rotation on Sheet** drop-down list in the **Options Bar**. You can edit the type properties of the selected view in the sheet.

Tip: *A view can also be added by simply dragging its name from the **Project Browser** into the sheet view.*

To do so, choose the **Edit Type** button in the **Properties** palette; the **Type Properties** dialog box will be displayed, refer to Figure 13-8. In this dialog box, you can use various parameters to control the visibility of the title and extension lines associated with the view in the sheet. In the **Type Properties** dialog box, you can also modify the line weight color, and line pattern of the label line associated with the view.

Figure 13-6 Parameters in the label line of the viewport

*Figure 13-7 The **Properties** palette for the viewport*

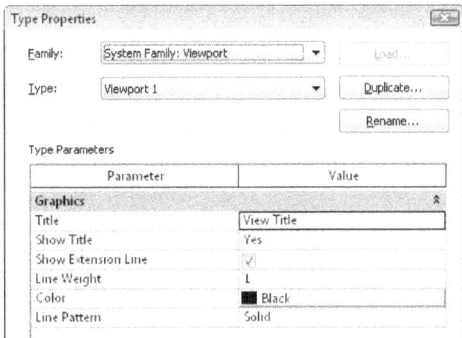

*Figure 13-8 The partial view of the **Type Properties** dialog box for the viewport*

In the **Properties** palette, you can click in the **Value** field corresponding to the **Detail Level** parameter and select any of the options coarse, medium and fine from the drop-down list to specify the level of details in the view.

> **Tip:** *The modifications made to the visibility of the elements in the viewport are also reflected in the actual view. To retain the visibility settings for the original view, make its copy and then add it to the drawing sheet. One project view cannot be added to more than one drawing sheet. However, its copy can be created and added to different drawing sheets.*

Panning the Viewports Added to the Sheet

In Revit, you can pan or move the views that are added in the sheet to place them accurately. To pan the view, select a viewport, right-click, and choose **Activate View** from the shortcut menu. You will notice that only the view, which is selected in the drawing is activated (You will learn more about it in the next section). Now, right-click again to display a shortcut menu. Choose the **Pan Active View** option from the displayed shortcut menu; the cursor will convert into a symbol with four arrows. Press and hold the left mouse button and drag the mouse to move the entities in the viewport. Once you have panned and placed the entities at the appropriate location in the sheet, choose **Deactivate View** from the shortcut menu to revert to the sheet.

> **Tip:** *The **Visibility/Graphics Overrides** tool is used effectively in the project drawings. Using the same building model, you can create multiple viewports in the drawing sheet and display or hide different categories of elements in each viewport. For example, you can create multiple viewports for a residence plan and selectively display certain elements such as flooring pattern, false ceiling layout, furniture arrangement, and so on in each viewport.*

Adding Schedules to a Drawing Sheet

You can easily add the schedules created in a project to a drawing sheet. To do so, drag the schedules created (required schedules) from **Project Browser** and drop them into the drawing sheet; the preview image of the schedule will be attached to the cursor. Move the cursor and click at the desired location in the drawing to place the schedule. The selected schedule will appear with blue triangles for each column and a break line on the right side, as shown in Figure 13-9.

You can modify the appearance and properties of a schedule. The blue triangles representing the controls for the column width can be dragged to modify the width of each column in the schedule. The break line in the right border represents the split control. It can be used to split the schedule table into multiple sections. When the split control is used, the schedule is split into two sections, as shown in Figure 13-10. These sections are placed adjacent to each other. In this manner, the schedule can be split into a number of sections that fit into the drawing sheet.

The sections of a schedule can be moved using the move control available in the center of the schedule section. Moreover, the sections of a schedule can be resized by dragging the blue dot at its end. When the schedule section is resized, the additional or reduced rows are automatically adjusted between the sections. However, the last section cannot be resized as it contains the remaining rows.

> **Note**
> *The schedule sections can neither be deleted individually nor moved from one drawing sheet to another. For these operations, the entire schedule is treated as a single entity.*

The split sections of a schedule can be rejoined again. As they are sequential, therefore a section can be joined only to its previous or next section. To join a split section, drag a section using the move control over the previous or the next section; the two schedule sections will be merged together into a single schedule section.

Creating Drawing Sheets and Plotting 13-9

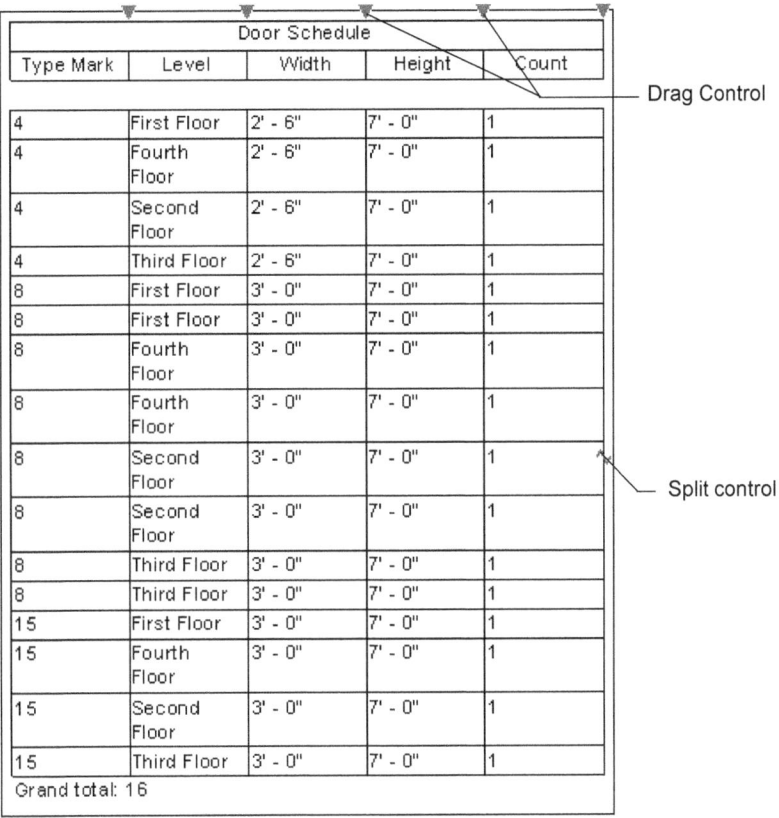

Figure 13-9 Schedule with controls added to a drawing sheet

Figure 13-10 The schedule table split into two sections

As already mentioned, you can adjust the width of the columns in a schedule by dragging the blue triangle control for the respective columns. When a column width is modified, the column width of all schedule sections will be modified automatically.

If a building model is modified after making the schedule, then the schedule will be updated automatically. To edit it, right-click on the schedule in the drawing sheet and then choose the **Edit Schedule** option from the shortcut menu.

Modifying a Building Model in a Drawing Sheet

You can modify a building model directly from the views added in a drawing sheet. To do so, you need to activate a view and make the desired modifications in it. To activate a view from a drawing sheet, select the viewport; the **Modify | Viewports** tab will be displayed. In this tab, choose the **Activate View** button from the **Viewport** panel; the view in the selected viewport will be activated. In the activated view, you can work on the building model as in any other project view. The desired elements can be edited using the editing tools. New elements can also be added to the model. When the building model is edited, the parametric change engine of Autodesk Revit Architecture modifies other project views immediately. As a result, all the project views are updated automatically. For example, the modifications made to the location of a furniture item in an activated viewport of the drawing sheet are also made in the corresponding floor plan, sections, and other associated views.

> **Tip:** *Another method to activate or deactivate a viewport is to move the cursor over the project view and right-click; a shortcut menu will be displayed. From the shortcut menu, you can choose the **Activate View** or **Deactivate View** option to activate or deactivate the specified viewport.*

After making the necessary modifications, choose the **Deactivate View** tool from **View > Sheet Composition > Viewports** drop-down to return to the drawing sheet view.

New views can also be added to the project when the viewport is activated. You can create a new plan, elevation, section, callout, detail view, and so on, while working in the activated view. The activated view can then be deactivated. Also, the newly created views can be added to the drawing sheet.

CREATING GUIDE GRIDS

Guide Grid is a customizable grid, available in Revit sheets. It is used to place the drawing view in place in the sheet. To create a Guide Grid, choose the **Guide Grid** tool from the **Sheet Composition** panel of the **View** tab; the **Assign Guide Grid** dialog box will be displayed, as shown in Figure 13-11. In this dialog box, the **Create new** radio button is selected by default. You can enter a name for guide grid in the **Name** edit box and choose the **OK** button; the Guide Grid will be displayed over the sheet in the drawing area, as shown in Figure 13-12. On creating a Guide Grid, it gets added as an instance property under the **Other** head in the **Properties** palette. Now, select the Guide Grid from the drawing area; the drag controls will be displayed. You can use the drag controls to resize the Guide Grids in the drawing area.

Figure 13-11 The *Assign Guide Grid* dialog box

Creating Drawing Sheets and Plotting

The **Properties** palette displays the instance properties of the selected Guide Grid. In the **Properties** palette, you can specify guide spacing in the **Guide Spacing** edit box to increase or decrease the spacing of the grids. You can also rename the guide name under the identity data in the **Name** edit box in the **Properties** palette.

Figure 13-12 *The Guide Grid displayed over the sheet*

Note
*In the current project, you can place the existing Guide Grid in new sheet. To place an existing Guide Grid, open new sheet and select an option from the **Guide Grid** drop-down list in the **Properties** palette .*

DUPLICATING DEPENDENT VIEWS

You can create multiple copies of the project views in Revit Architecture. These multiple views are called duplicate views. All duplicate views are dependent on the original view from which they are created. Therefore, these dependent views are automatically updated if any changes are made in the original view. Dependent views are useful when you want to use or place the same view on more than one sheet. It is also useful in case of huge projects when the overall project view is too large to fit in a single sheet. In such cases, you can crop the parent view into small segments using the crop regions, create dependent views from them, and then place the cropped dependent views on the sheet.

Creating Dependent Views

You can create a dependent view from a plan, elevation, section, and callout view. To create a dependent view, open the view from which you want to create duplicate views and choose the **Duplicate as Dependent** tool from **View > Create > Duplicate View** drop-down. Alternatively, select the required view name in the **Project Browser** and right-click; a shortcut menu will be displayed. Choose **Duplicate View > Duplicate as Dependent** from the shortcut menu; the primary view will display a crop region boundary, which will be added to the **Project Browser** as a dependent view under the primary view. Select the crop region boundary to display the drag controls. Now, using the drag controls, resize and crop the primary view to include only the required portion of the view in the dependent view. Next, select the name of the dependent view in the **Project Browser** and right-click; a shortcut menu will be displayed. Choose the **Rename** option from the shortcut menu; the **Rename View** dialog box will be displayed. Enter a name for the dependent view in the dialog box and choose the **OK** button; the duplicate view will be renamed. Again, open the primary view and choose the **Show Crop Region** button from **View Control Bar** to display the crop region boundary. Similarly, create another dependent view. In this way, you can crop the primary view and create multiple dependent views. Figure 13-13 shows the primary view and Figures 13-14 and 13-15 show two dependent views with the crop boundaries.

Tip: *The views added to the drawing sheet are displayed in the **Project Browser** below the sheet name under the **Sheets** subhead. You can delete a selected view from the sheet view. To do so, highlight the view name and right-click. Next, choose the **Remove From Sheet** option from the shortcut menu and delete the selected view*

Note
When you duplicate a view, the view will open in the drawing area and the default name for the duplicate view will be <view name>-Duplicate 1.

Figure 13-13 The primary view

Creating Drawing Sheets and Plotting 13-13

Figure 13-14 The left dependent view showing the left portion of the drawing with crop regions

Figure 13-15 The right dependent view showing the right portion of the drawing with crop regions

To navigate to the primary view from the dependent view, select the crop region boundary of the dependent view and right-click; a shortcut menu will be displayed. Choose the **Go to Primary View** option from the shortcut menu; the primary view will be displayed on the screen. You can also navigate to the dependent views from the primary view. To do so, choose the **Show Crop Region** button from the **View Control Bar**, if the crop regions are not displayed in the primary view. On doing so, the crop regions for all dependent views will be displayed. Select the crop region of the required dependent view and right-click; a shortcut menu will be displayed. Choose **Go to View** from the shortcut menu; the respective dependent view will open. You can display the primary or the dependent views by double-clicking on their respective view names in the **Project Browser**.

Adding Matchline to Dependent Views

Matchlines are the graphical representation of a split in views. These are the sketch lines that indicate the area where a view is split. To add a matchline, open the primary view from which the dependent views are created. Next, choose the **Show Crop Region** button from the **View Control Bar**; the crop regions of both the primary and dependent views will be displayed. Choose the **Matchline** tool from the **Sheet Composition** panel in the **View** tab; the **Modify | Create Matchline Sketch** tab will be displayed and the screen will enter the sketch mode. Sketch a matchline using the sketching tools in the **Draw** panel of the **Modify | Create Matchline Sketch** tab to show the split. After sketching the matchline, choose the **Finish Edit Mode** button from the **Mode** panel of the **Modify | Create Matchline Sketch** tab; the matchline will be displayed, as shown in Figure 13-16. You can also edit the length and shape of the matchline. To do so, select the matchline; the **Modify | Matchline** tab will be displayed. In this tab, choose the **Edit Sketch** button from the **Mode** panel; the **Modify | Matchline > Edit Sketch** tab will be displayed. On invoking this tab, the screen will enter the sketch mode. Modify the sketch of the matchline as required and then choose the **Finish Edit Mode** button from the **Mode** panel in the **Modify | Matchline > Edit Sketch** tab.

Figure 13-16 Matchline showing the area where you want to split the drawing

To modify the display of the matchline, select the matchline and right-click in the drawing; a shortcut menu will be displayed. Choose **Override Graphics in View > By Element** from the shortcut menu; the **View-Specific Element Graphics** dialog box will be displayed. You can modify the display properties of matchlines such as **Weight**, **Pattern**, and **Color** in the dialog box and choose the **OK** button.

In Revit Architecture, you can configure the settings of the matchline upto a certain level. For example, there may be a building with 35 floors and you want the same settings of the floor upto level 30. To do so, select the matchline. Then, in the **Properties** palette click in the **Value** column for the **Top Constraint** parameter and select the **Level 30** option from the drop-down list. On doing so, you will notice that the matchline is displayed only upto level 30. From level 31 onward, you can again configure different settings for the building model.

Adding Views to Sheet

In Revit, you can add one or more views of a building model to a sheet. The building model includes floor plans, ceiling plans, elevations, sections, 3D views, rendered views and so on. These views can be added on sheet. To add a view to a sheet, first open the sheet view and then choose the **Place View** tool from the **Sheet Composition** panel of the **View** tab. On choosing this tool, the **Views** dialog box will be displayed, as shown in Figure 13-17. The **Views** dialog box will display various views of a building model. Select the required view from this dialog box and then choose the **Add View to Sheet** button; the selected view will get attached to the cursor. Now, click anywhere on the sheet in the drawing area to place the view.

Creating Drawing Sheets and Plotting 13-15

Figure 13-17 The Views dialog box

Adding View Reference

You can add a view reference in the primary view after you have placed the cropped dependent views on the sheet. A view reference is a symbol that is used to refer the dependent view available in the same or different sheet.

To add a view reference, select the primary view on the sheet and right-click; a shortcut menu will be displayed. Now, choose the **Activate View** option from the shortcut menu; the selected view will be highlighted. Next, invoke the **View Reference** tool from the **Tag** panel of the **Annotate** tab. Now, select the dependent view to be referred to from the **Target View** drop-down list available in the **Options Bar** and then click in the selected drawing view to add the view reference. After adding the required view references, right-click, and then choose Deactivate View from the shortcut menu to deactivate the selected view. Now, if you double-click on the view reference tag, the respective referred view will open.

Note
If a plan view is split into two views, left and right duplicate views, then on selecting the left duplicate view to add a view reference to a right side view, the view reference tag will be visible in all views except the left view (referred view).

PRINTING IN Autodesk Revit Architecture

The created building model and project views can be stored in the computer's hard disk or on a temporary media. It also becomes imperative to print these views as a hard copy at various stages of the project. During the initial stages of the project development, you may need to print certain project views and discuss them with the others in your organization or with the clients. As the project progresses, other professional agencies such as structural, electrical, plumbing, HVAC, landscape, and so on become involved with the project. The printed drawings assist in a proper coordination between these agencies. The project may also require approval from statutory bodies and other departments. Printed drawings and project views explain the project and can be submitted as a complete set to obtain their approval.

Another important use of the printed drawings is during the construction process. The printed views such as plans, section, elevations, details, and 3D views convey the architect's or interior designer's concept of the project to all the executing agencies involved. These views provide the information and necessary details to materialize the project on the site. They can also explain the procedure for executing the job and the level of detailing/finishing that is desired by the designers.

Using Autodesk Revit Architecture, you can easily print the created project views or composed drawing sheets at any time during the project development. This section explains the general procedure for printing. You can print the current window, visible portion of the current window, or the selected view/sheet using the **Print** tool. The printing process involves selecting the correct output device (printer or plotter), specifying the area to be plotted, specifying the paper size, and other settings.

Printing Drawing Sheets and Project Views

The **Print** tool is used to print project views and drawing sheets. You can invoke this tool from the **Application Menu**. On invoking the **Print** tool, the **Print** dialog box will be displayed, as shown in Figure 13-18.

*Figure 13-18 The **Print** dialog box*

You have the option of using the default values in this dialog box. In case, the values conform to your requirements, you can choose the **OK** button and start printing directly. Otherwise, you can alter the print specifications using the options provided in the **Print** dialog box. The print options available in this dialog box are explained next.

Selecting and Modifying the Printer Settings

You can select a printing device from the **Name** drop-down list in the **Print** dialog box. This dialog box displays the information regarding the selected printer in the **Status**, **Type**, **Where**, and **Comment** fields below the printer name. The **Properties** button is used to set various printer properties. If you choose this button, a dialog box with the set of printer properties corresponding to the selected printer will be displayed, refer to Figure 13-19.

Figure 13-19 *The dialog box for the* **Microsoft XPS Document Writer** *printer*

The printer properties depend on the type of printer selected from the **Name** drop-down in the **Print** dialog box. In Figure 13-19, the **Layout** tab, displays the options related to the **Orientation** of the paper. Choose the **Advanced** button in this tab; the Microsoft XPS Document Writer Advanced Options dialog box will be displayed. You can modify and set printing preferences, such as **Paper Size**, refer to Figure 13-20. Some of the major options used for printing are discussed next.

Note

The appearance and options available in the **Print** *dialog box depend on the type of printer selected and the operating system used.*

*Figure 13-20 The **Microsoft XPS Document Writer Advanced Options** dialog box displayed for the selected printer*

Setting the Print Range

The **Print Range** area in the **Print** dialog box has three radio buttons: **Current window**, **Visible portion of current window**, and **Selected views/sheets**. You can select any of these radio buttons to specify the parameters of the view to be printed. The **Current window** radio button can be selected to print the project view that is currently displayed in the drawing window while the **Visible portion of current window** radio button is used to print only the portion of the view that is currently displayed in the drawing window.

You can select the **Selected views/sheets** radio button to select project views or drawing sheets for printing. On selecting this radio button, the **Select** button that is located below it will be activated. Choose this button; the **View/Sheet Set** dialog box will be displayed, as shown in Figure 13-21. It contains a list of views that have been created and also the drawing sheets in the project. This dialog box can be used to select project views and create drawing sets. You can select views by selecting their corresponding check boxes. Now, to save the settings, choose the **Save As** button; the **New** dialog box will be displayed. In this dialog box, enter the name of the setting and choose **OK**; the **Name** dialog box will close. The name of the new selection set can be selected from the **Name** drop-down list in the **View/Sheet Set** dialog box. You can choose the **Rename** button to rename a set. You can delete a set by choosing the **Delete** button. Similarly, you can choose the **Check All** and **Check None** buttons to select and deselect all the listed views and sheets. You can also control the display of views and sheets by using their respective check boxes in the **Show** area placed at the bottom of the **View/Sheet Set** dialog box.

Creating Drawing Sheets and Plotting 13-19

*Figure 13-21 The **View/Sheet Set** dialog box displaying the created views and sheets*

Using the Print Setup Dialog Box

Application Menu: Print > Print Setup

In Revit Architecture, you can specify various options for printing a drawing sheet. To do so, invoke the **Print Setup** dialog box by choosing **Print > Print Setup** from **the Application Menu** or choose the **Setup** button in the **Settings** area of the **Print** dialog box; the **Print Setup** dialog box will be displayed, as shown in Figure 13-22. This dialog box displays various setup options related to the printing procedure. The selected printer name is displayed on the top of the **Print Setup** dialog box. The **Name** drop-down list displays the name of the print settings that have been saved in the project. The **Size** drop-down list in the **Paper** area displays a list of paper sizes available for the selected printer. From this drop-down list, you can select the required size of paper to print the project view such as A5, A4, A3, and so on. From the **Source** drop-down list, you can select an option to specify the source of the paper. The **Portrait** or **Landscape** radio button can be selected to specify the orientation of the paper.

*Figure 13-22 The **Print Setup** dialog box*

The **Paper Placement** area specifies the placement or location of the view on the paper. The **Center** radio button can be selected for printing the view in the center of the paper. Selecting the **Offset from corner** radio button enables you to specify the offset distance of the view from the corner. You can select any of the three options, **No Margin**, **Printer limit**, or **User defined** to specify the offset distance. When the **User defined** option is selected, the **x** and **y** edit boxes get enabled where you can enter the X and Y offset distances. In the **Hidden Line Views** area, you can choose an option to increase the print performance for printing hidden lines in various views such as elevations, sections, 3D, and so on. When the **Vector Processing** radio button is selected in this area, the time taken to hide the lines will depend on the number and complexity of the views processed. This option produces smaller print files and decreases the print time. On the other hand, if the **Raster Processing** radio button is selected, the actual dimension of the print will be considered. As a result, larger print files will be produced, which will take more processing time.

Tip: *You can also invoke the* **Print Setup** *dialog box by choosing the* **Setup** *button from the* **Print** *dialog box.*

Note
In a view, the elements that are hidden using the **Temporary Hide/Isolate** *tool will be shown in print.*

The **Fit to page** radio button in the **Zoom** area can be selected to fit the view to the selected paper size. The **Zoom** radio button can be used to enlarge or reduce the view to a specified percentage. The **Appearance** area of the **Print Setup** dialog box displays the options for specifying the print quality and color. The **Raster quality** drop-down list in the **Appearance** area, displays the **Low**, **Medium**, **High**, and **Presentation** options that enable you to select the required quality of print. Note that a higher quality of print will take more time to print. The **Colors** drop-down list in this area is used to specify whether the view is to be printed as **Black Lines**, **Grayscale**, or **Color**. When you select the **Black Lines** option, all text, lines, pattern lines, and edges will be printed in black. However, all raster images and solid patterns will be printed in grayscale. To print all elements in grayscale, select the **Grayscale** option. The **Color** option can be used to print the project views in color. The printer, however, must support colored printing.

The **Options** area provides other print setting options. By default, the view links are printed in black. The **View links in blue** check box can be used to print the view links in blue. The options for hiding various annotations and elements such as scope boxes, reference/work planes, and crop boundaries are also provided in this section of the **Print Setup** dialog box.

Previewing the Print Setup

Before printing a project view or a drawing sheet, you can preview it using the **Print Preview** tool. This tool can be invoked by choosing the **Preview** button in the **Print** dialog box. When you invoke this tool, Autodesk Revit Architecture displays a draft version of the drawing sheet in the preview window, as shown in Figure 13-23. The displayed image acts as a preview of the hard copy that will be printed and is based on the set print parameters. If the displayed image does not conform to the desired result, you can use the **Close** button to close the preview and make the necessary modifications in the print setup till the desired result is achieved. While in the preview window, you can use the **Zoom In** and **Zoom Out** buttons to enlarge or reduce the view. On achieving the desired preview image, proceed to print the drawing using the **Print** tool.

*Figure 13-23 Previewing the print settings displayed using the **Print Preview** tool*

TUTORIAL

Tutorial 1 — Apartment 1

In this tutorial, you will create a drawing sheet for the *Apartment 1* project created in Tutorial 2 of Chapter 12, and then add the first floor plan, north elevation, longitudinal section, room schedule, and door schedule to the sheet, as shown in Figure 13-24. You will also add the following project and sheet information in the sheet title block:

(Expected time: 30 min)

1. Drawing sheet parameters:
   Titleblock to be used-
       For Imperial   **C17 x 22 Horizontal** from the **US Imperial > Titleblocks** folder.
       For Metric   **A2 metric** from the **US Metric > Titleblocks** folder.

2. Project information:
   Owner name: **Apartment Society**
   Sheet title: **Apartment 1**
   Sheet name: **Plan, Elevation and Schedules**
   Sheet number: **Apt-1-01**

Creating Drawing Sheets and Plotting 13-23

The following steps are required to complete this tutorial:

a. Add a sheet by using the **New Sheet** tool and by loading the specified titleblock.
b. Add the project information to the sheet titleblock, refer to Figure 13-25.
c. Add views to the sheet view and compose the drawing sheet, refer to Figure 13-26.
d. Modify the visibility settings of the added views using the **Activate View** tool.
e. Add schedules to the sheet.
f. Edit schedules to compose them on the sheet, refer to Figure 13-27.

Figure 13-24 Sheet layout for creating a drawing sheet for the Apartment 1 project

Adding a Sheet to the Project

First, you need to open the project file and create a new sheet view. You can load the titleblock from the specified folder.

1. Choose **Open > Project** from the **Application Menu** and open the *c12_Apartment1_tut2.rvt* (for Metric *M_c12_Apartment1_tut2.rvt*) file created in Tutorial 2 of Chapter 12. You can also download this file from *http://www.cadcim.com*. The path of the file is as follows: *Textbooks > Civil/GIS > Revit Architecture > Autodesk Revit Architecture 2015 for Architects and Designers*.

2. Choose the **Sheet** tool from the **Sheet Composition** panel in the **View** tab; the **New Sheet** dialog box is displayed.

3. Choose the **Load** button; the **Load Family** dialog box is displayed. In this dialog box, choose the titleblock **C 17 x 22 Horizontal** from **US Imperial > Titleblocks** folder (for Metric **A2 metric** from the **US Metric > Titleblocks** folder). On doing so, the specified titleblock is added to the list in the **Select titleblocks** area in the **New Sheet** dialog box.

4. Choose the **OK** button to close the **New Sheet** dialog box and create the sheet view by using the loaded titleblock.

Adding the Project Information to the Sheet Titleblock

In this section, you need to add the project information to the titleblock using the **Properties** palette. Further, you need to directly enter other project parameters in the title block.

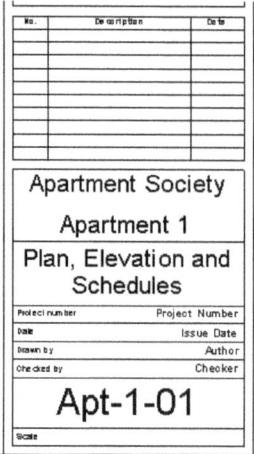

1. Select the titleblock from the drawing window. Then, in the **Properties** palette, click in the value fields for the **Sheet Name** and **Sheet Number** parameters and enter **Plan, Elevation and Schedule** and **Apt-1-01**, respectively.

2. Choose **Apply**. You will notice that the values entered in the **Properties** palette are displayed in the sheet.

3. Next in the titleblock, click in the **Owner** field and enter **Apartment Society** in the edit box. Now, press ENTER to view the new value in the sheet.

4. Similarly, you need to click on the **Project Name** field in the titleblock in the drawing area and enter **Apartment 1** in the edit box and then press ENTER. Now, the project details appear in the titleblock, as shown in Figure 13-25.

Figure 13-25 Project information in the titleblock of the sheet view

Adding Project Views to the Drawing Sheet

In this section, you need to add the specified project views by dragging their name from the **Project Browser** in the sheet. Further, you need to place the project views at their designated place in the sheet, based on the sheet layout, refer to Figure 13-24.

1. Drag **First Floor** from the **Floor Plans** head in the **Project Browser** into the drawing sheet. The view appears as a rectangle in the sheet view.

2. Next, move the cursor to the lower left area of the titleblock such that the corner of the rectangle is close to the lower left corner of the drawing sheet. Next, click to place the view. The first floor plan view is added to the sheet and appears enclosed in a rectangle.

3. In the **Project Browser**, click on the **North** elevation node under the **Elevations(Building Elevation)** head and then right-click to display the shortcut menu. From the shortcut menu, choose the **Rename** option; the **Rename View** dialog box is displayed. In the **Name** edit box of this dialog box, enter **North Elevation** and then choose the **OK** button; the **Rename View** dialog box is closed and the view is renamed.

Creating Drawing Sheets and Plotting 13-25

4. Drag **North Elevation** and **Section X** from the **Project Browser** and add them to the specified locations in the sheet, refer to Figure 13-24. The three views are added to the sheet, as shown in Figure 13-26.

5. Next, drag the **Door Jamb Detail** view from the **Project Browser** and add it to the desired location in the sheet, refer to Figure 13-26.

Note
You may need to hide the annotations that are not needed to be viewed in the sheet.

Figure 13-26 Project views added to the drawing sheet view

Modifying the Visibility of the Added Project Views

Notice that the project views in the drawing sheet given for this tutorial do not show the grids and section lines but show the complete section view. You can access each project view directly from the drawing sheet using the **Activate View** tool. Then, you can modify their visibility settings.

1. Select the **North Elevation** view from the drawing or highlight the view and then right-click to display the shortcut menu. Choose the **Activate View** option from the shortcut menu. On doing so, all other views except the selected view become grey. You can now use the editing tools to modify the building model and the visibility settings of the activated view.

2. Choose the **Visibility/Graphics** tool from the **Graphics** panel in the **View** tab; the **Visibility/Graphics Overrides for Elevation: North Elevation** dialog box is displayed.

3. In the **Annotation Categories** tab, clear the check boxes for Grids and Sections in the **Visibility** column. Choose **OK** to close the dialog box and return to the drawing window.

4. Right-click in the drawing window, and then choose the **Deactivate View** option from the shortcut menu.

5. Repeat step 1 for activating the **Section X** view from the sheet. Next, repeat steps 2 to 4 to turn off the display of grids and section in the activated view.

6. In the **Properties** palette for the **Section X** view, ensure that the check box corresponding to the **Crop Region Visible** parameter is selected. Next, in the sheet, select the boundary of the section view to display the view range controls.

7. Increase the size of the view range and display the entire section view by using the drag control located on the top as shown in the drawing sheet for this tutorial. You may use the **Zoom** tool to zoom into the section view. Next, right-click and choose **Deactivate View** from the shortcut menu.

Adding Schedules to the Drawing Sheet

Next, you need to add schedules to the drawing sheet in the same manner as you did in the case of the project view. Autodesk Revit Architecture, however, gives you the flexibility to divide larger schedules into smaller panels to accommodate them in the drawing sheet.

1. Drag **Room Schedule** from the **Schedules/Quantities** head in the **Project Browser**.

2. Move the cursor to the top left corner of the titleblock. The schedule is displayed and moves along with the cursor. Click to drop and add the room schedule at the location shown in the drawing sheet.

3. Similarly, drag and drop **Door Schedule** from the **Project Browser** to the drawing sheet.

   The door schedule is long and therefore you can use the **Split Schedule Table** tool to split it into two parts.

4. Click on the **Split Schedule Table** control available in the middle of the right edge of the door schedule, as shown in Figure 13-27. The schedule is divided into two parts and the second part is placed on the right of the first part, refer to Figure 13-24.

*Figure 13-27 Using the **Split Schedule Table** tool to split the table into two parts*

Creating Drawing Sheets and Plotting

This completes the tutorial for adding views and schedules to create a drawing sheet.

5. Choose **Save As > Project** from the **Application Menu**; the **Save As** dialog box is displayed. Enter **c13_Apartment1_tut1 (M_c13_Apartment1_tut1** for Metric) in the **File name** edit box and then choose **Save**.

6. Next, choose **Close** from the **Application Menu** to close the project file.

Self-Evaluation Test

Answer the following questions and then compare them to those given at the end of this chapter:

1. You can load additional titleblocks from the Autodesk Revit Architecture's Library. (T/F)

2. You can enter the project information directly in the titleblock. (T/F)

3. A view can be added to a sheet by using the dragging method. (T/F)

4. Once a view is added to a sheet, its parameters and properties cannot be modified. (T/F)

5. You can preview a print document before printing it. (T/F)

6. The _____ tool is used to activate a view added to a sheet.

7. The _____ control is used to split a schedule table into multiple parts.

8. You can access the **Type Properties** dialog box for a sheet by choosing the _____ button from the **Properties** palette.

9. The _____ option in the **Print** dialog box enables you to create a print file.

10. The _____ radio button in the **Print Setup** dialog box needs to be selected to fit the view to the selected paper size.

Review Questions

Answer the following questions:

1. The elements edited in a project view are automatically updated in a sheet view. (T/F)

2. The schedules added to one sheet can be moved to another sheet. (T/F)

3. When you edit a building parameter, the schedules added to a sheet are automatically updated. (T/F)

4. You can modify the **View Scale** parameter of a project view after adding it to a sheet. (T/F)

5. The visibility settings of a view are modified after adding it to a sheet. (T/F)

6. You can create your own titleblock by modifying the titleblock available in Autodesk Revit Architecture's library. (T/F)

7. Apart from printing sheet views, you can also print project views directly. (T/F)

8. Which of the following parameters cannot be used to specify the print range of a project view for printing?

    a) **Selected views/sheets**   b) **Visible portion of current window**
    c) **Size**   d) **Current window**

9. Which of the following tools can be used to add a project view to a sheet?

    a) **Callout**   b) **Sheet**
    c) **Drafting View**   d) **Add View**

10. Which of the following tools can be used to adjust the location of an added schedule in a sheet view?

    a) **Move**   b) **Offset**
    c) **Align**   d) **Array**

11. Which of the following step is required to place a schedule on a sheet ?
    a) Click on the schedule in the project browser and drag it onto the sheet
    b) Right-click on the schedules in the Project Browser and click Send to Sheet.
    c) Define the schedule as a hosted view in the sheets properties
    d) Define the schedules sheet location in its view properties.

12. Which of the following option is displayed in the Section Tag after placing a section view?

    a) The view scale   b) The view name
    c) The sheet number   d) All sheets referenced.

Exercises

Exercise 1   Club

Create a drawing sheet for the *Club* project created in Exercise 3 of Chapter 12. Add the first floor and roof plan, north elevation, sections, and room schedule to the sheet, as shown in Figure 13-28. Use the following project and sheet information parameters:

(Expected time: 30 min)

1. Drawing sheet parameters:
    Title block to be used:
        For Imperial   **C 17 x 22 Horizontal** from **US Imperial > Titleblocks** folder.
        For Metric   **A2 metric** from **US Metric > Titleblocks** folder.

Creating Drawing Sheets and Plotting 13-29

2. Project information:
   Owner name: **Club House**
   Sheet title: **Club Building**
   Sheet name: **Project Drawings**
   Sheet number: **Club-01**

3. Name of the file to be saved-
   For Impeial   **c13_Club_ex1**
   For Metric   **M_c13_Club_ex1**

Note
The Club project has been created using the Commercial-Default.rte template and therefore it already contains various sheet views. Some of the views have already been placed in them. You need to create a copy of the views and then add them to the new sheet that you create. You may also need to modify the view scale.

Figure 13-28 Sheet view for creating a drawing sheet for the Club project

Exercise 2 — Urban House

Create a drawing sheet for the *i_Urban_House.rvt* project. You can download the *i_Urban_House.rvt* file from *http://www.cadcim.com*. The path of the file is as follows: *Textbooks > Civil/GIS > Revit Architecture > Autodesk Revit Architecture 2015 for Architects and Designers*. In the drawing sheet, add the ground floor plan, first floor plan, second floor plan, south elevation, east elevation, and the 3D View 1, as shown in Figure 13-29. Use the titleblock **E1: 30 X 42 Horizontal** (for Metric **A0 metric** titleblock) for this exercise. All the views, except the 3D view, should be 1/8"=1'0"(for metric 1:100) view scale.

(Expected time: 30 min)

Save the file as-
    For Imperial   *c13_UrbanHouse_ex2.rvt*
    For Metric   *M_c13_UrbanHouse_ex2.rvt*

Figure 13-29 Sheet view for creating a drawing sheet for the Urban House project

Answers to Self-Evaluation Test
1. T, **2.** T, **3.** T, **4.** F, **5.** T, **6.** Activate View, **7.** Split Schedule Table, **8.** Edit Type, **9.** Print to File, **10.** Fit to Page

Chapter 14

Creating 3D Views

Learning Objectives

After completing this chapter, you will be able to:
- *Understand the usage of 3D views in a project.*
- *Generate orthographic views of a building model.*
- *Use the Navigation tools to view a building model.*
- *Generate perspective views using the Camera tool.*
- *Modify the properties of perspective views.*
- *Lock and unlock 3D views.*

INTRODUCTION

A three-dimensional view is a powerful medium of developing and presenting architectural and interior design concepts. Viewing a building model in all the three dimensions helps the architects and interior designers to visualize various building forms and shapes. It also conveys their vision of project to the clients, who, in most cases, are unable to understand the architectural drawings. The exterior 3D views of a building not only depict its overall scale, shape, and volume but can also represent the proposed exterior finishes as envisaged by the architects. The interior 3D views can be used to represent various interior elements such as interior partitions, furniture, plants, and interior finishes.

The use of computer graphics in the preparation of three-dimensional exterior and interior views gives numerous advantages to designers. The inevitable alterations in a building model during the design development can easily be studied with respect to their implications on the three-dimensional aspect of design. Software also enables the designers to develop design alternatives with different exterior and interior materials.

As described in the previous chapters, a building model of a project created using Autodesk Revit Architecture is an amalgamation of various three-dimensional elements such as walls, doors, windows, floor, roof, stairs, furniture, and so on. Each of these elements is a three-dimensional parametric entity. Autodesk Revit Architecture's powerful parametric technology enables the designers to create and edit these elements, and study them in all the three dimensions simultaneously. Autodesk Revit Architecture provides various tools to view these elements in 3D.

This chapter deals with the tools related to viewing building in three dimensions. It describes the procedure for generating new orthographic and perspective views for a building model. The ease of generating 3D views in Autodesk Revit Architecture gives a major advantage to all the users. They can also easily modify the view properties to achieve the desired effect in the exterior or interior 3D views.

THREE-DIMENSIONAL (3D) VIEWS

In Autodesk Revit Architecture, you can display a variety of three-dimensional (3D) views. There are two basic types of 3D views that can be created and viewed.

Orthographic View: An orthographic view is a 3D view of a building model in which all the elements are displayed in their actual sizes, irrespective of their distance from the source. This view is displayed automatically as a default 3D view. Once this view has been displayed, you can then use various tools to modify its properties.

Perspective View: A perspective view is displayed by placing a camera and specifying its eye elevation and target position.

Generating Orthographic View

Ribbon: View > Create > 3D View drop-down > Default 3D View

 In Autodesk Revit Architecture, the default 3D view is an orthographic view. To view a building model in orthographic projection, invoke the **Default 3D View** tool from the **Create** panel; the current view will change into the default 3D view.

Note
*In Revit Architecture, there is no default {3D} view in the **Project Browser**. However, when you invoke the **Default 3D View** tool from the **Create** panel, the default {3D} view is added to the **Project Browser**.*

When you create an orthographic 3D view for the first time in a project, a camera is automatically placed at the default position (southeast corner) and the corresponding view is displayed in the drawing window. The default view is named as **{3D}** and is added under the **3D Views** head of the **Project Browser**. Figure 14-1 shows an example of the 3D view of a building model displayed using the **Default 3D View** tool.

*Figure 14-1 3D view of a building model displayed using the **Default 3D View** tool*

Tip: *You can rename the default 3D view. After renaming it, when the **Default 3D View** tool is invoked, Autodesk Revit Architecture will create another default view.*

Dynamically Viewing Models Using Navigation Tools

The 3D environment of Revit Architecture has two important tools for navigation: **SteeringWheels** and **ViewCube**. You can use these tools to navigate through 3D views easily. These tools have already been discussed in brief in Chapter 2.

The **SteeringWheels** tool, as shown in Figure 14-2, is a tracking menu that enables you to navigate easily within the exterior and interior faces of a model. The **ViewCube** tool helps you simplify the switching of views from one point to another, as shown in Figure 14-3.

*Figure 14-2 The **SteeringWheels** tool*   *Figure 14-3 The **ViewCube** tool*

 Note
*If the **SteeringWheels** tool is not displayed by default, press F8 or invoke it from the **Navigation Bar**. You can also display or hide the **SteeringWheels** navigation by pressing Shift+W keys.*

Using the Navigation Tools in SteeringWheels

In Autodesk Revit Architecture, you can invoke nine navigation tools from the SteeringWheels. These tools are **CENTER, FORWARD, LOOK, ORBIT, PAN, REWIND, UP/DOWN, WALK,** and **ZOOM**. The availability of these tools depends upon the type of wheels being used. Different types of **SteeringWheels** have been discussed in Chapter 2. Various tools in the **SteeringWheels** are discussed next.

CENTER Tool

The **CENTER** tool is used to specify a point on a model as the center of the current view. While using this tool, you can adjust the location of the center of the current view by clicking and dragging the cursor to the defined point. As you drag the cursor, the appearance of the cursor changes to a sphere, as shown in Figure 14-4. Next, click at the desired place to specify the center of the view. When you release the mouse button, the model pans until the sphere is centered in the view and you return to the **SteeringWheels**.

Creating 3D Views

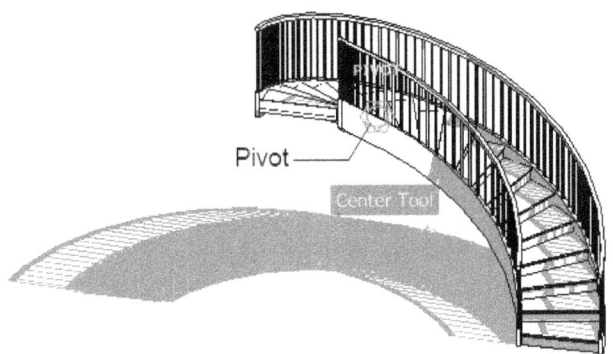

*Figure 14-4 Using the **CENTER** tool of **SteeringWheels***

After specifying the new center, you can revert to the original center. To do so, right-click on the **CENTER** button in the **SteeringWheels**, and then choose the **Restore Original Center** option from the shortcut menu displayed; the original center will be restored.

FORWARD Tool

The **FORWARD** tool is used to navigate a view forward and backward in the current viewport with respect to a pivot point, as shown in Figure 14-5. To invoke the tool, right-click on **SteeringWheels** and choose **Basic Tour Building Wheel** from the shortcut menu. Next, you need to fix the pivot point. To fix the pivot point, move the cursor close to the proposed point and then press and hold the left mouse button in such a way that the forward wedge in the **SteeringWheels** tool encompasses the proposed pivot point. As a result, the slider will be displayed in the 3D view. This slider is called **Drag Distance Indicator**. It has two marks: **START** and **SURFACE**. The **START** mark shows the starting distance of the navigation from the current viewpoint whereas the **SURFACE** mark shows the end distance from the current viewpoint. When you change the distance using the **Drag Distance Indicator**, the current distance is shown by the bright orange indicator. Move the cursor over the slider up and down to navigate the view. If you release the left mouse button, the slider will disappear.

*Figure 14-5 Using the **FORWARD** tool of **SteeringWheels***

Note
*When the **Forward** tool is clicked once, the model moves forward by 50% of the distance between the current location and the pivot point.*

LOOK Tool

The **LOOK** tool is used to rotate a view horizontally or vertically about a fixed point. The fixed point is defined by the center of the current view.

To invoke the **LOOK** tool, select **Full Navigation Wheel** or **Basic Tour Building Wheel**. Next, choose the **LOOK** option from the wheel and then hold the left mouse button until you notice the look cursor, as shown in Figure 14-6. Drag the look cursor along different directions to view the model.

*Figure 14-6 Using the **LOOK** tool from **SteeringWheels***

ORBIT Tool

The **ORBIT** tool is used to orbit or rotate a model about a fixed point. To use the **ORBIT** tool, you need to fix the pivot point that serves as the base point around which the model will rotate. Figure 14-7 shows the pivot point in the model while using the **ORBIT** tool. There are several ways to fix the pivot point for the **ORBIT** tool. One of the ways is to use the **CENTER** tool from **SteeringWheels**. In this case, the center that you fix up becomes the pivot point of the **ORBIT** tool. Alternatively, set the pivot point by pressing and holding the CTRL key and invoking the **ORBIT** tool from the **SteeringWheels**. Next, drag the cursor to the proposed pivot point on the model; this will change the cursor to a sphere indicating the new pivot point.

Creating 3D Views

*Figure 14-7 Using the **ORBIT** tool from **SteeringWheels***

You can also set the pivot point by selecting elements about which you want to orbit before using the **ORBIT** tool from **SteeringWheels**. The pivot point is calculated on the basis of the extent of the selected elements.

If you have not set the pivot point for the **ORBIT** tool by any of these ways, then by default, the target point of the current view will act as the pivot point.

As you invoke the **ORBIT** tool from the **SteeringWheels**, the cursor will change to the orbit cursor. You can drag the cursor to rotate your model about a pivot point. After dragging the cursor and then fixing a view, you can change the position of the pivot point in various ways.

PAN Tool

The **PAN** tool is used to scroll or move a view along the horizontal and vertical direction in the drawing area. To do so, invoke the **PAN** tool from **SteeringWheels** and hold the left mouse button; the cursor will change to a four-sided arrow, as shown in Figure 14-8. Drag the arrow in the required direction to scroll the model.

*Figure 14-8 Using the **PAN** tool from **SteeringWheels***

REWIND Tool

The **REWIND** tool holds a collection of previous views that have been navigated using various tools such as **ZOOM, PAN, LOOK, ORBIT**, and so on. The collection of the previous views is temporarily saved in the navigation history. The navigation history contains the representation of the navigated views of a model in the form of thumbnails, as shown in Figure 14-9. The navigation history of the **REWIND** tool is view-specific and has different saving options for different views.

*Figure 14-9 Using the **REWIND** tool from **SteeringWheels***

UP/DOWN Tool

Using the **Up/Down** tool, you can slide the current view of a model along the vertical axis of the screen. This sliding movement allows the current view plane to move vertically up and down. To invoke this tool, press and hold the **UP/DOWN** button; a graphical element will be displayed, showing the range of the vertical movement. The graphical element, which is called **Vertical Distance indicator**, has one mark on its each end: **TOP** and **BOTTOM**, as shown in Figure 14-10. The **TOP** and **BOTTOM** marks show the highest and lowest elevation of the view. On changing the elevation of the view with the **Vertical Distance indicator**, the current elevation will be shown by the bright orange indicator whereas the previous elevation will be shown by the dim orange indicator.

WALK Tool

The **WALK** tool gives you a visual sensation of walking through the space of a model. Using the **WALK** tool, you can virtually traverse through the space and gain a real time experience of navigating in a virtual 3D environment.

 Note
*Using the **WALK** tool, you can navigate only in a 3D perspective view.*

To invoke the **WALK** tool from **SteeringWheels**, press and hold the left mouse button over it; the cursor will change into a blue circle with a black dot at its center and eight arrows pointing in different directions, as shown in Figure 14-11. These arrows indicate the

Creating 3D Views　14-9

direction of movement while using the **WALK** tool. Now as you drag the cursor away from the blue circle, a single arrow will replace the cursor, which informs you or indicates the direction of the movement. If you want to change the direction of movement at any time during the navigation, drag the mouse in the specified direction as shown in the arrows.

Figure 14-10 *Using the **UP/DOWN** tool from **SteeringWheels***

Figure 14-11 *Using the **WALK** tool from **SteeringWheels***

While navigating through the space, you will observe that by default, the viewing plane is fixed to the horizontal plane. You can remove this restriction in order to view the model freely. To do so, right-click on **SteeringWheels**; a shortcut menu will be displayed. Choose the **Options** option from the shortcut menu; the **Options** dialog box will be displayed with the **Steering Wheels** tab chosen. In the **Walk Tool** area of the **Steering Wheels** tab, clear the **Move parallel to ground plane** check box. Next, choose the **OK** button in the

Options dialog box to return to the navigation. Now, you can navigate through the space without any restriction of the movement angle.

While you walk or fly through the space in the model, the speed of the movement is controlled by the **SpeedFactor** slider that is available in the **SteeringWheels** tab of the **Options** dialog box. When you move the slider toward right, the value of the **SpeedFactor** increases and when you move toward left, its value decreases. You can enter any value from 0.1 to 10 in the text box displayed next to the **SpeedFactor** slider. As you move the slider, you will notice the change in the value of the text box. Alternatively, you can use the period (.) and comma (,) keys in the keyboard to accelerate and decelerate the movement of navigation while using the **WALK** tool.

Note
*To increase or decrease the speed of navigation while using the **WALK** tool, right-click on the **WALK** option in the **Steering Wheels** and then choose **Increase Walk Speed** or **Decrease Walk Speed** from the shortcut menu displayed.*

While using the **Walk** tool, you can press and hold the SHIFT key to change the **Up/Down** tool. This tool can, in turn, be used to change the elevation of the viewing plane.

ZOOM Tool

The **ZOOM** tool is used to zoom in and zoom out a view. This tool is controlled by a magnification factor related to the amount of zooming done with respect to the current view scale, as shown in Figure 14-12.

*Figure 14-12 Using the **ZOOM** tool from **SteeringWheels***

Tip: *You can use the **ZOOM** tool to zoom in or zoom out the generated 3D perspective view. You can also stretch its extent by dragging the blue dots available in the view box.*

Creating 3D Views

Using the **ZOOM** tool, you can zoom and alter the magnification of your current view in several ways. To zoom out the current view, press and hold the SHIFT key before clicking on the **ZOOM** tool in **SteeringWheel**; the current view scale of the model will be reduced by 25 percent. Similarly, to increase the view scale of the current view by 25 percent, press and hold the CTRL key before clicking the left mouse button on the **ZOOM** tool. Alternatively, if you simply click the left mouse button once on the **ZOOM** tool, the magnification of the current view will increase by a factor of 25 percent. You can also make the zooming function dynamic by using the **ZOOM** tool. To do so, click the left mouse button on the **ZOOM** tool and drag the cursor up and down until you achieve the desired view on your screen.

Note

*When you are using the **Full Navigation Wheel** tool for zooming, the single-click zooming option will work provided the **Zoom in one increment with each mouse click** check box is selected in the **SteeringWheels** tab of the **Options** dialog box.*

Tip: *While using the **ZOOM** tool from the **Full Navigation Wheel** or **View Object Wheel** tool, the pivot point of the last zoom operation becomes the center point for the future orbit operations unless you use the **Center** tool after the zooming function.*

Using the Orient Tool

Autodesk Revit Architecture enables you to view the building model from certain predefined orientations such as north, south, east, west, northwest, southeast, and so on. These orientations are created by a camera placed in the respective directions and at a certain elevation. You can easily view the building model from these orientations using the **Orient** tool. To invoke this tool, right-click on the **ViewCube** tool; a shortcut menu will be displayed. Next, choose the **Orient to View** or **Orient to a Direction** option from the shortcut menu. You can choose the **Orient to View** option from the shortcut menu to transform the current view of the project to any of the views of floor plans or elevations. You can use the **Orient to a Direction** option from the shortcut menu to change the direction of the current project view to any of the orthographic or isometric view directions such as **North**, **South**, and **Northeast Isometric**. Similarly, you can use the **Orient to a Plane** option from the shortcut menu to change the orientation of the current project view to any of the specified workplanes in the project.

Note

*By default, a building plan is oriented in the north direction toward the top of the screen. You can, however, choose the **Location** tool from the **Project Location** panel in the **Manage** tab to modify its orientation.*

Orienting the 3D View to a Direction

To use the **Orient to a Direction** option, first you need to invoke the **ViewCube** tool. To do so, open the 3D view of the model; the **ViewCube** will be displayed. Next, right-click on the **ViewCube** to display a shortcut menu. Choose the **Orient to a Direction** option from the shortcut menu and then choose the required direction from the cascading menu, as shown in Figure 14-13.

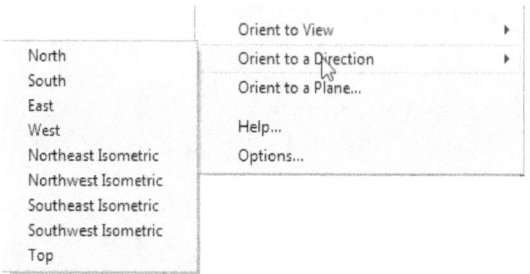

Figure 14-13 Choosing the **Orient to a Direction** option to open a 3D View

Note
*You can display the top view of a building model by right-clicking on the **ViewCube** tool and then choosing **Orient to a Direction** > **Top** from the shortcut menu displayed.*

Orienting the 3D View to a View

In Autodesk Revit Architecture, you can orient your current project view to a specified saved floor plan or elevation. To do so, open the 3D view to display **ViewCube**. Next, right-click on it and then choose **Orient to View** from the shortcut menu; a cascading menu will be displayed, as shown in Figure 14-14. You can choose the required Floor Plan/Elevation from the cascading menu.

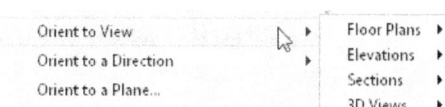

Figure 14-14 Choosing the **Orient to View** option from the shortcut menu

You can also orient the 3D view to a desired view using **SteeringWheels**. To do so, right-click on **SteeringWheels**, and then choose **Orient to View** from the shortcut menu; a cascading menu will be displayed. You can select the required Floor Plan/Elevation from this cascading menu.

Orienting the 3D View to a Plane

You can orient your current project view to a specified work plane. To do so, invoke the **SteeringWheels** tool by pressing the F8 key and then right-click on **SteeringWheels**; a shortcut menu will be displayed. In the shortcut menu, choose the **Orient to a Plane** option; the **Select Orientation Plane** dialog box will be displayed, as shown in Figure 14-15. Next, select the required radio button from this dialog box to specify the orientation plane.

Generating Perspective Views

Perspective views provide a realistic view of the exterior or interior space of a building model. Whenever you see an exterior or an interior view of a building with naked eye, it appears as the perspective view with the wall edges of the building converging at imaginary points. Using Autodesk Revit Architecture, you can easily create perspective views of a building model by defining the camera location and the target point. In most building projects, you will find it easier to use the floor plan view to define these points (camera location and camera target). You can then modify the view parameters to achieve the desired result.

Creating 3D Views

Figure 14-15 Specifying the orientation plane in the **Select Orientation Plane** *dialog box*

Generating Exterior Perspective Views

Ribbon: View > Create > 3D View drop-down> Camera

The **Camera** tool is used to create both exterior and interior perspective views of a building model. To create a perspective view, first open the floor plan or the ceiling plan view of the building model. Next, in the floor plan or in the ceiling plan view, invoke the **Camera** tool from the **Create** panel. On invoking the **Camera** tool, the **Options Bar** will display various related options for the camera to be placed in the view. Ensure that the **Perspective** check box is selected. The level of the eye point can be selected from the **From** drop-down list in the **Options Bar**. The **Offset** edit box can be used to enter the value of the offset level of the eye point from the selected level. For example, to generate a 3D perspective view from an eye point located at **5'0"** above level 1, you need to select **Level 1** from the **From** drop-down list and enter the value **5'0"** in the **Offset** edit box in **Options Bar**. This process should be followed before selecting the eye point.

As you move the cursor in the drawing window, a camera will be attached to it. Autodesk Revit Architecture will prompt you to specify the location of the eye point or the point from where you want to view the model. Next, click to specify location, as shown in Figure 14-16. In order to generate the exterior 3D views, the eye point must be placed outside the building model. Next, you need to specify the target point. To do so, move the cursor away from the camera location; you will notice that three rays are generated from the location point, as shown in Figure 14-17. These rays depict the field of the view for the selected camera point. You can use the **Offset** and **From** options in the **Options Bar** to specify the level and the offset elevation of the target point. Move the cursor and specify its location. The target point must be placed inside or beyond the building model for the camera to capture the model. Once you have selected the target point, Autodesk Revit Architecture will automatically generate the 3D perspective view of the building model and display it in the drawing window, as shown in Figure 14-18. The generated view will be added to the **3D Views** subhead of the **Project Browser**. Autodesk Revit

Architecture will name the generated 3D views as **3D View 1**, **3D View 2**, and so on. You can, however, rename them using the **Rename** option from the shortcut menu that is displayed on right-clicking on the newly created 3D view in the **Project Browser**.

 Tip: *The locations of the eye point and the target point define the amount of distortion in the perspective view. The closer the eye point to the building, the more is the distortion. To generate a realistic perspective view with minimum distortions, ideally, a building model or the portion of a building model to be viewed must fall within the field of view of the camera.*

Figure 14-16 Specifying the camera point to create a perspective view

Figure 14-17 Specifying the target point to create a perspective view

Creating 3D Views

*Figure 14-18 3D perspective view generated using the **Camera** tool*

You can also create orthographic views using the **Camera** tool. To do so, clear the **Perspective** check box in the **Options Bar** and then select the eye and the target points. Next, from the **Scale** drop-down list, select an option to specify the scale of the view. On doing so, an orthographic 3D view will be displayed with a specified scale.

Generating Interior Perspective Views

The procedure of creating an interior perspective view is similar to that of creating an exterior view. The **Camera** tool is also used to generate an interior view. However, in the case of an interior view, the eye point and the target point must be specified within the building model. Figure 14-19 shows the example of the eye point and the target point being specified for generating an interior perspective view.

 Note
If you select two different levels for the eye point and the target point, Autodesk Revit Architecture will display four lines indicating the field of view for both levels

Figure 14-19 *Specifying the eye point and the target point to generate an interior view*

Autodesk Revit Architecture generates the interior perspective view and displays it in the drawing window, as shown in Figure 14-20. To increase its extent, you can select any one of the blue dots at the four edges of the view box and drag them to the desired extent. This modifies the field of view for the camera. An example of the extended interior view is shown in Figure 14-21.

Figure 14-20 *The interior perspective view generated*

Creating 3D Views

Figure 14-21 Modified extent of the perspective view using the drag controls

Modifying Perspective View Properties

After creating the perspective view, you can modify its properties to achieve the desired effect. To do so, select the perspective view displayed and modify the desired instance properties in the **Properties** palette. The instance properties of the 3D view displayed in the **Properties** palette are described next.

In the **Properties** palette, the **View Name** instance parameter under the **Identity Data** head is used to rename a view. The **Detail Level** instance parameter is used to set the level of details desired in a view. The **Edit** button in the value column of the **Visibility/Graphics Overrides** instance parameter is used to set the visibility of models and annotations. On choosing this button, the **Visibility/Graphics Overrides <view name>** dialog box will be displayed. In this dialog box, you can set the visibility parameters of the model. Autodesk Revit Architecture generates a perspective view using the value 5'6" as the default elevation of the eye and also the target points from their respective specified levels. To modify the elevation of the eye point, enter the new value in the value column of the **Eye Elevation** instance parameter. Similarly, you can enter a new value for the **Target Elevation** instance parameter in its corresponding value column. As soon as you choose the **Apply** button, the perspective view is modified in the drawing window.

Locking and Unlocking 3D Views

In Revit Architecture, you can lock, unlock, and save the orientation of a 3D view. By locking a 3D view, you can add annotations and element tags to it. To view the options for locking, unlocking, and saving the 3D views, choose the **Unlocked 3D View** option from the **View Control Bar**. Note that the **Unlocked 3D View** option will be displayed in the 3D and camera views only. On choosing the **Unlocked 3D View** option, a flyout will be displayed, as shown in Figure 14-22. In the flyout, the following options are displayed: **Save Orientation and Lock View**, **Restore Orientation and Lock View**, and **Unlock View**. Note that the **Restore Orientation and Lock View** and the **Unlock View** options are inactive by default.

*Figure 14-22 Flyout displayed on choosing the **Unlocked 3D View** option*

On choosing the **Save Orientation and Lock View** option, the **Rename Default 3D View To Lock** dialog box will be displayed. In this dialog box, enter a name in the **Name** edit box and choose the **OK** button; the current view will be renamed, saved, and locked. After you save and lock the orientation of the 3D view, you can also tag the elements. After tagging the elements you can unlock the view. To do so, choose the **Unlock View** option from the flyout; the tags added will disappear and you can re-orient the 3D view. After re-orienting the view, you can restore the previous locked view that was saved. To do so, choose the **Restore Orientation and Lock View** option from the flyout.

Note
*In the Camera view, on choosing the **Save Orientation and Lock View** option from the **View Control Bar**; the **Rename Default 3D View To Lock** dialog box will not be displayed.*

Using the Section Box

A section box is used to limit the model geometry in a file that you want to export to other program such as Autodesk 3ds Max or Autodesk 3ds Max Design. It helps you clip unwanted content in a file. By adjusting the extent of a section box using drag controls, you can clip the unwanted portion of a model in the 3D view, thereby reducing the file size. This helps in easy and fast export of heavy files. Note that a section box can be enabled in a 3D view only.

To enable a section box, open the required 3D view and in the **Properties** palette, select the check box in the Value column corresponding to the **Section Box** parameter. Now, choose the **Apply** button in the **Properties** palette; a section box will be displayed in the 3D view as shown in Figure 14-23. Select the section box to display the blue color arrow controls. Drag the blue arrow controls and modify the extent of the section box to clip the unwanted portion of the model.

Note
*To hide the section box, clear the check box for the **Section Box** parameter in the **Properties** palette.*

Autodesk Revit Architecture allows you to modify the extents of a section box from the views other than the 3D view such as a plan view or elevation views. To do so, select the section box in a 3D view and then open the required plan or the elevation view. The blue arrow controls will be displayed in the respective view as well. Modify the extent of the section box and then open the 3D view again to see the change. If required, you can modify the extent of the scope box again in the 3D view. To hide the scope box, select the scope box and right-click; a shortcut menu will be displayed. Choose **Hide in view > Elements** from the shortcut menu; the scope box is visible in the view. To save the view, duplicate the view and rename it.

Creating 3D Views

Figure 14-23 Section Box generated for the 3D view

 Tip: *To modify the camera and target locations, open the view in which the camera was placed. Right-click the **3D view** name in the **Project Browser** that was created by using the camera. Choose the **Show Camera** option from the shortcut menu to display the location of the camera and the target points in the drawing window. The camera and target points can now be dragged to a new location. Autodesk Revit immediately regenerates the 3D view for the new location.*

 Note
The extents of a section box are not affected by the crop regions.

TUTORIALS

Tutorial 1   Apartment 1

In this tutorial, you will create two interior perspective views for the first floor of the *Apartment 1* project created in Chapter 13 of this textbook, refer to Figures 14-24 and 14-25. The first figure shows the living room and the second figure shows the view of the lobby area from the living room. The exact view angle and height are not important for this tutorial.

(Expected time: 20 min)

Figure 14-24 *3D view of the living room for the Apartment 1 project*

Figure 14-25 *3D view of the lobby area for the Apartment 1 project*

The following steps are required to complete this tutorial:

a. Open the project file and the ground floor plan view.
b. Generate the interior perspective view of the living room using the Camera tool, refer to Figure 14-26.
c. Generate the interior perspective view of the lobby room, refer to Figures 14-28 and 14-29.

Creating 3D Views

Opening the Project File and Invoking the Camera Tool

1. Choose **Open > Project** from the **Application Menu** and open the *c13_ Apartment 1_tut1.rvt* file created in Tutorial 1 of Chapter 13. You can also download this file from *http://www.cadcim.com*. The path of the file is as follows: *Textbooks > Civil/GIS > Revit Architecture > Autodesk Revit Architecture 2015 for Architects and Designers*.

2. Double-click on **First Floor** in the **Floor Plans** head of the **Project Browser** to open the corresponding floor plan in the drawing window.

3. Invoke the **Camera** tool from **View > Create > 3D View** drop-down; the **Options Bar** is displayed.

Generating the Interior Perspective View of the Living Room

In this section of the tutorial, you will specify the camera and the target points for the camera. You will use the default value **5'6"** (eye level) for both these points.

1. Select the **Perspective** check box in the **Options Bar**, if it is not selected by default.

2. Move the cursor to the lower right corner of the living room and click to specify the camera point.

3. Now, move the cursor toward the diagonally opposite ends of the living room and click when the field of view resembles the graphic shown in Figure 14-26. The drawing window shows the 3D interior view, as shown in Figure 14-27.

Figure 14-26 Specifying the camera point and the target point of the interior view

Figure 14-27 The 3D interior view of the living room

4. The selected 3D view shows the drag controls (blue dots at the midpoint of the four sides of the rectangle). Right-click in the drawing window and then choose **Zoom Out (2x)** from the shortcut menu.

5. Use the drag controls to increase the view extents based on the 3D view given for the living room. Next, press ESC to exit the **Modify | Cameras** tab.

6. In the **Project Browser**, right-click on **3D View 1** under **3D Views**; a shortcut menu is displayed. From the shortcut menu, choose the **Rename** option; the **Rename View** dialog box is displayed. In the **Name** edit box of the dialog box, enter the **Living Area** text and choose the **OK** button; the **3D View 1** view is renamed to **Living Area**.

Generating the Interior Perspective View of the Lobby

You can use similar steps to generate the 3D interior view of the lobby area.

1. Right-click on the **First Floor** view in the **Floor Plans** head in the **Project Browser** and choose **Open** from the shortcut menu to open the view.

2. Invoke the **Camera** tool from **View > Create > 3D View** drop-down. Ensure that the **Perspective** check box is selected in the **Options Bar** (default setting).

3. Move the cursor near the center of the opening between the lobby area and the living room, refer to Figure 14-28, and click to specify the camera point.

Creating 3D Views   14-23

4. Move the cursor horizontally toward the left and click when the field of view resembles the graphic shown in Figure 14-28. The drawing window shows the 3D interior view of the lobby area, as shown in Figure 14-29.

Figure 14-28 Specifying the camera point and the target point for generating the lobby interior view

5. Right-click in the drawing window and then choose **Zoom Out (2x)** from the shortcut menu displayed. Use the drag controls to increase the view extents.

6. Now, choose **Visual Style > Shaded** from the **View Control Bar**; the current view is shaded.

7. Use the drag controls to increase the view extents based on the 3D view given for the lobby area, refer to Figure 14-29.

8. Right-click on **3D View 1** in the **Project Browser** under **3D Views** and rename it to **Lobby Area** by using the **Rename** option from the shortcut menu.

9. Now, choose **Save As > Project** from the **Application Menu**; the **Save As** dialog box is displayed. Enter **c14_Apartment1_tut1** in the **File name** edit box and choose **Save**; the project file is saved.

10. Choose **Close** from the **Application Menu** to close the project file.

Figure 14-29 *The 3D interior view of the lobby area*

Tutorial 2   Club

Create an exterior 3D perspective view and an orthographic view for the *Club* project created in Exercise 1 of Chapter 13, refer to Figures 14-30 and 14-31. Note that the exterior 3D perspective view is from the main entrance. The exact view and height are not important for this tutorial.

(Expected time: 20 min)

The following steps are required to complete this tutorial:

a. Open the project file and the ground floor plan view.
b. Invoke the **Camera** tool to generate the exterior 3D view.
c. Generate the exterior perspective view of the Main Entrance, refer to Figure 14-32.
d. Generate the orthographic view of the building, refer to Figure 14-34.
e. Use the **SteeringWheels** tool and the **ORBIT** tool to display the orthographic view.

Creating 3D Views

Figure 14-30 3D exterior view of the main entrance of the club building

Figure 14-31 Orthographic view of the Club building

Opening the Project File and Invoking the Camera Tool

1. Choose **Open > Project** from the **Application Menu** and open the *c13_Club_ex1.rvt* file created in Exercise 1 of Chapter 13. You can also download this file from *http://www.cadcim.com*. The path of the file is as follows: *Textbooks > Civil/GIS > Revit Architecture > Autodesk Revit Architecture 2015 for Architects and Designers*.

2. Double-click on **First Floor** in the **Floor Plans** head of the **Project Browser** to open the corresponding floor plan in the drawing window.

3. Invoke the **Camera** tool from **View > Create > 3D View** drop-down; the options for inserting the camera are displayed in the **Options Bar**.

Generating the Exterior Perspective View of the Main Entrance

You need to specify the camera and target points. Also, you will use the default value 5'6" (eye level) for both these points.

1. Select the **Perspective** check box in the **Options Bar** if it is not selected by default.

2. Move the cursor vertically above the main entrance door and click to specify the camera point, as shown in Figure 14-32.

3. Move the cursor vertically downward and click when the field of view resembles the graphic shown in Figure 14-32; the drawing window shows the 3D exterior view of the main entrance, as shown in Figure 14-33.

Figure 14-32 *Specifying the camera and the target points for the exterior view*

4. Right-click in the drawing window and choose **Zoom Out (2x)** from the shortcut menu.

5. Ensure that the crop region of the 3D view is selected in the drawing and it displays the drag controls (blue dots at the midpoint of the four sides of the rectangle).

6. Use the drag controls to increase the view extents based on the 3D view given for the entrance view. Press ESC to exit the **Camera** tool.

7. Rename **3D View 1** to **Entrance View** by using the **Rename** option from the shortcut menu displayed on right-clicking in the view name in the **Project Browser**.

Creating 3D Views

Figure 14-33 *3D exterior view of the main entrance*

Generating the Orthographic View of the Club Building

You need to display the orthographic view of the club building using the **SteeringWheels** tool.

1. Invoke the **Default 3D View** tool from **View > Create > 3D View** drop-down.

2. Move the cursor toward the **ViewCube** and right-click on it; a shortcut menu is displayed.

3. Choose **Orient to a Direction > Northeast Isometric** from the shortcut menu; the northeast isometric view is displayed, as shown in Figure 14-34.

Figure 14-34 *Northeast isometric view of the Club building*

4. Press the F8 key to display **SteeringWheels**.

5. Next, press and hold the **ORBIT** tool in **SteeringWheels** and drag the cursor to display a view similar to the one specified for the project. Release the mouse button when the appropriate view is displayed, refer to Figure 14-35. Press ESC to exit.

Figure 14-35 Orthographic view of the Club project

6. In the **Project Browser**, right-click on **{3D}** under **3D Views** and rename **{3D}** to **Orthographic View** by using the **Rename** option from the shortcut menu displayed.

7. Double-click on **First Floor** in the **Floor Plans** head of the **Project Browser** to open the corresponding floor plan in the drawing window.

8. Choose **Save As > Project** from the **Application Menu**; the **Save As** dialog box is displayed.

9. Enter **c14_Club_tut2** in the **File name** edit box and choose **Save** to save the project file.

10. Choose **Close** from the **Application Menu** to close the project file.

Self-Evaluation Test

Answer the following questions and then compare them to those given at the end of this chapter:

1. The 3D views displayed are added under the **Floor Plans** head in the **Project Browser**. (T/F)

2. The last change made in the orientation of a view can be undone using the **Undo view orientation changes** tool. (T/F)

3. The **Save View** tool can be used to save the 3D view within a project file. (T/F)

4. A building model can be viewed in 3D from the predefined camera locations using the **Orient** tool. (T/F)

5. While using the **Camera** tool, the **Offset** edit box can be used to specify the height of the camera from the selected level. (T/F)

6. Once a 3D perspective view has been created, its camera location cannot be modified. (T/F)

7. You can save the current view displayed as the **Home** view of the **ViewCube**. (T/F)

8. The _____ tool is used to orient a 3D view to a plane.

9. To create an orthographic view using the **Camera** tool, the _____ check box must be cleared in the **Options Bar**.

10. The _____ tool can be used to display a 3D perspective view.

11. The _____ instance parameter indicates the height of the camera from the selected level.

12. You can choose the **Unlock View** option from the _____ to unlock a 3D View.

Review Questions

Answer the following questions:

1. The field of view can be modified after creating a 3D view. (T/F)

2. The height of the target point of the camera from the selected level is specified by the **Target Elevation** instance parameter. (T/F)

3. The **Visibility/Graphics** tool can be used to modify the visibility of elements in the 3D view generated. (T/F)

4. The **Perspective** check box in the **Options Bar** needs to be cleared in order to display a perspective view. (T/F)

5. A 3D perspective view can be created by using two different levels for the camera and target points. (T/F)

6. The **Display Model** tool can be used to set the level of detail in a project view. (T/F)

7. Which of the following tools can be used to view a 3D view with shading and edges?

    a) **Shading**   b) **Shaded with edges**
    c) **Wireframe**   d) **Hidden**

8. Which of the following **SteeringWheels** types has the **Look** tool available in it?

   a) **Full Navigation Wheel**   b) **View Object Wheel**
   c) **Mini Full Navigation Wheel**   d) **Tour Building Wheel**

9. Which of the following tools can be used to magnify a view?

   a) **Orient**   b) **Zoom**
   c) **Scroll**   d) **Spin**

10. Which of the following tools is used to move the camera point keeping the target point intact?

    a) **Pan**   b) **Look**
    c) **Forward**   d) **Slide**

Exercises

Exercise 1   Apartment 1

In this exercise, display the 3D exterior views using the file *c14-revit-2015-exr01.rvt* (for Metric *M_c14-revit-2015-exr01.rvt*) after downloading it from the website *www.cadcim.com*. Create two exterior perspective views, one from the front and the other from the side of the building model, as shown in Figures 14-36 and 14-37, respectively. Use an appropriate camera location, target point, eye elevation, and target elevation to achieve the given perspective view.

(Expected time: 30 min)

Save the file as *c14_Apartment-1_ex1.rvt* (for Metric *M_c14_Apartment-1_ex1.rvt*)

Figure 14-36 3D exterior front view for Exercise 1

Figure 14-37 *3D exterior side view for Exercise 1*

Exercise 2   Office Building 1

In this exercise, display a 3D exterior front view using the file *c14-revit-2015-exr02.rvt* (for Metric *M_c14-revit-2015-exr02.rvt*) after downloading it from the website *www.cadcim.com*, as shown in Figure 14-38. Use an appropriate camera location, target point, eye elevation, and target elevation to achieve the given perspective view.

(**Expected time: 15 min**)

Save the file as *c14_Office-1_ex2.rvt* (for Metric *M_c14_Office-1_ex2.rvt*)

Figure 14-38 *3D exterior front view for Exercise 2*

Exercise 3   Office Building 2

In this exercise, display an exterior 3D view using the *c10_Office-2_tut1.rvt* (for Metric *M_c10_Office-2_tut1.rvt*) project created in Tutorial 1 of Chapter10, as shown in Figure 14-39. Use an appropriate camera location and target point for using. The eye elevation and target elevation for the view are 15'0" and 35'0", respectively.

(Expected time: 15 min)

Save the file as *c14_Office-2_ex3.rvt* (for Metric *M_c14_Office-2_ex3.rvt*)

Creating 3D Views

Figure 14-39 *3D exterior view for Exercise 3*

Exercise 4   Hotel Building

In this exercise, display the 3D exterior views using the file *c14-revit-2015-exr04.rvt* (for Metric *M_c14-revit-2015-exr04.rvt*) after downloading it from the website *www.cadcim.com*, refer to Figures 14-40 through 14-42. Use an appropriate camera location, target point, eye elevation, and target elevation to achieve the given perspective views.

(Expected time: 25 min)

Save the file as *c14_Hotel_ex4.rvt* (for Metric *M_c14_Hotel_ex4.rvt*)

Figure 14-40 *Camera view 1 of the hotel building*

Figure 14-41 Camera view 2 of the hotel building

Figure 14-42 Camera view 3 of the hotel building

Answers to Self-Evaluation Test

1. F, **2.** T, **3.** T, **4.** T, **5.** T, **6.** F, **7.** T **8. Orient to Plane, 9. Perspective, 10. Camera, 11. Eye Elevation, 12. View Control Bar**

Chapter 15

Rendering Views and Creating Walkthroughs

Learning Objectives

After completing this chapter, you will be able to:
- *Create a rendered scene.*
- *Set natural and artificial lighting.*
- *Use different materials and textures.*
- *Create and render a walkthrough.*
- *Add people and vehicles to a building model.*
- *Use the Decal tool.*
- *Know about Autodesk 360 / Rendering.*

RENDERING IN REVIT ARCHITECTURE

Rendering is an art and a process of generating digital image from a three-dimensional model containing geometry, texture, light, and shading information through a computer program.

The rendering process helps you give a clear picture of the final outcome of an architectural project that you are working on. It bridges the gap between the final outcome and the two-dimensional working drawing, thereby giving you and your client the freedom to select the final finish with reduced cycle time for the approval and finalization of the design. Also, rendering with its rich photorealistic images helps you generate the actual bill of material for a project.

As described in the previous chapter, creating three-dimensional views of a building model enables you to visualize the interior and exterior of a building. However, to give a realistic effect to the view, it is necessary to apply materials to the building elements and render the view. The rendered exterior views of a building not only depict its overall scale, shape, and volume, but also represent the proposed exterior finish as envisaged by the architect. Similarly, a rendered interior three-dimensional view can be used to represent various interior elements such as interior partitions, furniture, plants, and interior finishes.

Revit Architecture, with its powerful drafting tool and Building Information Modeling, is capable of generating rich photorealistic images of a three-dimensional model. You can add texture, color, light, and various realistic elements to add life to your three-dimensional models.

In Revit Architecture, the mental ray rendering engine is used for rendering views. Mental ray is one of the most popular rendering engines that is used by Autodesk products such as AutoCAD, Autodesk Maya, Autodesk 3dsMax.

The mental ray was developed by mental images (Berlin, Germany) for the production of quality rendering application. It supports the ray tracing technique to deliver rich photorealistic images.

The inclusion of mental ray in Autodesk Revit Architecture has made it more powerful for generating high quality rendering images with improved lighting effects and more accurate render appearances for materials.

In Autodesk Revit Architecture, the user-interface for rendering images has been designed to accommodate fewer dialog boxes and a simplified workflow with specified defaults. It helps you generate presentations with high quality images with a little effort and less experience. You can also improve and refine the quality of the output by controlling several advanced settings that are discussed later in this chapter.

Rendering Workflow

In this chapter, you will learn about various methods and techniques used in a rendering workflow. A rendering workflow is a process chart that shows the flow of the rendering process to achieve the end result in the form of high quality rendered image, refer to Figure 15-1.

Rendering Views and Creating Walkthroughs

Figure 15-1 The rendering workflow chart

 Note
In the Rendering workflow, you can alter the order of steps from step1 to step 4.

The steps mentioned above are briefly discussed next.

Step 1 - Creating a Three-Dimensional View
To start with the rendering process, the first step is to generate a three-dimensional view of the exterior or interior of the building model that you have created. You have already learned the methods of creating three-dimensional views of a building model in Chapter 14.

Step 2 - Specifying Render Appearance and Applying Material
A material defines the exact look and finish of elements present in a building model. In Revit Architecture, you can create your own material or use in-built materials from the **Render Appearance Library** to apply to specific element. The Revit material defines the texture, color, and exact appearance of an element and also allows you to control various parameters required to define specific material. For example, to define a glass, you can define its transparency, reflection, color, and so on.

The materials provided in Autodesk Revit Architecture have been assigned the mental ray material properties, and therefore, they appear more realistic than the standard materials in the previous version. The materials and their applications are discussed later in this chapter.

Step 3 - Applying Lights

You can light a three-dimensional model by using natural illumination from daylight or using artificial light sources such as electric lights, gas lights, lamps, candles, or oil lamps.

While placing artificial lights in a three-dimensional model, you can define lighting fixtures and their light sources to attain the best effect. As you render, Autodesk Revit Architecture provides you the facility to control the visibility of these lights in a particular rendered image while defining the setting for rendering the scene. Details about lighting in Revit Architecture are discussed later.

Step 4 - Using Entourages and Decals

In Revit Architecture, you can use entourages to add additional features such as trees, people, cars, and so on. These features do not represent the main model but contribute toward making the rendered image more realistic. The entourage objects are defined as families and include Archvision's RPC (Rich Photorealistic Contents) objects that can add more realism, when added in a model and rendered.

Similarly, you can use decals to place images on the surfaces of a building model. Decals are generally used to depict signage, paintings, and signboards in a rendered image. In Revit Architecture, you can place decals only on a flat or cylindrical surface.

Step 5 - Defining Render Settings

After applying materials, lights, entourages, and creating a three-dimensional view, you need to start the rendering process. To do so, choose the **Show Rendering Dialog** button from the **View Control Bar** or type RR; the **Rendering** dialog box will be displayed. In this dialog box, you can specify the view area for rendering, lighting controls, background, render quality specifications, and size of the rendered image.

Step 6 - Creating the Rendered Image

After specifying all parameters for the rendering, you need to run the render engine using the **Rendering** dialog box to create a rendered image. To do so, choose the **Render** button from the **Rendering** dialog box. You will learn the process of rendering an image using the options in this dialog box later in this chapter.

Step 7 - Exporting the Rendered Image

After finishing the rendering process, you can save it in a file or as a project view. To export the rendered image to a file, choose the **Export** button from the **Image** area in the **Rendering** dialog box; the **Save Image** dialog box will be displayed. You can save the image file to the required location using the appropriate file format. Alternatively, if you want to save the rendered image in your project view, choose the **Save to Project** button from the **Image** area in the **Rendering** dialog box; the **Save To Project** dialog box will be displayed, where you can specify the name of the rendered image by entering a name in the **Name** edit box. Next, choose the **OK** button to save the image and exit the **Save To Project** dialog box. To open the rendered image in the project, you need to select the image by choosing **Views (all) > Renderings** in the **Project Browser**.

Introduction to Materials

In Revit Architecture, managing material, which is an important part of rendering process, includes creating and adding of various materials. Material specifies the actual look of the model elements as they appear in the rendered images. Materials convey the structural and descriptive information of model elements. In Revit Architecture, you can apply materials to individual elements in a building model or apply materials to elements at the time of defining their families.

Before you learn how to assign materials to the elements, you should be familiar with some of the concepts that are discussed next.

Color in Shaded View
You can define the color of an element in a shaded project view.

Pattern and Color on the Surface
You can specify the pattern and color of the surface of an element while defining a material.

Color and Fill Pattern when the Element is Cut
You can also specify the color and the pattern of a material that appears in the sectioned surface of an element when it is cut and viewed in a sectional view.

Render Appearance for Rendering
You can define materials by assigning textures and properties as the render appearance, which appears in the rendered image.

Description about Manufacturer, Cost, and Keynotes
Descriptive information such as details of manufacturer, cost of the material, and keynotes can also be added while defining a material.

Structural Information
While defining a material, you can add information about various properties. For example, you can define physical properties such as **Young's modulus**, **Shear modulus**, **Poisson ratio** and others, which may be required at the time of structural analysis.

Now, after learning the concept about material, you will now learn how to assign materials to the building elements. You can create, edit and assign the material by using the **Material Browser** dialog box and the **Material Editor** pane, as shown in Figure 15-2, that are discussed next.

*Figure 15-2 The **Material Browser** dialog box along with the **Material Editor** pane*

Material Browser Dialog Box

The **Material Browser** dialog box can be used to organize materials into separate groups so that they can be easily edited as per the requirement of the project. In this dialog box, you can add new material, create libraries, and edit the properties of the existing materials. To invoke the **Material Browser** dialog box, choose the **Materials** tool from the **Settings** panel of the **Manage** tab.

Materials that are available in the current project, whether they are applied to the objects or not, are displayed in the **Project Materials: All** area of the **Material Browser** dialog box. From this area, select a material and right-click; a shortcut menu will be displayed. You can choose an option from the shortcut menu to rename or duplicate the selected material, or to add the selected material to the desired library.

In the **Project Materials: All** area, you can also customize the display of materials. To do so, click on the double arrow placed at the bottom right corner of the **Project Materials: All** area. Next, click on the down arrow in the menu displayed; a flyout will be displayed. In this flyout, there are following sections: **Document Materials**, **View Type**, **Sort,** and **Thumbnail Size**. You can choose any option from these sections. For example, you can choose the **Show In Use** option from the **Document Materials** section to display only those elements that have been used in the project.

Rendering Views and Creating Walkthroughs 15-7

In the **Material Browser** dialog box, you can customize the **Autodesk Material-Library** list. To do so, choose the **Shows/Hides library panel** button located at the top right of the **Project Materials: All** area; the **Autodesk Materials-Library List** area will be displayed. In this area, there are three material libraries: **Autodesk Materials**, **Favorites**, and **AEC Materials**. Notice that lock icons appear next to the **Autodesk** and **AEC** libraries, which indicate that these libraries are protected and therefore, you cannot modify, add, or delete materials from their content. In the **Autodesk Materials-Library List** area, click on the arrow displayed on the left of any of the libraries; the categories of the materials will be displayed. Select a category; various materials belonging to the selected category will be displayed on the right. For example, if you choose **Concrete** from the **Autodesk Materials** library, you will find various materials such as GFRC (Glass Fibre Reinforced Concrete), Concrete Precast Panels, Concrete Panels, Concrete Lightweight and so on. You can add any of the library materials to the **Project Materials: All** area. This can be done either by clicking on the **Adds material to document** button which is displayed after placing the cursor on the material or by dragging and dropping the desired material in the **Project Materials: All** area.

In the material browser toolbar of the **Material Browser** dialog box, refer to Figure 15-2, the **Creates, opens, and edits user-defined libraries** button is used to open or edit an existing library, or to create a new library. The **Creates or Duplicates material** button is used to create a new material or generate a duplicate of the existing material. The **Opens/closes asset browser** button is used to open or close the **Asset Browser** dialog box. Similarly, the **Opens/closes material editor** button is used to display or hide the **Material Editor** pane.

Material Editor Pane

By default, the **Material Editor** pane is displayed along with the **Material Browser** dialog box. As discussed in the above section, you can choose the **Opens/closes material editor** button in the **Material Browser** dialog box to display or hide the **Material Editor** pane, refer to Figure 15-3. Alternatively, you can also display the hidden **Material Editor** pane by choosing the **Edits material, including properties and information** button, refer to Figure 15-4. This button will be displayed along with the name of the selected material in the **Project Materials: All** area of the **Material Browser** dialog box.

On selecting a material from the **Material Browser** dialog box, various properties of the selected material will be displayed in the **Material Editor** pane. You can edit these properties by using the options available in the following tabs: **Identity**, **Graphics**, **Appearance**, **Physical**, and **Thermal**. The options in these tabs are discussed next.

Identity Tab

The options in the **Identity** tab help you to define the material, so that whenever you perform a search operation, the material can be recognized by the values specified in this tab.

The **Name** edit box in this tab displays the name of the selected material. You can enter a new name by entering the desired text in this edit box. The other options in this tab are displayed under the following areas: **Descriptive Information**, **Product Information**, and **Revit Annotation Information**. These areas are discussed next.

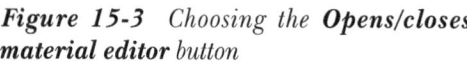

*Figure 15-3 Choosing the **Opens/closes material editor** button*

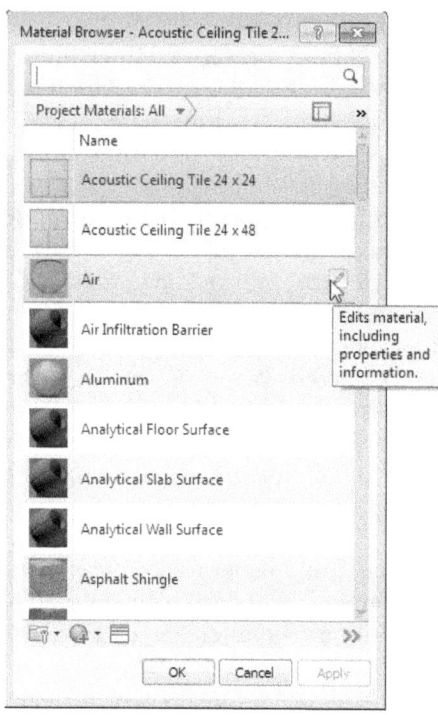

*Figure 15-4 Choosing the **Edits material, including properties and information** button*

Descriptive Information. The **Descriptive Information** area contains the **Description**, **Comments**, and **Keywords** edit boxes and the **Class** drop-down list. The **Description** edit box is used to describe the utility and importance of the material. The **Class** drop-down list is used to specify the type of material. The **Comments** edit box, is used for entering the general or specific comments regarding the material. The **Keywords** edit box is used for entering specific keywords for the material.

Product Information. The options in the **Product Information** area are used to define the product details such as manufacturer, model, cost, and URL. The **Manufacturer** text box in this area is used to enter the name of the company producing the selected material. Similarly, you can enter price, model number, and important web link of the vendor or manufacturer of the material in the **Cost**, **Model**, and **URL** text boxes, respectively.

Revit Annotation Information. The **Revit Annotation Information** area contains two text boxes: **Keynote** and **Mark**. In the **Keynote** text box, you can enter a specific keynote or choose the browse button next to it to select a standard keynote for the material. Similarly, you can enter a unique identification number for the material in the **Mark** text box.

Graphics Tab

You can use the options in the **Graphics** tab to control the display properties of the material assigned to an object. The **Graphics** tab consists of the following areas: **Shading**, **Surface Pattern**, and **Cut Pattern**, refer to Figure 15-5.

Rendering Views and Creating Walkthroughs 15-9

Shading. In the **Shading** area, select the **Use Render Appearance** check box to assign the color of the rendered appearance to the shaded view. In this case, the **Color** edit box and the **Transparency** slider will be deactivated. To assign a color to the shaded view, clear the **Use Render Appearance** check box; the **Color** button and the **Transparency** slider get activated. Choose the **Color** button; the **Color** dialog box will be displayed. From the **Color** dialog box, select the color that you want to assign to the material for its shaded view and then choose the **OK** button to close it. You can also make the shaded element appear opaque, semi-transparent, or transparent. To make the shading completely opaque, move the **Transparency** slider toward the left till it shows 0% in the text box. Similarly, move the slider towards the right to make the material appear transparent.

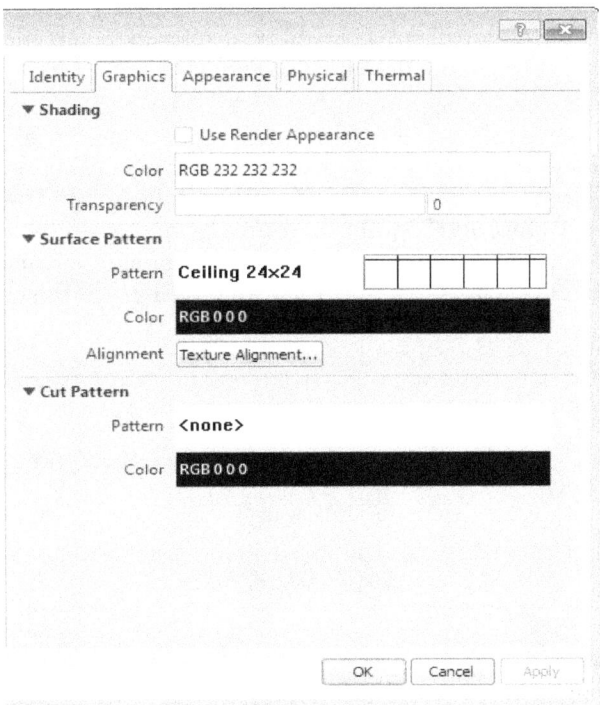

Figure 15-5 The **Graphics** tab displaying graphical properties of material

Surface Pattern. Expand the **Surface Pattern** area to display the options in it. The options in the **Surface Pattern** area allows you to assign hatch patterns of different colors to the surface of an element. To assign a hatch pattern, choose the swatch next to the **Pattern** parameter; the **Fill Patterns** dialog box will be displayed. Using the options in this dialog box, you can modify, create, or delete a pattern. After setting the required parameters in the **Fill Patterns** dialog box, choose the **OK** button to close it. Next, to assign a color to the selected hatch pattern, click on the color swatch next to the **Color** parameter; the **Color** dialog box will be displayed. Select the desired color from this dialog box and then choose the **OK** button to close it. You can also align the render appearance relative to the surface pattern using the options in the **Surface Pattern** area. To do so, choose the **Texture Alignment** button corresponding to the **Alignment** parameter, in the **Surface Pattern** area; the **Align Render Appearance to Surface Pattern** window will be displayed. In this window, the preview of the render appearance of the material is displayed along with the assigned surface pattern. You can use the four arrows displayed around the preview of the render appearance to align it with the surface pattern. After aligning the surface pattern, choose the **OK** button to close the **Align Render Appearance to Surface Pattern** window.

Cut Pattern. The **Cut Pattern** area displays various options under it. These options help you to edit the view of the cut surface of the material. When you click on the **Pattern** option in the **Cut Pattern** area, the **Fill Pattern** dialog box will appear. You can then assign any fill pattern to the element using the options in this dialog box. You can assign any color to the cut pattern of the element. To do so, click on the **RGB** button corresponding to the **Color** parameter; the **Color** dialog box will be displayed. Select the desired color from this dialog box and then choose the **OK** button to close it.

Appearance Tab

The **Appearance** tab displayed in the **Material Editor** pane, as shown in Figure 15-6, consists of the following area: **Information**, **Generic**, **Reflectivity**, **Transparency**, **Cutouts**, **Self Illumination**, **Bump**, and **Tint**. In these areas, you can assign different textures and colors to the material for changing the appearance of a rendered image, you can also edit existing material, and create a new material using the areas in the tab.

*Figure 15-6 The options displayed under the **Appearance** tab*

Information. You can use the options in the **Information** area to edit the name and description of the material, and also enter keywords related to the appearance of the material.

Generic. In the **Generic** area, you can change the color of the surface of the material. To do so, click on the **Color** swatch; the **Color** dialog box will appear. To make the elements look realistic, their texture can be edited using the **Texture Editor** dialog box. To invoke this dialog box, choose the drop-down next to the **Image** swatch in the **Generic** area, the **Texture Editor** dialog box will be displayed. The brightness of the image can also be controlled using this dialog box.

The **Image Fade** option in the **Generic** area is used to change the complexity of the appearance of the preview by distinguishing it from its base color. The **Glossiness** option helps you to change the brightness of the preview image. For example, the image can be made dull or bright. You can select the **Metallic** or **Non-metallic** option from the **Highlights** drop-down list to assign the required texture to the material.

Reflectivity. The reflectivity of the element can be changed by using the **Direct** and **Oblique** options in the **Reflectivity** head. On selecting the **Reflectivity** check box, the **Direct** and **Oblique** options get activated and these options help you when light is falling at it directly or at an angle respectively. Similarly, the **Transparency, Cutouts, Self Illumination, Bump,** and **Tint** options in this tab can be used to edit the texture of the image.

Physical Tab

The **Physical** tab in the **Material Editor** pane consists of various options that define the physical state of a material. This tab comprises of the following areas: **Information** and **Mechanical**, refer to Figure 15-7. The options available in these areas are discussed next.

Information. The **Information** area contains the **Name, Description, Keywords, Type,** and **Sub-class** edit boxes. The name of the selected material is displayed in the **Name** edit box of this area. In the **Description** edit box, you can write about the utility and importance of the material. To quicken and refine your search process, you may need to add keywords to the material. You can do so by entering the specific text in the **Keywords** edit box. The **Type** parameter, which is a read-only parameter, displays a value to specify the type of the material in context of its physical properties.

Mechanical. The **Mechanical** area contains the **Density** edit box. You can enter a value in this edit box to specify the density of the selected material.

Thermal Tab

The **Thermal** tab, as shown in Figure 15-8, contains options that describe the material as well define the thermal state and thermal behavior of materials such as thermal conductivity, specific heat, and so on. To edit the parameters, you can click on the **Opens/closes asset browser** button from the **Material Browser** dialog box.

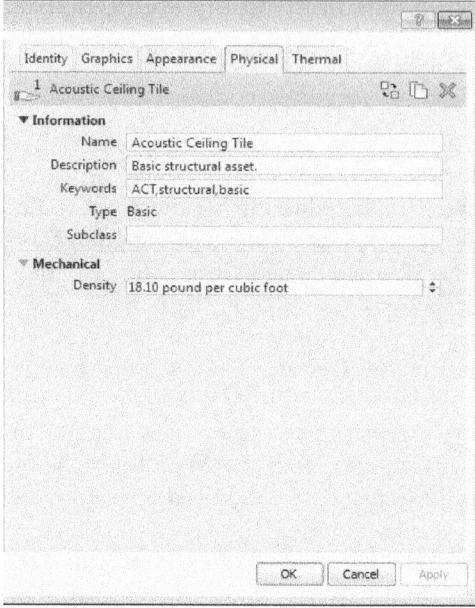

*Figure 15-7 The **Physical** tab displaying physical properties of a material*

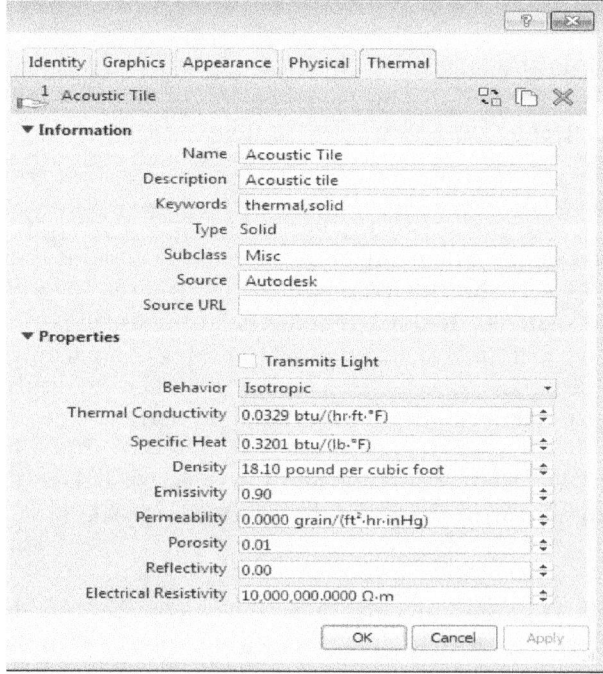

*Figure 15-8 The options under the **Thermal** tab*

Rendering Views and Creating Walkthroughs 15-13

Assigning Materials to Elements

After searching and selecting materials in the **Materials Browser** dialog box, you need to assign that material to an element. The materials can be assigned to a category or a subcategory of an element by using the **Object Styles** dialog box. You can also assign material directly to a model element, to the selected face of an element, or to various parts in an element using the family editor. The different methods to assign material in a project are discussed next.

Assigning Materials Using the Object Styles Dialog Box

In Autodesk Revit Architecture, you can apply materials to elements based on their categories or subcategories. For example, if you want to assign a material to a window, its category will be window and its subcategories will be frame/mullion, glass, trim, and so on.

To assign the selected material to a category or a subcategory of an element, choose the **Object Styles** tool from the **Settings** panel of the **Manage** tab; the **Object Styles** dialog box will be displayed, as shown in Figure 15-9. Choose the **Model Objects** or **Imported Objects** tab from the dialog box based on the status of the object to which you want to assign the material. Select the required category or expand the category to view its subcategories. Next, click on the cell of the **Material** column corresponding to the subcategory of the expanded category; the browse button will become available on the right of the field. Choose the browse button; the **Material Browser** dialog box will be displayed. Select the appropriate material and choose the **OK** button to exit the **Material Browser** dialog box. Choose **OK** again to close the **Object Styles** dialog box.

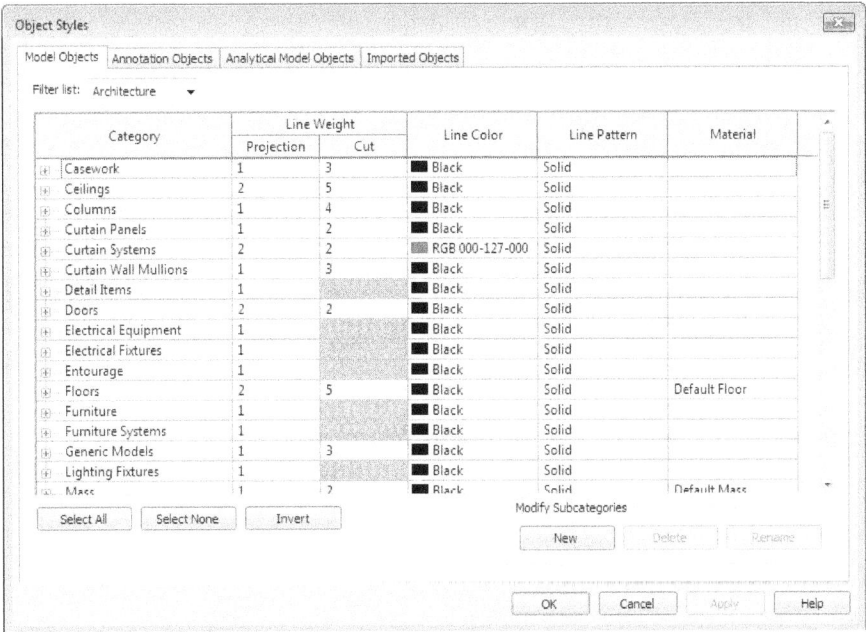

Figure 15-9 The **Object Styles** dialog box

Assigning Material Using the Family Editor

Using the family editor, you can assign materials to different parts of an element. To assign material to a particular part of an element, open the family in the family editor. Next, select the part to which you want to apply the material; the properties of the selected part will be displayed in the **Properties** palette. Next, choose the button in the value column corresponding to the **Material** instance parameter under the **Material and Finishes** heading to open the **Associate Family Parameter** dialog box, as shown in Figure 15-10. In this dialog box, you can select or add a parameter.

Figure 15-10 The Associate Family Parameter dialog box

Note

*The parameters displayed in the **Existing family parameters of compatible type** area of the **Associate Family Parameter** dialog box may vary depending on the type of element selected.*

To add a parameter, choose the **Add parameter** button in the **Associate Family Parameter** dialog box; the **Parameter Properties** dialog box will be displayed. In this dialog box, select the **Materials and Finishes** option from the **Group parameter under** drop-down list, if it is not selected by default. Next, select the **Instance** or **Type** radio button located on the right of the **Parameter Data** area to define the material of an element as an instance parameter or as a type parameter. In the **Name** edit box, enter the name of the parameter and choose the **OK** button; the created parameter is selected and added to the **Associate Family Parameter** dialog box and the **Parameter Properties** dialog box will be closed. Next, choose the **OK** button twice to exit.

Assigning Materials Directly to Model Elements

In Autodesk Revit Architecture, you can assign a material directly to model elements. To do so, select the model element in a view; the properties of the selected element will be displayed in the **Properties** palette. The assignment of material depends on whether the material parameter is defined as instance, type, or structural.

If the material of an element is defined as the instance parameter, click on the value field corresponding to the parameter whose material you need to change in the **Materials and Finishes** area of the **Properties** palette. As you click on the value field, the browse button will appear. Choose this button; the **Material Browser** dialog box will be displayed. Select the material and then choose the **OK** button twice to exit.

If the material of an element is defined as the type parameter, you can change the material in the **Type Properties** dialog box. In this dialog box, click on the **Value** column; the browse button will appear. Choose this button; the **Material Browser** dialog box will be displayed. Select the material and then choose the **OK** button to exit.

If the material of an element is defined as the structural parameter, as in the case of a wall, select the element and choose the **Edit Type** button from the **Properties** palette to invoke the **Type Properties** dialog box. In this dialog box, choose the **Edit** button in the **Value** field corresponding to the **Structural** parameter; the **Edit Assembly** dialog box will be displayed. Click on the **Material** column for the layer whose material you need to change, and then choose the browse button available in the cell to display the **Materials** dialog box. Now, select the appropriate material and choose the **OK** button twice to return to the drawing area.

Assigning Materials to Faces Using the Paint Tool

The **Paint** tool is used to apply a material to the face of an element without modifying its material properties. The elements that can be painted include walls, floor, ceiling, roof, and so on. To apply material to the face of an element, invoke the **Paint** tool from **Modify > Geometry > Paint** drop-down; the **Modify | Paint** tab will be displayed. Select the type of material from the **Material Browser** dialog box and move the cursor to the element to highlight it. Next, click to apply the selected paint to the face of the element. Now, choose the **Done** button in the **Material Browser** dialog box to close it. You can remove the material applied to a face of the element. To do so, choose the **Remove Paint** tool from **Modify > Geometry > Paint** drop-down and click on the desired face of the element.

Note
*The texture of the material assigned to the face of element will be visible only in the **Realistic** visual style.*

Applying Lights
Light is an important factor of the rendering process. It affects the overall appearance of elements and materials in the rendered view. It not only enables you to view the building model, but also helps you express its mood along with its ambience. For example, for the exterior of a shopping mall, a vibrant mood can be created by using bright afternoon lights with sharp shadows. On the contrary, for the exterior of a residential building, soft evening lights can be used to give a relaxing ambience. Similarly, an interior view of a showroom can be brightly lit and a bar interior view can be given an accent lighting. Autodesk Revit Architecture enables you to add and control the properties of a variety of artificial lighting fixtures based on the project requirement.

Controlling the Natural Lighting
In Revit Architecture, natural light is defined by the direction of sunlight or the location, date, and time of day to achieve a realistic ambience of sunlight on a building model. To set

the natural light before the rendering process, choose the **Sun Settings** tool from **Manage > Settings > Additional Settings** drop-down or type **SU**; the **Sun Settings** dialog box will be displayed in Figure 15-11. In this dialog box, you can select the predefined sunlight settings or define a new setting as per the project requirement.

*Figure 15-11 The **Sun Settings** dialog box*

The **Sun Settings** dialog box contains three areas: **Solar Study**, **Presets**, and **Settings**. In the **Solar Study** area, you can select the mode as per your requirement. To specify the sun settings based on a specified geographic location, you can select either **Still**, **Single Day**, or **Multi-Day**. In case you want to define the sun settings based on azimuth and altitude, select the **Lighting** radio button.

From the list box in the **Presets** area, select one of the predefined sun settings (such as a solstice). Next, to define a new sunlight setting, choose the **Duplicate** button in the **Presets** area of the **Sun Settings** dialog box; the **Name** dialog box will be displayed. In this dialog box, enter the desired name for the sunlight settings in the **Name** edit box and choose the **OK** button to exit the **Sun Settings** dialog box. In the **Settings** area of the **Sun Settings** dialog box, you can set the sunlight based on its geographical location or **Azimuth** and **Altitude**.

Next, if you need to cast shadows on a ground plane, select the **Ground Plane at Level** check box and then select the required level from the drop-down list below the check box. Autodesk Revit Architecture will cast shadow on the specified level for both the two-dimensional and three-dimensional views. On clearing the **Ground Plane at Level** check box, the shadow casting on levels will be disabled, except on the toposurface. Choose **Apply** and then **OK**; the **Sun Settings** dialog box will be closed.

Note
The options for the shadow, as discussed in the previous section, do not affect the settings of the shadow in the rendered image.

Adding Artificial Lights to a Project

Artificial lights can easily be added to a building model by using light fixture families. To do so, choose the **Place a Component** tool from **Architecture > Build > Component** drop-down; the **Modify | Place Component** tab will be displayed. Now, choose the **Load Family** tool from the **Mode** panel in the **Modify | Place Component** tab; the **Load Family** dialog box will be displayed. You can select various families of lighting fixtures by browsing the **US Imperial > Lighting > Architectural** folder. In the **Architectural** folder, you can select the lighting fixture from the **Internal** or **Externa**l sub-folders. After selecting the desired family of light, choose **Open** to load it into the project file. To select the loaded light fixture and add it to a view, select the desired light type from the **Type Selector** drop-down list and then click at the desired location in the ceiling or floor plan of the required level.

Note

Light fixtures can be added to an appropriate plan only. The exterior floor mounted lighting fixtures such as street lights and bollard lights can be added to the floor plan whereas other ceiling mounted fixtures can be added only to the corresponding ceiling plan (with a false ceiling). Fixtures are visible only when appropriate plan is displayed in the drawing window.

Modifying Properties of the Lighting Fixture

You can modify the properties of a lighting fixture before or after adding them to the project. To modify the lighting fixtures after you add them in the project, select the lighting fixture to be modified; the **Modify | Lighting Fixtures** tab will be displayed. In the **Properties** palette, certain instance parameters such as **Level**, **Phase Created**, and so on can be modified. To modify the type properties of the light fixture, choose the **Edit Type** button; the **Type Properties** dialog box will be displayed. Based on the fixture selected, its type properties are displayed and they can be modified. One of the most important parameter types is the **Initial Intensity** parameter displayed under the **Photometric** head in the **Type Properties** dialog box. Choose the button in its **Value** field; the **Initial Intensity** dialog box will be displayed. In this dialog box, you can set the values of **Wattage**, **Luminous Flux**, **Luminous Intensity**, and **Illuminance** in their respective spinners. After setting the values, choose **OK**; the **Initial Intensity** dialog box will be closed. In the **Type Properties** dialog box, you can also change the other properties associated with the light fixture such as lamp, material of fixture, and so on.

Using Decals and Entourages

The **Decal** tool is used to place an image on the face of a flat or a cylindrical element in the building model. This tool can also be used to represent signals, posters, billboards, and paintings in a rendered view. A decal is an external graphic file that is linked to the project file. The file formats that can be used as decal are *jpeg*, *targa*, *tiff*, and *bmp*. Since the decal files are linked to the project file and are not saved with it, the size of the project file does not increase. It is, however, recommended to save decals along with a project file so that the link is maintained. Entourages are the collection of people, trees, cars, parking elements, and other site components that can be inserted in the model to give a realistic look to the rendered image.

In Revit Architecture, entourages are family-based and are available as a library of entourage families. You can add additional entourages to an existing family if you want to use them in your scene. They are displayed in simple line drawings as placeholders in the project views. The photorealistic representations of entourages are displayed only in rendered images.

In a project, the people, plants, vehicles, and office clutters are parts of Archvision's RPC (Rich Photorealistic Content) product family. In Autodesk Revit Architecture, you can insert people in floor plans and three-dimensional views, where each people family is displayed as a placeholder.

You cannot place a people family in the elevation and section views. You can see the actual detail of these RPC in a rendered image.

Revit Architecture provides two people families: **RPC Male** and **RPC Female**. Each family type provides different render appearances for males and females. The other families of entourages that are available for placing in your project are: **RPC Beetle**, **RPC Chair**, **RPC Notebook Computer**, **RPC Picture Frame**, and **Semi Truck**.

A Revit plant family can be placed in the surrounding of a model. The Revit plant family uses a RPC file to specify the render appearance. In Autodesk Revit Architecture, you are provided with several RPC families for trees and plants. Different species of trees and plants are available as types in each family.

Creating Decal Type

Before placing a decal in a view, you need to create a new decal type. To do so, choose the **Decal Types** tool from **Insert > Link > Decal** drop-down; the **Decal Types** dialog box will be displayed. Now, choose the **Create new decal** button at the bottom left corner of the **Decal Types** dialog box; the **New Decal** dialog box will be displayed. Enter a suitable name in the **Name** edit box for the new decal type and choose the **OK** button to exit. On doing so, a decal will be added to the **Decal Types in Project** area of the **Decal Types** dialog box, as shown in Figure 15-12. Next, you need to add an image and the associated attributes to the new decal type by using the options in the **Settings** area of the **Decal Types** dialog box. To add an image, choose the Browse button next to the **Source** text box; the **Select File** dialog box will be displayed. Select an image file from this dialog box and choose the **Open** button. You can preview it in the preview area. Next, set the desired values in the corresponding lists for various attributes. After selecting various attributes, choose the **OK** button to return to the drawing area. Various attributes for **Decal Types** are described in the table given next.

Attributes	Definition
Brightness	Defines the brightness or darkness of the decal
Reflectivity	Measures the quantity of light reflected from the surface of a decal. Enter a value between 0 and 99 to define reflection
Transparency	Measures the quantity of light passing through a decal. Enter a value between 0 (completely opaque) and 1 (completely transparent)

Rendering Views and Creating Walkthroughs 15-19

Finish	Defines the finished condition of decal surfaces. Select the **Matte**, **Semi-gloss**, **Gloss**, **High Gloss**, or **Custom** option from the **Finish** drop-down list. If you select the **Custom** option, enter a value between 0 and 1 in the text box available next to it
Luminance (cd/m^2)	Defines the light emitted by a decal surface. It is measured in candela per meter square. Select various options from the **Luminance** drop-down list or select **Custom** to enter a value
Bump Pattern	Defines a texture that is added in addition to the texture applied to a decal. This texture is placed on the top of the texture that is already applied to the decal
Bump Amount	Reflects the amount of irregularities that can be created on the decal surface due to the **Bump Pattern** parameter. Enter any value between 0 and 100%
Cutouts	Defines the shapes cut on the surface of the decal. Select an image file to define the cut-outs

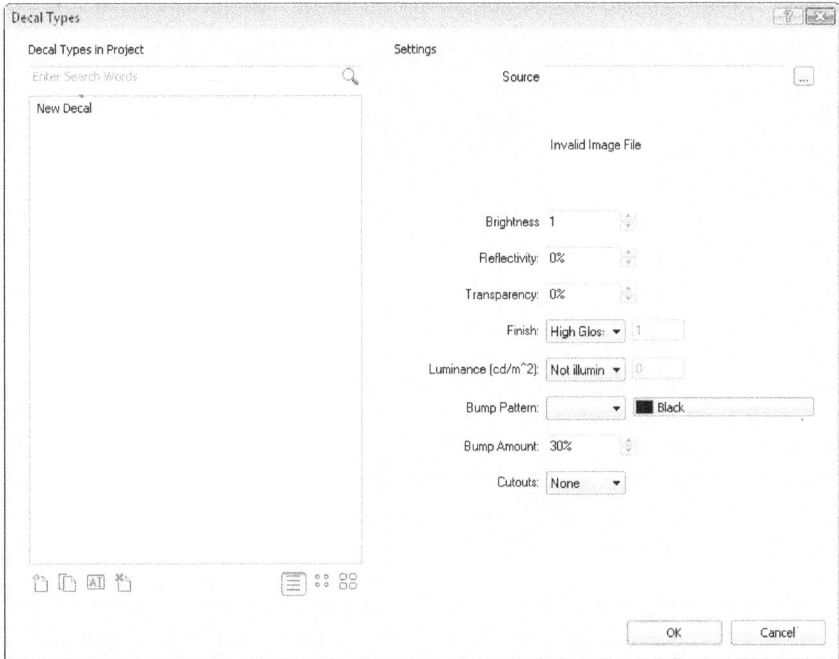

Figure 15-12 The decal added to the **Decal Types** dialog box

Placing a Decal

To place a decal in your scene, choose the **Place Decal** tool from the **Link** panel; the **Modify | Decal** tab will be displayed. Now, select the appropriate decal type from the **Type Selector** drop-down list and set the size of the decal in the **Width** and **Height** text boxes in the **Options Bar**. By default, the **Lock Proportions** check box is selected in the **Options Bar**, which indicates that the width to height ratio is set to one. You can clear this check box to remove the restriction, so that the width and height are independent of each other. Now, move the cursor near the surface over which the decal is to be placed. After the desired surface or the edge is highlighted, click to place the decal. The decal will appear as a rectangle with two diagonal lines in all views, except the rendered view.

Note

If no decal is loaded in the Decal Types dialog box, then on choosing the Place Decal tool, the Decal Types dialog box will be displayed and will prompt you to insert a decal.

Editing a Decal

To edit a decal, select it from the drawing. On doing so, the **Modify | Generic Models** tab along with the **Options Bar** will be displayed. Now, modify its size using the **Width** and **Height** edit boxes in the **Options Bar**. Alternatively, you can also use the drag controls at the four corners of the decal. The **Lock Proportions** check box in the **Options Bar** can be cleared to resize the decal to a different aspect ratio. Choose the **Reset** button in the **Options Bar** to reset the size of the decal to the original size. In the **Properties** palette, you can change the instance parameters such as **Height**, **Width**, and **Lock Proportions** from their corresponding **Value** fields. From the **Properties** palette, choose the **Edit Type** button to invoke the **Type Properties** dialog box. In this dialog box, you can modify the type properties of the decal such as **Decal Attributes**, **Keynotes**, and others. To modify the attributes of the decal such as image, brightness, reflectivity, transparency, and others, choose the **Edit** button in the **Value** field of the **Decal Attributes** parameter; the **Decal Types** dialog box will be displayed. In this dialog box, you can change the attributes of the decal by specifying values in the spinners, edit boxes, buttons and drop-down lists that will be displayed for various parameters in this dialog box.

Placing Entourages

To place entourages and plants in a building model, first you need to load the entourage family types in the drawing. To do so, choose the **Place a Component** tool from **Architecture > Build > Component** drop-down; the **Modify | Place Component** tab will be displayed. In this tab, choose the **Load Family** tool from the **Mode** panel; the **Load Family** dialog box will be displayed. In this dialog box, browse to the folder location **US Imperial > Entourage**. The **Entourage** folder contains the families of the people and vehicles. Alternatively, browse to the **US Imperial > Planting** folder location that contains the families of plants, trees, and shrubs. Select the desired family to be loaded into the **Load Family** dialog box and then choose the **Open** button to load it into the project file.

Next, in the **Modify | Place Component** tab, select the desired entourage from the **Type Selector** drop-down list and select the **Rotate after placement** check box from the **Options Bar**, if you need to rotate the element at the time of insertion. Select the desired floor level for the entourage from the drop-down list displayed next to the **Rotate after placement** check box. Next, move the cursor to the drawing window and click to add the selected element to the appropriate floor plan or the 3D view.

Rendering Views and Creating Walkthroughs

Rendering Settings

After creating three-dimensional view for rendering, applying lights and materials to elements, and placing entourages and decals, you need to do render settings before the final rendering. To render and create the presets for the rendering process, choose the **Show Rendering Dialog** button from **View Control Bar** or type RR; the **Rendering** dialog box will be displayed, as shown in Figure 15-13.

In the **Rendering** dialog box, you can define the view area for rendering, specify the quality of output, specify the light settings, set the background of the rendered image, adjust the rendered image exposure quality, and save the rendered image to a project view or export it as an external image file. Various settings are discussed next.

Setting the View Area

After creating the three-dimensional view and invoking the **Rendering** dialog box, you need to set the view area to be rendered by any one of the following methods, Render region, Crop region, Section Box, and Camera clipping plane. To set the view area by using the Render region method, select the **Region** check box in the **Rendering** dialog box; a red colored rectangular region boundary will be displayed in the drawing area. This boundary is called the render region boundary and is used to determine the enclosed area within which the elements displayed will be rendered. On selecting the render region boundary, the blue colored dots will be visible on all four edges of the rectangle. These dots are called control grips. Click on any one of the control grips and drag to the extent to resize the rectangular area. Similarly, you can use other methods such as Crop region, Section box, and Camera Clipping plane to determine the view area for rendering. These methods have already been discussed in the previous chapters.

*Figure 15-13 The **Rendering** dialog box*

Specifying Output Settings

After selecting the view area, now you need to set the resolution or the image size of the output image.

You can use various options from the **Output Settings** area of the **Rendering** dialog box to set the image size and the pixel quality of the output image. In the **Output Settings** area, there are two radio buttons, **Screen** and **Printer**. These radio buttons can be used to set the resolution or the image quality of the rendered image. On selecting the **Screen** radio button, you can set the final rendered image size in accordance with the screen display. In this case, you can use various methods as discussed in the previous topic to adjust the size of the final rendered image.

Similarly, you can also set the resolution of the output image in accordance with printer. To do so, select the **Printer** radio button in the **Output Settings** area of the **Rendering** dialog box. For setting the resolution of the output image, you need to set the printing quality in dots per inches (DPI). This is the standard unit of printing for all applications. Higher value of DPI determines better quality of the image and increases the render time. You can set the quality of the rendered image to 75 DPI, 150 DPI, 300 DPI, and 600 DPI by selecting the option from the drop-down list in the **Output Settings** area of the **Rendering** dialog box.

Controlling Lights

While specifying the settings for rendering, it is important to control the lights in a scene externally or internally. To make the lighting process easy, Autodesk Revit Architecture has provided you with an integrated control of lights in the scene. The lighting control appears in the **Lighting** area of the **Rendering** dialog box in the form of schemes, position of Sun, and control of artificial light. To set the light scheme for rendering images, select any of the six options, **Exterior: Sun only**, **Exterior: Sun and Artificial**, **Exterior: Artificial only**, **Interior: Sun only, Interior: Sun and Artificial**, and **Interior: Artificial only** from the **Scheme** drop-down list available in the **Lighting** area.

To set the position of the Sun, you can select an option from the **Sun Setting** drop-down list only if you select **Exterior: Sun only**, **Exterior: Sun and Artificial**, **Interior: Sun only**, or **Interior: Sun and Artificial** from the **Scheme** drop-down list. To set your own sun and shadow, select the **Choose a sun location** button placed next to the **Sun Setting** text box; the **Sun Settings** dialog box will be displayed. In this dialog box, you can use different types of presets that define the position of the sun on the basis of its location, date, and time. You can also set your own presets in the **Sun Settings** dialog box.

You can control the intensity and visibility of light in a view by setting the corresponding parameters in the **Rendering** dialog box. In the **Lightings** area, the **Artificial Lights** button is deactivated by default. To activate this button, select any scheme that contains artificial light from the **Scheme** drop-down list; the button will be activated. Now, choose this button; the **Artificial Lights - {3D}** dialog box will be displayed, as shown in Figure 15-14. This dialog box contains a list that displays the name of all the lighting fixtures that are placed in a building model. This list of lighting fixtures is divided into **Grouped Lights** and **Ungrouped Lights**. You can create a new group or edit an existing group to add or remove an individual light fixture from the group. In the **Artificial Lights - {3D}** dialog box, you can also set the intensity of individual or group lights by setting the dimming value in the **Dimming (0-1)** column between **0** and **1**. Similarly, you can turn on or off the visibility of the individual light or grouped light fixtures by selecting or clearing the corresponding check boxes in the **On/Off** column of the **Artificial Lights - {3D}** dialog box. A light group is an essential tool in the rendering process which helps you control the light fixtures in a scene collectively as well as individually. To create a new group of lights, choose the **New** button in the **Group Options** area of the **Artificial Lights-{3D}** dialog box. On doing so, the **New Light Group** dialog box will be displayed. Enter the name of the light group in **Name** edit box and choose the **OK** button to return to the **Artificial Lights - {3D}** dialog box. You will notice that a new group has been added under **Grouped Lights** with a default dimming value of 1. Next, you need to add light fixtures to the group. There are several methods by which you can add light fixtures to the group. Some of these methods are discussed next.

Figure 15-14 *The Artificial Lights - {3D} dialog box*

In the **Artificial Lights - {3D}** dialog box, select the group name to which you want to add light fixtures. After selecting the desired group, choose the **Edit** button in the **Group Options** area to display the **Light Group** panel in the **Architecture** tab. You will notice that all the model elements and the lighting fixtures belonging to another light group are displayed in halftone, the lighting fixtures belonging to the selected light group are displayed in green, and lighting fixtures that are not currently assigned to any light group are displayed normally in the drawing area. To add a light fixture to the group, choose the **Add** button, select a light fixture from the drawing area, and then choose the **Finish** button. To remove a light fixture from the group using the **Light Group** toolbar, choose the **Remove** button and select the light fixture from the group, and then choose the **Finish** button.

Alternatively, you can add a light fixture to the group using the **Artificial Lights - {3D}** dialog box. To do so, first select the required light fixtures from the **Ungrouped Lights** hierarchy. Then, choose the **Move to Group** button; the **Light Groups** dialog box will be displayed. In this dialog box, select various light groups from the **Light Group** drop-down list to assign the selected light fixture to the light group. To remove a light from a group, select the name of the light fixture that you want to remove from the **Artificial Lights - {3D}** dialog box and then choose the **Remove from Group** button. This will result in the transition of the light fixture from the **Grouped Lights** to **Ungrouped Lights** area.

Adding a Background to a Scene

You can add a suitable background to the rendered scene using the **Rendering** dialog box. The background that you specify can be of a solid color or a combination of sky and clouds.

Setting the Background of the Rendered Image

To set the background of a rendered image, select an option from the **Style** drop-down list in the **Background** area of the **Rendering** dialog box. After setting the background, you can use the **Haze** slider in the **Background** area to control the haziness of the rendered image. Note that the **Haze** slider will not be displayed in the **Background** area if you select the **Color** or **Image** option from the **Style** drop-down list. You can select the **Color** option from this drop-down list to assign a color to the background. On doing so, the **Color Swatch** button will be activated. Choose this button to display the **Color** window from where you can select the desired color for the background. Alternatively, you can select the **Image** option from the **Style** drop-down list to display an image in the background of the rendered scene. On doing so, the **Background Image** dialog box will be displayed. By default, no image file is assigned in the dialog box. As a result, all the options are disabled. To assign an image file for the background, choose the **Image** button; the **Import Image** dialog box will be displayed. You can use this dialog box to import an image to be used as a background for the rendered scene.

Note

In an interior view, including natural light and the sky and cloud background can affect the quality of illumination on the rendered image. It is recommended to use more clouds for better diffuse lighting.

Creating the Rendered Image

After creating 3D view, applying lights, and assigning desired materials to elements, you need to view them in the final rendered image. To start the rendering process, choose the **Render** tool from the **Graphics** panel of the **View** tab; the **Rendering** dialog box will be displayed. Choose the **Render** button from the dialog box; the **Rendering Progress** dialog box will be displayed and Autodesk Revit Architecture will begin the rendering process using the mental ray rendering engine that renders one block of an image at a time. While rendering, the **Rendering Progress** dialog box displays information about the progress of the rendering process along with the number of daylight portals and artificial lights used.

If the **Close dialog when Rendering is complete** check box is selected in the **Rendering Progress** dialog box, the dialog box will automatically be closed after the completion of the rendering process and the final rendered image will be displayed on the screen.

Adjusting the Exposure

You can improve the quality of a rendered image before saving it. To do so, choose the **Adjust Exposure** button in the **Image** area of the **Rendering** dialog box; the **Exposure Control** dialog box will be displayed, as shown in Figure 15-15.

Rendering Views and Creating Walkthroughs

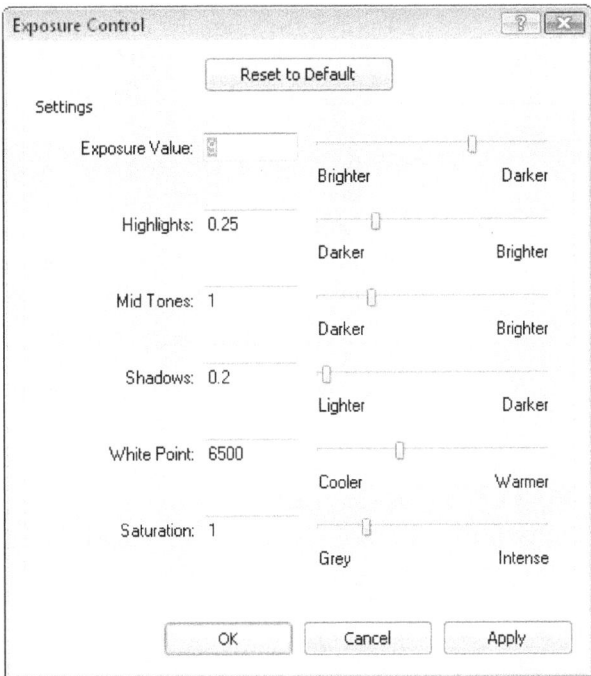

*Figure 15-15 The **Exposure Control** dialog box*

Various settings for the exposure control of an image are discussed in the table given next.

Settings	Description
Exposure Value	Enter a value between –6 and 16. The lesser value results in a brighter image and the higher value results in a darker image.
Highlights	Controls the level of the brightest area of the rendered image. You can enter a value between 0 (darkest) and 1 (brightest) highlights. The default value is 0.25.
Mid Tones	Controls the level of areas whose brightness lies between **Highlights** and **Shadows**. Enter a value between 0.1 (darkest) and 4 (brightest) midtones. The default value is 1.
Shadows	Controls the level of the darkest area of the rendered image. You can enter a value between 0.1 (lightest) and 4 (darkest) for the shadows. The default value is 0.2.

Saturation	Defines the intensity of colors in the rendered image. Enter a value between 0 (gray/black/white) and 5 (more intense colors) The default value is 1.
White Point	Defines the color temperature of light sources that display white color in the rendered images. Reduce the value if the rendered image looks orange. Increase its value if it looks blue. Use the value of 6500 for the scene illuminated with daylight.

Choose the **Apply** button each time you change the settings in the **Exposure Control** dialog box to see the updated image on your screen.

CREATING A WALKTHROUGH

A well rendered walkthrough can make a project presentation impressive. Using the **Walkthrough** tool, you can easily generate a walkthrough for a building model by rendering a series of 3D views defined by camera frames. The process of generating a walkthrough involves specifying a walkthrough path, editing it, and finally recording the walkthrough.

Creating the Walkthrough Path

Ribbon: View > Create > 3D View drop-down > Walkthrough

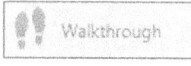

The first step for creating a walkthrough is to define the walkthrough path that a camera follows through the building model. In most cases, this path is defined in the plan view. But, you can also use the section, elevation, and 3D views to define the path.

The walkthrough path is defined by specifying the points that form a spline in the project view. The specified points become key frames in the walkthrough. Autodesk Revit Architecture automatically generates additional intermediate frames between these key frames.

To create a walkthrough path, first open the view in which it is to be defined. Next, invoke the **Walkthrough** tool from **View > Create > 3D View** drop-down; the **Modify | Walkthrough** tab will be displayed and the options related to the path creation will be displayed in the **Options Bar**, as shown in Figure 15-16.

*Figure 15-16 The **Options Bar** displaying the options for creating a walkthrough*

By default, the **Perspective** check box is selected to create walkthrough using perspective views from the camera positions. You can clear the **Perspective** check box to create walkthroughs as orthographic 3D views. Additionally, you can select the required view scale from the **Scale** drop-down list. The **Offset** edit box in the **Options Bar** is used to specify the height of the camera from the selected level. Using this edit box, you can move the camera upward or

Rendering Views and Creating Walkthroughs

downward while specifying the key frames along the walkthrough path. For example, by setting higher values for the **Offset** parameter, you can move the camera upward along a ramp or a flight of stairs. The **From** drop-down list displays all the defined levels in the project. You can select the level from which the offset camera height is specified. This parameter can be effectively used while creating an interior walkthrough at multiple levels.

To create the walkthrough path, click at the first point of the camera location; the point will define the first key frame of the walkthrough. As you move the cursor in the drawing area, Autodesk Revit Architecture will display three lines indicating the direction of the camera. Click to specify other points to create a spline to define the path of the camera. You can use the **Offset** and **From** options from **Options Bar** to modify the camera height, if required. After specifying the last point, choose the **Finish Walkthrough** button in the **Walkthrough** panel of the **Modify Walkthrough** tab; the **Modify | Cameras** tab will be displayed and the path of the camera for the walkthrough will be completed. The walkthrough path will be displayed in a different color in the drawing window. An example of the walkthrough path is shown in Figure 15-17.

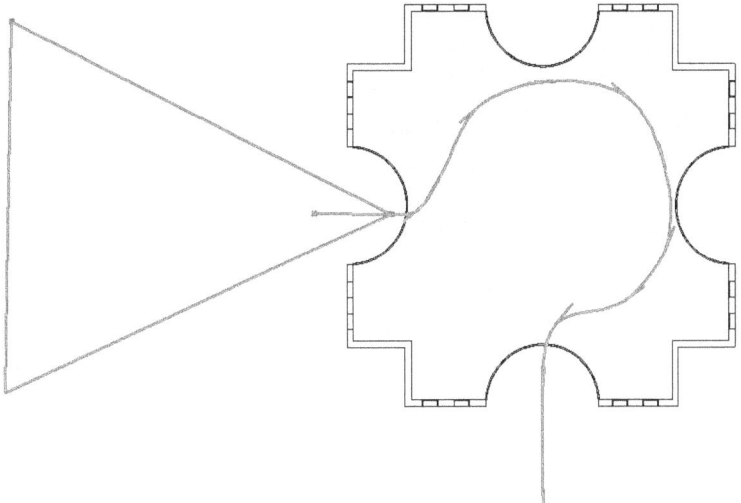

Figure 15-17 An example showing the walkthrough path

Note
After creating a complete walkthrough path you must first create the complete path and then edit it as per your requirement.

Editing and Playing the Walkthrough

When you create a walkthrough path, Autodesk Revit Architecture assigns **Walkthrough 1** as its name by default and then it is added to the **Project Browser** under the **Walkthroughs** heading.

To view the created walkthrough, double-click on its name in the **Project Browser** or right-click over the name and then choose **Open** from the shortcut menu; the drawing window will display the 3D view of the last frame. Select the frame from the drawing window; the **Modify | Cameras** tab will be displayed and the crop boundary with the grips will also be displayed. You can use the grips to resize the crop region. Alternatively, if you choose the **Size Crop** button in the **Crop** panel of the **Modify | Cameras** tab, the **Crop Region Size** dialog box will be displayed. In this dialog box, enter the new values for the **Width** and **Height** parameters of the crop region. The **Field of view** radio button in this dialog box is selected to modify the aspect ratio of the crop region. The **Scale** radio button is selected to scale the crop region by locking its aspect ratio. Note that while scaling the crop region, you can modify its width and height without affecting the field of view of the scene. After specifying the desired values, choose **OK**; the **Crop Region Size** dialog box will be closed and the crop region will be resized according to the parameters specified.

Now, to display the walkthrough path, double-click on the level name in which the path was created. While the walkthrough path is displayed in the drawing area, choose the **Edit Walkthrough** button in the **Modify | Cameras** tab; the **Edit Walkthrough** tab will be displayed, as shown in Figure 15-18. The options in the **Edit Walkthrough** tab are used to play or edit a walkthrough. The key frames specified to create the path are highlighted with dots in the drawing.

*Figure 15-18 The options for editing and playing a walkthrough in the **Edit Walkthrough** tab*

In **Options Bar**, the options in the **Controls** drop-down list are used to select the type of editing for the walkthrough. It has four options: **Active Camera**, **Path**, **Add Key Frame**, and **Remove Key Frame**. These options are discussed next.

The **Active Camera** option is used to drag a camera along a path to the desired frame or key frame. As you move the camera, it snaps to the key frame. While using this option, you can also drag the target point and the far clip plane of the camera at the key frames. At other additional frames, you can only modify the far clip plane.

 Tip: *After creating the walkthrough path, if you press the ESC key or click anywhere in the drawing area, it no longer remains visible. To display the path again, right-click on the name of the walkthrough and then choose the **Show Camera** option from the shortcut menu; the walkthrough path will be displayed in the current view. You can edit this path using the tools such as **Move**, **Copy**, **Mirror**, and so on.*

The **Path** option in the **Controls** drop-down list is used to edit a walkthrough path. When you select this option, key frames get converted into drag controls. You can drag them to modify the walkthrough path.

Rendering Views and Creating Walkthroughs   15-29

Select the **Add Key Frame** option to add key frames to the created path. Move the cursor over the path and click at the desired locations to add them. The **Remove Key Frame** option is used to remove the corresponding key frames by clicking over them.

The **Frame** edit box in the **Options Bar** displays the frame for the current location of the camera. You can enter a new frame number in this edit box to view the location of the camera at that frame. The **Frame Settings** button displayed next to the **Frame** edit box is used to set the properties of the frames. When you choose this button, the **Walkthrough Frames** dialog box will be displayed, as shown in Figure 15-19. The options in this dialog box are discussed next.

Figure 15-19 The **Walkthrough Frames** *dialog box*

The total number of frames in a walkthrough can be set by entering the value in the **Total Frames** edit box. Based on the values entered in this edit box, Autodesk Revit Architecture automatically divides frames along the created walkthrough path.

The **Uniform Speed** check box is selected by default. As a result, the camera traverses the walkthrough path at a uniform speed. You can change the speed of the walkthrough by entering a new value in the **Frames per second** edit box. Its default value is **15**. Lower the value in this edit box, slower will be the walkthrough. You can also vary the speed of the walkthrough by clearing the **Uniform Speed** check box in the **Walkthrough Frames** dialog box. This dialog box displays a table that contains five columns. These columns display the frame properties that are automatically generated based on the parameters specified for the walkthrough. When you clear the **Uniform Speed** check box, the **Accelerator** column in the table becomes editable. The **Accelerator** column displays the numerical values that change the speed of the walkthrough at specific key frames. You can enter values in the range of 0.1 and 10 to vary the speed of walkthrough. You can click on the **Key Frame** column to trace the key frame on the walkthrough path. A camera icon is also displayed at the selected key frame.

The **Indicators** check box is used to display the intermediate camera indicators along the walkthrough path. This helps in visualizing the distribution of frames along the path. The increment at which indicators are displayed can be set in the **Frame Increment** edit box.

After setting the required parameters in the **Walkthrough Frames** dialog box, you can play the walkthrough using the buttons in the **Edit Walkthrough** tab, refer to Figure 15-18. First, in the **Options Bar**, enter the frame number in the **Frame** edit box for the frame you wish to view in the drawing window. Next, in the **Edit Walkthrough** tab, choose the **Open Walkthrough** button to display the perspective view for the specified frame. To select the view type, choose the **Visual Style** button from **View Control Bar**; a cascading menu will be displayed. Now, select an option from this menu. Finally, choose the **Play** button from the **Edit Walkthrough** tab to play the walkthrough in the drawing window; the walkthrough starts playing based on the view type selected and the walkthrough parameters specified.

Note
When you create a walkthrough, it becomes a part of the project file and is not saved to the disk as a separate file. To save it to a disk, you need to record the walkthrough.

Tip: *The value specified in the **Frames per second** edit box indicates the speed of the walkthrough. You can enter a value in this edit box based on the total number of frames in the walkthrough. The **Total Time** edit box displays the total walkthrough time based on the total frames and the frames per second. Lower values of the **Frames per second** parameter may result in a jerky walkthrough.*

Recording a Walkthrough

Autodesk Revit Architecture enables you to record the walkthrough as **AVI** files and to export these files to a disk. The **AVI** files can be used to export the walkthrough. To export these files, open the walkthrough and choose **Export > Images and Animations > Walkthrough** from the **Application Menu**; the **Length/Format** dialog box will be displayed providing you with various options for exporting the walkthrough. The **Output Length** area of this dialog box enables you to select the frames to be exported. The **All frames** radio button in this area can be selected to export all the frames in the walkthrough. Alternatively, you can select the **Frame range** radio button and specify the number of frames to be exported by entering suitable values in the **Start** and **End** edit boxes. The **Frames/second** edit box is used to specify the speed at which the frames will be recorded.

The **Format** area of the **Length/Format** dialog box provides you with the options to specify the type and quality for the recording of the walkthrough. You can select the view type to be used for generating and recording the walkthrough from the **Visual Style** drop-down list. To record the rendered view of frames, select the **Rendering** option from this drop-down list. You can also specify the quality for the recording by setting the **Dimensions** and **Zoom to** spinners. Next, choose the **OK** button to invoke the **Export Walkthrough** dialog box, as shown in Figure 15-20. This dialog box is used to save a walkthrough. Enter a suitable name in the **File name** edit box and select the **AVI Files** option from the **Files of type** drop-down list. Next, choose the **Save** button from the **Export Walkthrough** dialog box to start recording the walkthrough. Now, Autodesk Revit Architecture will display the **Video Compression** dialog

Rendering Views and Creating Walkthroughs

box that enables you to select a video compressor from a list of compressors installed on your computer. When you choose the **OK** button, the dialog box will be closed and Autodesk Revit Architecture will start recording the walkthrough. The progress indicator and **Status Bar** at the bottom of the screen will display the progress of the processes being executed.

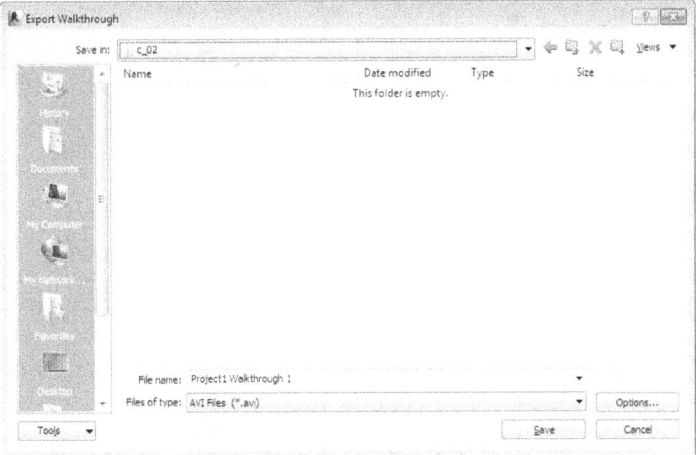

*Figure 15-20 The **Export Walkthrough** dialog box*

Note
The recorded file can be viewed using any of the media players. Note that this animation can now be viewed even without opening Autodesk Revit Architecture.

AUTODESK 360 | RENDERING

Autodesk 360 | Rendering is a cloud based rendering service that helps you to create photorealistic images and panoramic views for your project. It is a user interactive platform that provides a broad set of features including online cloud services , and related products.

The main features of the **Autodesk 360 | Rendering** service are:

1. Using the **Autodesk 360 | Rendering** service, you can render your Revit projects from any computer. Note that in Revit 2015, you can have direct access to the **Autodesk 360 | Rendering** rendering service.

2. Using the **Autodesk 360 | Rendering** service, you can access multiple versions of your renderings, render images as panoramas, change rendering quality, and apply background environments to rendered scenes.

3. Using this service, the design files can be reviewed even without the Revit software by accessing the **Autodesk @ 360** account online or even on mobile applications. The design files can be shared among users and the file updates and e-mail notifications reach the users whenever the file is edited.

4. The rendered views generated by the **Autodesk 360 | Rendering** application are grouped as collection in the render gallery. You can also create and view panoramic views. Panoramic views can be accessed from the render gallery.

5. Using the **Autodesk 360 | Rendering** service, you can adjust the exposure of the rendered image directly without having to re-render from the original desktop application.

6. The **Autodesk 360 | Rendering** service helps you to preview the rendered image of a single day or multi-day solar studies.

Rendering in Cloud

To render an image in the cloud, open a view in Revit interface. Next, choose the **Render in Cloud** tool from the **Graphics** panel of the **View** tab; the **Render in Cloud** dialog box will be displayed, as shown in Figure 15-21. Choose the **Continue** button; the **Render in Cloud** dialog box will be displayed again with the rendering options, as shown in Figure 15-22. In this dialog box, the 3D view to be rendered is to be chosen from the **3D View** drop-down list. You can specify the image type to be displayed, still or panoramic, from the **Output Type** drop-down list. You can specify the quality of rendered image as draft, standard, high, or best by selecting from the **Render Quality** drop-down list. You can specify image size for rendering by selecting an option from the **Image Size** drop-down list. From the **Exposure** drop-down list, you can select an option to specify whether the exposure being adjusted for the rendered image will be in advanced or native mode. After setting the required parameters, you can choose the **Start Rendering** button to render the image in the cloud. The estimated wait time to render a view is displayed at the right corner of this dialog box.

Note

*If a project is not saved in Revit, and the **Render in Cloud** tool is used to render the image, then the **Render in Cloud** message box will be displayed, prompting you to save the project and proceed.*

*Figure 15-21 The **Render in Cloud** dialog box*

Rendering Views and Creating Walkthroughs 15-33

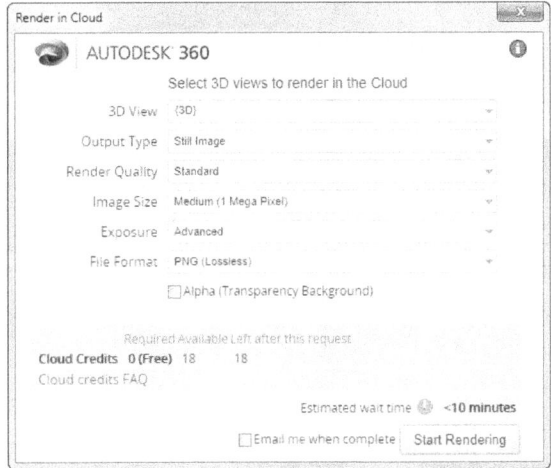

*Figure 15-22 The **Render in Cloud** dialog box*

 Tip: *The **Autodesk 360 / Energy Analysis** and **Autodesk 360 / Structural Analysis** cloud based services are available on subscription. The **Autodesk 360 / Energy Analysis** service helps in checking the energy efficiency of a building project whereas the **Autodesk 360 / Structural Analysis** service helps in performing structural analysis of the building elements.*

Accessing Render Gallery

The rendered images and the images being rendered are available online on **Render Gallery** page. The images are arranged in such a way that the newest image is displayed first. The grouping of images is done on the basis of file extension such as *.rvt* or *.dwg*. To access the Render gallery from Revit, choose the **Render Gallery** tool from the **Graphics** panel of the **View** tab; the **Autodesk 360 | Rendering** page will be opened. You need to sign in to your account to access the Render gallery from the **Autodesk 360 | Rendering** page.

TUTORIALS

Tutorial 1   Apartment 1

Using the project file *c14_Apartment1_tut1.rvt*, created in Tutorial 1 of Chapter 14, render the interior view of the living room at first floor, as shown in Figure 15-23. Replace the existing finish of materials assigned to the floor, wall, ceiling, and chair with new materials/textures (given with their path). Also, create a 200-frame interior walkthrough at eye level using the path shown in Figure 15-24. **(Expected time: 1 hr)**

The rendered image can be downloaded from *http://www.cadcim.com*. The path of the file is as follows: *Textbooks > Civil/GIS > Revit Architecture > Autodesk Revit Architecture 2015 for Architects and Designers*

 Note
The expected time of completing the tutorial does not include the rendering time. The rendering time will depend upon the system configuration.

Figure 15-23 *The interior view of the living room after rendering*

The materials used for rendering the scene are as follows:

1. New material for walls: **Finishes - Interior - Gypsum Wall Board** with **Wall-Paint Matte** render appearance.
2. New material for ceiling: **Finishes - Interior - Gypsum Wall Board - Ceiling**
3. New material for floor: **Finishes - Interior - VCT - Vinyl Composition Tile**
4. New cushion material for **Chair Corbu: Textile - Brown Leather**

Figure 15-24 *Sketch plan showing the walkthrough path for the Apartment 1 project*

Rendering Views and Creating Walkthroughs

Add lights based on the following parameters given below and as shown in Figures 15-25 and 15-26. Their exact location is not important in this tutorial.

1. Light Fixtures to be loaded and used from the **US Imperial > Lighting Fixture** folder:
   Table Lamp - Standard
   Pendant Light - Disk

The following steps are required to complete this tutorial:

a. Open the specified project file and the first floor plan view.
b. Use the **Paint** tool to apply materials to the floor.
c. Use the **Material Browser** dialog box to change the finish of the ceiling, walls, and textile of the chair.
d. Load lighting fixtures and add them to the floor and ceiling plan, refer to Figures 15-27 through 15-30.
e. Add RPC to the view, refer to Figures 15-31 and 15-32.
f. Set the rendering scene and generate the rendered image, refer to Figure 15-33.
g. Specify the walkthrough path and create a walkthrough, refer to Figures 15-34 through 15-36.

Figure 15-25 Sketch floor plan for adding table lamps to the living room

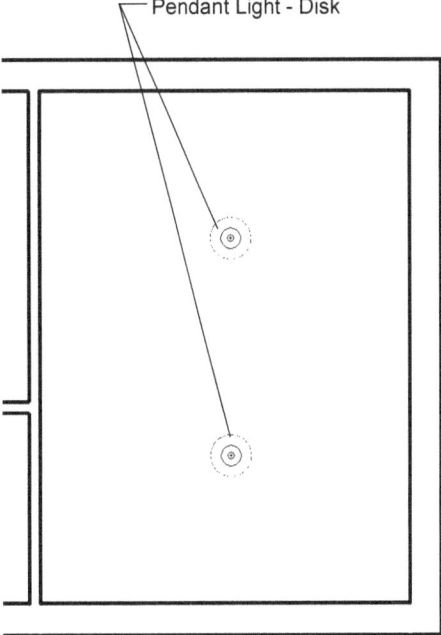

Figure 15-26 Sketch ceiling plan for adding ceiling lights to the living room

Opening the Project File and the First Floor Plan View

1. To open the specified file, choose **Open > Project** from the **Application Menu** and then open the *c14_Apartment1_tut1.rvt* file created in Tutorial 1 of Chapter 14. You can also download this file from *http://www.cadcim.com*. The path of the file is as follows: *Textbooks > Civil/GIS > Revit Architecture > Autodesk Revit Architecture 2015 for Architects and Designers*.

2. Now, double-click on **First Floor** in the **Floor Plans** head of the **Project Browser** to open the corresponding floor plan in the drawing window.

    As dimensions and tags are not required for this tutorial, you can turn off their visibility by using the **Visibility/Graphics** tool.

3. Choose the **Visibility/Graphics** tool from the **Graphics** panel of the **View** tab; the **Visibility/Graphic Overrides for Floor Plan: First Floor** dialog box is displayed. Choose the **Annotation Categories** tab and clear the check boxes for **Callouts**, **Dimensions**, **Furniture Tags**, and **Room Tags**.

4. Next, choose the **Apply** button and then the **OK** button to view the changes in the drawing area and to close the dialog box.

Modifying the Floor Material Using the Paint Tool

In this section of the tutorial, you will modify the finishes of the materials used in the building model. Also, you will use the **Paint** tool to apply the material to the floor in the section view.

1. Double-click on **Section X** under the **Sections (Building Section)** head in the **Project Browser** to display the section in the drawing window.

2. Choose the **Paint** tool from **Modify > Geometry > Paint** drop-down; the **Material Browser <default material name>** dialog box is displayed.

3. In the **Search** edit box of the **Material Browser** dialog box, type the **Vinyl Composition Tile** text; the **Finishes - Interior - VCT - Vinyl Composition Tile** is displayed in the area.

4. Select the **Finishes - Interior - VCT - Vinyl Composition Tile** material.

5. Now, in the drawing area, move the cursor near the top of the floor at the **First Floor** level in the section view and click when it is highlighted; the selected material is applied to the floor top. Choose the **Done** button in the **Material Browser** dialog box to close it.

Modifying the Finish of the Materials Using the Material Editor

In this section, you will modify the finish of other elements by using the **Material Browser** dialog box.

1. To start, first choose the **Modify** button from the **Select** panel and then move the cursor over the left exterior wall. Next, click to select it when it is highlighted.

2. Now, choose the **Type Properties** button in the **Properties** panel of the **Modify | Walls** tab; the **Type Properties** dialog box is displayed.

3. Next, choose the **Edit** button in the **Value** column for the **Structure** parameter to display the **Edit Assembly** dialog box, refer to Figure 15-27.
The finishes and structure of the selected wall type are displayed in the **Layers** area and are arranged with the exterior finish as the first and the interior finish as the last layer, refer to Figure 15-27. As the material properties of the interior finish need to be modified, you will modify the last layer (**Finish 2 [5]**).

4. Click in the **Material** column for the **Finish 2 [5]** layer and choose the browse button; the **Materials Browser** dialog box along with the **Material Editor** pane is displayed.

5. In the **Material Browser** dialog box, ensure that the **Gypsum Wall Board** option is selected in the **Project Materials: All** area and its parameters are displayed in the **Material Editor** pane.

6. Choose the **Appearance** tab, the preview of the selected material and its properties are displayed. Now, choose the **Replaces this asset** button from this tab; the **Asset Browser** dialog box is displayed, as shown in Figure 15-28.

7. In the **Asset Browser** dialog box, choose **Wall Paint > Matte > Biege** option from **Appearance Library**; a double arrow button is displayed.

Figure 15-27 The **Edit Assembly** *dialog box for the exterior wall type*

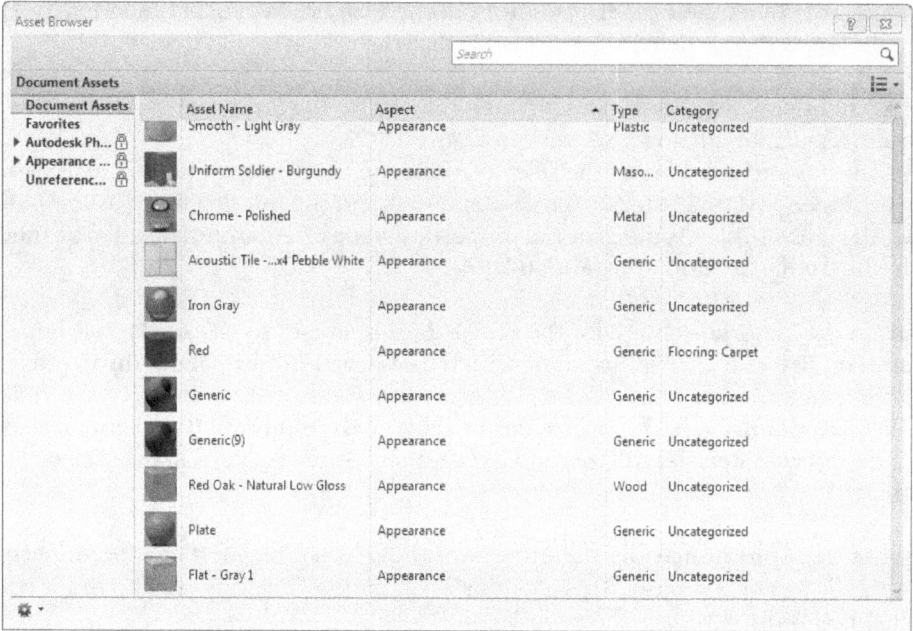

*Figure 15-28 The **Asset Browser** dialog box*

8. Choose the **Replaces this current asset in the editor with this asset** button to replace the current asset from the selected option. Close the **Asset Browser** dialog box and then choose the **OK** button in the **Material Browser** dialog box; the **Material Browser** dialog box along with the **Material Editor** pane is closed.

9. Close all the dialog boxes and return to the drawing window. Now, press ESC to exit the selection.

   Next, modify the appearance of the ceiling material.

10. Open the first floor ceiling plan and select the complete plan; the **Modify | Multi-Select** tab is displayed. Choose the **Filter** tool from the **Selection** panel of this contextual tab; the **Filter** dialog box is displayed. By default, all the check boxes are selected. Clear all the check boxes except the check box corresponding to the **Ceiling** parameter.

11. Choose the **OK** button; the **Filter** dialog box is closed; the **Modify | Ceiling** contextual tab is displayed.

12. Now, choose the **Type Properties** tool from the **Properties** panel of the **Modify | Ceilings** tab; the **Type Properties** dialog box is displayed.

13. Choose the **Edit** button in the **Value** field of the **Structure** parameter; the **Edit Assembly** dialog box is displayed with different layers of the selected ceiling.

Rendering Views and Creating Walkthroughs 15-39

14. Next, click in the **Material** column for the **Finish 2 [5]** layer and then choose the browse button to display the **Materials Browser** dialog box.

15. In the **Materials Browser** dialog box, the **Gypsum Wall Board** option is selected in the **Project Materials: All** area. The **Material Editor** pane displays the properties of material. Choose the **Duplicate Selected Material** option from the **Creates or duplicates material** drop-down located at the lower left corner of the **Material Browser** dialog box; the name **Gypsum Wall Board(1)** is displayed in the edit box in the **Material Browser** dialog box. Enter the name **Finish - Interior - Gypsum Wall Board - Ceiling** in this edit box.

16. Now, choose the **Replaces this asset** button from the **Appearance** tab; the **Asset Browser** dialog box is displayed. In this dialog box, choose **Paint > White** from **Appearance Library**. Click on double-arrow button to replace the current asset.

17. Close the **Asset Browser** dialog box. Choose the **Apply** and then the **OK** button to close the **Material Browser** dialog box. Choose the **OK** button in the **Edit Assembly** and the **Type Properties** dialog boxes to close them.

    Next, you will modify the texture of the chair textile.

18. Open the first floor plan view in the drawing window using the **Project Browser**.

19. Select the **Chair-Corbu** in the living room and then choose the **Edit Type** button from the **Properties** palette; the **Type Properties** dialog box is displayed.

20. In this dialog box, click in the **Value** column for the **Cushion Material** type parameter and choose the browse button; the **Material Browser** dialog box is displayed. In this dialog box, the **Textile - Black** option in the **Project Materials: All** area is selected. The **Material Editor** pane displays the properties of selected material.

21. In the **Material Browser** dialog box, choose the **Duplicate Selected Material** option from the **Creates or Duplicates Material** drop-down at the lower left corner of the **Material Browser** dialog box. Enter the name **Textile - Brown Leather** in the **Name** edit box and press ENTER.

22. Choose the **Replaces this asset** button from the **Appearance** tab in the **Material Editor** pane; the **Asset Browser** dialog box is displayed. In the **Asset Browser** dialog box, choose **Fabric > Leather** option from the **Appearance Library**.

23. Next, select the **Brown** material in the right pane of the **Appearance Library** area and click on the double arrow button to replace the current asset.

24. Now, close the **Asset Browser** dialog box and choose the **Graphics** tab from the **Materials Browser** dialog box; the **Graphic Properties** will be displayed in the **Material Editor** pane. Select the **Use Render Appearance** check box in the **Shading** area and then choose the **OK** button in the **Material Browser** dialog box and the **Type Properties** dialog box to close them. Now, press ESC to exit from selection of the chair. The **Leather** material is assigned to the cushion.

Loading and Adding Light Fixtures to the Building Model

In this section of the tutorial, you will load the light fixtures and then add them to the floor and ceiling plan.

1. Choose the **Place a Component** tool from **Architecture > Build > Component** drop-down; the **Modify | Place Component** tab is displayed.

2. Now, choose the **Load Family** tool from the **Mode** panel; the **Load Family** dialog box is displayed.

3. Navigate through the **US Imperial > Lighting > Architectural > Internal** folder and load the **Table Lamp - Standard** and **Pendant Light - Disk** fixtures using the CTRL key. Choose the **Open** button to return to the drawing area.

4. From the **Type Selector** drop-down list, select the **Table Lamp-Standard : 60W - 120V** fixture.

5. Move the cursor near the center of the side table placed at the lower right of the living room and click when the **Midpoint and Midpoint** object snap is displayed, as shown in Figure 15-29. Now, choose the **Modify** button to exit the selection mode.

6. Next, select the added table lamp; the instance parameters for the component are displayed in the **Properties** palette.

7. Enter the value **1'3"** in the value column for the **Offset** instance parameter and then choose the **Apply** button.

8. Use the **Copy** tool in the **Modify** panel to copy the added lamp to the other three side tables, as shown in Figure 15-30 (Select the **Multiple** check box in the **Options Bar**). Now, press ESC twice to exit from the current selection.

Rendering Views and Creating Walkthroughs 15-41

Figure 15-29 Adding lamp to the side table

Figure 15-30 Creating multiple copies of the table lamp component

9. Double-click on **First Floor** under the **Ceiling Plans** head in the **Project Browser** to display the ceiling plan view.

10. Next, choose the **Place a Component** tool from **Architecture > Build > Component > drop-down**; the **Modify | Place Component** tab is displayed. Select the **Pendant Light - Disk: 100W - 120V** fixture from the **Type Selector** drop-down list.

11. Move the cursor over the sitting area in the living room and click to add the light fixture at the approximate location, as shown in Figure 15-31.

12. Similarly, add the same fixture to the other side of the living room, as shown in Figure 15-32 and then press ESC twice to exit from the **Modify | Place Component** tab.

Figure 15-31 Adding the first light fixture in the ceiling plan

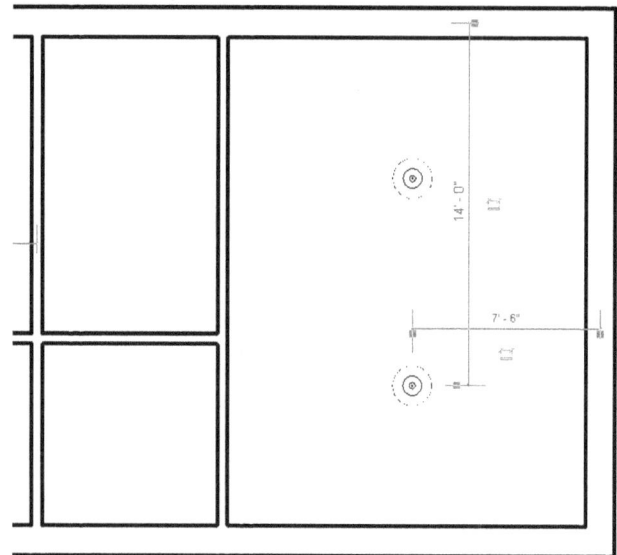

Figure 15-32 Adding the second light fixture in the ceiling plan

Adding RPC to the Interior Scene

In this section of the tutorial, you will use the **Place a Component** tool to load and add the specified RPC to the interior scene. The specified RPC (Rich Photorealistic Content) can be added at the location shown in Figure 15-33.

1. Open the first floor plan view from the **Floor Plans** heading in the drawing window using the **Project Browser**.

Rendering Views and Creating Walkthroughs

2. Now, choose the **Place a Component** tool from **Architecture > Build > Component** drop-down; the **Modify | Place Component** tab is displayed.

3. Choose the **Load Family** tool from the **Mode** panel; the **Load Family** dialog box is displayed.

4. Navigate through the **US Imperial > Entourage** folder, select the **RPC Female** family file and then choose **Open**; the selected family file is now loaded.

5. Next, select the **RPC Female : Cynthia** option from the **Type Selector** drop-down list.

6. Now, select the **Rotate after placement** check box from the **Options Bar** and then click on the sofa and move the cursor counterclockwise. Next, click to place and align the RPC in the view, as shown in Figure 15-33.

Figure 15-33 RPC added to the view

7. Press the ESC key twice to exit from the insertion process. Double-click on **Living Area** under the **3D Views** head in the **Project Browser** to view the 3D view after adding the lighting fixtures and RPC, refer to Figure 15-34.

8. Choose **Visual Style > Shaded** from **View Control Bar**; the current view will be shaded.

Note
*You can set the position of the RPCs by selecting the required elevation or section views from the **Project Browser**.*

Figure 15-34 The interior 3D view of the living room with the added lighting fixtures and RPC

Setting Up the Interior Rendering Scene

In this section of the tutorial, you will invoke the **Rendering** dialog box and specify the settings to render the interior scene.

1. Invoke the **Rendering** dialog box by choosing the **Show Rendering Dialog** button from **View Control Bar**. Alternatively, you can press RR to display the **Rendering** dialog box.

2. In the **Quality** area of the **Rendering** dialog box, select the **Best** option from the **Setting** drop-down list.

3. In the **Lighting** area, select the **Interior : Sun and Artificial** option from the **Scheme** drop-down list.

4. Choose the Browse button displayed next to the **Sun Setting** text box; the **Sun Settings** dialog box is displayed.

5. Select the **Still** radio button in the **Solar Study** area.

6. Choose the button next to the **Location** parameter in the **Settings** area to invoke the **Location Weather and Site** dialog box.

7. In the **Location** tab, select the **Default City List** option from the **Define Location by** drop-down list. Select **Chicago, IL** from the **City** drop-down list and choose the **OK** button.

8. Set the date **11/4/2014** in the **Date** drop-down list and then set the time to **10:00 PM** in the **Time** spinner.

9. Clear the **Ground Plane at Level** check box, if selected.

10. Choose **Apply** and **OK**; the specified settings are applied to the scene and the **Sun Settings** dialog box is closed.

11. Next, in the **Image** area of the **Rendering** dialog box, choose the **Adjust Exposure** button to invoke the **Exposure Control** dialog box.

12. In the **Exposure Control** dialog box, set the values of the parameters as given below:

Exposure Value: **6.5**   Highlights: **0.45**
Mid Tones: **1**   Shadows: **0.2**
White Points: **4000**

13. Choose **Apply** and **OK**; the specified settings are applied to the scene and the **Exposure Control** dialog box is closed.

14. In the **Rendering** dialog box, choose the **Render** button; Autodesk Revit Architecture starts the rendering process using the mental ray rendering engine for the interior view. The **Rendering Progress** dialog box is displayed on your screen. On completion of the process, the rendered image is displayed in the drawing area, as shown in Figure 15-35.

Figure 15-35 The interior 3D view of the living room rendered using mental ray

15. After the rendering process is complete, choose the **Save to Project** button in the **Image** area; the **Save to Project** dialog box is displayed. Enter **Living Area** in the **Name** edit

box and choose the **OK** button. This will add the rendered image under the **Renderings** head in the **Project Browser**. Now, close the **Rendering** dialog box.

The rendered image can be downloaded from *http://www.cadcim.com*. The path of the file is as follows: *Textbooks > Civil/GIS > Revit Architecture > Autodesk Revit Architecture 2015 for Architects and Designers*.

Note
*Depending on the hardware configuration of the system, it might take considerable time to render. To do a quick render, select **Draft** or **Low** from the **Setting** drop-down list in the **Rendering** dialog box.*

Generating the Walkthrough

In this section you will specify the walkthrough path in the floor plan view.

1. Double-click on **First Floor** under the **Floor Plans** head in the **Project Browser**.

2. Choose the **Walkthrough** tool from **View > Create > 3D View** drop-down; the **Modify | Walkthrough** tab is displayed. Note that the cursor changes into a **+** mark and different options related to creating a walkthrough path are displayed in the **Options Bar**.

3. Now, start sketching the walkthrough path by clicking at the first point near the center of the main entrance door of the apartment. Ensure that the first point is specified inside the lobby area and not outside the entrance door. Move the cursor toward the living room and click to specify multiple points in such a manner that they form a counterclockwise loop around the center table in the living room, as shown in Figure 15-36.

4. Similarly, move the cursor across the lobby and inside the bed room. Next, click to specify multiple points of the walkthrough path, refer to Figure 15-36. The exact location of these points is not critical.

5. After specifying the last point, choose the **Finish Walkthrough** button from the **Walkthrough** panel of the **Modify | Walkthrough** tab; walkthrough path is now complete and the **Modify | Cameras** tab is displayed.

Note
The dots indicate the specified points and are shown only for illustration. They are not displayed when the walkthrough path is being specified.

Note that the generated walkthrough is now added to the **Project Browser** as **Walkthrough 1** under the new **Walkthroughs** head. You can now modify the total frames for the walkthrough using the **Edit Walkthrough** button.

Figure 15-36 Sketch plan showing the walkthrough path for the Apartment 1 project

6. Double-click on **Walkthrough 1** under the **Walkthroughs** head in the **Project Browser**. Choose the **Edit Walkthrough** button from the **Walkthrough** panel of the **Modify | Cameras** tab; the **Edit Walkthrough** contextual tab is displayed.

7. Next, in the **Options Bar**, ensure that the **Active Camera** option is selected from the **Controls** drop-down list and **300** is displayed in the **Frame** edit box. Now, choose the **Frame Settings** button next to the **Frame** edit box; the **Walkthrough Frames** dialog box is displayed.

8. In the **Walkthrough Frames** dialog box, enter the value **200** in the **Total Frames** edit box and choose the **OK** button; the specified setting are now assigned to the walkthrough and the **Walkthrough Frames** dialog box closes. This modifies the total number of frames in the walkthrough from **300** to **200**, as specified for this tutorial.

Recording the Walkthrough

In this section of the tutorial, you will open the walkthrough, adjust the field of view of the camera and then record it by exporting it using the **AVI** file format.

1. In the **Options Bar**, enter **1** in the **Frame** edit box. Now, choose the **Edit Walkthrough** tab and then choose the **Open Walkthrough** button from the **Walkthrough** panel. The first frame is opened in the drawing window.

2. Right-click inside the drawing window and choose **Zoom Out (2x)** from the shortcut menu displayed.

3. Drag the extents of the rectangle to modify the field of view for the camera such that the view resembles the illustration given in Figure 15-37.

4. Right-click again and choose **Zoom To Fit** to enlarge the view.

5. Next, you will export the walkthrough as an AVI file. To do so, from the **Application Menu**, choose **Export > Images and Animations > Walkthrough**; the **Length/Format** dialog box is displayed, as shown in Figure 15-38.

Figure 15-37 *First frame of the walkthrough with the modified field of view*

Figure 15-38 The **Length/Format** *dialog box*

6. In the **Length/Format** dialog box, ensure that the **All frames** radio button is selected and then set **10** in the **Frames/sec** spinner.

7. In the **Format** area, select **Rendering** from the **Visual Style** drop-down list.

8. Next, set the value in the **Zoom to** spinner to **43** and choose the **OK** button; the **Length/Format** dialog box closes and the **Export Walkthrough** dialog box is displayed.

9. In the **Export Walkthrough** dialog box, specify an appropriate path, enter **c15_Apartment1_tut1_Walkthrough 1** in the **File name** edit box, and then make sure that **AVI Files** is the default file format selected in the **Files of type** drop-down list. Now, choose the **Save** button; the rendering and recording process starts. After rendering the first frame, the **Video Compression** dialog box will be displayed. Keep the **Full Frames (Uncompressed)** option selected in the **Compressor** drop-down list and choose the **OK** button to continue.

   Now, the rendering and recording process starts for each frame of the walkthrough and the **Rendering Progress** dialog box is displayed. When the procedure is completed, the file is recorded at the specified location. You can then use any media player to view the walkthrough file.

10. Choose **Save As > Project** from the **Application Menu**; the **Save As** dialog box is displayed.

11. Enter **c15_Apartment1_tut1** in the **File name** edit box and then choose **Save**.

12. Choose **Close** from the **Application Menu** to close the project file.

    This completes the tutorial for rendering the interior view and generating a walkthrough for the Apartment 1 project.

Tutorial 2 — Office Building 2

Render the exterior view of the *Office Building 2* project using the file created in Exercise 3 of Chapter 14. Replace the existing finishes of materials assigned to the exterior walls with the new materials/textures, add trees, and add entourages to the project based on the first floor plan view, as shown in Figure 15-39. Render the 3D view 1 based on the rendered view shown in Figure 15-40.   **(Expected time: 30 min)**

The rendered image can be downloaded from *http://www.cadcim.com*. The path of the file is as follows: *Textbooks > Civil/GIS > Revit Architecture > Autodesk Revit Architecture 2015 for Architects and Designers*.

1. New material for the exterior wall finish: **Finishes - Exterior- Cladding**
2. New material for toposurface: **Site - Grass**
3. Trees to be loaded and used from **US Imperial\Planting\RPC Tree - Deciduous** (for Metric **US Imperial\Planting\RPC Tree - Deciduous**)

   The following steps are required to complete this tutorial:

   a. Open the specified project file and the first floor plan view.
   b. Use the **Paint** tool to apply materials to the exterior walls.
   c. Add a toposurface to the building model and assign material to it.
   d. Add trees to the exterior view.

e. Add entourages to the building model.
f. Set up the rendering scene and render.

Figure 15-39 Sketch plan for adding toposurface, trees, and entourages to the Office Building 2

Figure 15-40 Rendered exterior view for Office Building 2 project

Opening the Project File and the First Floor Plan View

1. To open the specified file, choose **Open > Project** from the **Application Menu** and then open the *c14_Office-2_ex3.rvt* file created in Exercise 3 of Chapter 14. You can also download this file from *http://www.cadcim.com*. The path of the file is as follows: *Textbooks > Civil/GIS > Revit Architecture > Autodesk Revit Architecture 2015 for Architects and Designers*.

2. Double-click on **First Floor** in the **Floor Plans** head of the **Project Browser** to open the corresponding floor plan in the drawing window.

Modifying the Finishes of the Exterior Wall Using the Paint Tool

In this section of the tutorial, you will first create a new material and then use the **Paint** tool to apply it over the exterior walls.

1. Choose the **Materials** tool from the **Settings** panel of the **Manage** tab; the **Material Browser** dialog box is displayed.

2. In the **Materials Browser** dialog box, double-click on the **Metal Deck** from the **Project Materials: All** area; the **Material Editor** pane displays properties of **Metal Deck**. In this dialog box, choose the **Duplicate Selected Material** tool from the **Creates and Duplicates a Material** drop-down; a duplicate material name will be displayed in the edit box.

3. In the edit box, enter **Finishes-Exterior-Cladding** and choose the **Appearance** tab in the **Editor** pane. Choose the **Replaces this asset** button; the **Asset Browser** dialog box is displayed.

4. Click on the **Appearance Library** in the **Assets Browser** dialog box and select **Masonry/Brick** option from the expanded list.

5. Next, choose the **Non-Uniform Running-Red** material from the material list in the right pane of the **Asset Browser** dialog box and click on the double arrow button to assign material.

6. Now, close the **Asset Browser** dialog box and you can see the updated preview in the material preview box.

7. Next, choose the **Graphics** tab then select the **Use Render Appearance** check box in the **Shading Area**. Choose the **Apply** and **OK** buttons; the **Material Browser** dialog box is closed.

   You can now use the **Paint** tool to apply the created texture to the exterior walls.

8. Use the **Zoom in Region** tool from the **Navigation Bar** to enlarge the main building in the first floor plan.

9. Now, choose the **Paint** tool from **Modify > Geometry > Paint** drop-down; the **Modify | Paint** tab and the **Materials Browser** dialog box are displayed.

10. From this dialog box, select the **Finishes - Exterior-Cladding** material.

11. In the drawing area, move the cursor over the exterior face of the wall of the center building; the face gets highlighted. Next, click on the highlighted exterior face; the selected material gets applied to it.

12. Apply the selected texture to the exterior faces of the other exterior walls that are visible in the plan view and then choose the **Done** button in the **Materials Browser** dialog box to close it.

You can open the 3D view and then choose **Visual Style > Shaded** from the **View Control Bar**, if it is not selected, to display the shaded view of the modified exterior finish. Then, return to the plan view.

Creating a Toposurface and Adding Material to It

In this section of the tutorial, you will create a toposurface to add a base to the building and then add a material to it.

1. Double-click on **Site** in the **Floor Plans** head of the **Project Browser** to open the site plan. Now, hide the elevation symbol by using the **Visibility/Graphics** tool from the **View** tab.

2. Next, choose the **Massing & Site** tab and then choose the **Toposurface** tool from the **Model Site** panel.

3. Now, add points to the drawing area to create the toposurface, refer to Figure 15-39.

Note
The size of the toposurface can vary and is based on the extent of its visibility in the 3D view.

4. Next, choose the **Finish Surface** button from the **Surface** panel of the **Modify | Edit Surface** tab. Next, select the toposurface so that the instance parameters for the surface are displayed in the **Properties** palette.

5. Click on the value field of the **Material** parameter and then choose the browse button to display the **Materials Browser** dialog box.

6. In the dialog box, choose the **Earth** option from the **Project Material: All** list area.

7. Choose the **Duplicate Selected Material** option from the **Creates or duplicates material** drop-down at the lower left corner of the **Material Browser** dialog box; the name **Earth(1)** is displayed in the list under the **Project Material: All** area. Enter the name **Site - Grass** in the edit box.

8. Choose the **Replaces this asset** button in the **Appearance** tab; the **Asset browser** dialog box is displayed. Now, expand the **Appearance Library** in the left pane of the **Asset Browser** dialog box and select **Sitework > Grass-Bermuda**. Next, click on the double arrow button to update the material.

Rendering Views and Creating Walkthroughs   15-53

9. Next, close the **Asset Browser** dialog box to return to the **Material Browser** dialog box. Choose the **Graphics** tab from this dialog box; the graphic properties of the material will be displayed. Select the **Use Render Appearance** check box in the **Shading** area and then choose the **Apply** and then **OK** buttons in the **Material Browser** dialog box.

10. Now, press ESC to exit the selection.

    You will now use the **Site Component** tool to load and add the specified planting elements and people to the building model. The trees and people can be added to the location given in the sketch plan, refer to Figure 15-39.

11. Next, choose the **Site Component** tool from the **Model Site** panel of the **Massing & Site** tab; the **Modify | Site Component** tab is displayed.

12. Now choose the **Load Family** tool from the **Mode** panel; the **Load Family** dialog box is displayed.

13. Navigate through the **US Imperial > Planting** folder and select **RPC Tree - Deciduous** and then choose the **Open** button; the selected family type is loaded.

14. Now, from the **Type Selector** drop-down list, select **RPC Tree - Deciduous : Lombardy Poplar - 40'**.

15. Move the cursor near the location shown in the sketch plan for this tutorial and click to add the planting element.

    Similarly, click again at the diagonally opposite corner of the office building to add another instance of the planting element based on the given sketch plan. Further add more planting elements, refer to Figure 15-39.

16. Next, to add people to the building model, repeat steps 11 and 12 and invoke the **Load Family** dialog box.

17. Navigate through the **US Imperial > Entourage** folder and load the **RPC Male** and **RPC Female** families.

18. From the **Type Selector** drop-down list, select **RPC Male : Jay**, **RPC Male : Dwayne**, **RPC Male : LaRon**, **RPC Male : Alex**, **RPC Female : Cathy**, **RPC Female : YinYin**, **RPC Female : Tina**, and **RPC Female : Lisa** individually and then add them to the building model as per the site plan, refer to Figure 15-39.

Note
The locations of the RPCs are not fixed. You can change them according to the clarity of view and the requirement of the image.

Setting Up the Exterior Rendering Scene
You will now provide the information required to set up the rendering scene. To make the rendering tools available, open the 3D view of the project.

1. Open the **{3D}** view from the **3D Views** head in the **Project Browser**.

2. Choose the **Show Rendering Dialog** button from the **View Control Bar** to invoke the **Rendering** dialog box.

3. In the **Quality** area of the **Rendering** dialog box, select the **Best** option from the **Setting** drop-down list. Select the **Screen** radio button in the **Resolution** area, if it is not selected.

Note

*The rendering process may take considerable time if you select the **Best** option from the **Settings** drop-down list. To render quickly, select the **Low** or **Draft** option from the **Settings** drop-down list in the **Rendering** dialog box.*

4. Select the **Exterior: Sun only** option from the **Scheme** drop-down list in the **Lighting** area.

5. Next in this area, choose the browse button from the **Sun Setting** drop-down list to display the **Sun Settings** dialog box.

6. In the **Solar Study** area of the **Sun Settings** dialog box, ensure that the **Lighting** radio button is selected.

7. Ensure that **135.00°** is displayed in the **Azimuth** edit box. Next, enter **60.00°** in the **Altitude** edit box and then choose the **OK** button; the **Rendering** dialog box is displayed.

8. In the **Background** area, select the **Sky: Few Clouds** option from the **Style** drop-down list.

Rendering the Exterior View

In this section of the tutorial, you will render the exterior view using the mental ray rendering engine.

1. In the **Rendering** dialog box, choose the **Render** button to start the rendering process.

2. When you finish the rendering process, choose the **Adjust Exposure** button in the **Image** area to invoke the **Exposure Control** dialog box.

3. Enter the **Exposure Value** as **13.5** and **Shadows** as **0.3** in their respective edit boxes.

4. Choose the **OK** button to return to the **Rendering** dialog box.

5. Choose the **Save to Project** button in the **Image** area; the **Save to Project** dialog box is displayed.

6. Enter the name of the rendered view as **Exterior View 1** in the **Name** edit box and choose the **OK** button to return to the **Rendering** dialog box. Next, close the **Rendering** dialog box. Now, expand the **Renderings** head in the **Project Browser** and double-click on the **Exterior View 1**; the rendered view is displayed in the drawing area.

7. After viewing the rendered image, double-click on **First Floor** under the **Floor Plans** head in the **Project Browser**.

This completes the tutorial for rendering the exterior view of the Office Building 2 project.

Rendering Views and Creating Walkthroughs 15-55

8. Choose **Save As > Project** from the **Application Menu**; the **Save As** dialog box is displayed. Enter **c15_Office-2_tut2** in the **File name** edit box and then choose **Save**; the project file is saved.

9. Choose **Close** from the **Application Menu**; the project file closes.

Self-Evaluation Test

Answer the following questions and then compare them to those given at the end of this chapter:

1. In Autodesk Revit Architecture 2015, mental ray is used as the rendering engine. (T/F)

2. In the **Graphics** tab, you can assign different colors to the material for its shaded view. (T/F)

3. You cannot modify the predefined materials in the **Autodesk Library**. (T/F)

4. While generating a walkthrough, the height of the camera cannot be modified. (T/F)

5. The _____ attribute controls the brightness of the decal.

6. The _____ area of the **Identity** tab is used to specify the manufacturer, model, cost, and URL of the material selected.

7. The _____ tool is used to render only a portion of the 3D view.

8. In a project, the people, plants, vehicles, and office clutters are a part of _____ product family.

9. The _____ check box in the **Sun Settings** dialog box controls the visibility of shadows on the toposurface.

10. By choosing the _____ option, you can add keyframes to the path created.

Review Questions

Answer the following questions:

1. The mental ray rendering is used for the quality rendering. (T/F)

2. Each Autodesk Revit Architecture building element has a predefined material associated with it. (T/F)

3. The **Decal** tool is used to add 3D text to a plane. (T/F)

4. While generating a walkthrough, Autodesk Revit Architecture automatically generates intermediate frames between the specified keyframes. (T/F)

5. You can vary the speed of the camera while creating a walkthrough. (T/F)

6. You can create a new material using the **Material Browser** dialog box. (T/F)

7. The options in the **Style** drop-down list help you to set the background of the rendered image. (T/F)

8. Which of the following parameters controls the light output of a lighting fixture?

   a) **Lumen**
   c) **Light fixture height**
   b) **Wattage**
   d) **Assembly Code**

9. Which of the following dialog boxes is used to control the Daylight Portals?

   a) **Render Quality Settings**
   c) **Sun Settings**
   b) **Image Quality Settings**
   d) **Manage Place and Locations**

10. Which of the following parameters affects the speed of a walkthrough?

    a) **Offset**
    c) **Frames per second**
    b) **Indicators**
    d) **Total Time**

Exercises

Exercise 1   Club

Using the *c14_Club_tut2.rvt* (for Metric *M_c14_Club_tut2.rvt*) project file created in Tutorial 2 of Chapter 14, render the entrance view, as shown in Figure 15-41. Assume all the information required for this exercise.   **(Expected time: 30 min)**

Save the file as *c15_Club_ex1.rvt* (for Metric *M_c15_Club_ex1.rvt*)

Figure 15-41 Rendered exterior view of the Club project

Exercise 2   Apartment 1 - Night View

Using the project file created in Tutorial 1 of this chapter, render the morning time scene of the living room, as shown in Figure 15-42. You need to modify the time settings to 6:00A.M.
(Expected time: 30 min)

Save the file as *c15_Apartment-1_ex2.rvt* (for Metric *M_c15_Apartment-1_ex2.rvt*)

The rendered image can be downloaded from *http://www.cadcim.com*. The path of the file is as follows: *Textbooks > Civil/GIS > Revit Architecture > Autodesk Revit Architecture 2015 for Architects and Designers*

Rendering Views and Creating Walkthroughs

Figure 15-42 Rendered interior view of the living room

Exercise 3   Hotel Building - Walkthrough

Download *c15-revit-2015-ex03.rvt* file from the *CADCIM* website and create a walkthrough of a hotel building project, refer to Figures 15-43 through 15-45. The walkthrough of 1000 frames will be created of 1000 frames and at a frame rate of 15 frames per second. Use the camera at an eye level and move it along the path as shown in Figure 15-43.

(Expected time: 25 min)

Save the file as *c15_Hotel_ex3.rvt* (for Metric *M_c15_Hotel_ex3.rvt*)

Figure 15-43 The walkthrough path

Figure 15-44 *The walkthrough view at Frame 100*

Figure 15-45 *The walkthrough view at Frame 500*

Answers to Self-Evaluation Test

1. T, **2.** T, **3.** F, **4.** F, **5.** Intensity, **6.** Product Information, **7.** Region, **8.** RPC, **9.** Ground Plane at Level, **10.** Add Key Frames

Student Project

Student Project   City Mall

In this project, you will download the *city_mall.rvt* file and then perform the following:

- Create two section views, namely Sec_X and Sec_Y, refer to Figures 1, 2, and 3.
- Create a callout view, refer to Figures 1 and 4.
- Create a camera view, namely Cam01, refer to Figure 1 and 5.
- Perform rendering on the Cam01 view. You can assign materials and lights of your choice. For a sample rendering, refer to Figure 6. Note that you can also download the rendered sample image from *www.cadcim.com*
- Create a walkthrough of 1500 frames at a frame rate of 15 frames per second. For the path of the camera and the walkthrough views, refer to Figures 7, 8, and 9.

Figure 1 The architectural plan at **GF** level

Figure 2 The **Sec_X** *project view*

Figure 3 The **Sec_Y** *project view*

Figure 4 The *Callout view*

Figure 5 The **Cam01** *project view in the* **Shaded** *view style*

Figure 6 *The rendered view*

Figure 7 The **GF** *plan view showing the walkthrough path*

Figure 8 *The walkthrough view at Frame 100*

Figure 9 *The walkthrough view at Frame 500*

Index

A

Annotation Categories 1-5
Autodesk Revit Project 1-4
Autodesk Revit user interface screen 1-12, 1-13
Autodesk Help 1-21
Area Unit 2-5
Adding a Door to a Wall 4-7
Adding a Window to a Wall 4-13
Align tool 5-26
Array tool 5-21
Adding a Plan View 6-30
Adding Levels 6-6
Applying the Scope Box 6-40
Area and Volume Computations tool 7-28
Attach/Detach tool 7-32
Adding Components 8-2
Adding Curtain Grids 8-26
Adding Mullions 8-29
Adding Labels to Contours 9-18
Adding Slope to the Building Pads 9-15
Adding Other Building Elements 10-24
Adding Alternate Dimension Units 11-25
Adding Permanent Dimensions 11-21
Adding Tags 11-2
Angular Dimensions 11-22
Adding an Insulation Barrier 12-12
Adding a Revision Tag 12-27
Adding Detail Components 12-11
Adding Detail Lines 12-8
Adding Text notes 12-19
Annotation Crop Region 12-9

Adding Drawing Sheet to a Project 13-2
Adjusting the Exposure 15-24
Applying Lights 15-15
Artificial Lights- {3D} dialog box 15-22
Assemblies 5-40
Assigning Material to an Element Category 15-13
Assigning Material Using the Family Editor 15-14
AUTODESK 360 | Rendering 15-31
AVI tool 15-30
Adding Multiple Structural Columns 16-6
Adding Structural Beams and Braces 16-7
Import/Link RVT dialog box 16-31
Animated Solar Study 16-51
Animation Preview 16-52
Area Plan tool 16-13
Area Schedules 16-15
Area Schemes 16-12

B

Basic Concepts and Principles 1-3
Big SteeringWheels 2-29
Building Pads 9-13
building maker tools 10-20
Background 15-23
Binding Links 16-33

C

Contents Tab 1-23
Coordinating with Consultants 1-9
Creating an Architectural Drawing Set 1-8
Creating an Unusual Building Geometry 1-8
Creating a building project in Autodesk Revit 3-2
Curtain Walls 3-4
Changing the Temporary Dimensions 5-7
Copy tool 5-10
Create Similar tool 5-36
Creating a Selection 5-2
Creating Groups 5-30
Creating Groups Using the Group Editor 5-30

Index

Cutting and Pasting Elements 5-14
Cutting Elements 5-14
Cut to Clipboard tool 5-14
Controlling the Visibility of the Scope Box 6-40
Controlling Visibility of Grids 6-22
Controlling Visibility of Work Planes 6-24
Creating a Detail and a Wall Section View 6-38
Creating a Scope Box 6-39
Creating a Section View 6-34
Creating a Segmented Section 6-37
Creating Grids Using the Draw Tool 6-11
Creating Grids Using the Pick Tool 6-15
Ceiling tool 7-21
Creating Roofs by Extrusion 7-10
Creating the Roof by Footprint 7-7
Cutting Openings in the Floor, Roof, and Ceiling 7-29
Component tool 8-2
Creating a Curtain Wall 8-24
Curtain System by Face tool 8-25
Creating Property Lines Using Distances and Bearing 9-11
Creating Topographical Subregions 9-5
Conceptual Design Environment 10-15
Controlling Visibility of Massing Geometry 10-23
Creating a Blend 10-8
Creating an Extrusion 10-4
Creating a Revolved Geometry 10-5
Creating Curtain Systems by Selecting Faces 10-21
Creating Cuts in the Massing Geometry 10-11
Creating Floors by Selecting Faces 10-21
Creating the Massing Geometry 10-3
Creating Walls by Selecting Faces 10-21
Controlling the Dimension Arrow Display 11-29
Creating Automatic Linear Wall Dimensions 11-30
Callout View 12-3
Controlling the Visibility of the Revision Tag 12-27
Creating a Legend View 12-34
Creating a Model Text 12-23
Creating a Revision Cloud 12-26
Creating Details using the Building Model 12-2
Creating Drafted Details 12-15
Creating Drawing Sheets 13-2
Camera tool 14-13
Center tool 14-4

Creating Orthograhic Views 14-3
Controlling Natural Lighting 15-16
Color Scheme Legends 16-19
Color Schemes 16-17
Creating Phases and Setting Phase Filters 16-25
Creating Structural Columns 16-5
Creating Structural Components 16-2
Creating Structural Walls 16-3
Cutting Openings in Beams 16-8

D

Dimension Snaps 2-6
Delete tool 5-27
Deleting Elements 5-27
Diagnostic tools 5-38
Dormer Opening 7-31
Dimension Line 11-20
Dimension Text 11-20
Detail Component tool 12-11
Detail Lines tool 12-8
Drafting View tool 12-15
Default 3D View tool 14-3
Dynamically Viewing Models 14-4
Decal tool 15-17
Decal Type 15-18
Demolish tool 16-26
Design Options tool 16-10
Displaced View 16-23

E

Exterior Walls 3-4
Extracting Project Information 1-8
Edit Assembly dialog box 3-10
Exterior Walls 3-3
Element IDs of Selection text box 5-40
Elevation View 6-31
Editing the Massing Geometry 10-10
Editing Dimensions 11-27
Editing Text Notes 12-21
Entourages 15-17, 15-20

Index

Export Walkthrough dialog box 15-31
Exposure 15-24
Element Ownership Concepts 16-44
Exporting Drawing to SketchUp 16-56

F

File Locations Tab 2-15
Floor tool 7-2
Floor Slab Edge tool 7-6
Families 10-25
Families Using the Family Templates 10-26
Filled Region tool 12-10
Forward tool 14-5
Family Workset 16-42

G

General tab 2-12
Go To View dialog box 6-33
Grid Type Properties 6-18
Generating Exterior Perspective Views 14-13
Grouped Lights 15-22
Generating Design Options for a Project 16-10
Generating Shadows 16-47
Gross Building 16-13

H

History of Computer Aided Design 1-2
Hidden Line 2-31

I

Interior Walls 3-3
In-Place Families 10-26
Interface of the Conceptual Design Environment 10-15
Insulation tool 12-12
Interoperability with Autodesk 3ds Max and Max Design 16-55

K

Keyboard Accelerators 1-18
Keynote Legend 11-15
Keynotes 11-11

L

Levels in a Building Model 1-5
Length Unit Settings 2-4
Level Properties 6-3
Level tool 6-6
Label Contours tool 9-18
Linear Dimensions 11-22
Loading Tags 11-3
Locking Dimensions 11-30
Legend tool 12-34
Line Patterns dialog box 12-19
Line Patterns tool 12-18
Line Style Settings 12-16
Line Styles tool 12-16
Line Weights tool 12-17
Look tool 14-6
Light Group toolbar 15-23
Layer Mapping File 16-57
Linking Building Models and Sharing Coordinates 16-26
Linking Revit Models 16-30

M

Model Categories 1-5
Mini SteeringWheels 2-29
Model and Attached Detail Groups 5-31
Modifying Groups 5-33
Move tool 5-9
Multiple Copies of an Element 5-10
Modifying the Plan View Properties 6-31
Modifying the Section View 6-35
Modifying the Room Properties 7-27
Modifying Railing Properties 8-20
Modifying Stairs Properties 8-18
Merging Toposurfaces 9-7

Massing Concepts 10-2
Modifying Dimension Parameters 11-27
Model Crop Region 12-9
Model Text tool 12-23
Modifying the Model Text Properties 12-24
Matchline 13-13
Modifying Perspective View Properties 14-17
Material Browser dialog box 15-6
Material Editor Pane 15-7
Materials 15-5
Mental Ray 15-2
Manage Links dialog box 16-36
Masking Regions 16-21
Masking Regions to a Detail Family 16-22
Masking Regions to a Model Family 16-23
Masking Regions to a Project 16-22
Modifying the Color Scheme 16-21

N

New Project dialog box 2-2
Next Pan/Zoom 2-26
New Drafting View dialog box 12-15
New Schedule dialog box 12-29
New Subcategory dialog box 12-17
Navigation tools 14-4
New Area Plan dialog box 16-14
Number Parameter for Areas 16-15

O

Open tool 2-22
Offset tool 5-19
Ordinate Dimensions 11-26
Orienting the 3D view to a Direction 14-11
Orienting the 3D View to a Plane 14-12
Orienting the 3D View to a View 14-12
Orient tool 14-11
Object Styles dialog box 15-13

P

Project Browser 1-18
Project Units dialog box 2-4
Paste from Clipboard tool 5-15
Pin tool 5-37
Projection Lines 6-26
Paste Aligned tool 8-30
Parking Components 9-18
Parking Component tool 9-18
Property Line Creation dialog box 9-10
Property Lines Using Distances and Bearings 9-11
Property Line tool 9-10
Place Mass tool 10-13, 10-14
Placing the Massing Geometry 10-13
Profiles 10-19
Placing a Spot Dimension 11-31
Project Detailing in Autodesk Revit 12-2
Previewing the Print Setup 13-21
Print dialog box 13-16
Printing Drawing Sheets and Project Views 13-16
Printing in Autodesk Revit 13-15
Print Preview tool 13-21
Print Range 13-18
Print Setup dialog box 13-20
Print tool 13-16
Pan tool in SteeringWheels 14-7
Paint tool 15-15
Phases tool 16-25
Phasing dialog box 16-25
Point Cloud 16-54
Process of Worksharing 16-38
Purge Unused tool 16-45
Purging Unused Element Families 16-45

R

Revit Server 1-23
Retaining Walls 3-3
Rotate tool 5-15
Reference Planes 6-23

Index

Roof Boundary Line Properties 7-14
Roof by Extrusion tool 7-10
Roof Instance Properties 7-14
Roof Reference Level and Offset dialog box 7-11
Roofs 7-7
Roof Type Properties 7-14
Room Instance Parameters 7-27
Rooms 7-24
Room Schedules 7-26
Ramp tool 8-21
Resizing the Massing Geometry Using the Drag Control 10-10
Roof by Face tool 10-22
Radial Dimensions 11-23
Room Separation tool 11-9
Room Tags 11-9
Revision Clouds 12-25
Revision Cloud tool 12-25
Rendering dialog box 15-21
Rendering in Revit Architecture 15-2
Rendering Workflow 15-2
Reloading Files in Worksets 16-44
Rentable 16-12

S

Search Tab 1-23
Starting Autodesk Revit 1-9
Subdivisions of Elements into Categories and Subcategories 1-5
Save tool 2-11
Shaded 2-31
Snap Settings 2-6
Sequence of Creating a Building Model 3-2
Sketching Circular Wall Profiles 3-15
Sketching tools 3-12
Saving and Loading Groups 5-34
Select Element by ID dialog box 5-40
Selecting Elements Using Advanced tools 5-3
Selecting Multiple Elements 5-2
Spilt Elements tool 5-27
Split with Gap 5-29
Scope Box tool 6-39
Setting the Work Plane 6-23
Shaft Opening 7-31
Shape Editing tools for Floors 7-18

Sketching a Ceiling 7-21
Site Components 9-16
Site Component tool 9-16
Split Surface tool 9-6
Splitting a Toposurface 9-6
Subregion tool 9-6
Swept Blend tool 10-9
Symbol tool 11-16
Schedule Properties dialog box 12-30
Schedule/Quantities tool 12-28
Selecting and Modifying the Printer Settings 13-17
Sheet 13-2
Section Box 14-18
SteeringWheels tool 14-4
Setting the Background 15-24
Schedule Properties dialog box 16-16
Select Items To Copy dialog box 16-46
Sharing Coordinates 16-26
Sketching Foundation Walls 16-4
Sketching Retaining Walls 16-34
Solar Studies 16-47
Specifying Phases for the Project Views 16-26
Still Solar Study 16-48
Stacked Wall 3-17
Structural Beams and Braces 16-2
Structural Columns 16-2
Structural Walls 16-2

T

Title Bar 1-12
Trim/Extend Multiple Elements option 5-13
Trim/Extend Single Element option 5-12
Trimming and Extending Elements 5-18
Temporary Hide/Isolate tool 6-29
Types of Families 10-25
Tag All Not Tagged dialog box 11-7
Tag All Not Tag tool 11-7
Tagging All Elements in a View 11-6
Temporary Dimensions 11-18

Index

Tick Marks 11-20
Types of Dimensions 11-18
Text tool 12-14
Three-Dimensional Views 14-2
Transfer Project Standards tool 16-45
Transferring Project Standards 16-45

U

Understanding Autodesk Revit Terms 1-4
User Interface 1-12
Understanding Wall Types 3-3
Using the Scope Box tool 6-39
Using the Attach/Detach tool 7-32
Using components in Project 8-2
Understanding the Massing Concepts 10-2
Using Line Patterns 12-18
Using Schedules in Project 12-28
Up/Down Tool 14-8
User-Created Workset 16-42
Using Point Cloud File in a Project 16-55
Using the Worksets Tools 16-39

V

View Categories 1-5
View Control bar 1-16, 1-17
Visibility/Graphics Settings, Scale and Detail Level 1-17
ViewCube 2-27
Volume and Angle Unit Settings 2-5
View-Specific Element Graphics dialog box 6-26
Visibility of Grids 6-22
Void Revolve 10-12
View Reference 13-15
View/Sheet Set dialog box 13-19
Video Compression dialog box 15-30
View Workset 16-42

W

Wireframe 2-31
Work Plane Grid Snap 2-8
Wall Reveals 3-23
Wall Sweeps 3-21
Wall tool 3-4
Wall Types 3-3
Window 4-10
Working with Levels 6-2
Work Plane dialog box 6-24, 7-11
Wall by Face tool 10-21
Witness Lines 11-20
Line Weights dialog box 12-18
Walk Tool 14-8
Walkthrough 15-26
Walkthrough Frames dialog box 15-29
Walkthrough Path 15-26
Worksets dialog box 16-40

X

X-Ray 10-14
X-Ray tool 10-18

Z

Zoom tool 2-25
Zoom All to Fit 2-26
Zoom in Region 2-25
Zoom Tool in SteeringWheels 14-10

Other Publications by CADCIM Technologies

The following is the list of some of the publications by CADCIM Technologies. Please visit www.cadcim.com for the complete listing.

Autodesk Revit Architecture Textbooks
- Autodesk Revit Architecture 2014 for Architects and Designers
- Autodesk Revit Architecture 2013 for Architects and Designers

Autodesk Revit Structure Textbooks
- Exploring Autodesk Revit Structure 2015
- Exploring Autodesk Revit Structure 2014
- Exploring Autodesk Revit Structure 2013

Autodesk Navisworks Textbook
- Exploring Autodesk Navisworks 2015
- Exploring Autodesk Navisworks 2014

AutoCAD Civil 3D Textbooks
- Exploring AutoCAD Civil 3D 2015
- Exploring AutoCAD Civil 3D 2014
- Exploring AutoCAD Civil 3D 2013

AutoCAD Map 3D Textbooks
- Exploring AutoCAD Map 3D 2014
- Exploring AutoCAD Map 3D 2013

AutoCAD Textbooks
- AutoCAD 2015: A Problem Solving Approach, Basic and Intermediate
- AutoCAD 2015: A Problem Solving Approach, 3D and Advanced

NX Textbooks
- NX 9 for Designers
- NX 8.5 for Designers
- NX 7 for Designers
- NX 6 for Designers
- NX 5 for Designers

SolidWorks Textbooks
- SolidWorks 2014 for Designers
- SolidWorks 2014: A Tutorial Approach
- SolidWorks 2013 for Designers
- SolidWorks 2012 : A Tutorial Approach
- Learning SolidWorks 2011: A Project Based Approach

EdgeCAM Textbooks
- EdgeCAM 11.0 for Manufacturers
- EdgeCAM 10.0 for Manufacturers

CATIA Textbooks
- CATIA V5-6R2013 for Designers
- CATIA V5-6R2012 for Designers

Creo Parametric and Pro/ENGINEER Textbooks
- Creo Parametric 2.0 for Designers
- Creo Parametric 1.0 for Designers
- Pro/ENGINEER Wildfire 5.0 for Designers
- Pro/ENGINEER Wildfire 4.0 for Designers

ANSYS Textbooks
- ANSYS Workbench 14.0: A Tutorial Approach
- ANSYS 11.0 for Designers

3ds Max Design Textbooks
- Autodesk 3ds Max Design 2015: A Tutorial Approach
- Autodesk 3ds Max Design 2014: A Tutorial Approach

3ds Max Textbooks
- Autodesk 3ds Max 2015: A Comprehensive Guide
- Autodesk 3ds Max 2014: A Comprehensive Guide

Coming Soon from CADCIM Technologies
- Primavera P6
- Bentley's STADD.Pro.
- Energy Analysis Using Vasari and Green Building Studio
- Autodesk Raster Design
- The Foundry NukeX 8 for Compositors
- NX Nastran 9.0 for Designers

Online Training Program Offered by CADCIM Technologies

CADCIM Technologies provides effective and affordable virtual online training on various software packages including computer programming languages, Computer Aided Design and Manufacturing (CAD/CAM), animation, architecture, and GIS. The training will be delivered 'live' via Internet at any time, any place, and at any pace to individuals, students of colleges, universities, and CAD/CAM training centers. For more information, please visit the following link: *http://www.cadcim.com*

www.ingramcontent.com/pod-product-compliance
Lightning Source LLC
Chambersburg PA
CBHW081140290426
44108CB00018B/2395